CW01498729

Information Systems:
A Socio-Technical Perspective

Compiled from selected chapters from the following publications:

INTRODUCTION TO INFORMATION SYSTEMS,
R. Kelly Rainer, Jr., Efraim Turban, and Richard E. Potter

**LEARNING FOR ACTION: A SHORT DEFINITIVE ACCOUNT OF SOFT SYSTEMS
METHODOLOGY AND ITS USE FOR PRACTITIONERS, TEACHERS AND STUDENTS,**
Peter Checkland and John Poulter

**INFORMATION TECHNOLOGY FOR MANAGEMENT: TRANSFORMING
ORGANIZATIONS IN THE DIGITAL ECONOMY, 6TH EDITION,**
Efraim Turban, Dorothy Leidner, Ephraim McLean, and James Wetherbe

WEB DESIGN: A COMPLETE INTRODUCTION,
Nigel Chapman and Jenny Chapman

TEACH YOURSELF VISUALLY™ MACROMEDIA® DREAMWEAVER® 8,
Janine Warner

 **WILEY**
CUSTOM SERVICES

A Wiley Custom Services Publication
Prepared for: Brighton Business School, University of Brighton

Contents

From *Introduction to Information Systems*
R. Kelly Rainer, Jr., Efraim Turban, and Richard E. Potter. ISBN 978-0-471-73636-3
© 2007 John Wiley & Sons, Inc.

Contents vii

From *Learning for Action: A Short Definitive Account of Soft Systems Methodology and its use for Practitioners, Teachers and Students*
Peter Checkland and John Poulter. ISBN 978-0-470-02554-3 © 2006 John Wiley & Sons, Ltd

From *Information Technology for Management: Transforming Organizations in the Digital Economy, 6th Edition*
Efraim Turban, Dorothy Leidner, Ephraim McLean, and James Wetherbe. ISBN 978-0-471-78712-9 © 2008 John Wiley & Sons, Inc.

CHAPTER 7   TRANSACTION PROCESSING, FUNCTIONAL APPLICATIONS, AND INTEGRATION   **384**

From *Web Design: A Complete Introduction*
Nigel Chapman and Jenny Chapman. ISBN 978-0-470-06089-6
©2006 Nigel Chapman and Jenny Chapman

CHAPTER 10   WEB PAGE DESIGN   427

From *Teach Yourself VISUALLY*™ *Macromedia® Dreamweaver® 8*
Janine Warner. ISBN 978-0-7645-9998-9 © 2006 Wiley Publishing Inc.

CHAPTER 2   SETTING UP YOUR WEB SITE   491

CHAPTER 7   CREATING HYPERLINKS   501

CHAPTER 8 USING TABLES TO DESIGN A WEB PAGE   **521**

Chapter 1

Chapter Preview

In Chapter 1 we introduce you to the basic concepts of information systems in organizations. Information systems collect, process, store, analyze, and disseminate information for a specific purpose.

The two major determinants of information systems support are organizational structure and the functions that employees perform within organizations. As this chapter shows, information systems tend to follow the structure of organizations, and they are based on the needs of individuals and groups.

Information systems are located everywhere inside organizations, as well as among organizations. This chapter looks at the types of support that information systems provide to organizational employees. Because

these systems are so diverse, managing them can be quite difficult. Therefore, this chapter also briefly considers how organizations manage their IT systems.

The two terms, information systems and information technology, can be confusing. **Information technology (IT)** can have several meanings. In this book we use the term, *IT*, in its broadest sense—to describe an organization's collection of information resources, to identify the users of these resources, and to examine the management that oversees them. Typically, though, the term *information technology* is used interchangeably with *information system*, and we use the two terms interchangeably in this book. The purpose of this book is to acquaint you with all aspects of information systems/information technology.

Information Systems: Concepts and Management

Introduction to Information Systems
R. Kelly Rainer, Jr., Efraim Turban, and Richard E. Potter. ISBN 978-0-471-73636-3
©2007 John Wiley & Sons, Inc.

Chapter Outline

1.1 Information Systems: Concepts and Definitions
1.2 Types of Information Systems
1.3 Examples of Information Systems
1.4 Managing Information Resources
1.5 The Plan of This Book

Learning Objectives

1. Differentiate among data, information, and knowledge.
2. Differentiate between information technology infrastructure and information technology architecture.
3. Describe the components of computer-based information systems.
4. Describe the various types of information systems, by breadth of support.
5. Identify the major information systems that support each organizational level.
6. Describe how information resources are managed, and discuss the roles of the information systems department and the end users.

What's in  for me? ACC FIN MKT POM HRM MIS

3

The Boston Red Sox: World Champions!

The Business Problem

Ever since Boston Red Sox (*www.redsox.com*) owner Harry Frazee sold Babe Ruth to the Yankees following the 1919 season, the Sox had not won a World Series—an affliction known throughout baseball as the "Curse of the Bambino." But 2004 was going to be different, and the numbers said so.

The Red Sox's business problem is to identify the best players available, acquire them before their rivals do, and then figure out how long to keep them before they stop pro-

Source: Dorothy Littell Greco/The Image Works

ducing. The process is human capital management at its best. The ultimate goals for Theo Epstein, general manager of the Sox: Beat the New York Yankees and win the World Series.

The IT Solution

Baseball is a business where employee performance can be measured down to every swing, throw, or step taken. Baseball analysts can easily establish baselines on every facet of the athlete's physical characteristics, such as height, weight, and medical condition. This observation extends even to minutely defined activities such as arm strength, hitting discipline, and mental errors. Today, teams chronicle every season of every player's career, from school play onward, in minute detail. The Rex Sox go so far as to require players in their farm system to keep a log of their every at-bat.

The Red Sox are practitioners of Sabermetrics, a term derived from the acronym SABR, the Society of American Baseball Research. Sabermetricians argue that traditional measures of ballplayers' performances are not precise. For example, runs batted in (RBIs) is heavily dependent on where a player hits in the batting order. Therefore, sabermetricians have developed measures that more accurately reflect a player's value toward achieving a win. One such measure is "runs created." This statistic counts the number of times a batter gets on base, be it by walk or hit, and factors in an added value for the power of a hit, be it a single or a home run.

To use Sabermetrics the Red Sox must have extensive data. The team uses a software package called ScoutAdvisor (*www.scoutadvisor.com*), which keeps track of player talent from the minors to the pros. The heart of the system is housed in a data center in Tampa, Florida. There, computers store raw data on baseball players, such as high school and college records, family backgrounds, psychological profiles, and medical histories.

The system gathers data daily from a range of sources. The Major League Baseball Scouting Bureau provides the results from its Athletic Success Profile test of prospects, asking 110 questions designed to uncover athletes' psychological profile. SportsTicker (*www.sportsticker.com*) provides game reports, while STATS, Inc. (*www.stats.com*) employs a small army of "reporters" at games to gather statistics such as the pitch count at the end of an at-bat, types of pitches, and where balls land in the field after being hit. The huge advantage of ScoutAdvisor is that the system can slice and dice player data any way the team wants. In essence, ScoutAdvisor allows the Rex Sox to analyze the data to produce actionable business information. For example, the Red Sox put the system to good use when the team paid a large amount of money for All-Star pitcher Curt Schilling and traded All-Star shortstop Nomar Garciaparra to the Chicago Cubs.

The Results

The Red Sox can now decide which players to go after and how much to pay for each one. The ultimate result: In 2004, the Red Sox won the World Series for the first time in 86 years!

The Red Sox used information systems to support their goal of winning a World Series. For example, the team's entire scouting and player evaluation system has changed from paper-based to computer-based (ScoutAdvisor). Every team in baseball has access to the same data as the Red Sox, but perhaps the Red Sox used their information systems to collect and analyze these data more effectively than the other teams. After all, Boston now has a World Series title. In this chapter we describe how information systems of different kinds are structured, organized, and managed so that they can support businesses in the twenty-first century.

Sources: Compiled from M. Duvall, "Boston Red Sox: Backstop Your Business," *Baseline Magazine*, May 14, 2004; and *eWeek*, May 21, 2004.

What We Learned From This Case

1.1 Information Systems: Concepts and Definitions

It has been said that the purpose of information systems is to get the right information to the right people at the right time in the right amount and in the right format. Because information systems are intended to supply useful information, we begin by defining information and two closely related terms, data and knowledge.

Data, Information, and Knowledge

One of the primary goals of information systems is to economically process data into information or knowledge. Let's take a closer look at these concepts.

Data items refer to an elementary description of things, events, activities, and transactions that are recorded, classified, and stored but are not organized to convey any specific meaning. Data items can be numbers, letters, figures, sounds, or images. Examples of data items are a student grade in a class and the number of hours an employee worked in a certain week.

Information refers to data that have been organized so that they have meaning and value to the recipient. For example, a grade point average is data, but a student's name coupled with his or her grade point average is information. The recipient interprets the meaning and draws conclusions and implications from the information.

Knowledge consists of data and/or information that have been organized and processed to convey understanding, experience, accumulated learning, and expertise as they apply to a current business problem. For example, a company recruiting at your school has found over time that students with grade point averages (GPAs) over 3.0 have had the most success in its management program. Based on its experience, that company may well decide to interview only those students with GPAs over 3.0. Organizational knowledge, which reflects the experience and expertise of many people, has great value to all employees.

Now that we have a better idea of what information is and how it can be organized to convey knowledge, we shift our focus to the ways that organizations organize and use information. To do this we must look closely at an organization's information technology architecture and information technology infrastructure. These concepts underlie all information systems within the organization.

Information Technology Architecture

An organization's **information technology (IT) architecture** is a high-level map or plan of the information assets in an organization. It is both a guide for current operations and a blueprint for future directions. The IT architecture integrates the entire organization's business needs for information, the IT infrastructure (discussed in the next section), and all applications. The IT architecture is analogous to the architecture of a house. An architecture

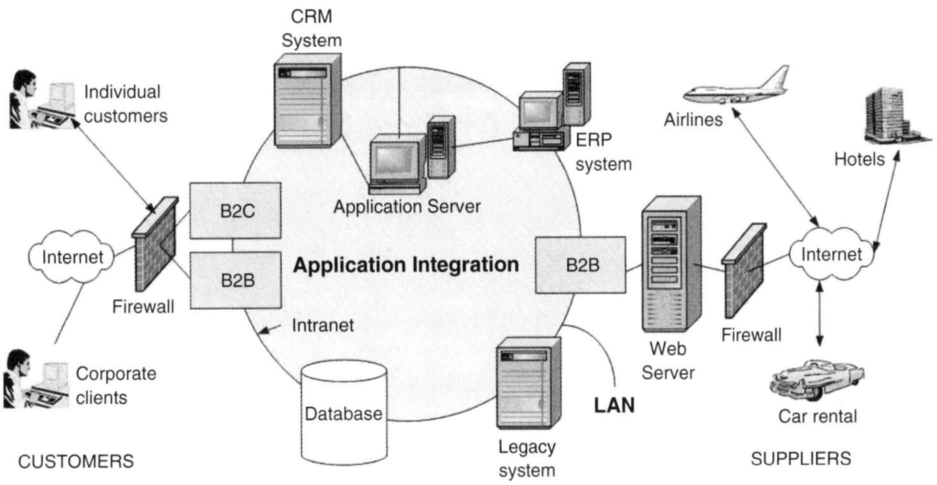

FIGURE 1.1
Architecture of an
online travel agency.

plan describes how the house is to be constructed, including how the various components of the house, such as the plumbing and electrical systems, are to be integrated. Similarly, the IT architecture shows how all aspects of information technology in an organization fit together. Figure 1.1 illustrates the IT architecture of a travel agency. We discuss each part of this figure in subsequent chapters.

Information Technology Infrastructure

An organization's **information technology (IT) infrastructure** consists of the physical facilities, IT components, IT services, and IT personnel that support the entire organization (see Figure 1.2). Starting from the bottom of Figure 1.2, we see that *IT components* are the computer hardware, software, and communications technologies that provide the foundation for all of an organization's information systems. As we move up the pyramid in Figure 1.2, we see that *IT personnel* use IT components to produce *IT services*, which include data management, systems development, and security concerns. To illustrate this model, IT's About Business 1.1 shows how the Queen Mary 2 uses her IT infrastructure to ensure a pleasant, memorable cruise for her passengers.

Computer-Based Information Systems

The IT architecture and IT infrastructure provide the basis for all information systems in the organization. An **information system (IS)** collects, processes, stores, analyzes, and disseminates information for a specific purpose. A **computer-based information system (CBIS)** is an information system that uses computer technology to perform some or all of its intended tasks. Although not all information systems are computerized, most are. For this reason the term "information system" is typically used synonymously with "computer-based information system." The basic components of information systems are listed below. Note that in Figure 1.2 the hardware, software, and networks are IT components, and the database is an IT service.

- **Hardware** is a device such as the processor, monitor, keyboard, and printer. Together, these devices accept data and information, process them, and display them.
- **Software** is a program or collection of programs that enable the hardware to process data.
- A **database** is a collection of related files or tables containing data.
- A **network** is a connecting system (wireline or wireless) that permits different computers to share resources.

IT's About Business

1.1 Passengers Get Royal Treatment on the Queen Mary 2

The Queen Mary 2 (QM2) is the first ship built by the Cunard Line since it launched the Queen Elizabeth 2 (QE2) in 1969. The QM2 is the largest passenger ship in history. She cost more than $780 million, including $8 million for her IT infrastructure. She has more than 1,300 cabins and can carry more than 2,600 passengers. For a tour of the QM2, see *www.cunard.com/QM2/home.asp*.

The Cunard Line had to ensure that the ship's information systems matched the expectations of passengers who paid anywhere from $2,800 to $37,499 for their voyage. The QM2 has a first-class IT infrastructure. The ship has three communications rooms, each located in a different fire zone. Significantly, the major computer systems are duplicated among the communications rooms, and fiber-optic cabling is deployed in parallel connections. This arrangement ensures that every major component of the network has a backup.

The QM2 also has an interactive TV system. Every cabin has an interactive TV controller hidden in its cabinetry. Whereas the interactive TV systems on most cruise ships use computer-controlled racks of videocassette players to deliver pay-per-view movies, the QM2 treats movies like any other digital content, storing them on hard disks. This system provides passengers with greater viewing flexibility. For example, passengers can stop playback of a movie before dinner and resume at the same spot later in the evening. The system also enables passengers to send and receive e-mail, make restaurant reservations, and order a bottle of wine for dinner. The interactive TV e-mail accounts have proven to be popular among passengers, which is good news for Cunard at $1.50 per message.

In addition, every shop and restaurant aboard the ship has personal computers and point-of-sale terminals. The QM2 also offers passengers network services through an Internet café and wireless access points throughout its public areas.

Unfortunately, the deployment of information technology on the QM2 was not without its glitches. For example, when the ship had its shakedown cruises, passengers reported being locked out of their rooms. It turned out that something was wrong with the QM2's system for controlling the electronic door locks. For cabins with more than one passenger, the door lock system was generating a separate key code for each person. However, the door lock recognized only one combination at a time. This software problem took two days to fix.

One passenger took advantage of the QM2's technology this way. She used the interactive TV to order photos taken by the ship's photographers, make restaurant reservations, and exchange e-mail with her dog sitter. She also avoided making trips to the purser's office and other distant locations on the ship.

Sources: Compiled from D. Carr, "Cunard Line: Royal Treatment." *Baseline Magazine*, August 1, 2004; and *www.cunard.com*, accessed March 1, 2005.

QUESTIONS

1. Describe the information technology infrastructure on the QM2.
2. What extra considerations might be involved in installing an IT infrastructure on a ship versus on land? How would you address those considerations?

- **Procedures** are the set of instructions about how to combine the above components in order to process information and generate the desired output.
- **People** are those individuals who use the hardware and software, interface with it, or use its output.

Computer-based information systems have many capabilities. Table 1.1 summarizes the most important ones.

Table 1.1

Major Capabilities of Information Systems

- Perform high-speed, high-volume, numerical computations.
- Provide fast, accurate communication and collaboration within and among organizations.
- Store huge amounts of information in an easy-to-access, yet small, space.
- Allow quick and inexpensive access to vast amounts of information, worldwide.
- Facilitate the interpretation of vast amounts of data.
- Increase the effectiveness and efficiency of people working in groups in one place or in several locations, anywhere.
- Automate both semiautomatic business processes and manual tasks.

Application Programs

An **application program** is a computer program designed to support a specific task or business process. Each functional area or department within a business organization employs dozens of application programs. Note that application programs are synonymous with applications. For instance, the human resources department sometimes uses one application for screening job applicants and another for monitoring employee turnover. The collection of application programs in a single department is usually referred to as a *departmental information system*. For example, the collection of application programs in the human resources area is called the *human resources information system* (*HRIS*). We can see in Figure 1.2 that there are collections of application programs—that is, information systems—in the other functional areas as well, such as accounting and finance. IT's About Business 1.2 shows how a variety of applications enable Commerce Bank to successfully serve its customers.

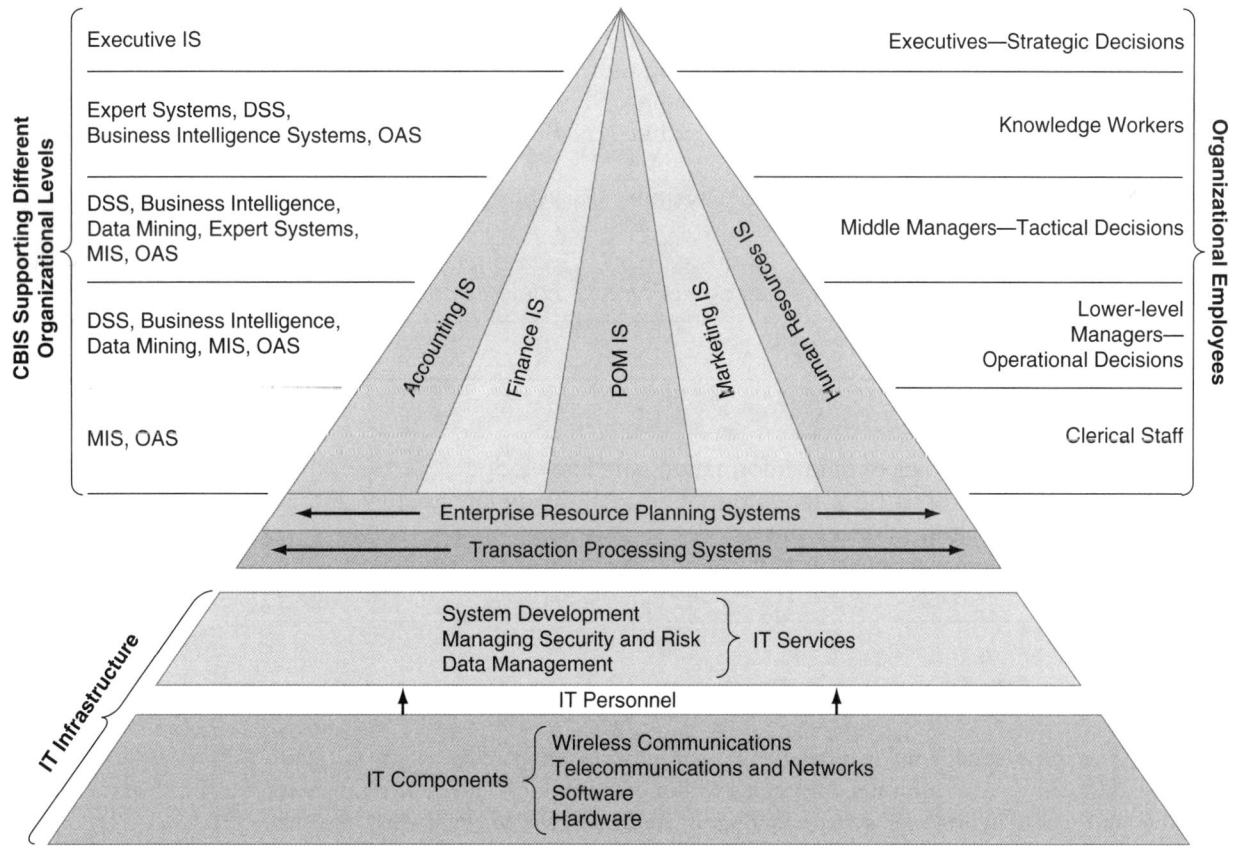

FIGURE 1.2 Information technology inside your organization.

IT's About Business

1.2 IT Helps Commerce Bank Branch Out

Commerce Bank (*www.commerce online.com*) is expanding its number of branches dramatically. The bank's focus on retail customers comes at a time when most banks are trying to close their branches. Bank branches require buildings, staff, and maintenance—all areas that cost more than ATMs and online banking. Yet surveys show that customers like doing business in person, and branch banking remains the largest single channel of business for banks.

Commerce Bank uses IT extensively to provide customers with very efficient service, including quick access to tellers. The typical Commerce branch handles 45,000 transactions per month, and some handle twice that number. However, the lobby never fills up because Commerce Bank tellers average less than 11 seconds for each customer transaction.

Commerce employees are delighted with IT systems such as the "signature upon screen" system. "Signature upon screen" pulls up a scanned image of a customer's signature as soon as the customer enters an account number, thus verifying his or her identity very quickly. Employees also like the bank's WOW Answer Guide. This is an online help system designed to make sure that anyone who is working with customers can find the answers to questions without having to walk away from the customers or

ask someone else for help. Further, the new Browser Teller System enables the head teller to settle the branch's books for the day in just four keystrokes. The IT systems enable Commerce Bank to comply with the new Check Clearing for the Twenty-First Century Act (Check 21), which requires banks to make deposited funds available the next business day. Check 21 eliminates the float period—that time between when customers deposit a check and when they have access to the money.

IT has certainly contributed to Commerce Bank's bottom line. In the most recent quarter, bank revenues were up 31 percent, profits increased 42 percent, deposits rose 34 percent, and total assets grew 33 percent.

Sources: Compiled from M. Fitzgerald, "Branching Out," *CIO Insight*, January 5, 2005; and *www.commerceonline.com*, accessed March 3, 2005.

QUESTIONS

1. How do the information systems at Commerce Bank provide the bank with a competitive advantage?
2. What issues other than speed should Commerce consider when planning customer service? Can you offer any suggestions as to how Commerce could address these concerns?

Before you go on. . .

1. Provide other examples of data, information, and knowledge.
2. Describe the difference between information technology architecture and information technology infrastructure.
3. What is the difference between applications and computer-based information systems?

1.2 Types of Information Systems

Today, organizations employ many different types of information systems. Figure 1.2 illustrates the different types of information systems within organizations, and Figure 1.3 shows the different types of information systems among organizations. We briefly discuss information systems in the next section. In doing so we highlight the numerous and diverse types of support these systems provide, both within a single organization and among organizations.

Breadth of Support of Information Systems

Certain information systems support parts of organizations, others support entire organizations, and still others support groups of organizations. We discuss each of these types of systems in this section.

As we have seen, each department or functional area within an organization has its own collection of application programs, or information systems. These **departmental information systems**, or **functional area information systems**, are located at the top of Figure 1.2. Each information system supports a particular functional area in the organization. Examples are accounting IS, finance IS, production/operations management (POM) IS, marketing IS, and human resources IS.

Just below the functional area IS are two information systems that support the entire organization: enterprise resource planning systems and transaction processing systems. **Enterprise resource planning (ERP) systems** are designed to correct a problem within the functional area IS. ERP systems were an important innovation because the various functional area ISs were often developed as standalone systems and did not communicate effectively (if at all) with one another. ERP systems resolve this problem by tightly integrating the functional area IS via a common database. In doing so they enhance communications among the functional areas of an organization. For this reason, experts credit ERP systems with greatly increasing organizational productivity.

In contrast to an ERP system, a **transaction processing system (TPS)** supports the monitoring, collection, storage, and processing of data from the organization's basic business transactions, each of which generates data. For example, when you are checking out of Wal-Mart, each time the cashier swipes an item across the bar code reader, that is one transaction. The TPS collects data continuously, typically in *real time*—that is, as soon as the data are generated—and provides the input data for the corporate databases. The TPSs are considered critical to the success of any enterprise because they support core operations. We discuss both TPSs and ERP systems in detail in Chapter 8.

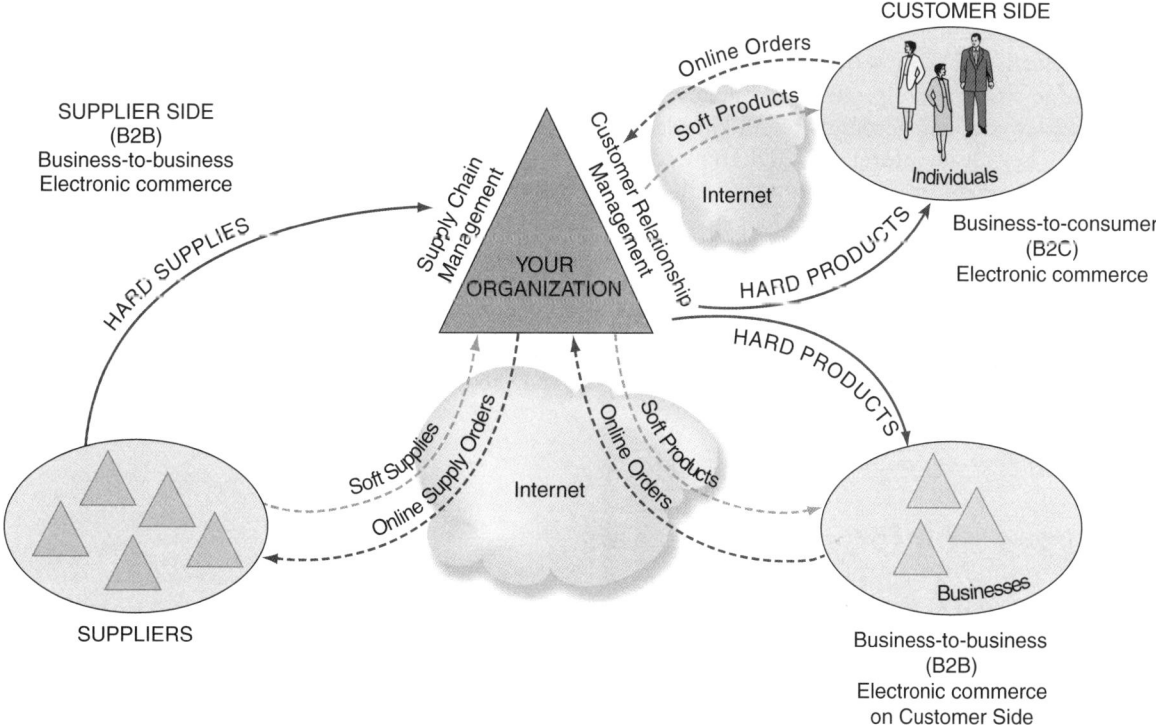

FIGURE 1.3 Information technology outside your organization (your supply chain).

Information systems that connect two or more organizations are referred to as **interorganizational information systems (IOSs)**. IOSs support many interorganizational operations, of which supply chain management is the best known. An organization's **supply chain** describes the flow of materials, information, money, and services from raw material suppliers through factories and warehouses to the end customers.

Note that the supply chain in Figure 1.3 shows both physical flows and information flows. Information flows and digitizable products (e.g., music and software) go through the Internet, whereas physical products are shipped. For example, when you order a computer from *www.dell.com*, your information goes to Dell via the Internet. When your transaction is complete (i.e., your credit card is approved and your order is processed), Dell ships your computer to you. Figure 1.3 represents information flows and digitizable products (soft products) with dotted lines and physical products (hard products) as solid lines. Digitizable products are those that can be represented in electronic form, such as music and software.

Electronic commerce systems are another type of interorganizational information system. These systems enable organizations to conduct transactions, called business-to-business (B2B) electronic commerce, and customers to conduct transactions with businesses, called business-to-consumer (B2C) electronic commerce. They are typically Internet-based. Figure 1.3 illustrates B2B and B2C electronic commerce. Electronic commerce systems are so important that we discuss them at length throughout the book. For example, IT's About Business 1.3 shows how Pratt & Whitney uses the Internet to collaborate with its customers and suppliers.

Support for Organizational Employees

So far we've concentrated on information systems that support specific functional areas and operations. We now consider information systems that support particular employees within the organization. The right side of Figure 1.2 identifies these employees. Note that they range from clerical workers all the way up to executives.

Clerical workers, who support managers at all levels of the organization, include bookkeepers, secretaries, electronic file clerks, and insurance claim processors. *Lower-level managers* handle the day-to-day operations of the organization, making routine decisions such as assigning tasks to employees and placing purchase orders. *Middle managers* make tactical decisions, which deal with activities such as short-term planning, organizing, and control. **Knowledge workers** are professional employees such as financial and marketing analysts, engineers, lawyers, and accountants. All knowledge workers are experts in a particular subject area. They create information and knowledge, which they integrate into the business. Knowledge workers act as advisors to middle managers and executives. Finally, *executives* make decisions that deal with situations that can significantly change the manner in which business is done. Examples of executive decisions are introducing a new product line, acquiring other businesses, and relocating operations to a foreign country. IT support for each level of employee appears on the left side of Figure 1.2.

Office automation systems (OASs) typically support the clerical staff, lower and middle managers, and knowledge workers. These employees use OAS to develop documents (word

UPDATE: THE PAPERLESS OFFICE

IN   OUT

MANKOFF

IT's About Business

1.3 Pratt & Whitney Collaborates with Customers

Even during flight, commercial airline engines are constantly transmitting information about the status of their parts. On the ground, data recorders at Pratt & Whitney (www.pratt-whitney.com), which builds and maintains these engines for carriers such as Delta Air Lines, capture this information and compare it to required standards to ensure the ongoing health of the engines.

Gaining access to this information used to be both complicated and time consuming. If you were an airline customer of Pratt & Whitney, you had to telephone the company to get an update on your engine. Pratt then had to look up your engine, find your records, and get back to you. To speed up this process, Pratt decided to install entirely secure cable lines that gave its airline customers direct access to Pratt systems. However, this process had its own drawbacks. First, at $2.6 million per year, it was quite expensive. Perhaps more important, because the data were dispersed over 400 different information systems, the new system was nearly as time consuming for customers as the old one.

To streamline the search process, Pratt brought all the data under one virtual, Web-based umbrella. It then customized the experience, depending on who—from the maintenance worker to the airline executive—was looking at the information. In short, Pratt created an "outward-facing" portal that gave customers and suppliers access to the same "inward-facing" portal used by Pratt's 12,000 employees.

Pratt also opted for software that allows users to customize their browsers. This means that in some cases the content is tailored to a customer who is authorized to make purchases. For other users—for example, an engineer—the screen will emphasize information on maintenance and will offer a way to track the upgrade history of any particular engine or part. Further, more than 400 suppliers now have access to drawings and documents for the parts they build for Pratt. Finally, partner companies and clients participate more closely in contract bids in the "Virtual Proposal Center," where engineers, suppliers, and partners collaborate on a proposal. Time saved: 45 days out of a typical 90-day proposal process.

Sources: Compiled from L. Rich, "Case Study: Pratt & Whitney." *CIO Insight,* June 1, 2004; and www.pratt-whitney.com, accessed February 27, 2005.

QUESTIONS

1. How do Pratt's information systems enable the company to get closer to its customers?
2. Is it a good idea to allow Pratt's customers to customize their browsers? What problems might this customization process generate? For example, could it lead to control issues? Explain.

---

processing and desktop publishing software), schedule resources (electronic calendars), and communicate (e-mail, voice mail, videoconferencing, and groupware).

Management information systems (MISs) summarize data and prepare reports, primarily for middle managers, but sometimes for lower-level managers as well. Because these reports typically concern a specific functional area, MISs are an important type of functional area IS.

Decision support systems (DSSs) provide computer-based support for complex, nonroutine decisions, primarily for middle managers and knowledge workers. (They also support lower-level managers, but to a lesser extent.) Two types of DSS—business intelligence (BI) systems and data mining—are used with a data warehouse and allow users to perform their own data analysis. We discuss DSS in Chapter 9 and data warehouses, BI systems, and data mining in Chapter 4.

Expert systems (ES) attempt to duplicate the work of human experts by applying reasoning capabilities, knowledge, and expertise within a specific domain. These systems are primarily designed to support knowledge workers. In contrast, **executive information systems (EIS)** support the top managers of the organization. EIS provide rapid access to timely information and direct access to structured information in the form of reports. We discuss both ES and EIS in Chapter 9. Table 1.2 provides an overview of the different types of information systems used by organizations.

Types of Organizational Information Systems

Type of System	Function	Example
Functional area IS	Support the activities within specific functional area.	System for processing payroll
Transaction processing system	Process transaction data from business events.	Wal-Mart checkout point-of-sale terminal
Enterprise resource planning system	Integrate all functional areas of the organization.	Oracle, SAP
Office automation system	Support daily work activities of individuals and groups.	Microsoft Office
Management information system	Produce reports summarized from transaction data, usually in one functional area.	Report on total sales for each customer
Decision support system	Provide access to data and analysis tools.	"What-if" analysis of changes in budget
Expert system	Mimic human expert in a particular area and make a decision.	Credit card approval analysis
Executive information system	Present structured, summarized information about aspects of business important to executives.	Status of production by product
Supply chain management system	Manage flows of products, services, and information among organizations.	Wal-Mart Retail Link system connecting suppliers to Wal-Mart
Electronic commerce system	Enable transactions among organizations and between organizations and customers.	www.dell.com

Table 1.2

Before you go on. . .

1. Explain how information systems provide support for knowledge workers.
2. As we move up the organization's hierarchy from clerical workers to executives, how does the type of support provided by information systems change?

1.3 Examples of Information Systems

Millions of different information systems are in use throughout the world. The following examples show the diversity of IT applications and the numerous benefits they provide.

IT Helps Your Local 7-Eleven Upscale. 7-Eleven (*www.7-eleven.com*) is searching for wealthier customers and larger profit margins. Therefore, 7-Eleven is banking on a new set of products.

In 1927, 7-Eleven invented the concept of convenience stores. By the 1980s, however, the company was experiencing serious problems. First, they found themselves competing

Examples

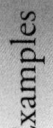

with oil companies that began turning their gas stations into mini convenience stores. In addition, 7-Eleven's supply chain was chaotic. Stores sometimes received more than 80 deliveries per week, with everything from milk to magazines arriving separately and often during prime shopping hours. To make matters worse, the "old guard" executives at 7-Eleven saw the chain's customers as blue-collar, truck-driving men and did not think the company could appeal to a broader customer base. These problems became so severe that in 1990 the company declared bankruptcy.

To regain its competitive status, 7-Eleven has spent more than $500 million on information technology over the past decade. The company has developed sophisticated systems for predicting demand and sales and for filling orders. For example, it has equipped each store with handheld computers that store operators use to place orders each morning for items that need replenishing the next day. These orders are then forwarded to one of the 23 third-party distribution centers with which 7-Eleven has partnered. The data also go to headquarters to be analyzed. At the distribution centers, suppliers drop off their inventory for sorting. Each afternoon, the orders are divided up by store and route. By 5 a.m. the next day, all products have reached their destinations.

Thanks to this updated system, the store manager can obtain real-time data on which products are selling best either at his or her location or across the country in a matter of seconds. He or she can also access instant weather reports. Depending on these forecasts, the store might stock up on umbrellas or on muffins that sell particularly well when the temperature falls below 40 degrees. In addition, 7-Eleven trains managers to stay current on upcoming sporting events or school functions to prepare for a surge in beer purchases or notebook purchases.

7-Eleven's technological overhaul has helped the company regain control over distribution and product decisions that for decades had been dictated by its major suppliers. Traditionally, large suppliers such as Anheuser-Busch and Coca-Cola had exerted enormous influence over which products a convenience store could carry, how much of them it got and when, and even how they were displayed. Now, 7-Eleven is getting suppliers to play by its rules, in part because the precise sales data it generates help the suppliers predict demand for their products nationwide.

The overall results? In 2004, the 7-Eleven company reported revenue of $12 billion, up 12 percent from the previous year. Profits totaled $106 million. The company has enjoyed 32 consecutive quarters of revenue growth, and its stock has achieved a post-bankruptcy high. (*Sources:* Compiled from Elizabeth Esfahani, "7-Eleven Gets Sophisticated," *Business 2.0*, January/February 2005; and *www.7-eleven.com*, accessed March 10, 2005.)

IT's About the Bike, Too. Lance Armstrong is the only person to win the world's most difficult bicycle race, the Tour de France, seven times. To that end, Armstrong spends six hours or more per day training on his bike, mostly in Spain and southern France, to be in shape to beat younger riders. He is his own engine, but the vehicle does matter. Saving the 32-year-old Armstrong as little as 10 watts of energy over the course of a 120-mile stage of the Tour will speed his trip by one minute. Can a single minute actually make a difference in such a long contest? Consider that in his record-tying fifth Tour win in 2003, Armstrong edged German rival Jan Ullrich by a total of 61 seconds after 2,125 miles of racing.

Saving this energy is where Trek Bicycle Corporation (*www.trekbikes.com*) comes in. When the company tests its bikes, it attaches sensors to various parts of the frame. These sensors, which are strain gauges, are wired to a data acquisition unit that is also attached to the frame. This system feeds the output of each ride into a database of more than 5,000 rides taken by Trek testers. Trek's ride database helps its designers understand what happens to the air that flows past and through Armstrong's legs as well as parts of the bike. The database also allows Trek's team to identify the exact locations of stress on the carbon fibers that make up the frame. Employing a combination of three-dimensional modeling software and mechanical design software, Trek designers use this data to design their bikes.

Trek actually designs two bikes for Armstrong. The first is for the "daily drive" in the race pack, or peloton, and the second is designed specifically to race uphill. Indeed, Lance won the toughest stage of the 2004 Tour de France, the L'Alpe d'Huez, the steepest mountain stage of the entire race. His performance was so dominant that he overtook his main rival, Ivan Basso, even though Basso started the time trial two minutes before Lance.

Ten years ago, a typical high-end Trek road bike sold for $2,200. This year, a typical price tag is $4,800. In 2003, Trek produced 3,800 of the Madone bikes (Lance model) for commercial sale. In 2004, Trek produced in excess of 30,000 bikes. Lance's victories and worldwide visibility, at least partly attributable to his computer-designed bikes, are really stimulating sales at Trek. (*Sources:* Compiled from T. Steinart-Threlkeld, "Trek Bicycle Corp: Tour de Force." *Baseline Magazine*, June 28, 2004; and *www.trekbikes.com*, accessed March 3, 2005.)

The Impact of Sarbanes–Oxley on Blue Rhino. Blue Rhino (*www.bluerhino.com*), an independent subsidiary of Ferrellgas Partners (*www.ferrellgas.com*), is the country's largest supplier of propane gas cylinder exchange for backyard grills. (When you run out of propane, you take your empty cylinder back to your supplier and exchange it for a cylinder full of propane.) In the summer of 2002, an event occurred that dramatically affected the company. Congress passed the Sarbanes–Oxley Act, which makes corporate executives more accountable for their company's income statements and balance sheets. Specifically, the law requires chief executives and chief financial officers to vouch for the accuracy of their company's quarterly and annual reports. Further, these executives face prison time if the financial statements turn out to be falsified. To make certain that they are protected from internal fraud and sabotage, companies with a market capitalization greater than $75 million must, at the end of their current fiscal year, issue a management report, signed by its outside auditor, attesting that they have put into place adequate controls on all financially related systems.

Sarbanes–Oxley is forcing Blue Rhino to tone down the aggressive attitude it adopted in building its business. The company's major problem is the large number of people who have to sign off on almost every initiative. For example, to alter a process in the financial system, programmers must obtain three separate approvals. (Prior to Sarbanes–Oxley, only one was required.) Moreover, according to the new rules, a separate programmer must manage each step of the modification. As a result, completing even a minor change can take up to three times as long as previously.

On the positive side, however, Blue Rhino's efforts to meet the demands of Sarbanes–Oxley have produced some benefits for the company. For example, the law lent urgency to a financial reengineering effort that the company had already begun. Faced with a growing retail network, Blue Rhino was drowning in inventory. This problem developed because distributors sent data on receivables and payables to headquarters piecemeal at the end of each month. Accounting staff members had to plug the data into spreadsheets manually and then integrate those spreadsheets into the centralized corporate network. Under this system, closing the books could take a week or more. During this interval, inventory levels in the field were not monitored with sufficient timeliness.

To solve this problem, Blue Rhino documented each process and its associated safeguards to ensure that information could not be changed without appropriate levels of permission. Implementing this solution cost $400,000 and took months of effort.

Efforts to comply with Sarbanes–Oxley also helped Blue Rhino to uncover processes that desperately needed to be fixed even though they were not directly related to financial systems. As one example, human resources traditionally had provided information about each new hire, such as start date and position, to the IT group via telephone or e-mail. This informal procedure slowed down the process of getting an employee into the flow of his or her job. To speed up this process, the company generated an automated human resources application that immediately sends details about a new hire to IT.

Blue Rhino has also changed its purchasing system from a manual process to online forms. Distributors can enter their requests on these forms, which are automatically sent to central purchasing. If the order is approved, based on spending limits and other criteria, it will be filled instantly. In addition, the data pertaining to the order will be shared with accounting, inventory, supply-chain management, and the company's executives.

All this effort had an interesting result. When Blue Rhino was acquired by Ferrellgas Partners in April 2004, it sold for a 22 percent premium over its stock price at the time. (*Sources:* Compiled from J. Rothfelder, "Better Safe Than Sorry: Blue Rhino Corp," *CIO Insight,* February 1, 2004; and *www.bluerhino.com,* accessed March 4, 2005.)

1.4 Managing Information Resources

Clearly, then, a modern organization possesses many information resources. Information resources is a general term that includes all the hardware, software (information systems and applications), data, and networks in an organization. In addition to the computing resources, numerous applications exist, and new ones are continuously being developed. Applications have enormous strategic value. Firms rely on them so heavily that, in some cases, when they are not working (even for a short time), an organization cannot function. In addition, these information systems are very expensive to acquire, operate, and maintain. Therefore, it is essential to manage them properly.

However, it is becoming increasingly difficult to manage an organization's information resources effectively. The reason for this difficulty comes from the evolution of the MIS function in the organization. When businesses first began to use computers in the early 1950s, the *information systems department* (*ISD*) owned the only computing resource in the organization, the mainframe. At that time, end users did not interact directly with the mainframe.

Today, computers are located throughout the organization, and almost all employees use computers in their work. This system is known as *end user computing*. As a result of this change, the ISD no longer owns the organization's information resources. Instead, a partnership has developed between the ISD and the end users. The ISD now acts as more of a consultant to end users, viewing them as customers. In fact, the main function of the ISD is to use IT to solve end users' business problems.

Which IT Resources Are Managed and by Whom

As we just saw, the responsibility for managing information resources is now divided between the ISD and the end users. This arrangement raises several important questions: Which resources are managed by whom? What is the role of the ISD, its structure, and its place within the organization? What is the appropriate relationship between the ISD and the end users? In this section we provide brief answers to these questions.

There are many types of information systems resources. In addition, their components may come from multiple vendors and be of different brands. The major categories of information resources are hardware, software, databases, networks, procedures, security facilities, and physical buildings. These resources are scattered throughout the organization, and some of them change frequently. Therefore, they can be difficult to manage.

To make things more complicated, there is no standard menu for how to divide responsibility for developing and maintaining information resources between the ISD and end users. Instead, that division depends on many things: the size and nature of the organization, the amount and type of IT resources, the organization's attitudes toward computing, the attitudes of top management toward computing, the maturity level of the technology, the

The Changing Role of the Information Systems Department

Manager's Checklist 1.1

Traditional Major IS Functions

- ☐ Managing systems development and systems project management
- ☐ Managing computer operations, including the computer center
- ☐ Staffing, training and developing IS skills
- ☐ Providing technical services
- ☐ Infrastructure planning, development, and control

New (Consultative) Major IS Functions

- ☐ Initiating and designing specific strategic information systems
- ☐ Incorporating the Internet and electronic commerce into the business
- ☐ Managing system integration including the Internet, intranets, and extranets
- ☐ Educating the non-IS managers about IT
- ☐ Educating the IS staff about the business
- ☐ Supporting end-user computing
- ☐ Partnering with the executives
- ☐ Managing outsourcing
- ☐ Proactively using business and technical knowledge to seed innovative ideas about IT
- ☐ Creating business alliances with vendors and IS departments in other organizations

amount and nature of outsourced IT work, and even the country in which the company operates. Generally speaking, the ISD is responsible for corporate-level and shared resources and the end users are responsible for departmental resources.

It is important that the ISD and the end users work closely together and cooperate regardless of who is doing what. Let's begin by looking at the role of the ISD within the organization.

The Role of the IS Department

The role of the director of the ISD is changing from a technical manager to a senior executive, who is often called the **chief information officer (CIO)**. As Manager's Checklist 1.1 shows, the role of the ISD is also changing from a purely technical one to a more managerial and strategic one. For example, the ISD is now responsible for managing the outsourcing of projects and for creating business alliances with vendors and IS departments in other organizations. Because its role has expanded so much, the ISD now reports directly to a senior vice president of administration or even to the CEO. (Previously it reported to a functional department such as accounting.) In its new role, the ISD must be able to work closely with external organizations such as vendors, business partners, consultants, research institutions, and universities.

Inside the organization, the ISD and the end-user units must be close partners. The ISD has the responsibility for setting standards for hardware and software purchases, as well as for information security. The ISD also monitors user hardware and software purchases, and it serves as a gatekeeper in regard to software licensing and illegal downloads (e.g., music files).

IT Offers Career Opportunities

Because information technology is vital to the operation of modern businesses, it offers many employment opportunities. The demand for traditional IT staff—such as programmers, business analysts, systems analysts, and designers—is substantial. In addition, many well-paid jobs exist in emerging areas such as the Internet and e-commerce, mobile commerce, network security, object-oriented programming, telecommunications, and multimedia design. For details about careers in IT, see *www.computerworld.com/careertopics/careers* and *www.monster.com*. In addition, Table 1.3 provides a list of IT jobs along with a description of each one.

Table 1.3

Information Technology Jobs

Position	Job Description
Chief Information Officer	Highest-ranking IS manager; responsible for strategic planning in the organization
IS Director	Responsible for managing all systems throughout the organization and day-to-day operations of the entire IS organization
Information Center Manager	Manages IS services such as help desks, hot lines, training, and consulting
Applications Development Manager	Coordinates and manages new systems development projects
Project Manager	Manages a particular new systems development project
Systems Manager	Manages a particular existing system
Operations Manager	Supervises the day-to-day operations of the data and/or computer center
Programming Manager	Coordinates all applications programming efforts
Systems Analyst	Interfaces between users and programmers; determines information requirements and technical specifications for new applications
Business Analyst	Focuses on designing solutions for business problems; interfaces closely with users to show how IT can be used innovatively
Systems Programmer	Writes the computer code for developing new applications or maintaining existing applications
Emerging Technologies Manager	Forecasts technology trends and evaluates and experiments with new technologies
Network Manager	Coordinates and manages the organization's voice and data networks
Database Administrator	Manages the organization's databases and oversees the use of database management software
Auditing or Computer Security Manager	Manages ethical and legal use of information systems
Webmaster	Manages the organization's World Wide Web site
Web Designer	Creates World Wide Web sites and pages

Before you go on. . .

1. How important are end users to the management of the organization's information resources?
2. Where do you think the IT staff should be located? Should they be decentralized in the functional areas? Centralized at corporate level? A combination of the two? Explain your answer.

1.5 The Plan of This Book

Now that we've covered the basics of information technology and information systems, we'll briefly consider how this book will address these issues. A major objective of this book is to help you understand the roles of information technologies in today's digital organizations. The book is also designed to help you think strategically about information systems. That is, we want you to be able look into the future and see how these tools can help you, your organization, and your world. Finally, the book demonstrates how IT supports all of the functional areas of the organization.

This chapter has introduced you to the basic concepts of information systems in organizations. Chapter 2 will discuss how organizations are using information systems to gain a strategic advantage in an extremely competitive business environment.

Chapter 3 addresses three critical and timely topics: ethics, security, and privacy. Recent corporate scandals such as Enron and Worldcom have emphasized the importance of ethics. Attacks on our information systems (e.g., viruses, worms, identity theft) make it essential that we keep security in mind at all times. Finally, the miniaturization and spread of surveillance technologies leads many people to wonder if they have any privacy left at all.

The amount of data available to us is increasing exponentially, meaning that we have to find methods and tools to manage the deluge. Chapter 4 discusses how to manage data so that we can use them effectively to make decisions.

Chapter 5 looks at telecommunications and networks, including the Internet. We live in a networked world, and the importance of computer networks cannot be overstated.

Electronic commerce, facilitated by the Internet, has revolutionized how businesses operate today. Chapter 6 covers this important topic. One of the newest technologies to impact organizations is wireless communications. We explore this technology in Chapter 7. Chapter 8 provides a detailed picture of the various types of information systems that are used in organizations today. Chapter 9 discusses the various information systems that support managerial decision making. Chapter 10 notes how organizations acquire or develop new applications. Finally, Technology Guides 1 (hardware), and 2 (software) provide a detailed look at the two most fundamental IT components that are the foundation for all information systems.

What's in IT for me?

Now that you have a sense of how this book is structured and organized, we'll conclude the chapter by discussing how and why IT is relevant to students with various business-related majors. As you review this section, keep in mind that technology will play an increasingly vital role in every function and department of modern business organizations.

For the Accounting Major

Data and information are the lifeblood of accounting. Transaction processing systems—which are now Web-based—capture, organize, analyze, and disseminate data and information throughout organizations, often through corporate intranets. The Internet has vastly increased the number of transactions (especially global) in which modern businesses engage. Transactions such as billing customers, preparing payrolls, and purchasing and paying for materials provide data that the accounting department must record and track. These transactions, particularly with customers and suppliers, now usually take place online, through extranets. In addition, accounting information systems must share information with information systems in other parts of a large organization. For example, transactional information from a sales or marketing IS is now input for the accounting system as well.

For the Finance Major

The modern financial world turns on speed, volume, and accuracy of information flow. Information systems and networks make these things possible. Finance departments use information systems to monitor world financial markets and to provide quantitative analyses (e.g., for cash flow projections and forecasting). They use decision support systems to support financial decision making (e.g., portfolio management). Financial managers now use business intelligence software to analyze information in data warehouses. Finally, large-scale information systems (e.g., enterprise resource planning packages) tightly integrate finance with all other functional areas within a wide-ranging enterprise.

For the Marketing Major

Marketing now uses customer databases, decision support systems, sales automation, data warehouses, and business intelligence software to perform its functions. The Internet has created an entirely new global channel for marketing from business-to-business and business-to-consumer. It also has dramatically increased the amount of information available to customers, who can now compare prices quickly and thoroughly. As a result, shoppers have become more knowledgeable and sophisticated. In turn, marketing managers must work harder to acquire and retain customers. To accomplish this goal they now use customer relationship management software. The Internet helps here, because it provides for much closer contact between the customer and the supplier.

For the Production/Operations Management Major

Organizations are competing on price, quality, time (speed), and customer service—all of which are concerns of productions and operations management. Every process in a company's operations that adds value to a product or service (e.g., purchasing inventory, quality control, receiving raw materials, and shipping products) can be enhanced by the use of Web-based information systems. Further, information systems have enabled the production and operations function to link the organization to other organizations in the firm's supply chain. From computer-aided design and computer-aided manufacturing through Web-based ordering systems, information systems support the production and operations function.

For the Human Resources Management Major

Information systems provide valuable support for human resources management. For example, record keeping has greatly improved in terms of speed, convenience, and accuracy as a result of technology. Further, disseminating HR information throughout the company via intranets enables employees to receive consistent information and handle much of their personal business (e.g., configuring their benefits) themselves, without help from HR personnel. The Internet makes a tremendous amount of information available to the job seeker, increasing the fluidity of the labor market. Finally, many careers require skills in the use of information systems. HR professionals must have an understanding of these systems and skills to support hiring, training, and retention within an organization.

The MIS Function

The MIS department directly supports every one of the other functional areas in an organization. The overall objective of MIS personnel is to solve users' business problems using information technology. Often, the MIS function is stereotyped as being only computer programming, but this is not the case.

Some MIS employees actually write computer programs. More often, however, they act as analysts, interfacing between business users on one hand and the programmers on the other. For example, if a marketing manager needs to analyze data that are not in the company's data warehouse, she would forward her information requirements to an MIS analyst. The analyst would then work with MIS database personnel to obtain the needed data and input them into the data warehouse.

1. Differentiate among data, information, and knowledge.

Data items refer to an elementary description of things, events, activities, and transactions that are recorded, classified, and stored, but are not organized to convey any specific meaning. Information is data that have been organized so that they have meaning and value to the recipient. Knowledge consists of data and/or information that have been organized and processed to convey understanding, experience, accumulated learning, and expertise as they apply to a current business problem.

2. Differentiate between information technology infrastructure and information technology architecture.

An organization's information technology *architecture* is a high-level map or plan of the information assets in an organization. The IT architecture integrates the information requirements of the overall organization and all individual users, the IT infrastructure, and all applications. An organization's information technology *infrastructure* consists of the physical facilities, IT components, IT services, and IT management that support the entire organization.

3. Describe the components of computer-based information systems.

A computer-based information system (CBIS) is an information system that uses computer technology to perform some or all of its intended tasks. The basic components of a CBIS are hardware, software, database(s), telecommunications networks, procedures, and people. Hardware is a set of devices that accept data and information, process them, and display them. Software is a set of programs that enable the hardware to process data. A database is a collection of related files, tables, relations, and so on that stores data and the associations among them. A network is a connecting system (wireline or wireless) that permits different computers to share resources. Procedures are the set of instructions about how to combine the above components in order to process information and generate the desired output. People are those individuals who work with the information system, interface with it, or use its output.

4. Describe the various types of information systems by breadth of support.

The departmental information systems, also known as functional area information systems, each support a particular functional area in the organization. Two information systems support the entire organization: enterprise resource planning (ERP) systems and transaction processing systems (TPSs). ERP systems tightly integrate the functional area IS via a common database, enhancing communications among the functional areas of an organization. A TPS supports the monitoring, collection, storage, and processing of data from the organization's basic business transactions.

Information systems that connect two or more organizations are referred to as interorganizational information systems (IOSs). IOSs support many interorganizational operations, of which supply chain management is the best known. Electronic commerce systems enable organizations to conduct business-to-business (B2B) and business-to-consumer (B2C) electronic commerce. They are generally Internet-based.

5. Identify the major information systems that support each organizational level.

At the clerical level, employees are supported by office automation systems and management information systems. At the operational level, managers are supported by office automation systems, management information systems, decision support systems, and business intelligence systems. At the managerial level, functional area management information systems (often called simply MISs) provide the major support. Middle managers are also supported by office automation systems, decision support systems, and business intelligence systems. At the knowledge-worker level, expert systems, decision support systems, and business intelligence systems provide support. Executives are supported mainly by executive information systems.

6. Describe how information resources are managed, and discuss the roles of the information systems department and the end users.

The responsibility for managing information resources is divided between two organizational entities: the information systems department (ISD), which is a corporate entity, and the end users, who are located throughout the organization. Generally speaking, the ISD is responsible for corporate-level and shared resources, while the end users are responsible for departmental resources.

Chapter Glossary

application program (also called **program**) A computer program designed to support a specific task or business process. (8)

chief information officer (CIO) The executive in charge of the information systems department in an organization. (17)

computer-based information system (CBIS) An information system that uses computer technology to perform some or all of its intended tasks. (6)

database A collection of related files, tables, relations, and so on that stores data and the associations among them. (6)

data items An elementary description of things, events, activities, and transactions that are recorded, classified, and stored but are not organized to convey any specific meaning. (5)

decision support systems (DSSs) Information systems that provide computer-based support for complex, non-routine decisions, primarily for middle managers and knowledge workers. (12)

departmental information systems (see functional area information systems) (10)

electronic commerce systems A type of interorganizational information system that enables organizations to conduct transactions with other businesses and with customers. (11)

enterprise resource planning (ERP) systems Systems that tightly integrate the functional area information systems via a common database. (10)

executive information systems (EISs) Information systems that support the top managers of the organization by providing rapid access to timely information and direct access to structured information in the form of reports. (12)

expert systems (ES) Information systems that attempt to duplicate the work of human experts by applying reasoning capabilities, knowledge, and expertise within a specific domain. (12)

functional area information systems (also called departmental information systems) Information systems designed to summarize data and prepare reports for the functional areas, such as accounting and marketing. (10)

hardware A set of devices (e.g., processor, monitor, keyboard, printer) that together accept data and information, process them, and display them. (6)

information Data that have been organized so that they have meaning and value to the recipient. (5)

information system (IS) A process that collects, processes, stores, analyzes, and disseminates information for a specific purpose; most ISs are computerized. (6)

information technology (IT) An organization's collection of information resources, the users of these resources, and the management that oversees these resources. (2)

information technology architecture A high-level map or plan of the information assets in an organization. (5)

information technology infrastructure The physical facilities, IT components, IT services, and IT personnel that support the entire organization. (6)

interorganizational information system (IOS) Information systems that connect two or more organizations. (10)

knowledge Data and/or information that have been organized and processed to convey understanding, experience, accumulated learning, and expertise as they apply to a current problem or activity. (5)

knowledge workers Professional employees who are experts in a particular subject area and create information and knowledge. (12)

management information systems (MISs) Information systems that summarize data and prepare reports, primarily for middle managers, but sometimes for lower-level managers as well. (12)

network A connecting system (wireline or wireless) that permits different computers to share their information. (6)

office automation systems (OASs) Information systems that typically support the clerical staff, lower and middle managers, and knowledge workers. (12)

people Those individuals who use the hardware and software, interface with it, or use its output. (7)

procedures The set of instructions about how to combine components of information systems in order to process information and generate the desired output. (7)

software A set of programs that enables the hardware to process data. (6)

supply chain The flow of materials, information, money, and services from raw material suppliers through factories and warehouses to the end customers. (10)

transaction processing system An information system that supports the monitoring, collection, storage, processing, and dissemination of data from the organization's basic business transactions. (10)

Discussion Questions

For review and practice questions and self-quizzes, go to www.wiley.com/college/rainer

1. Discuss the logic of building information systems in accordance with the organization's hierarchical structure.
2. Describe how IT architecture and IT infrastructure are interrelated.
3. Is the Internet an infrastructure, an architecture, or an application program? Why? If none of the above, then what is it?
4. Knowledge workers comprise the largest segment of the workforce in U.S. business today. However, many industries need skilled workers who are not knowledge workers. What are some examples of these industries? What might replace these skilled workers? When might the U.S. economy need more skilled workers than knowledge workers?
5. Using Figure 1.3 as your guide, draw a model of a supply chain with your university as the central focus. Keep in mind that every university has suppliers and customers.
6. Explain how office automation systems, management information systems, and decision support systems can support multiple levels of the organization.

Problem-Solving Activities

1. Characterize each of the following systems as one (or more) of the IT support systems:
   a. A student registration system in a university.
   b. A system that advises physicians about which antibiotics to use for a particular infection.
   c. A patient-admission system in a hospital.
   d. A system that provides a human resources manager with reports regarding employee compensation by years of service.
   e. A robotic system that paints cars in a factory.

2. Review the systems of the following companies, presented in this chapter, and identify the support provided by IT:
   - The Boston Red Sox
   - 7-Eleven
   - The Cunard Line
   - Commerce Bank
   - Pratt & Whitney
   - Trek Bicycle
   - Blue Rhino
   - Albertson's

Internet Activities

1. Enter the site of *Dell.com*, and find the current information systems used by the company. Explain how the systems' innovations contribute to Dell's success.
2. Surf the Internet for information about Homeland Security. Examine the available information, and comment on the role of information technologies in Homeland Security.
3. Access Truste (*www.truste.org*), and find the guidelines that Web sites displaying its logo must follow. What are the guidelines? Why is it important for Web sites to be able to display the Truste logo on their sites?
4. Enter *cio.com* and find recent information on the changing role of the CIO and the ISD. What is the role of the CIO in organizations today?

Team Assignments

1. Observe your local Wal-Mart checkout counter. Find material on the Web that describes how the scanned code is translated into the price that the customers pay. (Hint: Look at *www.howstuffworks.com*.)
   a. Identify the following components of the Wal-Mart system: inputs, processes, and outputs.
   b. What kind of a system is the scanner (TPS, DSS, EIS, ES, etc.)? Why did you classify it as you did?
   c. Having the information electronically in the system may provide opportunities for additional managerial uses of that information. Identify such uses.
   d. Checkout systems are now being replaced by self-service checkout kiosks and scanners. Compare the two in terms of speed, ease of use, and problems that may arise (e.g., an item that the scanner does not recognize).
2. Divide the class into teams. Each team will select a country government and visit its official Web site (e.g., try the United States, Australia, New Zealand, Singapore, Norway, Canada, the United Kingdom, the Netherlands, Denmark, Germany, and France). For example, the official Web portal for the U.S. government is *www.firstgov.gov*. Review and compare the services offered by each country. How does the United States stack up? Are you surprised at the number of services offered by countries through Web sites? Which country offers the most services? The least?

Can IT Save Albertson's from Wal-Mart?

THE BUSINESS PROBLEM Wal-Mart has changed the rules of competition in the grocery business. It uses its massive purchasing power, cheap labor, big-box stores, and automated distribution centers to outsell existing grocery store chains. The company now sells $56 billion of groceries per year.

Wal-Mart is threatening Albertson's, a grocery store chain with $36 billion in revenue (*www.albertsons.com*). Wal-Mart makes a profit of 3.3 cents on each dollar of sales, compared to only 1.4 cents for Albertson's. To make matters worse, Albertson's distribution and transportation costs are 3 to 5 percent higher than Wal-Mart's.

Albertson's used to contend that their stores were smaller than Wal-Mart's. As a result, customers could find items more quickly and have a better shopping experience. However, to compete with traditional grocery stores, Wal-Mart has responded with Wal-Mart Neighborhood Markets, which are the size of Albertson's and are much smaller than Wal-Mart Supercenters. Neighborhood Markets have fewer live cashiers than Albertson's. Instead they rely heavily on self-checkout registers where customers can scan and bag their own groceries.

The reality is that, compared to Wal-Mart, Albertson's costs are higher, its wages are higher, its prices are higher, and its profit margins are lower. Wal-Mart can also negotiate better prices with suppliers and get those products to stores faster and less expensively.

THE IT SOLUTION Albertson's is implementing many IT initiatives:
- To speed up checkout, the company is installing 4,500 NCR self-checkout terminals in its 2,300 stores at an estimated cost of about $18 million. The terminals will help get customers out of stores faster and will reduce Albertson's staffing costs.

- Albertson's wants to fill a bigger portion of every shopping basket. To do that it has to know its customers better. To accomplish this goal the company has installed an NCR Teradata data warehouse at headquarters to analyze corporate and customer data. Using data from customer-loyalty cards, Albertson's can match individual buying preferences against store inventories. Albertson's can also launch preemptive strikes against its competition by rewarding its best customers with special promotions and pricing.
- Albertson's is building iSupplier Web portals that enable suppliers to view and accept purchase orders as well as create shipping notices. The company wants to eliminate mailing purchase orders and to cut down on costly phone and fax inquiries.
- Albertson's has implemented retail-pricing software from KhiMetrics (*www.khimetrics.com*) to keep its prices competitive with Wal-Mart while maximizing profits.
- IBM is providing a repository for standardized product information for Albertson's. Further, Albertson's has asked all its suppliers to synchronize their product information through UCCnet (*www.uccnet.org*), a nonprofit industry organization. UCCnet has created a Web database of 14-character product codes that it hopes will eventually replace Universal Product Codes (UPCs). The goal is to create one global language for retailers and suppliers. This way, Albertson's buyers can talk to and "be on the same page with" suppliers all over the world.
- At its head office, Albertson's has consolidated financial operations into Oracle enterprise applications. The

company has deployed PeopleSoft (now owned by Oracle) software for all its human resources functions.

THE RESULTS Despite all of these IT initiatives, the results for Albertson's are not promising. Even though the company has been able to cut costs by more than $500 million, administrative and operating expenses have continued to rise. Meanwhile, Wal-Mart continues to improve its Retail Link Network, which provides its suppliers with information on how their products are being sold in Wal-Mart stores. Wal-Mart now sells 50 percent more groceries than Albertson's. In fact, it opened 30 Wal-Mart Neighborhood Markets and 210 Supercenters in 2004 alone. As a result, despite heavy investment in information technologies, Albertson's long-term future is in doubt.

Sources: Compiled from M. Duvall and K. Nash, "Albertson's: A Shot at the Crown," *Baseline Magazine*, February 5, 2004; and *www. albertsons.com*, accessed January 19, 2005.

QUESTIONS

1. What information systems is Albertson's developing in its attempt to compete with Wal-Mart?
2. Do you think that, in the long run, Albertson's will be able to compete with Wal-Mart? Why or why not? (Hints: Consider many variables such as wage and benefit levels, suppliers, store name and reputation, number and accessibility of stores. Also, the Supercenters attract customers who are shopping for nonfood items.)

Interactive Learning

Information Systems: Concepts and Management

Go to the Interactivities section on the WileyPLUS Web site and access Chapter 1: Information Systems: Concepts and Management. There, you will *find some animated, hands-on activities that visually explain the concepts in this chapter.*

Starting Your Internship at Club IT

Go to the Club IT link on the *WileyPLUS* Web site. There you will find a description of your internship at this downtown music venue, as well as some as- signments that will help you learn how to apply IT solutions to a virtual business.

wiley.com/college/rainer

Chapter 2

Chapter Preview

In Chapter 1 we discussed the concept of information technology and how businesses use IT in every facet of their operations. In this chapter we focus more specifically on the fundamental and powerful roles that information technologies play in helping businesses survive and prosper in today's dynamic, competitive, global environment. To do this we first examine how business is done at the beginning of the twenty-first century. We also describe how various pressures are forcing businesses to transition from the Old Economy to the New Economy. We then demonstrate that any information system can be *strategic*, meaning that it can provide a competitive advantage, if it is used properly. At the same time, we also provide examples of information systems that have failed, often at a great cost to the enterprise. We finish up the chapter by considering why you should learn about information technology.

The Modern Organization in the Digital Economy

Introduction to Information Systems
R. Kelly Rainer, Jr., Efraim Turban, and Richard E. Potter. ISBN 978-0-471-7363-3

Learning Objectives

1. Describe the characteristics of the digital economy and e-business.

2. Discuss the relationships among business pressures, organizational responses, and information systems.

3. Describe strategic information systems (SISs), and explain their advantages.

4. Describe Porter's competitive forces model and how IT helps companies improve their competitive positions.

5. Describe five strategies that companies can use to achieve competitive advantage in their industries.

What's in IT for me?   ACC   FIN   MKT   POM   HRM   MIS

27

CASE **Can IT Help Congestion at Major Airports?**

The Business Problem

If you have ever stood for hours in seemingly endless lines at an airport, this case about Toronto International Airport (*www.gtaa.com*) offers hope. The federal government's deregulation of the airline industry in 1978 led to the development of the "hub-and-spoke" system of airline flights. A hub is a central airport through which flights are routed. From that hub, the spoke flights take passengers to their destinations. Most major airlines have multiple hubs (for example, Delta has hubs in Atlanta, Cincinnati, and Salt Lake City). They claim that hubs allow them to offer more flights for passengers.

Would-be competitors challenge the argument that the hub-and-spoke is efficient. They charge that although the skies have been deregulated, the ground has not. The major airlines, especially in their hub airports, typically occupy entire terminals and therefore have sole access to all of the gates in those terminals. As a result, when a dominant carrier is not using one of its gates, no

© AP/Wide World Photos

other airline can use it either. Instead, the gate sits idle while competitors' planes either are stuck on the tarmac or are forced to dock at gates leased at a smaller, less-convenient airport located nearby. This inefficient system has generated major scheduling problems regarding available gates. In turn, these problems have led to endless lines at check-in and security.

At their hub airports, major airlines can lease gates for as long as 30 years at a stretch. They are then free to install their own computer networks, run their own telephone systems, and set up proprietary computer terminals. As a result, major airports must accommodate different proprietary systems from multiple airlines. This arrangement also creates major inefficiencies.

One solution to the problems at major airports is the "common-use airport," which we describe below. However, airlines that dominate their hubs often resist switching to common-use airports for fear of losing their competitive advantage. To understand how common-use airports could make air travel more efficient, let's take a look at the new Terminal 1 at Toronto's Pearson International Airport. (See *http://www.airport-technology.com/projects/toronto/images/overhead_13.jpg.*)

The IT Solution

In common-use airports, the airport—not the airlines—manages the telecommunications network, telecommunications, video feeds, check-in counters, gates, security, and baggage systems. Hardware, software, and telecommunications are standardized throughout the airport. In addition, the check-in counters and gates can be switched around seamlessly, and passengers and planes move more fluidly in and around the airport.

At Terminal 1 in Toronto, the airport installed 50 express check-in kiosks, 40 passenger information phones on four different levels of the terminal, 250 passenger check-in counter stations, 450 flight and baggage displays (all flat-panel monitors), 300 electronic message boards, and 9,700 directional signs. The single most important aspect of the huge project was the use of the Internet Protocol (IP) for telephones, ticketing terminals, and self-service passenger kiosks. Thousands of security cameras, providing video feeds, transmit over the IP network, as do the television broadcasts. Passengers and airport officials can view this information on monitors located in the waiting areas, baggage claims, and bars and restaurants. This information includes flight number, destination, boarding time, and the weather at the destination. Passengers know when to go to their gates, and when their row will be boarding.

The cost of these information technologies? Approximately $1 billion and four years of effort.

Terminal 1 opened in April 2004. By the end of June, the airport already reported a 15 percent increase in total passengers. Terminal 1 handles passengers from as many as 800 daily flights from 57 airlines, totaling about 10 million passengers a year. The common-use model saves money for both the airlines and the airports. Airlines save the costs and problems of managing their proprietary IT systems in every city they serve. At the same time, airports can create an entirely new source of revenue. In fact, the common-use system in Terminal 1 is saving the Toronto airport approximately $3 million per gate.

The Results

This case illustrates how an organization can use information technology to achieve a competitive advantage in the digital age. The new information system at Toronto International Airport illustrates the following points.

- It is sometimes necessary to change business models and strategies to succeed in the digital economy.

- IT enables organizations to gain competitive advantage and to survive in the face of serious business pressures.

- IT may require a large investment over a long period of time.

- An extensive networked computing infrastructure is necessary to support large organizations today.

- Internet-based applications can be used to provide superb customer service.

This case has shown us how fierce competition can drive even large organizations in mature industries to find ways to reduce costs, increase productivity, and improve customer service. These efforts are best achieved by using Internet-based systems, which are the major enablers in the transformation to an e-business in the digital economy. Toronto International Airport now performs various functions electronically in order to enhance its operations. The airport uses its new information systems in Terminal 1 to reduce costs, increase profits, and improve the passenger experience. All of these changes ultimately will increase customer satisfaction.

In the next section, we describe the pressures under which businesses operate in today's extremely competitive environment. We also examine the steps that companies are taking to counter these pressures.

What We lLearned From This Case

Sources: Compiled from Dan Briody, "Seize the Gate," *CIO Insight*, July 1, 2004; D. Grossman, "Disappearing Hub: It's a Myth," *USA Today*, March 14, 2005; and *www.gtaa.com*, accessed February 22, 2005.

2.1 Doing Business in the Digital Economy

In the twenty-first century, all organizations—for-profit, nonprofit, private sector, public sector—operate in the **digital economy**, which is an economy based on digital technologies. The digital economy is also called the *Internet economy*, the *new economy*, or the *Web economy*.

In this new economy, digital infrastructures provide a global platform over which people and organizations interact, communicate, collaborate, and search for information. This global platform includes:

- A huge number of digitizable products; that is, products that can be converted to digital format. The most common digitizable products are books, magazines, television and radio programs, movies, electronic games, music CDs, and computer software.

- Consumers and firms that conduct financial transactions digitally.

- Physical goods such as home appliances and automobiles that contain embedded computer chips and connectivity capabilities.

Within the digital economy, businesses increasingly perform their basic functions—buying and selling goods and services, servicing customers, and collaborating with business partners—electronically. This process is known as **e-business** or **e-commerce**. Organizations and individuals use digital technologies to access information stored in many places and to communicate and collaborate with others, all from their desktop or mobile computers. Their computers may be connected to the global networked environment, known as the *Internet*, or to its counterpart within organizations, called an *intranet*. In addition, many companies link their intranets to those of their business partners over networks called *extranets*. These connections typically are done via wireline systems. Since 2000, though, more and more communication and collaboration are being done via wireless systems.

The New Economy versus the Old Economy

Information technologies have brought significant changes to the way organizations do business. In fact, these technologies have paved the way for the transformation to the new, digital economy from the old economy. Here are a few examples that illustrate the differences.

Example #1: Registering for Classes

Old Economy (the way your parents' generation registered)   You must visit each department in person to obtain a computer punchcard with the course information on it. You then go to the Registrar's Office to turn in the cards. There you wait in long lines to have the cards processed by a clerk.

New Economy   To register for classes, you access your campus Web site, log into the registration site, and electronically register for classes without leaving your room. The registration Web site automatically checks for prerequisites, overloads, full classes, and other constraints.

Example #2: Photography

Old Economy   You use a camera with film, which you have to purchase and have developed. In addition, you must make multiple trips to the store if you want reprints. If family and friends want copies, then you also must go to the Post Office to mail them. Of course, if you want to take movies, then you need a different type of camera.

New Economy   First-generation digital photography allows you to scan the photos that were produced by the old economy process. After scanning your photos, you can enlarge them or send them to family or friends via e-mail.

In the second generation of digital photography, digital cameras are now capable of taking both photos and movies with no film or processing required. You can view the results immediately and then edit them on your home computer. Finally, you can forward them to family and friends, who can receive them on their personal computers, personal digital assistants (PDAs), or cell phones.

In the third generation of digital photography, your digital camera is now integrated into your cell phone, palmtop computer, or binoculars. You can take pictures wherever you are and then transmit them within a few seconds to any destination on the Internet for either viewing or reprints. The paparazzi use this technology to sell pictures of celebrities to the tabloids.

Example #3: Paying for Gasoline

Old Economy   You drive up to the gas station, fill up your tank, and then go inside to stand in line to pay for your gas, using either cash or a credit card.

New Economy.   Travelers insert their credit cards in the card-swipe slot on the pump, receive authorization for the charge, pump gas, and receive a receipt before driving away.

The Exxon Mobil (*www.exxonmobil.com*) Speedpass is an example of the newest generation of pay-at-the-pump systems. You simply wave the Speedpass token, which you carry on a key ring, across a sensor. The short-range wireless link starts an automatic activation and authorization process, and the total purchase is then charged to a preapproved credit card. You never have to take your credit cards or cash out of your car. You can enroll online to get your Speedpass at *https://www.speedpass.com/care/signup.jsp.*

Example #4: Paying for Transportation in New York City

Old Economy   New Yorkers have been using tokens for more than 50 years for bus and subway transportation. The tokens replaced cash, thereby eliminating long waiting lines. However, they cost more than $6 million per year to manufacture, collect, and process.

New Economy   Bus and subway riders now use MetroCards, which are offered at discounts. Chicago and Washington, D.C., as well as Paris and London, have converted to transit cards. In Hong Kong, millions of commuters use contactless cards not only for transportation but also for telephone, Internet access, food in vending machines, and much more. Contactless cards have no battery or power. When they are near a reader, they are "awakened" by the reader's electromagnetic waves. A small radio transmitter in the card transmits account information to the reader. We discuss contactless cards in Chapter 7.

Photo courtesy of MTA. Metrocard is a Metropolitan Transportation Authority Trademark.

In the next generation, travelers will use wireless devices, perhaps carried on a key chain. They will walk past a reader that will automatically debit their credit cards, debit cards, or bank accounts.

Example #5: Paying for Goods: The Checkout Experience

Old Economy   In the "old-old" economy, the customer selects goods, waits in line for the cashier to key in the price of each item, and then pays in cash. Neither the store nor the customer retains any information regarding the purchase.

In the first generation of digital checkout, the customer takes the items to checkout, and a clerk swipes the bar code of each item over a reader to capture the price and description of each item. The register then prints an itemized list with a total price. The shopper pays with cash, credit card, or debit card. Information scanned into the store's database is available almost instantly for analysis by the organization. This system is an example of *source-data automation*, which minimizes the role of people in inputting data.

In the second generation of digital checkout, shoppers take their items to a self-service kiosk and swipe the barcode of each item themselves. They then pay with cash, credit card, or debit card. Information is gathered for future use as in the previous generation of digital checkout.

IT's About Business

2.1 The Real Estate Industry in the New Economy

The Internet is dramatically changing how people look for new homes. Today, more than 70 percent of homebuyers shop online before buying a home, up from 41 percent in 2000. The shopper makes a few mouse clicks, and up pop photographs, floor plans, and often video clips for all types of properties.

What is less obvious is how all these Web-surfing home-buyers are changing the real estate industry. With a flood of data at their fingertips, they are becoming more knowledgeable. In turn, they are using this knowledge to chip away at the 6 percent commission that real estate brokers collect on each home they sell. Companies are responding to the needs of these new Internet-savvy customers. For example, by using the Web to cut costs, ZipRealty Inc. (*www.ziprealty.com*) can refund 20 percent of its commission to buyers and 25 percent to sellers. ZipRealty cuts costs by having its agents work via the Internet from home, rather than in offices. Agents get online training and sales tools, which help them sell two to three times as many homes than typical realtors.

In addition, HomeGain.com (*www.homegain.com*) and LendingTree (*www.lendingtree.com*), two leading mortgage providers, will also have a large impact on the real estate industry. These companies are using the Web to identify home sellers and buyers and funnel them to realtors. The companies are giving potential clients' names to several real estate agents and letting them fight it out. This process pressures the realtors to be more competitive, offer better service, and cut rates. In exchange for helping them find clients more cheaply and quickly, brokers pay HomeGain and LendingTree up to 35 percent of their commissions when they close a sale.

Better service and reduced rates affect consumer expectations. As a result, many real estate agents are cutting rates, amid pressure from customers.

Sources: Compiled from T. J. Mullaney, "Real Estate's New Reality," *BusinessWeek*, May 10, 2004, pp. 88, 90; *www.ziprealty.com, www.homegain.com,* and *www.lendingtree.com,* accessed March 3, 2005.

QUESTIONS

1. How should traditional realty companies compete in the digital economy?
2. As commission rates continue to fall due to pricing pressures, what will the real estate industry look like in five years? Can the industry survive in its present form? If not, what might replace the industry?

New Economy   Wireless technology affixed to each item allows you to select items and pass through the scanner. The scanner will read the wireless signals from each item simultaneously and generate an itemized account of the purchases. It will then total the prices and automatically debit the account you have designated for payment. Checkout lines are eliminated, and you proceed to your car.

In each of the above examples, we can see the advantages of the new economy over the old economy in terms of at least one of the following: cost, quality, speed, innovation, and customer service. However, the transformation from the Old Economy to the New Economy can be painful in some industries, as we see in IT's About Business 2.1.

Now that we have considered various aspects of doing business in the digital economy, we turn our attention to the business pressures that companies are facing, as well as some responses to those pressures.

Before you go on. . .

1. What are examples of digital technologies?
2. What are the major differences between the old economy and the new economy?
3. What are some other examples of the new economy versus the old economy?

2.2 Business Pressures, Organizational Responses, and IT Support

Modern digital organizations must compete in a challenging marketplace—one that is rapidly changing, unpredictable, complex, global, hypercompetitive, and customer-focused. Companies must react rapidly to problems and opportunities arising from this dynamic environment.

Business Pressures

The *business environment* is the combination of social, legal, economic, physical, and political factors that affect business activities. Significant changes in any of these factors are likely to create business pressures on organizations. Organizations typically respond to these pressures with activities supported by IT. Figure 2.1 shows the relationships among business pressures, organizational responses, and IT. We will focus on three types of business pressures that organizations face: market, technology, and societal pressures.

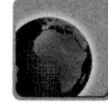

Market Pressures   Market pressures come from the global economy and strong competition, the changing nature of the workforce, and powerful customers. We'll look at each of these in turn.

Global Economy and Strong Competition   The move to a global economy has been facilitated by advanced telecommunications networks, particularly by the Internet. Regional agreements such as the North American Free Trade Agreement (NAFTA, which includes the United States, Canada, and Mexico) and the creation of a unified European market with a single currency—the euro—have contributed to increased world trade.

One important pressure that exists for businesses in a global market is the cost of labor, which varies widely among countries. In general, labor costs are higher in developed countries like the United States and Japan than in developing countries such as China and El Salvador.

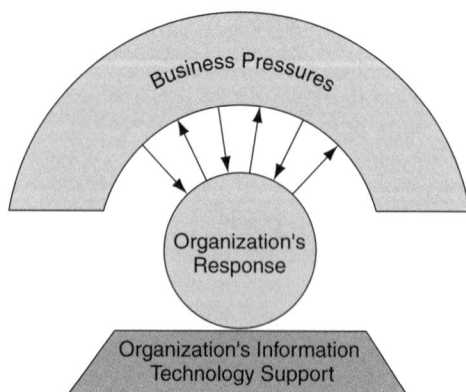

FIGURE 2.1   Relationships among business pressures, organizational responses, and IT.

Also, developed countries usually offer greater benefits, such as health care, to employees, which makes the cost of doing business even higher. Therefore, many labor-intensive industries have moved their operations to countries with low labor costs. IT has made such moves much easier to implement.

Changing Nature of the Workforce   The workforce, particularly in developed countries, is becoming more diversified. Increasing numbers of women, single parents, minorities, and persons with disabilities now work in all types of positions. IT is easing the integration of these employees into the traditional workforce. It is also allowing people to work from home.

Powerful Customers   Consumer sophistication and expectations increase as customers become more knowledgeable about the availability and quality of products and services. Customers can use the Internet to find detailed information about products and services, compare prices, and purchase items at electronic auctions.

The importance of customers has forced organizations to increase efforts to acquire and retain customers. An effort to do just that across an entire enterprise is called **customer relationship management (CRM)**. We address this topic in Chapter 8.

Technology Pressures   The second category of business pressures consists of those pressures related to technology. Two major technology-related pressures are technological innovation and information overload.

Technological Innovation and Obsolescence   New and improved technologies rapidly create or support substitutes for products, alternative service options, and superb quality. As a result, today's state-of-the-art products may be obsolete tomorrow. For example, how fast are thin-screen televisions and computer monitors replacing the bulky TVs and monitors of just a short time ago? How fast are you replacing your old, standard cell phones with the new camera-phones? These changes mean that businesses must keep up with consumer demands.

Information Overload   The amount of information available on the Internet more than doubles every year, and much of it is free. The Internet and other telecommunications networks are bringing a flood of information to managers. To make decisions effectively and efficiently, managers must be able to access, navigate, and utilize these vast stores of data, information, and knowledge. Information technologies, such as search engines and data mining (discussed in Chapter 4), provide valuable support in these efforts.

Societal Pressures   The third category of business pressures includes social responsibility, government regulation/deregulation, spending for social programs, spending to protect against terrorism, and ethics. In this section we consider how all of these elements affect business today.

Social Responsibility   Social issues that affect businesses range from the state of the physical environment to companies' contributions to education (e.g., by allowing interns to work in companies). Some corporations are willing to spend time and/or money on solving various social problems. These efforts are known as *organizational social responsibility*.

One social problem that affects modern business is the digital divide. The *digital divide* refers to the wide gap between those who have access to information and communications technology and those who do not. This gap exists both within and among countries.

According to reports by the United Nations, more than 90 percent of all Internet hosts are located in developed countries, although these countries contain only 15 percent of the world's population. Nearly 60 percent of the U.S. population has Internet access. Further, this distribution is highly correlated with household income. That is, the greater a household's income, the more likely they are to have Internet access. The U.S. federal and state governments are attempting to close the digital divide within the country by encouraging training and by supporting education and infrastructure improvements.

One of the developments that can help close the digital divide is Internet kiosks in public places and cybercafés. In the United States, computers with Internet access usually are also available at public libraries.

Cybercafés are public places such as coffee houses in which Internet terminals are available, usually for a small fee. Cybercafés come in all shapes and sizes, ranging from a chain of cafés (*www.easyeverything.com* and *www.easy.com*) that include hundreds of terminals in one location (e.g., 760 in one New York setting) to a single computer in a corner of many restaurants. According to *www.cybercaptive.com*, in 2005 there were approximately 6,000 cybercafés, public Internet access points, and kiosks located in 161 countries.

Computers have popped up in many other public locations: laundromats, karaoke bars, bookstores, CD stores, hotel lobbies, and convenience stores. Some facilities give free access to patrons; others charge a small fee.

Many other government and international organizations are also trying to close the digital divide around the world. As technologies develop and become less expensive, the speed at which the gap can be closed will accelerate. In the following example, the Media Lab at the Massachusetts Institute of Technology (MIT) responds to this problem (*www.media.mit.edu*).

"Grab some lederhosen, Sutfin. We're about to climb aboard the globalization bandwagon."

© The New Yorker collection 2001 Robert Weber from cartoonbank.com. All Rights Reserved.

MIT Helps Bridge the Digital Divide. O Siengle is a town in the remote northeastern corner of Cambodia, where individual incomes average $1 a day. At the elementary school in O Siengle, solar panels have been powering three computers. Once a day, an Internet "Motoman" rides a Honda motorcycle slowly past the school. On the passenger seat is a gray metal box with a short antenna. The box holds a wireless Wi-Fi setup that allows the box to exchange e-mail with the three computers. For this short period, then, this schoolyard with a hand-cranked water well becomes an Internet hot spot.

Five days a week, five Motomen ride their routes, downloading and uploading e-mail in several towns. This system has been called a "digital pony express." The system uses a receiver powered by the motorcycle's battery. The driver need only roll slowly past the school to download all the village's outgoing e-mail and deliver incoming e-mail. At dusk, the motorcycles converge on the provincial capital. There, an advanced school is equipped with a satellite dish that allows a bulk e-mail exchange with the outside world. The Media Lab at MIT provides the technology used by the Motomen.

Users say the Motoman system is starting to change the lives of people in Cambodia. For example, Cambodian doctors now have access to telemedicine to help them in their diagnoses. The doctors can send photographs of patients, X-rays, ultrasounds, and electrocardiograms to specialists in Boston at Partners Telemedicine. Doctors from Massachusetts General Hospital and Harvard Medical School then review the files and send diagnoses, all pro bono. (*Sources:* Compiled from J. Brooke, "Rural Cambodia, Though Far Off the Grid, Is Finding Its Way Online," *New York Times*, January 26, 2004; and *www.media.mit.edu*, accessed March 12, 2005.)

Government Regulations and Deregulation Other business pressures are related to government regulations regarding health, safety, environmental control, and equal opportunity. Businesses tend to view government regulations as expensive constraints on their activities. In general, government deregulation intensifies competition.

Protection Against Terrorist Attacks Since September 11, 2001, organizations have been under increased pressure to protect themselves against terrorist attacks. In addition, employees who are in the military reserves may be called up for active duty, creating personnel problems. Information technology can help protect businesses by providing security systems and possibly identifying patterns of behavior associated with terrorist activities that will help to prevent terrorist attacks (including cyberattacks) against organizations. The next example illustrates one weapon in the global attack on terrorism, facial-recognition software, that has many privacy advocates worried.

Example

Facial-Recognition Software Helps Fight Terrorism But Worries Privacy Advocates. The United States is moving closer to requiring citizens to have an identity card that could be scanned from a distance. By the end of 2005, U.S. passports may come with embedded radio-tag chips. Congress is considering mandating similar technology in driver's licenses. The government argues that the changes will make the nation safer from terrorists. However, privacy advocates fear that the information could be stolen or misused.

In 2002, Congress passed the Enhanced Border Security Act. One provision of this law requires that new passports be equipped with a chip with personal identification information. For this information, the government has chosen facial recognition, which privacy advocates consider to be less reliable than alternatives such as retina scans. Facial recognition software maps certain points on your face so that you can be recognized even if you try to alter your appearance, say by growing a beard, dyeing your hair, or wearing glasses. Retinal scans beam light to the back of your eye and map the pattern of blood vessels in your retina. Retinal scans are extremely reliable because blood vessel patterns in the retina are unique to each individual. Further, chips with this information would enable the government to read your personal information from more than 50 feet away. If airport and border security guards can secretly read everyone's identity cards, so can anyone with a radio-chip reader, from terrorists to identity thieves. (*Sources:* Compiled from J. Carey, "Big Brother's Passport to Pry," *BusinessWeek Online*, November 5, 2004; and "LAPD May Use Facial Recognition Software," *NewsMax Wires*, December 26, 2004.)

Ethical Issues Ethics relates to general standards of right and wrong. *Information ethics* relates specifically to standards of right and wrong in information-processing practices. Ethical issues are very important because, if handled poorly, they can damage an organization's image and destroy the morale of its employees. The use of IT raises many ethical issues, ranging from monitoring e-mail to invading the privacy of millions of customers whose data are stored in private and public databases. Chapter 3 covers ethical issues in detail.

Clearly, then, the pressures on organizations are increasing, and organizations must be prepared to take responsive actions if they are to succeed. We explore these organizational responses in the next section.

Organizational Responses

Organizations are responding to the pressures we just discussed by implementing IT such as strategic systems, customer focus, make-to-order and mass customization, and e-business. The Toronto International Airport case at the beginning of the chapter illustrated all of these responses. We discuss each type in greater detail in this section.

Strategic Systems   Strategic systems provide organizations with advantages that enable them to increase their market share and/or profits, to better negotiate with suppliers, or to prevent competitors from entering their markets. In IT's About Business 2.2, the merger of Kmart and Sears illustrates the relationship between business strategy and strategic information systems. We discuss strategic systems in detail in the next section of this chapter.

Customer Focus   Organizational attempts to provide superb customer service can make the difference between attracting and keeping customers on the one hand and losing them to competitors on the other. Numerous IT tools and business processes have been designed to keep customers happy. For example, consider Amazon. When you visit Amazon's Web site anytime after your first visit, the site welcomes you back by name and presents you with

IT's About Business

2.2 Ignore Your Information Systems at Your Peril

Kmart and Sears (*www.sears.com*) announced an $11 billion merger at the end of 2004. Amid all the talk of real estate divestment and converting Kmart stores to the Sears nameplate information systems received only a passing mention. In the words of Sears CEO A. J. Lacy, "We've got about $12 billion of sales, general, and administrative expenses, and I think in the areas of supply chain, IT, and administration we see some opportunity there." In reality the combined company is probably two years away from even beginning to figure out how to make effective use of IT to save money or bolster sales.

The combined company, Sears Holdings, is expected to convert hundreds of Kmart's nearly 1,500 stores to the Sears nameplate. Analysts maintain that Sears Holdings needs to decide what its business strategy will be: a mid-level retailer in malls? a megastore operator in rural areas? both? After the company makes these strategy decisions, it then must design merchandising, pricing, payment, and other processes to support the new strategy. Finally, it must decide which information systems are needed to support the processes and strategy.

Analysts warn, however, that the company cannot delay integrating the information systems for too long because the task is so enormous. According to one research firm, Kmart has three inventory management systems, five logistics management systems, five supply chain management systems, and four systems for merchandise planning. Meanwhile, Sears has five inventory management systems, four

logistics applications, five supply chain systems, and six merchandise planning systems. Just for that part of the two retailers' operations, then, the two companies currently have 37 systems, which are supplied by a wide range of vendors.

Just leaving existing systems alone will not work, either. Sears Holdings must compete with companies like Wal-Mart and Target that operate efficiently in the modern business environment. By purchasing goods globally, managing information effectively, and instituting efficient supply chain processes, Wal-Mart has been able to undercut rivals in nearly every category. Wal-Mart and Target will keep pressing the strategic advantages they have established through IT. By the time Sears Holdings plots its strategy, Wal-Mart and Target will both be well along in their use of radio frequency identification tagging (discussed in Chapter 7), which will boost in-stock rates and sales.

Sources: Compiled from L. Dignan, "Oh, Yeah, the Computers," *Baseline Magazine*, December 6, 2004; *www.sears.com*, accessed March 21, 2005; and "Sears Holding Corporation," *http://premium.hoovers.com*, accessed March 14, 2005.

QUESTIONS

1. Discuss the reasons why IT integration between Sears and Kmart will be delayed. Is this the correct procedure? Why or why not?
2. What advantages does Wal-Mart have over Sears Holdings?

information on books that you might like, based on your previous purchases. In another example, Dell guides you through the process of buying a computer by providing information and choices that help you make an informed buying decision.

Make-to-Order and Mass Customization   **Make-to-order** is a strategy of producing customized products and services. The business problem is how to manufacture customized goods efficiently and at a reasonably low cost. Part of the solution is to change manufacturing processes from mass production to mass customization. In mass production, a company produces a large quantity of identical items. In **mass customization**, it also produces a large quantity of items, but it customizes them to fit the desires of each customer. The next example shows how IT facilitates the process of mass customization in women's clothing.

Example

Finding Jeans That Fit. Finding a pair of jeans that best suits an individual's body shape can be a shopping nightmare. Now, Bodymetrics (*www.bodymetrics.com*) has developed the Full Body 3-D Scanner Structure Light System, which allows designers to create perfect-fitting clothes. When a customer steps into the body scanner, it captures more than 200,000 data points in less than 10 seconds from the shopper's physical appearance through the reflection of a white light. From these data points the scanner extracts more than 100 body measurements with exacting accuracy. Finally, it converts them to a 3-D simulation on a computer screen. The results are then e-mailed to the manufacturing unit. British designer Tristan Webber has come up with a new denim range of clothing, Digital Couture, in conjunction with Bodymetrics. His clothes are so tailor-made to the wearer's body shape that they have the customer's name and scan date on the label. (*Sources:* Compiled from P. Hancocks, "Scanner Creates Perfect-Fit Jeans," *CNN.com*, January 7, 2005; and *www.bodymetrics.com*, accessed March 21, 2005.

E-Business and E-Commerce   As we saw in the opening case on the Toronto International Airport, companies are transforming part or all of their operations into e-businesses. Doing business electronically is the newest and perhaps the most promising strategy that many companies can pursue. Chapter 5 will focus extensively on this topic. In addition, e-commerce applications appear throughout the book.

We have described the pressures that affect companies in today's business environment and the responses that organizations take to manage these pressures. To plan for the most effective responses, companies formulate strategies. In the new digital economy, these strategies rely heavily on information technology, especially strategic information systems. In the next section, we discuss corporate strategy and strategic information systems.

Before you go on. . .

1. Describe some of the pressures that characterize the modern global business environment.
2. What are some of the organizational responses to these pressures? Are any of the responses specific to a particular pressure? If so, which ones?

2.3 Competitive Advantage and Strategic Information Systems

A competitive strategy is a statement that identifies a business's strategies to compete, its goals, and the plans and policies that will be required to carry out those goals (Porter, 1985). Through its competitive strategy, an organization seeks a **competitive advantage** in an industry. That is, it seeks to outperform its competitors in some measure such as cost, quality, or speed. Competitive advantage helps a company control a market and generate larger-than-average profits.

Competitive advantage is even more important in the digital economy than in the old economy, as we demonstrate throughout the book. In most cases, the digital economy has not changed the *core business* of companies. That is, information technologies simply offer the tools that can increase an organization's success through its traditional sources of competitive advantage, such as low cost, excellent customer service, and superior supply chain management. **Strategic information systems (SISs)** provide a competitive advantage by helping an organization implement its strategic goals and increase its performance and productivity. Any information system that helps an organization gain a competitive advantage *or* reduce a competitive disadvantage is a strategic information system.

Porter's Competitive Forces Model

The best-known framework for analyzing competitiveness is Michael Porter's **competitive forces model** (Porter, 1985). Companies use Porter's model to develop strategies to increase their competitive edge. Porter's model also demonstrates how IT can make a company more competitive.

Porter's model identifies five major forces that could endanger a company's position in a given industry. Figure 2.2 highlights these forces. Over the past decade or so, the Internet

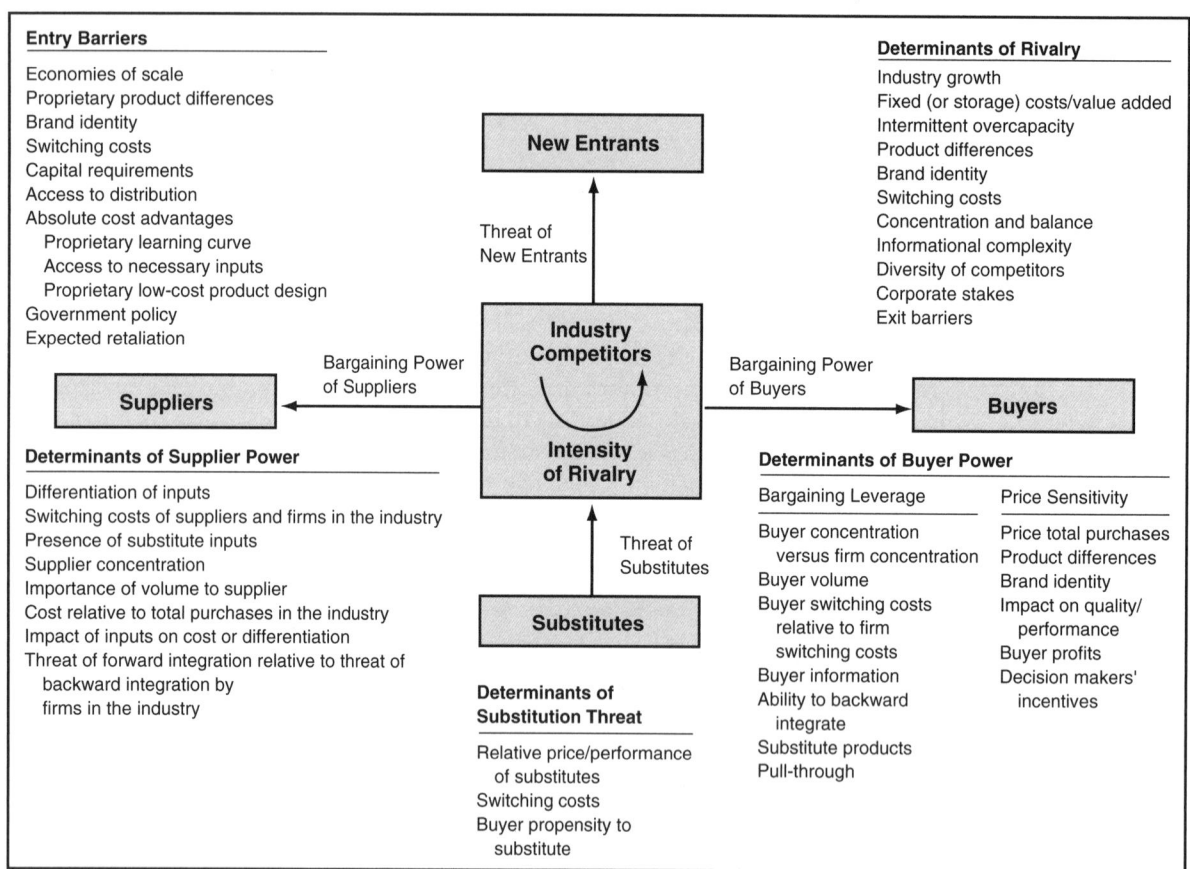

FIGURE 2.2   Porter's five forces model, including the major determinants of each force. (*Source:* Adapted with permission of the Free Press, a division of Simon & Schuster, Inc., from Michael Porter, *Competitive Advantage: Creating and Sustaining Superior Performance*, p. 6. © 1985, 1998 by Michael Porter.)

has changed the nature of competition, and Porter (2001) concludes that the *overall* impact of the Internet is to increase competition, which negatively impacts profitability. Let's examine the five forces and the ways that the Internet influences them.

1. ***The threat of entry of new competitors.*** For most firms, the Internet *increases* the threat that new competitors will enter the market. The Internet sharply reduces traditional barriers to entry, such as the need for a sales force or a physical storefront to sell goods and services. Now, competitors frequently need only to set up a Web site. This threat is particularly acute in industries that perform an intermediation role, which is a link between buyers and sellers (e.g., stock brokers and travel agents) as well as in industries where the primary product or service is digital (e.g., the music industry). In addition, the geographical reach of the Internet enables distant competitors to compete more directly with an existing firm.

2. ***The bargaining power of suppliers.*** The Internet's impact on suppliers is mixed. On the one hand, buyers can find alternative suppliers and compare prices more easily, reducing the supplier's bargaining power. On the other hand, as companies use the Internet to integrate their supply chains, participating suppliers prosper by locking in customers.

3. ***The bargaining power of customers (buyers).*** The Web greatly increases a buyer's access to information about products and suppliers. Internet technologies can reduce customers' *switching costs*, which are the costs, in money and time, of a decision to buy elsewhere, and buyers can more easily buy from other suppliers. In these ways the Internet greatly increases customers' bargaining power.

4. ***The threat of substitute products or services.*** Information-based industries are in the greatest danger from substitutes. Any industry in which digitized information can replace material goods (e.g., music, books, software) must view the Internet as a threat because the Internet can convey this information efficiently and at low cost.

5. ***The rivalry among existing firms in the industry.*** The visibility of Internet applications on the Web makes proprietary systems more difficult to keep secret. The result is fewer differences among competitors. In simple terms, when I see my competitor's new system online, I will rapidly match its features in order to remain competitive. In many other ways, Internet-based systems are changing the nature of competition and even industry structure. For example, bookseller Barnes & Noble, The Home Depot, and other companies have created independent online divisions that are competing against the parent companies' physical stores. Companies that have both online and offline sales operations are termed "click-and-mortar" firms because they combine both "brick-and-mortar" and e-commerce operations.

Competition also is being affected by the extremely low variable cost of digital products. That is, once the product has been developed, the cost of producing additional "units" approaches zero. Consider the music industry. When artists record, their songs are captured in digital format. Producing physical products, such as CDs or DVDs, with the songs on them for sale in music stores involves costs. The costs in a physical distribution channel are much higher than the costs involved in delivering the songs over the Internet in digital form.

In fact, some products might be given away for free. For example, some analysts predict that commissions for online stock trading will approach zero because investors can access the necessary information via the Internet to make their own decisions regarding buying and selling stocks. Consumers no longer need brokers to give them information that they can obtain themselves, virtually for free.

Strategies for Competitive Advantage

Organizations continually try to develop strategies to counter Porter's five forces. We discuss five of those strategies here.

1. ***Cost leadership strategy:*** Produce products and/or services at the lowest cost in the industry. An example is Wal-Mart's automatic inventory replenishment system, which enables Wal-Mart to reduce inventory storage requirements. As a result, Wal-Mart stores use floor space to sell products, not store them, thereby reducing inventory costs.

2. ***Differentiation strategy:*** Offer different products, services, or product features. Southwest Airlines, for example, has differentiated itself as a low-cost, short-haul, express airline. This has proved to be a winning strategy for competing in the highly competitive airline industry. Also, Dell has differentiated itself in the personal computer market through its mass-customization strategy.

3. ***Innovation strategy:*** Introduce new products and services, add new features to existing products and services, or develop new ways to produce them. A classic example is the introduction of automated teller machines (ATMs) by Citibank. The convenience and cost-cutting features of this innovation gave Citibank a huge advantage over its competitors. Like many innovative products, the ATM changed the nature of competition in the banking industry. Today an ATM is a competitive *necessity* for any bank.

4. ***Operational effectiveness strategy:*** Improve the manner in which internal business processes are executed so that a firm performs similar activities better than its rivals. Such improvements increase quality, productivity, and employee and customer satisfaction while decreasing time to market. For example, improvements in Terminal 1 of Toronto's International Airport have saved both the airport and the airlines millions of dollars.

5. ***Customer-orientation strategy:*** Concentrate on making customers happy. Web-based systems are particularly effective in this area because they can provide a personalized, one-to-one relationship with each customer. Interestingly, the customer-orientation strategy can be a two-edged sword, as shown in IT's About Business 2.3.

IT's About Business

2.3 IT Helps Create Demon Customers

J. E. is a demon customer, a retailer's worst nightmare. When he decided to buy a video camera, he researched the product online, did the rounds of the retail electronics stores, asked countless questions of in-store sales reps, and rigorously tested several models. Then he went home and bought a camera online, at a substantial discount. J. E. is not concerned with brand loyalty or customer service. He carries out research at brick-and-mortar stores, tying up sales reps for hours. He might even purchase a product, test it at home for a week, and return it for a full refund. Then he will find the cheapest possible source from which to buy it, whether online or offline. He is a multichannel shopper.

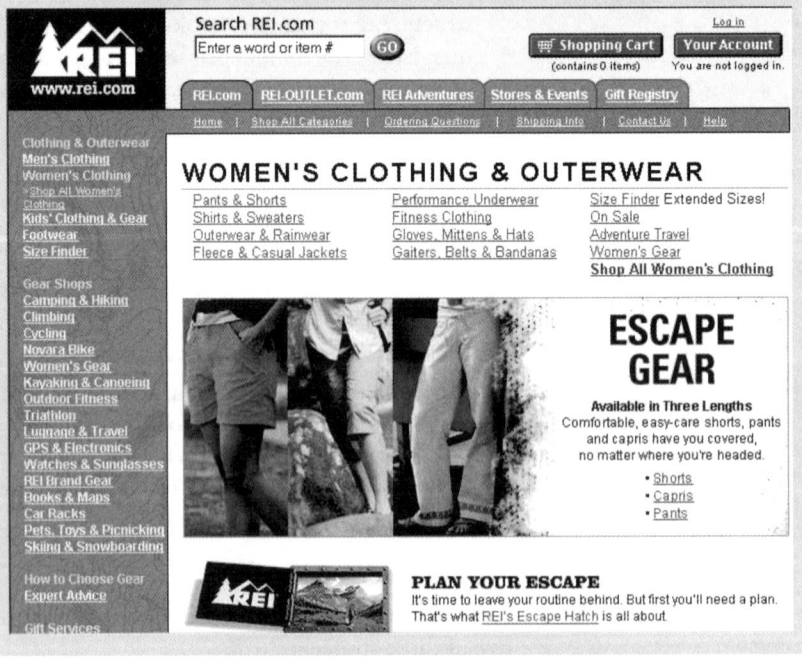

J. E. is not alone. Over the course of a single purchase, customers frequently cross over between the online and offline worlds. In fact, from the time they start their research until they make their purchase, half of all multichannel shoppers switch brands. One reason for this behavior is that most retailers have made little or no attempt to coordinate their online and in-store operations. In many cases, they treat the two as completely separate business units. Some retailers, such as Victoria's Secret Direct, will not even allow online purchases to be returned at stores. Toys "Я" Us farms out its entire online operation to Amazon.com.

Multichannel shoppers also use Web sites such as www.cnet.com, www.shoplocal.com, www.froogle.com, www.slickdeals.com, and www.nextag.com to do research online. These sites provide price comparisons, detailed product information, insider tips, and consumer feedback. They have now added more confidential information, such as which items a retailer is currently selling at a loss, which retailers have the most favorable return policies, and which retailers have planned upcoming sales.

Retailers are fighting back. At The Gap, if a regular-priced item is not available in the right size or color at a store, the company will ship it to the customer's home from another store, at no extra charge. Customers can also place online orders from within Gap stores themselves.

Recreational Equipment Inc. (REI) (www.rei.com) has made the IT investment to integrate its online and offline customer databases and inventory systems. When online customers want to forgo shipping charges—which are significant for large items, such as canoes—they can pick up the items at their local store. REI's efforts have met with tremendous success. In-store pickups from online sales now account for one-third of the company's annual online sales. REI also offers retail-store customers access to product information via kiosks.

Best Buy (www.bestbuy.com) and Circuit City (www.circuitcity.com) both enable customers to buy products online and then immediately go to the local store to pick up their purchases. Best Buy will even reply with an e-mail, send a sales assistant to pick out the item from the shelf, and hold it until the customer arrives to buy it. That way, customers are assured that their trip to the local store will not be fruitless.

Sources: Compiled from N. McKay, "Two-Faced and Tight-Fisted," *CIO Insight*, December 1, 2004; and J. Freed, "The Customer Is Always Right? Not Anymore," *www.sfgate.com*, July 5, 2004.

QUESTIONS

1. Are demon customers necessarily a bad thing for retailers? Support your answer.
2. Explain how you would manage demon customers.
3. Explain how information technology creates demon customers.

Before you go on. . .

1. What are strategic information systems?
2. What are the five forces that Porter says could endanger a firm's position in its industry or marketplaces?
3. What strategies might companies use to gain competitive advantage?

Failures of Information Systems

So far, we have introduced you to many success stories. You may wonder, though, "Is IT all success?" The answer is, "Absolutely not." There are many failures, and we can learn as much from failures as from successes. We will provide examples of information systems' failures throughout the book. Our next example describes an IT failure.

 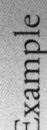

IRS Information System Performs Poorly. A software program designed to let the Internal Revenue Service (IRS) detect and analyze cases of unauthorized access to taxpayer data has not been functioning properly since the IRS took delivery of the program. According to the Treasury Department's Inspector General for Tax Administration, these software problems create security risks, and they cost the public hundreds of thousands of dollars each year.

In November 2002, Computer Sciences Corporation delivered the Security Audit and Analysis System (SAAS) to the IRS. The application was intended to gather audit information from IRS systems and store this information in a central database that IRS management could access. The IRS wanted the system to allow managers to generate reports and to create custom queries to detect unauthorized activities. It also planned to use the system to reconstruct events when unauthorized activities occurred. However, the Inspector General's team found that SAAS does not let users access its data once they have been collected. It also revealed that the IRS knew that SAAS was incomplete but accepted delivery anyway.

The problems with SAAS are proving to be costly. Auditors determined that the IRS will spend almost $600,000 in maintenance costs through fiscal year 2006 to continue using the system that SAAS was intended to replace. In addition, the IRS will spend $400,000 in fiscal 2004 and 2005 to pay employees whose jobs are to support the current system. (*Sources:* Compiled from L. Greenemeier, "Report Says IRS Software Program Is Not Doing the Job," *InformationWeek*, August 31, 2004; and *www.irs.gov*, accessed March 31, 2005.)

It is also possible that too much IT can be "too much of a good thing." In fact, Dollar General feels that less IT is better. As IT's About Business 2.4 shows, however, that approach can cause problems.

IT's About Business

2.4 Is Dollar General Really Thriving with Minimal IT?

Now that Wal-Mart sells wide-screen televisions and vacation packages along with its low-priced detergent, there is room underneath for chains devoted only to small-ticket goods. These chains are commonly called "dollar stores." Of course, not everything at a dollar store costs just a buck. However, the combination of $1 shampoo and $3 bug killer is big business. In 2004 shoppers spent $16.6 billion at the five leading dollar stores, up from $12.2 billion in 2003.

Dollar General (*www.dollargeneral.com*) leads the low-cost market, generating more than $7 billion per year in sales from more than 7,000 stores located in 30 states. In 2004, Wal-Mart earned 3.5 cents on each dollar of sales. That same year, Dollar General earned 4.3 cents, making the company 12 percent more profitable than the world's largest retailer. Profits come from frugality at the store level.

Although Dollar General's seven distribution centers have radio-frequency scanners and warehouse management and logistics software, its stores have very limited IT. There are no store network, no e-mail, and no local servers keeping track of inventory. A mainframe computer at headquarters polls each store's IBM cash registers via satellite network every night, recording how many of which items were sold and at what price.

Each register comes loaded with a simple software program that tracks sales. The company vetoed a graphical application because it considered it to be too slow and complicated to reboot after a power outage. This is a frequent problem for Dollar General in rural areas in the South and Midwest. In addition, Dollar General selected satellite communications after slow and spotty dial-up connections in small towns prevented between 5 and 8 percent of its stores from connecting to headquarters each night for mandatory sales reporting.

Dollar General spends less on technology per employee every year—about $3,000—than any of its dollar-store competitors. This policy helps keep store operating costs low. However, it also has negative consequences. About 3 percent of sales disappeared in 2004 due to *shrinkage*, that is, theft and loss. Items are bar-coded, but store employees do not have readers or software to verify shipments and check in products as they move hundreds of cartons off delivery trucks every week. The company also has no store-level inventory system.

Dollar General's shrink rates have grown steadily since 1998. A Loss Prevention application installed to flag unusual cash register transactions has not made any difference. The company has installed video cameras at "watch stores" with high shrink rates. Significantly, the lenses are pointed at registers, the stockroom, and the manager's office. Senior executives clearly believe that employees, rather than shoplifters, are responsible for the shrinkage.

However, some store managers claim that the big problem is the way products are checked in. Because employees have no scanners or software to check incoming goods, anything can happen to cartons after they leave the distribution center. In addition, the Loss Prevention application does nothing to catch either shoplifters or people who steal cases en route from the distribution center.

Sources: Compiled from Kim Nash, "Dollar General: 8 Days to Grow," *Baseline Magazine*, July 1, 2004; *www.dollargeneral. com* and *http://company.monster.com/dgcorp/*, accessed March 30, 2005.

QUESTIONS

1. Can Dollar General survive with minimal IT? Support your answer.
2. You are the CIO of Dollar General. Should you expand IT functions at your stores? Which ones should you add, if any?

Although there are many reasons why an IT project can fail, one of the most critical is our inability to predict the future of IT with any accuracy. Information technology is evolving and continuously changing in a rapid fashion, as we discussed in Chapter 1.

Before you go on. . .

1. Why do SISs support many corporate strategies?
2. Besides our inability to predict the future, what are other reasons why IT projects might fail?

2.4 Why Should You Learn About Information Technology?

Throughout this chapter we have seen that we live in a digital economy and that the ways we live and do business are changing dramatically. The organizational impacts of IT are growing rapidly, especially with the introduction of the Internet and e-commerce. We are becoming more and more dependent on information systems. We now focus more carefully on why people in various business positions should become more knowledgeable concerning information technology.

IT Is Essential for Work in Organizations

Simply put, organizations cannot operate without information technology. For this reason, every manager and professional staff member should learn about IT within his or her specialized field as well as across the entire organization and among organizations.

You will be more effective in your chosen career if you understand how successful information systems are built, used, and managed. You also will be more effective if you know how to recognize and avoid unsuccessful systems. Finally, becoming knowledgeable about IT can improve your chances of landing a good job. Even though computerization eliminates some jobs, it creates many more.

IT Will Reduce the Number of Middle Managers

IT makes managers more productive, and it increases the number of employees who can report to a single manager. In these ways it ultimately decreases the number of managers and experts. It is reasonable to assume, then, that fewer managerial levels will exist in many organizations, and there will be fewer staff and line managers.

IT Will Change the Manager's Job

One of the most important tasks of managers is making decisions. As we will see in Chapter 7, IT can change the manner in which many decisions are made. In this way it ultimately can change managers' jobs.

Many managers have reported that IT has finally given them time to get out of the office and into the field. They also have found that they can spend more time planning activities instead of "putting out fires." Managers now can gather information for decision making much more quickly by using search engines and intranets.

IT tends to reduce the time necessary to complete any step in the decision-making process. By using IT properly, then, managers today can complete tasks more efficiently and effectively.

Another possible impact on the manager's job is a change in managerial requirements. The use of IT might lead organizations to reconsider what qualities they want in a good manager. For example, much of an employee's work is typically performed online and stored electronically. For these employees, electronic or "remote" supervision could become more common. Remote supervision places greater emphasis on completed work and less on personal contacts and office politics. Managerial supervision becomes particularly difficult when employees work in geographically dispersed locations, including homes, away from their supervisors.

Will My Job Be Eliminated?

One of the major concerns of every employee, part-time or full-time, is job security. Due to difficult economic times, increased global competition, demands for customization, and increased consumer sophistication, many companies have increased their investments in IT. In fact, as computers gain in intelligence and capabilities, the competitive advantage of replacing people with machines is increasing rapidly. For this reason, some people believe that society is heading toward higher unemployment. Others disagree.

Another concern for all employees is outsourcing, also called offshoring, to foreign countries such as India, China, and Mexico that have much lower wage rates. We discuss outsourcing in detail in Chapter 10.

IT Impacts Employees at Work

Many people have experienced a loss of identity because of computerization. They feel like "just another number" because computers reduce or eliminate the human element that was present in noncomputerized systems.

The Internet threatens to have an even more isolating influence than computers and television. If people are encouraged to work and shop from their living rooms, then some unfortunate psychological effects, such as depression and loneliness, could develop. Our next example shows that some people have become so addicted to the Web that they have dropped out of their regular social activities at school, work, or home.

Internet Addiction Affects Finnish Army. Some soldiers in Finland have been excused from their full term of military service because they are addicted to the Internet, according to the Finnish Defense Forces. Doctors have found that the young men miss their computers so much that they can't cope with their compulsory six months in the armed forces.

One commander noted, "For people who play Internet games all night and do not have any friends, and no hobbies, coming into the Army is a very big shock." There are no official figures for the "Internet addict" dropout rate.

The army sends the young men home for three years. After that they have to come back. (*Sources:* Compiled from "Web Addiction Gets Conscripts Out of Army," *Reuters*, August 3, 2004; and "Finnish Army Drops Web Addicts," *BBC News*, August 5, 2004.)

Example

Another possible psychological impact relates to home schooling, which is much easier to conduct through the Internet (see *www.homeschool.com*). Opponents of home schooling argue that the lack of social contacts can damage the social, moral, and cognitive development of school-age children who spend long periods of time working alone on the computer.

IT Impacts Employees' Health and Safety   Computers and information systems are a part of the environment that may adversely affect individuals' health and safety. To illustrate this point, we will discuss the effects of job stress, video display terminals, and long-term use of the keyboard.

An increase in an employee's workload and/or responsibilities can trigger *job stress*. Although computerization has benefited organizations by increasing productivity, it has also created an ever-expanding workload for some employees. Some workers feel overwhelmed and become increasingly anxious about their job performance. These feelings of stress and anxiety can diminish workers' productivity. Management's responsibility is to help alleviate these feelings by providing training, redistributing the workload among workers, or hiring more workers.

Exposure to *video display terminals* (*VDTs*) raises the issue of radiation exposure, which has been linked to cancer and other health-related problems. For example, some experts charge that exposure to VDTs for long periods of time can damage an individual's eyesight.

Finally, the long-term use of keyboards can lead to *repetitive strain injuries* such as backaches and muscle tension in the wrists and fingers. *Carpal tunnel syndrome* is a particularly painful form of repetitive strain injury that affects the wrists and hands.

Designers are aware of the potential problems associated with prolonged use of computers. To address these problems, they have attempted to design a better computing environment. **Ergonomics**, the science of adapting machines and work environments to people, focuses on creating an environment that is safe, well lit, and comfortable. For example, antiglare screens have helped alleviate problems of fatigued or damaged eyesight. Also, chairs that contour the human body have helped decrease backaches. Figure 2.3 displays some sample ergonomic products.

IT Provides Opportunities for People with Disabilities   Computers can create new employment opportunities for people with disabilities by integrating speech and vision recognition capabilities. For example, individuals who cannot type are able to use a voice-operated keyboard, and individuals who cannot travel can work at home.

Adaptive equipment for computers permits people with disabilities to perform tasks they would not normally be able to do. Figure 2.4 shows a PC for a visually challenged user, a PC for a user with a hearing impairment, and a PC for a motor-disabled user.

Other devices help improve the quality of life for people with disabilities in more mundane, but useful, ways: a two-way writing telephone, a robotic page turner, a hair brusher, and a hospital-bedside video trip to the zoo or the museum. Several organizations deal with IT designed for people with disabilities.

IT Provides Quality-of-Life Improvements

On a broader scale, IT has significant implications for our quality of life. The workplace can be expanded from the traditional 9 to 5 job at a central location to 24 hours a day at any location. IT can provide employees with flexibility that can significantly improve the quality of leisure time, even if it doesn't increase the total amount of leisure time. However, IT can also place employees on "constant call" where they are never truly away from the office.

Robot Revolution on the Way   Once restricted largely to science fiction movies, robots that can do practical tasks are becoming more common. In fact, "cyberpooches," nursebots, and other mechanical beings may be our companions before we know it. Around the world, quasi-autonomous devices have become increasingly common on factory floors, in

FIGURE 2.3
Ergonomic products
protect computer users.
(a) Wrist support.
(b) Back support.
(c) Eye-protection filter
(optically coated glass).
(d) Adjustable foot rest.
[(a), (b), and (d)
courtesy of Ergodyne;
(c) courtesy of
3M.com)]

(a)   (b)   (c)

FIGURE 2.4   Enabling people with disabilities to work with computers. (a) A PC for a blind or sight-impaired user, equipped with an Oscar optical scanner and a Braille printer, both by TeleSensory. The optical scanner converts text into ASCII code or into proprietary word processing format. Files saved on disc can then be translated into Braille and sent to the printer. Visually impaired users can also enlarge the text on the screen by loading a TSR software magnification program. (b) The deaf or hearing-impaired user's PC is connected to a telephone via an Ultratec Intele-Modem Baudolt/ASCH modem. The user is sending and receiving messages to and from someone at a remote site who is using a telecommunications device for deaf people (right). (c) This motor-disabled person is communicating with a PC using a Pointer Systems optical head pointer to access all keyboard functions on a virtual keyboard shown on the PC's display. The user can "strike" a key in one of two ways. He can focus on the desired key for a user-definable time period (which causes the key to be highlighted), or he can click an adapted switch when he chooses the desired key. (*Source:* J. J. Lazzaro, "Computers for the Disabled," Byte, June 1993.)

hospital corridors, and in farm fields. Carnegie Mellon University in Pittsburgh, for example, has developed self-directing tractors that harvest hundreds of acres of crops around the clock in California. These "robot tractors" use global positioning systems combined with video image processing that identifies rows of uncut crops.

Many robotic devices are also being developed for military purposes. For example, the Pentagon is researching self-driving vehicles and bee-like swarms of small surveillance robots, each of which would contribute a different view or angle of a combat zone.

It probably will be a long time before we see robots making decisions by themselves, handling unfamiliar situations, and interacting with people. Nevertheless, robots are extremely helpful in various environments, as we see in IT's About Business 2.5.

IT's About Business

POM

2.5 Here Come the Robots

The first great wave of industrial robots began appearing in factories in the 1980s. Most of these devices were stationary, arm-like machines assigned to the "three D's"—dull, dirty, or dangerous jobs, such as spray painting or spot welding. Today, instead of working on tasks presented to them by moving conveyors, mobile robots are going where the work needs doing.

Cleaning Ship Hulls

The traditional way to remove old paint from a ship's hull involves erecting a scaffold from which workers blast garnet grit propelled by compressed air. It is a filthy, dangerous task. Workers risk falling off multistory scaffolding, and the process spews toxic dust downwind.

To reduce the labor involved in the process, Ultrastrip Systems (*www. ultrastrip.com*) decided to automate the process by building a self-propelled stripping robot. The robot moves on steerable rubber wheels and features powerful permanent magnets that cling to a ship's hull. The robot is operated by a worker using a joystick. Each robot replaces about 10 men, and the quality of the stripped surface is superior to that obtained from traditional grit blasting. Ultrastrip robots keep Carnival Cruise Lines ships looking spiffy. They also worked on the USS *Cole* after it was damaged in a terrorist attack.

Photo courtesy of Ultrastrip Systems

Finding Underground Leaks

As the nation's buried-pipe infrastructure ages, utility companies face the challenge of locating and fixing a growing number of underground leaks. Pinpointing a leak can be surprisingly difficult. This is why utilities must frequently dig multiple holes to locate a single problem.

Suppliers of natural gas in the Northeast concluded that they could reduce their maintenance costs if they did more preventive maintenance and less emergency response. That is the idea behind Explorer, a segmented pipe-inspecting robot that looks like a string of metal sausages. Thanks to its multiple joints, the 45-pound Explorer robot has the impressive ability to make 90-degree turns in the six- and eight-inch gas mains through which it crawls. The battery-powered robot has wide-angle video-cameras at both ends. It propels itself using motorized rollers attached to flipper-like legs that push against the inner walls of a pipe. (See *http://electronicosonline.com/imagenes/noticias/18082004.jpg*.)

Home Robots

Robots have begun appearing in the household for a variety of purposes: repetitive chores such as vacuuming and mowing the lawn, guarding our homes, and providing playmates for our children. Though not at the level of C-3PO and R2-D2 in *Star Wars*, today's home robots are surprisingly sophisticated. Here are a few examples.

Sony's robot dog, Aibo, can fetch, respond to its owner's voice, take photos, and find its recharger when its batteries run low. (See *http://www-2.cs. cmu.edu/~robosoccer/image-gallery/legged/2003/aibo-with-ball12.jpg*.)

Roomba is a self-propelled vacuum cleaner that is shaped like a thick Frisbee. An ultrasound monitor helps it avoid banging into furniture, and an infrared eye keeps it from falling down stairs. (See *http://techdigestuk.typepad.com/tech_digest/roomba_virtual.JPG*.)

From Yujin Robotics, the iRobi robot sings, dances, and even teaches English to young children. When Mom is out, she can use a wireless link to peek in on things through the robot's video camera eyes. She also can send video messages to the kids through an embedded monitor. (See *http://www.liputan6.com/ln/img/070304aLnRobot.jpg*.)

Wow Wee's Robosapiens robot has 67 preprogrammed moves controlled by a remote. (See *http://www.solarbotics.net/albums/Wowwee-Robosapien/comdex_robosapiens_001.jpg*.)

Honda Motor Co. has developed new technologies for the next-generation ASIMO humanoid robot. The new version will function more effec-

tively by quickly processing information and acting more nimbly in real-world environments. ASIMO can run in a human-like way, and it can take flexible routes to a destination. (See *http://world.honda.com/HDTV/ASIMO/200412-run/index.html*.)

Sources: Compiled from S.F. Brown, "Send in the Robots," *Fortune*, January 24, 2005, pp. 140 [C]–140 [L]; and C. Edwards, "Ready to Buy a Home Robot?" *BusinessWeek*, July 19, 2004, pp. 84–90.

QUESTIONS

1. What will be the impact on employment as robots take over more and more tasks previously performed by humans?
2. What additional functions do you think robots will be able to perform in the future?

Improvements in Health Care   IT has brought about major improvements in healthcare delivery. Medical personnel use IT to make better and faster diagnoses and to monitor critically ill patients more accurately. IT also has streamlined the process of researching and developing new drugs. Expert systems now support diagnosis of diseases, and machine vision is enhancing the work of radiologists. Recently, surgeons started to use virtual reality to plan complex surgeries. They have also used a surgical robot to perform long-distance surgery, by controlling the robot's movements. Cardiologists can interpret the vital signs from their patients' hearts from a distance (see *http://www.micromedtech.com/real/micromed01.html*). Finally, doctors can now discuss complex medical cases not only on the telephone, but also with the support of pictures and sound.

The medical industry has long been using advanced technologies to diagnose and treat health problems. For example, there is an "ingestible camera" pill that, when swallowed, takes color images from inside the intestines. It then transmits the images wirelessly to a device worn on a patient's belt for later examination (go to *www.givenimaging.com*, and see the PillCam). In addition, new computer simulations recreate the sense of touch, allowing doctors-in-training to perform virtual procedures without risking harm to an actual patient. The following example demonstrates the use of IT to combat hospital infections.

Hospitals Fight Infections with Data. Every year, 2 million patients contract infections in U.S. hospitals, and about 90,000 of them die as a result. Despite the severity of this problem, physicians have no systematic way to quickly and effectively identify infections that are spreading through a hospital. Now, U.S. hospitals are adopting data analysis technologies to alert doctors to problems they might otherwise miss.

One company that helps hospitals track infections is MedMined (*www.medmined.com*). Hospitals transmit encrypted data from patient records and laboratory tests to MedMined, which then uses data mining to discover unusual patterns in the hospital. For example, the data mining can discover traits that patients with the infection have in common. MedMined also analyzes data from emergency rooms and outpatient clinics for signs of community outbreaks and bioterrorism events.

Example

Hospitals have an incentive to pursue infection surveillance. Public scrutiny of hospital-acquired infections is increasing. For example, Illinois, Pennsylvania, and Missouri have passed laws requiring hospitals to publicly reveal their infection rates, and similar bills are pending in Florida and California. (*Sources:* Compiled from C. Lok, "Fighting Infections with Data," *MIT Technology Review*, October 2004, p. 24; and *www.medmined.com*, accessed March 17, 2005.)

Of the thousands of other applications related to health care, it is interesting to point out the administrative systems. These systems range from detecting insurance fraud to nursing scheduling to financial and marketing management.

The Internet contains vast amounts of medical information. For example, a site about cancer (*www.cancer.org*) features a huge array of documents, reviews, descriptions of personal experiences, suggested diets, and links to global resources for people who suffer from cancer. It also offers information on the latest research studies and on managing cancer pain. In addition, it helps families of cancer patients cope with their emotional and financial burdens.

There are numerous Web sites devoted to all kinds of specific health topics. The best-known health supersite is WebMD (*www.webmd.com*). Among the specific sites, iEmily (*www.iemily.com*) provides information on the physical and mental health of teenage girls. TeenGrowth (*www.teengrowth.com*) and KidsHealth (*www.kidshealth.org*) provide articles on general, sexual, and emotional health, as well as on fitness, sports, family, and safety issues. Organized like interactive magazines, these sites also offer discussion forums, chat rooms, and hyperlinks to related resources.

Finally, the outbreak of Severe Acute Respiratory Syndrome (SARS) demonstrated how IT can support the social and psychological needs of patients. Technologies such as Web cameras, audio/video phones, and Web-conferencing software enabled patients to stay in touch with their relatives and friends while they were under quarantine.

Crime Fighting and Other Benefits   Other quality-of-life improvements brought about by IT relate to crime fighting and other government services and benefits. Here are some examples of how computer applications can benefit society:

- Since 1997, information about sex offenders has been available on the Internet. People can now find out whether previously convicted offenders are living in their localities.

- Los Angeles County has a sophisticated computer program for reporting and tracking more than 150,000 gang members in the county. The program significantly helps reduce gang-related crimes.

- Electronic imaging and electronic fax enhance searches for missing children. In addition to its Web site (*www.missingkids.com*), which attracts more than a million hits each day, the Center for Missing and Exploited Children can send high-quality photos plus text to many fax machines and to portable machines in police cars. Computers have improved the quality of fax transmission and have increased the number of people who receive the announcements.

- A geographical information system helps the San Bernardino Sheriff's Department visualize crime patterns and allocate resources.

- Electronic sensors and computers reduce traffic congestion in many major cities, from Los Angeles to Tokyo.

- Police can now track emergency (911) calls made from cell phones equipped with GPS systems.

IT Is Used by All Departments

We saw in Chapter 1 that IT systems are integral to every functional area of an organization. In *finance* and *accounting*, for example, managers use IT systems to forecast revenues and business activity, to determine the best sources and uses of funds, and to perform audits to ensure that the organization is fundamentally sound and that all financial reports and documents are accurate. The next example illustrates how the Sarbanes–Oxley Act is helping Crown Media Holdings in two different ways.

Crown Media Complies with Sarbanes–Oxley. As we discussed in Chapter 1, the Sarbanes–Oxley Act of 2002 sets a series of deadlines for public companies to certify that their financial results are accurate, that all material information is reported in a timely fashion, and that they have ironclad process controls to protect the integrity of their financial data. Crown Media Holdings (*www.crownmedia.net*), the owner of the Hallmark Channel, had to produce its compliance report by the end of 2004. To meet this requirement, the company mapped in its balance sheet every major process it used to handle incoming and outgoing revenue and expenses. Much of these data had been located in standalone Excel spreadsheets, often without any safeguards to ensure that the numbers were not altered before being consolidated into overall company results.

Crown Media uploaded its Excel data and the processes used for recording each financial transaction into a software package called Movaris Certainty (*www.movaris.com*), which was specifically designed for Sarbanes–Oxley compliance. The software produced a hierarchy of preventive controls for every division and for every type of financial activity in the company. With these controls, when there is noncompliance or a possible misuse of internal data, executives receive an alert that pinpoints the problem and triggers possible disciplinary or mitigating action.

Examples

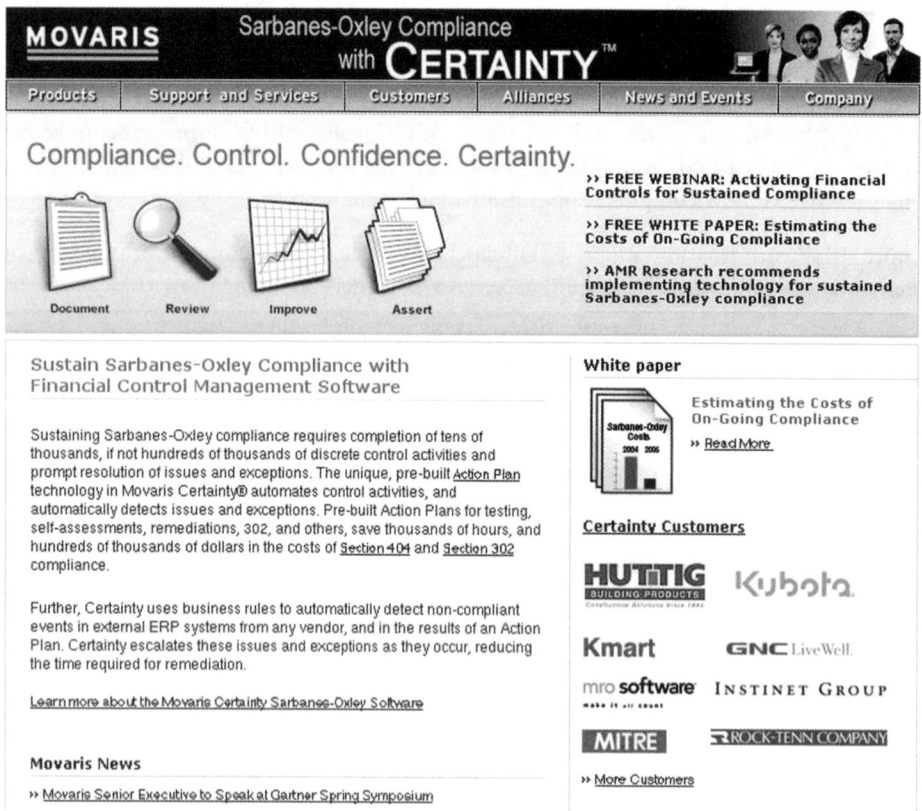

This process should satisfy Sarbanes–Oxley requirements. However, it also provides an added benefit to Crown Media. The new system has made internal financial data instantly available throughout the company. This availability lets Crown Media pursue marketing campaigns that larger companies have traditionally been able to pursue. (*Sources:* Compiled from J. Rothfeder, "Analysis: High Speed Compliance," *CIO Insight*, May 1, 2004; and *www.crownmedia.net* and *www.movaris.com*, accessed March 22, 2005.)

In *sales* and *marketing*, managers use information technology to perform the following functions:

- *Product analysis:* developing new goods and services
- *Site analysis:* determining the best location for production and distribution facilities
- *promotion analysis:* identifying the best advertising channels
- *Price analysis:* setting product prices to get the highest total revenues

Marketing managers also use IT to manage their relationships with their customers.

In *manufacturing*, managers use IT to process customer orders, develop production schedules, control inventory levels, and monitor product quality. They also use IT to design and manufacture products. These processes are called computer-assisted design (CAD) and computer-assisted manufacturing (CAM).

Managers in *human resources* use IT to screen job applicants, administer performance tests to employees, and monitor employee productivity. These managers also use legal IT to analyze product liability and warranties and to develop important legal documents and reports. The following example demonstrates how PriceWaterhouseCoopers uses its human resources software to achieve a competitive advantage.

Example

The Human Resources Management System at PWC. PriceWaterhouseCoopers (PWC) (*www.pwc.com*) is a large, global consulting company that saw the need to streamline its human resource management function across the globe. Many of the company's territories either had their own HR system or had no system at all. Not only did this inefficiency lead to higher costs, it left PWC with no common HR processes. This situation was a big challenge because, although PWC is global, its core operations tend to be at the country level.

PWC addresses this problem by instituting a common HR management system across 12 countries and in 12 languages. The first benefit to accrue from the new HR system was reduced costs and a common process for managing HR in the company. The second benefit was that PWC could now deliver better service to its clients. When PWC wins an assignment, the company often has to put a team together immediately. The new HR system lets PWC know which employees are available, which ones have the skills to meet the client's needs, and how the company can reach them. The third benefit was that the new system helps PWC manage risk and exposure in a tightening regulatory environment through improved compliance and tracking. PWC now has detailed information about what people are doing and the clients with whom they are working. (*Sources:* Compiled from *www.people soft.com* and *www.pwc.com*, accessed February 7, 2005.)

These are just a few examples of the roles of information technology in the various functional areas of an organization. We think it is important for students from the different functional areas to see the value of the information systems in their fields.

1. What are the major reasons why it is important for employees in all functional areas to become familiar with IT?
2. Why is it important to become knowledgeable about information technology if you are not working as an IT employee?

What's in IT for me?

In the previous section, we discussed IT in each of the functional areas. Here, we take a brief look at the MIS function.

The MIS Function

The MIS function is tasked with the responsibility for providing the information needed by each of the functional areas to make decisions. To provide this information, MIS personnel must understand the information requirements of managers from each functional area, as well as understand the technology. Therefore, we see that MIS personnel must think "business needs" first and "technology" second.

1. **Describe the characteristics of the digital economy and e-business.**

   Conducting e-business in the digital economy means using Web-based systems on the Internet and other electronic networks. The digital economy is based on digital technologies, including digital communications networks (the Internet, intranets, extranets, and others), computers, software, and other related information technologies. Digital networking infrastructures enable the digital economy by providing a global platform over which people and organizations interact, communicate, collaborate, and search for information.

2. **Discuss the relationships among business pressures, organizational responses, and information systems.**

   The business environment is the combination of social, legal, economic, physical, and political factors that affect business activities. Significant changes in any of these factors are likely to create business pressures. Organizations typically respond to these pressures with activities supported by IT. These activities include strategic systems, customer focus, make-to-order and mass customization, and e-business.

3. **Describe strategic information systems (SISs), and explain their advantages.**

   Strategic information systems support or shape a business unit's competitive strategy. An SIS can significantly change the manner in which business is conducted to help the firm gain a competitive advantage or reduce a competitive disadvantage.

Summary

4. Describe Porter's competitive forces model and how IT helps companies improve their competitive positions.

Companies use Porter's competitive forces model to develop strategies to gain a competitive advantage. Porter's model also demonstrates how IT can enhance a company's competitiveness. It identifies five major forces that could endanger a company's position in a given industry: (1) the threat of new competitors entering the market, (2) the bargaining power of suppliers, (3) the bargaining power of customers (buyers), (4) the threat of substitute products or services, and (5) the rivalries among existing firms in the industry. The Internet has changed the nature of competition. Porter concludes that the *overall* impact of the Internet is to increase competition, which has a negative impact on profitability.

5. Describe five strategies that companies can use to achieve competitive advantage in their industries.

The five strategies are as follows: (1) *cost leadership strategy*—produce products and/or services at the lowest cost in the industry; (2) *differentiation strategy*—offer different products, services, or product features; (3) *innovation strategy*—introduce new products and services, put new features in existing products and services, or develop new ways to produce them; (4) *operational effectiveness strategy*—improve the manner in which internal business processes are executed so that a firm performs similar activities better than rivals; and (5) *customer-orientation strategy*—concentrate on making customers happy.

Chapter Glossary

competitive advantage An advantage over competitors in some measure such as cost, quality, or speed; leads to control of a market and to larger-than-average profits. (38)

competitive forces model A business framework devised by Michael Porter, that analyzes competitiveness by recognizing five major forces that could endanger a company's position. (39)

customer relationship management (CRM) An enterprisewide effort to acquire and retain customers, often supported by IT. (34)

cybercafés Public places in which Internet terminals are available, usually for a small fee. (35)

digital economy An economy based on digital technologies, including communications networks (the Internet, intranets, and extranets), computers, software, and other related technologies. It is also called the Internet economy, the new economy, or the Web economy. (29)

e-business/e-commerce The conducting of business functions (e.g., buying and selling goods and services, servicing customers, collaborating with business partners) electronically in order to enhance an organization's operations. (30)

ergonomics The science of adapting machines and work environments to people, focusing on creating an environment that is safe, well lit, and comfortable. (46)

make-to-order The strategy of producing customized products and services. (38)

mass customization A production process in which items are produced in large quantities but are customized to fit the desires of each customer. (38)

strategic information systems (SISs) Systems that help an organization gain a competitive advantage by supporting its strategic goals and/or increasing performance and productivity. (39)

Discussion Questions

1. How has the digital economy affected competition?
2. Review the examples of the new versus old economy cases. In what ways did IT make the difference in each case?
3. Is IT a strategic weapon or a survival tool? Discuss.
4. Why might it be difficult to justify a strategic information system?

5. Describe the five forces in Porter's competitive forces model, and explain how the Internet has affected each one.
6. Why has the Internet been called the creator of new business models?
7. Discuss the idea that an information system by itself can rarely provide a sustainable competitive advantage.
8. Discuss the reasons why some information systems fail.

Problem-Solving Activities

1. Visit some Web sites that offer employment opportunities in IT. Prominent examples are: *www.hotjobs.com, www.monster.com, www.collegerecruiter.com, www.career builder.com, www.directemployers.com, www.job.com, www.career.com, www.truecareers.com.* Compare the IT salaries to salaries offered to accountants, marketing personnel, financial personnel, operations personnel, and human resources personnel. For other information on IT salaries, check *Computerworld's* annual salary survey.
2. Prepare a short report on the role of IT in government. Start with *www.whitehouse.gov/omb/egov, www.*

estrategy.gov, www.ctg.albany.edu, and *www.e-government. govt.nz.* Find e-government plans in Hong Kong and in Singapore (*www.info.gov.hk/digital21/e-gov/eng/index. htm* and *www.egov.gov.sg*).
3. Wal-Mart can offer "always low prices" largely as the result of the efficiency of its IT-enabled supply chain. Visit *www.wal-mart.com,* and examine the requirements to become a Wal-Mart supplier. How can Wal-Mart place such stringent requirements on its suppliers?

Internet Activities

1. Access the leading travel Web sites, such as *www. orbitz.com, www.travelocity.com, www.sidestep.com,* and *www.expedia.com.* Examine and compare the features of each site. Which site is the easiest to use? The most useful? Explain why. Next, find other travel sites, and compare them to these four.
2. Access *www.digitalenterprise.org.* Prepare a report regarding the latest electronic commerce developments in the digital age.

3. Access *www.x-home.com* and find information about the home of the future.
4. Experience customization by designing your own shoes at *www.nike.com,* your car at *www.jaguar.com,* your CD at *www.easternrecording.com,* and your business card at *www.iprint.com.* Summarize your experiences.

Team Assignments

1. Assign group members to each of the major car rental companies. Research their latest strategies regarding customer service. Visit their Web sites, and compare the findings. Have each group prepare a presentation on why its company should get the title of "best customer service provider." Also, each group should use Porter's competitive forces model to help make its case.

2. Assign group members to UPS, FedEx, DHL, and the U.S. Postal Service. Have each group study the e-commerce strategies of one organization. Then have members present the organization, explaining why it is the best.

CASE **Surviving in the Digital Age: Kodak's Story**

THE BUSINESS PROBLEM The fundamental challenge for Kodak (*www.kodak.com*) is replacing its high-margin film and film-processing business with a digital business that has very small profit margins and technical complexities that strong brand recognition alone cannot solve. Kodak's digital business will promise customers that they can order prints anywhere at any time. As photography shifts from traditional film to digits on networks, Kodak must develop an entirely new series of services to provide to retailers and other business partners. Otherwise, the company simply cannot survive.

Since 1990, Kodak has invested $7 billion in developing digital cameras, digital printing, and other digital businesses. In addition, in September 2003 the company cut its dividend to invest an additional $3 billion in developing these businesses. Despite this huge investment, Kodak's stock has fallen by 70 percent since 1998.

To further complicate matters, high-quality photo printers are now available—and affordable—for amateur as well as professional photographers. As a result, customers can now completely bypass Kodak in capturing, processing, and printing images. To meet this challenge, Kodak has to convince its increasingly independent customers that it remains the (best) source for low-cost yet high-quality prints. The company also wants to recapture its role as the central intermediary in print processing. To accomplish this goal it must develop a strategy to dominate global communications and printing standards. These standards will be open and shared not just among its retail and industrial customers but also among rival photo services, camera makers, and print producers.

THE IT SOLUTION Kodak is employing three strategies to move into the digital age. The company's first strategy is to serve the everyday snapshot artist through Ofoto.com. The service permanently stores photos for free and then charges customers for making and mailing out prints.

Kodak's second strategy is the development of the Common Picture Exchange Environment (CPXe). The CPXe is the set of standards that will enable Kodak and customers to transmit images from digital cameras, personal computers, and editing software to photofinishers anywhere. Photographers will be able to select from such photofinishers as stores or kiosks in malls, mini-labs in pharmacies, portals on the Internet, and a print factory maintained by Kodak itself. To make CPXe into a "common environment," Kodak will need many allies, from camera makers such as Olympus, Canon, and Nikon to rival print and film maker Fuji Photo Film to computer

and printer manufacturers such as Hewlett-Packard and Dell. Kodak's third strategy is to invest in medical imaging and digital applications for the growing commercial printing market.

THE RESULTS With respect to Kodak's first strategy, digital photographers take many images but make few prints. Ofoto now has more than 13 million registered users, but only 1 million of them have ever ordered a print. As a result, Kodak has yet to make a profit from Ofoto.

With respect to Kodak's second strategy, to this point few companies have been willing to participate in CPXe. Rather, many competitors are following similar strategies themselves. For example, camera makers from Canon to Sony believe that they can become as central to users of digital photography as Kodak. In addition, Hewlett-Packard generates almost 80 percent of its operating income from imaging and printing. Key suppliers of software for the exchange of documents over the Internet, such as Microsoft and Adobe Systems, are pursuing their own strategies for online photo ordering. Many companies say that Kodak's drive to be so thoroughly entrenched in all aspects of the digital imaging market is precisely why so few companies have joined CPXe. For example, camera manufacturers and photofinishers are entering into partnerships with one another based on proprietary hardware and software. As a result, almost 90 percent of all digital images are printed at home on ink-jet printers.

Kodak's third strategy has proved to be more successful. Sales and profits for capturing and processing images for hospitals and other health-care providers have increased. Overall, however, Kodak's gross profit margin dropped from 45 percent in 1998 to 32 percent in 2004. Digital cameras earn razor-thin margins, and Ofoto earns no margin at all. Despite all its efforts, Kodak has yet to show how it will make money in the digital era.

Sources: Compiled from L. Barrett, and D. F. Carr, "Eastman Kodak: Picture Imperfect," *Baseline Magazine*, September 1, 2004; and "Kodak Posts Loss, Citing Costs of Shifts to Digital Photography," *New York Times*, April 23, 2005.

QUESTIONS

1. Kodak is implementing three IT strategies to compete in the digital economy. Do you think they will work? Why or why not?
2. Draw an analogy between Kodak and music retailers. What impact has the digital age had on each? Can Kodak and the music retailers survive?

Interactive Learning

How Does UPS Track Its Orders?

Go to the Interactivities section on the *WileyPLUS* Web site, and access Chapter 2: The modern Organization in the Digital Economy. There you will find an interactive simulation of the UPS Tracking system, as well as some hands-on activities that visually explain business concepts in this chapter.

Identifying Information at Club IT

Go to the Club IT link on the *WileyPLUS* Web site. There you will find a description of your internship at this downtown music venue, as well as some assignments that will help you learn how to apply IT solutions to a virtual business.

wiley.com/college/rainer

Chapter 3

Information technologies, properly used, can have enormous benefits for individuals, organizations, and entire societies. In the first two chapters we discussed the diverse ways in which IT has made businesses more productive, efficient, and responsive to consumers. We also have explored areas such as medicine in which IT has improved people's health and well-being. Unfortunately, information technologies can also be misused, often with devastating consequences. Consider the following:

- Individuals can have their identities stolen.
- Organizations can have customer information stolen, leading to financial losses and erosion of customer confidence.
- Countries face the threat of cyberterrorism and cyberwarfare.

In fact, the misuse of information technologies has come to the forefront of any discussion of IT. Now that you are acquainted with the major capabilities of IT, we address the complex issues of ethics, privacy, and security.

Ethics, Privacy, and Information Security

Introduction to Information Systems
R. Kelly Rainer, Jr., Efraim Turban, and Richard E. Potter. ISBN 978-0-471-7363-3
©2007 John Wiley & Sons, Inc.

Student Web Site
- Web Quizzes
- Links to relevant Web sites
- Lecture Slides in PowerPoint

WileyPlus
- Virtual Company assignments and Club IT Web site
- Interactive Learning Sessions
- Microsoft Excel and Access Exercises
- Software Skills Tutorials
- e-book

Chapter Outline

3.1 Ethical Issues
3.2 Threats to Information Security
3.3 Protecting Information Resources

Learning Objectives

1. Describe the major ethical issues related to information technology, and identify situations in which they occur.

2. Identify the many threats to information security.

3. Understand the various defense mechanisms used to protect information systems.

4. Explain IT auditing and planning for disaster recovery.

What's in IT for me? ACC FIN MKT POM HRM MIS

What Sin City Can Teach the Department of Homeland Security

CASE

The Business Problem

No city has attracted more dubious characters than Las Vegas. "Sin City" is a most vigilant and diligent user of advanced surveillance, identification, background checking, and security technologies. The business problem is simple: Catch the bad guys. The technology solution is very complex, however, because casinos employ a vast number of information technologies in their security efforts.

Source: Andre Jenny/The Image Works

The IT Solutions

NORA and ANNA "Non-obvious relationship awareness" (NORA) software searches for obvious and non-obvious relationships among data stored in multiple databases. NORA flags high-risk individuals—from casino cheats to terrorists—and then compares what it knows about them with information in airline-reservation, passport, and other databases.

NORA is able to identify all types of relationships. Stated in technical terms, it can uncover connections that span more than 30 degrees of separation. The term "degree of separation" refers to the closeness of the relationship among various types of data. Generally, the smaller the degree, the closer the relationship. For example, two people who work at the same casino and also listed the same address on their resumes would represent 1 degree of separation. The second degree could be a third-party vendor providing chips to the casino who attended the same high school as one of those two employees. The third degree would be if all three of these individuals maintain checking accounts at the same bank. Because it can span more than 30 degrees, NORA can discover a wide-ranging number of connections that can indicate even remote possibilities of security risks.

"Anonymized data analysis" (ANNA) allows investigators to search databases without seeing names, addresses, and other information they are examining. With ANNA, owners of data send that data to a third party in a coded form. That third party acts as an independent holder of the data. It indexes the contents and then applies another level of coding that makes it impossible to read or restore the data to its original form.

Investigators then pose queries to the coded data, but cannot see or learn the original names, addresses, or information. If the investigators' queries produce matches, they ask the original holder of the data for the specific information underlying those matches. For example, casino employees who make many cell phone calls to known felons would be a suspicious match.

Customer Monitoring In addition to these systems, casinos use a number of high-tech devices to create profiles of suspected cheaters. Among these technologies are digital-video surveillance cameras, facial-recognition software, and transaction-tracking systems.

Digital-video surveillance enables casinos to record what goes on inside and outside their walls 24 hours a day, every day. Analysis software then searches and analyzes the images. Digital video makes it easier to program video systems to alert operators about suspicious activities. Compared to VHS tape, digital video also provides better facial images, and it reduces the time required to find specific frames of video from hours to seconds.

Facial-recognition software mathematically measures features such as the distance between a person's eyes or the structure of his or her cheekbone to compare a face to stored images. These systems are designed to see through disguises. Casinos admit, though, that the facial-recognition software alone is not enough. For this reason, they hire trained operators, including security guards, pit bosses, cheat spotters, and investigators, to make the actual decisions about persons they want to identify. These operators carry handheld digital assistants or laptop computers that receive images from the digital video via a wireless network.

The tracking systems used by casinos are very thorough. For example, if you arrive by rental car or taxi, these systems photograph both you and the vehicle's license plate. In fact, they will photograph you even if you arrive on foot. In addition, X-rays and bomb-sniffing dogs will check your bags, laptops, and parcels. If you purchase more than $1,000 in chips at one time, the casino secretly investigates you for money laundering. If you then win more than $600, you have to produce two legitimate forms of identification before you receive your payout. Your purchases from cocktail waitresses and the restaurant are recorded. If you use cash, the serial number on each bill is recorded. If you make calls from your room, even "free" local calls, the time, number dialed, and duration of the call are recorded. Room-service orders and movie choices also are recorded.

Some casinos are even using chips with embedded radio-frequency identification (RFID) tags in them. The casino can monitor betting patterns and detect attempts to cheat–such as moving chips after all bets have been placed.

Monitoring Employees Casinos realize that people and their circumstances change all the time. For this reason it's not enough to check employees' background or credit before the casino hires them. Casinos must know what is going on with employees right now. To accomplish this goal they employ the same technologies they use to monitor customers.

Sharing Information Casinos have been sharing their information on customers and employees with one another for years. They also share information with the Las Vegas Metropolitan Police Department and the FBI. In the other direction, the FBI e-mails a daily report to the casinos with names and descriptions of suspected terrorists.

According to the FBI, since 2001 Las Vegas has recorded the fewest crimes per thousand residents of any U.S. city with a population of more than 1 million residents. The Department of Homeland Security and other federal agencies now use the same security technologies to pursue terrorists. The question remains, however, whether the agencies will share information with one another to the necessary degree. The head of security at one Las Vegas casino noted that if government agencies had been using these technologies and sharing their information, they might have caught the 9/11 terrorists and prevented the attacks.

The events of September 11, 2001, led the Bush administration to establish the Department of Homeland Security. The attacks and the government reponse have fueled an intense debate over how much privacy U.S. citizens have to and are willing to give up in return for increased security. This debate involves both the government's strategies to provide that security and the ethical questions surrounding those strategies.

The lessons that can be learned from the Las Vegas casinos address the three major issues discussed in this chapter: ethics, privacy, and security. Each of these issues is closely related to IT and raises significant questions. For example, is it ethical for the casinos to gather so much information on each guest? Is such thorough monitoring necessary? Increased surveillance, by definition, leads to a loss of privacy at the same time that it increases security. Is it worth trading privacy for security? How much privacy will be and should be lost for how much additional security? Finally, who should make these decisions?

The answers to these and other questions are not clear. As we discuss ethics, privacy, and security in the context of information technology, you will acquire a better understanding of these issues, their importance, their relationships, and their trade-offs.

Sources: Compiled from L. Barrett, and S. Gallagher, "What Sin City Can Teach Tom Ridge," *Baseline Magazine*, April 4, 2004; R. Jarvis, "Casinos Bet Big on RFID," *Business 2.0*, March 23, 2005; and *http://lasvegas.about.com/cs/casinohoteljobs/a/Security.htm*, accessed March 3, 2005.

3.1 Ethical Issues

As we discussed in Chapter 2, ethics deals with what is considered to be right and wrong. Before we go any further, it is very important that you realize that what is *unethical* is not necessarily *illegal.* In most instances, then, an individual or organization faced with an ethical decision is not considering whether to break the law. This doesn't mean, however, that ethical decisions don't have serious consequences for individuals, organizations, or society at large.

Deciding what is right or wrong is not always easy or clear-cut. For this reason, many companies and professional organizations develop their own codes of ethics. A **code of ethics** is a collection of principles that are intended to guide decision making by members of the organization. The diversity and ever-expanding use of IT applications have created a variety of ethical issues. These issues fall into four general categories: privacy, accuracy, property, and accessibility.

1. *Privacy issues* involve collecting, storing, and disseminating information about individuals.
2. *Accuracy issues* involve the authenticity, fidelity, and accuracy of information that is collected and processed.
3. *Property issues* involve the ownership and value of information.
4. *Accessibility issues* revolve around who should have access to information and whether they should have to pay for this access.

Manager's Checklist 3.1 lists representative questions and issues for each of these categories. In addition, Online Appendix W3.1 presents 14 ethics scenarios for you to consider.

Protecting Privacy

In general, **privacy** is the right to be left alone and to be free of unreasonable personal intrusions. *Information privacy* is the right to determine when, and to what extent, information about yourself can be gathered and/or communicated to others. Privacy rights apply to individuals, groups, and institutions.

The definition of privacy can be interpreted quite broadly. However, court decisions in many countries have followed two rules fairly closely:

1. The right of privacy is not absolute. Privacy must be balanced against the needs of society.
2. The public's right to know is superior to the individual's right of privacy.

These two rules show why it is difficult in some cases to determine and enforce privacy regulations. The right to privacy is recognized today in all U.S. states and by the federal government, either by statute or common law. In the following section we explore some representative issues involving privacy.

Electronic Surveillance According to the American Civil Liberties Union (ACLU), tracking people's activities with the aid of computers has become a major privacy-related problem. The ACLU notes that this monitoring, or **electronic surveillance**, is rapidly increasing, particularly with the emergence of new technologies. IT's About Business 3.1 demonstrates that such monitoring may not be well received by employees.

In general, employees have very limited protection against surveillance by employers. Although several legal challenges are now underway, the law appears to support the right of employers to read their employees' e-mail and other electronic documents and to monitor their Internet use.

Surveillance is also a concern for private individuals regardless of whether it is conducted by corporations, government bodies, or criminals. Many Americans are still trying to determine the appropriate balance between personal privacy and electronic surveillance, especially where threats to national security are involved. The terrorist attacks of 9/11 and the subsequent anthrax attacks caused many Americans to change their positions toward allowing more government surveillance. The next example illustrates how technology can lead to increased surveillance of individuals.

(handwritten note in left margin:) (Lloyd) - 251 Example.

A Framework for Ethical Issues

Privacy Issues

☐ What information about oneself should an individual be required to reveal to others?
☐ What kind of surveillance can an employer use on its employees?
☐ What things can people keep to themselves and not be forced to reveal to others?
☐ What information about individuals should be kept in databases, and how secure is the information there?

Accuracy Issues

☐ Who is responsible for the authenticity, fidelity, and accuracy of information collected?
☐ How can we ensure that information will be processed properly and presented accurately to users?
☐ How can we ensure that errors in databases, data transmissions, and data processing are accidental and not intentional?
☐ Who is to be held accountable for errors in information, and how should the injured party by compensated?

Property Issues

☐ Who owns the information?
☐ What are the just and fair prices for its exchange?
☐ How should one handle software piracy (copying copyrighted software)?
☐ Under what circumstances can one use proprietary databases?
☐ Can corporate computers be used for private purposes?
☐ How should experts who contribute their knowledge to create expert systems be compensated?
☐ How should access to information channels be allocated?

Accessibility Issues

☐ Who is allowed to access information?
☐ How much should be charged for permitting accessibility to information?
☐ How can accessibility to computers be provided for employees with disabilities?
☐ Who will be provided with equipment needed for accessing information?
☐ What information does a person or an organization have a right or a privilege to obtain, and under what conditions and with what safeguards?

Car Insurance Rates Based on GPS Tracking. What if liability premiums were based not on demographics (e.g., your age and gender) and Department of Motor Vehicles (DMV) records (e.g., the number of speeding tickets you have had in the last three years), but on your actual driving habits? With the help of the Global Positioning System (GPS), the British insurance company Norwich Union (*www.norwichunion.com*) is attempting to do just that.

In a pilot test, Norwich Union tracked 5,000 of its customers by placing GPS receivers in the trunks of their cars. The company then used data from the devices to adjust drivers' premiums from month to month. In doing so it calculated everything from speed and acceleration to whether drivers were braking too early or too late at intersections. Overall, Norwich Union collected data on about 1 million journeys. Company statisticians are now using the data to recalculate its insurance tables. The company plans to make the technology available to the rest of its 3.5 million customers, hoping that the feedback will lead to fewer accidents—and thus higher profits. (*Sources:* Compiled from E. Schonfeld, "GPS-Tracked Car Insurance," *Business 2.0*, January/February 2005, p. 49; and "UK: Customised Car Insurance," *www.qualisteam.com/news/mar05/15-03-05-7.html*, accessed March 10, 2005.)

IT's About Business

3.1 Your Boss Is Watching

Many companies monitor employee e-mail and Internet usage, and Web-based security cameras are commonplace in many buildings. However, technologies such as the Global Positioning System (GPS) and employee badges with radio-frequency identification (RFID) tags promise to take employee monitoring to a new level. Today's tracking systems can record, display, and archive the exact location of any employee, both inside and outside the office, at any time, offering managers the unprecedented ability to monitor employee behavior.

On the surface, tracking employees seems like an obvious way to boost productivity. Monitoring the location of truck drivers on the road, for example, allows dispatch offices to route deliveries more effectively. On-the-road monitoring can make it easier to provide roadside assistance, reduce damage claims and lawsuits, and reduce excessive break times. Similarly, monitoring employees in the office using RFID technology can help management quickly locate key people and keep unauthorized personnel out of secure areas.

Despite the potential benefits, many employees find the tracking technologies to be extremely intrusive. As an example, consider the police department of Orlando, Florida. Every police officer's nightmare is to be wounded on the streets while alone. To address this fear, the Orlando Police Department pilot-tested new GPS units, which let the central office track the locations of their people. Instead of being grateful, as the Police Department anticipated, police officers resented being monitored 24/7. In addition, they did not see much benefit from the system in their daily work. After the unions strenuously objected, the project was canceled.

Sources: Compiled from G. James, "Can't Hide Your Prying Eyes," *Computerworld*, March 1, 2004; "A Post-Privacy Future for Workers," *BW Online*, April 13, 2004; and *www.privacyrights.org/fs/fs7-work.htm*, accessed March 7, 2005.

QUESTIONS

1. Describe how you would feel to be monitored at work with an RFID tag in your ID badge. Would it be overly intrusive? Why or why not?
2. Would monitoring your e-mails and Internet usage be overly intrusive? Why or why not?
3. What is the difference—if any—between monitoring your location and monitoring your computer usage? Would you feel differently about one than the other? Explain.

Personal Information in Databases Information about individuals is being kept in many databases. Perhaps the most visible locations of such records are credit-reporting agencies. Other institutions that store personal information include:

- Banks and financial institutions
- Cable TV, telephone, and utilities companies
- Employers
- Apartment companies
- Mortgage companies
- Equipment rental companies
- Hospitals; schools and universities
- Supermarkets, retail establishments, and mail-order houses
- Government agencies (Internal Revenue Service, Census Bureau, your state, your municipality)
- Libraries
- Insurance companies
- Data from questionnaires you fill out on the Internet (e.g., when you try to win a prize)

There are several concerns about the information you provide to these record-keepers. Some of the major concerns are:

- Do you know where the records are?
- Are the records accurate?
- Can you change inaccurate data?
- How long will it take to make a change?
- Under what circumstances will personal data be released?
- How are the data used?
- To whom are they given or sold?
- How secure are the data against access by unauthorized people?

Obviously, storing information in databases can generate serious problems The following example shows how these problems can arise.

Big Brother and Politics. Fundrace.org (*www.fundrace.org*) follows political money to your front door. Records of campaign contributions have long been available online. By simply plugging in any address, you can retrieve a list of all the contributors in a neighborhood, their addresses and occupations, the names of their favored candidates, and the amounts they gave. These basic data are part of the public record and are supplied by the Federal Election Committee (FEC).

The Fundrace Web site takes this information further, however, by subjecting the location data to geocoding. *Geocoding* is a process that assigns a latitude–longitude coordinate to each address. The site also presents several indexes that use census data to rank candidates by the characteristics of their contributors. A GrassRoots Index shows who has received small contributions from all over America. A Devotion Index shows who inspires repeat giving and financial sacrifice. Finally, a FatCats Index shows who gets large contributions from the wealthiest Americans. In May 2004, President Bush led in the GrassRoots and Devotion indexes, and Senator Kerry led in FatCats donations. Finally, the Web site features maps of the top 10 donating cities, showing Democratic and Republican contributions as blue or red circles superimposed on a map. Users can also use Fundrace to search contributors by name, which lends itself nicely to celebrity sleuthing.

Fundrace has received hundreds of complaints about the addresses, and dozens of people have asked Fundrace to remove their information. One donor wrote to the FEC complaining that the site was violating his civil rights. He stated, "A future employer could give a job I was applying for to someone that shares his or her political philosophy." Fundrace has declined to remove any addresses on the grounds that they are part of the public record and can be found at the FEC's Web

Example

site. (*Sources:* Compiled from T. McNichol, "Street Maps in Political Hues," *New York Times*, May 20, 2004; and *http://libraries.mit.edu/gis/teach/geocoding.html* and *www.fund race.org*, accessed March 8, 2005.)

Information on Internet Bulletin Boards and Newsgroups Every day we see more and more *electronic bulletin boards, newsgroups,* and *electronic discussions* such as chat rooms. These sites appear on the Internet, within corporate intranets, and on blogs. A *blog* (short for Weblog) is an informal, personal journal that is frequently updated and intended for general public reading. How does society keep owners of bulletin boards from disseminating information that may be offensive to readers or simply untrue? This is a difficult problem because it involves the conflict between freedom of speech on the one hand and privacy on the other. This conflict is a fundamental and continuing ethical issue in U.S. society.

Privacy Codes and Policies **Privacy policies** or **privacy codes** are an organization's guidelines with respect to protecting the privacy of customers, clients, and employees. In many corporations, senior management has begun to understand that when they collect vast amounts of personal information, they must protect it. Manager's Checklist 3.2 provides a sampling of privacy policy guidelines.

Having a privacy policy in place can help organizations avoid legal problems. However, criminals do not pay attention to privacy codes and policies, as IT's About Business 3.2 shows.

Manager's Checklist 3.2

Privacy Policy Guidelines: A Sampler

Data Collection

- Data should be collected on individuals only for the purpose of accomplishing a legitimate business objective.
- Data should be adequate, relevant, and not excessive in relation to the business objective.
- Individuals must give their consent before data pertaining to them can be gathered. Such consent may be implied from the individual's actions (e.g., applications for credit, insurance, or employment).

Data Accuracy

- Sensitive data gathered on individuals should be verified before it is entered into the database.
- Data should, where and when necessary, be kept current.
- The file should be made available so the individual can ensure that the data are correct.
- If there is disagreement about the accuracy of the data, the individual's version should be noted and included with any disclosure of the file.

Data Confidentiality

- Computer security procedures should be implemented to ensure against unauthorized disclosure of data. They should include physical, technical, and administrative security measures.
- Third parties should not be given access to data without the individual's knowledge or permission, except as required by law.
- Disclosures of data, other than the most routine, should be noted and maintained for as long as the data are maintained.
- Data should not be disclosed for reasons incompatible with the business objective for which they are collected.

IT's About Business

3.2 Company Required to Disclose Data Breach

ChoicePoint is a data aggregator. That is, the company retrieves, stores, analyzes, and delivers data to businesses of all sizes as well as to the federal, state, and local governments. In its privacy statement, ChoicePoint Inc. (*www.choicepoint.com*) asserts that it is "dedicated to protecting the privacy of individuals." To do this, the company adheres to "strict standards regarding the use and dissemination of personal information." These statements sound very reassuring. In reality, however, the company's safeguards against disseminating personal information proved highly inadequate. At one point, identity thieves set up 50 fictitious businesses and duped ChoicePoint into granting them access to nearly 150,000 consumer-data profiles. The scam was old-fashioned, simple, and did not involve hacking into ChoicePoint's computers. Each of the fake businesses collected just enough data to remain unnoticed by ChoicePoint. Taken together, however, the stolen pieces of information painted an almost complete financial portrait of the individuals involved.

ChoicePoint was alerted about the breach in October 2004. However, some 35,000 Californian consumers did not realize they were potential victims until ChoicePoint alerted them about the security breach the following February. Significantly, California law required ChoicePoint to disclose the incident. The company further agreed to send out 110,000 additional notifications to consumers outside California. We still don't know the extent of the fraud arising from the incident.

Sources: Compiled from T. Claburn, "Law Prompts Company to Disclose Data Breach," *InformationWeek*, February 21, 2005; "The ChoicePoint Incident," *Red Herring*, February 23, 2005; and B. Sullivan, "Database Giant Gives Access to Fake Firms," *MSNBC News*, February 14, 2005.

QUESTIONS

1. Do you think ChoicePoint should be legally liable for the stolen customer data? Support your answer.
2. Discuss possible ways to defend yourself against attacks by data aggregators like ChoicePoint. Hint: See Appendix 2.

International Aspects of Privacy   Privacy regulations vary greatly from country to country. The absence of consistent or uniform standards can obstruct the flow of information among countries. The European Union (EU), for one, has taken steps to overcome this problem. In 1998 the European Community Commission (ECC) issued guidelines to all its member countries regarding the rights of individuals to access information about themselves. The ECC data protection laws are stricter than U.S. laws and therefore may create problems for multinational corporations, which may face lawsuits for privacy violation.

The transfer of data in and out of a nation without the knowledge of either the authorities or the individuals involved raises a number of privacy issues. Whose laws have jurisdiction when records are stored in a different country for reprocessing or retransmission purposes? For example, if data are transmitted by a Polish company through a U.S. satellite to a British corporation, which country's privacy laws control the data, and when? Questions like these will become more complicated and frequent as time goes on. Governments must make an effort to develop laws and standards to cope with rapidly changing information technologies in order to solve some of these privacy issues.

Before you go on . . .

1. Define ethics and list its four categories as they apply to IT.
2. Describe the issue of privacy as it is affected by IT.
3. What does a code of ethics contain?
4. Describe the relationship between IT and privacy.

3.2 Threats to Information Security

Several factors are increasing the threats to information security today. First, computing devices have shrunk in size, increased in power, and decreased in cost. As a result, many more people can afford computers with significant processing power and storage capability. The more personal information they store on these computers, the greater the threat of theft and fraud. Also, because some of these devices are small enough for people to carry with them, they can be lost or misplaced.

Second, the Internet has brought millions of unsecured computer networks into communication with each other. Our ability to secure each computer's stored information is now influenced (or determined) by the security of every other computer to which it is connected. Networks improve productivity greatly, and they are essential to operations in today's business environment. At the same time, however, they make organizational data and information much more susceptible to threats.

As more and more members of the international community become computer literate and computing devices become available to most of the population, computer security becomes ever more critical. In today's networking and Internet environment, remote users can access computer systems quickly and easily and with very little expense. This means that malicious individuals can attack from anywhere in the world at any time.

Before we discuss the many threats to information security, let's look at some key terms. Organizations have many information resources. These resources are subject to a huge number of threats. A **threat** to an information resource is any danger to which a system may be exposed. The **exposure** of an information resource is the harm, loss, or damage that can result if a threat compromises that resource. A system's **vulnerability** is the possibility that the system will suffer harm by a threat. **Risk** is the likelihood that a threat will occur. **Information system controls** are the procedures, devices, or software aimed at preventing a compromise to the system. We discuss these controls in Section 3.3.

Information systems have many components in several locations. Thus, each information system is vulnerable to many potential hazards or threats. Figure 3.1 illustrates the major threats to the security of an information system. There are many threats, so the following outline should help you follow our discussion.

Threats to Information Systems

- Unintentional
- Intentional
  - Espionage or trespass
  - Information extortion
  - Sabotage or vandalism
  - Theft
  - Identity theft
  - Software attacks
    - Viruses
    - Worms
    - Trojan horses
    - Logic bombs
    - Back doors
    - Denial of service
    - Alien software (pestware, adware, spyware, spamware, spam, cookies, Web bugs)
    - Phishing
    - Pharming
  - Compromises to intellectual property

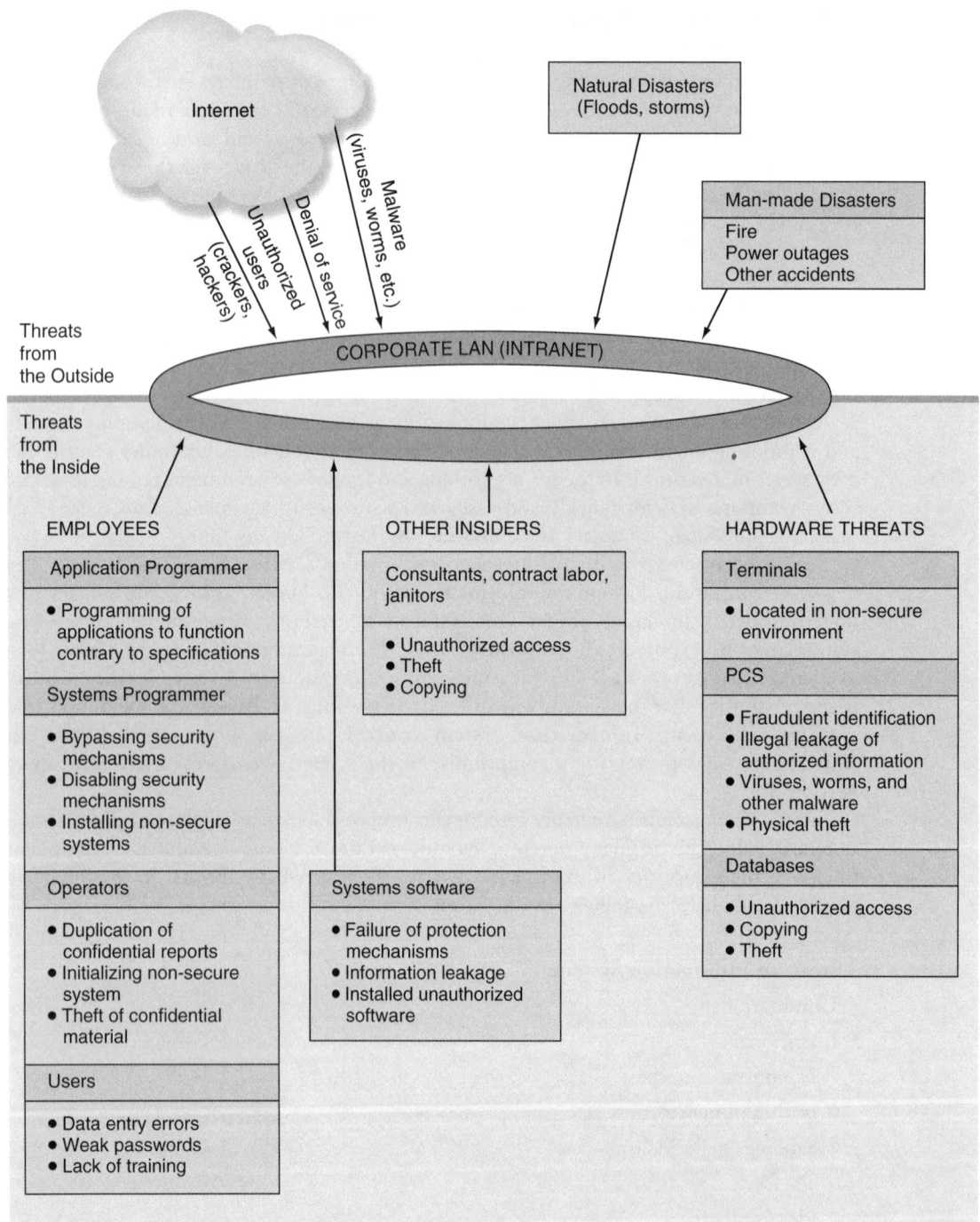

FIGURE 3.1   Security threats.

Unintentional Threats

Unintentional threats can be divided into three major categories: human errors, environmental hazards, and computer system failures. *Human errors* can occur in the design of the hardware and/or information system. They can also occur in the programming, testing, data collection, data entry, authorization, and procedures. Human errors contribute to more than half of the control- and security-related problems in many organizations.

Environmental hazards include earthquakes, severe storms, floods, power failures or strong fluctuations, fires (the most common hazard), defective air conditioning, explosions, radioactive fallout, and water-cooling-system failures. Such hazards can disrupt normal computer operations and result in long waiting periods and exorbitant costs while computer programs and data files are recreated.

Computer system failures can occur as the result of poor manufacturing or defective materials. Unintentional malfunctions can also happen for other reasons, ranging from lack of user experience to flawed testing.

Intentional Threats

Intentional threats are typically criminal in nature. **Cybercrimes** are fraudulent activities committed using computers and communications networks, particularly the Internet. Cybercrime is a serious problem in modern societies. According to the FBI, an average robbery involves about $3,000, and an average white-collar crime involves $23,000. In contrast, an average cybercrime involves about $600,000.

Cybercrimes can be committed by *outsiders* who penetrate a computer system or by *insiders* who are authorized to use the computer system but misuse their authorization. An outside person who has penetrated a computer system, usually with no criminal intent, is referred to as a **hacker**. A **cracker** is a *malicious hacker*, who may represent a serious problem for a corporation.

Crackers sometimes involve unsuspecting insiders in their crimes. For example, in a strategy called **social engineering**, computer criminals or corporate spies get around security systems by building an inappropriate trust relationship with insiders. These insiders then supply the crackers with sensitive information or unauthorized access privileges. For example, one enterprising cracker, posing as an employee in the IT department, called secretaries throughout a company. He told them that he needed their user names and passwords so that he could run a "security check" on their computers. Three-fourths of them provided the information without checking that he was who he said he was.

In addition to computer crimes against organizations, there is an alarming increase in fraud committed against individuals via the Internet. The Internet environment provides an extremely easy landscape for conducting illegal activities. Innovative criminals use hundreds of different methods and "tricks" to get money from innocent people, to buy without paying, to sell without delivering, to abuse or hurt people, and much more.

There are many types of intentional threats: espionage or trespass, information extortion, sabotage or vandalism, theft, identity theft, software attacks, and compromises to intellectual property. We discuss each in turn, with examples.

Espionage or Trespass When an unauthorized individual gains access to the information that an organization is trying to protect, that act is categorized as espionage or trespass. *Industrial espionage* occurs in areas where researching information about the competition is perfectly legal within certain limits. In cases of espionage the information gatherers go beyond these legal limits. Governments all over the world practice industrial espionage against companies in other countries. A low-technology type of espionage is *shoulder surfing*, where individuals observe information without authorization by looking at a computer monitor or ATM screen over another individual's shoulder.

Information Extortion Information extortion occurs when an attacker or formerly trusted employee steals information from a computer system and then demands compensation for its return or for an agreement to not disclose it. The following example illustrates extortion using instant messaging.

Example

Extortion with Spim. A teenager became the first person arrested in the United States for sending *spim*, or unsolicited instant messages. The teen was accused of sending approximately 1.5 million spim messages to the users of MySpace.com, an online community that caters to teenagers. After he sent the spim, he contacted MySpace officials, took responsibility for the spim flood, and proposed that he be given exclusive rights to send commercial messages to MySpace users. He also offered to protect MySpace against other spim advertisers for $150 per day. When MySpace did not respond, he threatened to show other advertisers how to send messages to MySpace users. He was arrested by the U.S. Secret Service when he traveled to Los Angeles to talk with MySpace corporate officials, who were cooperating with the Secret Service. (*Sources:* Compiled from R. Mark, "Teen's Extortion Plot Spims Out of Control," *Internetnews.com*, February 22, 2005; and C. Biever, "Spam Being Rapidly Outpaced by Spim," *www.NewScientist.com*, March 26, 2004.)

Sabotage or Vandalism   An organization's Web site is often its most visible "face" to the public. If the site is vandalized, then the organization's customers might lose confidence. In turn, loss of consumer confidence generally leads to reduced profits and income. A popular type of online vandalism is *hacktivist* or *cyberactivist* activities. Hacktivists and cyberactivists use technology for high-tech civil disobedience to protest the operations, policies, or actions of an individual, an organization, or a government agency.

For example, when the infamous hacker Kevin Mitnick (check out *www.mitnicksecurity.com*) was released from prison, he discovered that his personal Web site had been defaced by a hacker named BugBear. The message read, "Welcome to the free world. Your security skills are a little rusty, aren't they?" In another example, one of the political parties in New Zealand had Neo-Nazi slogans plastered over its Web site. The defacement led to a great deal of embarrassment and a quick shutdown of the site for a security review.

Cyberterrorism can be considered a more sinister form of cyberactivism. **Cyberterrorism** can be defined as a premeditated, politically motivated attack against information, computer systems, computer programs, and data that results in violence against noncombatant targets by subnational groups or clandestine agents. At this time, examples of cyberterrorism are limited to acts such as the defacement of NATO Web pages during the war in Kosovo.

There is increasing interest in the threat of **cyberwar**, in which a country's information systems could be paralyzed by a massive attack of destructive software. (We discuss cyberwar in the following sections.) The target systems can range from the information systems of business, government services, and the media to military command systems. In the United States, the Critical Infrastructure Protection Board (CIPB) is preparing protection plans, policies, and strategies to deal with cyberterrorism. For more details and debates, see *www.cdt.org/security/critinfra* and *www.ciaonet.org*.

Theft   Theft is the illegal taking of property that belongs to another individual or organization. Within an organization, that property can be physical, electronic, or intellectual. IT's About Business 3.3 describes a theft with an IT twist.

Identity Theft   The fastest growing white-collar crime is **identity theft**, in which a criminal poses as someone else. The thief steals Social Security numbers and credit card numbers, usually obtained from the Internet, to commit fraud (e.g., to buy products or consume services). The biggest problem for the person whose identity has been stolen is to restore his or her damaged credit rating. According to a 2003 survey by the Identity Theft Resource Center (*www.idtheftcenter.org*), the average identity theft victim spends at least 600 hours over several years and $16,000 in lost or potential income to recover from the crime. For other

IT's About Business

3.3 Using eBay to Fence Stolen Goods

Stealing the merchandise was the easy part. The ring of young men and women had become pros at snatching cashmere sweaters, perfumes, and other expensive items from stores such as Abercrombie & Fitch, Victoria's Secret, and the Pottery Barn. The problem was how to turn the stolen goods into cash. Any attempt to return the goods for refunds would probably not work without some proof of purchase.

The ring discovered that some stores would allow them to return the goods without receipts for store credit or gift cards. They then sold those vouchers on eBay. It was easy, instant, and anonymous. They received 76 cents per dollar of stolen merchandise, a huge amount considering that shoplifters traditionally net 10 percent or less of the retail value of stolen items. The group made more than $200,000 in 10 months.

Breaking up the scheme involved a massive, year-long sting operation that took authorities across five Northeast states. Authorities had to analyze hundreds of computer files, conduct secret surveillance at stores, and place an undercover agent to infiltrate the ring.

eBay states that it would be impossible to pinpoint a stolen good before it is reported to the company. eBay further notes, "We don't own it. We don't ship it. We never handle it." The company has increased its security team to 1,000 people, 13 percent of its total employees, to help combat the problem. eBay has also implemented a computer analysis system to flag suspicious auctions.

Sources: Compiled from A. Cha, "Thieves Find Exactly What They're Looking for on eBay," *Washington Post*, January 6, 2005; "Seller Charged over Stolen Goods on eBay," *ABC News Online*, February 2, 2005; and J. Morse "Pair Admit Selling Stolen Goods on eBay," *The Enquirer*, June 24, 2004.

QUESTIONS

1. Can eBay's security team defend the company and its customers against a theft ring like the one in this case? If so, how?
2. Would you be suspicious to buy gift cards on eBay at a discount? Why or why not?

information, see *www.identitytheft.org*. College students are not immune from this crime. Appendix 1 at the end of this chapter provides tips for securing your home computer and Appendix 2 provides tips on protecting your identity and recovering from identity theft.

Software Attacks The most familiar type of computer threat is the software attack. Deliberate software attacks occur when individuals or groups design software—called "malicious software" or "malware"—to attack computer systems. This software is designed to damage, destroy, or deny service to the targeted systems. The most common types of software attacks are viruses, worms, Trojan horses, logic bombs, back doors, denial-of-service, alien software, phishing, and pharming.

Viruses **Computer viruses** are segments of computer code that perform actions ranging from merely annoying to destructive. The virus attaches itself to an existing computer program and takes control of that program. The virus-controlled, infected program then replicates the virus into additional systems. One of the most common methods of virus transmission is through e-mail attachment files, as the following example shows.

Example

FBI Concerned over Fake E-Mail. A fake e-mail that purports to be from the FBI is circulating on the Internet, carrying a computer virus. The unsolicited e-mail tells users that "their Internet use has been monitored by the FBI's Internet Fraud Complaint Center and that they have accessed illegal Web sites." The fake message then asks recipients to click on an attachment and answer some questions about their alleged illegal Internet use. The attachment carries the virus. The FBI said that it never sends official unsolicited e-mails to citizens for any reason. Any e-mail messages supposed to be from the FBI should be ignored. (*Sources:* Compiled from T. Weiss, "New Virus Being Distributed in Fake FBI E-mail," *Computerworld*, February 23, 2005; and D. Sooman, "Fake FBI E-mail Carries Virus," *www.techspot.com*, February 24, 2005.)

A new type of virus has emerged, targeting mobile telephones. The world's first mobile phone virus began in the Philippines and had spread slowly into 12 countries as of March 2005. The virus, called Cabir, could one day disrupt the lives of many of the world's 1.5 billion mobile phone users. So far, the biggest impact of the relatively innocuous virus has been to drain mobile phone batteries. The mobile phone virus threat is predicted to increase in the future. Virus writers are becoming more sophisticated, and mobile phones increasingly are relying on standard technologies. These developments will make it easier for viruses to spread across not just specific devices but the entire industry.

Worms **Worms** are destructive programs that replicate themselves without requiring another program to provide a safe environment for replication. As an example, consider the Slammer (also called Sapphire) worm. This worm was the fastest computer worm in history. In January 2003, it began spreading throughout the Internet, doubling in size every 8.5 seconds. It infected more than 90 percent of vulnerable computers around the entire world within 10 minutes. The worm caused network outages and unforeseen consequences such as canceled airline flights and ATM failures.

Trojan Horses **Trojan horses** are software programs that hide in other computer programs and reveal their designed behavior only when they are activated. Trojan horses are often disguised as interesting, helpful, or necessary pieces of software, such as the README files included with shareware or freeware packages downloaded from the Internet.

Logic Bombs **Logic bombs** are segments of computer code that are embedded within an organization's existing computer programs, often by a disgruntled employee. The logic bomb is designed to activate and perform a destructive action at a certain time or date. For example, a terminated employee at one company inserted a logic bomb in his company's payroll system. The logic bomb was designed to activate in six months and check to see if he were still on the payroll. When the bomb activated, it found that he was not on the payroll and erased every payroll record in the company. Fortunately, the company had back-ups (copies) of its payroll files in another facility.

Back Doors or Trap Doors A virus or worm can install a **back door** to a computer system. The back door is typically a password, known only to the attacker, that allows an attacker to access the system at will, without having to go through any security procedures.

Denial of Service In a **denial-of-service attack**, the attacker sends so many information requests to a target system that the target cannot handle them successfully. In some cases a denial-of-service attack prevents the target system from performing ordinary functions. In more serious cases it causes the entire system to crash. In a **distributed denial-of-service (DDoS)** attack, a coordinated stream of requests is launched against a target system from many computers at the same time. Most DDoS attacks are preceded by a preparation phase in which many systems are compromised. The attacker remotely directs the compromised machines, known as *zombies*, toward the target.

Alien software Many personal computers have alien software running on them that the owners do not know about. The different types of alien software include pestware, adware, spyware, cookies, and Web bugs.

Pestware is clandestine software that is installed on your PC through duplicitous channels. In many cases the vendor or perpetrator tricks you into installing by claiming it will provide benefits to you. Pestware typically is not as malicious as a virus, but it does use up valuable system resources. In addition, it can report on your Web surfing habits and other personal behavior. Analysts estimate that up to 90 percent of all PCs are affected by pestware. One clear indication that software is pestware is that it does not come with an uninstaller program. An *uninstaller* is an automated program that removes a particular software package systematically and entirely.

The vast majority of pestware is **adware**—software that is designed to help pop-up advertisements appear on your screen. Adware producers often require you to consent to the installation of the adware by duping you into thinking you are downloading freeware (free software) such as an atomic clock program or a local weather forecasting program.

Why is there so much adware? The answer is, because it works. According to advertising agencies, for every 100 people who delete such an ad, 3 click on it. This hit rate is extremely high for Internet advertising. For example, the leader in the young adware industry, Claria Corporation (*www.claria.com*), had net profits of $35 million on sales of $90 million in 2003. Today, Claria's flagship product, Gator, is on 43 million personal computers.

Some pestware is **spyware**. Spyware programs include (1) keylogger programs that record your keystrokes, (2) password capture programs that record your passwords, and (3) **spamware** that is designed to use your computer as a launch pad for spammers.

Spam is unsolicited e-mail, usually for the purpose of advertising for products and services. Not only is spam a nuisance, but it wastes time and money. In fact, spam costs U.S. corporations more than $20 billion per year. These costs come from productivity losses, clogged e-mail systems, additional storage, user support, and antispam software. Companies and Internet service providers are fighting back with spam firewalls (firewalls are discussed in the next section), such as the Barracuda Spam Firewall (*www.barracudanetworks.com*). This firewall places any e-mail identified as spam in a quarantine folder. It also notifies users at regular intervals via e-mail if it has placed any messages in their quarantine. Users then visit their quarantine periodically and mark and delete spam messages. As users mark messages as spam, the firewall actually "learns" to identify the sources of these messages and automatically blocks any future messages from them.

Unfortunately, most antivirus programs do not remove or block pestware. However, there are *antipestware* products that actively prevent pestware from running in your computer's memory. These products include:

- Ad-aware (*www.lavasoft.com*)
- A-squared (*www.emsisoft.com/en/software/free*)
- PestPatrol (*www.ca.com/products/pestpatrol*)
- SpyBot Search & Destroy (*www.safer-networking.org*)
- SpySweeper (*www.webroot.com*)
- Xcleaner (*www.xblock.com/download-freeware.shtml*)

Cookies are small amounts of information that Web sites store on your computer, temporarily or more-or-less permanently. In many cases cookies are useful and innocuous. For example, some cookies are passwords and user IDs that you do not have to retype every time you load a new page at the site that issued the cookie. Cookies are also necessary if you want to shop online, as they are used for your shopping carts at various online merchants. Other cookies, however, can be used to track your path through a Web site, the time you spend there, what links you click on, and other details that the company wants to record, usually for marketing purposes.

Most cookies can be read only by the party that created them. However, some companies that manage online banner advertising are, in essence, cookie-sharing rings. These compa-

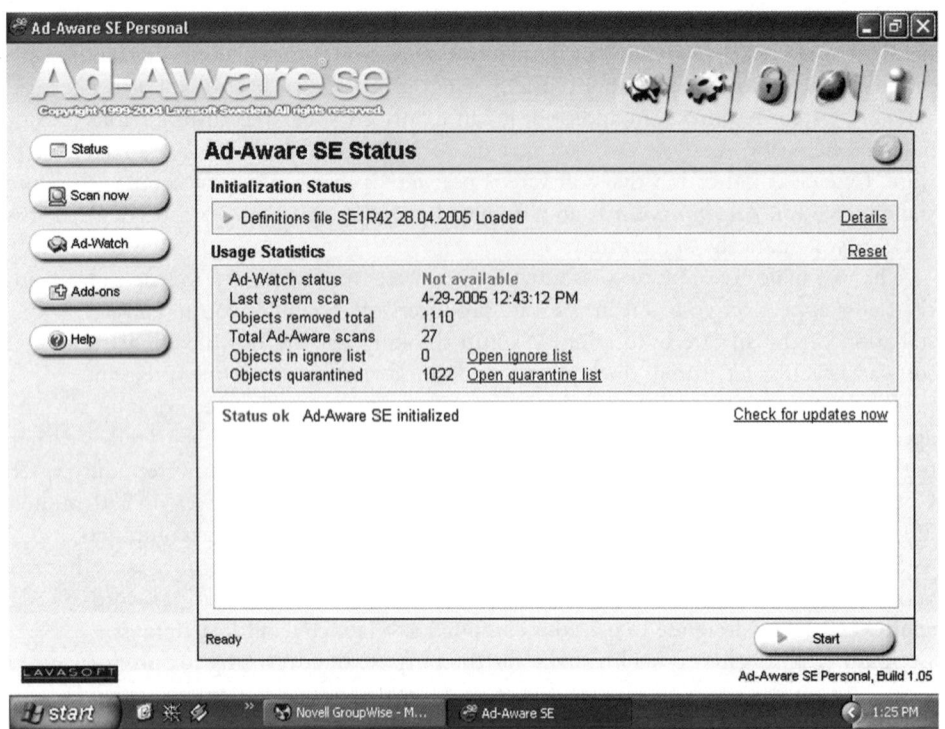

Antipestware products like Ad-aware help combat pestware.

nies can track information such as which pages you load and which ads you click on. They then share this information with all of their client Web sites (which may number in the thousands). Some examples of these cookie-sharing rings are DoubleClick, AdCast, and LinkExchange. For a cookie demonstration, see *http://privacy.net/track/*.

Finally, **Web bugs** are small, usually invisible, graphic images that are added to a Web page or an e-mail message. Companies use Web bugs to obtain statistics on Internet usage patterns and who is looking at particular documents. A more sinister use is when spammers hide them within e-mail messages. This technique allows spammers to know that your e-mail address is real and working. Once spammers know this for certain, they will sell your e-mail address over and over again.

Phishing   **Phishing** uses deception to acquire sensitive personal information such as account numbers and passwords by masquerading as an official-looking e-mail. In one instance, bogus e-mails, supposedly from AOL's billing center, urged subscribers to provide sensitive financial information before their accounts were canceled. The link embedded in these e-mails sent recipients to a stunningly realistic but phony AOL billing page, where they could input their credit card numbers. The data, however, went to the thieves' account. Phishers steal goods, services, and cash totaling $1.2 billion a year. They receive help from 50 or more gangs of professional criminals who operate primarily in Russia and Eastern Europe.

Pharming   In **pharming**, the attacker fraudulently acquires the Domain Name for a company's Web site. When people type in the Web site address, they actually are on the fake Web site of the attacker, which looks just like the real Web site. These people may enter sensitive information, thinking they are on the real Web site. In January 2005, the Domain Name of a large Internet Service Provider, *www.panix.com*, was hijacked to a Web site in Australia. (We discuss Domain Names and Internet Service Providers in Chapter 5.)

Many of these software attacks are interrelated and can occur together. IT's About Business 3.4 examines a series of attacks against one software company.

IT's About Business

3.4 MyDoom Attacks the SCO Group

The SCO Group, Inc. (SCO) is a provider of software solutions for small- to medium-sized businesses. SCO has been a frequent target of online attacks since it filed a multibillion-dollar lawsuit against IBM in March 2003, charging the giant company with misappropriating trade secrets and unfair competition. Among other things, SCO accused IBM of violating SCO's copyright on Unix System V by copying elements of that operating system into Linux, which IBM distributes for free. Based on this charge, SCO claims to own parts of Linux. Further, it has threatened to enforce its ownership through patent infringement lawsuits against Linux users. These threats irritated open-source enthusiasts. (We discuss open source software in Technology Guide 2.) Many people view SCO's legal actions as a threat to the spread of Linux, which they consider a possible rival to the dominance of Microsoft's proprietary desktop and server operating systems. These people are in favor of an alternative to Microsoft's Windows.

In January 2004, the MyDoom e-mail worm tore through the Internet, deluged e-mail systems with infected messages, and set records for infecting vulnerable computer systems. At the height of the MyDoom outbreak, the worm was found in 1 of every 12 messages intercepted by e-mail security vendor MessageLabs (*www.messagelabs.com*).

MyDoom installed a Trojan horse program on machines it infected. The infected machines were then used to launch a denial-of-service attack against the SCO Web site. Estimates are that between 25,000 and 50,000 computers took part in the attack. Not surprisingly, the site promptly crashed.

In a subsequent attack, malicious hackers compromised SCO's Web site by posting messages that mocked the company's claims to own parts of Linux. They inserted a banner image that read, "We own all your code. Pay us all your money." The image was removed the following morning.

The SCO suit against IBM is scheduled for court in November 2005.

Sources: Compiled from P. Roberts, "MyDoom One Year Later: More Zombies, More Spam," *Computerworld*, January 27, 2005; P. Roberts, "SCO Web Site Hack Mocks Company's Legal Claims," *Computerworld*, November 29, 2004.

QUESTIONS

1. Identify the integrated software attacks inflicted on the SCO Group.
2. If you were the chief information officer of SCO, what steps would you take to ensure that your Web site does not crash again from a denial-of-service attack?

Compromises to Intellectual Property Protecting intellectual property is a vital issue for people who make their livelihood in knowledge fields. **Intellectual property** is the property created by individuals or corporations which is protected under *trade secret, patent,* and *copyright* laws.

A **trade secret** is an intellectual work, such as a business plan, that is a company secret and is not based on public information. An example is a corporate strategic plan. A **patent** is a document that grants the holder exclusive rights on an invention or process for 20 years. **Copyright** is a statutory grant that provides the creators of intellectual property with ownership of the property for the life of the creator plus 70 years. Owners are entitled to collect fees from anyone who wants to copy the property.

The most common intellectual property related to IT deals with software. The U.S. Federal Computer Software Copyright Act (1980) provides protection for *source* and *object code* of computer software, but the law does not clearly identify what is eligible for protection. For example, copyright law does not protect similar concepts, functions, and general features such as pull-down menus, colors, and icons. However, copying a software program without making payment to the owner—including giving a disc to a friend to install on his or her computer—is a copyright violation. Not surprisingly, this practice, called **piracy**, is a major problem for software vendors. The global trade in pirated software amounted to over $30 billion in 2004. This value amounted to almost 60 percent of all legal global desktop software sales.

The Business Software Alliance (BSA) is an organization representing the world's commercial software industry that promotes legal software and performs research on software piracy in an attempt to eliminate it. The BSA (*www.bsa.org*) identifies Vietnam, China, Indonesia, Ukraine, and Russia as the countries with the highest percentage of illegal software. In those countries, more than 85 percent of the software used consists of illegal copies.

"Software pirates! Run for your lives!!"

Software companies are taking steps to combat software piracy. For example, Microsoft is selling a super-cut-rate edition of Windows called the Windows XP Starter Edition in three Asian countries: Malaysia, Thailand, and Indonesia. Industry experts predict that Brazil, China, India, and Russia are the next likely participants.

Why is it so difficult to stop cybercriminals? One reason is that the online commerce industry is not particularly willing to install safeguards that would make it harder to complete transactions. It would be possible, for example, to demand passwords or personal identification numbers for all credit card transactions. However, these requirements might discourage people from shopping online. Also, there is little incentive for victims like AOL to share leads on criminal activity either with one another or with the FBI. It is cheaper to block a stolen credit card and move on than to invest time and money on a prosecution.

What Companies Are Doing   Despite these difficulties, the information security industry is battling back. Companies are developing software and services that deliver early warnings of trouble on the Internet. Unlike traditional antivirus software, which is reactive, early-warning systems are proactive, scanning the Web for new viruses and alerting companies to the danger.

The new systems are emerging in response to ever-more-effective virus writers. As virus writers become more expert, the gap between the time when they learn of vulnerabilities and when they exploit them is closing quickly. For example, the Sasser worm hit just 17 days after Microsoft revealed a flaw in Windows in April 2004. Security experts predict that hackers will soon be producing new viruses and worms in a matter of hours.

Technicians at TruSecure (*www.cybertrust.com*) and Symantec (*www.symantec.com*) are working around the clock to monitor Web traffic. Symantec's team taps into 20,000 sensors placed at Internet hubs in 180 countries to spot e-mail and other data packets that seem to be carrying viruses. TruSecure sends technicians posing as hackers into online virus-writer chat rooms to find out what they are planning. TruSecure boasts that it even contributed to the arrests of the authors of the Melissa, Anna Kournikova, and Love Letter viruses.

Despite the difficulties defending against attacks, organizations spend a great deal of time and money protecting their information resources. We discuss the methods of protection in the next section.

Before you go on . . .

1. Give an example of one type of unintentional threat to a computer system.
2. Describe the various types of software attacks.
3. Define and give an example of cybercrime.
4. Describe the issue of intellectual property protection.

3.3 Protecting Information Resources

Risk Analysis

Before spending money to apply controls, organizations must perform risk management. A risk is the probability that a threat will impact an information resource. The goal of **risk management** is to identify, control, and minimize the impact of threats. In other words, risk management seeks to reduce risk to acceptable levels. There are three processes in risk management: risk analysis, risk mitigation, and controls evaluation.

Risk analysis is the process in which an organization assesses the value of each asset being protected, estimates the probability that each asset might be compromised, and compares the probable costs of each being compromised with the costs of protecting it. Organizations perform risk analysis to ensure that their information systems security programs are cost effective. The risk analysis process prioritizes the assets to be protected, based on each asset's value, its probability of being compromised, and the estimated cost of its protection. The organization then considers how to mitigate the risk.

In **risk mitigation**, the organization takes concrete actions against risks. Risk mitigation has two functions: (1) implementing controls to prevent identified threats from occurring, and (2) developing a means of recovery should the threat become a reality. There are several risk mitigation strategies that organizations may adopt. The three most common are risk acceptance, risk limitation, and risk transference.

- **Risk acceptance**: Accept the potential risk, continue operating with no controls, and absorb any damages that occur.
- **Risk limitation**: Limit the risk by implementing controls that minimize the impact of the threat.
- **Risk transference**: Transfer the risk by using other means to compensate for the loss, such as by purchasing insurance.

In **controls evaluation**, the organization identifies security deficiencies and calculates the costs of implementing adequate control measures. If the costs of implementing a control are greater than the value of the asset being protected, then control is not cost-effective.

For example, an organization's mainframe computers are too valuable for risk acceptance. As a result, organizations limit the risk to mainframes through controls, such as access controls. Organizations also use risk transference for their mainframes, by purchasing insurance and having off-site backups.

In another example, suppose that the old car you are driving is worth $2,000. Also suppose that you think the probability of an accident or other damage happening to your car is .01. The amount of your probable loss would be $20 ($2,000 × .01). If you live in a state that allows it, you might decide not to carry any insurance on your car. You are practicing risk acceptance. Or you might try to limit your risk by driving carefully. Finally, you could transfer the risk by purchasing insurance, but you would try to keep the cost of the insurance below $20, which is the amount you assigned to your probable loss.

Controls

Organizations protect their systems in many ways. One major strategy is to join with the FBI to form the *National Infrastructure Protection Center (NIPC)*. This partnership between government and private industry is designed to protect the nation's infrastructure—its telecommunications, energy, transportation, banking and finance, emergency, and governmental operations. The FBI has also established *Regional Computer Intrusion Squads*, which focus on intrusions to telephone and computer networks, privacy violations, industrial espionage, pirated computer software, and other cybercrimes. Another national organization is the *Computer Emergency Response Team (CERT)* at Carnegie Mellon University (*www.cert.org*).

The Difficulties in Protecting Information Resources

- ☐ Hundreds of potential threats exist.
- ☐ Computing resources may be situated in many locations.
- ☐ Many individuals control information assets.
- ☐ Computer networks can be outside the organization and difficult to protect.
- ☐ Rapid technological changes make some controls obsolete as soon as they are installed.
- ☐ Many computer crimes are undetected for a long period of time, so it is difficult to learn from experience.
- ☐ People tend to violate security procedures because the procedures are inconvenient.
- ☐ Many computer criminals who are caught go unpunished, so there is no deterrent effect.
- ☐ The amount of computer knowledge necessary to commit computer crimes is usually minimal. As a matter of fact, one can learn hacking, for free, on the Internet.
- ☐ The cost of preventing hazards can be very high. Therefore, most organizations simply cannot afford to protect against all possible hazards.
- ☐ It is difficult to conduct a cost-benefit justification for controls before an attack occurs because it is difficult to assess the value of a hypothetical attack.

Manager's Checklist 3.3 lists the major difficulties involved in protecting information. Because it is so important to the entire enterprise, organizing an appropriate defense system is one of the major activities of any prudent CIO and of the functional managers who control information resources. As a matter of fact, IT security is the business of *everyone* in an organization.

The most important strategy for protecting information is to insert *controls* (defense mechanisms). Controls are intended to prevent accidental hazards, deter intentional acts, detect problems as early as possible, enhance damage recovery, and correct problems. The important point is that defense should stress *prevention*. Defense does no good after the crime has been committed.

Because there are many security threats, there are also many defense mechanisms. *Security controls* are designed to protect all of the components of an information system, specifically data, software, hardware, and networks. A defense strategy may involve the use of several controls. We divide defense controls into two major categories: *general controls* and *application controls*. Both categories have several subcategories. Table 3.1 shows the various types of controls and Figure 3.2 illustrates these controls.

General Controls   **General controls** are established to protect the system regardless of the specific application. For example, protecting hardware and controlling access to the data center are independent of any particular application. The major categories of general controls are physical controls, access controls, data security controls, communications (network) controls, and administrative controls. In the following section, we discuss only physical, access, and communications controls. Data security controls and administrative controls are defined in Table 3.1.

Physical controls prevent unauthorized individuals from gaining access to a company's computer facilities. Common physical controls include walls, doors, fencing, gates, locks, badges, guards, and alarm systems. One weakness of physical controls is known as tailgating. *Tailgating* occurs when an authorized individual unlocks a door (with a key or badge) and other individuals enter with the authorized person.

Access controls restrict unauthorized individuals from using information resources and are concerned with user identification. There are many types of access controls, including something the user is, something the user has, something the user does, and something the user knows.

Table 3.1

General and Application Controls for Protecting Information Systems

Type of Control	Description of Purpose
General Controls	
Physical controls	Physical protection of computer facilities and resources.
Access controls	Restriction of unauthorized user access to computer resources; concerned with user identification.
Data security controls	Protecting data from accidental or intentional disclosure to unauthorized persons, or from unauthorized modification or destruction.
Administrative controls	Issuing and monitoring security guidelines.
Communications (network) controls	
Border security	Major objective is access control.
Firewalls	System that enforces access-control policy between two networks.
Virus controls	Antivirus software (see *www.trendmicro.com*, *www.cert.org, www.pgp.com, www.symantec.com, www.rsasecurity.com, www.mcafee.com,* and *www.iss.net*).
Intrusion detection	Major objective is to detect unauthorized access to network.
Virtual private networking	Uses the Internet to carry information within a company and among business partners but with increased security by use of encryption, authentication, and access control.
Authentication	Major objective is proof of identity.
Authorization	Permission issued to individuals and groups to do certain activities with information resources, based on verified identity.
Application Controls	
Input controls	Prevent data alteration or loss.
Processing controls	Ensure that data are complete, valid, and accurate when being processed and that programs have properly executed.
Output controls	Ensure that the results of computer processing are accurate, valid, complete, and consistent.

Something the User Is Also known as **biometrics**, these access controls examine a user's innate physical characteristics. Common biometric applications are fingerprint scans, palm scans, retina scans, iris recognition, and facial recognition. Of these, fingerprints, retina scan, and iris recognition provide the most definitive identification. Interestingly, iris recognition is already in use in Germany at the Frankfurt airport.

Something the User Has These access controls include regular ID cards, smart cards, and tokens. Regular ID cards have the user's picture and, probably, his or her signature. Smart cards have a chip embedded in them with pertinent information about the user. Tokens have embedded chips and a digital display that present a login number that the employee uses for access. The number changes with each login.

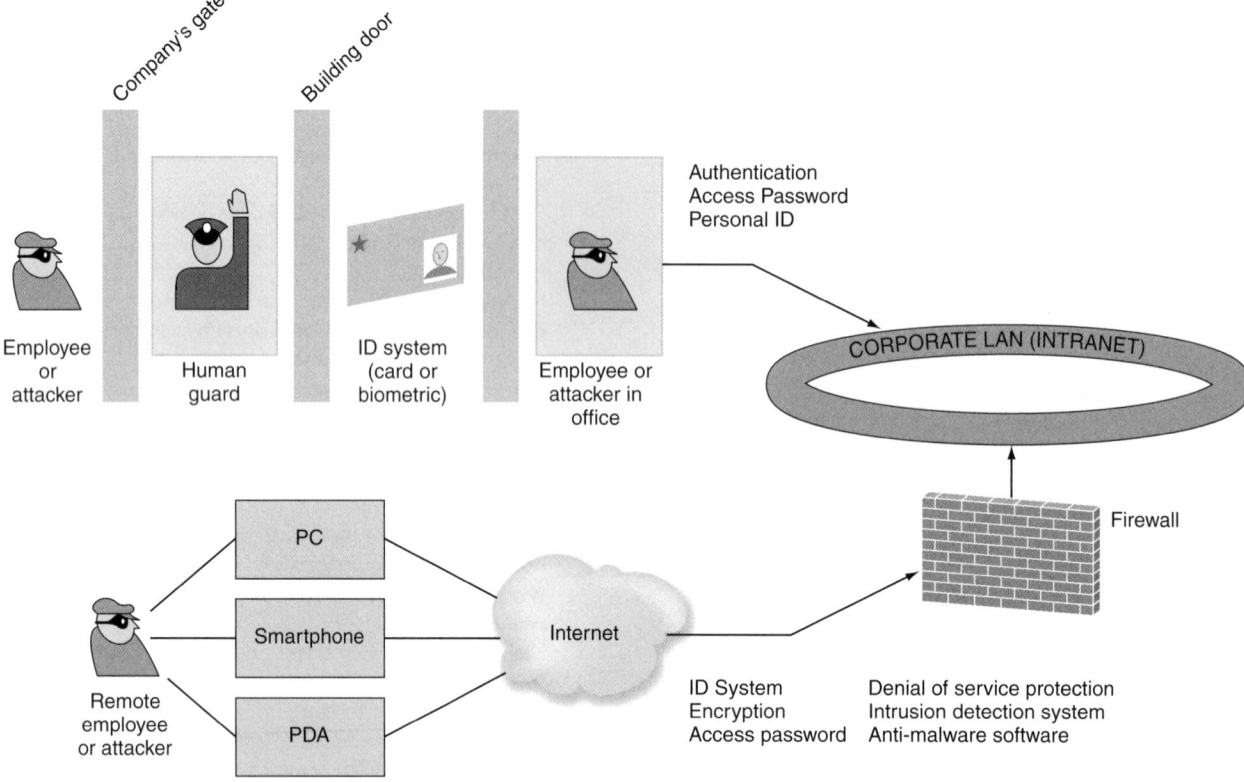

FIGURE 3.2   Where defense mechanisms are located.

Something the User Does   These access controls include voice and signature recognition. In voice recognition, the user speaks a phrase (e.g., his or her name and department) that has been previously recorded. The voice recognition system matches the two voice signals. In signature recognition, the user signs his or her name, and the system matches this signature with one previously recorded. Signature recognition systems also match the speed of the signature and the pressure of the signature.

Something the User Knows   These access controls include passwords and passphrases. A **password** is a private combination of characters that only the user should know. A **passphrase** is a series of characters that is longer than a password but can be memorized easily. Examples: "Maytheforcebewithyoualways," "goaheadmakemyday," "livelongandprosper," or "aman'sgottoknowhislimitations".

An effective password has the following characteristics:

- It should be difficult to guess.
- It should be longer rather than shorter.
- It should employ uppercase letters, lowercase letters, and special characters.
- It should not be the name of anything or anyone familiar, such as your family or pets.
- It should not be a recognizable string of numbers, such as a Social Security number or birthday.
- It should not be a recognizable word.

Passwords with these characteristics are called **strong passwords**.

Hackers can figure out weak passwords by using a *brute force dictionary attack.* The hacker simply uses a computer program that tries every word in the dictionary, including proper names, until it finds a match. Remember the axiom: Weak passwords always trump strong security. The next example illustrates the importance of passwords.

Example

Paris Hilton Gets Hacked. In late 2004, Paris Hilton's phone numbers were the hot search item on the Web. Surfers hoped to get the phone numbers of dozens of Hollywood celebrities whose contact information was leaked after somebody hacked Hilton's T-Mobile Sidekick II device. T-Mobile proposed that someone may have known her password.

T-Mobile has told its Sidekick users to use complex passwords and change them on a regular basis to improve their level of security. According to industry experts, in 2004 some 84 percent of organizations surveyed claimed that human error was partially responsible for security breaches. Many of those "human errors" involved poor password security. Experts recommend that passwords include a combination of numbers, letters, and punctuation marks. They also recommend that people change their passwords at least every 90 days. (*Sources*: Compiled from S. Kerner, "Hilton's T-Mobile Hack a Password Wake-Up," *www.internetnews.com*, February 22, 2005; and L. Sherriff, "Paris Hilton's Sidekick Hacked," *The Register*, February 21, 2005.)

Communications (network) controls deal with the movement of data across networks and include border security controls, authentication, and authorization. Authentication and authorization are defined in Table 3.1. Border security controls consist of firewalls, malware controls, intrusion detection controls, encryption, and virtual private networking. Virus controls and intrusion detection controls are defined in Table 3.1. We discuss firewalls, encryption, and virtual private networking in more detail here.

Firewalls A **firewall** is a system that prevents a specific type of information from moving between untrusted networks, such as the Internet, and private networks, such as your company's network. Put simply, firewalls prevent unauthorized Internet users from accessing private networks. Firewalls can consist of hardware, software, or a combination of both. All messages entering or leaving your company's network pass through the firewall. The firewall then examines each message and blocks those that do not meet specified security criteria.

Firewalls range from simple, for home use (see Figure 3.3a), to very complex, for organizations that need a high level of security (see Figure 3.3b). Figure 3.3a shows a basic firewall for a home computer. In this case, the firewall is implemented as software on the home computer. Figure 3.3b shows an organization that has implemented an external firewall and an internal firewall with a demilitarized zone (DMZ) between them. Messages from the Internet must first pass through the external firewall. If they conform to the defined rules, then they are sent to company servers located in the DMZ. These servers typically handle Web page requests and e-mail. Any messages designated for the company's internal network (e.g., its intranet) must pass through the internal firewall to gain access to the company's private network.

Encryption Millions of people around the world send e-mails; use wireless telephones to call friends, family, and business associates; and put sensitive information on computers. Until recently, they gave little thought to whether our communications and information were secure. Today, that is not the case.

When you do not have a secure channel for sending information, you should use encryption to stop unauthorized eavesdroppers. **Encryption** is the process of converting an original message into a form that cannot be read by anyone except the intended receiver.

All encryption systems use a key, which is the code that scrambles, and then decodes, the messages. In **symmetric encryption** the sender and the recipient use the same key. One

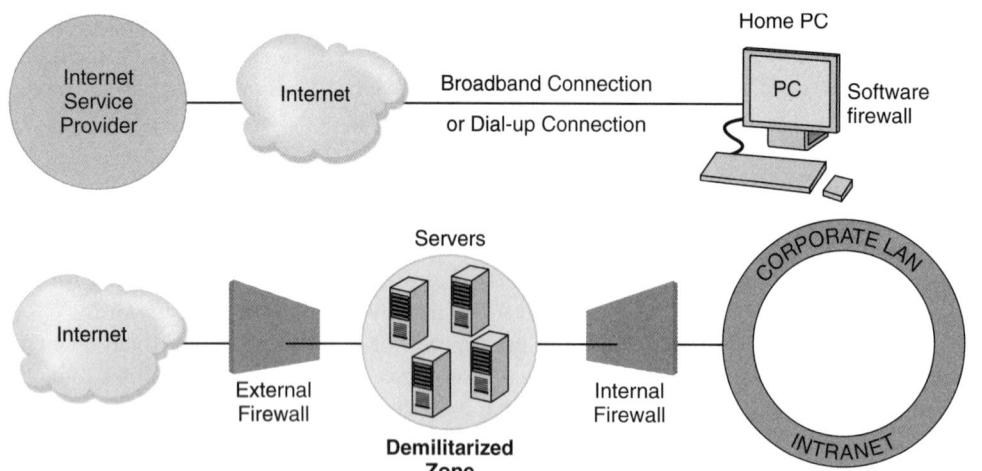

FIGURE 3.3
(A) Basic firewall for
home computer.

(B) Organization
with two firewalls and
demilitarized zone.

problem with symmetric encryption is that both the sender and recipient must know the key and keep it secret from everybody else. Further, if the sender uses different keys to send messages to different people, then key management becomes a problem.

Key management problems led to the development of public-key encryption. **Public-key encryption**—also known as asymmetric encryption—uses two different keys: a public key and a private key (see Figure 3.4). The public key and the private key are created simultaneously using the same mathematical formula (algorithm). Because the two keys are mathematically related, the data encrypted with one key can be decrypted by using the other key. The public key is publicly available in a directory that all parties can access. The private key is kept secret, never shared with anyone, and never sent across the Internet. In this system, if Alice wants to send a message to Bob (see Figure 3.4), she first obtains Bob's public key, which is available in a directory. Alice uses Bob's public key to encrypt (scramble) her message. When Bob receives Alice's message, he uses his private key to decrypt (unscramble) it.

Public key systems also show that a message is authentic. That is, if you encrypt a message using your private key, you have electronically "signed" it. A recipient can verify that the message came from you by using your public key to decrypt it.

Although this system is adequate for private correspondence, doing business over the Internet requires a more complex system. In this case, a third party, called a **certificate authority**, acts as a trusted intermediary between companies. As such, the certificate authority issues digital certificates and verifies the worth and integrity of the certificates. A **digital certificate** is an electronic document attached to a file certifying that the file is from the organization it claims to be from and has not been modified from its original format. As you can see in Figure 3.5, Sony requests a digital certificate from Verisign, a certificate authority, and uses this certificate when doing business with Dell. Note that the digital certificate contains an identification number, the issuer, validity dates, and the requester's public key. For examples of certificate authorities, see *www.entrust.com, www.verisign.com, www.cybertrust.com, www.secude.com,* and *www.thawte.com.*

Virtual Private Networking   A **virtual private network (VPN)** is a private network that uses a public network (usually the Internet) to connect users. Instead of using a proprietary wide-area network, a VPN uses "virtual" connections routed through the Internet from the company's private network to a remote site, an employee, or another company. VPNs use encryption for security. We discuss VPNs in more detail in Chapter 5.

Application controls   Whereas general controls protect an entire system, **application controls**, as their name suggests, are safeguards that protect specific applications. General controls do not protect the *content* of each specific application. Therefore, controls are

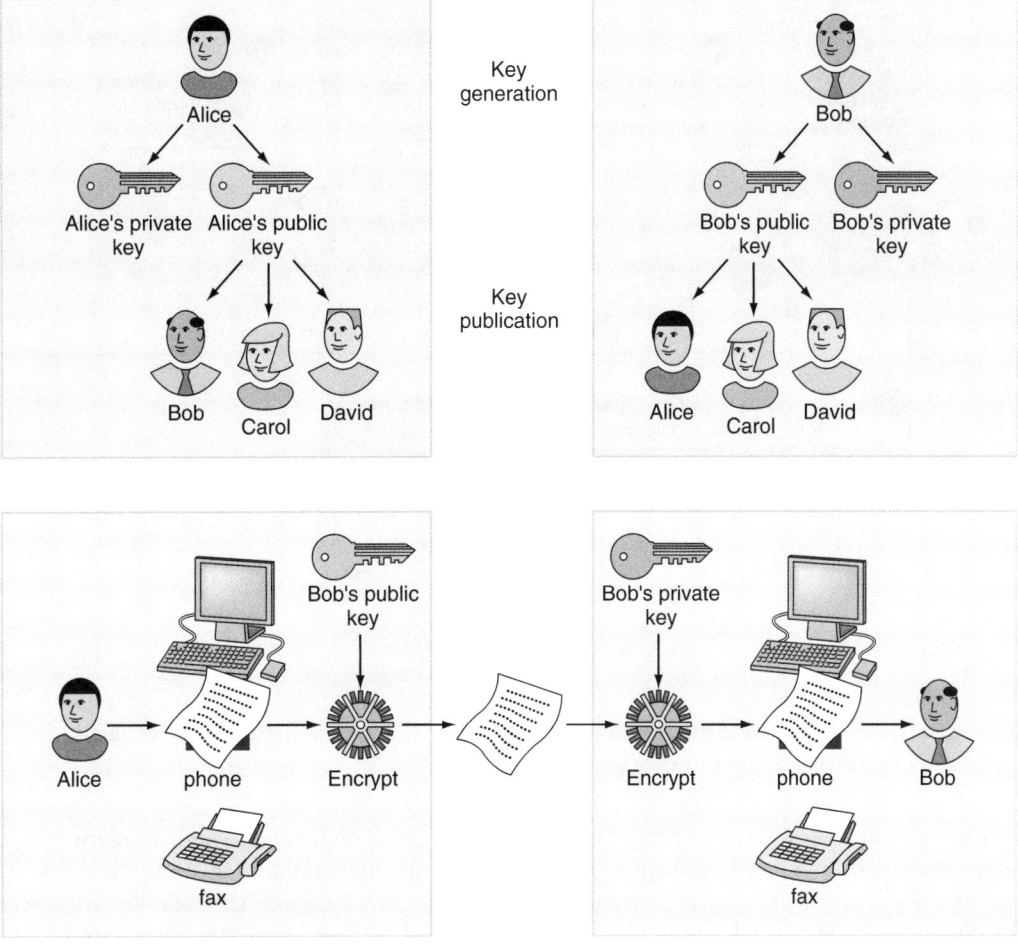

FIGURE 3.4   How public key encryption works. (*Source:* Omnisec AG.)

frequently built into the applications; that is, they are part of the software. Application controls include three major categories: input controls, processing controls, and output controls. Input controls include programmed routines that are performed to edit input data for errors before they are processed. For example, Social Security numbers should not contain any alphabetic characters. Processing controls, for example, might match employee time cards with a payroll master file and report missing or duplicate time cards. Processing controls also balance the total number of transactions processed with the total number of transactions input or output. An example of output controls is documentation specifying that authorized recipients have received their reports, paychecks, or other critical documents.

Information Systems Auditing

Companies implement security controls to ensure that information systems work properly. These controls can be installed in the original system, or they can be added after a system is in operation. Installing controls is necessary but not sufficient to provide adequate security. In addition, people responsible for security need to answer questions such as: Are all controls installed as intended? Are they effective? Has any breach of security occurred? If so, what actions are required to prevent future breaches?

These questions must be answered by independent and unbiased observers. Such observers perform the task of *information systems auditing.* In an IS environment, an **audit** is an examination of information systems, their inputs, outputs, and processing.

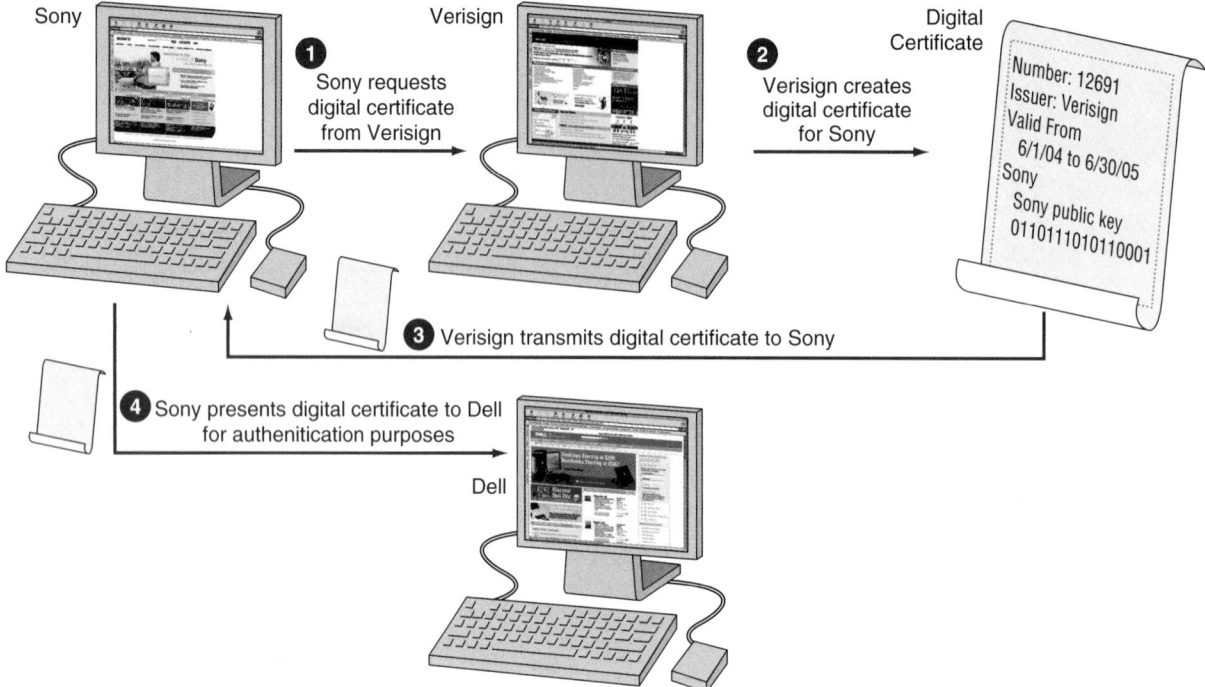

FIGURE 3.5 How digital certificates work. Sony and Dell, business partners, use a digital certificate from Verisign for authentication.

Types of Auditors and Audits There are two types of auditors and audits: internal and external. IS auditing is usually a part of accounting *internal auditing*, and it is frequently performed by corporate internal auditors. An *external auditor* reviews the findings of the internal audit as well as the inputs, processing, and outputs of information systems. The external audit of information systems is frequently a part of the overall external auditing performed by a certified public accounting (CPA) firm.

   IS auditing is a broad topic, so we present only its essentials here. Auditing considers all potential hazards and controls in information systems. It focuses on topics such as operations, data integrity, software applications, security and privacy, budgets and expenditures, cost control, and productivity. Guidelines are available to assist auditors in their jobs, such as those from the Institute of Internal Auditors (*www.theiia.org*).

How Is Auditing Executed? IS auditing procedures fall into three categories: (1) auditing around the computer, (2) auditing through the computer, and (3) auditing with the computer.

   Auditing around the computer means verifying processing by checking for known outputs using specific inputs. This approach is best used in systems with limited outputs. In *auditing through the computer*, inputs, outputs, and processing are checked. Auditors review program logic, test data, and controlling processing and reprocessing. *Auditing with the computer* means using a combination of client data, auditor software, and client and auditor hardware. It allows the auditor to perform tasks such as simulating payroll program logic using live data.

Disaster Recovery Planning

One important defense strategy is to be prepared for various eventualities. An important element in any security system is a *disaster recovery plan*. Destruction of most or all of an organization's computing facilities can cause significant damage. In fact, many organizations have trouble obtaining insurance unless they have a satisfactory disaster prevention and recovery plan for their information systems.

Disaster recovery is the chain of events linking planning to protection and to recovery. The purpose of a recovery plan is to keep the business running after a disaster occurs, a process called *business continuity*. Planning should focus first on recovering from a total loss of all computing capabilities. To do this the plan must identify all critical applications as well as their recovery procedures. The plan should be kept in a safe place and audited periodically. All managers should have a copy.

Disaster avoidance is oriented toward prevention. The idea is to minimize the chances of avoidable disasters such as arson or other human threats. For example, many companies use a device called *uninterrupted power supply (UPS)*, which provides backup power in case of a power outage.

In the event of a major disaster, it is often necessary to access a backup location while the central computing facility is inoperable. Many companies contract with external **hot sites** for access to fully configured data centers that have copies of their data and programs. The World Trade Center tragedy on September 11, 2001, illustrated the importance of backup arrangements, especially hot sites. IT's About Business 3.5 provides a dramatic illustration.

Before you go on . . .

1. Describe the two major types of controls for information systems.
2. What is information system auditing?
3. What is the purpose of a disaster recovery plan?

IT's About Business

3.5 Cantor Fitzgerald Gives Pop Quizzes

On September 11, 2001, the bond trading operations of Cantor Fitzgerald (www.cantor.com) were destroyed in the terrorist attacks on the World Trade Center, and 658 employees died. Nonetheless, the electronic markets supported by the company's eSpeed (www.espeed.com) subsidiary were restored within 48 hours.

Since the attacks, Cantor has launched new businesses, entered new markets, and turned its focus to equity trading and investment banking. However, because of its life-shattering experience, the company is constantly on the lookout for the next disruption. It has adopted a simple technique to make sure that it is prepared for disaster: the "pop quiz."

Instead of monthly, quarterly, or annual reviews, Cantor tests its systems, IT infrastructure, and continuity plans year-round at unexpected times. There is no formal pattern or schedule. The company knows that, for best results, it cannot announce a test and give employees time to prepare for it. Cantor also tests with groups that have not been directly involved with disaster recovery planning, because this is the only way to determine whether the procedures those planners have set out are clear and precise.

How does the pop quiz work? In one example, the CIO and his technology staff pick an inconvenient time to wake up the staff in Cantor's London data center. That could be dinnertime or 3 A.M. Then comes the mission: Rebuild a mortgage-backed securities trading system from scratch within a time limit of one hour.

Other quizzes may not be as extreme as the London example. Traders and managers working at Cantor's midtown Manhattan office may get a phone call before work telling them to move to a backup center in New Rochelle and operate from there. At New Rochelle, they will find 50 seats with workstations capable of toggling between job functions, from executive level to back-office transaction tracking.

On 9/11, Cantor's advanced disaster recovery planning saved the company in the wake of the destruction. Cantor had a hot back-up site that replicated all of its machines at both New Rochelle and the World Trade Center. It also had a well-drilled staff who could perform their jobs under extreme duress. Today, however, a single level of redundancy is no longer enough. Cantor now operates two data centers in the United States and two in London. In addition, the company is considering adding a third U.S. center. Meanwhile, the pop quizzes continue.

Sources: Compiled from "Pop Culture." *Baseline Magazine,* September 8, 2004 ; and E. Cone and S. Gallagher, "Cantor-Fitzgerald: Forty-Seven Hours," *Baseline Magazine,* October 29, 2001.

QUESTIONS

1. Could Cantor's pop quizzes cause a drop in productivity? Why or why not?
2. Should more organizations follow Cantor's lead, testing security anytime under varying conditions? Why or why not? What are the advantages of this policy? The disadvantages?

What's in IT for me?

For the Accounting Major

The accounting scandals of the past few years led to the passage of the Sarbanes–Oxley Act. This act gives accounting professionals increased responsibility for ethical reporting principles. Companies have to provide accurate financial statements, and they must submit to external examinations of internal systems. Firms must demonstrate that controls are in place to prevent fraudulent actions. As a result, information systems auditing is a growing area of special interest. Also, data security is a major concern to the accountant. Accountants are involved in fraud prevention and detection programs. They also assist with disaster recovery planning.

For the Finance Major

The finance and banking industry depends heavily on computers and their networks. Security is one of the major requirements for the development of new technologies such as electronic (home) banking and smart cards. Also, payment systems are critical for e-commerce, and their security and auditing are of the utmost importance. Finally, banking and financial institutions are prime targets for computer criminals. A related problem is fraud involving stocks and bonds that are sold over the Internet. Finance personnel must be aware of both the hazards and the available controls associated with these activities.

For the Marketing Major

Marketing professionals have new opportunities to collect data on their customers, for example, through business-to-consumer electronic commerce. Business ethics clearly state that these data should be used internally in the company and not sold to anyone else. Marketers clearly do not want to be sued because of invasion of privacy in data collected for the marketing database. At the same time they don't want their innovative marketing strategies to fall into the hands of their competitors. Also, because customers' privacy can be easily invaded while their data are kept in the marketing database or are collected at the point-of-sale, marketers must learn how to prevent such incidents.

For the Production/Operations Management Major

POM professionals decide whether to outsource (or offshore) manufacturing operations. In some cases, these operations are sent overseas to countries that do not have strict labor laws. This situation raises serious ethical questions. Is it ethical to hire people as employees in countries with poor working conditions in order to save on labor costs? POM managers must answer other difficult questions: To what extent do security efforts reduce productivity? Are incremental improvements in security worth the additional costs? To answer these and other questions, POM managers must be familiar with the topics discussed in this chapter.

For the Human Resources Management Major

Ethics is critically important to HR managers. HR policies describe the appropriate use of information technologies in the workplace. Questions arise such as: Can employees use the Internet, e-mail, or chat systems for personal purposes while at work? Is it ethical to monitor employees? If so, how? How much? How often? HR managers must formulate and enforce such policies while at the same time maintaining trusting relationships between employees and management.

The MIS Function

Ethics might be more important for MIS personnel than for anyone else in the organization, because they have control of the information assets. They also have control over a huge amount of personal information on all employees. As a result, the MIS function must be held to the highest ethical standards.

The MIS function provides the security infrastructure that protects the organization's information assets. This function is critical to the success of the organization, even though it is almost invisible until an attack succeeds.

Summary

1. Describe the major ethical issues related to information technology, and identify situations in which they occur.

The major ethical issues related to IT are privacy, accuracy, property (including intellectual property), and accessibility to information. Privacy may be violated when data are held in databases or are transmitted over networks. Privacy policies that address issues of data collection, data accuracy, and data confidentiality can help organizations avoid legal problems. Intellectual property is the intangible property created by individuals or corporations that is protected under trade secret, patent, and copyright laws. The most common intellectual property related to IT deals with software. Copying software without paying the owner is a copyright violation, and it is a major problem for software vendors.

2. Describe the many threats to information security.

There are numerous threats to information security, which fall into the general categories of unintentional and intentional. Unintentional threats include human errors, environmental hazards, and computer system failures. Intentional failures include espionage, extortion, vandalism, theft, software attacks, and compromises to intellectual property. Software attacks include viruses, worms, Trojan horses, logic bombs, back doors, denial of service, alien software, phishing, and pharming. A growing threat is cybercrime, which includes identity theft and phishing attacks.

3. Understand the various defense mechanisms used to protect information systems.

Information systems are protected with a wide variety of controls such as security procedures, physical guards, and detection software. These can be classified as controls used for prevention, deterrence, detection, damage control, recovery, and correction of information systems. The major types of general controls include physical controls, access controls, data security controls, administrative controls, and communications controls. Application controls include input, processing, and output controls.

4. Explain IT auditing and planning for disaster recovery.

Information systems auditing is done in a similar manner to accounting/finance auditing, around, through, and with the computer. A detailed internal and external IT audit may involve hundreds of issues and can be supported by both software and checklists. Related to IT auditing is the preparation for disaster recovery, which specifically addresses how to avoid, plan for, and quickly recover from a disaster.

Chapter Glossary

access controls Controls that restrict unauthorized individuals from using information resources and are concerned with user identification. (79)

adware Alien software designed to help pop-up advertisements appear on your screen. (74)

application controls Controls that protect specific applications. (83)

asymmetric encryption (see **public-key encryption**) (83)

audit An examination of information systems, their inputs, outputs, and processing. (84)

back door (also called trap door) Typically a password, known only to the attacker, that allows the attacker to access the system without having to go through any security procedures. (73)

biometrics The science and technology of authentication (i.e., establishing the identity of an individual) by measuring the subject's physiologic or behavioral characteristics. (80)

certificate authority A third party that acts as a trusted intermediary between computers (and companies) by issuing digital certificates and verifying the worth and integrity of the certificates. (83)

code of ethics A collection of principles that are intended to guide decision making by members of the organization. (62)

communications controls Controls that deal with the movement of data across networks. (82)

controls evaluation A process in which the organization identifies security deficiencies and calculates the costs of implementing adequate control measures. (78)

cookie Small amounts of information that Web sites store on your computer, temporarily or more-or-less permanently. (74)

copyright A grant that provides the creator of intellectual property with ownership of it for the life of the creator plus 70 years. (76)

cracker A malicious hacker. (70)

cybercrimes Illegal activities executed on the Internet. (70)

cyberterrorism Can be defined as a premeditated, politically motivated attack against information, computer systems, computer programs, and data that results in violence against noncombatant targets by subnational groups or clandestine agents. (71)

cyberwar War in which a country's information systems could be paralyzed from a massive attack by destructive software. (71)

denial-of-service (DoS) A cyberattack in which an attacker sends a flood of data packets to the target computer, with the aim of overloading its resources. (73)

digital certificate An electronic document attached to a file certifying that this file is from the organization it claims to be from and has not been modified from its original format or content. (83)

disaster avoidance A security approach oriented toward prevention. (86)

disaster recovery The chain of events linking planning to protection to recovery. (86)

distributed denial-of-service (DDoS) A denial-of-service attack that sends a flood of data packets from many compromised computers simultaneously. (73)

electronic surveillance Monitoring or tracking people's activities with the aid of computers. (62)

encryption The process of converting an original message into a form that cannot be read by anyone except the intended receiver. (82)

exposure The harm, loss, or damage that can result if a threat compromises an information resource. (68)

firewall A system (either hardware, software, or a combination of both) that prevents a specific type of information from moving between untrusted networks, such as the Internet, and private networks, such as your company's network. (82)

general controls Security controls established to protect a computer system regardless of the specific application. (79)

hacker An outside person who has penetrated a computer system, usually with no criminal intent. (70)

hot site A fully configured computer facility, with all information resources and services, communications links, and physical plant operations, that duplicate your company's computing resources and provide near real-time recovery of IT operations. (86)

identity theft Crime in which someone uses the personal information of others to create a false identity and then uses it for some fraud. (71)

information systems controls The procedures, devices, or software aimed at preventing a compromise to a system. (68)

intellectual property The intangible property created by individuals or corporations, which is protected under trade secret, patent, and copyright laws. (76)

logic bomb Segments of computer code embedded within an organization's existing computer programs. (73)

passphrase A series of characters that is longer than a password but that can be memorized easily. (81)

password A private combination of characters that only the user should know. (81)

patent A document that grants the holder exclusive rights on an invention or process for 20 years. (76)

pestware Clandestine, alien software installed on computers through duplicitous channels. (74)

pharming An attacker fraudulently acquires the Domain Name for a company's Web site so that when people enter the URL for that Web site, they go to the fake site. (75)

phishing An attack that uses deception to fraudulently acquire sensitive personal information by masquerading as an official-looking e-mail. (75)

physical controls Controls that restrict unauthorized individuals from gaining access to a company's computer facilities. (79)

piracy Copying a software program without making payment to the owner. (77)

privacy The right to be left alone and to be free of unreasonable personal intrusion. (62)

privacy policy (also called **privacy code**) An organization's guidelines with respect to protecting the privacy of customers, clients, and employees. (66)

public-key encryption (also called **asymmetric encryption**) A type of encryption that uses two different keys, a public key and a private key. (83)

risk The likelihood that a threat will occur. (68)

risk acceptance Where the organization accepts the potential risk, continues to operate with no controls, and absorbs any damages that occur. (78)

risk analysis The process in which an organization assesses the value of each asset being protected, estimates the probability that each asset might be compromised, and compares the probable costs of each being compromised with the costs of protecting it. (78)

risk limitation Where the organization limits its risk by implementing controls that minimize the impact of a threat. (78)

risk management A process that identifies, controls, and minimizes the impact of threats, in an effort to reduce risk to manageable levels. (78)

risk mitigation Where the organization takes concrete actions against risks, such as implementing controls and developing a disaster recovery plan. (78)

risk transference Where the organization transfers the risk by using other means to compensate for a loss, such as by purchasing insurance. (78)

social engineering Getting around security systems by tricking computer users inside a company into revealing sensitive information or gaining unauthorized access privileges. (70)

spam Unsolicited e-mail. (74)

spamware Alien software that uses your computer as a launch platform for spammers. (74)

spyware Alien software that can record your keystrokes and/or capture your passwords. (74)

strong password A password that is difficult to guess, longer rather than shorter, contains upper and lower case letters, numbers, and special characters, and is not a recognizable word or string of numbers. (81)

symmetric encryption A form of encryption where the sender and recipient use the same key. (82)

threat Any danger to which an information resource may be exposed. (68)

trade secret Intellectual work, such as a business plan, that is a company secret and is not based on public information. (76)

trap door (see back door) (73)

Trojan horse A software program containing a hidden function that presents a security risk. (73)

virtual private network A private network that uses a public network (usually the Internet) to securely connect users by using encryption. (83)

virus Malicious software that can attach itself to (or "infect") other computer programs without the owner of the program being aware of the infection. (72)

vulnerability The possibility that an information resource will suffer harm by a threat. (68)

Web bug Small, usually invisible, graphic image added to a Web page. (75)

worm Destructive programs that replicate themselves without requiring another program to provide a safe environment for replication. (73)

Discussion Questions

1. The Internal Revenue Service (IRS) buys demographic market research data from private companies. These data contain income statistics that could be compared to tax returns. Many U.S. citizens feel that their rights are being violated by the agency's use of such information. Is this unethical behavior on the part of the IRS? Discuss.

2. Northeast Utilities (Hartford, Connecticut) (*www. nu.com*) instructs its meter readers to gather information about services needed on its customers' homes, such as a driveway or fence in need of repair. The company then sells the data to other companies that would stand to gain from the information. In turn, these companies solicit Northeast customers via direct mail, telemarketing, and so on regarding these services. Although some customers welcome this approach, others consider it an annoyance because they are not interested in the particular repairs. Assess the value of Northeast Utilities' initiative against the potential negative effects of adverse public reaction.

3. Many hospitals, health maintenance organizations (HMOs), and federal agencies are converting patients' medical records from paper to electronic storage using imaging technology. After they make the conversion, they can use Web technology and electronic storage to access most records quickly and easily. However, making these records available in a database and on networks could also enable unauthorized people to view these data. However, implementing a system to fully protect patients' privacy could cost too much or slow down authorized access to the records. What types of policies could health-care administrators use in such situations?

4. Find your school's guidelines for ethical computer use at its Web site. Does it have restrictions as to the types of Web sites and material that can be viewed (e.g., gambling, pornography, etc.)? Are students allowed to change the programs on the hard drives of the lab computers or to download software for their own use? Does your school have rules governing personal use of computers and e-mail?

5. Should laws be passed to make spam a crime? If so, how should lawmakers deal with First Amendment rights? How would such laws be enforced?

6. Some insurance companies will not insure a business unless the firm has a computer disaster recovery plan. Explain why. Is this policy fair? Why or why not?

Problem-Solving Activities

1. Complete the computer ethics quiz at *http://web.cs.bgsu. edu/maner/xxicee/html/welcome.htm*. Also visit *http:// onlineethics.org/cases/robot/robot.html*. Discuss what you learned from the quiz and from the case on The Killer Robot.

2. An information security manager routinely monitored the contents of electronic correspondence among employees. She discovered that many employees were using the system for personal purposes. Some messages were love letters to fellow employees, and others related to a football betting pool. The security manager prepared a list of the employees, with samples of their messages, and gave them to management. Some managers punished their employees for having used the corporate e-mail for personal purposes. Some employees, in turn, objected to the monitoring, claiming that they should have the same right to privacy as they have using the company's interoffice mail system.
   a. Is monitoring of e-mail by managers ethical? (It is legal.) Support your answer.
   b. Is the use of e-mail by employees for personal communication ethical? Support your answer.
   c. Is the security manager's submission of the list of abusers to management ethical? Why or why not?

   d. Is punishing the abusers ethical? Why or why not?
   e. What should the company do in order to rectify the situation?

3. Mr. Jones worked as a customer support representative for a small software company but was fired in late 2004. In early 2005, the company discovered that someone was logging onto its computers at night via a modem and had altered and copied files. During the investigation, the police traced the calls to Mr. Jones's home and found copies there of proprietary information valued at several million dollars. Mr. Jones's access code was canceled the day he was terminated. However, the company suspects that he obtained the access code of another employee.
   a. How might the crime have been committed? Why were the controls ineffective? (State any relevant assumptions.) What other methods could Mr. Jones have used to access his old company's systems?
   b. What can the company, or any company, do in order to prevent similar incidents in the future?

4. What is the difference betweeen cyberterrorism and cyberwar? Should laws be passed to combat cyberterrorism? What should they enforce? How could they be

enforced? By whom? One country? An international body?

5. Frank Abignale, the criminal played by Leonardo di Caprio in the motion picture *Catch Me If You Can*, ended up in prison. However, when he left prison, he went to work as a consultant to many companies on matters of fraud. Why do so many companies not report computer crimes? Why do these companies hire the perpetrators (if caught) as consultants? Is this a good idea?

Internet Activities

1. Enter *www.scambusters.org*. Find out what the organization does. Learn about e-mail scams and Web site scams. Report your findings.

2. Download freeware from *www.junkbusters.com* and learn how to prohibit unsolicited e-mail (spam). Describe how your privacy is protected.

3. Enter the following Web sites: *http://www.consumer.gov/idtheft/*, *http://www.identitytheft. org*, and *http://www.fraud.org*. Learn all you can about identity theft and how to protect yourself.

4. Access The Computer Ethics Institute's Web site at *http://archive.cpsr.net/program/ethics/cei.html*. The site offers the "Ten Commandments of Computer Ethics." Study these 10 and decide if any should be added.

5. Software piracy is a global problem. Access the following Web sites: *http://www.bsa.org* and *http://www. microsoft.com/piracy/*. What can organizations do to mitigate this problem? Are some organizations dealing with the problem better than others?

Team Assignments

1. Access *www.consumer.gov/sentinel/* to learn more about how law enforcement agencies around the world work together to fight consumer fraud. Each team should obtain current statistics on one of the top five consumer complaint categories and prepare a report. Are any categories growing faster than others? Are any categories more prevalent in certain parts of the world?

2. The State of California maintains a database of people who allegedly abuse children. (The database also includes names of the alleged victims.) The list is made available to dozens of public agencies, and it is considered in cases of child adoption and employment decisions. Because so many people have access to the list, its content is easily disclosed to unauthorized persons.

In 1996, an alleged abuser and her child, whose case had been dropped but whose names had remained on the list, sued the State of California for invasion of privacy. With the class divided into groups, answer the following four questions in terms of a database of sex offenders.

   a. Is there a need to include names of people on the list in cases that were dismissed or declared unfounded?

   b. Who should make the decision about what names should be included and what the criteria should be for inclusion?

   c. What is the potential damage (if any) to the abusers?

   d. Should the State of California abolish the list? Why or why not?

CASE   ## What Are Universities to Do?

THE BUSINESS PROBLEM Recently, the CIO of Dartmouth College had to notify the college community that an unauthorized user had gained access to eight servers in a college laboratory and installed an unauthorized program. The hacker accessed human resources data of Dartmouth employees, research data, and student immunization information. In doing so, the hacker might have copied sensitive information. The CIO contacted all of the affected individuals either by e-mail or regular mail. He urged alumni, employees, and students to monitor their credit reports in case their identities had been stolen.

At the University of California, Berkeley, a hacker accessed names and Social Security numbers of about 1.4 million Californians after breaking into a university computer system. At the University of Michigan, a graduate student was accused of stealing the user names and passwords of 60 students and faculty members. At Eastern Connecticut State University, when students logged on at the beginning of the fall semester, they accidentally brought so many viruses with them that the entire network collapsed.

University IT staff members are trying to stay ahead of their own students. The threats from students include the introduction of viruses into school networks, improper use of file sharing services, hogging bandwidth when downloading huge graphic files such as movies, and outright theft of information about their school records. The problem is that at a university, IT security personnel have to deal with academic freedom and information exchange. At a university, then, nothing is secure unless it absolutely has to be.

THE IT SOLUTION Universities are working hard to solve these information security problems. Schools are separating student networks from administrative and other academic networks. For instance, student residential networks are able to connect to an academic research database at various points, but the connection can be quickly terminated by administrators.

Schools are requiring all students on residential networks to authenticate their identities with passwords. Schools are also ensuring that student computers are up to date with the latest antivirus software and patches. For example, if a student's Windows XP desktop does not have the latest security patches, that student will not be allowed access to the network until he or she installs the patches.

At one university, to access one of the school's academic or administrative networks, a student must (1) have a user name and password to access an application, (2) be at a location connected to the network, (3) pass through a firewall with intrusion detection, and (4) be registered into a database that records who accessed the software. During each student's session, all IP addresses and activities are logged for auditing.

THE RESULTS The results are mixed. Universities simply have too many students with diverse backgrounds and different levels of technology expertise to adequately secure networks. In fact, simply installing network monitoring software is difficult due to complications arising from academic freedom.

Some universities are turning to the students themselves for help. They are including students in technology decisions, listening to their input, and observing how they use such IT as messaging and PDAs. For example, when bandwidth usage got out of hand, one university went to students for help. The students' suggestion: Students either regulate themselves or face a tuition hike to pay for additional bandwidth. The bandwidth problem eased within a week.

Sources: Compiled from L. Dignan, "Hack to School," *Baseline Magazine*, September 1, 2004; "Hacker Hits California-Berkeley Computer," *CNN.com*, October 10, 2004.

QUESTIONS

1. Do you think universities should have the same stringent information security controls that corporations do? Why or why not?
2. Should universities segregate student networks? Support your answer.
3. What security measures does your university require?

Interactive Learning

Big Brother or Necessary Security Measures?

Go to the Interactivities section on the *WileyPLUS* Web site and access Chapter 3: Ethics, Privacy, and Information Security. There you will find some animated, hands-on activities that help you make some decisions about ethical issues like privacy and electronic tracking at a hospital, manufacturing plant, and office.

Information and Ethics at Club IT

Go to the Club IT link on the *WileyPLUS* Web site. On the Web site, you will find some assignments that will help you learn how to apply IT solutions to a business.

wiley.com/college/rainer

How-to Appendix 1

Protecting Your Own Computer

- Use strong passwords.
- Back up your important files and folders.
- Install and use antivirus programs.
  - See this Web site for free antivirus programs: *http://netsecurity.about.com/od/antivirus software/a/aafreeav.htm.*
- Keep your system up-to-date with the latest patches (e.g., patches for Microsoft Windows).
- Be very careful opening e-mail attachments.
- Be very careful downloading and installing programs from the Internet.
- Install and use a firewall program (software).
  - See this Web site for free personal firewall programs: *http://netsecurity.about.com/od/personalfirewalls/a/aafreefirewall.htm.*
  - Install and use a hardware firewall.
- Use encryption.
  - See this Web site for free encryption software: *http://netsecurity.about.com/cs/hacker-tools/a/aafreecrypt.htm.*
  - Pay particular attention to "pretty good privacy" at *www.pgp.com/downloads/freeware/index.html.*

How-to Appendix 2

Avoiding Identity Theft

- Carry only the credit cards and ID that you need to have with you. File others in a safe place.
- Sign your credit cards immediately.
- Do not carry your Social Security card with you. Keep it in a secure place.
- Do not attach a Personal Identification Number (PIN) or Social Security number to any cards that you carry with you.
- Do not attach or write a PIN or Social Security number on anything that you are going to discard (e.g., a receipt).
- Shred any document that contains your Social Security number or a credit card number. (Buy a shredder to use at home.)
- Check receipts and other documents to ensure that they pertain to you and not someone else.
- Alert any creditor if you do not receive your statement. Someone may have taken it from your mailbox.
- Immediately report the suspected theft or loss of a key identification document such as a driver's license, passport, or Social Security card to the issuing agency.

How to Recover if Your Identity Is Stolen

- First, prepare yourself for a long, difficult trip through a bureaucratic maze. Get organized—keep a file with all your paperwork, including the names and numbers of everyone you contact.

- File as detailed a police report as possible. Send copies to creditors and other agencies that may require proof of the crime. Get the phone number of your investigator and give it to creditors. In all communications, use certified, return receipt mail.

- Report that you are the victim of identity theft with the fraud divisions of all three major credit bureaus. If you notify one bureau, it is supposed to notify the other two. However, do not take a chance. Notify all three yourself.

  ○ Equifax (*www.equifax.com*) (800-525-6285)

  ○ Experian (*www.experion.com*) (888-397-3742)

  ○ TransUnion (*www.transunion.com*) (800-680-7289)

- Be sure to get your unique case number, and ask each bureau to send you a credit report. Read it carefully for suspicious activity.

- Tell the bureaus to issue a "fraud alert," which requires mortgage brokers, car dealers, credit card companies, and other lenders to scrutinize anyone who opens an account in your name for 90 days. Also, ask for the document you need to file a long-term fraud alert, which lasts for seven years, and can be canceled at any time.

- Ask the bureaus for names and phone numbers of lenders with whom fraudulent accounts have been opened (because this information may not be included on the credit report). Tell the bureaus to remove inquiries generated due to fraud, because even a large number of inquiries can harm your credit rating.

- Tell the bureaus to notify anyone who received your report in the last six months that you are disputing the information. The credit bureaus will alert any employer who has asked for the report in the last two years.

- Californians can order a "credit freeze" with all three major credit card bureaus. This requires lenders, retailers, utilities, and other businesses to get special access to your credit report through a PIN-based system. It also helps prevent anyone from getting any new loans and credit in your name. Vermont, Texas, and Louisiana have similar freeze laws going into effect in 2005, and bills have been introduced in 12 other states.

- Call credit card companies directly. Although financial institutions are supposed to see your fraud alerts, the data are not always shared immediately. Credit card companies generally forgive consumers for fraudulent transactions. However, late payments—even on credit cards you did not open—can damage your credit rating.

- Fill out fraud affidavits for creditors. The Federal Trade Commission provides a form that many creditors accept.

- If your credit cards have been used fraudulently, get replacements with new account numbers and close your old accounts.

- Monitor your mail for any suspicious increase or decrease in volume or strange bills, and be on the lookout particularly for change-of-address forms. The post office must send notifications to your old and new addresses. If someone tries to change your mailing address, it is a major tip-off that you have been victimized.

- If debt collectors demand payment of fraudulent accounts, write down the name of the company as well as the collector's name, phone number, and address. Tell the collector that you are a victim of fraud. Send a letter with a filled-out FTC form.

Chapter 4

During the last year, the world created the digital equivalent of 10 trillion novels of information. We are accumulating data at a frenzied pace from such diverse sources as e-mails, Web pages, credit card swipes, phone messages, stock trades, memos, address books, and radiology scans. We are awash in data, and yet we have to manage it and make sense of it.

Information technologies and systems support organizations in managing—that is, acquiring, organizing, storing, accessing, analyzing, and interpreting—data. When these data are managed properly, they become *information* and then *knowledge*. As we have seen, information and knowledge are valuable organizational resources that can provide a competitive advantage. In this chapter, we explore the process whereby data is transformed first into information and then into knowledge.

Few business professionals are comfortable making or justifying business decisions that are not based on solid information. This is especially true today, when modern information systems make access to that information quick and easy.

For example, we have technology that puts data in a form that managers and analysts can easily understand. These professionals can then access the data themselves and analyze them according to their needs with a variety of tools, thereby producing information. They can then apply their experience to place this information in the context of a business problem, thus producing knowledge. Knowledge management, enabled by information technology, captures and stores knowledge in forms that all organizational employees can access and apply, creating the flexible, powerful "learning organization."

We begin this chapter by discussing the problems in managing data and discuss the database approach that organizations use to solve those problems. We then show how database management systems enable us to access and use the data in databases. Data warehouses have become increasingly important as they provide the data that managers need to analyze to make decisions. Managers use business intelligence tools to analyze the data in data warehouses and use data visualization tools to make analysis results more understandable and attractive. We close the chapter with a look at knowledge management.

Data and Knowledge Management

Introduction to Information Systems
R. Kelly Rainer, Jr., Efraim Turban, and Richard E. Potter. ISBN 978-0-471-7363-3
©2007 John Wiley & Sons, Inc.

Student Web Site
- Web Quizzes
- Links to relevant Web sites
- Lecture Slides in PowerPoint

WileyPlus
- Virtual Company assignments and Club IT Web site
- Interactive Learning Sessions
- Microsoft Excel and Access Exercises
- Software Skills Tutorials
- e-book

Learning Objectives

1. Recognize the importance of data, issues involved in managing these data, and their life cycle.
2. Describe the sources of data, and explain how data are collected.
3. Explain the advantages of the database approach.
4. Explain the operation of data warehousing and its role in decision support.
5. Understand the capabilities and benefits of data mining.
6. Describe data visualization and explain geographical information systems and virtual reality.
7. Define knowledge, and describe the different types of knowledge.

What's in IT for me?

ACC   FIN   MKT   POM   HRM   MIS

CASE # Data Management Improves MetLife's Performance

MetLife (*www.metlife.com*), an insurance company worth nearly $36 billion, is transforming itself into a high-tech, high-response, fully networked financial services firm. This transition is difficult, however.

Throughout much of the early 1990s, MetLife was distracted by a scandal involving overly aggressive insurance sales practices that eventually cost the company nearly $2 billion in fines and penalties. Their return on assets hit a disturbingly low 0.1 percent, compared with an industry average of nearly 1 percent. Return on assets is a measure of an insurer's health because its assets are, in great measure, its policies. If MetLife was going to be ready to take advantage of new opportunities that were expected to come with the 1999 repeal of the Glass–Steagall Act, it had to catch up to the modern world of financial services quickly. This act, which was passed during the New Deal, prohibited companies from engaging in banking, securities, and insurance simultaneously.

Source: Christian Heeb/laif/Redux

MetLife decided to create a data management network that could connect the vast number of systems the company employed. The company implemented an enterprisewide client information file that for the first time made a centralized customer database available to all MetLife business units. These units use this database for cross-selling new business, handling service issues, and managing accounts. In effect, MetLife is making the customer the foundation of its business.

There were problems, though. The business units involved were engaged in different lines of business and offered different products. They had a vertical perspective. The new system required them to adopt a much broader outlook by providing the customer base with a wide range of services, not just a few related ones.

MetLife began with its Individual Business (IB) unit, which includes life and property insurance, annuities, mutual funds, and financial planning. In the IB unit, each product line had its own administrative system, and none of them were related. If a customer had two life insurance policies, an automobile policy, and a mutual funds account, he or she had four different client files of information, one for each contract.

The solution was to produce a single file for each client, regardless of how many policies he or she held. To accomplish this task the company turned to DWL (*www.dwl.com*), a company that provides software for integrating and managing data. DWL software integrates existing databases and acts as a single source for client files. The software not only supplies a single, readily accessible location for customer records, but it also turns these files into potential transactions. For example, when a customer's address is updated on a policy, the software can alert salespeople of the opportunity to sell that customer a homeowner's policy.

Unfortunately, implementing the DWL software caused at least two problems. First, it created a cultural change because it clashed with the traditional way of doing business. Second, the implications of data sharing caused friction, particularly when it involved cross-selling. MetLife's agents were concerned their customers would be inundated with offers for other MetLife products by other MetLife agents. This type of overkill could alienate customers from the company in general.

The new system has enabled MetLife's IB managers to help clients purchase more products. It also has allowed them to analyze the data in real time to target new customers. Finally, it has led to an overall increase in productivity. The system eliminates the need to enter new data every time a customer moves, changes account information, or signs up for another product offering. The system has resulted in significant cost savings.

The project is ongoing and is expected to continue at least until 2007. However, in 2003 MetLife's return on assets hit a 10-year high of 0.7 percent, and its net income rose 38 percent over the previous year.

The Results

The opening case about MetLife illustrates the importance of data to a large insurance company. To operate effectively and profitably the company must collect vast amounts of data, organize and store them properly, and then analyze them and use the results to make better marketing and other corporate decisions. The MetLife case also shows that data may be a source of problems in an organization, as people who "own" the data might be reluctant to share them.

As MetLife agents deal with their customers, the agents' experiences can be added to the customer database. This process creates knowledge. When this knowledge is properly disseminated, it can help to create a learning organization. In this chapter, we explain the process of managing data, transforming the data into usable information, and using the information in context to produce knowledge.

What We Learned From This Case

Sources: Compiled from J. Rothfeder, "Pay as You Go," *PC Magazine*, October 15, 2004; L. Mearian, "MetLife Building Giant Customer Relational Database," *Computerworld*, January 1, 2002; and *www.dwl.com*, *www.metlife.com*, accessed March 22, 2005.

4.1 Managing Data

As we have seen throughout this textbook, IT applications require data. Data should be of high quality, meaning that it should be accurate, complete, timely, consistent, accessible, relevant, and concise. However, there are increasing difficulties in acquiring, keeping, and managing data.

The Difficulties of Managing Data

Because data are processed in several stages and often in several places, they may be subject to some problems and difficulties. Managing data in organizations is difficult for various reasons:

- The amount of data increases exponentially with time. Much historical data must be kept for a long time, and new data are added rapidly.

- Data are scattered throughout organizations and are collected by many individuals using various methods and devices. Data are frequently stored in numerous servers and locations and in different computing systems, databases, formats, and human and computer languages.

- Data come from internal sources (e.g., corporate databases), personal sources (e.g., personal thoughts, opinions, experiences), and external sources (e.g., commercial databases, government reports, corporate Web sites).

"This is Fenton. Fenton does our really tricky spreadsheets."

- Data come from the Web, in the form of clickstream data. **Clickstream data** are those that visitors and customers produce when they visit a Web site. People move around a Web site by clicking on hyperlinks (described in Chapter 5). These clicks are recorded and are called clickstream data. Clickstream data provide a trail of the users' activities in the Web site, including user behavior and browsing patterns.

- An ever-increasing amount of external data needs to be considered in making organizational decisions.

- Data security, quality, and integrity are critical, yet they are easily jeopardized. In addition, legal requirements relating to data differ among countries and industries and change frequently.

Because data are difficult to manage, organizations might not always have high-quality data. IT's About Business 4.1 shows how "dirty data" causes problems at one company.

The Data Life Cycle

Businesses run on data that have been processed into information and knowledge. Managers then apply this knowledge to business problems and opportunities. Businesses transform data into knowledge and solutions in several ways. The general process is illustrated in Figure 4.1. It starts with the collection of data from various sources. The data are stored in a database(s). Selected data from the organization's databases are then processed to fit the format of a data warehouse or data mart. Users then access the data in the warehouse or data mart for analysis. The analysis is done with data-analysis tools, which look for patterns, and with intelligent systems, which support data interpretation. We discuss each of these concepts in this chapter.

These activities ultimately generate knowledge that can be used to support decision making. Both the data (at various times during the process) and the knowledge (derived at the end of the process) must be presented to users. This presentation can be accomplished by using different visualization tools. The created knowledge can also be stored in an organizational knowledge base and then used, together with decision-support tools, to provide solutions to organizational problems. The remaining sections of this chapter will examine the elements and the process shown in Figure 4.1 in greater detail.

The Data Hierarchy

Data are organized in a hierarchy that begins with bits and proceeds all the way to databases (see Figure 4.2). A *bit* (*b*inary dig*it*) represents the smallest unit of data a computer can process. The term "binary" means that a bit can consist only of a 0 or a 1. A group of eight

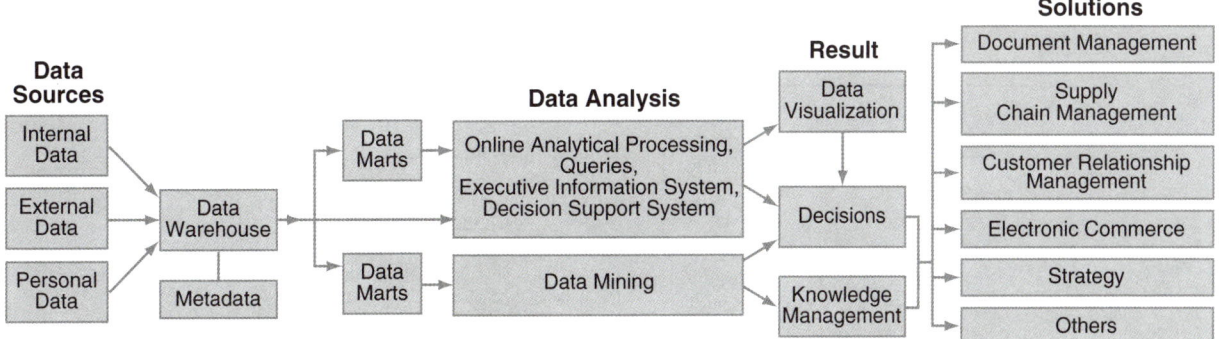

FIGURE 4.1   Data life cycle.

IT's About Business

4.1 How Clean Are Your Data?

Clean data means data without errors. However, as long as there have been data, there have been errors. But in the 1980s at least, there were less data to manage than today. At that time, the main source of customer data was basically the address to ship an item and an address to bill the customer. Today, data are considerably more complex. In addition to keeping track of vendors, suppliers, inventory, and financial records, companies now track customers' buying habits, preferences, and a host of other data.

Unfortunately, many companies simply assume that their data are accurate. This assumption can be highly inaccurate. In fact, Gartner (*www.gartner.com*), a research company, recently estimated that 25 percent of the critical data used in large corporations is flawed. The main causes of these flaws are human data-entry error, customer profile changes (such as a change of address), and a lack of proper corporate data standards. Gartner also said that through 2007, more than half of data-warehouse projects will experience problems or failure because they will not proactively address data-quality issues.

Consider, for example, Emerson Process Management (*www.compsys.com*). Emerson produces valves, pressure devices, and software for power plants, refineries, and food and beverage manufacturers. The company has 14 subdivisions, more than 10,000 employees, and more than 100,000 customers around the world. Each subdivision makes separate products, but their client bases often overlap. However, because each subdivision owns its own data, there was no way for managers to get an overall view of the company's business.

Three years ago, Emerson began an effort to consolidate and clean the company's customer database. The team first spoke to all the business unit heads in order to get a better understanding of their processes, the kind of data they needed, and how those data could best be delivered. Then the team began the long process of cleaning, consolidating, and "de-duplicating," using software from Group 1 Software (*www.g1.com*). Emerson now has an integrated view of each customer across all lines of business.

However, the effort did not end there. Keeping the data clean is a constant, ongoing effort. The system automatically processes 1.7 million addresses per month. Software does much of this work, but the reviewing process still requires human effort, particularly data that deal with information about companies in foreign countries. The Emerson data team notes that data quality degrades over time. It has a half-life, like radioactive material, depending on the business activity.

Sources: Compiled from D. D'Agostino, "Data Management: Getting Clean," *CIO Insight*, August 1, 2004; M. Wheatley, "Operation Clean Data," *CIO*, July 1, 2004; and B. Booth, "Clean Data Is Good Business," *ComputerWeekly.com*, February 8, 2005.

QUESTIONS

1. Why are clean data important to Accounting? Finance? Human Resources? Production/Operations? Marketing?
2. What types of data would have the shortest half-life (i.e., would degrade most quickly)?

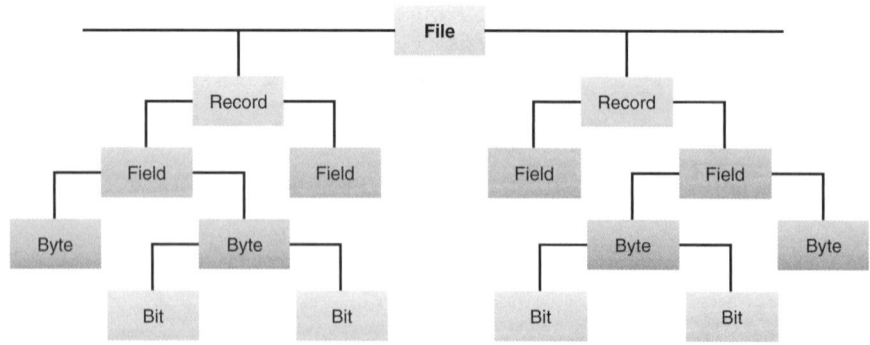

FIGURE 4.2
Hierarchy of data for a computer-based file.

bits, called a *byte*, represents a single character. A byte can be a letter, a number, or a symbol. A logical grouping of characters into a word, a small group of words, or an identification number is called a **field.** For example, a student's name in a university's computer files would appear in the "name" field, and her or his Social Security number would appear in the "Social Security number" field. A logical grouping of related fields, such as the student's name, the courses taken, the date, and the grade, comprise a **record**. A logical grouping of related records is called a **file** or **table**. For example, the records from a particular course, consisting of course number, professor, and students' grades, would constitute a data file for that course. A logical grouping of related files would constitute a **database**. Using the same example, the student course file could be grouped with files on students' personal histories and financial backgrounds to create a student database. The next section discusses the database approach in today's organizations.

Before you go on . . .

1. What are some of the difficulties involved in managing data?
2. Describe the data life cycle.
3. What are the various sources for data?
4. What are the units of the data hierarchy?

4.2 The Database Approach

Using databases eliminates many problems that arose from previous methods of storing and accessing data. Databases are arranged so that one set of software programs—the *database management system*—provides all users with access to all the data. This system minimizes the following problems:

- *Data redundancy:* The same data are stored in many places.
- *Data Isolation:* Applications cannot access data associated with other applications.
- *Data Inconsistency:* Various copies of the data do not agree.

In addition, database systems maximize the following issues:

- Data security.
- Data integrity: Data meet certain constraints, such as no alphabetic characters in a Social Security Number field.
- Data Independence: Applications and data are independent of one another (i.e., applications and data are not linked to each other, meaning that all applications are able to access the same data).

Figure 4.3 illustrates a university database. Note that university applications from the Registrar's office, the Accounting department, and the Athletics department access data through the database management system.

In the next section, we discuss how databases are designed. We focus on entity-relationship modeling and normalization procedures.

Designing the Database

Data must be organized so that users can retrieve, analyze, and understand them. A key to effectively designing a database is the data model. A **data model** is a diagram that represents entities in the database and their relationships. An **entity** is a person, place, thing, or event—such as a customer, employee, or product—about which information is maintained. Entities can typically be identified in the user's work environment. A record generally describes an entity. Each char-

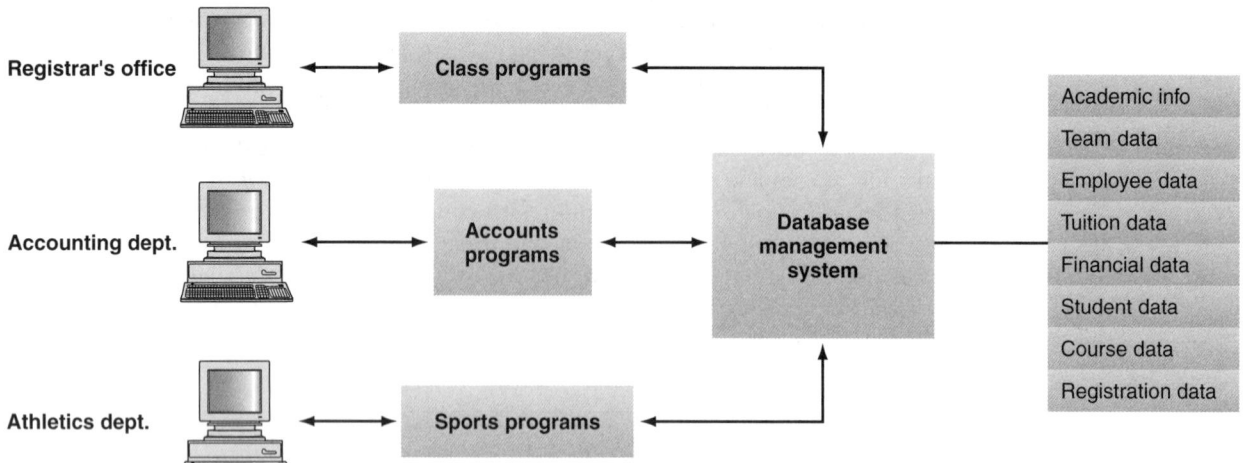

FIGURE 4.3   A database management system (DBMS) provides access to all data in the database.

acteristic or quality of a particular entity is called an **attribute**. Using the above examples, customer name, employee number, and product color would be considered attributes.

Every record in a file must contain at least one field that uniquely identifies that record so that it can be retrieved, updated, and sorted. This identifier field is called the **primary key**. For example, a student record in a U.S. college would probably use the Social Security number as its primary key. In some cases, locating a particular record requires the use of secondary keys. **Secondary keys** are other fields that have some identifying information but typically do not identify the file with complete accuracy. For example, the student's major might be a secondary key if a user wanted to find all students in a particular major field of study. It should not be the primary key, as more than one student can have the same major.

Entity-Relationship Modeling   Database designers plan the database design in a process called **entity-relationship (ER) modeling**, with an **entity-relationship diagram**. ER diagrams consist of entities, attributes, and relationships. Entities are pictured in boxes, and relationships are shown in diamonds. The attributes for each entity are listed next to the entity, and the primary key is underlined. Figure 4.4 shows an entity-relationship diagram.

As defined earlier, an *entity* is something that can be identified in the users' work environment. For example, consider student registration at a university. Students register for courses and register their cars for parking permits. In this example, STUDENT, PARKING PERMIT, COURSE, and PROFESSOR are entities, as shown in Figure 4.4.

Entities of a given type are grouped in **entity classes**. In our example, STUDENT, PARKING PERMIT, COURSE, and PROFESSOR are entity classes. An **instance** of an entity class is the representation of a particular entity. Therefore, a particular STUDENT (James Smythe, 145-89-7123) is an instance of the STUDENT entity class; a particular parking permit (91778) is an instance of the PARKING PERMIT entity class; a particular course (76890) is an instance of the COURSE entity class; and a particular professor (Margaret Wilson, 115-65-7632) is an instance of the PROFESSOR entity class.

Entity instances have **identifiers**, which are attributes that are unique to that entity instance. For example, STUDENT instances can be identified with StudentIdentification-Number; PARKING PERMIT instances can be identified with PermitNumber; COURSE instances can be identified with CourseNumber; and PROFESSOR instances can be identified with ProfessorIdentificationNumber. These identifiers (or primary keys) are underlined on ER diagrams, as in Figure 4.4.

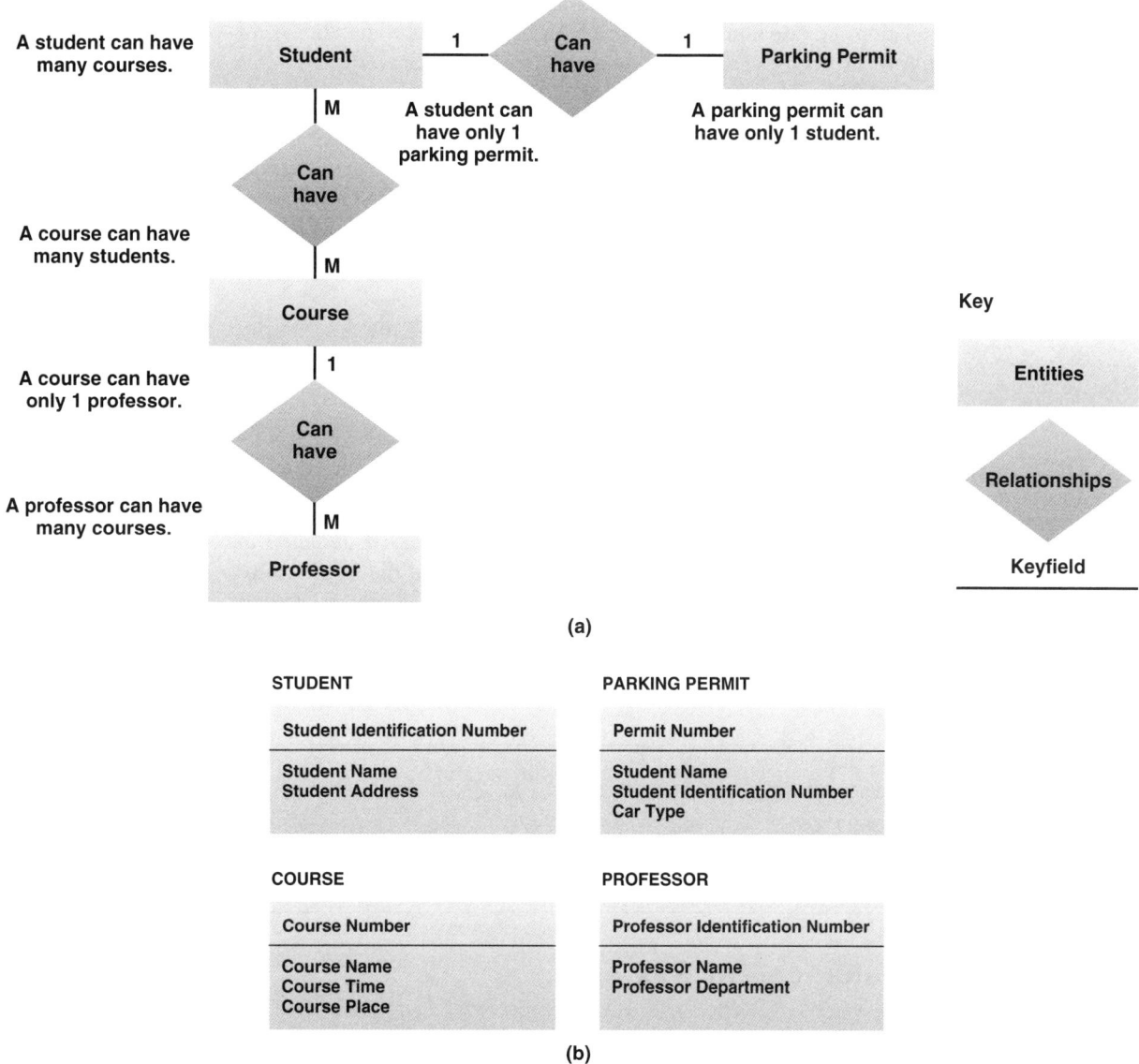

(a)

STUDENT

Student Identification Number
Student Name Student Address

PARKING PERMIT

Permit Number
Student Name Student Identification Number Car Type

COURSE

Course Number
Course Name Course Time Course Place

PROFESSOR

Professor Identification Number
Professor Name Professor Department

(b)

FIGURE 4.4 Entity-relationship diagram model.

Entities have attributes, or properties, that describe the entity's characteristics. In our example, examples of attributes for STUDENT would be StudentIdentificationNumber, StudentName, and StudentAddress. Examples of attributes for PARKING PERMIT would be PermitNumber, StudentName, StudentIdentificationNumber, and CarType. Examples of attributes for COURSE would be CourseNumber, CourseName, and CoursePlace. Examples of attributes for PROFESSOR would be ProfessorIdentificationNumber, ProfessorName, and ProfessorDepartment. (Note that each course at this university has one professor—no team teaching.)

Why are StudentName and StudentIdentificationNumber attributes of both the STUDENT and PARKING PERMIT entity classes? That is, why do we need the PARKING PERMIT entity class? If you consider all interlinked university systems, the PARKING PERMIT entity class is needed for other applications, such as fee payments, parking tickets, and external links to the state Department of Motor Vehicles.

Entities are associated with one another in relationships, which can include many entities. (Remember that relationships are noted by diamonds on ER diagrams.) The number of entities in a relationship is the degree of the relationship. Relationships between two items are called *binary relationships*. There are three types of binary relationships: one-to-one, one-to-many, and many-to-many. We discuss each one below.

1. In a *one-to-one (1:1)* relationship, a single-entity instance of one type is related to a single-entity instance of another type. Figure 4.4 shows STUDENT-PARKING PERMIT as a 1:1 relationship that relates a single STUDENT with a single PARKING PERMIT. That is, no student has more than one parking permit, and no parking permit is for more than one student.

2. The second type of relationship, *one-to-many (1:M)*, is represented by the COURSE–PROFESSOR relationship in Figure 4.4. This relationship means that a professor can have many courses, but each course can have only one professor.

3. The third type of relationship, *many-to-many (M:M)*, is represented by the STUDENT–COURSE relationship. This M:M relationship means that a student can have many courses, and a course can have many students.

Entity-relationship modeling is valuable because the process allows database designers to talk with users throughout the organization to ensure that all entities and the relationships among them are represented. This process underscores the importance of all users in designing organizational databases. Notice that all entities and relationships in our example above are in terms that users can understand. Now that we have taken a look at designing a database, we turn our attention to database management systems.

Before you go on . . .

1. What is a data model?
2. What is a primary key? A secondary key?
3. What is an entity? A relationship?

4.3 Database Management Systems

A **database management system (DBMS)** is a set of programs that provide users with tools to add, delete, access, and analyze data stored in one location. An organization can access the data by using query and reporting tools that are part of the DBMS or by using application programs specifically written to access the data. DBMSs also provide the mechanisms for maintaining the integrity of stored data, managing security and user access, and recovering information if the system fails. Because databases and DBMSs are essential to all areas of business, they must be carefully managed.

There are a number of different database architectures, but we focus on the relational database model because of its popularity and ease of use. Other database models (e.g., hierarchical and network) are the responsibility of the MIS function and are not used by organizational employees. Popular examples of relational databases are Microsoft Access and Oracle.

The Relational Database Model

Most business data—especially accounting and financial data—traditionally were organized into simple tables consisting of columns and rows. Tables allow people to compare information quickly by row or column. In addition, items are easy to retrieve by finding the point of intersection of a particular row and column.

The **relational database model** is based on the concept of two-dimensional tables. A relational database is not always one big table—usually called a *flat file*—that contains all of the records and attributes. Such a design would entail far too much data redundancy. Instead, a relational database is usually designed with a number of related tables. Each of these tables contains records (listed in rows) and attributes (listed in columns).

These related tables can be joined when they contain common columns. The uniqueness of the primary key tells the DBMS which records are joined with others in related tables. This feature allows users great flexibility in the variety of queries they can make. Yet, this model has some disadvantages. Because large-scale databases may be composed of many interrelated tables, the overall design may be complex and therefore have slow search and access times.

Consider the relational database example about students shown in Figure 4.5. The table contains data about the entity called students. Attributes of the entity are name, undergraduate major, and grade point average. The rows are the records on Sally Adams, John Jones, Jane Lee, Kevin Durham, Juan Rodriguez, Stella Zubnicki, and Ben Jones. Of course, your university keeps much more data on you than our example shows. In fact, your university's student database probably keeps hundreds of attributes on each student.

Query Languages Requesting information from a database is the most commonly performed operation. **Structured query language (SQL)** is the most popular query language used to request information. SQL allows people to perform complicated searches by using relatively simple statements or key words. Typical key words are SELECT (to specify a desired attribute), FROM (to specify the table to be used), and WHERE (to specify conditions to apply in the query).

To understand how SQL works, imagine that a university wants to know the names of students who will graduate with honors in May 2005. The university IS staff would query the student relational database with an SQL statement such as: SELECT (Student Name), FROM (Student Database), WHERE (Grade Point Average > 3.40 and < 3.59). The SQL query would return: John Jones and Juan Rodriguez.

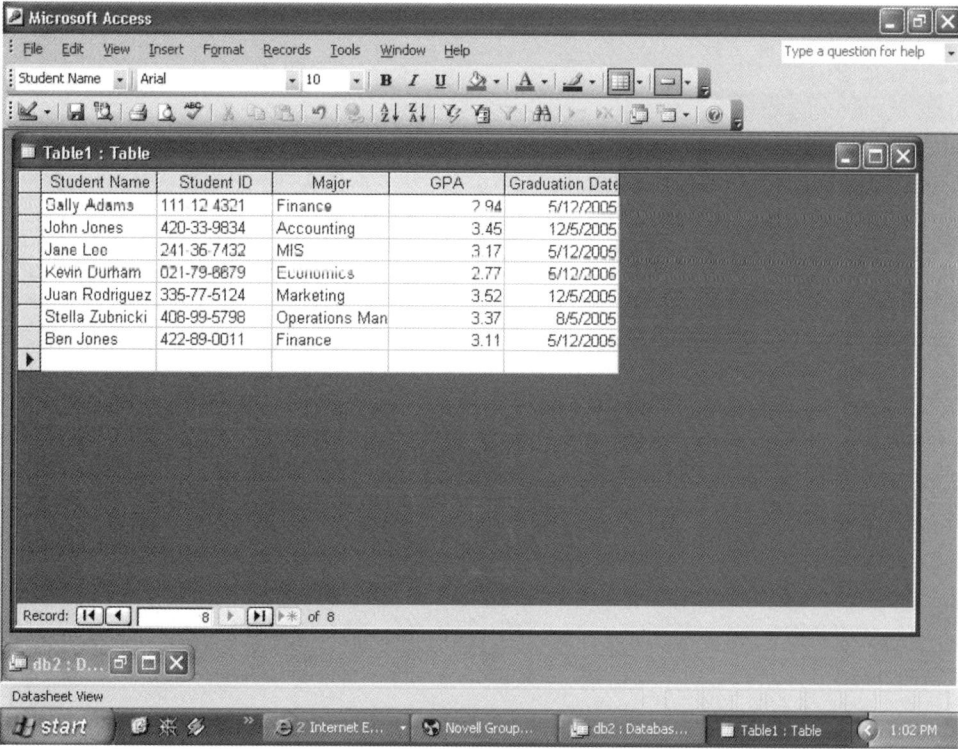

FIGURE 4.5
Student database
example.

Another way to find information in a database is to use **query by example (QBE)**. In QBE, the user fills out a grid or template (also known as a form) to construct a sample or description of the data he or she wants. Users can construct a query quickly and easily by using drag-and-drop features in a DBMS such as Microsoft Access. Conducting queries in this manner is simpler than keying in SQL commands.

Data Dictionary When a relational model is created, the **data dictionary** defines the format necessary to enter the data into the database. The data dictionary provides information on each attribute, such as its name, whether it is a key or part of a key, the type of data expected (alphanumeric, numeric, dates, etc.), and valid values. Data dictionaries can also provide information on how often the attribute should be updated, why it is needed in the database, and which business functions, applications, forms, and reports use the attribute.

Data dictionaries provide many advantages to the organization. Because they provide names and standard definitions for all attributes, they reduce the chances that the same attribute will be used in different applications but with a different name. In addition, data dictionaries enable programmers to develop programs more quickly because they don't have to create new data names.

Normalization In order to use a relational database management system effectively, the data must be analyzed to eliminate redundant data elements. **Normalization** is a method for analyzing and reducing a relational database to its most streamlined form for minimum redundancy, maximum data integrity, and best processing performance. When data are *normalized*, attributes in the table depend only on the primary key.

As an example of normalization, consider an automotive repair garage. This business takes orders from customers who want to have their cars repaired. In this example, ORDER, PART, SUPPLIER, and CUSTOMER are entities. In this example, there are many PARTS in an ORDER, but each PART can come from only one SUPPLIER. In a nonnormalized relation called ORDER (see Figure 4.6), each ORDER would have to repeat

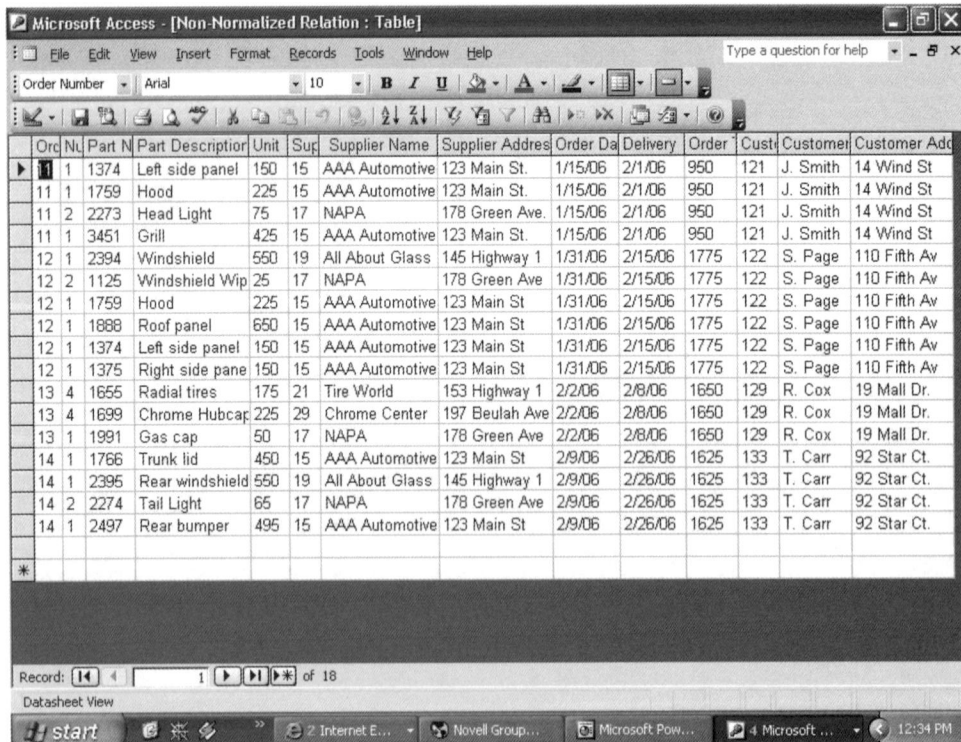

FIGURE 4.6
Non-normalized
relation.

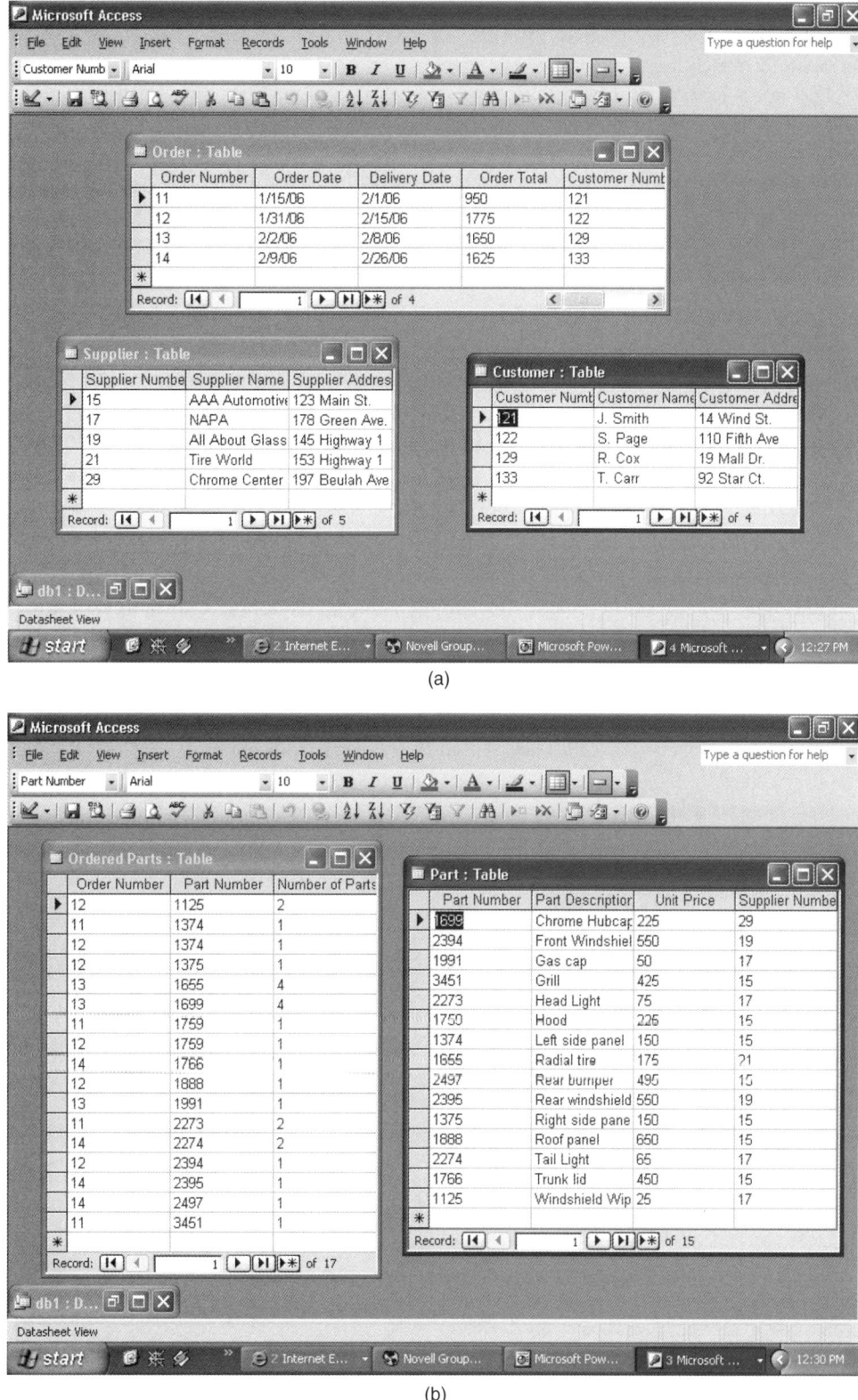

(a)

(b)

FIGURE 4.7 Smaller relationships broken down from the nonnormal relations. (a) Order, Supplier, Customer. (b) Ordered Parts, Part.

the name, description, and price of each PART needed to complete the ORDER, as well as the name and address of each SUPPLIER. This relation contains repeating groups and describes multiple entities.

The normalization process breaks down the relation, ORDER, into smaller relations: ORDER, PART, ORDERED-PARTS, SUPPLIER, and CUSTOMER. Each of these relations describes a single entity. This process is conceptually simpler, and it eliminates repeating groups (see Figures 4.7a and 4.7b). For example, consider an order at the automobile repair shop. The normalized relations can produce the order in the following manner (see Figure 4.8).

1. The ORDER relation provides the OrderNumber (the primary key), OrderDate, DeliveryDate, OrderTotal, and CustomerNumber.

2. The primary key of the ORDER relation (OrderNumber) provides a link to the ORDERED PARTS relation (the link numbered 1 in Figure 4.8).

3. The ORDERED PARTS relation supplies the NumberofParts information to ORDER.

4. The primary key of the ORDERED PARTS relation (PartNumber) provides a link to the PART relation (the link numbered 2 in Figure 4.8).

5. The PART relation supplies the PartDescription, UnitPrice, and SupplierNumber to ORDER.

6. The SupplierNumber in the PART relation provides a link to the SUPPLIER relation (the link numbered 3 in Figure 4.8).

7. The SUPPLIER relation provides the SupplierName and SupplierAddress to ORDER.

8. The CustomerNumber in ORDER provides a link to the CUSTOMER relation (the link numbered 4 in Figure 4.8).

9. The CUSTOMER relation supplies the CustomerName and CustomerAddress to ORDER.

The automotive repair shop order now has all the necessary information.

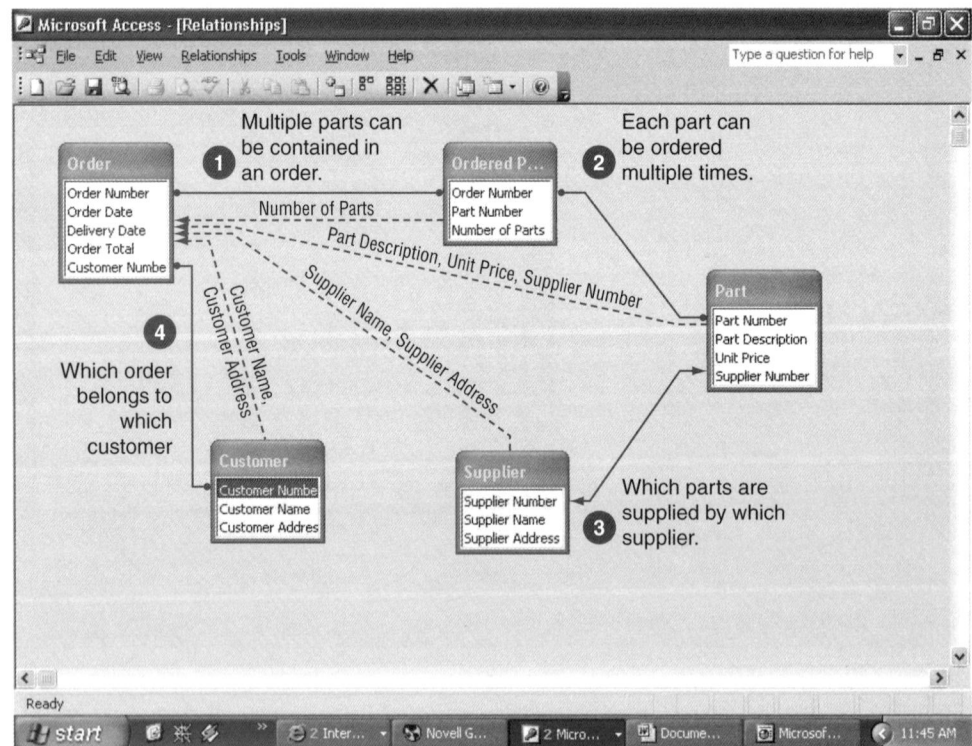

FIGURE 4.8
How normalized relations produce the order.

Virtual Databases

Organizations have data physically located anywhere on the corporate network and in a variety of formats. Multiple locations and formats often make it difficult for users to find the data that they need. **Virtual databases** are software applications that provide a way of managing many different data sources as though they were all one large database. Therefore to the user, it all looks like a single database. The benefits of virtual databases include lower development costs, faster development time, less maintenance, and a single point of entry into a company's data. IT's About Business 4.2 shows how virtual database software helps two companies obtain a single, integrated view of their data.

Before you go on . . .

1. What are the advantages and disadvantages of relational databases?
2. What are the benefits of data dictionaries?
3. Describe how structured query language works.

IT's About Business

4.2 Virtual Database Provides Relief

Since 2000 the typical big-business database has grown in size a hundredfold. This enormous expansion can be traced to the ever-growing numbers of computing systems and applications, Internet commerce, and recordkeeping mandated by government regulations. For management, the problem lies not only in the quantity of data but also in the lack of compatibility among the data. For example, financial information is different from personnel records, and Web content differs from call center logs. To deal with this compatibility problem, organizations are turning to virtual databases.

The DB2 Information Integrator (*www.ibm.com*) is a software application that provides IBM clients with a virtual database. The Integrator races through different databases, recognizing different types of data, mapping the entire system, and figuring what information needs to move where. The Integrator can piece together customer service records, photos, e-mails, and Web pages into a coherent whole. The diversity of the data remains, but the user now has a single, integrated view of all of the information.

Taikang Life, a Chinese insurance company, is using the Integrator to manage the several hundred new databases it has installed just since 2000. Formerly, to generate detailed customer histories and profiles, employees had to examine 200 data sources

from 30 offices. It took a team of 10 employees an entire week to produce a single massive report. Now, with the Integrator, employees can deliver the necessary information to a corporate desktop or a salesperson's mobile phone in just a few seconds.

Kawasaki uses the Integrator to generate production schedules and sales projections for its parts distribution network. The company had long relied on faxes, phone calls, and FedExes to and from thousands of dealers. As a result, its 100 databases took at least one day to produce just one report. Now, every night the Integrator scours databases for product information from Japan, updates from manufacturers, warehouse and local inventories, wholesale transactions with its dealers, and retail sales. Kawasaki can now do forecasting and troubleshooting in real time.

Sources: Compiled from Q. Hardy, "Data of Reckoning," *Forbes*, May 10, 2004; R. Kwon, "Primer: The Virtual Database," *Baseline Magazine*, May 1, 2003; and M. Songini,"IBM Pushes Out Virtual Database Technology," *Computerworld*, February 6, 2003.

QUESTIONS

1. Why do we need virtual databases?
2. What are the advantages of a virtual database?

4.4 Data Warehousing

Today, the most successful companies are those that can respond quickly and flexibly to market changes and opportunities. A key to this response is the effective and efficient use of data and information by analysts and managers, as shown in the chapter opening case on MetLife. The problem comes in providing users with access to corporate data so that they can analyze it. Let's look at an example.

If the manager of one of your local bookstores wanted to know the profit margin on used books at her store, she could find out from her database, using SQL or QBE. However, if she needed to know the trend in the profit margins on used books over the last 10 years, she would have a very difficult query to construct in SQL or QBE.

The bookstore manager's problem shows us two reasons why organizations are building data warehouses. First, the organization's databases do have the necessary information to answer her query, but it is not organized in a way that makes it easy for her to search for needed information and insight. Also, the organization's databases are designed to process millions of transactions per day. Therefore, complicated queries might take a long time to answer and might degrade the performance of the databases. As a result of these problems, companies are using data warehousing and data mining tools to make it easier and faster for users to access, analyze, and query data.

Describing the Data Warehouse

A **data warehouse** is a repository of historical data that are organized by subject to support decision makers in the organization. Data warehouses facilitate analytical processing activities, such as data mining, decision support, and querying applications. The basic characteristics of a data warehouse include:

- *Organized by business dimension or subject.* Data are organized by subject (e.g., by customer, vendor, product, price level, and region) and contain information relevant for decision support and data analysis.

- *Consistent.* Data in different databases may be encoded differently. For example, gender data may be encoded 0 and 1 in one operational system and "m" and "f" in another. In the data warehouse, though, they must be coded in a consistent manner.

- *Historical.* The data are kept for many years so that they can be used for trends, forecasting, and comparisons over time.

- *Nonvolatile.* Data are not updated after they are entered into the warehouse.

- *Use online analytical processing.* Typically, organizational databases are oriented toward handling transactions. That is, databases use **online transaction processing (OLTP)**, where business transactions are processed online as soon as they occur. The objective is speed and efficiency, which is critical to a successful Internet-based business operation. Data warehouses, which are not designed to support OLTP, but to support decision makers, use online analytical processing. **Online analytical processing (OLAP)** involves the analysis of accumulated data by end users.

- *Multidimensional.* Typically the data warehouse uses a multidimensional data structure. Recall that relational databases store data in two-dimensional tables. Data warehouses, though, store data in more than two dimensions. For this reason, the data are said to be stored in a **multidimensional structure**. A common representation for this multidimensional structure is the *data cube*.

    The data in the data warehouse are organized by *business dimensions*, which are the edges of the data cube and are subjects such as functional area, vendor, product, geographic area, or time period (look ahead briefly to Figure 4.11). Users can view and analyze data from

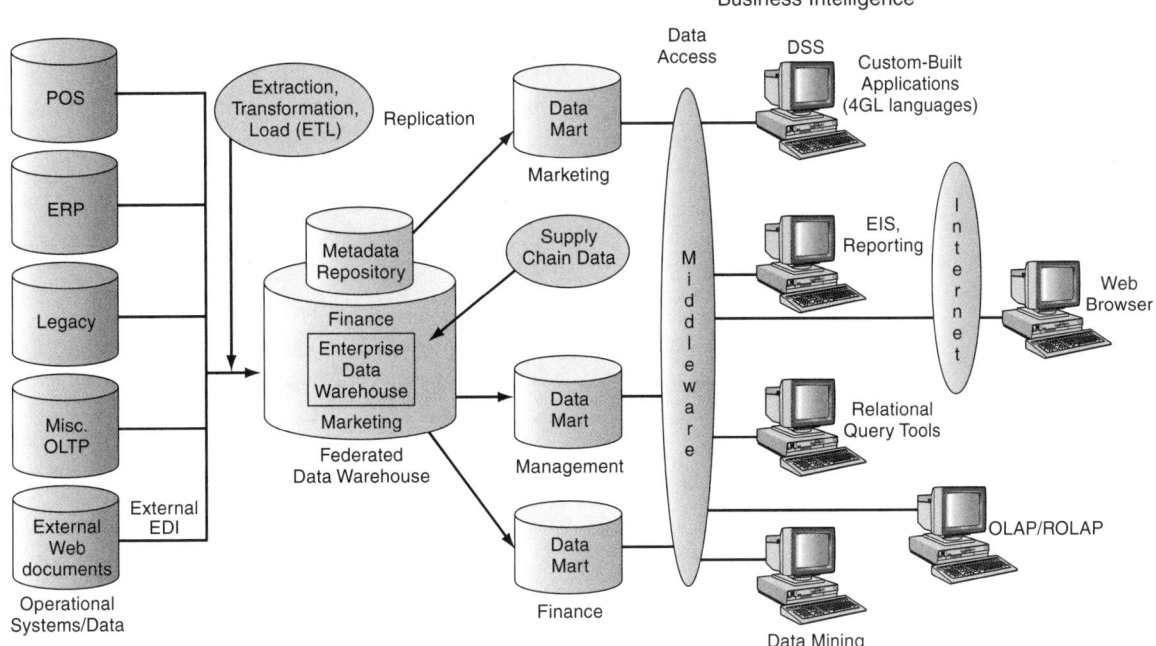

FIGURE 4.9 Data warehouse framework and views.

the perspective of the various business dimensions. This analysis is intuitive because the dimensions are in business terms, easily understood by users.

- **Relationship with relational databases.** The data in data warehouses come from the company's operational databases, which can be relational databases. Figure 4.9 illustrates the process of building and using a data warehouse. The organization's data are stored in operational systems (left side of the figure). Using special software called extract, transform, and load (ETL), the system processes data and then stores them in a data warehouse. Not all data are necessarily transferred to the data warehouse. Frequently only a summary of the data is transferred. Within the warehouse the data are organized in a form that is easy for end users to access.

To differentiate between relational and multidimensional databases, suppose your company has four products—nuts, screws, bolts, and washers—which have been sold in three territories—East, West, and Central—for the previous three years—2003, 2004, and 2005. In a relational database, these sales data would look like Figures 4.10a, b, and c. In a multidimensional database, these data would be represented by a three-dimensional matrix (or data cube), as shown in Figure 4.11. We would say that this matrix represents sales *dimensioned by* products and regions and year. Notice that in Figure 4.10a we can see only sales for 2003. Therefore, sales for 2004 and 2005 are shown in Figures 4.10b and 4.10c. Figure 4.12 shows the equivalence between these relational and multidimensional databases.

Hundreds of successful data-warehousing applications have been reported. For example, you can read client success stories and case studies at Web sites of vendors such as NCR Corp. (*www.ncr.com*) and Oracle (*www.oracle.com*). For a more detailed discussion visit the Data Warehouse Institute (*www.tdwi.org*). Some of the benefits of data warehousing include:

- End users can access needed data quickly and easily via Web browsers because they are located in one place.

(a) 2003

Product	Region	Sales
Nuts	East	50
Nuts	West	60
Nuts	Central	100
Screws	East	40
Screws	West	70
Screws	Central	80
Bolts	East	90
Bolts	West	120
Bolts	Central	140
Washers	East	20
Washers	West	10
Washers	Central	30

(b) 2004

Product	Region	Sales
Nuts	East	60
Nuts	West	70
Nuts	Central	110
Screws	East	50
Screws	West	80
Screws	Central	90
Bolts	East	100
Bolts	West	130
Bolts	Central	150
Washers	East	30
Washers	West	20
Washers	Central	40

(c) 2005

Product	Region	Sales
Nuts	East	70
Nuts	West	80
Nuts	Central	120
Screws	East	60
Screws	West	90
Screws	Central	100
Bolts	East	110
Bolts	West	140
Bolts	Central	160
Washers	East	40
Washers	West	30
Washers	Central	50

FIGURE 4.10   Relational databases.

- End users can conduct extensive analysis with data in ways that may not have been possible before.
- End users can have a consolidated view of organizational data.

These benefits can improve business knowledge, provide competitive advantage, enhance customer service and satisfaction, facilitate decision making, and streamline business processes. IT's about Business 4.3 demonstrates the benefits of data warehousing at a major British corporation.

Data warehouses do have problems. First, they can be very expensive to build and to maintain. Second, it may be difficult and expensive to incorporate data from obsolete mainframe systems. Finally, people in one department might be reluctant to share data with other departments.

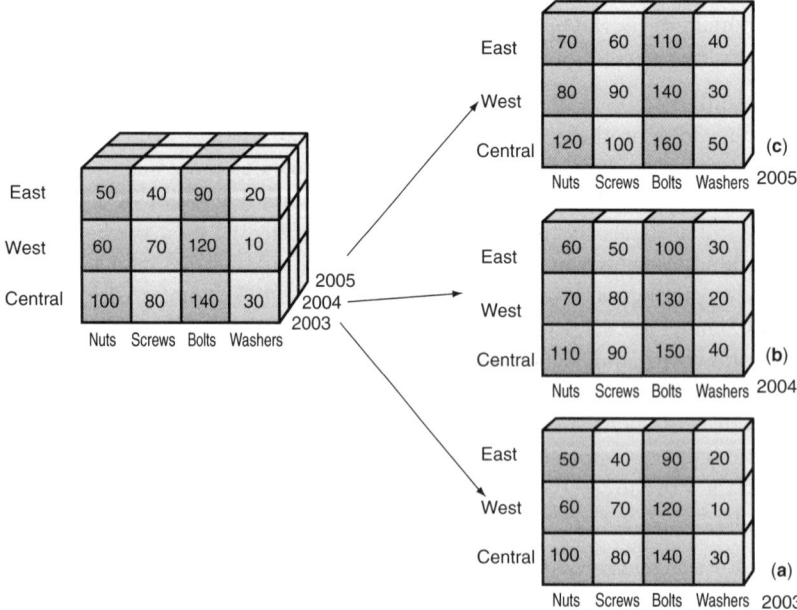

FIGURE 4.11
Multidimensional database.

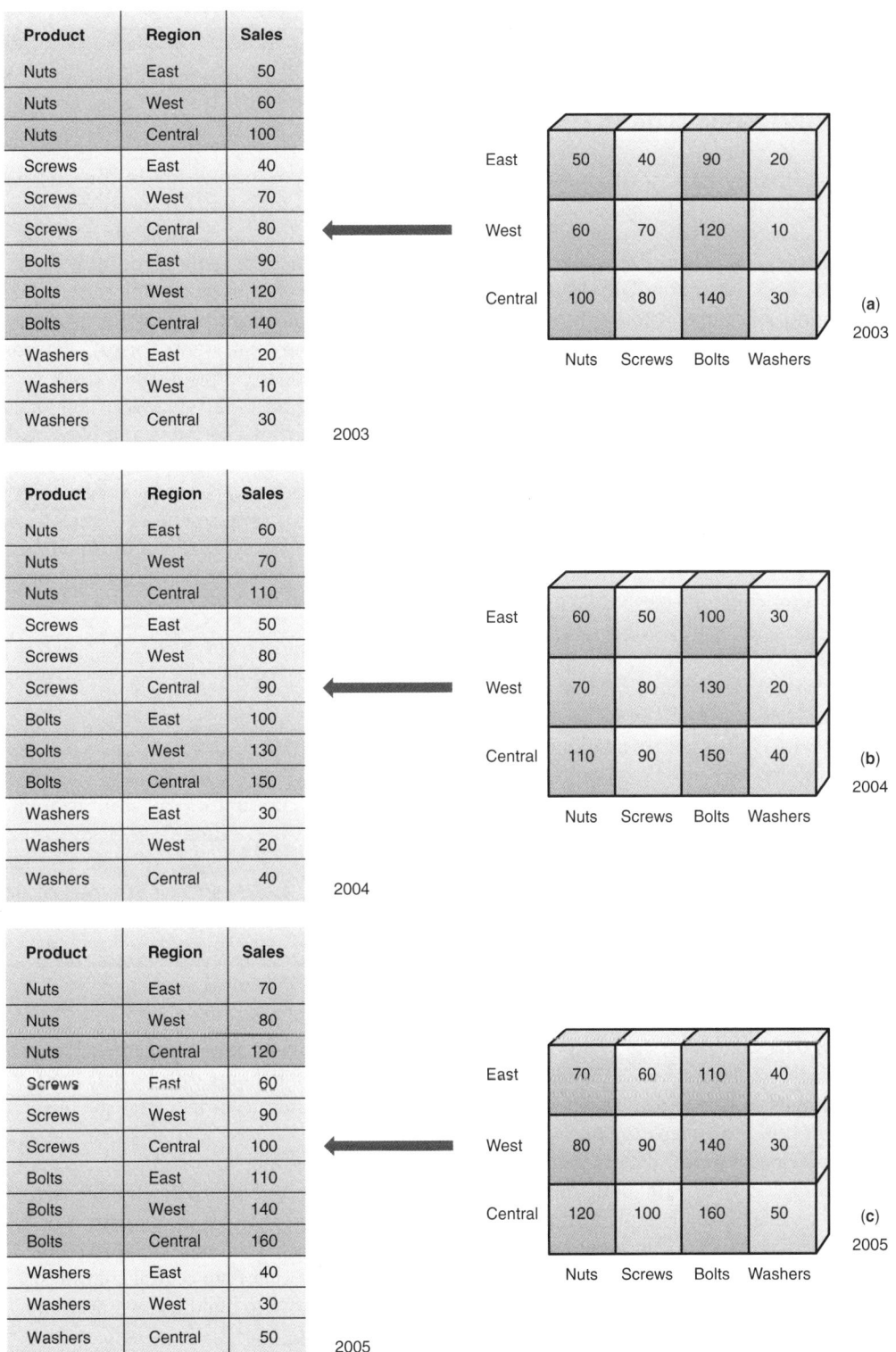

Product	Region	Sales
Nuts	East	50
Nuts	West	60
Nuts	Central	100
Screws	East	40
Screws	West	70
Screws	Central	80
Bolts	East	90
Bolts	West	120
Bolts	Central	140
Washers	East	20
Washers	West	10
Washers	Central	30

2003

Product	Region	Sales
Nuts	East	60
Nuts	West	70
Nuts	Central	110
Screws	East	50
Screws	West	80
Screws	Central	90
Bolts	East	100
Bolts	West	130
Bolts	Central	150
Washers	East	30
Washers	West	20
Washers	Central	40

2004

Product	Region	Sales
Nuts	East	70
Nuts	West	80
Nuts	Central	120
Screws	East	60
Screws	West	90
Screws	Central	100
Bolts	East	110
Bolts	West	140
Bolts	Central	160
Washers	East	40
Washers	West	30
Washers	Central	50

2005

FIGURE 4.12 Equivalence between relational and multidimensional databases.

IT's About Business

4.3 Diageo Tracks Its Spirits

Diageo (*www.diageo.com*), a British company, has eight priority brands—Smirnoff Vodka, Johnnie Walker Scotch, Guinness Ale, Baileys Irish Cream, J&B Scotch, Captain Morgan Rum, Jose Cuervo Tequila, and Tanqueray Gin. Marketing spirits is like marketing perfume. It is all about the imagery and emotional appeal. Age, income, and other data about customers, tied to records of the volume of sales of different products, will make promotions more effective.

However, Diageo North America has to deal with a confusing maze of state regulations, making it difficult to manage all this information. Requirements governing how and when alcoholic beverages can be sold in the United States vary from state to state. By comparison, in Europe, Diageo sells directly to retailers, and sales information can come back overnight. Another constraint in the United States is that beverage companies can make direct sales only to distributors. Therefore, Diageo can collect data only on its deliveries to distributors. It cannot track its products' arrival or departure from store shelves unless distributors or a third party report back. Diageo typically receives retail data only once a month from third-party trackers.

As a result, Diageo implemented a data warehouse to gain more timely sales information. This in-

formation will help the company to invest its money in the right promotions. The data warehouse provides sales and marketing executives with a scorecard containing monthly data on sales, volume, and profitability of different brands. The company can figure out how well a product is selling at Irish pubs, fine restaurants, or retail stores. Next, Diageo will include demographic data so the company can tell whether 28-year-old lawyers are inclined to buy a pint of Guinness at a New York pub.

Diageo is planning for direct data acquisition from, for example, handhelds at stores. However, the company must first determine exactly what information on sales and deliveries it needs in almost real time rather than for each month.

Sources: Compiled from "Procurement Perfected," *Infoconomy.com*, May 1, 2005; and L. Dignan, "Diageo: Kindred Spirits," *Baseline Magazine*, December 1, 2004.

QUESTIONS

1. Describe how state regulations interfere with Diageo's data collection.
2. What types of data will Diageo need on a daily basis, and what types of data will it need only on a monthly basis?

Data Marts

Because data warehouses are so expensive, they are used primarily by large companies. Many other firms employ a lower-cost, scaled-down version of a data warehouse called a data mart. A **data mart** is a small data warehouse, designed for the end-user needs in a strategic business unit (SBU) or a department.

As previously stated, data marts are far less costly than data warehouses. A typical data mart costs less than $100,000, compared with $1 million or more for data warehouses. Also, data marts can be implemented more quickly, often in less than 90 days. Further, because they contain less information than a data warehouse, they have a more rapid response and are easier to learn and navigate. Finally, they support local rather than central control by conferring power on the using group. They also empower an SBU to build its own decision support systems without relying on a centralized IS department.

Data Mining

Once the data are stored in the data warehouse and/or data marts, they can be accessed and analyzed by managers, analysts, and other users, using data mining. The objective of this analysis is to provide business intelligence. Business intelligence is simply knowledge about your competitors, your customers, your business partners, and your internal operations. This knowledge enables you to make better decisions, particularly about difficult, not easily understood problems.

Data mining derives its name from searching for valuable business information in a large database, data warehouse, or data mart. Data mining can perform two basic operations: (1) predicting trends and behaviors, and (2) identifying previously unknown patterns.

Regarding the first operation, data mining automates the process of finding predictive information in large databases. Questions that traditionally required extensive hands-on analysis can now be answered directly and quickly from the data. A typical example of a predictive problem is *targeted marketing*. Data mining can use data from past promotional mailings to identify people who are most likely to respond favorably to future mailings. Other predictive examples include forecasting bankruptcy and other forms of default.

Data mining can also identify previously hidden patterns in a single step. For example, it can analyze retail sales data to discover seemingly unrelated products that are often purchased together, such as diapers and beer.

One interesting pattern-discovery problem is detecting fraudulent credit card transactions. After you use your credit card for a time, a pattern emerges of the typical ways you use your card (e.g., places you use your card, amount spent, etc.). If your card is stolen and used fraudulently, this usage is often different than your pattern of use. Data mining tools can distinguish the difference in the two patterns of use.

There are a variety of data mining tools that managers and analysts use to analyze the data, including query-and-reporting tools, multidimensional analysis tools, and statistical tools. Query-and-reporting tools are similar to SQL and QBE. Multidimensional analysis tools allow users to "slice and dice" the data in any desired way. Within a data warehouse, this process looks like rotating the cube as users view it from different perspectives. Statistical tools provide users with mathematical models that can be applied to the data to gain answers to their queries.

We can refer back to Figure 4.11 for an example of slice and dice. Assume that a business has organized its sales force by regions—say Eastern, Western, and Central. These three regions might then be broken down into states. The VP of sales could slice and dice the data cube to see the sales figures for each region (i.e., the sales of nuts, screws, bolts, and washers). The VP might then want to see the Eastern region broken down by state so that he could evaluate the performance of individual state sales managers. Note that the business organization is reflected in the multidimensional data structure.

The power of data mining is in its ability to analyze the data in such a way as to allow users to quickly answer business questions. "How many bolts were sold in the Eastern region in 2005?" "What is the trend in sales of washers in the Western region over the past three years?" "Are any of the four products typically purchased together?"

Many vendors offer integrated packages of these tools, under the overall name of business intelligence (BI) software. Major BI vendors include SAS (*www.sas.com*), Hyperion (*www.hyperion.com*), Business Objects (*www.businessobjects.com*), Cognos Corp. (*www.cognos.com*), Information Builders (*www.informationbuilders.com*), DBMiner Technology (*www.dbminer. com*), and SPSS (*www.spss.com*).

Data Mining Applications   There are numerous data mining applications, both in business and in other fields. According to a Gartner report (*www.gartner.com*), most of the Fortune 1000 companies worldwide currently use data mining, as illustrated by the representative examples that follow. Note that in most cases the intent of data mining is to identify a business opportunity in order to create a sustainable competitive advantage.

- *Retailing and sales.* Predicting sales, preventing theft and fraud, and determining correct inventory levels and distribution schedules among outlets. For example, retailers such as AAFES (stores on military bases) use Fraud Watch from Triversity (*www.triversity.com*) to combat fraud by employees in their 1,400 stores.

- *Banking.* Forecasting levels of bad loans and fraudulent credit card use, predicting credit card spending by new customers, and determining which kinds of customers will best respond to (and qualify for) new loan offers.

- *Manufacturing and production.* Predicting machinery failures, and finding key factors that help optimize manufacturing capacity.

- *Insurance.* Forecasting claim amounts and medical coverage costs, classifying the most important elements that affect medical coverage, and predicting which customers will buy new insurance policies.

- *Policework.* Tracking crime patterns, locations, and criminal behavior; identifying attributes to assist in solving criminal cases.

- *Health care.* Correlating demographics of patients with critical illnesses, and developing better insights on how to identify and treat symptoms and their causes.

- *Marketing.* Classifying customer demographics that can be used to predict which customers will respond to a mailing or buy a particular product.

We can see that there are myriad opportunities to use data mining in organizations. IT's About Business 4.4 illustrates how Snyder's of Hanover uses data mining in its operation.

IT's About Business

4.4 Straightening Out a Pretzel Maker

Snyder's of Hanover (*www.snydersofhanover.com*) is the world's second largest pretzel maker. The company is revamping the way it collects and analyzes financial data. Under its old system the company's financial analyst would spend the last week of each month collecting Excel spreadsheets from more than 50 department heads scattered worldwide. Then she would consolidate and reenter all the data into a single spreadsheet. This spreadsheet served as the company's *de facto* monthly profit-and-loss (P&L) statement. It got worse at the end of each fiscal quarter, when three months' worth of data had to be collected and consolidated. The worst scenario, however, occurred when the year-end P&L statement and annual budget were prepared. The major problem was that any corrections or additions at any point during these report-closing periods would require the analyst to return the edited spreadsheets to the department heads. She then had to wait for them to resubmit the spreadsheets to her for further consolidation.

Snyder's turned to the Satori Group for its business intelligence software (see *www.satorigroupinc.com/products/bi_platform.html*), called ProCube. Snyder's had two goals in mind: (1) cut labor costs involved in creating financial reports and (2) obtain information on a timely basis to identify and eliminate money-losing brands.

The first phase of the ProCube implementation enabled Snyder's financial analyst to prepare company-wide P&L statements in a day or two each quarter. Department heads from across the country now enter daily sales and returns information into Excel spreadsheets, which are then fed into the ProCube software for consolidation. The second phase allows Snyder's to access P&L statements at the product level. This information will help the company to better manage the production and distribution of its products.

Sources: Compiled from L. Barrett, "Snyder's of Hanover: Twisted Logic," *Baseline Magazine*, January 16, 2004; and "Satori Group Tears Open Snack Food Manufacturing Sector: Snyder's of Hanover, the #1 National Brand of Specialty Pretzels, Rolls with ProCube," *Business Wire*, January 16, 2003.

QUESTIONS

1. What were the business advantages of the new software package? Can you think of other advantages that Snyder's might realize in the future?
2. Other than finance and accounting, what other functional areas did the ProCube software impact? Describe each one.

Before you go on . . .

1. What is a data warehouse, and what are its characteristics?
2. What is the multidimensional database model?
3. What is a data mart, and how is it different from a data warehouse?
4. Describe the capabilities of data mining.

4.5 Data Visualization Technologies

After data have been processed, they can be presented to users in visual formats such as text, graphics, and tables. This process, known as data visualization, makes IT applications more attractive and understandable to users. Data visualization is becoming more and more popular on the Web not only for entertainment but also for decision support. A variety of visualization methods and software packages that support decision making are available. The most popular technologies include digital images, geographic information systems, graphical user interfaces, multidimensional tables and graphs, virtual reality, three-dimensional presentations, videos, and animation.

Geographic Information Systems

A **geographic information system (GIS)** is a computer-based system for capturing, integrating, manipulating, and displaying data using digitized maps. Its most distinguishing characteristic is that every record or digital object has an identified geographical location. This process, called *geocoding*, enables users to generate information for planning, problem solving, and decision making. The graphical format makes it easy for managers to visualize the data.

Today, relatively inexpensive, fully functional PC-based GIS packages are readily available. Representative GIS software vendors are ESRI (*www.esri.com*), Intergraph (*www.intergraph.com*), and Mapinfo (*www.mapinfo.com*). GIS data are available from a wide variety of sources. Both government sources and private vendors provide diversified commercial data. Some of these packages are free; for example, CD-ROMs from Mapinfo and downloadable material from *www.esri.com* and *http://data.geocomm.com.*

There are countless applications of GISs to improve decision making in both the public and private sectors. The following are just a few examples.

- *Finding locations for new restaurants.* McDonald's uses a GIS system to overlay all kinds of demographic information on maps to identify the best locations for new restaurants.

- *Emerging GIS applications.* The integration of GISs and *global positioning systems (GPSs)* has the potential to help restructure and redesign the aviation, transportation, and shipping industries. GPSs are satellite-based systems for finding your location at any spot on the earth. These systems enable vehicles or aircraft equipped with a GPS receiver to pinpoint their locations as they move. GPSs are also being used in personal automobile mapping systems as well as to track vehicles and earth-moving equipment. The following example illustrates an application of GIS and GPS.

UPS Maps Drivers' Routes. United Parcel Service (UPS) is investing $600 million in software and hardware to analyze historical shipping trends, input actual shipping information, and create daily delivery routes. All this information promises to improve the efficiency of UPS workers who sort, load, and deliver almost 14 million packages each business day.

As packages roll off trucks onto conveyor belts at the distribution centers, a worker with a handheld scanner swipes each package's original shipping label. This scan reveals the package's weight, dimensions, and destination and forwards that data to a central database. The same worker prints a 2"×3" label with codes that spell out precisely which chute and conveyor belt will send that package to the proper shelf in its assigned truck. This technology has made UPS loaders more efficient. Each worker can now load 3 or 4 trucks, as opposed to 2.5 trucks in the old system. At the same time, it seems to have improved working conditions and employee morale. For example, the turnover of loaders fell dramatically from 45 percent to 8 percent in only two years.

The new system gives drivers immediate access to more information. Previously, each driver's handheld device noted only that he had a delivery at a certain address. Now, it provides the exact delivery route, and it specifies how many packages must be dropped off at that address and by what time. UPS drivers used to average 130 stops—deliveries and pickups—per day. That number has increased to 145, and the system is shaving eight miles off the average route. *Sources:* Compiled from A. M. Virzl, "United Parcel Service: Sticky Fix," *Baseline Magazine*, February 5, 2004; and *www.ups.com*, accessed March 25, 2005.)

Geographic information systems can also be coupled with business intelligence systems. The following example shows how business intelligence software, used with GIS software, helps combat fraud.

Business Intelligence Helps the State of Louisiana Save Money. On any given day in Louisiana, there are hundreds of impoverished people desperately attempting to sell their food stamps for 50 cents on the dollar. All it takes is a dishonest retailer who is willing to pay cash for the food stamps and then pocket the difference. Known as "discounting," food stamp fraud in Louisiana costs federal taxpayers about $28 million annually.

Past efforts at fraud detection by the government were largely low-tech. Basically, undercover agents from the U.S. Department of Agriculture and the Secret Service would walk into grocery stores and attempt to sell food stamps for cash. Even when these agents successfully conducted a "sting," by itself this was insufficient to build a prosecutable case against a retailer.

This situation changed dramatically with the adoption of electronic benefit transfer technology, in which debit cards with scanable magnetic strips replaced actual food stamp certificates. At that point the state began to collect large amounts of data from JPMorgan Chase, which runs the program for the state. Using WebFocus, a business intelligence product from Information Builders (*www.informationbuilders.com*), the state began to sift through data, looking for patterns that would direct federal agents to suspicious retailers. However, state investigators were not able to obtain enough detail in the data to get what they needed.

It was not until the state implemented geographic information software from ESRI (*www.esri.com*) that the data started to make sense. Plotting more than 100 million transactions annually on a map of the state, the investigators saw clear patterns, such as people traveling long distances to redeem their food stamps at particular stores. The investigators are now able to target suspicious stores much more accurately and to develop cases more likely to result in prosecutions. (*Sources:* Compiled from J. Soat, "Louisiana Fights Fraud with Mapping Software," *InformationWeek*, May 25, 2004; and D. Briody, "Business Intelligence Beats Back Food Stamp Fraud," *CIO Insight*, December 1, 2004.)

Virtual Reality

There is no standard definition of virtual reality. The most common definitions usually imply that **virtual reality (VR)** is interactive, computer-generated, three-dimensional graphics delivered to the user through a head-mounted display. In VR, a person "believes" that what he or she is doing is real even though it is artificially created.

More than one person and even a large group can share and interact in the same artificial environment. For this reason, VR can be a powerful medium for communication, entertainment, and learning. Instead of looking at a flat computer screen, the VR user interacts with a three-dimensional, computer-generated environment. To see and hear the environment, the user wears stereo goggles and a headset. To interact with the environment, control objects in it, or move around within it, the user wears a computerized display and hand-position sensors (gloves). VR displays achieve the illusion of a surrounding medium by updating the display in real time. The user can grasp and move virtual objects. Table 4.1 provides examples of the many different types of VR applications.

Before you go on . . .

1. Why is data visualization important?
2. What is a geographical information system?
3. What is virtual reality, and how does it contribute to data visualization?

Table 4.1

Examples of Virtual Reality Applications

Applications in Manufacturing	Applications in Business
Training	Real estate presentation and evaluation
Design testing and interpretation of results	Advertising
Safety analysis	Presentation in e-commerce
Virtual prototyping	Presentation of financial data
Engineering analysis	
Ergonomic analysis	
Virtual simulation of assembly,	
production, and maintenance	
Applications in Medicine	Applications in Research and Education
Training surgeons (with simulators)	Virtual physics lab
Interpretation of medical data	Representation of complex mathematics
Planning surgeries	Galaxy configurations
Physical therapy	
Applications in Amusement	Applications in Architecture
Virtual museums	Design of buildings and other structures
Three-dimensional racecar games (on PCs)	
Air combat simulation (on PCs)	
Virtual reality arcades and parks	
Ski simulator	

4.6 Knowledge Management

As we have discussed throughout the book, data and information are critically important organizational assets. Knowledge is a vital asset as well. Successful managers have always used intellectual assets and recognized their value. But these efforts were not systematic, and they did not ensure that knowledge was shared and dispersed in a way that benefited the overall organization. Moreover, industry analysts estimate that most of a company's knowledge assets are not housed in relational databases. Instead, they are dispersed in e-mail, Word documents, spreadsheets, and presentations on individual computers. This arrangement makes it extremely difficult for companies to access and integrate this knowledge. The result frequently is less-effective decision making.

Concepts and Definitions

Knowledge management (KM) is a process that helps organizations manipulate important knowledge that is part of the organization's memory, usually in an unstructured format. For organizational success, knowledge, as a form of capital, must exist in a format that can be exchanged among persons. In addition, it must be able to grow.

Knowledge   In the information technology context, knowledge is very distinct from data and information. Data are a collection of facts, measurements, and statistics; information is organized or processed data that are timely and accurate. As we have discussed, **knowledge** is information that is *contextual, relevant,* and *actionable*. Simply put, knowledge is *information in action*. **Intellectual capital** (or **intellectual assets**) is another term often used for knowledge.

To illustrate with an example, a bulletin listing all the courses offered by your university during one semester could be considered data. When you register, you process the data from the bulletin to create your schedule for the semester. Your schedule would be considered information. Awareness of your work schedule, your major, your desired social schedule, and characteristics of different faculty members could be construed as knowledge, because it can affect the way you build your schedule. We see that this awareness is contextual and relevant (to developing an optimal schedule of classes), as well as actionable (it can lead to changes in your schedule). The implication is that knowledge has strong experiential and reflective elements that distinguish it from information in a given context. Unlike information, knowledge can be exercised to solve a problem.

Explicit and Tacit Knowledge   **Explicit knowledge** deals with more objective, rational, and technical knowledge. In an organization, explicit knowledge consists of the policies, procedural guides, reports, products, strategies, goals, core competencies of the enterprise, and the IT infrastructure. In other words, explicit knowledge is the knowledge that has been codified (documented) in a form that can be distributed to others or transformed into a process or strategy. A description of how to process a job application that is documented in a firm's human resources policy manual is an example of explicit knowledge.

In contrast, **tacit knowledge** is the cumulative store of subjective or experiential learning. In an organization, tacit knowledge consists of an organization's experiences, insights, expertise, know-how, trade secrets, skill sets, understanding, and learning. It also includes the organizational culture, which reflects the past and present experiences of the organization's people and processes, as well as the prevailing values. Tacit knowledge is generally slow, imprecise, and costly to transfer. It is also highly personal. Finally, because it is unstructured, it is difficult to formalize or codify. For example, salespersons who have worked with particular customers over time know the needs of those customers quite well. This knowledge is typically not recorded. In fact, it might be difficult for the salesperson to put it into writing.

Knowledge Management Systems

The goal of knowledge management is to help an organization make the most effective use of the knowledge it has. Historically, management information systems have focused on capturing, storing, managing, and reporting explicit knowledge. Organizations now recognize the need to integrate both explicit and tacit knowledge in formal information systems. **Knowledge management systems (KMSs)** refer to the use of modern information technologies—the Internet, intranets, extranets, LotusNotes, data warehouses—to systematize, enhance, and expedite intrafirm and interfirm knowledge management. KMSs are intended to help an organization cope with turnover, rapid change, and downsizing by making the expertise of the organization's human capital widely accessible. IT's About Business 4.5 describes a knowledge management system used by the Department of Commerce.

Organizations can realize many benefits with KMSs. Most importantly, it makes **best practices**, which are the most effective and efficient ways of doing things, readily available to a wide range of employees. Enhanced access to best-practice knowledge improves overall organizational performance. For example, account managers can now make available their tacit knowledge about how best to handle large accounts. This knowledge can then be used to train new account managers. Other benefits include improved customer service, more efficient product development, and improved employee morale and retention.

IT's About Business

4.5 Who Ya' Gonna Call?

An international trade specialist for the U.S. Commercial Service division in the Department of Commerce was stumped. It was his job to help U.S. corporations conduct business overseas. However, when a U.S.-based software company called with a question, he did not know what to advise. The company wanted to close a deal with a customer in Poland, but the buyer wanted to charge the U.S. company a withholding tax of 20 percent. The buyer attributed this tax to Poland's recent admission into the European Union. Was the tax legitimate?

To find out, the DOC specialist turned to the division's knowledge management system (KMS), known as DOC Insider. After typing in his question, he found some documents that were related to his query. However, they did not explain the EU tax code completely. He next asked the system to search the database of the 1700 employees of the Commercial Service for a "live" expert. Within seconds, he received a list of 80 people who might be able to help him. From these names, he chose the six people he felt were most qualified. He then forwarded his query to them.

According to this specialist, before the DOC Insider was in place, it would have taken him three days to answer the same question. Now, thanks to the Insider, he received three responses within minutes and a complete answer within an hour. The result? The sale that went through the following morning.

The DOC Insider is helping his division meet its goals. In the first nine months the system was in place, it saved the department more than 1,000 employee hours.

For the most part, KMSs have depended heavily on employees to volunteer data. Often, knowledge databases relied on simple keyword searches of documents, but little else. In contrast, expertise-location systems (ELSs) like the DOC Insider let employees find and connect with colleagues, wherever they are, to solve critical business problems. ELS software trawls through your company's e-mails and documents, looking for specific search phrases to determine who is the most knowledgeable about certain topics. From those data, the software decides who is the best person to ask, and it automatically contacts that person. Once the query has been answered, the software logs the information and adds it to its growing knowledge database.

Sources: Compiled from D. D'Agostino, "Expertise Management: Who Knows About This?" *CIO Insight,* July 1, 2004; T. Kontzer, "Help Wanted: Expertise-Management Tools Locate Talent," *InformationWeek,* May 5, 2003.

QUESTIONS

1. Is an ELS a knowledge management system? Why or why not?
2. If your company implemented ELS software, would you feel that your privacy could be invaded?

At the same time, however, there are challenges to implementing effective KMSs. First, employees must be willing to share their personal tacit knowledge. To encourage this behavior, organizations must create a "knowledge management" culture that rewards employees who add their expertise to the knowledge base. Second, the knowledge base must be continually maintained and updated. New knowledge must be added, and old, outdated knowledge must be deleted. Companies must be willing to invest in the resources needed to carry out these operations.

The Knowledge Management System Cycle

A functioning KMS follows a cycle that consists of six steps (see Figure 4.13). The reason the system is cyclical is that knowledge is dynamically refined over time. The knowledge in an effective KMS is never finalized because the environment changes over time, and knowledge must be updated to reflect these changes. The cycle works as follows:

1. *Create knowledge.* Knowledge is created as people determine new ways of doing things or develop know-how. Sometimes external knowledge is brought in.

2. *Capture knowledge.* New knowledge must be identified as valuable and be represented in a reasonable way.

3. *Refine knowledge.* New knowledge must be placed in context so that it is actionable. This is where tacit qualities (human insights) must be captured along with explicit facts.

4. *Store knowledge.* Useful knowledge must then be stored in a reasonable format in a knowledge repository so that others in the organization can access it.

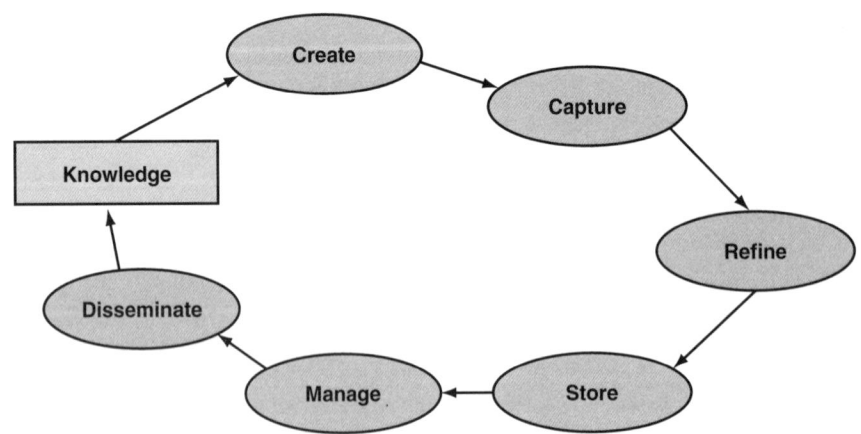

FIGURE 4.13
The knowledge management cycle.

5. *Manage knowledge.* Like a library, the knowledge must be kept current. It must be reviewed regularly to verify that it is relevant and accurate.

6. *Disseminate knowledge.* Knowledge must be made available in a useful format to anyone in the organization who needs it, anywhere and any time.

Before you go on . . .

1. What is knowledge management?
2. What is the difference between tacit knowledge and explicit knowledge?
3. Describe the knowledge management system cycle.

What's in IT for me?

For the Accounting Major

The accounting function is intimately concerned with keeping track of the transactions and internal controls of an organization. Modern data warehouses and data mining enable accountants to perform these functions more effectively. Data warehouses help accountants manage the flood of data in today's organizations so that they can keep their firms in compliance with the new standards imposed by Sarbanes–Oxley.

Accountants also play a role in cost-justifying the creation of a knowledge base and then auditing its cost-effectiveness. In addition, if you work for a large CPA company that provides management services or sells knowledge, you will most likely use some of your company's best practices that are stored in a knowledge base.

For the Finance Major

Financial managers make extensive use of computerized databases that are external to the organization, such as CompuStat or Dow Jones, to obtain financial data on organizations in their industry. They can use these data to determine if their organization meets industry benchmarks in return on investment, cash management, and other financial ratios.

Modern data mining techniques are effective in finance, particularly for the automated discovery of relationships in securities and portfolio management. Financial managers, who produce the organization's financial status reports, are also closely involved with Sarbanes–Oxley. Data warehouses help these managers comply with the new standards.

For the Marketing Major

Marketing personnel access data from the organization's marketing transactions (e.g., customer purchases) to plan targeted marketing campaigns and to evaluate the success of previous campaigns. They also link this information to geographical databases to determine where certain products will sell the best.

Data warehouses and data mining help marketing managers uncover many unanticipated relationships among some aspect of the buyer's "profile," the product, and the marketing and advertising campaigns. By exploiting these relationships, companies can increase sales substantially. In fact, marketing research is one of the most common applications of data mining.

Knowledge about customers can make the difference between success and failure. In many data warehouses and knowledge bases, the vast majority of information and knowledge concerns customers, products, sales, and marketing. Marketing managers certainly use an organization's knowledge base and often participate in its creation.

For the Production/Operations Management Major

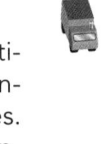

Production/operations personnel access organizational data to determine optimum inventory levels for parts in a production process. Past production data enable POM personnel to determine the optimum configuration for assembly lines. Firms also keep quality data that inform them not only about the quality of finished products but also about quality issues with incoming raw materials, production irregularities, shipping and logistics, and after-sale use and maintenance of the product.

Data warehousing and data mining automate discovery of previously undetected issues regarding production, logistics, and other activities. These issues can be located either within the organization or along the supply chain.

Knowledge management is extremely important for running complex operations. The accumulated knowledge regarding scheduling, logistics, maintenance, and other functions is very valuable. Innovative ideas are necessary for improving operations and can be supported by knowledge management.

For the Human Resources Management Major

Organizations keep extensive data on employees, including gender, age, race, current and past job descriptions, and performance evaluations. Human resources personnel access these data to provide reports to government agencies regarding compliance with federal equal opportunity guidelines. HR managers also use these data to evaluate hiring practices, evaluate salary structures, and manage any discrimination grievances or lawsuits brought against the firm.

Data warehouses and data mining can help the HR professional investigate relationships in the data that involve the health, safety, productivity, and retention of valuable human resources. Data warehouses also can help HR managers provide assistance to all employees as more and more decisions about their health care and retirement planning are turned over to the employees themselves. The employees can use the data warehouses for help in selecting the optimal mix among these critical choices.

Human resources managers need to use a knowledge base frequently to find out how past cases were handled. Consistency in how employees are treated not only is important, it protects the company against legal actions. Also, training for building, maintaining, and using the knowledge system sometimes is the responsibility of the HR department. Finally, the HR department might be responsible for compensating employees who contribute their knowledge.

The MIS Function

The MIS function manages the organization's data and the databases, data warehouses, and data marts where they are stored. MIS database administrators standardize data names by using the data dictionary. This ensures that all users understand which data are in the database. Database personnel also provide data for the data warehouse and provide the data mining tools to help users access and analyze needed data. MIS personnel—and users as well—can now generate reports with query tools much more quickly than was possible using old mainframe systems written in COBOL.

Summary

1. **Recognize the importance of data, issues involved in managing these data, and their life cycle.**

   IT applications cannot be done without using data. Data should be accurate, complete, timely, consistent, accessible, relevant, and concise. Managing data in organizations is difficult for various reasons: (1) the amount of data increases with time; (2) data are stored in various systems, databases, formats, and languages; and (3) data security, quality, and integrity are often compromised.

   The data life cycle starts with data collection. The data are stored in a database(s) and then preprocessed to fit the format of a data warehouse or data marts. Users then access data from the warehouse or data mart for analysis. Data analysis and mining tools look for patterns, and intelligent systems support data interpretation. The result of all these activities is the generation of decision support and knowledge.

2. **Describe the sources of data and explain how data are collected.**

   Data sources can be internal, personal, clickstream (from your company's Web transactions), and external (particularly the Internet). Internal data are usually located in corporate databases and are usually accessible via an organization's intranet. IS users create personal data by documenting their own expertise. These data can reside on the user's PC, or they can be placed on corporate databases or on corporate knowledge bases. Sources of external data range from commercial databases to sensors and satellites. Government reports constitute a major source of external data. Many thousands of databases all over the world are accessible through the Internet.

3. **Explain the advantages of the database approach.**

   A database, which is a group of logically-related files, eliminates the problems associated with a traditional file environment. In a database, data are integrated and related so that one set of software programs provides access to all the data. Therefore, data redundancy, data isolation, and data inconsistency are minimized, and data can be shared among all users of the data. In addition, data security and data integrity are increased, and applications and data are independent of one another.

4. **Explain the operation of data warehousing and its role in decision support.**

   A data warehouse is a repository of subject-oriented historical data that are organized to be accessible in a form readily acceptable for analytical processing activities. End users can access needed data in a data warehouse quickly and easily via Web browsers. They can conduct extensive analysis with data and can have a consolidated view of organizational data. These benefits can improve business knowledge, provide competitive advantage, enhance customer service and satisfaction, facilitate decision making, and help in streamlining business processes.

5. Understand the capabilities and benefits of data mining.

Data mining is a major tool for analyzing large amounts of data, usually in a data warehouse. Given databases or data warehouses of sufficient size and quality, data mining technology can generate new business opportunities by providing automated prediction of trends and behaviors and automated discovery of previously unknown patterns.

6. Describe data visualization, and explain geographical information systems and virtual reality.

Data visualization involves presentation of data by technologies such as digital images, geographical information systems, three-dimensional presentations, videos and animation, virtual reality, and other multimedia. A geographical information system (GIS) is a computer-based system for manipulating and displaying data using digitized maps. Virtual reality refers to interactive, computer-generated, three-dimensional graphics delivered to the user through a head-mounted display.

7. Define knowledge, and describe the different types of knowledge.

Knowledge is information that is contextual, relevant, and actionable. Explicit knowledge deals with more objective, rational, and technical knowledge. Tacit knowledge is usually in the domain of subjective, cognitive, and experiential learning. It is highly personal and difficult to formalize.

Chapter Glossary

attribute Each characteristic or quality describing a particular entity. (103)

best practices The most effective and efficient ways to do things. (122)

clickstream data Data collected about user behavior and browsing patterns by monitoring users' activities when they visit a Web site. (100)

database A group of logically related files that stores data and the associations among them. (102)

data dictionary Collection of definitions of data elements, data characteristics that use the data elements, and the individuals, business functions, applications, and reports that use this data element. (107)

database management system (DBMS) The software program (or group of programs) that provides access to a database. (105)

data mart A small data warehouse designed for a strategic business unit (SBU) or a department. (115)

data mining The process of searching for valuable business information in a large database, data warehouse, or data mart. (116)

data model Definition of the way data in a DBMS are conceptually structured. (102)

data visualization Visual presentation of data by technologies such as graphics, multidimensional tables and graphs, videos and animation, and other multimedia formats. (118)

data warehouse A repository of subject-oriented historical data that are organized to be accessible in a form readily acceptable for analytical processing. (111)

entity A person, place, thing, or event about which information is maintained in a record. (102)

entity-relationship modeling The process of designing a database by organizing data entities to be used and identifying the relationships among them. (103)

entity-relationship (ER) diagram Document that shows data entities and attributes and relationships among them. (103)

entity classes A grouping of entities of a given type. (103)

explicit knowledge The more objective, rational, and technical types of knowledge. (121)

field A grouping of logically related characters into a word, a small group of words, or a complete number. (102)

file A grouping of logically related records. (102)

geographic information system (GIS) A computer-based system for capturing, integrating, manipulating, and displaying data using digitized maps. (118)

identifier An attribute that identifies an entity instance. (103)

instance A particular entity within an entity class. (103)

intellectual capital (intellectual assets) Other terms for knowledge. (121)

knowledge Information that is contextual, relevant, and actionable. (121)

knowledge management (KM) A process that helps organizations identify, select, organize, disseminate, transfer, and apply information and expertise that are part of the organization's memory and that typically reside within the organization in an unstructured manner. (121)

knowledge management systems (KMSs) Information technologies used to systematize, enhance, and expedite intra- and interfirm knowledge management. (122)

multidimensional structure The manner in which data are structured in a data warehouse so that they can be analyzed by different views or perspectives, which are called dimensions. (111)

normalization A method for analyzing and reducing a relational database to its most streamlined form for mini-

mum redundancy, maximum data integrity, and best processing performance. (107)

online analytical processing (OLAP) The analytical processing of data as soon as transactions occur. (111)

online transaction processing (OLTP) A type of computer processing where business transactions are processed as soon as they occur. (111)

primary key The identifier field or attribute that uniquely identities a record. (103)

query by example (QBE) Database language that enables the user to fill out a grid (form) to construct a sample or description of the data wanted. (107)

record A grouping of logically related fields. (102)

relational database model Data model based on the simple concept of tables in order to capitalize on characteristics of rows and columns of data. (106)

secondary key An identifier field or attribute that has some identifying information, but typically does not identify the file with complete accuracy. (103)

structured query language (SQL) Popular relational database language that enables users to perform complicated searches with relatively simple instructions. (106)

table A grouping of logically related records. (102)

tacit knowledge Te cumulative store of subjective or experiential learning; it is highly personal and hard to formalize. (121)

virtual database A database that consists only of software; manages data that can physically reside anywhere on the network and in a variety of formats. (110)

virtual reality (VR) Interactive, computer-generated, three-dimensional graphics delivered to the user through a head-mounted display. (118)

Discussion Questions

1. Explain the difficulties in managing data.
2. Describe the advantages of relational databases.
3. Describe the process of information and knowledge discovery, and discuss the roles of the data warehouse, data mining, and OLAP in this process.
4. Discuss the benefits of data warehousing to end users.
5. What is the relationship between a company's databases and its data warehouse?
6. Distinguish between data warehouses and data marts.
7. Differentiate between business intelligence, online analytical processing, and data mining.
8. Explain why it is important to capture and manage knowledge.
9. Compare and contrast tacit knowledge and explicit knowledge.

Problem-Solving Activities

1. Access various employment Web sites (e.g., *www.monster.com*), and find several job descriptions for a database administrator. Are the job descriptions similar? What are the salaries offered in these positions?
2. Access the Web sites of several real estate companies. Find the sites that take you through a step-by-step process for buying a home, that provide virtual reality tours of homes in your price range and location, that provide mortgage and interest rate calculators, and that offer financing for your home. Do the sites require that you register to access their services? Can you request that an e-mail be sent to you when properties in which you might be interested become available?

3. It is possible to find many Web sites that provide demographic information. Access several of these sites and see what they offer. Do the sites differ in the types of demographic information they offer? How? Do the sites require a fee for the information they offer? Would demographic information be useful to you if you wanted to start a new business? How?
4. The Internet contains many Web sites with information on financial aid resources for students. Access several of these sites. Do you have to register to access the information? Can you apply for financial aid on the sites, or do you have to request paper applications that you must complete and return?

Internet Activities

1. Access the Web sites of IBM (*www.ibm.com*), Sybase (*www.sybase.com*), and Oracle (*www.oracle.com*) and trace the capabilities of their latest products, including Web connections.
2. Access the Web sites of two of the major data warehouse vendors, such as NCR (*www.ncr.com*) and SAS (*www.sas.com*); describe their products and how they are related to the Web.

3. Enter *http://www.teradatauniversitynetwork.com*. Prepare a summary on resources available there. Is it valuable to a student?
4. Enter *www.visualmining.com* and review the support they provide to business intelligence. Prepare a report.

Team Assignments

1. Several applications now combine GIS and GPS.
   a. Survey such applications by conducting literature and Internet searches and query GIS vendors.
   b. Prepare a list of five applications.
   c. Describe the benefits of the integration of GIS and GPS.
2. Prepare a report on the topic of "data management and intranets." Specifically, pay attention to the role of the data warehouse, the use of browsers for query, and data mining. Each team will visit one vendor site, read the white papers, and examine products (see, for example, Oracle, IBM, Hyperion, NCR, SAS, and

SPSS). Also, visit the Web site of the Data Warehouse Institute (*www.tdwi.org*).
3. Each team will access the Web site of a GIS vendor (see for example, *www.esri.com*, *www.intergraph.com*, *www.bently.com*, *www.mapinfo.com*, and *www.autodesk.com*). Prepare a report on each vendor's applications in each of the functional areas. If available, download a demo.
4. Each team will access a Web site about data collection via the Web (see for example, *www.activewebsoftwares.com* and *www.clearlearning.com*). Prepare a report about the methods for data collection that each company uses.

CASE **Data Management Helps Save Toyota U.S.A.**

THE BUSINESS PROBLEM Just 10 years ago, Toyota Motor Sales U.S.A. was suffering with a hopelessly backward IT infrastructure. Toyota U.S.A. was rapidly generating massive amounts of sales and market data, but it had no way to use the information strategically. Internal departments were stuck in a "mainframe mindset" and did not share information. By the time the departments did generate reports that could be acted upon, it was too late to do anything about the company's problems.

Toyota U.S.A. takes ownership of the vehicles from the moment they leave the factories until the moment they reach the dealers. In other words, it essentially purchases the vehicles from its corporate parent in Japan and then resells them to dealers across the United States. This process requires Toyota U.S.A. to carry a finance charge of about $8 a day per car until they can unload the cars on the dealers. Multiply that by about 2 million cars per year and an average delivery time of nine days, and it is easy to see how manually compiled Quicken spreadsheets and a lack of data integration were costing Toyota U.S.A. millions of dollars.

THE IT SOLUTION One of the most critical applications for Toyota U.S.A. is the Toyota Logistics System (TLS). The functions of TLS are precision tracking and supply chain management to ensure that the right cars get to the right dealers in a predictable and timely fashion.

The company decided to implement a data warehouse for TLS, based on seven key areas in which Toyota management needed real-time, accurate data. Even with the data warehouse, however, executives discovered that the information coming out was often inaccurate. It turned out that years of human error had gone unchecked. Incorrect data therefore returned illogical analysis results. Further, there were severe problems in transferring files from Toyota's old systems into the new data warehouse. As a result, the data warehouse was helping to store and integrate the data, but it was not having a measurable impact on the business executives. IT employees rather than the business executives themselves still had to run the reports, a time-consuming process.

Faced with these problems, the company decided to switch to another data warehouse. This time, the executives saw positive results. The new data warehouse included a dashboard feature that allows executives to see hot spots in their business units and investigate further to identify the problem. The dashboard works like a stoplight, with lights that display green (good), yellow (acceptable but questionable), and red (danger). The gauges on the dashboard can be programmed to a variety of data sets, including accessory revenues, order management, and expenses.

In just one example, an analyst found that Toyota was getting billed twice for rail shipments of vehicles out of a particular rail yard. The problem was that the railcars were being scanned twice—an honest mistake—but Toyota executives had no way to access data that were detailed enough to enable them to discover the duplicate entries. The new information saved the company $800,000.

THE RESULTS The painful evolution in Toyota's data-management strategy was driven by the business needs of the organization, and the results have been impressive. Toyota U.S.A. increased the volume of cars it handles by 40 percent in just eight years while increasing the number of employees by just 3 percent. This success has helped Toyota Motor Corporation reach the highest profit margins in the automobile business, and its stock is a perennial high performer.

Sources: Compiled from D. Briody, "Toyota's Business Intelligence: Oh! What a Feeling," *CIO Insight*, October 1, 2004; and Nucleus Research, "ROI Case Study: Brio and Toyota Motor Sales," *Computerworld*, December 2003.

QUESTIONS

1. Describe the mainframe mindset at Toyota U.S.A. and the problems it caused with respect to data and information.
2. Describe the benefits that Toyota U.S.A. received from its data warehouse implementation.

Interactive Learning

Following Cherry Garcia: A Look at Tracking at Ben and Jerry's

Go to the Interactivities section on the *WileyPLUS* Web site and access Chapter 4: Data and Knowledge Management. There you will find an animated simulation of the technologies used to track the life of ice creams at Ben and Jerry's, as well as some hands-on activities that visually explain business concepts in this chapter.

Go to the Club IT link on the *WileyPLUS* Web site. There you will find assignments that will ask you to advise the club owners on how they can use databases to track information for their business.

wiley.com/college/rainer

Chapter 5

Chapter Preview

Without networks, the computer on your desk would be merely another productivity enhancement tool, just as the typewriter once was. The power of networks, however, turns your computer into an amazingly effective tool for discovery, communication, and collaboration, vastly increasing your productivity and your organization's competitive advantage. Regardless of the type of organization (profit/not-for-profit, large/small, global/local) or industry (manufacturing, financial services, health care), networks have transformed the way we do business.

Networks support new ways of doing business, from marketing, to supply chain management, to customer service, to human resources management. In particular, the Internet and its private organizational counterpart, intranets, have an enormous impact on our lives, both professionally and personally. In fact, for all organizations, having an Internet strategy is no longer just a source of competitive advantage; it is necessary for survival.

In the Appendix to this chapter, we discuss how networks function. First, we describe the basic telecommunications system. Understanding this system is important because it is the way all networks function, regardless of size. We continue with a discussion of network services, network protocols, and types of network processing.

In the chapter itself, we define the types of networks, from local area networks, to wide area networks, to the Internet. We conclude the chapter with network applications (i.e., what networks help us to do).

Network Computing

Introduction to Information Systems
R. Kelly Rainer, Jr., Efraim Turban, and Richard E. Potter. ISBN 978-0-471-7363-3
©2007 John Wiley & Sons, Inc.

Web Resources   wiley.com/college/rainer

Student Web Site
- Web Quizzes
- Links to relevant Web sites
- Lecture Slides in PowerPoint

WileyPlus
- Virtual Company assignments and Club IT Web site
- Interactive Learning Sessions
- Microsoft Excel and Access Exercises
- Software Skills Tutorials
- e-book

Chapter Outline

5.1 Types of Networks
5.2 The Internet
5.3 The World Wide Web
5.4 Network Applications
5.5 E-Learning and Distance Learning
5.6 Telecommuting

Learning Objectives

1. Describe the two major types of networks.
2. Differentiate among the Internet, the World Wide Web, intranets, and extranets.
3. Describe the four major network applications.
4. Describe groupware capabilities.
5. Differentiate between e-learning and distance learning.
6. Understand the advantages and disadvantages of telecommuting for both employers and employees.

What's in IT for me?   ACC   FIN   MKT   POM   HRM   MIS

133

132   Information Systems: A Socio-Technical Perspective

This Bud's For You

The Business Problem

As recently as 1998, the beer industry was a technological laggard. Distributors and sales reps would return from their daily routes with stacks of invoices and sales orders. They would then have to type the details into a PC and dial in to a central computer at the brewery to upload the information. The breweries, in turn, would compile the data into monthly reports to see which brands were the hottest. This approach was much too slow and cumbersome to allow Anheuser-Busch (*www.anheuser-busch.com*) to respond to rapidly changing market conditions.

© AP/Wide World Photos

The IT Solution

Anheuser began amending its contracts with wholesalers to demand that they collect data on (a) how much shelf space their retailers devoted to all beer brands, (b) which brands had the most visible displays, and (c) the locations of those displays. At first, the company left it up to the distributors to figure out how to collect and deliver the data to Anheuser. Many distributors submitted Excel spreadsheets. This approach did not work well, as Anheuser had to combine thousands of spreadsheets. Anheuser then had its distributors equip their sales reps with handheld computers, which they could use to collect information and immediately upload it over their cell phones.

The Results

When Dereck Gurden pulls up at one of his customer's stores, he carries a brick-sized, handheld PC. First, he checks the accounts receivable to make sure that everything is current. Then his handheld shows him an inventory screen with a four-week history. He gets past sales, package placements—facts and numbers on how much of the sales occurred when they had a display in a certain location. Next, he "walks the store," inputting data about his competitors' product displays. When he is finished, he plugs the handheld into his cell phone and sends orders to the warehouse, along with any data that he has gathered.

Dereck is a sales rep for Sierra Beverage, one of about 700 U.S. distributors that work for Anheuser. He and several thousand reps and drivers serve as the eyes and ears of a data network through which distributors report, in excruciating detail, on sales, shelf stocks, and displays at thousands of outlets.

Called BudNet, this network is the primary reason why Anheuser's share (by volume) of the $74.4 billion U.S. beer market inched up to 50.1 percent from 48.9 percent during 2003. This was a huge gain at a time when a weak economy, lousy weather, and the threat of higher state taxes and tighter drinking laws kept sales of Coors, Miller, and other brewers flat. Anheuser uses the data to constantly change marketing strategies, to design promotions that suit the ethnic makeup of its markets, and to detect where rivals might have an edge.

Anheuser collects the data in a nightly nationwide sweep of its distributors' servers. In the morning, the company is able to see which brands are selling, in which packages, using which displays, discounts, and promotions. Anheuser then sends marching orders to its distributors.

Today, Anheuser is the only major brewer to rely heavily on data from Information Resources, Inc. (*www.infores.com*), which tracks every bar-coded product swiped at checkout and performs consumer surveys. Integrating that data with its own, Anheuser can determine which images or ideas to push in its ads and which new products to unveil. All these data, integrated with U.S. Census figures on the ethnic and economic makeup of neighborhoods, also help Anheuser tailor marketing campaigns with local precision. Anheuser can see those data by city, neighborhood, holiday, and socioeconomic class.

The ultimate result? Beginning in 1999, Anheuser posted double-digit profit gains for 20 straight quarters.

The opening case about Anheuser-Busch illustrates three fundamental points about network computing. First, computers do not work in isolation in modern organizations. Rather, they constantly exchange data. Second, this exchange of data—facilitated by telecommunications technologies—brings a number of very significant advantages to companies. Third, this exchange can take place over any distance and over networks of any size. The case also demonstrates how networks enable discovery, communications, and collaboration, not only within Anheuser-Busch, but also among individual stores, distributors, and Anheuser-Busch. Networks in general, and the Internet in particular, have fundamentally altered the ways we do business and the way we live.

Sources: Compiled from K. Kelleher, "66,207,896 Bottles of Beer on the Wall," *Business 2.0*, February 1, 2004; L. Dignan, "Diageo: Kindred Spirits," *Baseline Magazine*, December 1, 2004; and *www.anheuser-busch.com*, and *www.infores.com/public/us/newsEvents/press*, accessed March 3, 2005.

5.1 Types of Networks

A **computer network** is a system that connects computers via communications media so that data can be transmitted among them. Computer networks are essential to modern organizations for many reasons. First, networked computer systems enable organizations to be more flexible so they can adapt to rapidly changing business conditions. Second, networks enable companies to share hardware, computer applications, and data across the organization and among organizations. Third, networks make it possible for geographically dispersed employees and work groups to share documents, ideas, and creative insights. This sharing encourages teamwork, innovation, and more efficient and effective interactions. Finally, networks are a critical link between businesses and their customers.

There are various types of computer networks, ranging from small to worldwide. Types of networks include (from smallest to largest) local area networks, wide area networks, and the Internet. Here we discuss local area and wide area networks. We consider the Internet in the next section.

Local Area Networks

A **local area network (LAN)** connects two or more devices in a limited geographical region, usually within the same building, so that every device on the network has the potential to communicate with every other device. A LAN consists of the following components:

- A file server
- A number of client machines, called **nodes**
- Wired or wireless communications media that connect the devices on a network
- Network interface cards, which are special adapters that link an individual device to the communications medium
- Software to control LAN activities

The LAN **file server** is a repository of various software and data files for the network. The server determines who gets access to which files and in what sequence. Servers can be powerful microcomputers with large, fast-access hard drives. They also can be workstations,

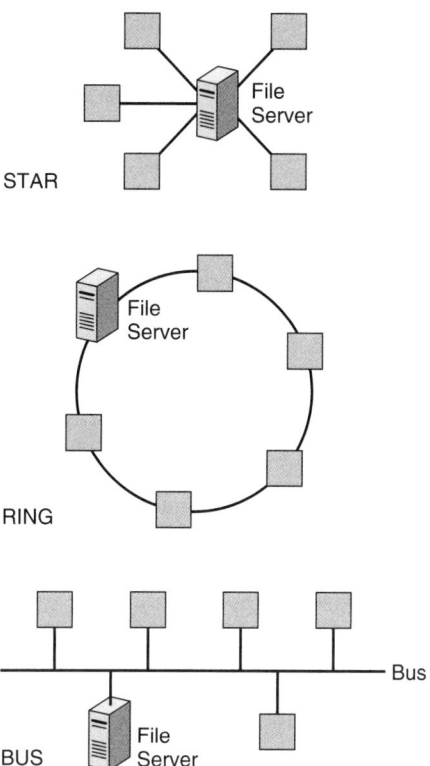

FIGURE 5.1
LAN topologies.

minicomputers, or mainframes. The server typically houses the LAN's network operating system, which manages the server and routes and manages communications on the network. The LAN **network interface card** specifies the rate of data transmission, the size of the message units, the addressing information attached to each message, and the network topology.

LANs come in an assortment of topologies. The **topology** of a network refers to its physical layout and connectivity. Figure 5.1 illustrates three basic LAN topologies: star, bus, and ring.

In a *star topology*, all network nodes connect to a single computer, typically the file server. In a *bus topology*, all network nodes connect to the *bus*, which is a single communications channel, such as twisted pair, coaxial cable, or fiber-optic cable. In a *ring topology*, network nodes are connected to adjacent nodes to form a closed loop. Table 5.1 shows the advantages and disadvantages of the three network topologies.

Advantages and Disadvantages of Network Topologies

Table 5.1

Topology	Advantages	Disadvantages
Star	It is easy to add a node. It provides fast communications, with only two hops from one node to another.	If the central computer is lost, so is the network. With too many nodes in the star, central computer performance is degraded.
Bus	It is easy to add a node.	If the bus is lost, so is the network. Too many nodes will overload the bus.
Ring	It can cover larger distances than the other two topologies.	Too many nodes will degrade network performance. It is more difficult to add a node than with the other two topologies.

The network gateway connects the LAN to external networks—either public or corporate—so that it can exchange information with them. A **gateway** is a communications processor that connects dissimilar networks by translating from one set of protocols (rules that govern the functioning of a network) to another. A processor that connects two networks of the same type is called a **bridge**. A **router** routes messages through several connected LANs or to a wide area network.

As we mentioned earlier, because a LAN is restricted to a small area, the nodes can be connected either through cables or via wireless technologies. *Wireless local area networks (WLANs)* provide LAN connectivity over short distances, typically less than 150 meters. We discuss WLANs and other wireless technologies in Chapter 7.

Wide Area Networks

When businesses have to transmit and receive data beyond the confines of the LAN, they use wide area networks. **Wide area networks (WANs)** are networks that cover large geographic areas. WANs typically connect multiple LANs. WANs generally are provided by common carriers, such as telephone companies and the international networks of global communications services providers. WANs have large capacity, and they typically combine multiple channels (e.g., fiber optic cables, microwave, and satellite). The Internet, which we discuss in the next section, is an example of a WAN. The following example focuses on a network that covers a very wide area: it stretches from the Earth to Mars!

A 100-Million-Mile Wide Area Network. Eighteen days after landing on Mars in 2004, the robotic explorer named Spirit squawked in distress and went silent for nearly 24 hours. Scientists at the Jet Propulsion Laboratory in Pasadena had to fix a broken interplanetary communications link that reached more than 100 million miles and kept increasing as the orbits of Earth and Mars drew apart. To transmit signals to Spirit, the JPL scientists use three Earth stations spaced roughly one-third of the way around the Earth from one another. The stations are located in California, Spain, and Australia. They are specially situated so that, as the Earth rotates, at least one station can communicate with Spirit at any given moment.

The problem was traced to a software glitch in Spirit's programs. The scientists were able to send a patch to Mars, correcting the problem and bringing Spirit back into operation. (*Sources:* Compiled from D. Carr, "The 100-Million-Mile Network," *Baseline Magazine*, February 6, 2004; and *http://marsrovers.jpl.nasa.gov/home/*, accessed March 24, 2005.)

Example

One important type of WAN is the **value-added network (VAN)**. VANs are private, data-only networks managed by outside third parties that provide telecommunication and computing services to multiple organizations. Many companies use VANs to avoid the expenses of creating and managing their own networks.

Enterprise Networking

Organizations today have multiple LANs and may have multiple WANs, which are interconnected to form an **enterprise network**. Figure 5.2 shows a model of enterprise computing. Note that the enterprise network in the figure has a backbone network composed of fiber-optic cable. Corporate **backbone networks** are high-speed central networks to which multiple smaller networks (such as LANs and smaller WANs) connect. The LANs are called *embedded LANs* because they connect to the backbone WAN.

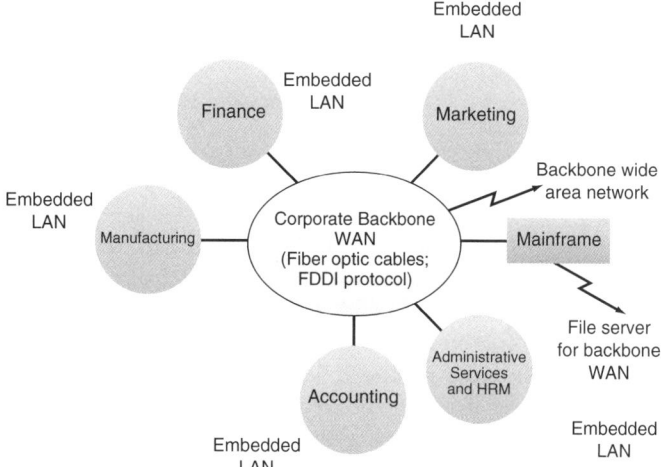

FIGURE 5.2
Enterprise computing network.

---

1. What are the main business reasons for using networks?
2. What is the difference between LANs and WANs?
3. Describe an enterprise network.

5.2 The Internet

The Internet ("the Net") is a global WAN that connects approximately 1 million organizational computer networks in more than 200 countries on all continents, including Antarctica. Participating computer systems, called nodes, include PCs, LANs, databases, and mainframes. As a network of networks, the Internet enables people to access data in other organizations and to communicate, collaborate, and exchange information seamlessly around the world, quickly and inexpensively. Thus, the Internet has become a necessity in the conduct of modern business.

The Internet grew out of an experimental project of the Advanced Research Project Agency (ARPA) of the U.S. Department of Defense. The project began in 1969 as the *ARPAnet*. Its purpose was to test the feasibility of a WAN over which researchers, educators, military personnel, and government agencies could share data, exchange messages, and transfer files.

Today, Internet technologies are being used both within and among organizations. An **intranet** is a network designed to serve the internal informational needs of a single organization. Intranets support discovery (easy and inexpensive browsing and search), communication, and collaboration. For the numerous uses of intranets, see *www.intranetjournal.com*.

In contrast, an **extranet** connects parts of the intranets of different organizations and allows secure communications among business partners over the Internet using virtual private networks. Extranets offer limited accessibility to the intranets of participating companies, as well as necessary interorganizational communications. They are widely used in the areas of business-to-business (B2B) electronic commerce (see Chapter 6) and supply chain management (SCM).

Extranets require additional technology to ensure secure transmission of information between business partners. Virtual private networks provide this technology. **Virtual private networks (VPNs)** are private communications networks that use the Internet for trans-

FIGURE 5.3
Virtual private network and tunneling.

mission. Therefore, VPNs integrate the global connectivity of the Internet with the security of a private network. VPNs are labeled "virtual" because the connection between organizations is created when a transmission needs to be made and terminated when the transmission has been sent. VPNs are handled by common carriers (i.e., telephone service providers).

To provide secure transmissions, VPNs use a process called tunneling. **Tunneling** encrypts the data packet to be sent, and places it inside another packet. In this manner, the packet can travel across the Internet with confidentiality, authentication, and integrity. Figure 5.3 depicts a VPN and tunneling.

Darknets are private networks that run on the Internet but are open only to users who belong to the network. Typically, relatively few people or organizations have access to a darknet, due to security concerns. These users swap passwords or digital keys so they can communicate securely with one another. The data flowing between computers often are encrypted, making darknets more secure than typical corporate intranets, because companies usually do not encrypt data located inside corporate firewalls.

There are three major uses for darknets:

1. Freedom of speech in countries where censorship exists

2. Corporate security where companies create highly secure networks to protect sensitive data

3. Copyright infringement: file-sharing software connecting people who share music, movies, and software

Operation of the Internet

The set of rules used to send and receive packets from one machine to another over the Internet is known as the **Internet Protocol (IP)**. Other protocols are used in connection with IP. The best-known of these is the *Transmission Control Protocol* (*TCP*). The IP and TCP protocols are so commonly used together that they are referred to as the *TCP/IP protocol*.

The Internet is a packet-switching network. **Packet switching** is a transmission technology that breaks up blocks of text into small, fixed bundles of data called packets. Figure 5.4

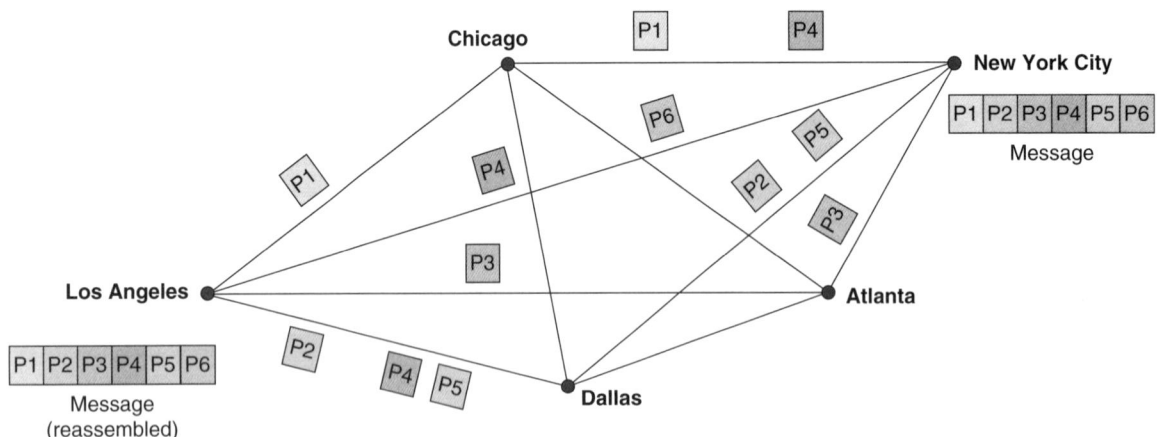

FIGURE 5.4 Packet switching.

illustrates a message being sent from New York City to Los Angeles over a packet-switching network. Each packet travels independently through the network, and each can be routed through different paths in the network. The packets are reassembled into the original message when they reach their destination.

The computers and organizational nodes on the Internet can be of different types and makes. They are connected to one another by data communications lines of different speeds. The main network connections and telecommunications lines that link the nodes are referred to as the backbone. For the Internet, the backbone is a fiber-optic network that is operated mainly by large telecommunications companies.

No central agency manages the Internet. Instead, the cost of its operation is shared among hundreds of thousands of nodes. Thus, the cost for any one organization is small. Organizations must pay a small fee if they wish to register their names, and they need to have their own hardware and software for the operation of their internal networks. The organizations are obliged to move any data or information that enter their organizational network, regardless of their source, to their destination, at no charge to the senders. The senders, of course, pay the telephone bills for using either the backbone or regular telephone lines.

Accessing the Internet   There are several ways to access the Internet. From your place of work or your university, you can access an Internet-connected file server on your organization's LAN. A campus or company backbone connects all the various LANs and servers in the organization to the Internet. Another option is to use a modem you can connect to your campus or company network from any place that offers a dial tone. (We discuss modems in the Appendix at the end of the chapter.) You can also log onto the Internet from your home or on the road, and wireless connections are also possible.

Connecting via an Online Service   You can also access the Internet by opening an account with an Internet service provider. An **Internet service provider (ISP)** is a company that offers Internet connections for a fee. Large ISPs include America Online (*www.aol.com*), Juno (*www.juno.com*), Earthlink (*www.earthlink.com*), and NetZero (*www.netzero.net*). In addition, many telephone providers and cable companies sell Internet access, as do computer companies such as Microsoft. To use this service you need a modem and standard communications software. To find a local ISP, access *www.thelist.com*. There, you can search by your telephone area code for an ISP that services your area.

ISPs connect to one another through **network access points (NAPs)**. NAPs are an exchange point for Internet traffic. They determine how traffic is routed. NAPs are key components of the Internet backbone. Figure 5.5 shows a schematic of the Internet. Note that the white links at the top of the figure represent the Internet backbone.

Connecting via Other Means   There have been several attempts to make access to the Internet cheaper, faster, and easier. For example, **Internet kiosks** are terminals located in public places like libraries and airports (and even in convenience stores in some countries) for use by people who do not have their own computers. Accessing the Internet from cell phones and pagers is also becoming more common. It is also possible to connect to the Internet via satellite, which we discuss in Chapter 7.

Addresses on the Internet   Each computer on the Internet has an assigned address, called the **Internet Protocol (IP) address**, that distinguishes it from all other computers. The IP address consists of numbers, in four parts, separated by dots. For example, the IP address of one computer might be 135.62.128.91.

Most computers also have names, which are easier for people to remember than IP addresses. These names are derived from a naming system called the **domain name system**

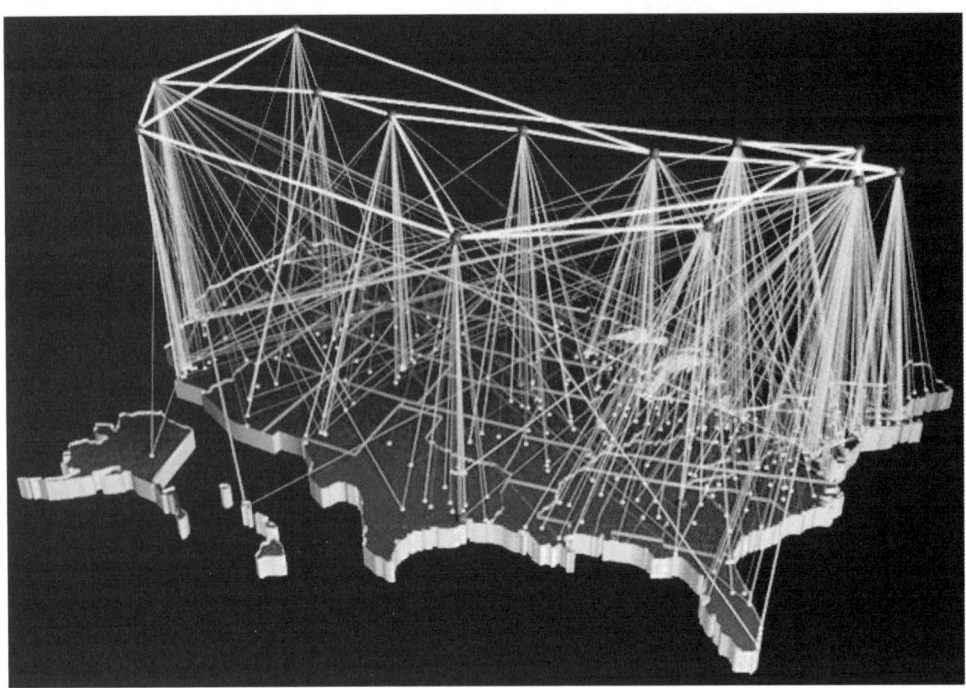

FIGURE 5.5
Internet (backbone
in white)
Source: neosoft.com.

(DNS). Currently, 82 companies, called *registrars*, are accredited to register domain names from the Internet Corporation for Assigned Names (ICANN) (*www.internic.net*). **Domain names** consist of multiple parts, separated by dots, which are read from right to left.

For example, consider the domain name *software.ibm.com*. The rightmost part of an Internet name is its **top-level specification**, or the zone. It designates the type of organization that owns the site. The letters "com" in *software.ibm.com* indicate that this is a commercial site. Popular zones are:

com   commercial sites
edu   educational sites
mil   military sites
gov   government sites
org   organizations

To finish our domain name example, "ibm" is the name of the company (IBM), and "software" is the name of the particular machine (computer) within the company to which the message is being sent.

In some domain names, you will find two letters to the right of the top-level specification. These two letters represent the country of the Web site. For example, "us" stands for the United States, "de" for Germany, "it" for Italy, and "ru" for Russia. There are some 300,000 registered domain names, and these domain names have commercial value in themselves. This value has led to the practice of *cybersquatting*—buying a potentially coveted domain name and hoping someone wants that name enough to pay for it. The practice of cybersquatting grew out of the early policy of registering domain names on a first-come, first-served basis. This policy resulted in companies or individuals registering a domain name associated with an established firm before the established firm did, which resulted in disputed names and legal actions. Dreams of six-figure payouts all but ended when the U.S. Congress passed the Anti-Cybersquatting Consumer Protection Act in November 1999.

The Future of the Internet

Despite the massive scope and potential of the Internet, in some cases it is too slow for data-intensive applications. Examples of such applications include full-motion video files (movies) or large medical files (X-rays). In addition, the Internet is unreliable and not secure. As a result, three initiatives are underway to improve today's Internet: the Internet2, the Next Generation Internet (NGI), and the Very-High-Speed Backbone Network Service (vBNS). Led by more than 200 U.S. universities working with industry and government, **Internet2** develops and deploys advanced network applications such as remote medical diagnosis, digital libraries, distance education, online simulation, and virtual laboratories. Internet2 is not a separate physical network from the Internet. For more detail, see *http://www.internet2.edu.*

The **Next Generation Internet (NGI)** initiative is a U.S. federal government research and development program that aims to create an Internet that is fast, always on, everywhere, natural, intelligent, easy, and trusted. For more detail, see *http://www.ngi.gov.* The **vBNS** is a high-speed network designed to support the academic Internet2 and the government-sponsored NGI initiatives. The goal is to increase the bandwidth of the vBNS backbone to 2.4 gigabits per second.

Before you go on . . .

1. Describe the evolution of the Internet, and discuss three future initiatives for the Internet.
2. Describe the various ways that you can connect to the Internet.
3. Describe the parts of an Internet address.

5.3 The World Wide Web

Many people equate the Internet with the World Wide Web. However, they are not the same thing. The Internet functions as a transport mechanism, whereas the World Wide Web is an application that uses those transport functions. Other applications, such as e-mail, also run on the Internet.

The **World Wide Web (the Web, WWW, or W3)** is a system of universally accepted standards for storing, retrieving, formatting, and displaying information via a client/server architecture. The Web handles all types of digital information, including text, hypermedia, graphics, and sound. It uses graphical user interfaces, so it is very easy to use.

Offering information through the Web requires establishing a **home page**, which is a text and graphical screen display that usually welcomes the user and explains the organization that has established the page. In most cases, the home page will lead users to other pages. All the pages of a particular company or individual are collectively known as a **Web site**. Most Web pages provide a way to contact the organization or the individual. The person in charge of an organization's Web site is its **Webmaster**.

To access a Web site, the user must specify a **uniform resource locator (URL)**, which points to the address of a specific resource on the Web. For instance, the URL for Microsoft is *http://www.microsoft.com.* HTTP stands for **hypertext transport protocol**, which is the communications standard used to transfer pages across the Web portion of the Internet. HTTP defines how messages are formatted and transmitted and indicates what actions Web servers and browsers should take in response to various commands. The remaining letters in this URL—www.microsoft.com—indicate the domain name that identifies the Web server storing the Web site.

Users access the Web primarily through software applications called **browsers**. Browsers provide a graphical front end that enable users to point-and-click their way across the Web, a process called **surfing**. Web browsers became a means of universal access because they deliver the same interface on any operating system under which they run. Leading browsers include Internet Explorer from Microsoft, Firefox from Mozilla (*www.mozilla.org*), and Netscape Navigator.

Before you go on . . .

1. What are the roles of browsers?

2. Describe the difference between the Internet and the World Wide Web.

3. What is a URL? Describe the different parts that make up a URL.

5.4 Network Applications

Hopefully you now have a working knowledge of what a network is and how you can access it. At this point, the key question is, How do businesses use networks to improve their operations? This section addresses that question. Stated in general terms, networks support businesses and other organizations in all types of functions. These functions fall into the following major categories: discovery, communication, collaboration, and Web services. We discuss each of these categories in the following sections.

Discovery

The Internet permits users to access information located in databases all over the world. By browsing and searching data sources on the Web, users can apply the Internet's discovery capability to areas ranging from education to government services to entertainment and to commerce.

In some ways, however, the Web's major strength is also its greatest challenge. The amount of information on the Web can be overwhelming, and it doubles approximately each year. This makes navigating through the Web and gaining access to necessary information more and more difficult. The solution is the use of search engines, directories, software agents, toolbars, and portals.

Search Engines and Directories   Search engines and directories are two different types of search facilities available on the Web. A **search engine** (e.g., *www.altavista.com, www.google.com, www.mamma.com*) is a computer program that searches for specific information by key words and reports the results. A search engine maintains an index of hundreds of millions of Web pages (more than 8 billion pages in the case of Google). It uses that index to find pages that match a set of user-specified keywords. Such indexes are created and updated by software robots called *softbots*, which execute routine tasks for the benefit of their users.

Directories differ slightly from search engines. A **directory** (e.g., Yahoo, About.com) is a hierarchically organized collection of links to Web pages. Directories are compiled manually, unlike search engine indexes, which are generated by computers.

Search engines and directories often present users with links to thousands or even millions of pages. It is quite difficult to find information of interest within such a large number of links. In these cases we can use additional tools to refine the search. Three of these tools are metasearch engines, software agents, and toolbars.

Metasearch engines   **Metasearch engines** search several engines at once and integrate the findings of the various search engines to answer queries posted by users. Examples include Surfwax (*www.surfwax.com*), Metacrawler (*www.metacrawler.com*), Ungoogle (*www.ungoogle.com*), Ixquick (*www.ixquick.com*), and Dogpile (*www.dogpile.com*). Figure 5.6 shows the SurfWax home page.

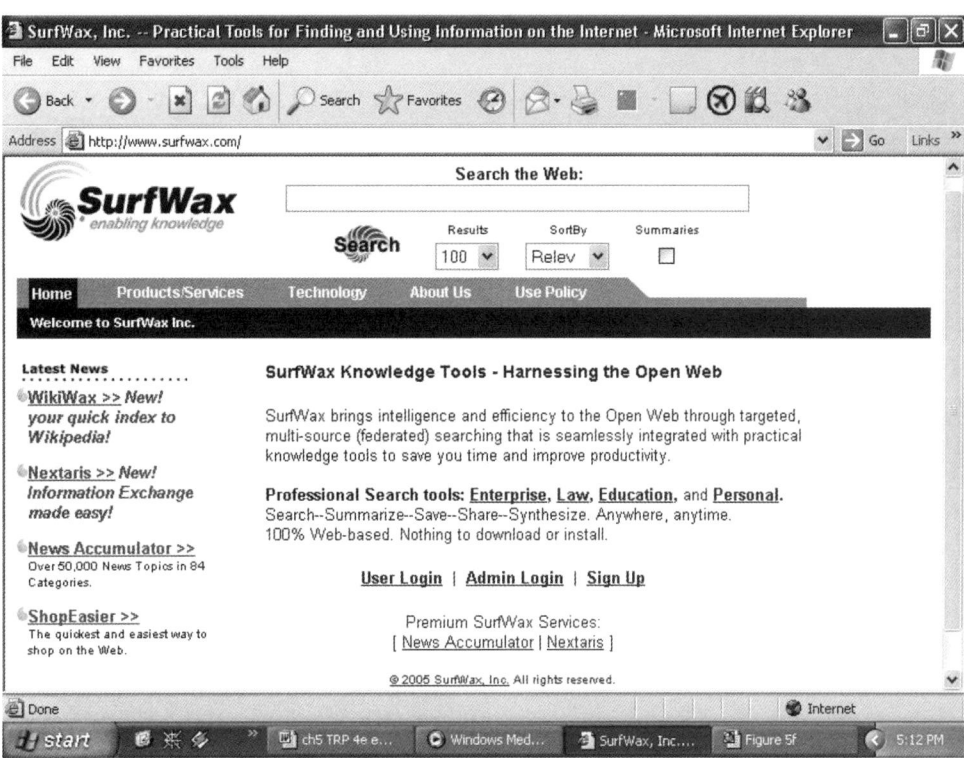

FIGURE 5.6
SurfWax.

Software Agents A large number of Internet software agents can be used to automate and expedite discovery. **Software agents** are computer programs that carry out a set of routine computer tasks on behalf of the user and in so doing employ some sort of knowledge of the user's goals. Agents that help us access information include Web-browsing-assisting agents, frequently-asked-questions (FAQ) agents, and intelligent-indexing agents.

Web-browsing-assisting agents, known as tour guides, facilitate browsing by offering the user a tour of the Internet. For example, NetCaptor (*www.netcaptor.com*) is a custom browser application that makes browsing more productive. In contrast, FAQ agents guide people to the answers to frequently asked questions. AskJeeves (*www.ask.com*) is a popular FAQ agent that makes it easy to find answers on the Internet to questions asked in plain English. Finally, intelligent-indexing agents—also called Web robots and spiders—can carry out a massive autonomous search of the Web for a user. These agents retrieve requested pages, as well as all other pages referencing the requested page.

Toolbars To get the most out of search engines, you may use add-on toolbars and special software. A **toolbar** is a horizontal row or vertical column of selectable image icons or buttons. By clicking on an icon, the user can access desktop or other application functions, such as saving or printing a document or moving pages forward or backward within a Web browser. The toolbar also reminds users of what functions are available. Figure 5.7 illustrates the Microsoft Internet Explorer toolbar.

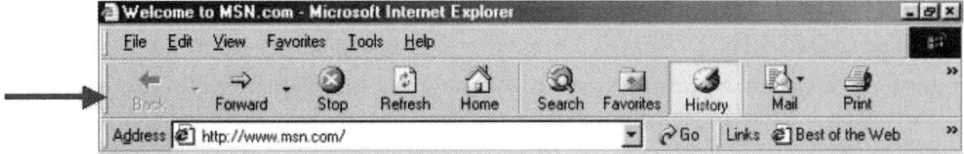

FIGURE 5.7
Microsoft Internet
Explorer toolbar.

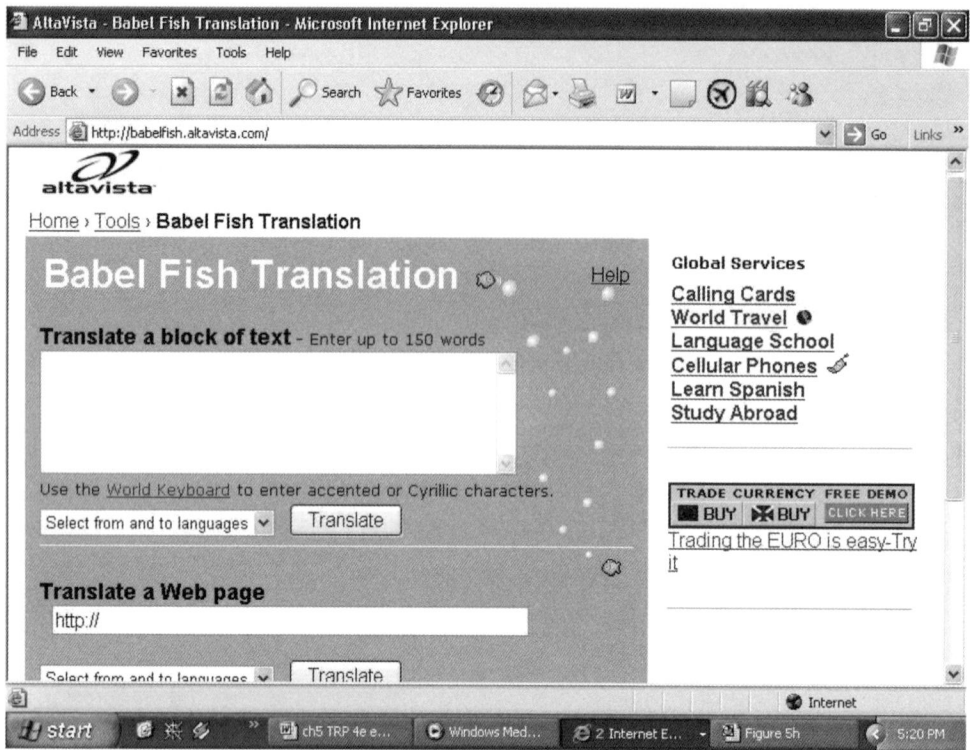

FIGURE 5.8
AltaVista translator.

Some toolbars are attached to the popular search engines, and others are independent. Most are free. Examples are Google Toolbar (*www.toolbar.google.com*), Copernic Agent Basic (*www.copernic.com*), KartOO (*www.kartoo.com*), Yahoo Companion (*http://companion.yahoo.com*), and Grokker (*www.groxis.com*).

Discovery of Material in Foreign Languages   Not only is there a huge amount of information on the Internet, but it is written in many different languages. How, then, do you access this information? The answer is that you use an *automatic translation* of Web pages. Such translation is available, to and from all major languages, and its quality is improving with time. Some major translation products are Altavista (*http://babelfish.altavista.com*) and Google (*www.google.com/language_tools*), and products and services available at *http://www.trados.com* and *http://www.translationzone.com*.

For translation, you enter the text of what you want translated. You then select the "from–to" languages for the translation (e.g., from English to German). The Web site then presents the translated text. See Figure 5.8. However, problems remain, as the following example shows.

How Not to Translate Your Web Page   Language has the power to bring marketing directors to their knees. Consider the following translation faux pas:

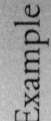

- Mercedes-Benz shortened the name of its Grand Sports Tourer to GST. In Canada, however, the acronym stands for the widely loathed goods and services tax, also known as the "gouge and screw tax."

- Ikea, the $7 billion household products company that is headquartered in Denmark, sells a workbench called Fartfull and a computer table named Jerker. These are common names in Danish.

- Coca-Cola's attempt to render its name in Chinese characters came off as "Bite the Wax Tadpole."
- The Perdue Farms slogan, "It takes a tough man to make a tender chicken," translated into Spanish as, "It takes a sexually aroused man to make a chicken affectionate."

To survive, companies should not rely on translator products. They should find native speakers who know dialects and slang. Companies also should hire foreign marketing people because translations can be perfect but have no cultural resonance. Finally, when in doubt, be original. Try a new foreign name when adaptations are not working. (*Sources:* Compiled from M. Lasswell, "Lost in Translation," *Business 2.0,* August 2004; and *http://babelfish. altavista.com* and *www.google.com,* accessed March 25, 2005.)

Portals   Most organizations and their managers encounter information overload. Information is scattered across numerous documents, e-mail messages, and databases at different locations and systems. Finding relevant and accurate information is often time-consuming and may require access to multiple systems.

One solution to this problem is to use portals. A **portal** is a Web-based, personalized gateway to information and knowledge that provides relevant information from different IT systems and the Internet using advanced search and indexing techniques. We distinguish among five types of portals below.

1. **Commercial (public) portals** offer content for diverse communities, and they are the most popular portals on the Internet. They are intended for broad audiences, and they offer fairly routine content, some in real time (e.g., a stock ticker). Examples are *www.yahoo.com, www.lycos.com,* and *www.msn.com.*

2. **Affinity portals** support communities such as a hobby group or a political party. They offer a single point of entry to an entire community of affiliated interests. For example, your university most likely has an affinity portal for its alumni. Figure 5.9 shows the affinity portal for the Auburn University Alumni Association. Other examples include *www.techweb.com* and *http://www.zdnet.com.*

3. **Mobile portals** are portals that are accessible from mobile devices. One example is i-mode from DoCoMo (*www.nttdocomo.com*) in Japan. We discuss mobile portals, including i-mode, in Chapter 7.

4. **Corporate portals** offer a personalized, single point of access through a Web browser to critical business information located inside and outside an organization. They are also known as *enterprise portals, information portals,* or *enterprise information portals.* In addition to making it easier to find needed information, corporate portals offer customers and employees self-service opportunities. Figure 5.10 provides a framework for corporate portals and IT's About Business 5.1 discusses a corporate portal at British Aerospace.

5. **Industrywide portals.** In addition to single-company portals, there are also portals for entire industries. An example is *www.chaindrugstore.net,* which links retailers and product manufacturers and provides product and industry news and recall and promotional information. The site has an offshoot for independent pharmacies (called *Community-DrugStore.net*). The service reaches more than 130 retailers representing 32,000 stores. The service is free to the retailers. Suppliers pay annual fees in exchange for being able to use the portal to communicate information to retailers (e.g., to advertise special deals, to notify retailers about price changes). The portal also provides industry news, and it can be personalized for individual retailers.

Communication

The second major category of network applications is communication. There are many types of communications, including e-mail, call centers, chat rooms, voice, blogging, and Wikis. We discuss each one in this section.

FIGURE 5.9
Auburn University
affinity portal.

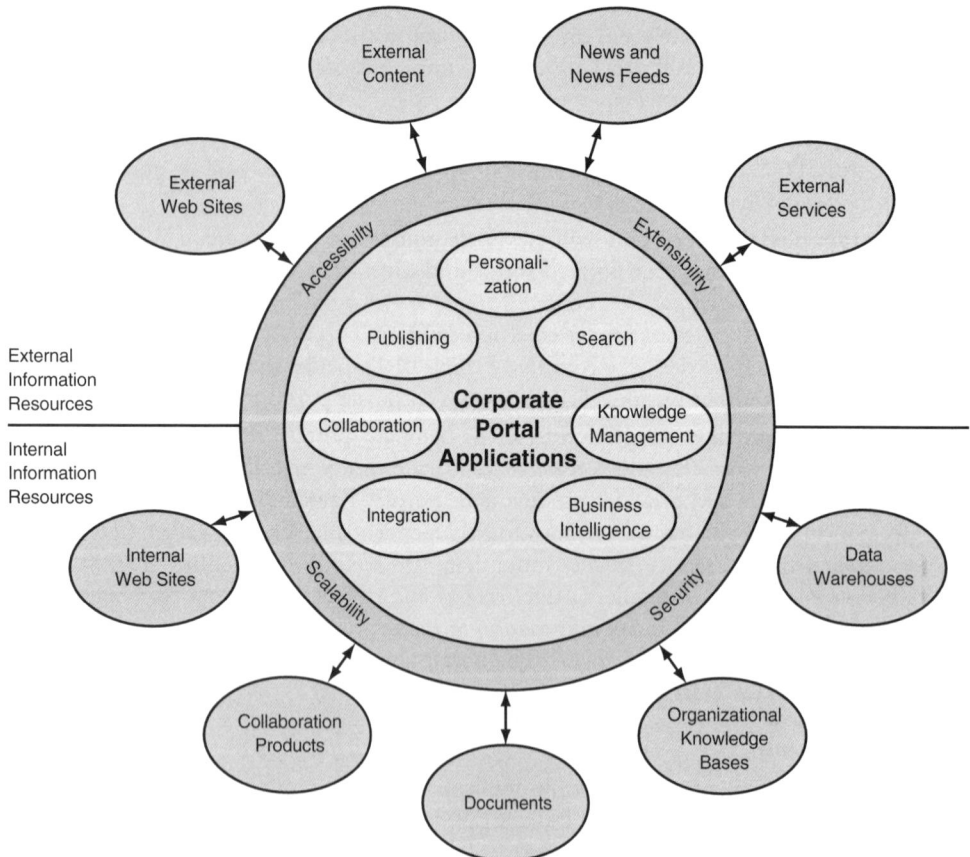

FIGURE 5.10
A corporate portal
framework. (*Sources:*
Compiled from A. Aneja
et al., "Corporate Portal
Framework for
Transforming Content
Chaos on Intranets,"
Intel Technology Journal,
Q1, 2000, and from
T. Kounandis, "How to
Pick the Best Portal,"
e-Business Advisor,
August 2000.)

IT's About Business

5.1 Corporate Portal Improves Productivity at British Aerospace

According to some estimates, more than 80 percent of employees waste, on average, 30 minutes of each day simply retrieving information. British Aerospace (*www.baesystems.com*) believes this. The defense and aerospace company knew it was sitting on an information gold mine. Unfortunately, the wealth of information sources available to its employees was hampering, not enhancing, productivity. To address this problem, the company decided to develop a corporate portal that would be so easy to navigate that employees would no longer waste time searching for the information they needed.

The first step was to make the information easier to find. To accomplish this, British Aerospace used Autonomy's (*www.autonomy.com*) software to integrate all internal and external information resources. The result was easy-to-navigate, Yahoo-like topical directories. To make it even simpler for employees to hone in on what they were looking for, British Aerospace used hypertext links throughout the portal. Finally, the company used personalized reports and alerts to keep employees up to speed on job-related developments.

The corporate portal has already improved access to the wealth of information available from the Web and within British Aerospace's databases, file servers, and desktops. The portal has also markedly improved the productivity of British Aerospace's employees.

Sources: Compiled from "Big Challenges, Big Rewards," *www.cio.com*, March 9, 2005; "NewsEdge Desktop Applications Real-Time News Keeps British Aerospace Professionals On Top of Their World," *www.dialog.com/products/case studies/ british.shtml*, accessed March 29, 2005; and *www. baeportal.datathree.com/*, accessed April 3, 2005;

QUESTIONS

1. What are the problems in deciding which information to put in the portal? In finding the information to put in the portal? In formatting the information in the portal?

2. How would British Aerospace's portal improve the decision making of its employees?

Electronic Mail   Electronic mail (e-mail) is the largest-volume application running over the Internet. However, e-mail is beginning to have serious problems. In the spring of 2003, for example, spam (unsolicited e-mail) accounted for more than half of all e-mail traffic. Even worse, MessageLabs (*www.messagelabs.com*), a leading provider of e-mail security services, maintains that in 2004, the ratio of virus-infected messages to other e-mail traffic increased by nearly 85 percent. These viruses caused PCs to serve as "open relays," giving spammers still more launchpads for their anonymous attacks. For many users, e-mail has all but replaced the telephone. However, people can waste as much as one hour every week simply managing their e-mail. Despite the problems, a recent study found that almost 90 percent of companies conduct business transactions via e-mail, and nearly 70 percent confirm that e-mail is tied to their means of generating revenue.

"Got your e-mail, thanks."

Web-Based Call Centers   Effective personalized customer contact is becoming an important aspect of Web-based customer support. Such service is provided through *Web-based call centers*, also known as *customer care centers*. For example, if you need to contact a software vendor for technical support, you will usually be communicating with the vendor's Web-based call center, using e-mail, a telephone conversation, or a simultaneous voice/Web session. Web-based call centers may be located in countries such as India. Such *outsourcing* has lately become an issue for U.S. companies.

Electronic Chat Rooms

Electronic chat refers to an arrangement whereby participants exchange conversational messages in real time. A **chat room** is a virtual meeting place where groups of regulars come to "gab." Chat programs allow you to send messages to people who are connected to the same channel of communication at the same time. Anyone can join in the online conversation. Messages are displayed on your screen as they arrive, even if you are in the middle of typing a message.

Two major types of chat programs exist. The first type is a Web-based chat program, which allows you to send messages to Internet users by using a Web browser and visiting a Web chat site (e.g., *http://chat.yahoo.com*). The second type is an e-mail-based (text-only) program called *Internet Relay Chat (IRC)*. A business can use IRC to interact with customers, provide online experts' answers to questions, and so on.

Voice Communication

When people need to communicate with one another from a distance, they use the telephone more frequently than any other communication device. With the Plain Old Telephone System (POTS), every call opened up a dedicated circuit for the duration of the call. (A dedicated circuit connects you to the person you are talking with and is devoted only to your call.) In contrast, as we discussed, the Internet divides data into packets, which traverse the Internet in random order and are reassembled at their destination.

With **Internet telephony (voice-over IP or VoIP)**, phone calls are just another kind of data. Your analog voice signals are digitized, sectioned into packets, and then sent over the Internet. VoIP significantly reduces your monthly phone bills. In addition, it allows you to customize your phone service to do exactly what you want. For example, you can forward your calls to any phone you desire (including your cell phone), and you can set up a conference call online by entering the other numbers on a Web site. In addition, with VoIP, your area code no longer has to correspond with your physical address. (Vonage, *www.vonage.com*, and other VoIP providers claim that 212 (Manhattan) and 310 (Beverly Hills) are in high demand.)

In the past, VoIP required a computer with a sound card and a microphone. Today, however, you do not need special phones or headsets for your computer. Vonage sells do-it-yourself kits through retailers such as Best Buy and Radio Shack. Skype (*www.skype.com*) even provides voice-over IP services for free. Figure 5.11 shows the Skype interface. VoIP has the potential to revolutionize corporate communications, as IT's About Business 5.2 demonstrates.

Weblogging (Blogging)

Blogs and blogging enable individuals to publish personal materials on the Internet. A **Weblog** (**blog** for short) is a personal Web site, open to the public, in which the site creator expresses his or her feelings or opinions. *Bloggers*—people who create and maintain blogs—write stories, tell news, and provide links to other articles and Web sites that are of interest to them.

The simplest method to create a blog is to sign up with a blogging service provider, such as *www.blogger.com* (see Figure 5.12), *www.pitas.com*, *www.livejournal.com*, and *http://www.moveabletype.com*.

Bloggers are creating their own rich terminology. For a blogger's dictionary, see *www.marketingterms.com/dictionary/blog*. Blogs are becoming powerful business tools, as IT's About Business 5.3 shows.

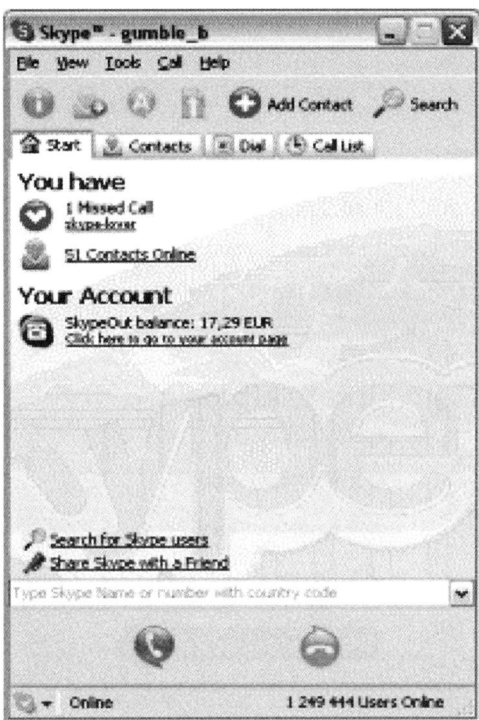

FIGURE 5.11
Skype interface.

IT's About Business

5.2 H. J. Heinz Becomes Its Own Phone Company

Traditional telephone companies may soon find that their best and biggest customers are their biggest competitors. Let's look at the European operations of H. J. Heinz, the Pittsburgh condiments maker.

Heinz has installed VoIP systems at eight sites in the Netherlands and five sites in the United Kingdom. The company has deployed 7,000 VoIP phones on the Continent and another 1,000 at its U.S. headquarters. The Wincanton Group in Wigan, England, sits next to the Heinz factory. Wincanton moves bottles of Heinz ketchup around the United Kingdom. When Wincanton built its distribution center next to the ketchup factory, the two companies paid about 7.5 cents (U.S.) per minute to talk with one another.

So, Heinz decided to bypass the public phone network altogether. It laid its own fiber line to the distribution center and put 100 VoIP phones on Wincanton's site. Now, Heinz managers pay nothing to talk with their logisticians at Wincanton. Both companies save money.

Heinz even gave Wincanton a new main phone number and its own local data network. Therefore, Heinz linked the two companies not only in voice communications, but also in exchanging purchase orders, voice mail, and video messages.

Heinz has 37 sites across Europe. It is in the process of replacing its existing contracts with numerous communications companies with as few as one master contract with a single ISP. The economics are very persuasive.

Sources: Compiled from T. Steinert-Threlkeld, "Say Hello to Your New Phone Company: You," *Baseline Magazine*, October 1, 2004; and L. Kelly, "Online Buying Means Business for Heinz," *Computing*, October 15, 2003.

QUESTIONS

1. How does VoIP affect traditional telephone companies?
2. What concerns would you have about communicating over the Internet?

FIGURE 5.12
Blogger.com.

IT's About Business

5.3 Blogs Mean Business

Blogs can be good news for businesses, or bad news. But they can no longer be ignored. Consider the case of Kryptonite (*www.kryptonite.com*), a manufacturer of bicycle locks. On September 12, 2004, a blogger posted something unusual that he or she had noticed in a group discussion site for bicycle enthusiasts. According to the blogger, the ubiquitous, U-shaped Kryptonite lock could be easily picked with a Bic ballpoint pen. Two days later a number of blogs, including the consumer electronics site Engadget, posted videos demonstrating the trick. On September 16, Kryptonite issued a bland statement saying the locks remained a "deterrent to theft" and promising that a new line would be "tougher." That was not enough. "Trivial empty answer," wrote another blogger. Every day new bloggers began writing about the issue and talking about their experiences, and hundreds of thousands of people were reading about it. Prompted by the blogs, on September 17 the *New York Times* and the Associated Press published stories about

the problem—articles that set off a new chain of blogging. Two days later, Technorati (*www.technorati.com*), a site that keeps track of the world of Weblogs, estimated that some 1.8 million people saw postings about Kryptonite.

Finally, on September 22, Kryptonite announced that it would exchange any affected lock free. The company sent out more than 100,000 new locks, at a cost of $10 million. That is $10 million in 10 days—a victory for the blogosphere.

Sources: Compiled from D. Kirkpatrick and D. Roth, "Why There's No Escaping the Blog," *Fortune*, January 10, 2005; and P. Rojas, "Kryptonite Offers Free Upgrades for Easily Picked Bike Locks," *www.engadget.com*, September 19, 2004.

QUESTIONS

1. Was blogging good news or bad news for Kryptonite? Defend your answer.
2. In general, how does blogging affect the relationship between businesses and their customers?

Wikis A **Wiki** is a Web site on which anyone can post material and make changes quickly, without using difficult commands. Volunteers have posted more than 280,000 English-language articles since 2001 to the online encyclopedia Wikipedia (*www.wikipedia.org*). Wikis have an "edit" link on each page that allows anyone to add, change, or delete material, fostering easy collaboration. For example, Kodak's Ofoto uses wikis to help teams develop prototypes of new technologies, work with contractors, and coordinate other tasks. Voice Communications, a public-relations firm, uses wikis to keep clients informed about campaigns and schedules faster and more reliably than it could with e-mail exchanges.

Collaboration

The third major category of network applications is collaboration. An important feature of modern organizations is that people collaborate to perform work. **Collaboration** refers to efforts by two or more entities (individuals, teams, groups, or organizations) who work together to accomplish certain tasks. The term **work group** refers specifically to two or more individuals who act together to perform some task. If group members are in different locations, they constitute a **virtual group (team)**. Virtual groups conduct *virtual meetings*; that is, they "meet" electronically. **Virtual collaboration** (or *e-collaboration*) refers to the use of digital technologies that enable organizations or individuals to collaboratively plan, design, develop, manage, and research products, services, and innovative applications.

As one example of virtual collaboration, organizations interact with customers, suppliers, and other business partners to improve productivity and competitiveness. IT's About Business 5.4 shows how Dannon collaborates with its customers.

As we discussed earlier, a variety of tools are available to support collaboration. In this section we consider two of them: workflow technologies and groupware tools.

Workflow Technologies **Workflow** is the movement of information as it flows through the sequence of steps that make up an organization's work procedures. Workflow management makes it possible to pass documents, information, and tasks from one participant to another in a way that is governed by the organization's rules or procedures. Workflow systems are tools for automating business processes. One key benefit of these tools is that they place system controls in the hands of user departments. The following example illustrates a workflow system.

Example

Workflow Software Helps Document Management at Brazos. The Brazos Higher Education Services Corporation provides financing and loan-management services for higher education in the United States. The Brazos Group is the nation's fifth largest holder of student loans, with total assets in excess of $5 billion. Brazos implemented a networked workflow solution to eliminate the distribution of paper documents while ensuring that the electronic documents can be viewed, searched, tracked, secured, archived, and readily available for verification. Brazos personnel (regardless of their location) have the capability to perform a global search to determine where applicable documents reside on the company's network. Paper documents received via the mailroom are prepared by qualified personnel. They are then electronically scanned, indexed, processed, and managed by the workflow system for their respective local repositories or remote scanning to other Brazos locations via the company's network. Once documents are successfully scanned into the system, paper documents are prepped for on/off-site storage or distribution. (*Sources:* Compiled from *http://www.workflowsystems.com*, accessed February 17, 2005; and *www.bhesc.org*, accessed February 19, 2005.)

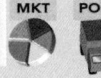

IT's About Business

5.4 Speak, Customer!

Should companies let amateurs design their products? The answer is not clear. Nevertheless, many companies are letting customers have input into cars, insurance products, fast food, toys, and appliances. These companies have concluded that instant feedback is one way to cope with the high failure rate—about 80 percent—of new products.

Dannon U.S.A. (*www.dannon.com*) was experiencing such a problem. Its reduced-fat Light 'n' Fit yogurts were being squeezed by rivals. The company turned to consumers for help. The company was looking specifically for diet-conscious yogurt eaters who were responsible for grocery shopping in their households. Dannon's director of market research needed a quick read on what features customers felt were essential. She called in Affinnova (*www.affinnova.com*), a marketing research company. Affinnova e-mailed 40,000 men and women and asked them to visit a Web site to help create a new product. All respondents would be eligible to win $10,000. The e-mailing resulted in 705 people qualifying for the test.

Affinnova presented the respondents a series of yogurt containers so that they could evaluate different combinations of name, package design, nutritional labeling, and size. There were 11,268 possible combinations, but each "player" in this game was asked to choose among only a few. The test changed as more people took it, and a statistics program highlighted frequently selected features.

In just six days of Web activity, Affinnova had reached the following conclusions:

- The new yogurt should be called Carb Control.
- It should come in a red container.
- It should be sold in a four-pack of 4-ounce cups.
- It should highlight its nutritional information for dieters: "80% less sugar" and "3 grams of carbs."

Dannon had the new product on store shelves six months after the test. The results? In 2004, sales hit $70.5 million, a marked increase.

Sources: Compiled from M. Wells, "Have It Your Way," *Forbes*, February 14, 2005; J. Fitzgerald, "Marketer's First Breakthrough: Itself," *Boston Herald*, January 24, 2005; and P. Reynolds, "Packaging for Kids at Kellogg and Dannon," *www.packworld.com*, accessed March 31, 2005.

QUESTIONS

1. What are the benefits of collaborating with customers on products?
2. What might be disadvantages of collaborating with customers on products?

Groupware   **Groupware** refers to software products that support groups of people who share a common task or goal and who collaborate to accomplish it. Groupware uses networks to connect people, even if the people are in the same room. In this section we will describe some of the most common groupware products.

Groupware technologies are often integrated with other computer-based technologies to create *groupware suites*. (A *software suite* is created when several products are integrated into one system.) Lotus Notes/Domino is one of the most popular groupware suites.

The Lotus Notes/Domino suite (*www.ibm.com*) provides online collaboration capabilities, workgroup e-mail, distributed databases, bulletin whiteboards, text editing, (electronic) document management, workflow capabilities, instant virtual meetings, application sharing, instant messaging, consensus building, voting, ranking, and various application development tools. All these capabilities are integrated into one environment with a graphic, menu-based user interface.

Two types of groupware technologies include electronic teleconferencing and real-time collaboration tools. A discussion of each type follows.

Participating in a desktop videoconference.
Source: thinkstock/Getty

Electronic Teleconferencing **Teleconferencing** is the use of electronic communication that allows two or more people at different locations to hold a simultaneous conference. There are several types of teleconferencing. The oldest and simplest is a telephone conference call, where several people talk to each other from multiple locations. The biggest disadvantage of conference calls is that they do not allow for face-to-face communication. Also, participants in one location cannot see graphs, charts, and pictures at other locations. One solution is *video teleconferencing*, in which participants can see one another as well as the documents.

In a **videoconference**, participants in one location can see participants at other locations. With videoconferencing, participants can share data, voice, pictures, graphics, and animation by electronic means. They can also transmit data along with voice and video, making it possible to work on documents together and to exchange computer files. This technology allows geographically dispersed groups to work on the same project and to communicate simultaneously by video. When videoconferencing is conducted over the Internet, it is called **Web conferencing**.

Real-Time Collaboration Tools The Internet, intranets, and extranets offer tremendous potential for real-time and synchronous interaction of people working in groups. *Real-time collaboration* (*RTC*) tools help companies bridge time and space to make decisions and to collaborate on projects. RTC tools support synchronous communication of graphical and text-based information. These tools are being used in distance training, product demonstrations, customer support, and sales applications.

For example, computer-based **whiteboards** enable all participants to join in. During meetings, each user can view and draw on a single document "pasted" onto the electronic whiteboard on a computer screen. Computer-based whiteboards can be used by participants in the same room or across the world. Digital whiteboarding sessions can also be saved for later reference or other use.

Web Services

The fourth major category of network applications is Web Services. **Web Services** are applications, delivered over the Internet, that users can select and combine through almost any device (from personal computers to mobile phones). By using a set of shared protocols and standards, these applications permit different systems to "talk" with one another—that is, to share data and services—without requiring human beings to translate the conversations.

Specifically, a Web Service fits the following three criteria: (1) It is able to announce and describe itself to other applications, allowing those applications to understand what the service does. (2) It can be located by other applications via an online directory, if it has been registered. (3) It can be invoked by the originating application by using standard protocols.

Web Services have great potential because they can be used in a variety of environments: over the Internet, on an intranet inside a corporate firewall, on an extranet set up by business partners. In addition, they can be written using a wide variety of development tools. Web Services perform a wide variety of tasks, from automating business processes to integrating components of an enterprisewide system to streamlining online buying and selling. IT's About Business 5.5 shows how Citigroup used Microsoft's .NET to provide a Web Services application for its employees.

Web Services are based on four key standards, or protocols: XML, SOAP, WSDI, and UDDI. We discuss each one below.

- *XML.* *Extensible Markup Language* makes it easier to exchange data among a variety of applications and to validate and interpret such data. An XML document describes a Web

IT's About Business

5.5 Citigroup Creates a Global, Web-Based Information Delivery System

Citigroup is the largest financial services group in the world. Its 120 million clients are served by 280,000 employees in 103 countries. More than 90 percent of Citigroup employees are local to the territory that they serve. This arrangement makes delivering and distributing information a particularly difficult, yet vital task for the company.

In order to serve their clients, Citigroup employees must have globally accessible, real-time information that is integrated from many sources in a readily understandable format. This information must also be delivered with collaboration tools, so that employees anywhere can interact with one another. Employees should share a common set of information. At the same time, however, they must be able to personalize the information for their needs. As one Citigroup executive put it, "We have the information available in a variety of sources and formats around the world; we just need a 'master key' to unlock it all."

To meet these requirements, Citigroup used Microsoft's .NET Web Services technology to build a corporate portal, which came to be called Citigroup CitiVision. The portal integrates 270 information sources, including internal and external sources, and makes this information available to Citigroup's global user base in real time. Users now have access to a wide range of information with a single-password logon. This information includes market data, internal company data, live streaming video, and customer profiles. With the CitiVision portal, Citigroup employees can now make better, faster decisions.

Sources: Compiled from C. Babcock, "Software's Next Step," *Wall Street Technology,* November 29, 2004; and *www.microsoft.com/resources/casestudies,* accessed March 23, 2005.

QUESTIONS

1. Why is it important to have a "common core" of information that is available to all employees?
2. Why is it important for employees to be able to customize some of that information?

Service, and it includes information detailing exactly how the Web Service can be run. (We describe XML in more detail in Technology Guide 2.)

- ***SOAP.*** *Simple Object Access Protocol* is a set of rules that facilitate XML exchange among network applications. SOAP defines a common standard that allows different Web Services to interoperate. That is, it enables communications, such as allowing Visual Basic clients to access a Java server. SOAP runs on all hardware and software systems. It defines how messages can be sent among systems through the use of XML.

- ***WSDL.*** The *Web Services Description Language* is used to create the XML document that describes the tasks performed by Web Services. Tools such as VisualStudio.Net automate the process of accessing the WSDL, reading it, and coding the application to reference the specific Web Service.

- ***UDDI.*** *Universal Description, Discovery, and Integration* allows for the creation of public or private searchable directories of Web Services. It is the registry of Web Services descriptions. UDDI allows users and applications to search for needed Web Services.

Before you go on . . .

1. Describe the four major network applications and the tools and technologies that support each one.
2. Describe the protocols underlying Web Services.

5.5 E-Learning and Distance Learning

E-learning and distance learning are not the same thing, but they do overlap each other. **E-learning** refers to learning supported by the Web. It can take place inside classrooms as a support to conventional teaching, such as when students work on the Web during class. It also can take place in *virtual classrooms*, in which all coursework is done online and classes do not meet face-to-face. In these cases, e-learning is a part of distance learning. **Distance learning (DL)** refers to any learning situation in which teachers and students do not meet face-to-face.

Today, the Web provides a multimedia interactive environment for self-study. Web-enabled systems make knowledge accessible to those who need it, when they need it, any time, anywhere. For this reason, E-learning and DL can be useful both for formal education and for corporate training.

The Benefits of E-Learning

There are many benefits to e-learning. For example, online materials can deliver very current content that is of high quality (created by content experts) and consistent (presented the same way every time). It also gives students the flexibility to learn from any place, at any time, and at their own pace. In corporate training centers that use e-learning, learning time generally is shorter, which means that more people can be trained within a given time frame. This system reduces training costs as well as the expense of renting facility space.

Despite these benefits, e-learning has some drawbacks. To begin with, students must be computer literate. Also, they may miss the face-to-face interaction with instructors. Finally, assessing students' work can be problematic because instructors really do not know who completed the assignments.

E-learning does not usually replace the classroom setting. Rather, it enhances it by taking advantage of new content and delivery technologies. Advanced e-learning support environments, such as Blackboard (*www.blackboard.com*) and WebCT (*www.webct.com*), add value to traditional learning in higher education.

Virtual Universities

Virtual universities are online universities from which students take classes from home or at an off-site location, via the Internet. A large number of existing universities offer online education of some form. Some universities, such as the University of Phoenix (*www.phoenix.edu*), California Virtual Campus (*www.cvc.edu*), and the University of Maryland (*www.umuc.edu/distance*), offer thousands of courses and dozens of degrees to students worldwide, all online. Other universities offer limited online courses and degrees but use innovative teaching methods and multimedia support in the traditional classroom.

Before you go on . . .

1. Differentiate between e-learning and distance learning.
2. Describe virtual universities.

5.6 Telecommuting

Telecommuting refers to an arrangement whereby employees can work at sites other than their office. These sites include their home, the customer's premises, and special work places. Telecommuters can also perform their jobs while traveling, for example, on an airplane flight. They generally use a computer that is linked to their place of employment via the Internet.

Telecommuting has a number of potential advantages for employees, employers, and society. For employees, the benefits include reduced stress and improved family life. In addition, telecommuting offers employment opportunities for housebound people such as single parents and persons with disabilities. Employer benefits include increased productivity, the ability to retain skilled employees, and the ability to attract employees who don't live within commuting distance. For example, in 2004 Cigna's 6,000 "E-workers" delivered 4 to 12 percent more output than office workers doing similar work. In addition, the company saved $3,000 per employee on reduced office space.

However, telecommuting also has some potential disadvantages. For employees, the major disadvantages are increased feelings of isolation, possible loss of fringe benefits, lower pay (in some cases), no workplace visibility, the potential for slower promotions, and lack of socialization. The major disadvantages to employers are difficulties in supervising work, potential data security problems, training costs, and the high cost of equipping and maintaining telecommuters' homes.

Before you go on . . .

1. What is telecommuting? Do you think you would like to telecommute?

2. What are the advantages and disadvantages of telecommuting from the viewpoint of the employee? From the viewpoint of the organization?

What's in IT for me?

For the Accounting Major

Accounting personnel use corporate intranets and portals to consolidate transaction data from legacy systems to provide an overall view of internal projects. This view contains the current costs charged to each project, the number of hours spent on each project by individual employees, and how actual costs compare to projected costs. Finally, accounting personnel use Internet access to government and professional Web sites to stay informed on legal and other changes affecting their profession.

For the Finance Major

Corporate intranets and portals can provide a model to evaluate the risks of a project or an investment. Financial analysts use two types of data in the model: historical transaction data from corporate databases via the intranet, and industry data obtained via the Internet. In addition, financial services firms can use the Web for marketing and to provide services.

For the Marketing Major

Marketing managers use corporate intranets and portals to coordinate the activities of the sales force. Sales personnel access corporate portals via the intranet to discover updates on pricing, promotion, rebates, customer information, and information about competitors. Sales staff can also download and customize presentations for their customers. The Internet, particularly the Web, opens a completely new marketing channel for many industries. Just how advertising, purchasing, and information dispensation should occur appears to vary from industry to industry, product to product, and service to service.

For the Production/Operations Management Major

Companies are using intranets and portals to speed product development by providing the development team with three-dimensional models and animation. All team members can access the models for faster exploration of ideas and enhanced feedback. Corporate portals, accessed via intranets, provide for close management of both inventories and real-time production on assembly lines. Extranets are also proving valuable as communication formats for joint research and design efforts among companies. The Internet is also a great source of cutting-edge information for POM managers.

For the Human Resources Management Major

Human resources personnel use portals and intranets to publish corporate policy manuals, job postings, company telephone directories, and training classes. Many companies deliver online training obtained from the Internet to employees through their intranets. Via intranets, human resources departments offer employees health care, savings, and benefit plans, as well as the opportunity to take competency tests online. The Internet supports worldwide recruiting efforts, and it can also be the communications platform for supporting geographically dispersed work teams.

The MIS Function

As important as the networking technology infrastructure is, it is invisible to users (unless something goes wrong). The MIS function is responsible for keeping all organizational networks up and running all the time. MIS personnel, therefore, provide all users with an "eye to the world" and the ability to compute, communicate, and collaborate any time, anywhere. For example, organizations have access to experts at remote locations without having to duplicate that expertise in multiple areas of the firm. Virtual teaming allows experts physically located in different cities to work on projects as though they were in the same office.

Summary

1. Describe the two major types of networks.

The two major types of networks are local area networks and wide area networks. LANs encompass a limited geographic area and are usually composed of one communications medium. WANs encompass a broad geographical area and are usually composed of multiple communications media.

2. Differentiate among the Internet, the World Wide Web, intranets, and extranets.

The *Internet* is a global network of computer networks, using a common cmmunications protocol, TCP/IP. The *World Wide Web* is a system that stores, retrieves, formats, and displays information accessible through a browser. An *intranet* is a network designed to serve the internal informational needs of a company, using Internet concepts and tools. An *extranet* connects portions of the intranets of different organization and allows secure communications among business partners over the Internet.

3. Describe the four major network applications.

Networks support discovery, communication, collaboration, and Web Services. Discovery involves browsing and information retrieval, and provides users the ability to view information in databases, download it, and/or process it. Discovery tools include search engines, directories, software agents, toolbars, and portals. Networks provide fast, inexpensive communications, via e-mail, call centers, chat rooms, voice communications, and blogs. Collaboration refers to mutual efforts by two or more entities (individuals, groups, or companies) who work together to accomplish tasks. Collaboration is enabled by workflow systems and groupware. Web Services are self-contained, self-describing applications, delivered over the Internet, that users can select and combine through almost any device (from personal computers to mobile phones). By using a set of shared protocols and standards, these applications permit different systems to talk with one another—that is, to share data and services—without requiring human beings to translate the conversations.

4. Describe groupware capabilities.

Groupware products provide a way for groups to share resources and opinions. For example, the Lotus Notes/Domino suite provides online collaboration capabilities, work group e-mail, distributed databases, bulletin whiteboards, text editing, (electronic) document management, workflow capabilities, instant virtual meetings, application sharing, instant messaging, consensus building, voting, ranking, and various application development tools.

5. Differentiate between e-learning and distance learning.

E-learning refers to learning supported by the Web. It can take place inside classrooms as a support to conventional teaching, such as when students work on the Web during class. It also can take place in *virtual classrooms*, in which all coursework is done online and classes do not meet face-to-face. In these cases, e-learning is a part of distance learning. Distance learning refers to any learning situation in which teachers and students do not meet face-to-face.

6. Understand the advantages and disadvantages of telecommuting for both employers and employees.

For employees who telecommute, there is less stress, improved family life, and employment opportunities for housebound people. Telecommuting can provide the organization with increased productivity, the ability to retain skilled employees, and the ability to tap the remote labor pool.

The major disadvantages for the employees are increased feelings of isolation, possible loss of fringe benefits, lower pay (in some cases), no workplace visibility, the potential for slower promotions, and lack of socialization. The major disadvantages to employers are difficulties in supervising work, potential data security problems, training costs, and the high cost of equipping and maintaining telecommuters' homes.

Discussion Questions

1. What are the implications of having fiber-optic cable going to everyone's home?
2. Do you feel that satellite telephones will eventually replace today's cell phones? Support your answer.
3. Should the Internet be regulated? If so, by whom?
4. Discuss the pros and cons of delivering this book over the Internet.
5. List the types of communication tools you use each day (e.g., e-mail, voice mail, fax, instant messages, pagers, telephone, cell phone, etc.). Which do you use the most? What are the strengths and weaknesses of each?
6. Explain how the Internet works. Assume you are talking with someone who has no knowledge of information technology (i.e., keep it very simple).
7. When you access Web pages, do some take longer to download than others? Why? Explain your answer.
8. How are the network applications of communication and collaboration related? Do communication tools also support collaboration? Give examples.
9. Is telecommuting a good idea? Elaborate on the pros and cons.

Problem-Solving Activities

1. You plan to take a two-week vacation in Austria this year. Using the Internet, find information that will help you plan the trip. Such information includes, *but is not limited to*, the following:
   a. Geographical location and weather conditions at the time of your trip.
   b. Major tourist attractions and recreational facilities.
   c. Travel arrangements (airlines, approximate fares).
   d. Car rental; local tours.
   e. Alternatives for accommodation (within a moderate budget) and food.
   f. Estimated cost of the vacation (travel, lodging, food, recreation, shopping, etc).
   g. Country regulations regarding the entrance of your dog that you would like to take with you.
   h. Shopping.
   i. Passport information (either to obtain one or renew one).
   j. Information on the country's language and culture.
   k. What else do you think you should research before going to Austria?

2. From your own experience or from the vendor's information, list the major capabilities of Lotus Notes/Domino. Do the same for Microsoft Exchange. Compare and contrast the products. Explain how the products can be used to support knowledge workers and managers.

3. Visit *www.polycom.com* and sites of other companies that manufacture conferencing products for the Internet. Prepare a report. Why are conferencing products considered part of video commerce?

4. Access the Web site of your university. Does the Web site provide high-quality information (right amount, clear, accurate, etc.)? Do you think a high-school student who is thinking of attending your university would feel the same way?

Internet Activities

1. Access the Web site of the Recording Industry Association of America (*www.riaa.com*). Discuss what you find there regarding copyright infringement (i.e., downloading music files). How do you feel about the RIAA's efforts to stop music downloads? Debate this issue from your point of view and from the RIAA's point of view.

2. Visit *www.cdt.org*. Find what technologies are available to track users' activities on the Internet.

3. Research the companies involved in Internet telephony (voice-over IP). Compare their offerings as to price, necessary technologies, ease of installation, etc. Which company is the most attractive to you? Which company might be the most attractive for a large company?

4. Access the Web sites of companies entering the satellite market and obtain the latest information regarding the status of their satellite constellations. Prepare a report detailing the current status of these constellations.

Team Assignments

1. Assign each group member to an integrated group support tool kit (Lotus Notes, Exceloncorp, GroupWise, etc.). Have each member visit the Web site of the commercial developer and obtain information about this product. As a group, prepare a comparative table of the major similarities and differences among the kits.

2. Assign each team to a college collaborative tool such as Blackboard, WebCT, etc. Establish common evaluative criteria. Have each team evaluate the capabilities and limitations of its tool, and convince each team that its product is superior.

3. Have each team download a free copy of Groove from *www.groove.net*. Install the software on the members' PCs and arrange collaborative sessions. What can the free software do for you? What are its limitations?

CASE **Network Pulls a Company Together**

THE BUSINESS PROBLEM Advance Auto Parts (*www.advanceautoparts.com*) has been around since 1932. In 1998, an investment firm purchased the company and began a period of rapid expansion, opening hundreds of new outlets and buying out competitors. The company ended up with more than 2,500 stores. Unfortunately, it also ended up with different sales strategies, systems, and management philosophies. As a result, the company faced a big challenge in integrating new employees into its operations and promoting brand recognition among its consumers. Employees had to quickly become familiar with Advance's products, sales systems, and corporate culture.

THE IT SOLUTION Advance decided to use an in-store media network with programming showing on television screens around the stores. Programming is delivered to stores via satellite, with appropriate video feeds targeted to specific stores. For example, stores in centers with large Hispanic populations receive programming in Spanish, and newly opened stores receive a specific feed. Programming can also be delivered to individual flat screens in stores, because each screen has its own IP address.

The satellite feeds also transmit other corporate data between the stores and the head office, such as the electronic parts catalog. In the morning before the store opens, the network delivers information on training seminars, new in-store computer systems, and product introductions, as well as company news. After the doors open, the programming switches to sports scores, car parts and accessories, and repair tips.

THE RESULTS Originally, Advance believed they could make money by selling advertising on the network. This has not yet turned out to be the case. Although Advance sells ads to suppliers such as Halvoline Motor Oil and Bondo Filler, advertisers have been slow to embrace the concept.

The system makes its greatest impact when the stores are busy and customers are waiting in line. For some products such as a new carburetor, the customer has a definite need and is not subject to impulse advertising on the screens. However, for other items, such as motor oil, Advance's network has had success in driving in-store sales. For example, a recent promotion for Bosch windshield wipers increased sales by 62 percent.

The network's biggest impact to date, however, had nothing to do with the bottom line. The network's programming includes spots for the National Center for Missing and Exploited Children with "America's Most Wanted." In June 2003, an employee spotted an abductor with a child in an Advance store and called the police. As a result of the employee's actions, the boy was reunited with his mother after four years.

Sources: Compiled from T. Serafin, "Hoping for a Bad Winter," *Forbes*, January 10, 2005; M. Duvall, "Screening Rooms," *Baseline Magazine*, March 1, 2004; and "Advanced Auto Parts Opens," *Chesterton Tribune*, August 5, 2004.

QUESTIONS

1. Do you feel that in-store media advertising is effective or just annoying?
2. Should stores collect feedback from their customers about in-store media? If so, then what types of information should they collect? How should they use this information?

Interactive Learning

From Tokyo to Atlanta: How Does an International Bank Stay Connected?

Go to the Interactivities section on the *WileyPLUS* Web Site and access Chapter 5: Network Computing. There you will find an interactive simulation of the technologies used for communication between the headquarters and regional offices of an international bank, as well as some hands-on activities that visually explain business concepts in this chapter.

Telecommunications at Club IT

Go to the Club IT link on the *WileyPLUS* Web site. There you will find assignments that will ask you to advise the club owners on how they can use databases to track information for their business.

wiley.com/college/rainer

Telecommunications Appendix

Learning Objectives

1. Understand the basic telecommunications system.
2. Describe the eight basic types of communications media, including their advantages and disadvantages.
3. Identify the major types of network services.
4. Describe the Ethernet and TCP/IP protocols.
5. Differentiate between client/server computing and peer-to-peer computing.

The Telecommunications System

A **telecommunications system** consists of hardware and software that transmit information from one location to another. These systems can transmit text, data, graphics, voice, documents, or full-motion video information. They transmit this information with two basic types of signals, analog and digital. **Analog signals** are continuous waves that transmit information by altering the characteristics of the waves. Analog signals have two parameters, amplitude and frequency. For example, voice and all sound are analog, traveling to human ears in the form of waves. The higher the waves (or amplitude), the louder the sound; the more closely packed the waves, the higher the frequency or pitch. **Digital signals** are discrete pulses that are either on or off, representing a series of *bits* (0s and 1s). This quality allows them to convey information in a binary form that can be clearly interpreted by computers. See Figure 5.A1 for a graphic representation of analog and digital signals.

The major components of a telecommunications system include the following: servers, communications processors, communications channels and media, and client computers. **Servers** are computers that provide access to various services available on the network, such as printing, data, and communications. There are many types of servers, one of which is the

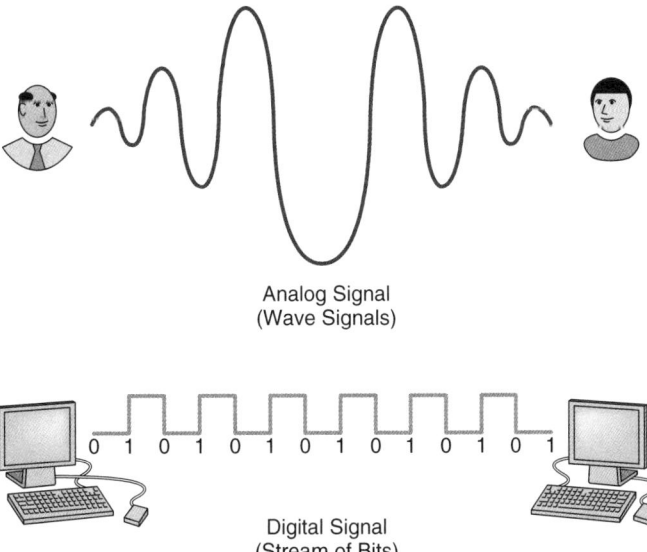

Analog Signal
(Wave Signals)

Digital Signal
(Stream of Bits)

FIGURE 5.A1
Analog and digital signals.

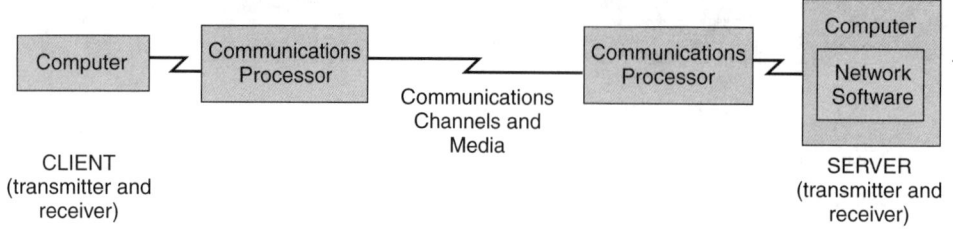

FIGURE 5.A2
Typical
telecommunications
system.

LAN file server. **Clients** are computers, such as a user's personal computer, that use any of the services provided by servers. Figure 5.A2 shows a typical telecommunications system. Note that these systems communicate in both directions, so clients and servers are both transmitters and receivers.

Communications Processors

Communications processors are hardware devices that support data transmission and reception across a telecommunications system. These devices include modems, multiplexers, and front-end processors.

Modem   The U.S. public telephone system (called POTS, for "Plain Old Telephone Service") was designed as an analog network to carry voice signals or sounds in an analog wave format. In order for this type of circuit to carry digital information, that information must be converted into an analog wave pattern. The conversion from digital to analog is called *modulation*, and the reverse is *demodulation*. The device that performs these two processes is called a **modem**, a contraction of the terms *mo*dulate/*dem*odulate (see Figure 5.A3).

Modems are used in pairs. The modem at the sending end converts a computer's digital information into analog signals for transmission over analog lines. At the receiving end, another modem converts the analog signal back into digital signals for the receiving computer. Like most communications equipment, a modem's transmission speed is measured in bits per second (bps). Modem speeds range up to 56,600 bps.

Multiplexer   A **multiplexer** is an electronic device that allows a single communications channel to carry data transmissions simultaneously from many sources. Multiplexing can be accomplished by dividing a high-speed channel into multiple channels of slower speeds or by assigning each transmission source a very small amount of time for using the high-speed channel. Multiplexers lower communication costs by allowing devices to share communications channels. Multiplexing thus makes more efficient use of these channels by merging the transmissions of several computers (e.g., personal computers) at one end of the channel, while a similar unit separates the individual transmissions at the receiving end (e.g., a mainframe).

FIGURE 5.A3
Twisted-pair wire.

Front-End Processor With most mainframe and minicomputers, the central processing unit (CPU) must communicate with multiple computers at the same time. Routine communication tasks can absorb a large proportion of the CPU's processing time, leading to degraded performance on more important jobs. In order not to waste valuable CPU time, many computer systems have a small secondary computer dedicated solely to communication. Known as a **front-end processor**, this specialized computer manages all routing communications with peripheral devices.

Communications Media and Channels

For data to be communicated from one location to another, some form of pathway or medium must be used. These pathways are called **communications channels**. The communications channels, in two types of media, are shown below.

Cable Media	**Broadcast Media**	
1. Twisted-pair	4. Microwave	7. Cellular radio
2. Coaxial cable	5. Satellite	8. Infrared
3. Fiber optic	6. Radio	

Cable or **wireline media** use physical wires or cables to transmit data and information. Twisted-pair wire and coaxial cable are made of copper, and fiber-optic cable is made of glass. The alternative is communication over **broadcast** or **wireless media**. The key to mobile communications in today's rapidly moving society is data transmissions over electromagnetic media—the "airwaves." We discuss wireless media in Chapter 7. Manager's Checklist 5.A1 summarizes the advantages and disadvantages of the various wireline communications channels. We discuss each of the wireline channels in this section.

Twisted-Pair Wire **Twisted-pair wire** is the most prevalent form of communications wiring; it is used for almost all business telephone wiring. Twisted-pair wire consists of strands of copper wire twisted in pairs. It is relatively inexpensive to purchase, widely available, and easy to work with. It can be made relatively unobtrusive by running it inside walls,

Manager's Checklist 5.A1

Advantages and Disadvantages of Wireline Communications Channels

Channel	Advantages	Disadvantages
Twisted-pair wire	Inexpensive. Widely available. Easy to work with. Unobtrusive.	Slow (low bandwidth). Subject to interference. Easily tapped (low security).
Coaxial cable	Higher bandwidth than twisted-pair. Less susceptible to electromagnetic interference.	Relatively expensive and inflexible. Easily tapped (low-to-medium security). Somewhat difficult to work with.
Fiber-optic cable	Very high bandwidth. Relatively inexpensive. Difficult to tap (good security).	Difficult to work with (difficult to splice).

floors, and ceilings. However, twisted-pair wire has some significant disadvantages. It is relatively slow for transmitting data, it is subject to interference from other electrical sources, and it can be easily tapped for gaining unauthorized access to data by unintended receivers.

Coaxial Cable **Coaxial cable** (Figure 5.A4) consists of insulated copper wire. It is much less susceptible to electrical interference than is twisted-pair wire, and it can carry much more data. For these reasons, it is commonly used to carry high-speed data traffic as well as television signals (thus the term cable TV). However, coaxial cable is more expensive and more difficult to work with than twisted-pair wire. It is also somewhat inflexible.

Fiber Optics **Fiber-optic cables** (Figure 5.A5) consist of thousands of very thin filaments of glass fibers that transmit information via light pulses generated by lasers. The fiber-optic cable is surrounded by cladding, a coating that prevents the light from leaking out of the fiber.

Fiber-optic cables are significantly smaller and lighter than traditional cable media. They also can transmit far more data, and they provide greater security from interference and tapping. Optical fiber has reached data transmission rates of 6 trillion bits (terabits) per second. Fiber-optic cable is typically used as the backbone for a network, while twisted-pair wire and coaxial cable connect the backbone to individual devices on the network.

Attenuation is the reduction in the strength of a signal. It occurs for both analog and digital signals, and is also a problem for fiber optics. Attenuation requires manufacturers to install equipment to receive the weakened or distorted signals and send them out amplified to their original strength.

Transmission Speed

Bandwidth refers to the range of frequencies available in any communications channel. Bandwidth is a very important concept in communications because the transmission capacity of any channel (stated in bits per second or bps) is largely dependent on its bandwidth. In general, the greater the bandwidth, the greater the channel capacity.

The speeds of particular communications channels are as follows:

- Twisted-pair wire: up to 100 Mbps (million bits per second)
- Microwave: up to 200 Mbps
- Satellite: up to 200 Mbps
- Coaxial cable: up to 200 Mbps
- Fiber-optic cable: up to 6 Tbps (trillion bits per second)

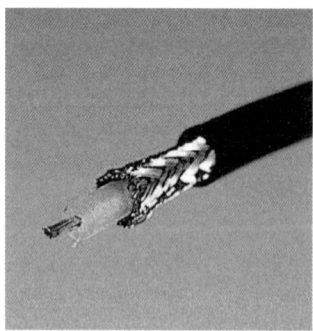

FIGURE 5.A4 Coaxial cable.

FIGURE 5.A5 Fiber-optic cable.

Before you go on . . .

1. Describe the basic telecommunications system.
2. Compare and contrast the wireline communications channels.

Network Fundamentals

This section addresses three topics: network services, network protocols, and types of network processing. These topics describe how networks actually transmit and process data and information over the basic telecommunications system.

Network Services

Networks provide a number of services designed to enable rapid, high-volume, accurate data transmission over any type of network.

Integrated Services Digital Network **Integrated services digital network (ISDN)** is a high-speed, digital data-transmission technology that uses existing telephone lines and allows users to transfer voice, video, image, and data simultaneously at high speed. ISDN transmission is a popular upgrade with firms whose transmission requirements exceed standard telephone capacity. Because ISDN is digital, you can use it to connect your PC to the Internet.

Digital Subscriber Line **Digital subscriber lines (DSL)** provide high-speed, digital data transmission from homes and businesses over existing telephone lines. Because the existing lines are analog and the transmission is digital, you need a modem to use DSL technology. DSL is a popular alternative to ISDN.

Cable Modems **Cable modems** are modems that operate over coaxial cable (e.g., cable TV). They offer high-speed access to the Internet or corporate intranets at speeds of up to 4 Mbps. Cable modems use a shared line. Therefore, when large numbers of users access the same modem, they can slow down the access speed.

Asynchronous Transfer Mode **Asynchronous transfer mode (ATM)** networks allow for almost unlimited bandwidth on demand. These networks are packet-switched, eliminating the need for protocol conversion. ATM creates a virtual connection for the packet transmission, which disappears on the completion of a successful transmission.

ATM offers several advantages. It makes possible large increases in bandwidth. It provides support for data, video, and voice transmissions on a single communications line. It offers virtual networking capabilities, which increase bandwidth utilization and simplify network administration. ATM currently requires fiber-optic cable, but it can transmit up to 2.5 gigabits per second. On the downside, ATM is more expensive than ISDN and DSL.

Switched-Hub Technologies **Switched-hub technologies** are often used to boost local area networks. A switched hub can turn many small LANs into one big LAN. A network need not be rewired nor adapter cards replaced when changes are made. Instead, all that is needed is the addition of a switching hub. Switched-hub technology can also add an ATM-like packet-switching capability to existing LANs, essentially doubling their bandwidth.

Synchronous Optical Network **Synchronous optical network (SONET)** is an interface standard for transporting digital signals over fiber-optic lines that allows the integration of transmissions from multiple vendors. SONET defines optical line rates, known as optical carrier (OC) signals. The base rate is 51.84 Mbps (OC-1), and higher rates are direct multiples of the base rate. For example, OC-3 runs at 155.52 Mbps, or three times the rate of OC-1.

T-Carrier System   The **T-carrier system** is a digital transmission system that defines circuits that operate at different rates, all of which are multiples of the basic 64 Kbps used to transport a single voice call. These circuits include T1 (1.544 Mbps, equivalent to 24 channels); T2 (6.312 Mbps, equivalent to 96 channels); T3 (44.736 Mbps, equivalent to 672 channels); and T4 (274.176 Mbps, equivalent to 4,032 channels).

Network Protocols

Computing devices that are connected to the network access and share the network to transmit and receive data. These components are often referred to as "nodes" of the network. They work together by adhering to a common set of rules that enable them to communicate with one another. This set of rules and procedures that govern transmission across a network is a **protocol**.

The principal functions of protocols in a network are line access and collision avoidance. *Line access* concerns how the sending device gains access to the network to send a message. *Collision avoidance* refers to managing message transmission so that two messages do not collide with each other on the network. Other functions of protocols are to identify each device in the communication path, to secure the attention of the other device, to verify correct receipt of the transmitted message, to verify that a message requires retransmission because it cannot be correctly interpreted, and to perform recovery when errors occur.

Ethernet   The most common network protocol is **Ethernet**. Ethernet 10BaseT means that the network has a speed of 10 Mbps. Fast Ethernet is 100BaseT, meaning that the network has a speed of 100 Mbps. The most common protocol in large corporations is the gigabit Ethernet. That is, the network provides data transmission speeds of one billion bits per second. However, 10-gigabit Ethernet is becoming the standard (10 billion bits per second).

TCP/IP   The **Transmission Control Protocol/Internet Protocol (TCP/IP)** is a file transfer protocol that can send large files of information across sometimes-unreliable networks with assurance that the data will arrive in uncorrupted form. TCP/IP is the protocol of the Internet. It allows efficient and reasonably error-free transmission between different systems. TCP/IP is very popular with business organizations due to its reliability and the ease with which it can support intranets and related functions.

The International Standards Organization Open Systems Interconnection Protocol   Network devices from different vendors must communicate with one another by following the same protocols. Unfortunately, commercially available data communication devices follow a number of different protocols, causing substantial problems with data communications networks.

Attempts at standardizing data communications have been somewhat successful. Nevertheless, standardization in the United States has lagged behind other countries in which the communications industry is more closely regulated. Various organizations, including the Electronic Industries Association (EIA), the Consultative Committee for International Telegraph and Telephone (CCITT), and the International Standards Organization (ISO), have developed electronic interfacing protocols that are widely used within the industry.

Typically, the protocols required to achieve communication on behalf of an application are actually multiple protocols that exist at different levels or layers. Each layer defines a set of functions that are provided as services to upper layers, and each layer relies on services provided by lower layers. At each layer, one or more protocols define precisely how software on different systems interacts to accomplish the functions for that layer. This layering notion has been formalized in several architectures. The most widely known is the Open Systems Interconnection (OSI) model of the International Standards Organization (ISO). The *ISO-OSI model* defines how software on different systems communicates at different layers. The model has seven layers, each having its own well-defined function.

> *Layer 1: Physical layer.* Defines the mechanism for communicating with the transmission media and interface hardware.
> *Layer 2: Data link layer.* Validates the integrity of the flow of data.
> *Layer 3: Network layer.* Defines the protocols for data routing to ensure that information arrives at the correct destination.
> *Layer 4: Transport layer.* Defines the protocols for structuring messages.
> *Layer 5: Session layer.* Coordinates communications and maintains the session for as long as needed, including security and log-on functions.
> *Layer 6: Presentation layer.* Defines the way data are formatted, converted, and encoded.
> *Layer 7: Application layer.* Defines the way that application programs such as e-mail interact with the network.

Types of Network Processing

Organizations typically use multiple computer systems across the firm. **Distributed processing** divides processing work among two or more computers. This process enables computers in different locations to communicate with one another via telecommunications links. A common type of distributed processing is client/server processing. A special type of client/server processing is peer-to-peer processing.

Client/Server Computing   **Client/server computing** links two or more computers in an arrangement in which some machines (called servers) provide computing services for user PCs (called clients). Usually, an organization does the bulk of its processing or application/data storage on suitably powerful servers that can be accessed by less powerful client machines. The client requests applications, data, or processing from the server, which acts on these requests by "serving" the desired commodity.

Client/server computing leads to the ideas of "fat" clients and "thin" clients. *Fat clients* have large storage and processing power and can still run local programs (e.g., Microsoft Office) if the network is down. *Thin clients* may have no local storage and limited processing power. Thus, they must depend on the network to run applications. Network computers are popular thin clients.

Peer-to-Peer Processing   **Peer-to-peer (P2P) processing** is a type of client/server distributed processing where each computer acts as *both* a client and a server. Each computer can access (as assigned for security or integrity purposes) all files on all other computers.

There are three basic types of peer-to-peer processing. The first accesses unused CPU power among networked computers. A well-known application of this type is SETI@home (*http://setiathome.ssl.berkeley.edu*) (Figure 5.A6). These applications are from open-source projects and can be downloaded at no cost.

The second form of peer-to-peer is real-time, person-to-person collaboration, such as America Online's Instant Messenger. Companies such as Groove Networks (*www.groove.net*) have introduced P2P collaborative applications that use buddy lists to establish a connection, then allow real-time collaboration within the application. The third peer-to-peer category is advanced search and file sharing. This category is characterized by natural-language searches of millions of peer systems and lets users discover other users, not just data and Web pages. One example of this is Madster (*www.madster.com*), which allows searching of the major Internet file-sharing services, such as AOL and Gnutella. In the example below, BitTorrent shows that P2P software continues to evolve.

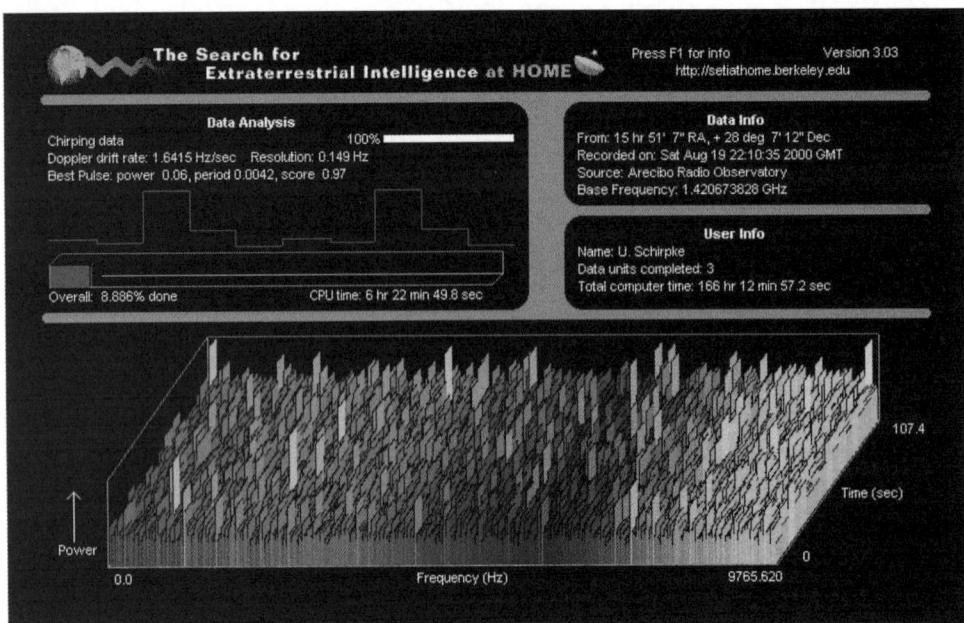

FIGURE 5.A6
SETI@home.

P2P: Good News and Bad News BitTorrent (*www.bittorrent.com*) is an open-source, free, peer-to-peer file-sharing application that is able to simplify the problem of sharing large files by dividing them into tiny pieces, or "torrents." BitTorrent addresses two of the biggest problems of file sharing: (1) Downloading bogs down when lots of people access a file at once, and (2) some people leech, downloading content but refusing to share. BitTorrent eliminates the bottleneck by having everyone share little pieces of a file at the same time—a process called *swarming*. The program prevents leeching because users must upload a file while they download it. This means that the more popular the content, the more efficiently it zips over a network. According to CacheLogic (*www.cachelogic.com*), more than 30 million people are using BitTorrent, and the software now accounts for about one-third of all Internet traffic.

One problem with BitTorrent is that users have to connect to other users through a "tracker" site. The operators of those tracker sites are, therefore, targets for the Motion Picture Association of America (MPAA) and the Recording Industry Association of America (RIAA). The MPAA has filed dozens of civil suits against tracker sites in the United States and Britain. However, BitTorrent may be a step ahead of the lawyers. For every tracker site that is legally challenged and shut down, another pops up. As open-source software, BitTorrent does not reside on a central site that can be shut down. In addition, it continually evolves as software writers enhance the code.

A recent upgrade, Exeem (*www.exeem.com*), blends the swarming technology with robust search capabilities. Instead of visiting tracker sites, users enter a title in a search box, and Exeem scours the Web for the file.

BitTorrent does have legitimate uses. A software firm like Red Hat (*www.redhat.com*) uses it to send out updates of its Linux products, lowering its bandwidth costs. Nonprofit sites like etree (*www.etree.org*) use it to distribute live concerts, with the blessings of the musicians. (*Sources:* Compiled from D. Fonda, "Downloading Hollywood," *Time*, February 14, 2005; "Torrentspy.com," *PC Magazine*, April 6, 2005; and C. Metz, "The New Peer-to-Peer Players," *PC Magazine*, November 16, 2004.)

Example

Before you go on . . .

1. Compare and contrast the ATM, SONET, and T-carrier systems.
2. What is a network protocol?
3. Describe the Ethernet and TCP/IP protocols.
4. What is the ISO/OSI model?
5. Differentiate between client/server computing and peer-to-peer processing.

1. Describe the basic telecommunications system.

Telecommunications systems are composed computers, which act as transmitters and receivers of information; communications processors (e.g., modems, multiplexers, and front-end processors); communications channels and media; and networking software.

2. Describe the eight basic types of communications media, including their advantages and disadvantages.

The eight basic types of communications media are twisted-pair wire, coaxial cable, fiber-optic cable, microwave, satellite, radio, cellular radio, and infrared transmission. The first three media are cable media, and the remaining five are broadcast (wireless) media. Manager's Checklist 5.A1 describes the advantages and disadvantages of each wireline medium.

3. Describe the major types of network services.

Integrated services digital network (ISDN) technology allows users to transfer voice, video, image, and data simultaneously at high speed, using existing telephone lines. *Digital subscriber lines* provide high-speed, digital data transmission, also over existing telephone lines. *Cable modems* operate over coaxial cable (e.g., cable TV). *Asynchronous transfer mode (ATM)* networks are packet-switched and allow for almost unlimited bandwidth on demand. *Switched-hub technologies* boost local area networks by turning many small LANs into one big LAN. *Synchronous optical network (SONET)* is an interface standard for transporting digital signals over fiber-optic lines, allowing integration of transmissions from multiple vendors. The *T-carrier system* is a digital transmission system, whose circuits operate at different rates, all of which are multiples of 64 Kbps.

4. Describe the Ethernet and TCP/IP protocols.

The most common network protocol is *Ethernet*. Ethernet 10BaseT means that the network has a speed of 10 Mbps. Fast Ethernet is 100BaseT, meaning that the network has a speed of 100 Mbps. The most common protocol in large corporations is the gigabit Ethernet, which provides data transmission speeds of one billion bits per second. The 10-gigabit Ethernet (10 billion bits per second) is becoming the standard. The *Transmission Control Protocol/Internet Protocol (TCP/IP)* is a file transfer, packet-switching, protocol that can send large files of information with assurance that the data will arrive in uncorrupted form. TCP/IP is the communications protocol of the Internet.

5. Differentiate between client/server computing and peer-to-peer computing.

Client/server architecture divides processing between clients and servers. Both are on the network, but each processor is assigned functions it is best suited to perform. In a client/server approach, the components of an application (i.e., presentation, application, and data management) are distributed over the enterprise rather than being centrally controlled. Peer-to-peer processing is a type of client/server distributed processing that allows two or more computers to pool their resources, so that each computer acts as both a client and a server.

Chapter Glossary

analog signal Continuous waves that transmit information by altering the amplitude and frequency of the waves. (162)

affinity portal Web site that offers a single point of entry to an entire community of affiliated interests. (146)

asynchronous transfer mode (ATM) Data transmission technology that uses packet switching and allows for almost unlimited bandwidth on demand. (166)

backbone network The main fiber-optic network that links the nodes of a network. (137)

bandwidth The range of frequencies available in a communications channel, stated in bits per second. (165)

broadcast (wireless) media Communications channels that use electromagnetic media (the "airwaves") to transmit data. (164)

bridge A communications processor that connects two networks of the same type. (137)

browsers Software applications through which users primarily access the Web. (142)

cable (wireline) media Communications channels that use physical wires or cables to transmit data and information. (164)

cable modem A modem that operates over coaxial cable and offers high-speed access to the Internet or corporate intranets. (166)

chat room A virtual meeting place where groups of regulars come to "gab" electronically. (149)

client Computers, such as users' personal computers, that use any of the services provided by servers. (163)

client/server computing Form of distributed processing in which some machines (servers) perform computing functions for end-user PCs (clients). (168)

coaxial cable Insulated copper wire; used to carry high-speed data traffic and television signals. (165)

collaboration Mutual efforts by two or more individuals who perform activities in order to accomplish certain tasks. (152)

commercial (public) portal Web site that offers fairly routine content for diverse audiences; offers customization only at the user interface. (146)

communications processors Hardware devices that support data transmission and reception across a telecommunications system. (163)

communications channel Pathway for communicating data from one location to another. (164)

computer network A system connecting communications media, hardware, and software needed by two or more computer systems and/or devices. (135)

corporate portal Web site that provides a single point of access to critical business information located inside and outside of an organization. (146)

darknet A private network that runs on the Internet but is open only to users who belong to it. (139)

directory A hierarchically organized collection of links to Web pages, compiled manually; an example is Yahoo. (143)

digital signal A discrete pulse, either on or off, that conveys information in a binary form. (162)

digital subscriber line (DSL) A high-speed, digital data-transmission technology using existing analog telephone lines. (166)

distance learning (DL) Learning situations in which teachers and students do not meet face-to-face. (156)

distributed processing Network architecture that divides processing work between two or more computers, linked together in a network. (168)

domain name The name assigned to an Internet site, consisting of multiple parts, separated by dots, which are translated from right to left. (141)

domain name system (DNS) The system administered by the Internet Corporation for Assigned Names (ICANN) that assigns names to each site on the Internet. (140)

e-learning Learning supported by the Web; can be done inside traditional classrooms or in virtual classrooms. (156)

enterprise network Interconnected multiple LANs and WANs. (137)

Ethernet The most common network protocol. (167)

extranet A network that connects parts of the intranets of different organizations. (138)

fiber-optic cable Thousands of very thin filaments of glass fibers, surrounded by cladding, that transmit information via light pulses generated by lasers. (165)

file server A repository of various software and data files for the network, which determines who gets access to what and in what sequence. (135)

front-end processor A small secondary computer, dedicated solely to communication, that manages all routing communications with peripheral devices. (164)

gateway A communications processor that connects dissimilar networks by translating from one set of protocols to another. (137)

groupware Software products that support groups of people who collaborate on a common task or goal and that provide a way for groups to share resources. (153)

home page A text and graphical screen display that welcomes users and describes the organization that has established the page. (142)

hypertext transport protocol (HTTP) The communications standard used to transfer pages across the WWW portion of the Internet; defines how messages are formulated and transmitted. (142)

industrywide portal A Web-based gateway to information and knowledge for an entire industry. (146)

integrated services digital network (ISDN) A high-speed technology that allows users to transfer voice, video, image, and data simultaneously, over existing telephone lines. (166)

The Internet ("the Net") The massive network that connects computer networks of businesses, organizations, government agencies, and schools around the world, quickly, seamlessly, and inexpensively. (138)

Internet2 A new, faster telecommunications network with limited access, devoted exclusively to research purposes. (142)

Internet kiosks Terminals for public Internet access. (140)

Internet Protocol (IP) The set of rules used to send and receive packets from one machine to another over the Internet. (140)

Internet service providers (ISPs) Companies that provide Internet connections for a fee. (140)

Internet telephony (voice-over IP or VoIP) The use of the Internet as the transmission medium for telephone calls. (149)

intranet A private network that uses Internet software and TCP/IP protocols. (138)

IP address An assigned address that uniquely identifies a computer on the Internet. (140)

local area network (LAN) Network that connects communications devices in a limited geographical region (e.g., a building), so that every user device on the network can communicate with every other device. (135)

metasearch engine A computer program that searches several engines at once and integrates the findings of the various search engines to answer queries posted by users. (143)

mobile portal Web site that is accessible from mobile devices. (146)

modem Device that converts signals from analog to digital and vice versa. (163)

multiplexer Electronic device that allows a single communications channel to carry data transmissions simultaneously from many sources. (163)

network access points (NAPs) Computers that act as exchange points for Internet traffic and determine how traffic is routed. (140)

network interface card Hardware that specifies the data transmission rate, the size of message units, the addressing information attached to each message, and network topology. (136)

Next-Generation Internet (NGI) A multiagency, U. S. federal government research and development program that is developing revolutionary applications that require advanced networking. (142)

nodes Computing devices that are connected to a network, including the Internet. (135)

packet switching Data transmission technology that breaks up blocks of text into small, fixed bundles of data (packets) that are sent independently through the network. (139)

peer-to-peer processing A type of client/server distributed processing that allows two or more computers to pool their resources, making each computer both a client and a server. (168)

portal A Web-based personalized gateway to information and knowledge that provides information from disparate information systems and the Internet, using advanced search and indexing techniques. (146)

protocol The set of rules and procedures governing transmission across a network. (167)

router A communications processor that routes message through several connected LANs or to a wide area network. (137)

search engine A computer program that can contact other network resources on the Internet, search for specific information by key words, and report the results; an example is Google. (143)

server A computer that provides access to various network services, such as printing, data, and communications. (162)

software agents Computer programs that carry out a set of routine computer tasks on behalf of the user and in so doing employ some sort of knowledge of the user's goals. (144)

surfing The process of navigating around the Web by pointing and clicking a Web browser. (143)

switched-hub technology Data transmission technology that boosts local area networks by adding an ATM-like packet-switching capability. (166)

synchronous optical network (SONET) An interface standard for transporting digital signals over fiber-optic lines; allows the integration of transmissions from multiple vendors. (166)

T-carrier system A digital transmission system that defines circuits that operate at different rates, all of which are multiples of the basic 64 Kbps used to transport a single voice call. (167)

telecommunications system Combination of hardware and software that transmits information (text, data, graphics, and voice) from one location to another. (162)

telecommuting Arrangement whereby employees work at home, at the customer's premises, in special workplaces, or while traveling, usually using a computer linked to their place of employment. (156)

teleconferencing The use of electronic communication that allows two or more people at different locations to have a simultaneous conference. (154)

toolbar A horizontal row or vertical column of selectable image icons or buttons. (144)

top-level specification (zone) The rightmost part of an Internet name, indicating the type of organization that owns the site. (141)

topology The physical layout and connectivity of a network. (136)

Transmission Control Protocol/Internet Protocol (TCP/IP) A file transfer protocol that can send large files of information across sometimes unreliable networks with assurance that the data will arrive uncorrupted. (167)

tunneling The process of sending data over the Internet in encrypted form. (139)

twisted-pair wire Strands of copper wire twisted together in pairs. (164)

uniform resource locator (URL) Set of letters that identify the address of a specific resource on the Web. (142)

value-added network (VAN) a private, data-only network that is managed by an outside third party and used by multiple organizations to obtain economies in the cost of network service and network management. (137)

vBNS (Very-High-Speed Backbone Network Service) A high-speed network designed to support the academic Internet2 and the government-sponsored Next-Generation Internet (NGI) initiative. (142)

videoconference Virtual meeting in which participants in one location can see and hear participants at other locations and can share data and graphics by electronic means. (154)

virtual collaboration The use of digital technologies that enable organizations or individuals to collaboratively plan, design, develop, manage, and research products, services, and innovative information systems and electronic commerce applications. (152)

virtual group (team) A work group whose members are in different locations and who meet electronically. (152)

virtual private network (VPN) A WAN operated by a common carrier; provides a gateway between a corporate LAN and the Internet. (138)

virtual universities Online universities from which students take classes from home or an off-site location, via the Internet. (156)

Web conferencing Video teleconferencing that is conducted solely on the Internet (not on telephone lines). (154)

Web Services Self-contained business/consumer modular applications delivered over the Internet. (154)

Weblog (blog) A personal Web site, open to the public, in which the site owner expresses his or her feelings or opinions. (149)

Web site Collectively, all of the Web pages of a particular company or individual. (142)

webmaster The person in charge of an organization's Web site. (142)

whiteboard (electronic) An area on a computer display screen on which multiple users can write or draw; multiple users can use a single document "pasted" onto the screen. (154)

wide area network (WAN) A network, generally provided by common carriers, that covers a wide geographic area. (137)

wiki A Web site on which anyone can post material and make changes quickly, without using difficult commands. (152)

work group Two or more individuals who act together to perform some task, on either a permanent or temporary basis. (152)

workflow The movement of information as it flows through the sequence of steps that make up an organization's work procedures. (152)

World Wide Web (the Web) System with universally accepted standards for storing, retrieving, formatting, and displaying information via a client/server architecture; uses the transport functions of the Internet. (142)

Chapter 6

Chapter Preview

One of the most profound changes in the modern world of business is electronic commerce, also known as e-commerce (EC) and e-business. E-commerce is changing all business functional areas and their important tasks, from advertising to paying bills. Its impact is so widespread that it is affecting almost every organization. In addition, it is drastically changing the nature of competition, due to new online companies, new business models, and the diversity of EC-related products and services. E-commerce provides unparalleled opportunities for companies to expand worldwide at a small cost, to increase market share, and to reduce costs. In this chapter we will explain the major applications of e-business and what services are necessary for its support. We look at the major types of electronic commerce: business-to-consumer (B2C), business-to-business (B2B), consumer-to-consumer (C2C), business-to employee (B2E), and government-to-citizen (G2C). We conclude by examining several legal and ethical issues that have arisen as a result of the rapid growth of e-commerce.

E-Business and E-Commerce

Introduction to Information Systems
R. Kelly Rainer, Jr., Efraim Turban, and Richard E. Potter. ISBN 978-0-471-7363-3
©2007 John Wiley & Sons, Inc.

Chapter Outline

6.1 Overview of E-Business and E-Commerce

6.2 Business-to-Consumer (B2C) Electronic Commerce

6.3 Business-to-Business (B2B) Electronic Commerce

6.4 Electronic Payments

6.5 Ethical and Legal Issues in E-Business

Learning Objectives

1. Describe electronic commerce, including its scope, benefits, limitations, and types.
2. Distinguish between pure and partial electronic commerce.
3. Understand the basics of how online auctions work.
4. Differentiate among business-to-consumer, business-to-business, consumer-to-consumer, business-to-employee, and government-to-citizen electronic commerce.
5. Describe the major e-commerce support services, specifically payments and logistics.
6. Discuss some ethical and legal issues relating to e-commerce.

What's in IT for me?   ACC   FIN   MKT   POM   HRM   MIS

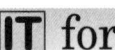    

175

Procter & Gamble Benefits from B2B Electronic Commerce

The Business Problem

Procter & Gamble (P&G) (*www.pg.com*), a $50 billion company, produces an extensive mix of household products in five major categories: (1) fabric and home care, (2) beauty care, (3) baby and family care, (4) health care, and (5) snacks and beverages. In the past, P&G used a "push" system of moving products to customers. Independent of what retailers were doing, P&G would forecast sales for its products. Then, the company would tweak sales throughout the year with various incentives designed to entice customers to buy. This process was highly inefficient, producing delays and excessive inventory. As a further problem, P&G's supply chain was not tightly integrated.

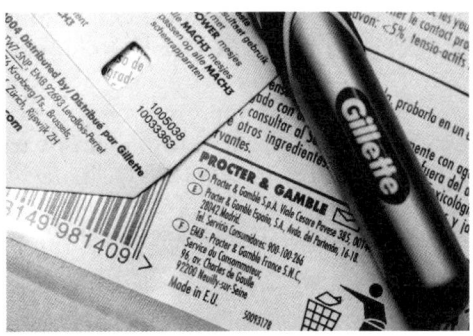
© H. De Oliveira/Expansion/Redux

P&G's mission is to get its products into the hands of 5 billion customers in 170 countries efficiently. To accomplish this mission, P&G must stock shelves in stores around the world more accurately by responding to what people want. That means that P&G must get 5,000 retailers and 30,000 suppliers to participate in a system that immediately signals which products are favored by customers. P&G's objective was to reduce inventories and produce only those products that customers were buying by developing a demand-driven system of supplying products to stores.

The IT Solution

P&G brought its retailers and suppliers into the planning and delivery process. The *signals* of customer demand came from the stores. The *responses* came from P&G manufacturing managers and suppliers, who linked the manufacture of products to sales reports coming in from the stores.

P&G implemented SAP's (*www.sap.com*) supply chain management system, which required retailers and suppliers to adhere to common conventions in feeding information in, and drawing information out of, the system. In effect, P&G integrated its retailers and suppliers into a large business-to-business (B2B) e-commerce network.

Establishing a B2B network led to major changes at P&G's factories. In the old build-to-forecast days, the plants would simply produce large numbers of items, move them to warehouses, and then let marketing sell the inventory. The company forbade changeovers of manufacturing lines because it believed that long product runs reduced per-unit costs. P&G failed to realize that per-unit costs actually rise if you are making products that customers are not buying. Today, P&G plans changeovers on its production lines every day, driven by information provided by its retailers. Retailers give P&G a count of all products flowing through the supply chain at any given moment, whether on store shelves, in back of the store, in warehouses, in trucks, or anyplace else.

The Results

Within one year, P&G reduced its out-of-stock conditions (i.e., products not being on shelves when customers want them) by almost one-half, representing a yearly savings of almost $100 million. The company reduced its *supply chain response time*—that is, the time from when a cash register records the sale of a product to the purchase of raw materials to produce its replacement—from 100 days to 50 days. Sales increased by 8 percent, and net profits rose by 19 percent.

The output of an information system is only as good as the input data. When data are inaccurate and/or delayed, the decisions based on the data are not the best. This clearly was the case with Procter & Gamble's old system, which generated high inventories, frequent out-of-stocks, and low customer satisfaction. The e-commerce system described in this case expedited and improved the flow of information from retailers to corporate headquarters and to suppliers, with dramatic results. This case illustrates a B2B application of e-commerce that involved P&G, its retailers, and its suppliers. There are several other types of e-commerce, all of which are discussed in this chapter. We begin, though, with a general overview of e-commerce and e-business.

Sources: Compiled from L. Barrett and T. Steinert-Threlkeld, "Procter & Gamble: Delivering Goods," *Baseline Magazine*, July 1, 2004; L. Kellam, "P & G Rethinks Supply Chain," *Optimize Magazine*, October 2003; and *www.pg.com*, accessed March 12, 2005.

What We Learned From This Case

6.1 Overview of E-Business and E-Commerce

This section examines the basics of e-business and e-commerce. We begin our discussion by defining these two concepts and then defining pure and partial electronic commerce. We then take a look at the various types of electronic commerce. Next, we note electronic commerce mechanisms, which are the ways that businesses and people buy and sell over the Internet. We end this section with the benefits and limitations of electronic commerce.

Definitions and Concepts

Electronic commerce (EC or e-commerce) describes the process of buying, selling, transferring, or exchanging products, services, or information via computer networks, including the Internet. **E-business** is a somewhat broader concept. In addition to the buying and selling of goods and services, it also refers to servicing customers, collaborating with business partners, and performing electronic transactions within an organization. However, because e-commerce and e-business are so similar, we use the two terms interchangeably throughout the book.

Pure versus Partial EC   Electronic commerce can take several forms depending on the *degree of digitization involved*. The degree of digitization refers to the extent to which the commerce has been transformed from physical to digital. It can relate to: (1) the product or service being sold, (2) the process by which the product or service is produced, or (3) the delivery agent or intermediary. In other words, the product can be physical or digital; the process can be physical or digital; and the delivery agent can be physical or digital.

In traditional commerce all three dimensions are physical. Purely physical organizations are referred to as **brick-and-mortar organizations**. In *pure EC* all dimensions are digital. Companies engaged only in EC are considered **virtual** (or pure-play) **organizations**. All other combinations that include a mix of digital and physical dimensions are considered *partial* EC (but not pure EC). **Click-and-mortar organizations** are those that conduct some e-commerce activities, yet their primary business is done in the physical world. E-commerce is now simply a part of traditional commerce, and people increasingly expect companies to offer some form of e-commerce.

"Sorry, but I get all the stuff I don't need on the Internet."

© The New Yorker Collection 2004 Michael Maslin from cartoonbank.com. All Rights Reserved.

For example, buying a shirt at Wal-Mart Online or a book from Amazon.com is *partial EC*, because the merchandise is physically delivered by FedEx. However, buying an e-book from Amazon.com or a software product from Buy.com is pure EC, because the product as well as its delivery, payment, and transfer are all conducted online. To avoid confusion, in this book we use the term EC to denote either pure or partial EC. IT's About Business 6.1 illustrates how a click-and-mortar company is impacting the traditional brick-and-mortar diamond industry.

IT's About Business

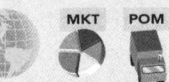

6.1 Electronic Commerce Threatens Traditional Jewelers

Companies are using the Internet to pull together complex information, condense it, and provide it to existing and potential customers. In addition, broadband connections help customers handle the large amounts of information that these companies deliver over the Internet. Consider, for example, the case of Blue Nile (*www.bluenile.com*).

Amy Smith is what happens when true love meets the Internet. Amy had long admired the engagement rings at the Tiffany & Co. near her home. When she got engaged, however, she checked the online jeweler Blue Nile. After using Blue Nile's guides to master the Four C's of diamonds (color, cut, clarity, carats), she picked out a $10,000 ring on their Web site (see Figure 6.1). She noted that Blue Nile charged $6,000 less than traditional jewelers.

Jewelers involved in e-commerce account for about $2 billion of the industry's $45 billion in U.S. revenues. Their strategy is to lower their costs by eliminating intermediaries and expensive stores. This leaves them free to slash prices. Blue Nile, for example, sells diamonds for up to 35 percent less than its rivals. Nevertheless, the company is highly profitable. In fact, it enjoys higher profit margins

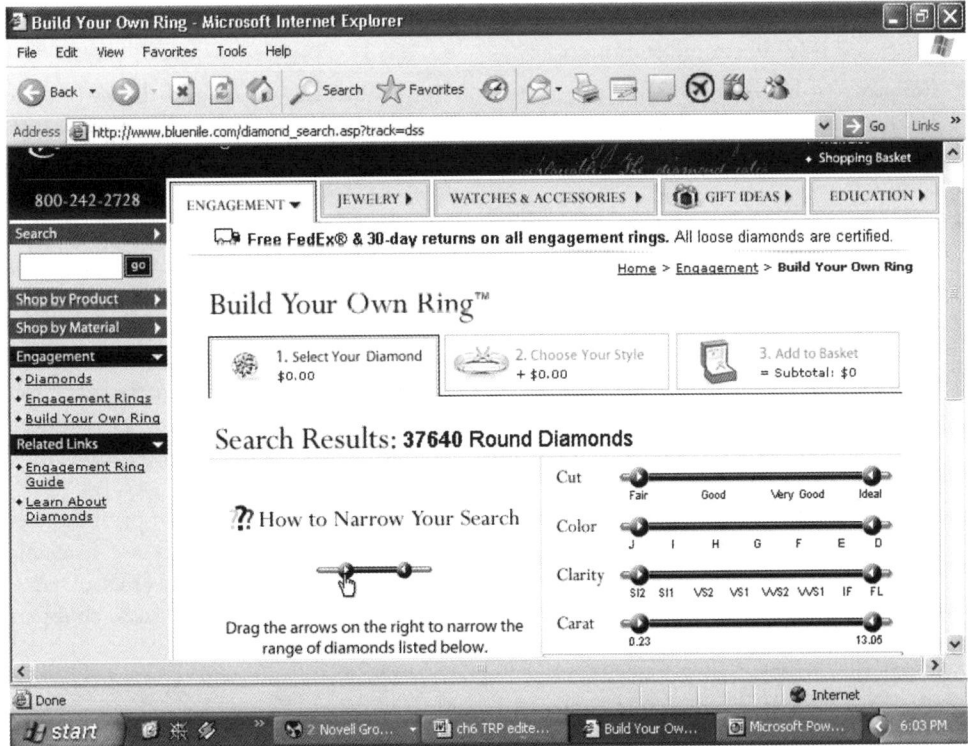

FIGURE 6.1
Building a custom engagement ring online.

than the top-ranked jewelry chain, Zale Corporation (*www.zale.com*).

Historically the jewelry business has been notoriously byzantine. For example, a South African diamond can pass through five different intermediaries, including rough-diamond brokers, cutters, and jewelry and diamond wholesalers. Blue Nile uses IT to streamline this process. It connects over the Internet to its key suppliers, who buy their stones directly from South Africa's powerful DeBeers Consolidated Mines Ltd. This process eliminates at least three intermediaries.

Blue Nile has just 115 full-time staffers and a single warehouse. To sell as many diamonds as Blue Nile, a chain would need 116 stores and more than 900 workers. In addition, Blue Nile gives prospective buyers the same information a jewelry expert would give them. Further, it offers its customers a 30-day, money-back guarantee.

This method of diamond selling is making it progressively harder for small jewelers to make money. That is one reason why 465 jewelry stores closed in 2003 alone. Even among survivors, profits are lean. In fact, many small jewelers now specialize in custom-crafted jewelry that does not contain diamonds.

Sources: Compiled from R. Berner and B. Grow, "Jewelry Heist," *Business Week*, May 10, 2004, pp. 82–83; "No One Will Know You Are a Procrastinator," *PRNewswire*, December 16, 2004; and *www.bluenile.com*, *www.debeers.com*, and *www.diamondhelpers.com*, accessed March 11, 2005.

QUESTIONS

1. How is Blue Nile impacting the traditional diamond industry?
2. What can the traditional diamond industry do to compete with Blue Nile?

Types of E-Commerce

E-commerce can be conducted between and among various parties. We define the common types of e-commerce here. We discuss C2C, B2E, and e-government here. As a result of their complexity, we have an entire section devoted to B2C and one to B2B.

- **Business-to-consumer (B2C):** In B2C, the sellers are organizations, and the buyers are individuals. We discuss B2C electronic commerce in Section 6.2. Recall that Figure 1.3 illustrated B2C electronic commerce.

- **Business-to-business (B2B):** In B2B transactions, both the sellers and the buyers are business organizations. The vast majority of EC volume is of this type. We discuss B2B electronic commerce in Section 6.3. Recall that Figure 1.3 illustrated B2B electronic commerce.

- **Consumer-to-consumer (C2C):** In C2C, an individual sells products or services to other individuals. (You also will see the term C2C used as "customer-to-customer." The terms are interchangeable, and we use both in this book.) The major ways that C2C is conducted on the Internet are auctions and classified ads.

  In dozens of countries, C2C selling and buying on auction sites is exploding. Most auctions are conducted by intermediaries, like eBay (*www.ebay.com*). Consumers can select general sites such as *www.800webmall.com* and *www.auctionanything.com*. In addition, many individuals are conducting their own auctions. For example, *www.greatshop.com* provides software to create online C2C reverse auction communities.

  The major categories of online classified ads are similar to those found in print ads: vehicles, real estate, employment, pets, tickets, and travel. Classified ads are available through most Internet service providers (AOL, MSN, etc.), at some portals (Yahoo!, etc.), and from Internet directories and online newspapers. On many of these sites, shoppers can use search engines to narrow their searches.

  Internet-based classified ads have one big advantage over traditional types of classified ads: They offer an international, rather than a local, audience. This wider audience greatly increases both the supply of goods and services and the number of potential buyers.

- **Business-to-employee (B2E):** In B2E, an organization uses EC internally to provide information and services to its employees. Companies allow employees to manage their benefits and to take training classes electronically. In addition, employees can buy discounted insurance, travel packages, and tickets to events on the corporate intranet. They also can order supplies and materials electronically. Finally, many companies have electronic corporate stores that sell the company's products to its employees, usually at a discount.

- **E-Government:** E-government is the use of Internet technology in general and e-commerce in particular to deliver information and public services to citizens (called government-to-citizen or G2C EC), and business partners and suppliers (called government-to-business or G2B EC). It is also an efficient way of conducting business transactions with citizens and businesses and within the governments themselves. E-government makes government more efficient and effective, especially in the delivery of public services. An example of G2C electronic commerce is electronics benefits transfer, in which governments transfer benefits, such as Social Security and pension payments, directly to recipients' bank accounts.

- **Mobile commerce (m-commerce):** The term *m-commerce* refers to e-commerce that is conducted entirely in a wireless environment. An example is using cell phones to shop over the Internet; we call it m-commerce. We discuss m-commerce in Chapter 7.

Each of the above types of EC is executed in one or more business models. A **business model** is the method by which a company generates revenue to sustain itself. The major EC business models are summarized in Manager's Checklist 6.1.

Major E-Commerce Mechanisms

There are a number of mechanisms through which businesses and customers can buy and sell on the Internet. The most widely used ones are electronic catalogs, electronic auctions, e-storefronts, e-malls, and e-marketplaces.

Catalogs have been printed on paper for generations. Today, however, they are available on CD-ROM and the Internet. Electronic catalogs consist of a product database, directory and search capabilities, and a presentation function. They are the backbone of most e-commerce sites.

An **auction** is a competitive process in which either a seller solicits consecutive bids from buyers or a buyer solicits bids from sellers. The primary characteristic of auctions is that prices are determined dynamically by competitive bidding. Electronic auctions (e-auctions) generally increase revenues for sellers by broadening the customer base and shortening the cycle time of the auction. Buyers generally benefit from e-auctions because they can bargain for lower prices. In addition, they don't have to travel to an auction at a physical location.

The Internet provides an efficient infrastructure for conducting auctions at lower administrative costs and with many more involved sellers and buyers. Individual consumers and corporations alike can participate in auctions. There are two major types of auctions: forward and reverse.

Forward auctions are auctions that sellers use as a channel to many potential buyers. Usually, sellers place items at sites for auction, and buyers bid continuously for them. The highest bidder wins the items. Both sellers and buyers can be individuals or businesses. The popular auction site eBay.com is a forward auction.

In **reverse auctions**, one buyer, usually an organization, wants to buy a product or a service. The buyer posts a request for quotation (RFQ) on its Web site or on a third-party Web site. The RFQ provides detailed information on the desired purchase. The suppliers study the RFQ and then submit bids electronically. Everything else being equal, the lowest-price bidder wins the auction. The buyer notifies the winning supplier electronically. The reverse auction is the most common auction model for large purchases (in terms of either quantities or price). Governments and large corporations frequently use this approach, which may provide considerable savings for the buyer.

Auctions can be conducted from the seller's site, the buyer's site, or a third party's site. For example, eBay, the best-known third-party site, offers hundreds of thousands of differ-

E-Commerce Business Models

EC Model	Description
Online direct marketing	Manufacturers or retailers sell directly to customers. Very efficient for digital products and services. Can allow for product or service customization. (*www.dell.com*)
Electronic tendering system	Businesses request quotes from suppliers. Uses B2B with a reverse auction mechanism.
Name-your-own-price	Customers decide how much they are willing to pay. An intermediary (e.g., *www.priceline.com*) tries to match a provider.
Find-the-best-price	Customers specify a need; an intermediary (e.g., *www.hotwire.com*) compares providers and shows the lowest price. Customers must accept the offer in a short time or may lose the deal.
Affiliate marketing	Vendors ask partners to place logos (or banners) on partner's site. If customers click on logo, go to vendor's site, and buy, then vendor pays commissions to partners.
Viral marketing	Receivers send information about your product to their friends. (Be on the watch for viruses.)
Group purchasing (e-coops)	Small buyers aggregate demand to get a large volume; then the group conducts tendering or negotiates a low price.
Online auctions	Companies run auctions of various types on the Internet. Very popular in C2C, but gaining ground in other types of EC. (*www.ebay.com*)
Product customization	Customers use the Internet to self-configure products or services. Sellers then price them and fulfill them quickly (*build-to-order*). (*www.jaguar.com*)
Electronic marketplaces and exchanges	Transactions are conducted efficiently (more information to buyers and sellers, less transaction cost) in electronic marketplaces (private or public).
Bartering online	Intermediary administers online exchange of surplus products and/or company receives "points" for its contribution, and the points can be used to purchase other needed items. (*www.bbu.com*)
Deep discounters	Company (e.g., *www.half.com*) offers deep price discounts. Appeals to customers who consider only price in their purchasing decisions.
Membership	Only members can use the services provided, including access to certain information, conducting trades, etc. (*www.egreetings.com*)

ent items in several types of auctions. Overall, more than 300 major companies, including Amazon.com and Dellauction.com, offer online auctions.

An **electronic storefront** is a Web site on the Internet representing a single store. An **electronic mall**, also known as a cybermall or e-mall, is a collection of individual shops under one Internet address. Electronic storefronts and electronic malls are closely associated with B2C electronic commerce. We discuss each one in more detail in Section 6.2.

An **electronic marketplace** (e-marketplace) is a central, virtual market space on the Web where many buyers and many sellers can conduct electronic commerce and electronic business activities. Electronic marketplaces are associated with B2B electronic commerce, and we discuss this topic in Section 6.3.

Benefits and Limitations of E-Commerce

Few innovations in human history have provided as many benefits to organizations, individuals, and society as e-commerce has. E-commerce benefits organizations by making national and international markets more accessible and by lowering the costs of processing, distributing, and retrieving information. Customers benefit by being able to access a vast number of products and services, around the clock. The major benefit to society is the ability to easily and conveniently deliver information, services, and products to people in cities, rural areas, and developing countries.

Despite all these benefits, EC has some limitations, both technological and nontechnological, that have slowed its growth and acceptance. Technological limitations include the lack of universally accepted security standards, insufficient telecommunications bandwidth, and expensive accessibility. Nontechnological limitations include a perception that EC is insecure, has unresolved legal issues, and lacks a critical mass of sellers and buyers. As time passes, the limitations, especially the technological ones, will lessen or be overcome.

Before you go on . . .

1. Define e-commerce, and distinguish it from e-business.
2. Differentiate between B2C, B2B, C2C, and B2E electronic commerce.
3. Define e-government.
4. Describe forward and reverse auctions.
5. List some benefits and limitations of e-commerce.

6.2 Business-to-Consumer (B2C) Electronic Commerce

Even though B2B EC is much larger by volume, B2C EC is more complex. The reason is that B2C involves a large number of buyers making millions of diverse transactions per day with a relatively small number of sellers. Consider Amazon, an online retailer (e-tailer) that offers thousands of products to its customers. Each customer purchase is relatively small, but Amazon must manage that transaction as if that customer were its most important. Each order must be processed quickly and efficiently and the products shipped to the customer. Returns also must be managed. Multiply this simple example by millions, and you get an idea of the complexity of B2C EC.

This section addresses the more important issues in B2C EC. We begin with a discussion of the two main ways for customers to access companies on the Web, electronic storefronts and electronic malls. In addition to purchasing products over the Web, customers also access online services. Our next section covers several online services, such as banking, securities trading, job search, travel, and real estate. The complexity of B2C EC leads to two major issues faced by sellers: channel conflict and order fulfillment. We examine these two topics in detail. Companies doing B2C EC must "get the word out" to prospective customers, so we conclude this section with a look at online advertising.

Electronic Storefronts and Malls

For generations home shopping from catalogs, and later from television shopping channels, has attracted millions of shoppers. Shopping online offers an alternative to catalog and television shopping. **Electronic retailing (e-tailing)** is the direct sale of products and services through electronic storefronts or electronic malls, usually designed around an electronic catalog format and/or auctions.

Like any mail-order shopping experience, e-commerce enables you to buy from home and to do so 24 hours a day, 7 days a week. However, EC offers a wider variety of products and services, including the most unique items, often at lower prices. Furthermore, within seconds, shoppers can get very detailed supplementary information on products. In addition, they can easily locate and compare competitors' products and prices. Finally, buyers can find hundreds of thousands of sellers. Two popular online shopping mechanisms are electronic storefronts and electronic malls.

Electronic Storefronts   Hundreds of thousands of solo storefronts (representing a single store), called *electronic storefronts*, can be found on the Internet. Each electronic storefront has its own uniform resource locator (URL), or Internet address, at which buyers can place orders. Some electronic storefronts are extensions of physical stores such as Home Depot, The Sharper Image, and Wal-Mart. Others are new businesses started by entrepreneurs who saw a niche on the Web. Among the best known are Amazon.com, CDNow.com, Uvine.com, Restaurant.com, and Alloy.com. Manufacturers (e.g., *www.dell.com*) as well as retailers (e.g., *www.officedepot.com*) use storefronts.

Electronic Malls   An *electronic mall*, also known as a cybermall or e-mall, is a collection of individual shops under one Internet address. The basic idea of an electronic mall is the same as that of a regular shopping mall—to provide a one-stop shopping place that offers many products and services. Each cybermall may include thousands of vendors. For example, *http://eshop.msn.com* includes tens of thousands of products from thousands of vendors (see Figure 6.2).

FIGURE 6.2
Electronic malls include products from thousands of vendors.

Two types of malls exist. First, there are *referral malls* (e.g., *www.hawaii.com*). You cannot buy in such a mall. Instead, you are transferred from the mall to a participating storefront. In the second type of mall (e.g., *http://shopping.yahoo.com*), you can actually make a purchase. At this type of mall, you might shop from several stores, but you make only one purchase transaction at the end. An *electronic shopping cart* enables you to gather items from various vendors and pay for them all together in one transaction. (The mall organizer, such as Yahoo, takes a commission from the sellers for this service.)

Online Service Industries

In addition to purchasing products, customers can also access needed services via the Web. Selling books, toys, computers, and most other products on the Internet can reduce vendors' selling costs by 20 to 40 percent. Further reduction is difficult to achieve because the products must be delivered physically. Only a few products (such as software or music) can be digitized to be delivered online for additional savings. In contrast, services, such as buying an airline ticket or purchasing stocks or insurance, can be delivered entirely through e-commerce, often with considerable cost reduction. Not surprisingly, then, online delivery of services is growing very rapidly, with millions of new customers being added each year. We take a look here at the leading online service industries: banking, trading of securities (stocks, bonds), job matching, travel services, real estate and really simple syndication.

Cyberbanking   *Electronic banking*, also known as **cyberbanking**, involves conducting various banking activities from home, a business, or on the road instead of at a physical bank location. Electronic banking has capabilities ranging from paying bills to applying for a loan. It saves time and is convenient for customers. For banks, it offers an inexpensive alternative to branch banking (for example, about 2 cents cost per transaction versus $1.07 at a physical branch). It also enables banks to enlist remote customers. In addition to regular banks with added online services, we are seeing the emergence of **virtual banks**, which are dedicated solely to Internet transactions. An example of a virtual bank is *www.netbank.com* (see Figure 6.3).

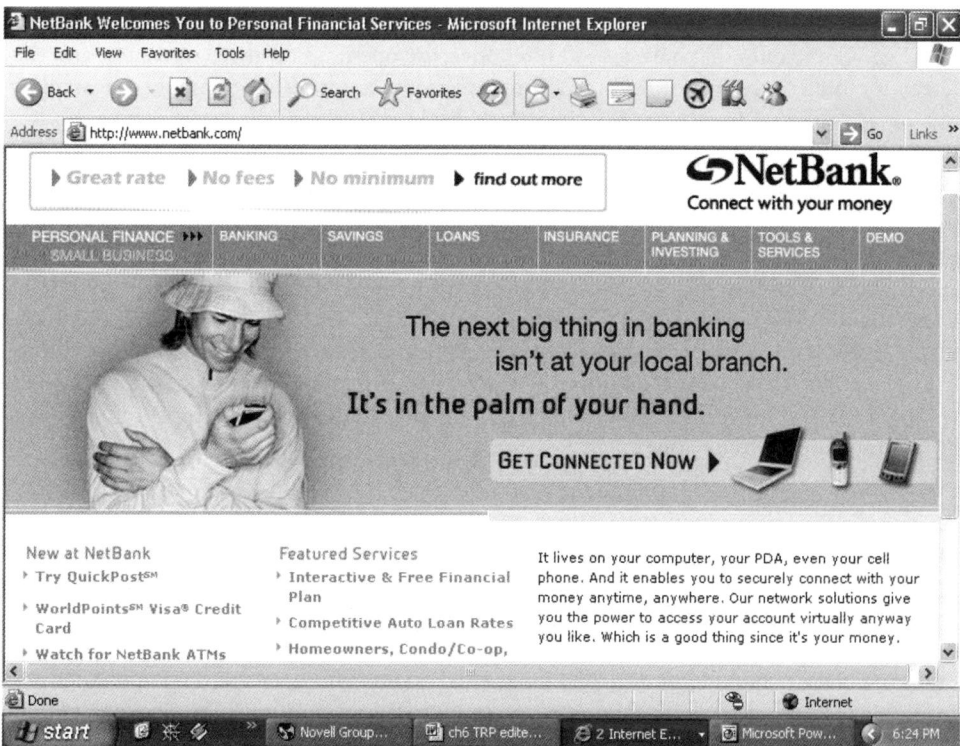

FIGURE 6.3
Virtual banks are devoted to online transactions.

International banking and the ability to handle trading in multiple currencies are critical for international trade. Transfers of electronic funds and electronic letters of credit are important services in international banking. An example of support for EC global trade is provided by TradeCard, in conjunction with MasterCard. TradeCard is an international company that provides a secure method for buyers and sellers to make digital payments anywhere on the globe (see the demo at *www.tradecard.com*). In another example, banks and companies such as Oanda (*www.oanda.com*) also provide conversions of more than 160 currencies.

Online Securities Trading   Emarketer.com estimates that some 40 million people in the United States use computers to trade stocks, bonds, and other financial instruments. In Korea, more than half of stock traders are already using the Internet for that purpose. Why? Because it is cheaper than a full-service or discount broker. On the Web, investors can find a considerable amount of information regarding specific companies or mutual funds in which to invest (e.g., *http://money.cnn.com, www.bloomberg.com*).

For example, let's say you have an account with Charles Schwab. You access Schwab's Web site (*www.schwab.com*) from your PC or your Internet-enabled mobile device, enter your account number and password to access your personalized Web page, and then click on "stock trading." Using a menu, you enter the details of your order (buy or sell, margin or cash, price limit, market order, and so on). The computer tells you the current "ask" and "bid" prices, much as a broker would do over the telephone. You can then approve or reject the transaction. Some well-known companies that offer only online trading are E*Trade, Ameritrade, and Suretrade.

The Online Job Market   The Internet offers a promising new environment for job seekers and for companies searching for hard-to-find employees. Thousands of companies and government agencies advertise available positions, accept resumes, and take applications via the Internet.

Job seekers use the online job market to reply online to employment ads, to place resumes on various sites, and to use recruiting firms (e.g., *www.monster.com* and *www.jobdirect.com*). Companies that have jobs to offer advertise openings on their Web sites, and they search the bulletin boards of recruiting firms. In many countries, governments must advertise job openings on the Internet.

Travel Services   The Internet is an ideal place to plan, explore, and arrange almost any trip economically. Online travel services allow you to purchase airline tickets, reserve hotel rooms, and rent cars. Most sites also offer a fare-tracker feature that sends you e-mail messages about low-cost flights. Examples of comprehensive online travel services are Expedia.com, Travelocity.com, and Orbitz.com. Online services are also provided by all major airline vacation services, large conventional travel agencies, car rental agencies, hotels (e.g., *www.hotels.com*), and tour companies. Priceline.com allows you to set a price you are willing to pay for an airline ticket or hotel accommodations. It then attempts to find a vendor that will match your price.

Real Estate   Real estate transactions are an ideal area for e-commerce. You can view many properties on the screen, and you can sort and organize properties according to your preferences and decision criteria. In some locations, brokers require that prospective buyers use real estate databases only in the brokers' offices. Nevertheless, considerable information is now available on the Internet. For example, Realtor.com allows you to search a database of more than 1.2 million homes across the United States. This database is composed of local "multiple listings" of all available properties, in hundreds of locations. People who are looking for an apartment can try Apartments.com.

Really Simple Syndication Another interesting service is called Really Simple Syndication (RSS). If you have personal interests such as news, particular kinds of music, or anything else, RSS lets you pull together a list of Web sites that you want to follow. The information that you requested, called a feed, comes to you through a piece of software called a newsreader. Several services let you set up your feed easily. Try Bloglines (*www.bloglines.com*), Feeddemon (*www.feeddemon.com*), Pluck (*www.pluck.com*), and My Yahoo! (*http://my.yahoo.com*).

Issues in E-Tailing

Despite e-tailing's ongoing growth, many e-tailers continue to face serious issues that can restrict their growth. Perhaps the two major issues are channel conflict and order fulfillment.

Click-and-mortar companies may face a conflict with their regular distributors when they sell directly to customers online. This situation, known as **channel conflict**, can alienate the distributors. Channel conflict has forced some companies (e.g., Ford Motor Company) to avoid direct online sales. An alternative approach for Ford allows customers to configure a car online but requires them to pick up the car from a dealer, where they arrange financing, warranties, and service.

Channel conflict can arise in areas such as pricing of products and services and resource allocation (e.g., how much to spend on advertising). Another potential source of conflict involves logistics services provided by the offline activities to the online activities. For example, how should a company handle returns of items bought online? Some companies have completely separated the "clicks" (the online portion of the organization) from the "mortar" or "bricks" (the traditional brick-and-mortar part of the organization). However, this approach can increase expenses and reduce the synergy between the two organizational channels. As a result, many companies are integrating their online and offline channels, a process known as **multichanneling**. IT's About Business 6.2 illustrates the process of multichanneling.

The second major issue is order fulfillment, which can also be a source of problems for e-tailers. Any time a company sells directly to customers, it is involved in various order-fulfillment activities. It must perform the following activities: Quickly find the products to be shipped; pack them; arrange for the packages to be delivered speedily to the customer's door; collect the money from every customer, either in advance, by COD, or by individual bill; and handle the return of unwanted or defective products.

It is very difficult to accomplish these activities both effectively and efficiently in B2C, because a company has to ship small packages to many customers and do it quickly. For this reason, companies involved in B2C activities often have difficulties in their supply chains.

Order fulfillment includes not only providing customers with what they ordered and doing it on time, but also providing all related customer service. For example, the customer must receive assembly and operation instructions for a new appliance. (Good examples are available at *www.livemanuals.com*.) In addition, if the customer is not happy with a product, an exchange or return must be arranged. (Visit *www.fedex.com* to see how returns are handled via FedEx.)

In the late 1990s, e-tailers faced continuous problems in order fulfillment, especially during the holiday season. The problems included late deliveries, delivering wrong items, high delivery costs, and compensation to unhappy customers. For e-tailers, taking orders over the Internet is the easy part of B2C e-commerce. Delivering orders to customers' doors is the hard part. Order fulfillment is less complicated in B2B. These transactions are much larger but fewer in number. In addition, these companies have had order fulfillment mechanisms in place for many years.

Online Advertising

Advertising is an attempt to disseminate information in order to influence a buyer–seller transaction. Traditional advertising on TV or in newspapers is impersonal, one-way mass communication. Direct-response marketing, or telemarketing, contacts individuals by direct

IT's About Business

6.2 Good News and Bad News about Multichanneling

New technologies are allowing retailers to remove the wall between online shopping and in-store shopping and to make gathering customer data easier and more valuable. The ultimate goal is more customized, personalized service. The best retailers have always tried to provide the most tailored service possible. The integration of online and offline shopping provides benefits, as we see at REI (*www.rei.com*). It can also cause problems, however, as we see at Staples (*www.staples.com*).

REI and Staples have adoped the "multichanneling" model of integrated retail sales. That is, both companies have integrated digital services with in-store, mail-order, and telephone sales, and with any other retail channels. The reasoning behind multichanneling is that the Internet works fine for some types of goods, such as books, computer products, and music. However, for other items—canoes, cars, clothes, and entertainment systems, for example—many shoppers do not want to purchase and pay shipping costs without first trying them out, trying them on, and talking with knowledgeable salespeople.

In 2003, REI began offering customers the option of ordering products online and picking them up at its stores. The concept grew out of an examination of the in-store Web kiosks that REI began using in 1998. The kiosks provided product information that the sales staff did not have access to. In addition, however, customers used the kiosks to place orders when stores did not have items they wanted. Apparently these customers were willing to pay shipping costs for goods they had intended to buy in person. Today, the kiosk orders that are trucked out of REI's central warehouse are wrapped distinctively. This way employees can easily tell which items should be held for customer pickup. When such an item comes in, its bar code is scanned to register its arrival, and an e-mail notification is sent to the buyer.

REI is making e-commerce far more interactive. This system has provided many benefits for REI customers. First, they can buy through any channel: offline at any of REI's 77 stores, online at in-store kiosks, online over the Internet, and so on. In addi-

tion, they can purchase items online but pick up or return them at a store. Discounts are the same in all locations. Finally, every item offered on the Web can be ordered through the store or catalogue, and vice versa.

For Staples, however, e-commerce has been a mixed blessing. Staples is trying to find a balance between offering superior customer service on the one hand and discouraging unethical or fraudulent behavior on the other. A particular concern is serial returning. Customers who engage in serial returning purchase a product, claim the manufacturer's rebate, and then return the product for a net gain. Customer behaviors such as this increase the company's operational costs. Staples does recognize that customers may need to return purchases, and the company does not want to deny those customers the service they deserve. On the other hand, Staples loses money on serial returners.

The solution is the Return Exchange (*www.returnexchange.com*), a company that operates like a credit bureau for store returns. The company keeps track of shoppers' returns and then uses a rules-based application to assess if they are acting in good faith. At Staples, if you return an item that you bought for cash and you have lost the receipt, the store will ask for your driver's license. Your name will then be stored on the computer system of the Return Exchange. That way, customers who show a pattern typical of fraudulent behavior will be flagged and possibly denied the right to return products.

Sources: Compiled from R. Buderi, "E-Commerce Gets Smarter," *MIT Technology Review*, April 2005, pp. 54–59; "Striking a Balance," *CIO Insight*, December 1, 2004; and *www.rei.com, www.staples.com,* and *www.returnexchange.com,* accessed March 10, 2005.

QUESTIONS

1. What are the advantages of multichanneling for retailers? The disadvantages?
2. What are the advantages of multichanneling for consumers? The disadvantages?

mail or telephone and requires them to respond in order to make a purchase. The direct-response approach personalizes advertising and marketing, but it can be expensive, slow, and ineffective. It can also be extremely annoying to the consumer.

Internet advertising redefines the advertising process, making it media-rich, dynamic, and interactive. It improves on traditional forms of advertising in a number of ways. First, Internet ads can be updated any time at minimal cost and therefore can be kept current. In addition, Internet ads can reach very large numbers of potential buyers all over the world. Further, they are generally cheaper than radio, television, and print ads. Internet ads can be interactive and targeted to specific interest groups and/or individuals. Despite all these advantages, it is difficult to measure the effectiveness and cost-justification of online ads. The following example illustrates the power of online advertising.

Example

Online Advertising Attracts Attention. In the golden age of television, they were called roadblocks. Advertisers ran the same commercial at the same minute on the three big networks. That way, the ad would blanket the entire medium, collaring viewers no matter what show they were watching. What about roadblocks online? Can a company do over the Internet what advertisers used to do on television?

The answer is yes. In mid-2005, Ford Motor Company unveiled a roadblock on the Internet to promote its F-150 truck. On the day of the launch, Ford placed bold banner ads for 24 hours on the three leading portals—AOL, MSN, and Yahoo! Some 50 million Web surfers saw Ford's banner. Millions of them clicked in, pouring onto Ford's Web site at a rate that reached 3,000 per second. Ford claimed that the traffic led to a 6 percent increase in sales over the first three months of the campaign.

Advertising roadblocks on the Internet can be powerful. Each of the three biggest portals attracts 70 percent of the Americans online to its properties monthly, according to comScore Networks, a traffic-tracking organization. As more companies realize the influence of these three portals, prices have been soaring. Last year, corporate buyers could land discounted space on the home pages of major portals for between $100,000 and $180,000 per 24 hours. The cost has since risen to $300,000. (*Sources:* Compiled from S. Baker, "The Online Ad Surge," *Business Week*, November 22, 2004, pp. 76–82; and *www.ford.com*, accessed February 21, 2005.)

Advertising Methods The most common online advertising methods are banners, pop-ups, and e-mail. **Banners** are simply electronic billboards. Typically, a banner contains a short text or graphical message to promote a product or a vendor. It may even contain video clips and sound. When customers click on a banner, they are transferred to the advertiser's home page. Banner advertising is the most commonly used form of advertising on the Internet (see Figure 6.4).

A major advantage of banners is that they can be customized to the target audience. If the computer system knows who you are or what your profile is, you may be sent a banner that is supposed to match your interests. A major disadvantage of banners is that they can convey only limited information due to their small size. Another drawback is that many viewers simply ignore them.

Pop-up and pop-under ads are contained in a new browser window that is automatically launched when you enter or exit a Web site. A **pop-up ad** appears in front of the current browser window. A **pop-under ad** appears underneath the active window: when users close the active window, they see the ad. Many users strongly object to these ads, which they consider intrusive.

E-mail is emerging as an Internet advertising and marketing channel. It is generally cost-effective to implement, and it provides a better and quicker response rate than other adver-

FIGURE 6.4
When customers click on a banner ad, they are transferred to the vendor's homepage.

tising channels. Marketers develop or purchase a list of e-mail addresses, place them in a customer database, and then send advertisements via e-mail. A list of e-mail addresses can be a very powerful tool because the marketer can target a group of people or even individuals.

However, there is a potential for misuse of e-mail advertising. In fact, some consumers receive a flood of unsolicited e-mail. This e-mail is called spam. **Spamming** is the indiscriminate distribution of electronic ads without the permission of the receiver. Unfortunately, spamming is becoming worse over time.

Two important responses to spamming are permission marketing and viral marketing. **Permission marketing** asks consumers to give their permission to voluntarily accept online advertising and e-mail. Typically, consumers are asked to complete an electronic form that asks what they are interested in and requests permission to send related marketing information. Sometimes, consumers are offered incentives to receive advertising.

Permission marketing is the basis of many Internet marketing strategies. For example, millions of users receive e-mails periodically from airlines such as American and Southwest. Users of this marketing service can ask to be notified of low fares from their hometown or to their favorite destinations. Users can easily unsubscribe at any time. Permission marketing is also extremely important for market research (e.g., see Media Metrix at *www.comscore.com*).

In one particularly interesting form of permission marketing, companies such as Click-dough.com, Getpaid4.com, and CashSurfers.com have built customer lists of millions of people who are happy to receive advertising messages whenever they are on the Web. These customers are paid $0.25 to $0.50 an hour to view messages while they do their normal surfing.

Viral marketing refers to online "word-of-mouth" marketing. The idea behind viral marketing is to have people forward messages to friends, suggesting that they "check this out." A marketer can distribute a small game program, for example, embedded with a sponsor's e-mail, that is easy to forward. By releasing a few thousand copies, vendors hope to reach many more thousands. Viral marketing allows companies to build brand awareness at a minimal cost. Unfortunately, though, several e-mail hoaxes have spread via viral marketing. Also, a more serious danger of viral marketing is that a destructive computer virus can be added to an innocent advertisement, game, or message.

Before you go on . . .

1. Describe electronic storefronts and malls.
2. Discuss various types of online services (e.g., cyberbanking, securities trading, job searches, travel services).
3. List the major issues relating to e-tailing.
4. Describe online advertising, its methods, and its benefits.
5. What are spamming, permission marketing, and viral marketing?

6.3 Business-to-Business (B2B) Electronic Commerce

In *business to business (B2B)* e-commerce, the buyers and sellers are business organizations. B2B comprises about 85 percent of EC volume. It covers a broad spectrum of applications that enable an enterprise to form electronic relationships with its distributors, resellers, suppliers, customers, and other partners. By using B2B, organizations can restructure their supply chains and their partner relationships.

There are several business models for B2B applications. The major ones are sell-side marketplaces, buy-side marketplaces, electronic exchanges, and electronic hubs.

Sell-Side Marketplaces

In the **sell-side marketplace** model, organizations attempt to sell their products or services to other organizations electronically from their own private e-marketplace Web site and/or from a third-party Web site. This model is similar to the B2C model in which the buyer is expected to come to the seller's site, view catalogs, and place an order. In the B2B sell-side marketplace, however, the buyer is an organization.

The key mechanisms in the sell-side model are electronic catalogs that can be customized for each large buyer and forward auctions. Sellers such as Dell Computer (*www.dellauction.com*) use auctions extensively. In addition to auctions from their own Web sites, organizations can use third-party auction sites, such as eBay, to liquidate items. Companies such as Ariba (*www.ariba.com*) are helping organizations to auction old assets and inventories.

The sell-side model is used by hundreds of thousands of companies. It is especially powerful for companies with superb reputations. The seller can be either a manufacturer (e.g., Dell, IBM), a distributor (e.g., *www.avnet.com*), or a retailer (e.g., *www.bigboxx.com*). The seller uses EC to increase sales, reduce selling and advertising expenditures, increase delivery speed, and reduce administrative costs. The sell-side model is especially suitable to customization. Customers can configure their orders online at many companies. For example, at Dell (*www.dell.com*), you can determine the exact type of computer that you want. You can choose the type of chip (e.g., Pentium 4), the size of the hard drive (e.g., 120 gigabytes), the type of monitor (e.g., 19-inch flat screen), and so on. At Jaguar (*www.jaguar.com*), you can customize the Jaguar you want on the Web site. Self-customization of orders generates fewer misunderstandings about what customers want while encouraging faster order fulfillment.

Buy-Side Marketplaces

The **buy-side marketplace** is a model in which organizations attempt to buy needed products or services from other organizations electronically. A major method of buying goods and services in the buy-side model is the reverse auction.

The buy-side model uses EC technology to streamline the purchasing process. The goal is to reduce the costs of items purchased as well as the administrative expenses involved in purchasing them. In addition, EC technology can shorten the purchasing cycle time. Procurements using a third-party, buy-side marketplace model are especially popular for medium and small organizations due to potentially lower costs of items purchased and lower administrative expenses. Procurement includes purchasing goods and materials, as well as sourcing, negotiating with suppliers, paying for goods, and making delivery arrangements. Organizations now use the Internet to accomplish all these functions.

Purchasing by using electronic support is referred to as **e-procurement**. E-procurement uses reverse auctions, particularly group purchasing. In **group purchasing**, the orders of many buyers are combined so that they constitute a large volume. This process allows them to attract more seller attention. In addition, when the combined orders are placed on a reverse auction, a volume discount can be negotiated. Typically, the orders of small buyers are aggregated by a third-party vendor, such as the United Sourcing Alliance (*www.usa-llc.com*).

Electronic Exchanges

Private exchanges have one buyer and many sellers. E-marketplaces, in which there are many sellers and many buyers, are called **public exchanges**, or just **exchanges**. Public exchanges are open to all business organizations. They frequently are owned and operated by a third party. Public exchange managers provide all the necessary information systems to the participants. Thus, buyers and sellers merely have to "plug in" in order to trade. B2B public exchanges are often the initial point for contacts between business partners. Once they make contact, the partners may move to a private exchange or to the private trading rooms provided by many public exchanges to do their subsequent trading activities.

Some electronic exchanges are for direct materials, and some are for indirect materials. *Direct materials* are inputs to the manufacturing process, such as safety glass used in automobile windshields and windows. *Indirect materials* are those items, such as office supplies, that are needed for maintenance, operations, and repairs (MRO).

Vertical exchanges connect buyers and sellers in a given industry. Examples of vertical exchanges include *www.plasticsnet.com* in the plastics industry, *www.papersite.com* in the paper industry, *www.chemconnect.com* in the chemical industry, and *www.isteelasia.com* in the steel industry.

Horizontal exchanges connect buyers and sellers across many industries and are used mainly for MRO materials. Examples of horizontal exchanges include EcEurope (*www.eceuroope.com*), Globalsources (*www.globalsources.com*), and Alibaba (*www.alibaba.com*).

In **functional exchanges**, needed services such as temporary help or extra office space are traded on an "as-needed" basis. For example, Employease (*www.employease.com*) can find temporary labor using employers in its Employease Network.

All types of exchanges offer diversified support services, ranging from payments to logistics. Vertical exchanges are frequently owned and managed by a *consortium*, a term for a group of big players in an industry. For example, Marriott and Hyatt own a procurement consortium for the hotel industry, and ChevronTexaco owns an energy e-marketplace. The vertical e-marketplaces offer services particularly suited to the community they serve.

Electronic Hubs

B2B exchanges are used mainly to facilitate trading among companies. In contrast, a hub is used to facilitate communication and coordination among business partners, frequently along the supply chain. Hubs allow each partner to access a Web site, usually a portal, that is used for an exchange of information. Each partner can deposit new information, make changes, and get and leave messages. Some hubs allow partners to conduct trade as well. For example, Asite (*www.asite.com*) is a B2B hub for the construction industry in the United Kingdom.

Before you go on . . .

1. Briefly differentiate between the sell-side marketplace and the buy-side marketplace.
2. Briefly differentiate among vertical exchanges, horizontal exchanges, and functional exchanges.

6.4 Electronic Payments

Implementing EC typically requires electronic payments. **Electronic payment systems** enable you to pay for goods and services electronically, rather than writing a check or using cash. Electronic payment systems include electronic checks, electronic credit cards, purchasing cards, and electronic cash. Payments are an integral part of doing business, whether in the traditional manner or online. Traditional payment systems have typically involved cash and/or checks. However, as IT's About Business 6.3 points out, traditional check writing is not fast enough to keep up with the speed of electronic commerce.

In most cases, traditional payment systems are not effective for EC, especially for B2B. Cash cannot be used because there is no face-to-face contact between buyer and seller. Not everyone accepts credit cards or checks, and some buyers do not have credit cards or checking accounts. Finally, contrary to what many people believe, it may be *less* secure for the buyer to use the telephone or mail to arrange or send payment, especially from another country, than to complete a secured transaction on a computer. For all of these reasons, a better way is needed to pay for goods and services in cyberspace. This better method is electronic payment systems. We now take a look at electronic checks, electronic credit cards, purchasing cards, and electronic cash.

Electronic Checks

Electronic checks (*e-checks*) are similar to regular paper checks. They are used mostly in B2B. First, the customer establishes a checking account with a bank. When the customer contacts a seller and buys a product or a service, he or she e-mails an encrypted electronic check to the seller. The seller deposits the check in a bank account, and funds are transferred from the buyer's account and into the seller's account.

Like regular checks, e-checks carry a signature (in digital form) that can be verified (see *www.echeck.net*). Properly signed and endorsed e-checks are exchanged between financial institutions through electronic clearinghouses (see *www.eccho.org* and *www.echecksecure.com* for details).

Electronic Credit Cards

Electronic credit (*e-credit*) cards allow customers to charge online payments to their credit card account (see Figure 6.5). Here is how e-credit cards work. When you buy a book from Amazon, for example, your credit card information and purchase amount are encrypted in your browser. This way the information is safe while it is "traveling" on the Internet. Furthermore, when this information arrives at Amazon, it is not opened. Rather, it is transferred automatically (in encrypted form) to a clearinghouse, where the information is

IT's About Business

6.3 The Check's in the Mail—Not!

A funny thing happens when you write a check at some Wal-Mart stores. Wal-Mart does not keep your check. In an effort to speed up payments, reduce costs, and combat fraud, the world's largest retailer now scans paper checks for pertinent information such as the bank and account number. It then gives the checks back to the customers in the checkout line.

Digital processing technologies and the increasing adoption of online bill payment are reshaping the $30 billion business of printing, transporting, and processing checks. Driving this transformation are banks, credit card companies, and merchants eager to simplify an antiquated system that involves as many as 28 intermediaries. They have plenty of motivation. Handling an online payment costs only 10 cents, roughly one-third the expense involved in processing a paper check. The result: The number of checks written annually should decline by about 25 percent by 2007.

The old practice of printing checks and carrying them around the country in armored cars is in upheaval. In fact, the nation's largest check printer—Deluxe Corporation (*www.deluxe.com*)—is closing 3 of its 13 printing plants. At the same time, it is attempting to increase its profits by promoting higher-priced check designs and fraud-prevention services. Another victim is AirNet Systems (*www.airnet.com*), which gets nearly 70 percent of its revenues from flying checks between cities on Learjets.

By 2007, 73 million U.S. consumers will be paying some of their bills online. Gartner estimates that an average company with 2 million customers can reduce costs by $26 million per year by persuading customers to receive and pay their bills online.

Going further, paper checks themselves are going digital. Behind this transformation is the Check Clearing for the Twenty-First Century Act (or Check 21). This act puts electronic images of checks on an equal legal footing with paper originals. For example, you have probably been receiving photocopies of your canceled checks for years. Now, those photocopies are legally equivalent to the paper originals.

These changes will allow large banks to compete with local banks. Local businesses typically have done business with local banks because they want to get credit for their daily deposits as quickly as possible. With digital check processing, proximity no longer matters. Merchants can choose banks that offer quick and secure processing for the lowest price—wherever they are located.

Sources: Compiled from T. Mullaney, "Checks Check Out," *Business Week*, May 10, 2004, pp. 83–84; "Plastic Overtakes Checks," *http://moneycentral.msn.com*, December 6, 2004; and *www.deluxe.com*, accessed March 5, 2005.

QUESTIONS

1. Do you still write checks? Would you feel comfortable with not being able to write checks at all? Why or why not?
2. List some advantages and disadvantages of traditional check writing for the consumer.

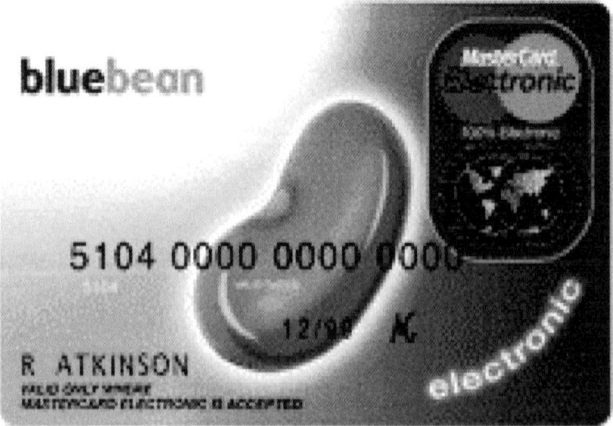

FIGURE 6.5
Electronic credit card.

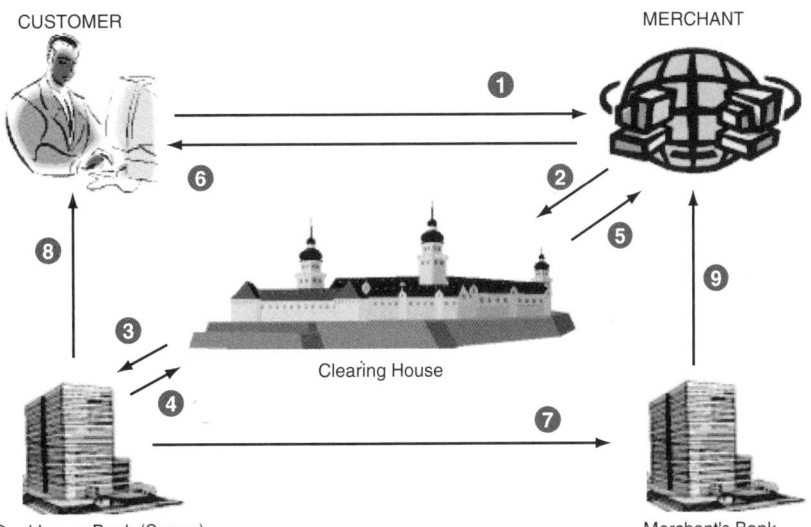

CUSTOMER

FIGURE 6.6
How e-credit cards
work. (The numbers
1–9 indicate the
sequence of activities.)
Source: Drawn by
E. Turban.

decrypted for verification and authorization. The complete process of how e-credit cards work is shown in Figure 6.6. Electronic credit cards are used primarily in B2C and in shopping by small-to-medium enterprises (SMEs).

Purchasing Cards

The B2B equivalent of electronic credit cards is *purchasing cards* (see Figure 6.7). In some countries companies pay other companies primarily by means of purchasing cards, rather than by paper checks. Unlike credit cards, where credit is provided for 30 to 60 days (for free) before payment is made to the merchant, payments made with purchasing cards are settled within a week.

Purchasing cards typically are used for unplanned B2B purchases, and corporations generally limit the amount per purchase (usually $1,000 to $2,000). Purchasing cards can be used on the Internet, much like regular credit cards.

Electronic Cash

Despite the growth of credit cards, cash remains the most common mode of payment in offline transactions. However, many EC sellers, and some buyers, prefer electronic cash. *Electronic cash (e-cash)* appears in four major forms: stored-value money cards, smart cards, person-to-person payments, and digital wallets.

FIGURE 6.7
Purchasing card.

Stored-Value Money Cards   Although they resemble credit cards, **stored-value money cards** actually are a form of e-cash. The cards that you use to pay for photocopies in your library, for transportation, or for telephone calls are stored-value money cards. They are called "stored-value" because they allow you to store a fixed amount of prepaid money and then spend it as necessary. Each time you use the card, the amount is reduced by the amount you spent.

Smart Cards   Although some people refer to stored-value money cards as "smart cards," they are not really the same. True **smart cards** contain a chip that can store a considerable amount of information (more than 100 times that of a stored-value money card) (see Figure 6.8). Smart cards are frequently *multipurpose*; that is, you can use them as a credit card, a debit card, or a stored-value money card. In addition, when you use a smart card in department store chains as a *loyalty card*, it may contain your purchasing information. However, as IT's About Business 6.4 demonstrates, smart cards do not always work.

Advanced smart cards can help customers transfer funds, pay bills, and purchase items from vending machines. Consumers can also use them to pay for services such as those offered on television or PCs. For example, the VISA Cash Card (see Figure 6.9) allows you to buy goods or services at participating gas stations, fast-food outlets, pay phones, discount stores, post offices, convenience stores, coffee shops, and even movie theaters. You can load money values onto advanced smart cards at ATMs and kiosks as well as from your PC.

IT's About Business

6.4 Target's Not-So-Smart Cards

Target's (*www.target.com*) new credit card was not a success story. The company knew that smart cards could store an account number and a personal identification number. This system would let Target understand the cardholder's buying habits and use this information to produce targeted electronic coupons. In Target's case, the coupon loyalty program did not pay off.

Although frequent-shopper perks were the Target card's main selling point, the loyalty capabilities were too complicated. That is, it was not clear how shoppers who used Target's card frequently could obtain perks. In an industry where a response rate of 1 percent to a newspaper coupon is considered high, technology works only if it makes coupon use effortless. However, the Target card technology made obtaining discounts more difficult. Shoppers had to order a special card reader from Target and install it on their home computers. They then used the reader to download coupons to their cards. As an alternative, they could obtain discounts at in-store kiosks located near customer service desks. Not surprisingly, neither harried parents—almost 40 percent of Target customers have young children—

nor technology neophytes gave the kiosks or balky peripherals more than limited use.

Second, Target also ignored another major benefit of smart cards: their ability to redeem points for rewards at a network of other retailers. Finally, the cards cost $3 apiece, which proved to be far too expensive.

Less than a year after the program was operational, Target pulled the plug on its smart card. That occurred after the company had spent two years and an estimated $40 million developing the card, retrofitting 37,000 cash registers to handle the new cards, and installing coupon kiosks at its 1,191 stores.

Sources: Compiled from I. Mount, "Target's Not-So-Smart Cards," *Business 2.0*, September 2004; "Target Taking Brains Out of Smart Cards," *Retail Merchandiser*, April 2004; and *www.target.com*, accessed March 17, 2005.

QUESTIONS

1. What were the reasons that the Target smart card failed?

2. What could Target executives have done to save their smart card?

FIGURE 6.8
Smart cards are
frequently
multipurpose.

Smart cards are ideal for *micropayments*, which are small payments of a few dollars or less. However, they have additional functions. In Hong Kong, for example, the transportation card called Octopus is a stored-value money card that can be used for trains and buses (see Figure 6.10). However, as its capabilities have expanded so that it can be used in stores and vending machines, it is moving to a smart card.

Person-to-Person Payments **Person-to-person payments** are a form of e-cash that enables two individuals or an individual and a business to transfer funds without using a credit card. They are one of the newest and fastest-growing payment mechanisms. This service can be used for a variety of purposes, such as sending money to students at college, paying for an item purchased at an online auction, or sending a gift to a family member.

One of the first companies to offer this service was PayPal (an eBay company). Today, AOL QuickCash, One's Bank eMoneyMail, Yahoo PayDirect, and WebCertificate (*www. webcertificate.com*) all compete with PayPal.

Virtually all of these person-to-person payment services work in a similar way. First, you select a service and open up an account. Basically, this entails creating a user name, selecting a password, and providing the service with a credit card or bank account number. Next, you add funds from your credit card or bank account to your new account. Now you're ready to send money to someone over the Internet. You access PayPal (for example) with your user name and password, and you specify the e-mail address of the person to receive the money,

FIGURE 6.9
Visa Cash Card.

FIGURE 6.10
Hong Kong's Octopus card is a stored-value money card for transportation.

along with the dollar amount that you want to send. An e-mail is sent to the payee's e-mail address. The e-mail will contain a link back to the service's Web site. When the recipient clicks on the link, he or she will be taken to the service. The recipient will be asked to set up an account to which the money that you sent will be credited. The recipient can then credit the money from this account to either a credit card or a bank account. The payer pays a small amount (around $1) per transaction.

Digital Wallets   **Digital wallets** (or **e-wallets**) are software mechanisms that provide security measures, combined with convenience, to EC purchasing. The wallet stores the financial information of the buyer, such as credit card number, shipping information, and more. Thus, sensitive information does not need to be reentered for each purchase. If the wallet is stored at the vendor's Web site, it does not have to travel on the Internet for each purchase, making the information more secure.

The problem is that you need an e-wallet with each merchant. One solution is to have a wallet installed on your computer (e.g., MasterCard Wallet or AOL Wallet). In that case, though, you cannot use the e-wallet to make a purchase from another computer, nor is it a totally secured system. Another solution is a universal e-wallet such as Microsoft's Passport.

Before you go on . . .

1. List the various electronic payment mechanisms. Which of these are most often used for B2B payments?
2. What are micropayments?

6.5 Ethical and Legal Issues in E-Business

Technological innovation often forces a society to reexamine and modify its ethical standards. In many cases the new standards are incorporated into law. In this section, we discuss two important ethical issues: privacy and job loss. We then turn our attention to various legal issues arising from the practice of e-business.

Ethical Issues

Many of the ethical and global issues related to IT also apply to e-business. Here we consider two basic issues, privacy and job loss.

By making it easier to store and transfer personal information, e-business presents some threats to privacy. To begin with, most electronic payment systems know who the buyers are. It may be necessary, then, to protect the buyers' identities. For example, this protection can be accomplished with encryption.

Another major privacy issue is tracking. For example, individuals' activities on the Internet can be tracked by cookies, discussed in Chapter 3. Programs such as cookies raise privacy concerns. The tracking history is stored on your PC's hard drive, and any time you revisit a certain Web site, the computer knows it (see NetTracker at *www.sane.com*). In response, some users install programs to have some control over cookies and restore their online privacy.

In addition to compromising employees' privacy, the use of EC may eliminate the need for some of a company's employees, as well as brokers and agents. The manner in which these unneeded workers, especially employees, are treated can raise ethical issues: How should the company handle the layoffs? Should companies be required to retrain employees for new positions? If not, how should the company compensate or otherwise assist the displaced workers?

One of the most pressing EC issues relating to job loss is **disintermediation**. Intermediaries, also known as middlemen, have two functions: (1) They provide information, or (2) they perform value-added services such as consulting. The first function can be fully automated. For this reason, it probably will be assumed by e-marketplaces and portals that provide information for free. In this case, the intermediaries who perform only (or mainly) this function are likely to be eliminated. This process is called disintermediation.

In contrast, performing value-added services requires expertise. Unlike the information function, then, it can be only partially automated. Thus, intermediaries who provide value-added services not only are likely to survive, they may actually prosper. The Web helps these employees in two situations: (1) when the number of participants is enormous, as with job finding; or (2) when the information that must be exchanged is complex.

Legal Issues Specific to E-Commerce

Many legal issues are related specifically to e-commerce. When buyers and sellers do not know one another and cannot even see one another, there is a chance that dishonest people will commit fraud and other crimes. During the first few years of EC, the public witnessed many such crimes. These illegal actions ranged from creating a virtual bank that disappeared along with the investors' deposits to manipulating stock prices on the Internet. Unfortunately, fraudulent activities on the Internet are increasing. In the following section we examine some of the major legal issues that are specific to e-commerce.

Fraud on the Internet Internet fraud has grown even faster than Internet use itself. In one case, stock promoters falsely spread positive rumors about the prospects of the companies they touted in order to boost the stock price. In other cases the information provided might have been true, but the promoters did not disclose that they were paid to talk up the companies. Stock promoters specifically target small investors who are lured by the promise of fast profits.

Stocks are only one of many areas where swindlers are active. Auctions are especially conducive to fraud, by both sellers and buyers. Other types of fraud include selling bogus investments and setting up phantom business opportunities. Thanks to the growing use of e-mail, financial criminals now have access to many more people. The U.S. Federal Trade Commission (*www.ftc.gov*) regularly publishes examples of scams that are most likely to be spread via e-mail or to be found on the Web. Later in this section we discuss some ways in which consumers and sellers can protect themselves from online fraud.

Domain Names Another legal issue is competition over domain names. Domain names are assigned by central nonprofit organizations that check for conflicts and possible infringement of trademarks. Obviously, companies that sell goods and services over the Internet want customers to be able to find them easily. This is most likely when the domain name matches the company's name.

Problems arise when several companies with similar names compete over a domain name. For example, if you want to book reservations at Holiday Inn hotels and you go to *www.holidayinn.com*, you get the Web site for Holiday Inn at the Falls, a hotel at Niagara Falls, New York. To get to the *hotel chain's* Web site, you have to go to *www.ichotelsgroup.com*. Several cases of disputed names are already in court.

Cybersquatting   **Cybersquatting** refers to the practice of registering domain names solely for the purpose of selling them later at a higher price. For example, the original owner of *www.tom.com* received about $8 million for the name. The case of *www.tom.com* was ethical and legal. In other cases, though, cybersquatting can be illegal or at least unethical. A domain name is considered to be legal when the person or business who owns the name has had a legitimate business under that name for some period of time. For example, the Holiday Inn at the Falls in Niagara, New York, had been operating under that name for some time, so that hotel's domain name was not cybersquatting. Companies such as Christian Dior, Nike, Deutsche Bank, and even Microsoft have had to fight or pay to get the domain name that corresponds to their company's name. The Anti-Cybersquatting Consumer Protection Act (1999) lets trademark owners in the United States sue for damages. Occasionally, companies can take their domain names too seriously. One example is Microsoft, as we explain in IT's About Business 6.5.

Taxes and Other Fees   In offline sales, most states and localities tax business transactions that are conducted within their jurisdiction. The most obvious example is sales taxes. Federal, state, and local authorities now are scrambling to figure out how to extend these policies to e-business. This problem is particularly complex for interstate and international e-commerce. For example, some people claim that the state in which the *seller* is located deserves the entire sales tax (or in some countries, value-added tax, VAT). Others contend that the state in which the *server* is located also should receive some of the tax revenues.

IT's About Business

6.5 Microsoft Goes After Student

Mike Rowe, a 17-year-old student from Canada, created a Web site to demonstrate his part-time Web design work. He named the site MikeRoweSoft.com. Rowe became a minor Web celebrity when Microsoft demanded he give up the domain name, accusing him of copyright infringement over the site's name. Microsoft lawyers insisted that he transfer the Web site to Microsoft as soon as possible. In return, he would receive about $10.

Mike responded that he had put a lot of work into his Web site and that the name was worth at least $10,000. He heard nothing more until he received a 25-page letter in the mail accusing him of planning to extort Microsoft all along. Mike went to the news media with the story. After a short while, Microsoft admitted that perhaps it took the case too seriously. After negotiations, Mike gave Microsoft control of the Web site. In return, Microsoft helped him get a new Web site, direct his traffic there, and fly him and his family to Redmond to attend the company's annual research Tech Fest. The company also agreed to pay for Mike's Microsoft certification training and give him a subscription to a Web site for Microsoft developers. Finally, Microsoft agreed to give Mike an Xbox video game console and let him choose some games from the company store.

Sources: Compiled from K. McCarthy, "Microsoft Lawyers Threaten Mike Rowe," *The Register*, January 19, 2004; "Microsoft Takes on Teen's Site MikeRoweSoft.com," *CNN.com*, January 19, 2004; and *www.microsoft.com* and *www.mikerowesoft.com*, accessed March 9, 2005.

QUESTIONS

1. Choose sides, and debate the issue from Mike Rowe's viewpoint and from Microsoft's viewpoint.
2. Could Microsoft simply have ignored Mike Rowe's Web site? Why or why not?

In addition to the sales tax, there is a question about where (and in some cases, whether) electronic sellers should pay business license taxes, franchise fees, gross-receipts taxes, excise taxes, privilege taxes, and utility taxes. Furthermore, how should tax collection be controlled? Legislative efforts to impose taxes on e-commerce are opposed by an organization named the Internet Freedom Fighters. Their efforts have been successful so far. At the time this edition was written, the United States and several other countries had imposed a ban on imposing a sales tax on business conducted on the Internet. This ban could remain valid until fall 2006. In addition, buyers were exempt from tax on Internet access.

Copyright   Recall from Chapter 3 that intellectual property is protected by copyright laws and cannot be used freely. Protecting intellectual property in e-commerce is very difficult, however. Hundreds of millions of people in some 200 countries with differing copyright laws having access to billions of Web pages makes it far too difficult to enforce copyright laws. For example, some people mistakenly believe that once they purchase a piece of software, they have the right to share it with others. In fact, what they have bought is the right to *use* the software, not the right to *distribute* it. That right remains with the copyright holder. Similarly, copying material from Web sites without permission is a violation of copyright laws.

Before you go on . . .

1. List some ethical issues in EC.
2. List the major legal issues of EC.
3. Describe buyer protection in EC.
4. Describe seller protection in EC.

What's in IT for me?

For the Accounting Major

Accounting personnel are involved in several EC activities. Designing the ordering system and its relationship with inventory management requires accounting attention. Billing and payments are also accounting activities, as are determining cost and profit allocation. Replacing paper documents by electronic means will affect many of the accountant's tasks, especially the auditing of EC activities and systems. Finally, building a cost-benefit and cost-justification system of which products/services to take online and creating a chargeback system are critical to the success of EC.

For the Finance Major

The worlds of banking, securities and commodities markets, and other financial services are being reengineered due to EC. Online securities trading and its supporting infrastructure are growing more rapidly than any other EC activity. Many innovations already in place are changing the rules of economic and financial incentives for financial analysts and managers. Online banking, for example, does not recognize state boundaries, and it may create a new framework for financing global trades. Public financial information is now accessible in seconds. These innovations will dramatically change the manner in which finance personnel operate.

For the Marketing Major

A major revolution in marketing and sales is taking place due to EC. Perhaps its most obvious feature is the transition from a physical to a virtual marketplace. Equally important, though, is the radical transformation to one-on-one advertising and sales and to customized and interactive marketing. Marketing channels are being combined, eliminated, or recreated. The EC revolution is creating new products and markets and significantly altering others. Digitization of products and services also has implications for marketing and sales. The direct producer-to-consumer channel is expanding rapidly and is fundamentally changing the nature of customer service. As the battle for customers intensifies, marketing and sales personnel are becoming the most critical success factor in many organizations. Online marketing can be a blessing to one company and a curse to another.

For the Production/Operations Management Major

EC is changing the manufacturing system from product-push mass production to order-pull mass customization. This change requires a robust supply chain, information support, and reengineering of processes that involve suppliers and other business partners. Using extranets, suppliers can monitor and replenish inventories without the need for constant reorders. In addition, the Internet and intranets help reduce cycle times. Many production/operations problems that have persisted for years, such as complex scheduling and excess inventories, are being solved rapidly with the use of Web technologies. Companies can now use external and internal networks to find and manage manufacturing operations in other countries much more easily. Also, the Web is reengineering procurement by helping companies conduct electronic bids for parts and subassemblies, thus reducing cost. All in all, the job of the progressive production/operations manager is closely tied in with e-commerce.

For the Human Resources Management Major

HR majors need to understand the new labor markets and the impacts of EC on old labor markets. Also, the HRM department may use EC tools for such functions as procuring office supplies. Also, becoming knowledgeable about new government online initiatives and online training is critical. Finally, HR personnel must be familiar with the major legal issues related to EC and employment.

The MIS Function

The MIS function is responsible for providing the information technology infrastructure necessary for electronic commerce to function. In particular, this infrastructure includes the company's networks, intranets, and extranets. The MIS function is also responsible for ensuring that electronic commerce transactions are secure.

1. Describe electronic commerce, its scope, benefits, limitations, and types.

E-commerce can be conducted on the Web and on other networks. It is divided into the following major types: business-to-consumer, business-to-business, consumer-to-consumer, business-to-employee, and government-to-citizen. E-commerce offers many benefits to organizations, consumers, and society, but it also has limitations (technological and non-technological). The current technological limitations are expected to lessen with time.

2. Distinguish between pure and partial electronic commerce.

In pure EC, the product or service, the process by which the product or service is produced, and the delivery agent are all digital. All other combinations that include a mix of digital and physical dimensions are considered partial EC.

3. Understand the basics of how online auctions work.

A major mechanism in EC is auctions. The Internet provides an infrastructure for executing auctions at lower cost, and with many more involved sellers and buyers, including both individual consumers and corporations. Two major types of auctions exist: forward auctions and reverse auctions. Forward auctions are used in the traditional process of *selling* to the highest bidder. Reverse auctions are used for *buying*, using a tendering system to buy at the lowest bid.

4. Differentiate among business-to-consumer (B2C), business-to-business (B2B), consumer-to-consumer (C2C), business-to-employee (B2E), and government-to citizen (G2C) electronic commerce.

B2C (e-tailing) can be pure or part of a click-and-mortar organization. Direct marketing is done via solo storefronts, in malls, via electronic catalogs, or by using electronic auctions. The leading online B2C service industries are banking, securities trading, job markets, travel, and real estate. The major B2B applications are selling from catalogs and by forward auctions (the sell-side marketplace), buying in reverse auctions and in group and desktop purchasing (the buy-side marketplace), and trading in electronic exchanges and hubs. EC also can be done between consumers (C2C), but should be undertaken with caution. Auctions are the most popular C2C mechanism. C2C also can be done by use of online classified ads. B2E provides services to employees, typically over the company's intranet. G2C takes place between government and citizens, making government operations more effective and efficient.

5. Describe the major e-commerce support services, specifically payments and logistics.

New electronic payment systems are needed to complete transactions on the Internet. Electronic payments can be made by e-checks, e-credit cards, purchasing cards, e-cash, stored-value money cards, smart cards, person-to-person payments via services like Pay-Pal, electronic bill presentment and payment, and e-wallets. Order fulfillment is especially difficult and expensive in B2C, because of the need to ship relatively small orders to many customers.

6. Discuss some ethical and legal issues relating to e-commerce.

There is increasing fraud and unethical behavior on the Internet, including invasion of privacy by sellers and misuse of domain names. The value of domain names, taxation of online business, and how to handle legal issues in a multicountry environment are major legal concerns. Protection of customers, sellers, and intellectual property is also important.

Chapter Glossary

auction A competitive process in which either a seller solicits consecutive bids from buyers or a buyer solicits bids from sellers, and prices are determined dynamically by competitive bidding. (180)

banners Electronic billboards, which typically contain a short text or graphical message to promote a product or a vendor. (188)

brick-and-mortar   organizations Organizations   in which the product, the process, and the delivery agent are all physical. (177)

business-to-business electronic commerce (B2B) Electronic commerce in which both the sellers and the buyers are business organizations. (179)

business-to-consumer electronic commerce (B2C) Electronic commerce in which the sellers are organizations and the buyers are individuals; also known as e-tailing. (179)

business-to-employee electronic commerce (B2E) An organization using electronic commerce internally to provide information and services to its employees. (180)

business model The method by which a company generates revenue to sustain itself. (180)

buy-side marketplace B2B model in which organizations buy needed products or services from other organizations electronically, often through a reverse auction. (191)

channel conflict The alienation of existing distributors when a company decides to sell to customers directly online. (186)

click-and-mortar organizations Organizations that do business in both the physical and digital dimensions. (177)

consumer-to-consumer electronic commerce (C2C) Electronic commerce in which both the buyer and the seller are individuals (not businesses). (179)

cyberbanking Various banking activities conducted electronically from home, a business, or on the road instead of at a physical bank location. (184)

cybersquatting Registering domain names in the hope of selling them later at a higher price. (199)

disintermediation Elimination of intermediaries in electronic commerce. (198)

e-business A broader definition of electronic commerce, including buying and selling of goods and services, and also servicing customers, collaborating with business partners, conducting e-learning, and conducting electronic transactions within an organization. (177)

e-government The use of electronic commerce to deliver information and public services to citizens, business partners, and suppliers of government entities, and those working in the public sector. (180)

e-procurement Purchasing by using electronic support. (191)

e-wallets (digital wallets) A software component in which a user stores secured personal and credit card information for one-click reuse. (197)

electronic commerce (e-commerce) The process of buying, selling, transferring, or exchanging products, services, or information via computer networks, including the Internet. (177)

electronic mall A collection of individual shops under one Internet address. (181)

electronic marketplace A virtual market space on the Web where many buyers and many sellers conduct electronic business activities. (182)

electronic payment systems Computer-based systems that allow customers to pay for goods and services electronically, rather than writing a check or using cash. (192)

electronic retailing (e-tailing) The direct sale of products and services through storefronts or electronic malls, usually designed around an electronic catalog format and/or auctions. (182)

electronic storefront The Web site of a single company, with its own Internet address, at which orders can be placed. (181)

forward auction An auction that sellers use as a selling channel to many potential buyers; the highest bidder wins the items. (180)

functional exchanges Electronic marketplaces where needed services such as temporary help or extra office space are traded on an "as-needed" basis. (191)

group purchasing The aggregation of purchasing orders from many buyers so that a volume discount can be obtained. (191)

horizontal exchanges Electronic marketplaces that connect buyers and sellers across many industries, used mainly for MRO materials. (191)

mobile commerce (m-commerce) Electronic commerce conducted in a wireless environment. (180)

multichanneling A process in which a company integrates its online and offline channels. (186)

permission marketing Method of marketing that asks consumers to give their permission to voluntarily accept online advertising and e-mail. (189)

person-to-person payment A form of electronic cash that enables the transfer of funds between two individuals, or between a individual and a business, without the use of a credit card. (196)

pop-up ad An advertisement that is automatically launched by some trigger and appears in front of the active window. (188)

pop-under ad An advertisement that is automatically launched by some trigger and appears underneath the active window. (188)

public exchanges (exchanges) Electronic marketplace in which there are many sellers and many buyers, and entry is open to all; frequently owned and operated by a third party. (191)

reverse auction An auction in which one buyer, usually an organization, seeks to buy a product or a service, and suppliers submit bids; the lowest bidder wins. (180)

sell-side marketplace B2B model in which organizations sell to other organizations from their own private e-marketplace and/or from a third-party site. (190)

smart card A card that contains a microprocessor (chip) that enables the card to store a considerable amount of information (including stored funds) and to conduct processing. (195)

spamming Indiscriminate distribution of e-mail without permission of the receiver. (189)

stored-value money card A form of electronic cash on which a fixed amount of prepaid money is stored; the amount is reduced each time the card is used. (195)

vertical exchanges Electronic marketplaces that connect buyers and sellers in a given industry. (191)

viral marketing Online word-of-mouth marketing. (189)

virtual bank A banking institution dedicated solely to Internet transactions. (184)

virtual organizations Organizations in which the product, the process, and the delivery agent are all digital; also called pure-play organizations. (177)

Discussion Questions

1. Discuss the major limitations of e-commerce. Which of them are likely to disappear? Why?
2. Discuss the reasons for having multiple EC business models.
3. Distinguish between business-to-business forward auctions and buyers' bids for RFQs.
4. Discuss the benefits to sellers and buyers of a B2B exchange.
5. What are the major benefits of G2C electronic commerce?
6. Discuss the various ways to pay online in B2C. Which one(s) would you prefer and why?
7. Why is order fulfillment in B2C considered difficult?
8. Discuss the reasons for EC failures.

Problem-Solving Activities

1. Assume you are interested in buying a car. You can find information about cars at numerous Web sites. Access five of them for information about new and used cars, financing, and insurance. Decide what car you want to buy. Configure your car by going to the car manufacturer's Web site. Finally, try to find the car from *www.autobytel.com*. What information is most supportive of your decision-making process? Write a report about your experience.
2. Consider the opening case about Procter & Gamble.
   a. How was the corporate decision making improved?
   b. Summarize the benefits to the company, retailers, suppliers, and customers.
3. Compare the various electronic payment methods. Specifically, collect information from the vendors cited in the chapter and find more with *google.com*. Pay attention to security level, speed, cost, and convenience.
4. Prepare a study on how to stop spam. Look at *http://find.pcworld.com/27401, http://find.pcworld.com/27424*, and *http://find.pcworld.com/27426*. Consider *www.intermute.com, www.guidescope.com*, and *www.synamtec.com*. Investigate what AOL and Yahoo offer. What is new in legislation regarding spamming in your country?

Internet Activities

1. Access the Stock Market Game Worldwide (*www.smgww.org*). You will be bankrolled with $100,000 in a trading account every month. Play the game and relate your experiences with regard to information technology.
2. Access *www.realtor.com*. Prepare a list of services available on this site. Then prepare a list of advantages derived by the users and advantages to realtors. Are there any disadvantages? To whom?

3. Enter *www.alibaba.com*. Identify the site's capabilities. Look at the site's private trading room. Write a report. How can such a site help a person who is making a purchase?

4. Enter *www.campusfood.com*. Explore the site. Why is the site so successful? Could you start a competing one? Why or why not?

5. Enter *www.dell.com*, go to "desktops," and configure a system. Register to "my cart" (no obligation). What calculators are used there? What are the advantages

of this process as compared with buying a computer in a physical store? What are the disadvantages?

6. Enter *www.checkfree.com* and find their services. Prepare a report.

7. Access various travel sites such as *www.travelocity.com, www.orbitz.com, www.expedia.com, www.sidestep.com,* and *www.pinpoint.com*. Compare these Web sites for ease of use and usefulness. Note differences among the sites. If you ask each site for the itinerary, which one gives you the best information and the best deals?

Team Assignments

1. Have each team study a major bank with extensive EC strategy. For example, Wells Fargo Bank is well on its way to being a cyberbank. Hundreds of brick-and-mortar branch offices are being closed (see *www.wellsfargo.com*). Other banks to look at are Citicorp (*www.citicorp.com*), Netbank (*www.netbank. com*), and HSBC (*www.hsbc.com*) in Hong Kong. Each team should attempt to convince the class that its e-bank activities are the best.

2. Assign each team to one industry. Each team will find five real-world applications of the major business-to-

business models listed in the chapter. (Try success stories of vendors and EC-related magazines.) Examine the problems they solve or the opportunities they exploit.

3. Have teams investigate how B2B payments are made in global trade. Consider instruments such as electronic letters of credit and e-checks. Visit *www.tradecard.com* and examine their services to small and medium size enterprises (SMEs). Also, investigate what Visa and MasterCard are offering. Finally, check Citicorp and some German and Japanese banks.

CASE

The San Francisco Giants Enhance Their Fans' Experience

MKT

THE BUSINESS PROBLEM The consortium that purchased the money-losing San Francisco Giants in 1993 realized that they had to build a new stadium to help stop the losses. However, the move from Candlestick Park and the building of the new SBC Park left the consortium $200 million in debt. To recoup their losses, the consortium had to find ways to attract as many fans as possible to the new ballpark. Ticket sales comprise the team's biggest revenue source—about 50 percent of the team's annual income.

THE IT SOLUTION Information technology is important to the Giants in three areas. The first is operations, meaning SBC Park itself. In addition to the Giants, the stadium plays host to soccer games, concerts, Monster Truck rallies, and many other events. IT helps in planning and scheduling these events.

The second area is baseball. For example, the players, coaches, and scouts rely on digital video to improve their hitting and pitching. In addition, the team's scouts all have laptops on which they enter information about prospects and opposing players.

The third area is the fan experience. In August 1996, more than a year before the first brick was laid at SBC Park, Giants fans were able to go online and check out the view of home plate from their prospective season seats. They could even purchase the rights to those seats for a lifetime.

One IT innovation for fans is the "Double Play" reselling auction, in which ticket holders can resell tickets when they cannot make a particular game. Market research had discovered that one of the major reasons that season-ticket holders do not renew is the "tickets-in-the-drawer" syndrome. At the end of a season, fans end up with a pile of unused tickets that they can't return. To address this issue, the Giants established a Web site for ticket holders to sell their tickets back to the Giants. The Giants take responsibility for the transactions. Fans do not have to meet a stranger, carry cash, mail a personal check, or give out a credit card number. Instead, the tickets are reassigned as e-tickets and printed out at the stadium kiosks when the purchaser arrives. The transaction is safe and secure. The Giants take a small transaction fee on each sale.

As a result of these policies, the Giants now sell out more games. Of course, the more fans who attend, the greater the opportunities for concession and souvenir sales.

THE RESULTS Twenty-eight thousand of the park's 42,000 seats—which amounts to 67%—are presold to season-ticket holders. –This is the highest percentage in professional baseball. Also, the renewal rate for season ticket holders is 90 percent. The Giants have almost tripled annual revenues, from $65 million to $170 million.

The ultimate goal is for SBC Park to be one of the most technologically advanced sports facilities in the world. As their next step, the Giants are planning a completely ticketless and cashless facility where even the turnstiles will be electronic.

Sources: Compiled from B. Schlough, "How IT Bolsters the Baseball Experience and Revenues," *CIO Insight,* October 1, 2004; "California Installs Wi-Fi Access at State Parks," *Reuters,* January 21, 2005; and *www.sfgiants.com,* accessed March 19, 2005.

QUESTIONS

1. Discuss the "Double Play" auction. Do you think it is a good idea, or is it just another form of scalping tickets? Support your answer.
2. Describe how information technology has helped triple the Giants' annual revenues.

Interactive Learning

Opening Up E-Wallets on Amazon.com

Go to the Interactivities section on the *WileyPLUS* Web site and access Chapter 6: E-Business and E-Commerce. There you will find an interactive simulation of the technologies used for the electronic wallets used by Amazon.com's customers, as well as some hands-on activities that visually explain business concepts in this chapter.

E-commerce at Club IT

Go to the Club IT link on the *WileyPLUS* Web site to find assignments that will ask you to help club IT's owner's leverage e-commerce.

wiley.com/college/rainer

How-To Appendix

Tips for Safe Electronic Shopping

- Look for reliable brand names at sites like *Wal-Mart Online, Disney Online*, and *Amazon.com*. Before purchasing, make sure that the site is authentic by entering the site directly and not from an unverified link.

- Search any unfamiliar selling site for the company's address and phone and fax numbers. Call up and quiz the employees about the seller.

- Check out the vendor with the local Chamber of Commerce or Better Business Bureau (*bbbonline.org*). Look for seals of authenticity such as TRUSTe.

- Investigate how secure the seller's site is by examining the security procedures and by reading the posted privacy policy.

- Examine the money-back guarantees, warranties, and service agreements.

- Compare prices with those in regular stores. Too-low prices are too good to be true, and some catch is probably involved.

- Ask friends what they know. Find testimonials and endorsements in community sites and well-known bulletin boards.

- Find out what your rights are in case of a dispute. Consult consumer protection agencies and the National Fraud Information Center (*fraud.org*).

- Check *consumerworld.org* for a listing of useful resources.

Chapter 7

In many situations the traditional working environment that requires users to come to a wired computer is either ineffective or inefficient. In these situations the solution is to build computers small enough to carry or wear, which can communicate via wireless networks. The ability to communicate any time, anywhere, provides organizations with strategic advantage by increasing productivity and speed and improving customer service.

Wireless computing provides the infrastructure for mobile commerce—conducting e-commerce wirelessly, any time, and from any place. Wireless computing enables location-based e-commerce, which is based on knowing where people are at any given time and on the ability to communicate with them. Wireless computing is also changing how IT is deployed and is creating the foundation of pervasive computing. This chapter explores all of these topics.

Wireless, Mobile Computing, and Mobile Commerce

Introduction to Information Systems
R. Kelly Rainer, Jr., Efraim Turban, and Richard E. Potter. ISBN 978-0-471-7363-3
©2007 John Wiley & Sons, Inc.

Chapter Outline

7.1 Wireless Technologies

7.2 Wireless Computer Networks and Internet Access

7.3 Mobile Computing and Mobile Commerce

7.4 Pervasive Computing

7.5 Wireless Security

Learning Objectives

1. Discuss the various types of wireless devices and wireless transmission media.
2. Describe Bluetooth, Zigbee, Wi-Fi, and WiMax.
3. Define mobile computing and mobile commerce.
4. Discuss the major m-commerce applications.
5. Define pervasive computing and describe two technologies underlying pervasive computing.
6. Discuss the four major threats to wireless networks.

What's in IT for me?

ACC    FIN   MKT   POM   HRM    MIS

CASE **What to Do at Philip Morris?**

The Business Problem

On November 16, 2004, a DHL express freight plane landed at New York's John F. Kennedy International Airport. Upon its arrival, agents from the U.S. Department of Justice's Bureau of Alcohol, Tobacco, Firearms, and Explosives (ATF) seized its cargo of 82,000 bootleg cartons of cigarettes, valued at more than $1 million. The cigarettes were earmarked for customers in the United States who had placed orders with Otamedia, an online tobacco retailer based in Switzerland. The majority of the

Source: James Leynse/Redux Pictures

cartons consisted of Marlboro and Marlboro Lights. These brands are produced by the world's largest tobacco manufacturer, Altria Group (*www.altria.com*), through two subsidiaries: Philip Morris International (PMI) (*www.philipmorrisinternational.com*) and Philip Morris USA (*www.pmusa.com*).

It is illegal to import cigarettes into the United States without paying appropriate taxes and import duties. These taxes and duties can increase the price of a carton of Marlboros at a U.S. grocery store to $50. In contrast, Otamedia's Internet customers were paying as little as $14 per carton—plus an additional $5 for shipping—to have their cigarettes delivered right to their door. How serious is the problem of cigarette smuggling? A conservative estimate is that it costs national, state, and local governments more than $30 billion per year in lost tax revenue.

Philip Morris denies it is responsible for this illegal cigarette trade. Instead, it maintains that the cartons are being shipped by an unauthorized distributor. It also claims that it has taken Otamedia to court to stop this illicit supply chain. Regulators in Europe, however, insist that none of this matters. Rather, they argue that it is the responsibility of a manufacturer to control its supply chain from start to finish, regardless of who puts its products in the hands of consumers. In July 2004, the European Union (EU) ordered Philip Morris to implement new information systems to track and trace its cigarettes all the way from the manufacturing line to the consumer.

More specifically, the EU is requiring Philip Morris to identify the date and place of manufacture of every pack of its cigarettes with embossed markings on the packaging. These markings must be able to identify the manufacturing facility, the individual machine used, and the production shift. In addition, on each pack of cigarettes Philip Morris must identify the country in which it will be sold. The company must also build and maintain a database of all pack information for the European antifraud investigating organization. This database will allow investigators to identify the products they find in any seizure as well as their last known purchasers.

The Possible IT Solution

Philip Morris has assembled a team of experts from its packaging, research and development, IT, and brand integrity departments to evaluate new technologies that could help it meet the EU's mandate. One option under consideration is radio frequency identification (RFID) technology. **RFID technology** allows manufacturers to attach tags with antennas and computer chips on goods and then track their movement through radio signals. Some experts, however, argue that RFID may be too expensive for Philip Morris to use in tracking individual cigarette packs.

It costs companies from $1 million to $3 million just to set up a basic RFID pilot system. For a full-scale installation, the readers, tags, and accompanying software will cost corporations about $20 million. However, these costs are typical of a supply chain in which

RFID tags are attached to pallets of goods. The expenses are far greater when tags have to be attached to individual packs of cigarettes.

How expensive would such a program be? Consider the following numbers. One product label with an embedded RFID tag can easily cost 50 cents. In 2003, Philip Morris sold 4.5 billion cartons of cigarettes. If the company put an RFID tag on each carton, the cost would be $2.25 billion. Keep in mind, too, that Philip Morris also would have to purchase readers to record the data from the RFID tags. If the company sells 4.5 billion cartons, then how many readers would it need, and where would it put them? Another issue is that RFID readers must be precisely tuned for the places in which they operate. For example, a reader at a receiving dock door must be tuned so that is does not accidentally retrieve codes from products arriving at an adjacent door.

Given all of these problems, why is Philip Morris even considering RFID technology? The answer is that more data can be encoded on an RFID chip than in a standard bar-code strip. So, an effective RFID system would enable the company to track every pack of cigarettes it produces. Unlike the 12-digit standard Universal Product Code (UPC), the 28-digit Electronic Product Code (EPC) being promoted for use with RFID can produce the information required by the EU.

The Results

Philip Morris has already spent millions of dollars to investigate how RFID technology can be implemented in its supply chain. The company has developed a database, integrated with its SAP supply-chain system, that contains all the information for first-tier distributors (the distributors who receive the cigarettes directly from the manufacturing facility). By itself, however, this innovation will not be enough for the EU. The reason is that this system cannot track cigarette packs past first-tier distributors, and the EU has mandated that Philip Morris track cigarette packs all the way to the consumer. The company faces severe fines from the EU if it does not meet the EU's mandate. It is probable that RFID technologies will decrease in cost in the near future. Even so, Philip Morris has not decided whether it will proceed with RFID.

What We Learned From This Case

Wireless is a term used to describe telecommunications in which electromagnetic waves (rather than some form of wire or cable) carry the signal between communicating devices (e.g., computers, personal digital assistants, cell phones, etc.). The opening case is an example of a wireless technology (RFID) that is a possible solution for a serious regulatory problem for Philip Morris. Philip Morris' problem also applies to other industries—for example, pharmaceuticals, food services, liquor, apparel, and hazardous materials—as government agencies from many countries try to stop counterfeiting, fraud, smuggling, and tax evasion. The case also demonstrates that wireless technology is in its beginning stages, with exciting potential but currently high costs.

Wireless technologies enable mobile computing, mobile commerce, and pervasive computing. We define these terms here and discuss each in more detail later in the chapter. **Mobile computing** refers to a real-time, wireless connection between a mobile device and other computing environments, such as the Internet or an intranet. **Mobile commerce**—also known as **m-commerce**—refers to e-commerce (EC) transactions that are conducted in a wireless environment, especially via the Internet. **Pervasive computing** (also called *ubiquitous computing*) means that virtually every object has processing power with wireless or wired connections to a global network.

Wireless technologies and mobile commerce are spreading rapidly, replacing or supplementing wired computing. In some cases, wireless technologies are allowing countries to build a communications infrastructure from scratch. For example, after two decades of civil war, technology is beginning to appear in Afghanistan. In 2002, the entire country had only one telephone line for every 1,000 people. In addition, in a country with approximately

25 million people, there were only 1,000 Internet users and 15,000 people with mobile phones. Today, Afghanistan has more than 650,000 people using mobile phones, and Internet cafés are springing up in Kabul, the nation's capital and largest city. Afghanistan received its Internet domain, *.af*, in March 2003.

The wireless infrastructure upon which mobile computing is built may reshape the entire IT field. The technologies, applications, and limitations of mobile computing and mobile commerce are the main focus of this chapter. We begin the chapter with a discussion of wireless devices and wireless transmission media. We continue by examining wireless computer networks and wireless Internet access. We then look at mobile computing and mobile commerce, which are made possible by wireless technologies. Next, we turn our attention to pervasive computing and conclude the chapter by discussing wireless security.

Sources: Compiled from D.F. Carr, and L. Barrett, "Philip Morris International: Smoke Screen," *Baseline Magazine*, February 1, 2005; M. Roberti, "Where RFID Is Happening." *RFID Journal*, January 26, 2004; B. Smith, "Raising the RFID Profile," *Wireless Week*, December 15, 2003.

7.1 Wireless Technologies

Wireless technologies include both wireless devices, such as pagers and cell phones, and wireless transmission media, such as microwave, satellite, and radio. These technologies are fundamentally changing the ways organizations are operating and doing business. As one example, IT's About Business 7.1 illustrates how wireless technologies are transforming law enforcement.

Wireless Devices

Individuals are finding it convenient and productive to use wireless devices for several reasons. First, they can make productive use of time that was formerly wasted (e.g., while commuting to work in their cars or on public transportation). Second, because they can take these devices

---

IT's About Business

7.1 Wireless Helps the Police in Two Cities

Tyler, Texas

In Tyler, Texas, digital video cameras in the city's 60 police cars are able to send TV images of police action back to headquarters. These images are sent in real time over a wireless network. This system represents a major innovation in law-enforcement IT. In contrast, many police forces continue to use an older technology, which consists of video cameras mounted on the car's dashboard. Unlike the digital cameras, these video cameras only record police stops on tape.

The digital technology collects and stores video on a hard drive in the police car. It automatically retrieves data starting four minutes prior to the officer's hitting "record" by flipping on the overhead pursuit lights. In this way the wireless network helps identify the probable cause for the police action. It actually enables headquarters to see events unfold

live. The computer record from each police car is downloaded each day and placed into computer storage. Data from the car, such as readings from the radar gun, are matched with the digital video. They also can be compared with information from the magnetic strip on the suspect's driver's license, which is swiped by police. The system allows the police to quickly retrieve the video and data of a police stop. The police can use these data as evidence in a court hearing. At the same time, the person who was stopped can use the information to charge the police with unlawful conduct.

Jersey City, New Jersey

Beat cops in the Jersey City Police Department walk, bike, and drive over their territory. To ensure that every officer has access to critical information in

---

real time, the department implemented a high-speed wireless mobile network and gave each officer a handheld computing device. An important goal was to provide data through wireless technology to officers who are not assigned to patrol cars. The handhelds have an integrated bar-code scanner, digital camera, digital video camera, and cell phone. The officers use these computers to remotely access information needed during investigations, including license-plate numbers, criminal histories, and outstanding warrants. The devices also allow officers to tap into existing video-surveillance cameras located throughout the city.

Sources: Compiled from J. Herskovitz, "Live, Digital Video Heading to U.S. Police Cars," *Reuters*, April 20, 2004; L. Greenemeier, "Jersey City Cops Add Video to Shoe Leather," *InternetWeek*, March 7, 2005; and B. Smith, "Police Drive into Next Gen," *Wireless Week*, August 1, 2003.

QUESTIONS

1. What are the advantages of these wireless technologies for the police?
2. What are the advantages of these wireless technologies for the public?
3. What are the privacy implications of these wireless technologies for the public?

with them, their work locations are becoming much more flexible. Third, wireless technology enables them to allocate their working time around personal and professional obligations.

Wireless devices are small enough to easily carry or wear, have sufficient computing power to perform productive tasks, and can communicate wirelessly with the Internet and other devices. These devices include pagers, e-mail handhelds, personal digital assistants (PDAs), cellular telephones, and smart phones. We discuss each of these technologies below. As you read each description, consider how the specific technology affects your working environment now and in the future.

The **Wireless Application Protocol (WAP)** is the standard that enables wireless devices with tiny display screens, low-bandwidth connections, and minimal memory to access Web-based information and services. (Recall that bandwidth refers to the amount of information that can be transmitted over a communications channel in a unit of time, typically seconds).

WAP-compliant devices contain **microbrowsers**, which are Internet browsers with a small file size that can work within the low-memory constraints of wireless devices and the low bandwidths of wireless networks. Figure 7.1a shows the full-function browser on Amazon's Web page, and Figure 7.1b shows the microbrowser on the screen of a cell phone accessing Amazon.com.

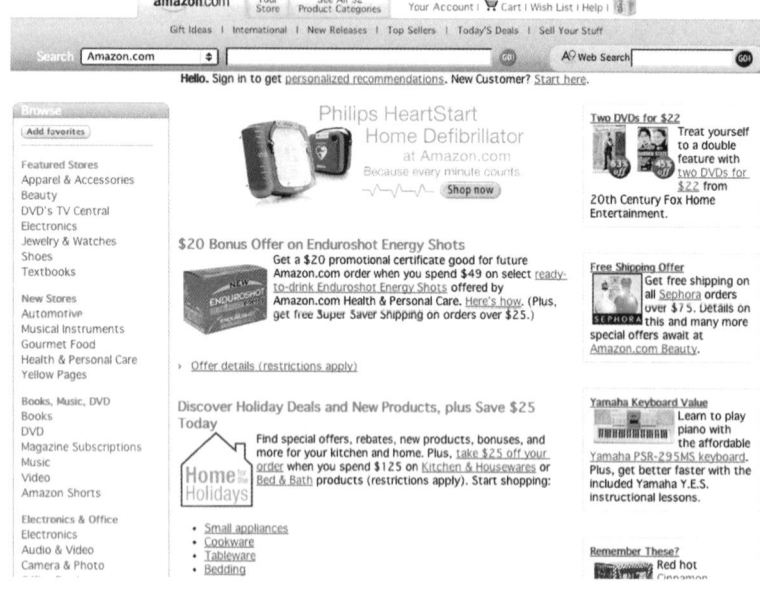

FIGURE 7.1A   Amazon Web page browser. *Source:* www.amazon.com

FIGURE 7.1B   Cell phone microbrowser.

FIGURE 7.2
Pager. *Source:* Brand X
Pictures/Media Bakery

FIGURE 7.2
Pager. *Source:* Brand X
Pictures/Media Bakery

FIGURE 7.3
BlackBerry.
Source: Research in
Motion (RIM)

Pagers.   A **pager** is a one-way, wireless messaging system. The pager alerts the user when it receives an incoming message. Pagers provide several kinds of messages: tone-only, numeric display, alphanumeric display, and tone-and-voice (see Figure 7.2). This pager is providing a traffic alert, so the driver can take an alternate route.

E-mail Handhelds.   E-mail handhelds, such as the BlackBerry (see *www.rim.com* and *www.blackberry.com*), have a small display screen and a keypad for typing short messages (see Figure 7.3). Newer versions also have an organizer as well as Web and voice transmission features. In addition, the user can integrate them with corporate applications. These devices make it easy to keep in touch with clients and the office.

Cellular Telephones (Cell Phones).   **Cellular telephones** use radio waves to provide two-way communication. The cell phone communicates with radio antennas (towers) placed within adjacent geographic areas called *cells* (see Figure 7.4). A telephone message is transmitted to the local cell (antenna) by the cell phone and then is passed from cell to cell until it reaches the cell of its destination. At this final cell, the message is either transmitted to the receiving cell phone or transferred to the public switched telephone system to be transmitted to a wireline telephone. This is why you can use a cell phone to call both other cell phones and standard wireline phones.

Cellular technology is quickly evolving, moving toward higher transmission speeds and richer features. The technology has progressed through four stages:

1. *First generation (1G)* cellular used analog signals and had low bandwidth (capacity).

2. *Second generation (2G)* uses digital signals primarily for voice communication, 2G provides data communication up to 10 Kbps. (*Note*: Kbps means 1,000 bits per second (kilo thousand).)

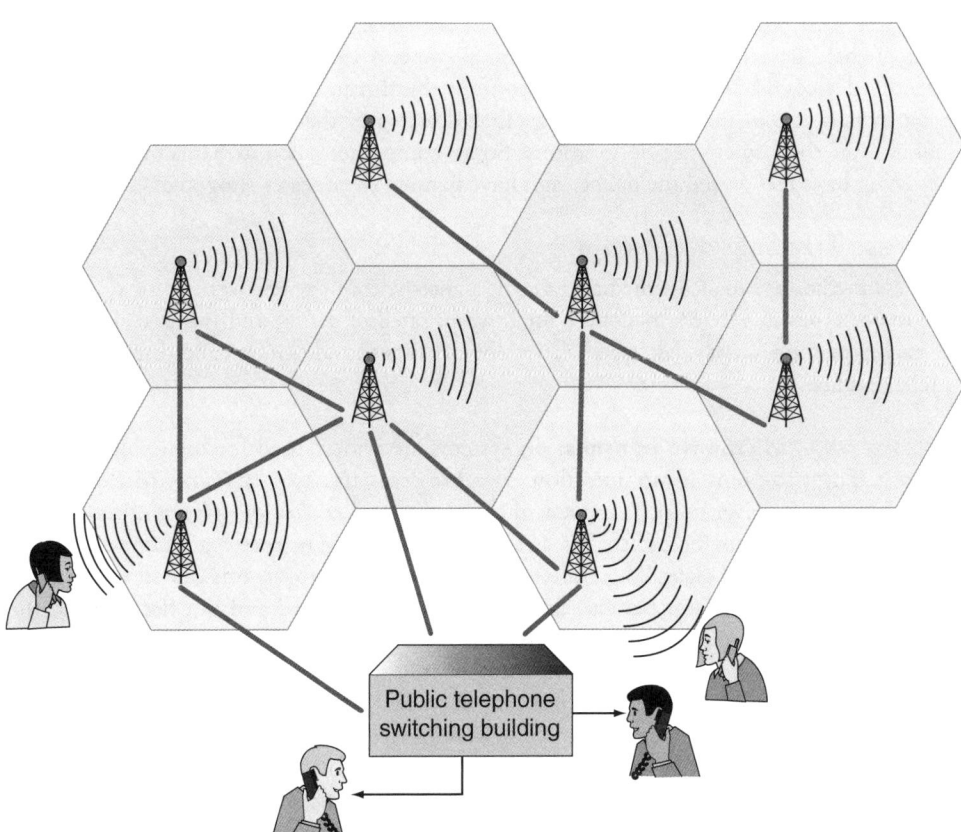

FIGURE 7.4
Cellular network.
Source: Adapted from
http://people.bu.edu/
storo/im1.gif

3. *2.5 G* uses digital signals and provides voice and data communication up to 144 Kbps.

4. *Third generation (3G)* uses digital signals and can transmit voice and data up to 384 Kbps when the device is moving at a walking pace, 128 Kbps when moving in a car, and up to 2 Mbps when the device is in a fixed location; 3G supports video, Web browsing, and instant messaging.

Cell phones are becoming cheaper and more powerful, and their use is exploding. In 2002 the number of cell phones surpassed that of wireline phones for the first time. Almost 2 billion cell phones are expected to be in use worldwide by 2007.

Digital cellular telephones are capable of sending and receiving short text messages (up to 160 characters in length), a process called **Short Messaging Service (SMS)**. These messages can be stored and forwarded.

Personal Digital Assistants (PDAs).   **Personal digital assistants** are small, handheld computers that can transmit digital communications. PDAs provide applications such as electronic schedulers and address books. Advanced models also display, compose, send, and receive e-mail messages, and they provide wireless access to the Internet. Some PDAs have built-in digital cameras and voice communication capabilities.

Smart Phones.   **Smart phones** are a new class of digital communication appliances that combine the functionality of a PDA with that of a digital cell phone. Smart phones provide many functions, which include an organizer, cell phone, digital camera, access to e-mail, Internet access, and short message service. Smart phones play music, play video, and allow the user to view photos. These devices have a color screen and a built-in keyboard (see the Treo 650 by *www.palmone.com* in Figure 7.5).

A downside is that smart camera phones can cause damage in the workplace. For example, if you were an executive at Intel, would you want workers snapping pictures of their colleagues with your secret new technology in the background? Unfortunately, managers think of these devices as phones, not as digital cameras that can transmit wirelessly. New jamming devices are being developed to counter the threat. For example, Iceberg Systems (*www.iceberg-ip.com*) provides technology that deactivates the imaging systems in camera phones after they enter specific locations. Some companies, such as Samsung (*www.samsung.com*), have recognized the danger and have banned the devices altogether.

Wireless Transmission Media

Wireless media, or broadcast media, transmit signals without wires over the air or in space. The major types of wireless media are microwave, satellite, radio, and infrared. Let's examine each type more closely. Manager's Checklist 7.1 lists the advantages and disadvantages of wireless media.

Microwave.   **Microwave transmission** systems are widely used for high-volume, long-distance, point-to-point communication. *Point-to-point* has two characteristics: first, the transmitter and receiver must be in view of each other (called *line-of-sight*); and second, the transmission itself must be tightly directed from transmitter to receiver. Microwave transmission requires line-of-sight. Therefore, adjacent microwave towers must be in view of each other. This creates problems because the earth's surface is curved and not flat. Due to this fact, microwave towers usually cannot be spaced more than 30 miles apart.

The fact that microwave requires line-of-sight transmission severely limits its usefulness as a large-scale solution to data communications needs, especially over very long distances. Additionally, microwave transmissions are susceptible to environmental interference during severe weather such as heavy rain or snowstorms. Although long-distance microwave data communications systems are still widely used, they are being replaced by satellite communications systems.

FIGURE 7.5
The 650 Smart phone.
Source: PalmOne, Inc.

Manager's Checklist 7.1

Advantages and Disadvantages of Wireless Media

Channel	Advantages	Disadvantages
Microwave	High bandwidth. Relatively inexpensive	Must have unobstructed line of sight. Susceptible to environmental interference.
Satellite	High bandwidth. Large coverage area.	Expensive. Must have unobstructed line of sight. Signals experience propagation delay. Must use encryption for security.
Radio	High bandwidth. Signals pass through walls. Inexpensive and easy to install.	Creates electrical interference problems. Susceptible to snooping unless encrypted.
Infrared	Low to medium bandwidth.	Must have unobstructed line of sight. Used only for short distances.

Satellite **Satellite transmission** systems make use of communication satellites. Currently, there are three types of satellites around the earth, each type in a different orbit. The three types of satellite are geostationary (GEO), medium-earth-orbit (MEO), and low-earth-orbit (LEO). In this section we examine the three different satellites. We then look at two major satellite applications: global positioning systems and Internet transmission via satellites.

As with microwave transmission, satellites must receive and transmit via line of sight. However, the enormous *footprint*—the area of the earth's surface reached by a satellite's transmission—overcomes the limitations of microwave data relay stations. Keep in mind: The higher the orbit of a satellite, the larger the footprint. So, middle-earth-orbit satellites have a smaller footprint than geostationary satellites, and low-earth-orbit satellites have the smallest footprint of all. Figure 7.6 compares the footprints of the three types of satellite.

As opposed to point-to-point transmission with microwave, satellites use *broadcast* transmission, which sends signals to many receivers at one time. So, even though satellites are line-of-sight like microwave, they are high enough for broadcast transmission, thus overcoming the limitations of microwave.

Types of orbits *Geostationary earth orbit (GEO)* satellites orbit 22,300 miles directly above the equator and maintain a fixed position above the earth's surface. These satellites are excellent for sending television programs to cable operators and broadcasting directly to homes. Another advantage is that receivers do not have to track GEO satellites. They have their limitations, though. Transmissions from GEO satellites take a quarter of a second to send and return. This brief pause, called **propagation delay**, makes two-way telephone conversations difficult. Also, GEO satellites are large, expensive, and require large amounts of power to launch.

Medium earth orbit (MEO) satellites are located about 6,000 miles above the earth's surface. MEO orbits require more satellites to cover the earth than GEO orbits, because MEO footprints are smaller. MEO satellites are less expensive than GEO satellites and do not have an appreciable propagation delay. One problem with MEO satellites is that they move with respect to a point on the earth's surface, meaning that receivers must track these satellites. (Think of a satellite dish slowly turning to remain oriented to a MEO satellite).

Low earth orbit (LEO) satellites are located 400 to 700 miles above the earth's surface. Because LEO satellites are much closer to the earth, they have little, if any, propagation delay.

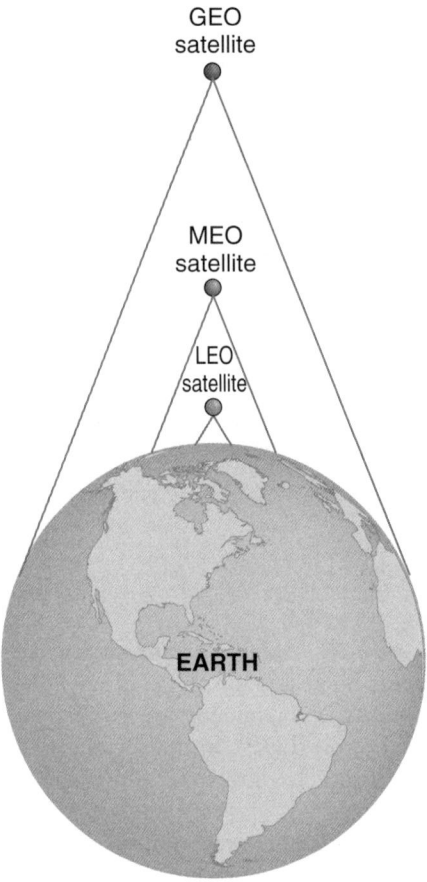

FIGURE 7.6
Comparison of satellite footprints.
Source: Drawn by Kelly Rainer

However, their low altitude means that LEO satellites move with respect to a point on the earth's surface. Therefore, receivers must track LEO satellites. Tracking LEO satellites is more difficult than tracking MEO satellites, because LEO satellites move much more quickly than MEO satellites relative to a point on the earth.

Unlike GEO and MEO satellites, LEO satellites can pick up signals from weak transmitters. This is important because handheld telephones that operate via LEO satellites need less power and can use smaller batteries. Another advantage of LEO satellites is that they consume less power and cost less to launch than GEO and MEO satellites.

However, the footprints of LEO satellites are small, which means that many of them are required to cover the earth. For this reason a single organization often produces multiple LEO satellites, known as *LEO constellations.* Two examples are Iridium and Globalstar.

Iridium (*www.iridium.com*) has placed a LEO constellation in orbit consisting of 66 satellites and 12 in-orbit spare satellites. The company says that it provides complete satellite communications coverage of the earth's surface, including the polar regions. Globalstar (*www.globalstar.com*) also has a LEO constellation in orbit, but with less coverage of the earth than Iridium. Figure 7.7 shows Globalstar's coverage.

Table 7.1 shows the differences among the three types of satellites.

Global Positioning Systems   The **global positioning system (GPS)** is a wireless system that uses satellites to enable users to determine their position anywhere on the earth. GPS is supported by 24 satellites that are shared worldwide. The exact position of each satellite is always known because the satellite continuously broadcasts its position along with a time signal. By using the known speed of the signals and the distance from three satellites (for

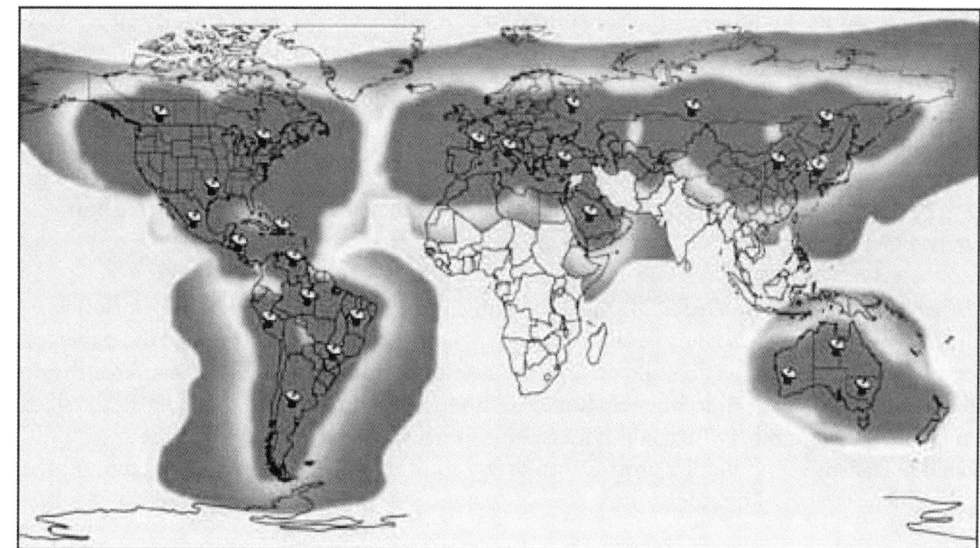

FIGURE 7.7
Globalstar LEO coverage.
Source: http://www. satphonestore.com/ servprod/globalstar/ Coverage/Coverage Mapgstar.jpg

Three Basic Types of Telecommunications Satellites

Table 7.1

Type	Characteristics	Orbit	Number	Use
GEO	• Satellites remain stationary relative to point on earth. • Few satellites needed for global coverage. • Transmission delay (approximately .25 second). • Most expensive to build and launch. • Longest orbital life (many years).	22,300 miles	8	TV signal
MEO	• Satellites move relative to point on earth. • Moderate number needed for global coverage. • Requires medium-powered transmitters. • Negligible transmission delay. • Less expensive to build and launch. • Moderate orbital life (6–12 years).	6,434 miles	10–12	GPS
LEO	• Satellites move rapidly relative to point on earth. • Large number needed for global coverage. • Requires only low-power transmitters. • Negligible transmission delay. • Least expensive to build and launch. • Shortest orbital life (as low as 5 years).	400–700 miles	Many	Telephone

two-dimensional location) or four satellites (for three-dimensional location), it is possible to find the location of any receiving station or user, within a range of 10 feet. GPS software can also convert the user's latitude and longitude to an electronic map. Figure 7.8 shows a smart phone giving directions obtained from a GPS system.

Commercial use of GPS has become widespread, including for navigation, mapping, and surveying, and particularly in remote areas. Cell phones in the United States now must have a GPS embedded in them so that the location of a caller to 911 can be detected immediately. For a GPS tutorial, see *www.trimble.com/gps*.

FIGURE 7.8
Smart phone and GPS system. ©AP/Wide World Photos

Internet over Satellite (IoS).   In many regions of the world, IoS is the only option available for Internet connections because installing the necessary cables is either too expensive or physically impossible. IoS allows users to access the Internet via GEO satellites from a dish mounted on the side of their homes. Although IoS makes the Internet available to many people who otherwise could not access it, it has its drawbacks. As we have seen, GEO satellite transmissions entail a propagation delay, and they can be disrupted by environmental influences such as thunderstorms.

Radio.   **Radio transmission** uses radio-wave frequencies to send data directly between transmitters and receivers. Radio transmission has several advantages. To begin with, radio waves travel easily through normal office walls. In addition, radio devices are fairly inexpensive and easy to install. Finally, radio waves can transmit data at high speeds. For these reasons, radio increasingly is being used to connect computers with both peripheral equipment and local area networks.

As with other technologies, however, radio transmission has its drawbacks as well. First, radio media can create electrical interference problems. Also, radio transmissions are susceptible to snooping by anyone who has similar equipment that operates on the same frequency.

Satellite Radio   One problem with radio transmission is that when you travel too far away from the source station, the signal breaks up and fades into static. Most radio signals can travel only about 30 or 40 miles from their source. However, **satellite radio**, also called **digital radio**, overcomes this problem. Satellite radio offers uninterrupted, near CD-quality music that is beamed to your radio, either at home or in your car, from space. In addition, satellite radio offers a broad spectrum of stations, types of music, news, and talk radio.

XM Satellite Radio (*www.xmradio.com*) and Sirius Satellite Radio (*www.sirius.com*) have launched satellite radio services. XM broadcasts its signals from GEO satellites; Sirius uses MEO satellites. Listeners subscribe to either service for a monthly fee.

Infrared   The final type of wireless transmission is infrared transmission. **Infrared** light is red light that is not commonly visible to human eyes. Common applications of infrared light are in remote control units for televisions, VCRs, DVDs, and CD players. In addition, like radio transmission, infrared transceivers are used for short-distance connections between computers and peripheral equipment and local area networks. A *transceiver* is a device that can transmit and receive signals. Many portable PCs have infrared ports, which are handy when cable connections with a peripheral (such as a printer or modem) are not practical.

Before you go on . . .

1. Describe the various types of wireless devices.
2. Describe the convergence of cell phones, e-mail messagers, and digital cameras. (*Hint:* Think about the TREO 650.)

7.2 Wireless Computer Networks and Internet Access

We have discussed various wireless devices and how these devices transmit wireless signals. These devices typically form wireless computer networks, and they provide wireless Internet access. We discuss these topics in this section.

We organize our discussion around a set of standards established by the Institute of Electrical and Electronics Engineers (IEEE) for wireless computer networks. We have ordered these standards by effective distance and bandwidth, from shortest distance and lowest bandwidth, to greatest distance and highest bandwidth. These standards include:

- IEEE 802.15 (Bluetooth) for wireless personal area networks (PANs)
- IEEE 802.11 (Wi-Fi) for wireless local area networks (WLANs)
- IEEE 802.16 (WiMax) for wireless metropolitan area networks (WMANs)
- IEEE 802.20 (proposed) for wireless wide area networks (WWANs)

We discuss the Bluetooth, Wi-Fi, and WiMax in this section, as IEEE 802.20 is still under development.

Bluetooth

Bluetooth (*www.bluetooth.com*), an industry specification, is used to create small personal area networks. A **personal area network** is a computer network used for communication among computer devices (e.g., telephones, personal digital assistants, and smart phones) close to one person. Bluetooth can link up to eight devices within a 10-meter area using low-power, radio-based communication. It can transmit up to 1 Mbps. 1 Mbps means one megabit per second, or 1 million bits per second ("mega" means million). Ericsson, the Scandinavian mobile handset company that developed this standard, called it Bluetooth, after the tenth-century Danish King Harald Blatan (Bluetooth). IT's About Business 7.2 illustrates a wireless application developed by UPS that integrates Bluetooth and Wi-Fi (discussed in the next section).

IT's About Business

7.2 UPS Integrates Bluetooth and Wi-Fi

United Parcel Service (*www.ups.com*), the $37 billion shipping and logistics company, has 55,000 sorting workers at 1,700 global facilities. Their task is to scan—by hand—the bar codes on 14.1 million parcels every day so that UPS and its customers know where those parcels are at all times.

Beginning in 1996, UPS sorters began using a scanner worn like a ring and linked by a cable to a terminal mounted on their forearms. This terminal wirelessly transmitted bar code data to a facility's server. These devices gave UPS almost-real-time package tracking—a service that UPS customers were beginning to demand. But the devices also led to millions of dollars in unforeseen expenses. The cables would get caught on the packages and get yanked out. Once the cables were disconnected, productivity stopped. UPS had to buy and store spare cables and other equipment for its global fa-

cilities, and maintenance workers were kept constantly busy fixing equipment.

As a result of these problems, in 2001 UPS turned to Symbol Technologies (*www.symbol.com*), a company that makes laser scanners and builds wireless networks for other companies. Symbol convinced UPS to invest $120 million in a new device. This device used Bluetooth's short-range radio capability to relay a package's bar code information from a worker's ring scanner to a wireless receiver worn on the worker's hip. As the name implies, the scanner was worn on the worker's finger, leaving his or her hands free.

The scanner could handle shipping data at up to 60 scans per minute, double the rate that UPS was getting with their previous scanners. In part, the speed increased because Symbol's belt terminal transmitted a package's bar code data to the shipping facility's server using Wi-Fi. This project represented the first viable combination of Bluetooth and Wi-Fi technology in one system.

There was one difficulty, however. In shipping facilities, sorters—and thus their wireless devices—work in close proximity to each other. Symbol therefore had to equip its scanners and terminals with software designed to prevent "data collision."

The new equipment will pay for itself within 16 months of full deployment (the end of 2006). About a third of the savings will come from increased productivity. The remainder will come from reductions in equipment repair costs and spare equipment purchases.

UPS is also incorporating Bluetooth and Wi-Fi connectivity into the handheld computers that UPS drivers carry. The drivers' new electronic clipboards,

first deployed in April 2005, allow drivers to receive last-minute delivery or route changes via a truck's wireless receiver.

Sources: Compiled from T. Mashberg, "Brown Goes Bluetooth," *MIT Technology Review*, June 2005; P. Judge, "Blending Wi-Fi and Bluetooth for a Tracking System," *Techworld*, July 2, 2004; and *www.ups.com* and *www.symbol.com*, accessed April 4, 2005.

QUESTIONS

1. What were the advantages of the new device to UPS sorters?
2. In what ways did UPS save money with the new devices?

Wireless phones, keyboards, computers, printers, and computing devices using Bluetooth can communicate with one another without wires. For example, Bluetooth can connect wireless keyboards and mice to PCs, and it can connect earpieces to a cell phone.

One interesting personal area network uses wireless sensors manufactured and sold by Fitsense Technology (*www.fitsense.com*), a developer of sports and fitness monitors. Runners clip a one-ounce sensor (called the Foot pod) to a shoelace and then use it to record their speed and the distance they have run. The device transmits the data via a Bluetooth signal to a wrist device. In turn, the wrist device transmits the data wirelessly to a desktop computer, where it can be analyzed. The PAN also includes a wireless heart monitor (see Figure 7.9).

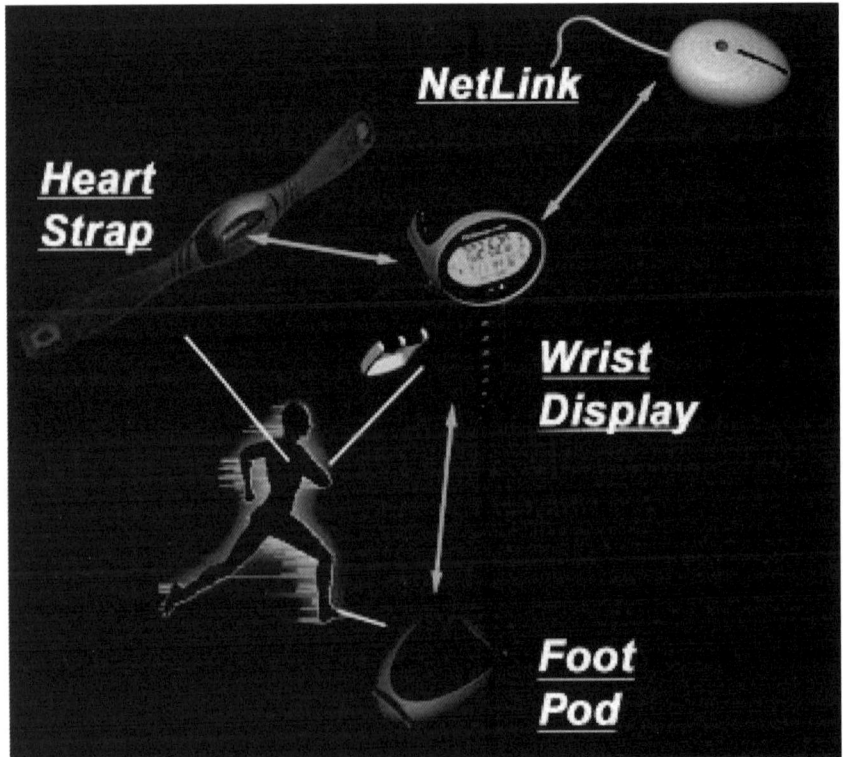

FIGURE 7.9
Fitsense devices.
Source:
www.fitsense.com

Wireless Local Area Networks

A **wireless local area network (WLAN)** is like a wired LAN but without the cables. In a typical configuration, a transmitter with an antenna, called a **wireless access point**, connects to a wired LAN or to satellite dishes that provide an Internet connection. Figure 7.10 shows a wireless access point. A wireless access point provides service to a number of users within a small geographical perimeter (up to a couple of hundred feet), known as a **hotspot**. See Figure 7.11 for the locations of hotspots in Brighton, England. To support a larger number of users across a larger geographical area, several wireless access points are needed. To communicate wirelessly, mobile devices, such as laptop PCs, often need an additional card called a **wireless network interface card (NIC)** that has a built-in radio and antenna.

WLANs provide fast and easy Internet or intranet broadband access from public hotspots located at airports, hotels, Internet cafés, universities, conference centers, offices, and homes. Broadband means high bandwidth. Users can access the Internet while walking across the campus, to their office, or throughout their homes (see *www.weca.net*). In addition, users can access a WLAN with their laptops, desktops, or PDAs by adding a wireless network card. Most PC and laptop manufacturers incorporate these cards directly in their PCs (as an option).

The IEEE standard for WLANs is the 802.11 family, known as **Wi-Fi**, for **wireless fidelity**. There are three standards in this family: 802.11a, 802.11b, and 802.11g.

FIGURE 7.10
Wireless access point.
Source: D-Link systems

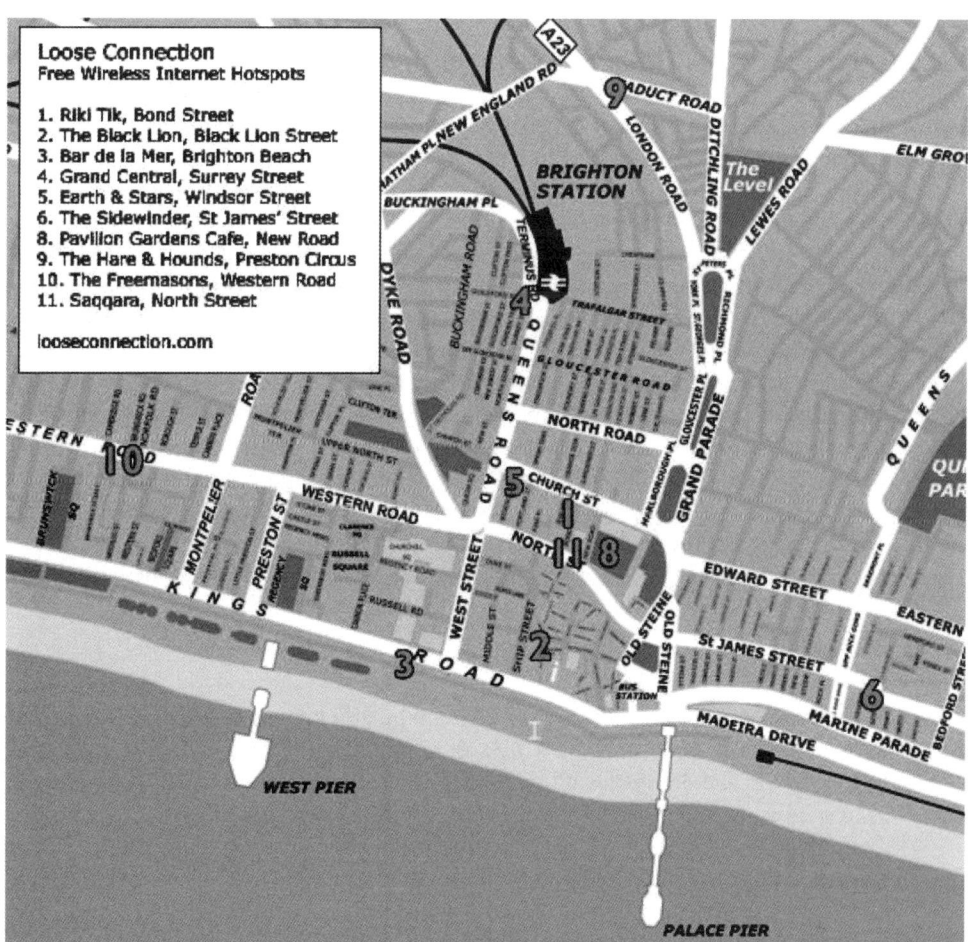

FIGURE 7.11
Wi-Fi hotspots in Brighton, England.
Source: http://wireless.
looseconnection.com/
brighton/

The 802.11a standard can transmit up to 54 Mbps with an effective distance of 10 to 30 meters. The 802.11b standard can transmit up to 11 Mbps with an effective distance of 30 to 50 meters, although this range can be extended outdoors by using tower-mounted antennas. Most of today's WLANs run on the 802.11b standard. The 802.11g standard can transmit up to 54 Mbps and is compatible with the 802.11b standard.

The major benefits of Wi-Fi are its low cost and its ability to provide simple Internet access. It is the greatest facilitator of the *wireless Internet*, that is, the ability to connect to the Internet wirelessly. Significantly, newer laptop PCs come equipped with chips that can send and receive Wi-Fi signals.

Corporations are using Wi-Fi to provide a broad range of services. Here are a few examples:

- American Airlines has installed Wi-Fi in its Admiral's Clubs, and it is partnering with T-Mobile, along with Delta Air Lines and United Airlines, to install Wi-Fi services at the gates of several major airports. American Airlines also uses Wi-Fi for curbside check-in, baggage handling, and cargo packages.

- Lufthansa Airlines and other airlines are equipping their planes with Wi-Fi so that passengers with laptop computers can access the Internet in flight.

- Starbucks and McDonalds are offering customers Wi-Fi in many of their stores, mainly for Internet access. They receive some revenue from their fees for Wi-Fi services, but their strategy is to encourage customers to spend more time in their stores and to choose their stores over those of competitors.

Problems with Wi-Fi.   Three factors are limiting even greater commercial Wi-Fi market growth: roaming, security, and cost. At this time, users cannot roam from hotspot to hotspot if the hotspots use different Wi-Fi network services. Unless the service is free, users have to log on to separate accounts for each service, each with its own fees.

Security is the second barrier to widespread acceptance of Wi-Fi. Because Wi-Fi uses radio waves, it is difficult to protect. We discuss Wi-Fi security in the last section of this chapter.

Even though Wi-Fi services come at a low cost, many experts question whether commercial Wi-Fi services can survive when so many free hotspots are available to users. For example, Freenetworks (*www.freenetworks.org*) is an organization that supports the creation of free community wireless network projects around the globe.

In some places, Wi-Fi Internet hubs are marked by symbols on sidewalks and walls. This practice is called *war chalking*. Certain war chalking symbols mean that there is an accessible Wi-Fi hotspot in the vicinity of a building. Therefore, if your laptop has a wireless network interface card, you can access the Internet for free. You could also access the wireless network of a company located in the building. Other symbols mean that the Wi-Fi hotspot around the building is closed. You can only access it if you were authorized. Despite these problems, MCI is expanding its use of Wi-Fi, as we see in IT's About Business 7.3.

WiMax

Worldwide Interoperability for Microwave Access, popularly known as WiMax, is the name for IEEE Standard 802.16. WiMax has a wireless access range of up to 31 miles, compared to 300 feet for Wi-Fi and 30 feet for Bluetooth. WiMax also has a data transfer rate of up to 75 Mbps. It is a secure system, and it offers features such as voice and video.

WiMax antennas can transmit broadband Internet connections to antennas on homes and businesses miles away. The technology can therefore provide long-distance broadband wireless access to rural areas and other locations that are not currently being served. IT's About Business 7.4 illustrates this use of WiMax.

IT's About Business

7.3 MCI Bets on Wi-Fi

MCI is increasing its Wi-Fi access by nearly doubling its hotspot coverage and by exploring new applications that will cater to corporate customers. The carrier will expand from 6,200 hotspots worldwide to about 11,000 through a deal with Boingo Wireless (www.boingo.com). This expansion will focus on cafés and public business centers rather than on hotels and airports. This strategy is directed toward business customers who will need wireless access for offsite excursions even if they are not flying somewhere.

MCI is also looking at several billing options for Wi-Fi. Customers now pay either a flat rate of $40 per month on top of existing dial-up services, or they pay $8 to $15 on a per-usage basis. To justify these fees, the company plans to support wireless services beyond basic Wi-Fi data access. For example, MCI software lets customers identify available hotspots. When none are available, customers can use the software to select among local dial-up options. The company also provides several encryption protocols.

MCI feels that charging for Wi-Fi access will work, despite the fact that free hotspots are popping up all over the United States. For instance, McCarran International Airport in Las Vegas offers free Wi-Fi access, as do most locations of Panera Bread Company and Schlotzsky's, a sandwich-shop chain.

Sources: Compiled from C. Nobel, "MCI Expands Wi-Fi Coverage," *eWeek*, March 22, 2005; P. Cohen, "Panera Bread Goes Wi-Fi For Free," *MacWorld*, August 12, 2003; and *www.mci.com* and *www.boingo.com*, accessed March 15, 2005.

QUESTIONS

1. Is MCI's strategy of focusing on cafés and business centers a good idea? If not, where should MCI offer Wi-Fi access?
2. Can MCI make money with its Wi-Fi offerings? Why or why not? Would you pay for the MCI service when so many free hotspots are available?

Before you go on . . .

1. What is Bluetooth? What is a WLAN?
2. Describe the members of the 802.11 family.

7.3 Mobile Computing and Mobile Commerce

In the traditional computing environment users come to a computer, which is connected with wires to other computers and to networks. The need to be linked by wires makes it difficult or impossible for people on the move to use them. In particular, salespeople, repair people, service employees, law enforcement agents, and utility workers can be more effective if they can use IT while in the field or in transit. Thus, mobile computing was designed for workers who travel outside the boundaries of their organizations or for any people traveling outside their homes.

Recall that mobile computing refers to a real-time, wireless connection between a mobile device and other computing environments, such as the Internet or an intranet. This innovation is revolutionizing how people use computers. It is spreading at work and at home, in education, health care, and entertainment, and in many other areas.

Mobile computing has two major characteristics that differentiate it from other forms of computing: mobility and broad reach. *Mobility* is based on the fact that users carry a mobile device with them and can initiate a real-time contact with other systems from wherever they

IT's About Business

7.4 Wi-Max Comes to Rural England

When a successful entrepreneur moved to rural southeast England, he discovered that the area had no cellular service, no satellite television, and no broadband. He realized that, even in a prosperous country like Great Britain, hundreds of thousands of people still lack high-speed Internet service. This problem is particularly acute in rural areas, where homes are just too far from telephone exchanges for broadband access. He estimated that only 16 percent of people living in rural English villages had broadband access. He further calculated that, in rural southeast England, there were 500,000 potential residential and small-business subscribers waiting for broadband access. These customers represented a potential market of $280 million in annual sales.

To access this market, he founded a company named Telabria (*www.telabria.com*). Telabria then linked up with Shepherd Neame, Britain's oldest brewer and the owner of 368 pubs, to build a Wi-Max network in three communities using antennas set on top of pubs as access points. This network allowed customers to access the Internet in the pubs themselves and throughout the villages.

The first hotspot was Chequers Inn in Doddington, once a stopping point for religious pilgrims en route to nearby Canterbury. Telabria now has about 500 hotspots in southeast England. Walk-up customers pay $5.60 per hour or $19 per day for the service.

BT Group (British Telecommunications at *www.btplc.com*) is now a competitor and Telabria knows its rates will have to fall. Telabria might also have to underwrite the $349 wireless WiMax receivers for residential customers.

Sources: Compiled from M. Freedman, "Untapped Market," *Forbes*, January 10, 2005; P. Durman, "WiMax Technology Goes Live in Southwest England." *The Times Online*, February 6, 2005; and *www.telabria.com* and *www.btplc.com*, last accessed March 21, 2005.

QUESTIONS

1. Are there alternatives to Telabria's plan to use WiMax technology? What are they?
2. Why would Telabria pay for WiMax receivers? Is this a good strategy? Why or why not?

happen to be. *Broad reach* refers to the fact that when users carry an open mobile device, they can be reached instantly.

These two characteristics, mobility and broad reach, create five value-added attributes that break the barriers of geography and time: ubiquity, convenience, instant connectivity, personalization, and localization of products and services. A mobile device can provide information and communication regardless of the user's location (*ubiquity*). With an Internet-enabled mobile device, it is easy and fast to access the Web, intranets, and other mobile devices without booting up a PC or placing a call via a modem (*convenience* and *instant connectivity*). Information can be customized and sent to individual consumers as an SMS (*customization*). Finally, knowing a user's physical location helps a company advertise its products and services (*localization*). Mobile computing provides the foundation for mobile commerce (m-commerce), which we discuss next.

Mobile Commerce

While the impact of mobile computing on our lives will be very significant, a similar impact is already occurring in the way we conduct business. Recall that mobile commerce refers to e-commerce (EC) transactions that are conducted in a wireless environment, especially via the Internet. Like regular EC applications, m-commerce can be transacted via the Internet, private communication lines, smart cards, or other infrastructures. M-commerce creates opportunities to deliver new services to existing customers and to attract new ones. To see how m-commerce applications are classified by industry, see *www.nordicwirelesswatch.com/wireless/* and *www.mobiforum.org.*

The development of m-commerce is driven by the following factors:

- *Widespread availability of mobile devices.* The number of cell phones throughout the world exceeded 1.5 billion in 2005 (see *http://cellular.co.za/stats/stats-main.htm*). It is estimated that within a few years about 70 percent of cell phones in the developed countries will have Internet access. Thus, a potential mass market is developing for mobile computing and m-commerce. Cell phones are also spreading quickly in developing countries. In China, for example, the number of cell phones exceeds 300 million. This growth enables developing countries to leapfrog to m-commerce.

- *No need for a PC.* Because the Internet can be accessed via a smart phone or other wireless devices, there is no need for a PC to go online. Even though the cost of a PC that is used primarily for Internet access can be less than $300, that amount is still a major expense for the vast majority of people in the world.

- *The "cell phone culture."* The widespread use of cell phones is a social phenomenon, especially among young people. The use of SMS and instant messaging has increased enormously in European and Asian countries. The members of the "cell phone culture" will constitute a major force of online buyers once they begin to make and spend more money.

- *Declining prices.* Over time, the price of wireless devices is declining. The per-minute pricing of mobile services is expected to decline by 50 to 80 percent by 2006.

- *Bandwidth improvement.* To properly conduct m-commerce, it is necessary to have sufficient bandwidth for transmitting text, voice, video, and multimedia; 3G cellular technology, Wi-Fi, and Wi-Max provide the necessary bandwidth.

Mobile computing and m-commerce include many applications. These applications result from the capabilities of various technologies. We examine these applications and their impact on business activities in the next section.

Mobile Commerce Applications

There are a large variety of mobile commerce applications. The most popular applications include financial services, intrabusiness applications, accessing information, location-based applications, telemedicine, and telemetry.

Financial Services Mobile financial applications include banking, wireless payments and micropayments, wireless wallets, bill-payment services, brokerage services, and money transfers. The bottom line for mobile financial applications is to make it more convenient for customers to transact business regardless of where they are or what time it is. Harried customers are demanding such convenience.

Mobile Banking In many countries, banks increasingly offer mobile access to financial and account information. For example, Citibank (*www.citibank.com*) alerts customers on their digital cell phones about changes in account information. Thailand's Bank of Asia provides a mobile service called ASIA M-Banking. Customers enrolled in the program can check account balances and transfer funds between accounts. See *www.bankasia4u.com/channels/channels-asia-m-banking.htm.*

Wireless Electronic Payment Systems Wireless payment systems transform mobile phones into secure, self-contained purchasing tools capable of instantly authorizing payments over the cellular network. In Italy, for example, DPS-Promatic (*www.dpspro.com*) has designed and installed the first parking meter payable by mobile telephone. In the United States, Cellbucks (*www.cellbucks.com*) offers a mobile payment service to participating sports stadiums. Any fan who is a member of the Cellbucks Network can dial a toll-free number, enter his or her password and seat location, and then select numbered items from the electronic menu of food, beverages, and merchandise. Once the purchase is authorized, it is passed on to stadium personnel, who deliver it to the fan's seat. An e-mail detailing the transaction is sent to the fan as further confirmation of the order. In Europe and Japan, wireless purchasing of tickets to movies and other events is popular.

Micropayments   If you took a taxi ride in Frankfurt, Germany, you could pay the taxi driver using your cell phone. Electronic payments for small-purchase amounts (generally less than $10) are called *micropayments*. The demand for wireless micropayments systems is fairly high. A study by research firm A.T. Kearney (*www.clickz.com/stats/*) found that more than 40 percent of mobile phone users surveyed would like to use their mobile phone for small cash transactions such as transit fares and vending machines.

The success of micropayment applications, however, ultimately depends on the costs of the transactions. Transaction costs will be small only when the volume of transactions is large. One technology that can increase the volume of transactions is wireless e-wallets.

Mobile (Wireless) Wallets   Various companies offer **mobile wallet** (*m-wallet*, also known as *wireless wallet*) technologies that enable cardholders to make purchases with a single click from their mobile devices. One example is the Nokia wallet. This application securely stores information (such as credit card numbers) in the customer's Nokia phone for use in making mobile payments. The information also can be used to authenticate transactions by signing them digitally. Microsoft also offers an m-wallet, Passport, for use in a wireless environment.

Wireless Bill Payments   A number of companies are now providing their customers with the option of paying their bills directly from a cell phone. HDFC Bank of India (*www.hdfcbank.com*), for example, allows customers to pay their utility bills through SMS.

Smartpay offers a service for people in Shanghai, China, to pay their utility bills by cell phone. Most people in China do not have checking accounts, and only 2 million people out of 1.3 billion have credit cards. As a result, customers typically have to stand in a line at a bank to pay their bills. The Smartpay system saves its customers from this hassle by sending a message to the subscriber's cell phone when a payment is due. The subscriber then enters a secret number to authorize the payment from his or her bank account.

Intrabusiness Applications   Although B2C m-commerce gets considerable publicity, most of today's m-commerce applications actually are used *within* organizations. In this section we will look at how companies use mobile computing to support their own employees.

Mobile devices are becoming an increasingly integral part of workflow applications. For example, nonvoice mobile services can be used to assist in dispatch functions, that is, to assign jobs to mobile employees, along with detailed information about the task. Target areas for mobile delivery and dispatch services include transportation (delivery of food, oil, newspapers, cargo, courier services, tow trucks, and taxis); utilities (gas, electricity, phone, water); field service (computer, office equipment, home repair); health care (visiting nurses, doctors, social services); and security (patrols, alarm installation). We now provide several examples of intrabusiness applications. For additional information on intrabusiness applications, see *www.mdsi-advantex.com* and *www.symbol.com*.

AirIQ (*www.airiq.com*) provides telematics applications for owners and managers of rental vehicle, commercial transport, and heavy equipment fleets. *Telematics* refers to the wireless communication of location-based information and control messages to and from vehicles and other mobile assets. AirIQ's applications combine Internet, wireless, GPS, and digital mapping. A device in each of the vehicles being tracked collects vital information about a vehicle's direction, speed, and location. Managers can view and access information about the fleet on digital maps. They can also monitor the location of their vehicles on the Internet. Companies using AirIQ applications can, for example:

- Receive daily location reports on fleet vehicles;
- Locate overdue and stolen vehicles;
- Disable stolen and overdue vehicles on demand;
- Know when a vehicle is traveling at an unsafe speed.

At Kemper Insurance Company (*www.kemperinsurance.com*), property adjusters use a wireless digital camera to take pictures at the scene of an accident and transmit them to a processing center. The cameras are linked to Motorola's StarTac data-enabled cellular phone service, which sends the information to a database. These applications eliminate delays in obtaining information and in film processing that exist with conventional methods.

Like many national franchises, Taco Bell employs "mystery customers" who visit restaurants to conduct a survey, unknown to the managers. Taco Bell provides these customers with handheld computers so that they can communicate their reports more quickly to the company's headquarters. The mystery customers answer 35 questions, ranging from the speed of the service to the quality of their food. Before they had these devices, they had to fill out paper forms and then send them to headquarters via overnight mail. The information was then scanned into computers for processing. The information flow using the handhelds is both faster, more accurate, and less expensive.

Accessing Information   Mobile portals and voice portals are designed to aggregate and deliver content in a form that will work with the limited space available on mobile devices. These portals provide information anywhere and anytime to users.

Mobile Portals   A **mobile portal** aggregates and provides content and services for mobile users. These services include news, sports, and e-mail; entertainment, travel, and restaurant information; community services; and stock trading.

The field of mobile portals is increasingly being dominated by a few big companies. The world's best known mobile portal—i-mode from NTT DoCoMo—has more than 40 million subscribers, mostly in Japan. Major players in Europe are Vodafone, O2, and T-Mobile. Some traditional portals—for example, Yahoo, AOL, and MSN—have mobile portals as well.

Voice Portals   A **voice portal** is a Web site with an audio interface. Voice portals are not Web sites in the normal sense because they can also be accessed through a standard or a cell phone. A certain phone number connects you to a Web site, where you can request information verbally. The system finds the information, translates it into a computer-generated voice reply, and tells you what you want to know. Most airlines provide real-time information on flight status this way.

An example of a voice portal is the voice-activated 511 travel-information line developed by Tellme.com. It enables callers to inquire about weather, local restaurants, current traffic, and other handy information. In addition to retrieving information, some sites provide true interaction. For example, iPing (*www.iping.com*) is a reminder and notification service that allows users to enter information via the Web and receive reminder calls. This service can even call a group of people to notify them of a meeting or conference call.

Location-Based Applications   As in e-commerce, m-commerce B2C applications are concentrated in three major areas—retail shopping, advertising, and providing customer service. Location-based mobile commerce is called **location-based commerce** or **L-commerce**.

Shopping from Wireless Devices   An increasing number of online vendors allow customers to shop from wireless devices. For example, customers who use Internet-ready cell phones can shop at certain sites such as *http://mobile.yahoo.com and www.amazon.com.*

Cell phone users can also participate in online auctions. For example, eBay offers "anywhere wireless" services. Account holders at eBay can access their accounts, browse, search, bid, and rebid on items from any Internet-enabled phone or PDA. The same is true for participants in Amazon.com auctions.

Location-Based Advertising   Imagine that you are walking near a Starbucks store, but you do not even know that one is there. Suddenly your cell phone beeps with a message: "Come inside and get a 15 percent discount." Starbucks used a location-based application to detect your wireless device and direct carefully targeted advertising to you.

When marketers know the current locations and preferences of mobile users, they can send user-specific advertising messages to wireless devices about nearby shops, malls, and restaurants. SMS messages and short paging messages can be used to deliver this type of advertising to cell phones and pagers.

One method of location-based advertising, already in use in a few places, involves putting ads on top of taxicabs. The ad changes based on the taxi's location. For example, a taxi cruising in the theater district in New York City might show an ad for a play or a restaurant in that area. When the cab goes to another neighborhood, the ad changes to one for a restaurant or business in that area.

Location-Based Services   Vodafone, an Italian company, provides information to its customers via cell phones, including traffic conditions and the locations of gas stations, hotels, and restaurants. In London, Zingo (*www.zingotaxi.com*) allows customers to use a mobile phone to hail taxicabs. The customer calls a certain telephone number and is connected to the closest available taxi driver. The caller speaks directly to the driver to confirm the trip specifics. IT's About Business 7.5 describes how location-based services can make life easier for shoppers.

Wireless Telemedicine   Telemedicine is the use of modern telecommunications and information technologies for the provision of clinical care to individuals located at a distance and for the transmission of information to provide that care. Today there are three different kinds of technology used for *telemedicine* applications. The first involves storing and transferring digital images from one location to another. The second allows a patient in one location to consult with a medical specialist in another in real time through videoconferencing. The third type uses robots to perform remote surgery. In most of these applications, the patient is in a rural area, and the specialist is in an urban location.

Wireless technology is also transforming the ways in which prescriptions are filled. Traditionally, physicians wrote out a prescription, and you took it to the pharmacy, where you either waited on line or returned later. Today, mobile systems allow physicians to enter a prescription onto a personal digital assistant. That information goes by cellular modem (or Wi-Fi) to a company such as Med-i-nets (*www.med i nets.com*). There, employees make certain that the prescription conforms to the insurance company's regulations. If everything checks out, then the prescription is transferred electronically to the appropriate pharmacy. For refills, the system notifies physicians when it is time for the patient to reorder. The doctor can then renew the prescription with a few clicks on the modem.

Another valuable application involves emergency situations that arise during airplane flights. In-flight medical emergencies occur more frequently than you might think. Alaska Airlines, for example, deals with about 10 medical emergencies every day. Many companies now use mobile communications to attend to these situations. For example, MedLink, a ser-

IT's About Business

7.5 Circuit City Improves the Shopping Experience

When customers walk into a Circuit City (*www.circuitcity.com*) store, the company wants to whisper customized sales pitches into their ears—literally. As customers walk into a store, they receive a very light wireless headset. As they walk through the store, the device uses sensors to learn where the customer is. When the customer stops in a certain area, the headset can explain items, present audio from a TV demonstration, and connect the customer with a centralized sales assistant. The sales assistant might be 2,000 miles away, if no one in the store is available.

Circuit City realizes that it cannot win on price, as it must compete with Best Buy and Wal-Mart. The alternative, then, is to dramatically improve the customer experience. This strategy is especially important when customers are shopping for products that are also sold by Circuit City's largest competitors. To implement this strategy, Circuit City is implementing many innovative location-based services. The wireless headsets described above are one illustration of this. As another example, the company is embedding RFID into loyalty cards. When customers enter the store, their card is scanned by a reader. A coupon dispenser at the door then dispenses specific coupons based on their past buying habits. Going further, when the customer's card is read, the store automatically knows that he or she was on the Circuit City Web site yesterday, evaluating plasma TVs. So, when the customer's card is read in the plasma TV section, Circuit City could offer him or her a $500 coupon right on the spot. Keep in mind that customer cards can be read throughout the store.

Sources: Compiled from E. Schuman, "Circuit City's New Approach to Customer Service," *eWeek*, January 17, 2005; L. Ulanoff, "Bargain Hunting Online." *PC Magazine*, November 17, 2004; and *www.circuitcity.com*, accessed March 3, 2005.

QUESTIONS

1. Is Circuit City's RFID technology too intrusive? Would you feel comfortable shopping with it? Why or why not?
2. In what other ways could Circuit City use wireless technology to improve their customers' shopping experience?

vice of MedAire (*www.medaire.com*), provides around-the-clock access to board-certified physicians. These mobile services can also remotely control medical equipment, like defibrillators, that are located on the plane.

Telemetry Applications **Telemetry** is the wireless transmission and receipt of data gathered from remote sensors. Telemetry has numerous mobile computing applications. For example, technicians can use *telemetry* to identify maintenance problems in equipment. Also, as we just saw, doctors can monitor patients and control medical equipment from a distance.

Car manufacturers use telemetry applications for remote vehicle diagnosis and preventive maintenance. For example, drivers of many General Motors cars use its OnStar system (*www.onstar.com*) in numerous ways. For example, OnStar automatically alerts an operator when an air bag deploys; drivers may have questions about a warning light that appeared on their dashboard; and there are many other examples. Also, Nokia (*www.nokia.com*) has developed the Smart Traffic Terminal that is incorporated in the car. This technology provides the driver with traffic information and navigation, automated emergency functions, in-car security, and car maintenance functions.

One particularly important application of telemetry involves 911 emergency calls. If someone dials 911 from a regular wireline phone, the emergency service can pinpoint the location of the phone. But what happens if someone places a 911 call from a mobile phone? Can the emergency service locate the caller? A few years ago, the U.S. Federal Communications Commission (FCC) issued a directive to wireless carriers, requiring that they establish services to handle **wireless 911 (e-911)** calls. To give you an idea of the magnitude of this requirement, consider that more than 156,000 wireless 911 calls are made *every day*. In fact, this number represents more than half the 911 calls made daily in the United States. In 2003, 66 million emergency calls were made from cell phones in the United States.

Before you go on . . .

1. What are the major drivers of mobile computing?
2. Describe mobile portals and voice portals.
3. Describe wireless financial services.
4. List some of the major intrabusiness wireless applications.

7.4 Pervasive Computing

A world in which virtually every object has processing power with wireless or wired connections to a global network is the world of **pervasive computing**, also called *ubiquitous computing*. Pervasive computing is invisible "everywhere computing" that is embedded in the objects around us—the floor, the lights, our cars, the washing machine, our cell phones, our clothes, and so on.

For example, in a *smart home*, your home computer, television, lighting and heating controls, home security system, and many appliances can communicate with one another via a home network. These linked systems can be controlled through various devices, including your pager, cellular phone, television, home computer, PDA, or even your automobile. One of the key elements of a smart home is the *smart appliance*, an Internet-ready appliance that can be controlled by a small handheld device or a desktop computer via a home network (wireline or wireless) or the public Internet (see *www.internethomealliance.com*). Two technologies provide the infrastructure for pervasive computing: radio-frequency identification (RFID) and wireless sensor networks (WSNs).

Radio-Frequency Identification — OYSTER GARD Application

Recall that *RFID technology* allows manufacturers to attach tags with antennas and computer chips on goods and then track their movement through radio signals. Radio-frequency identification (RFID) was developed to replace bar codes. A typical bar code, known as the *Universal Product Code (UPC)*, is made up of 12 digits, in various groups. The first two digits show the country where it was issued, the next four represent the manufacturer, and the remaining six are the product code assigned by the manufacturer. Bar codes have worked well, but they do have limitations. First, they require line-of-sight to the scanning device. This is fine in a store, but it can pose substantial problems in a manufacturing plant or a warehouse or on a shipping/receiving dock. Second, because bar codes are printed on paper, they can be ripped, soiled, or lost. Third, the bar code identifies the manufacturer and product, but not the item.

Auto-ID overcomes these limitations (*www.autoidcenter.org*). The mission of the Auto-ID Center is to create an **Internet of "things"**; that is, a network that connects computers to objects. These objects can range from boxes of laundry detergent to pairs of jeans to airplane engines. This Internet of things will provide the ability to track *individual* items as they move from factories to store shelves to recycling facilities. This will make possible near-perfect supply chain visibility. One of the tools of Auto-ID is RFID.

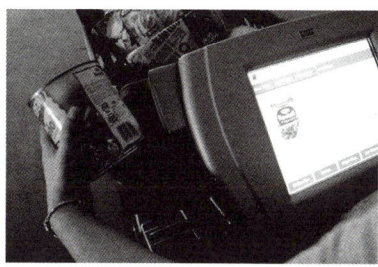

FIGURE 7.12
Small RFID reader and RFID tag.
Source: Kruell/laif/Redux Pictures

RFID systems use tags with embedded microchips, which contain data, and antennas to transmit radio signals over a short distance to RFID readers. The readers pass the data over a network to a computer for processing. The chip in the RFID tag is programmed with information that uniquely identifies an item. It also contains information about the item such as its location and where and when it was made. Figure 7.12 shows an RFID reader and an RFID tag on a pallet.

The problem with RFID has been the expense. Tags currently cost about 50 cents, which makes them unusable for low-priced items. A California company called Alien Technology (*www.alientechnology.com*) has invented a way to mass-produce RFID tags for less than 10 cents apiece for large production runs.

Wireless Sensor Networks (WSNs)

Wireless sensor networks are networks of interconnected, battery-powered, wireless sensors called *motes* (analogous to nodes) that are placed into the physical environment. The motes collect data from many points over an extended space. Each mote contains processing, storage, and radio frequency sensors and antennas. The motes provide information that enables a central computer to integrate reports of the same activity from different angles within the network. Therefore, the network can determine with much greater accuracy information such as the direction a person is moving, the weight of a vehicle, or the amount of rainfall over a field of crops.

A new type of wireless sensor network is mesh networking. A **mesh network** is composed of motes, where each mote "wakes up" or activates for a fraction of a second when it has data to transmit and then relays that data to its nearest neighbor. So, instead of every mote transmitting its information to a remote computer at a base station, an "electronic bucket brigade" moves the data mote by mote until it reaches a central computer where it can be stored and analyzed. An advantage of a mesh network is that, if one mote fails, another one can pick up the data. This process makes a mesh network very efficient and reliable. Also, if more bandwidth is needed, it is easy to boost performance by placing new motes when and where they are required. There are many diverse uses for WSNs, as the following examples indicate:

Examples

WSN Provides 3-D Picture of Redwoods. A biologist deployed 80 motes to sunlight, temperature, and humidity i This network eliminated miles of wiring cent. In addition, the motes gave him h microclimate. He is now moving his m to better understand how the loss and f and water resources. (*Sources:* Compiled *ence & Society*, February 16, 2004; T. E 2003; and *www.dust-inc.com*, accessed N

WSN Enhances Security. Science A is using motes from Dust Networks (*w* other sensitive areas. This application co ple, vehicles, voices, and motion, with a ing on applications to use motes on ship nuclear weapon emitted during transit. (where," *InformationWeek*, January 24, : cessed March 11, 2005.)

WSNs Monitor Business Processes. British Petroleum (BP) is using motes at its Cherry Point refinery in Washington to monitor the temperature inside giant on-site fans. This system costs about $1,000 per mote. In contrast, the old monitoring system cost $10,000 per measuring point. BP is also using motes to measure conditions in the engine room of an oil tanker, to remotely adjust lighting and heat in office buildings, to test soil for pollutants, and to detect whether chemicals are stored properly. (*Sources:* Compiled from A. Ricadela, "Sensors Everywhere," *Information Week*, January 24, 2005; and *www.xbow.com*, accessed March 12, 2005.)

One kind of mesh network is Zigbee. Zigbee (*www.zigbee.org*) is a set of wireless communications protocols that target applications requiring low data transmission rates and low power consumption. Zigbee can handle hundreds of devices at once. Its current focus is to wirelessly link sensors that are embedded into industrial controls, medical devices, smoke and intruder alarms, and building and home automation.

A promising application of Zigbee is meter reading. Zigbee sensors embedded in utility meters would send wireless signals that could be picked up by utility employees driving by your house. The employees would not even have to get out of their trucks.

Before you go on . . .

1. Define pervasive computing, RFID, and wireless sensor networks.
2. Explain the benefits of auto-ID and RFID.

7.5 Wireless Security

Clearly, wireless networks provide numerous benefits for businesses. However, they also present a huge challenge to management. This challenge is their inherent lack of security. Wireless is a broadcast medium, and transmissions can be intercepted by anyone who is close enough and has access to the appropriate equipment. There are four major threats to wireless networks: rogue access points, war driving, eavesdropping, and RF jamming.

A *rogue access point* is an unauthorized access point to a wireless network. The rogue could be someone in your organization who sets up an access point meaning no harm but fails to tell the IT department. In more serious cases the rogue is an "evil twin," someone who wishes to access a wireless network for malicious purposes.

In an evil twin attack, the attacker is in the vicinity with a Wi-Fi-enabled computer and a separate connection to the Internet. Using a hotspotter, a device that detects wireless networks and provides information on them (see *www.canarywireless.com*), the attacker simulates a wireless access point with the same wireless network name, or SSID, as the one that authorized users expect. If the signal is strong enough, users will connect to the attacker's system instead of the real access point. The attacker can then serve them a Web page asking for them to provide confidential information such as user names, passwords, and account numbers. In other cases the attacker simply captures wireless transmissions. These attacks are more effective with public hotspots (e.g., McDonald's or Starbucks) than in corporate networks.

War driving is the act of locating WLANs while driving around a city or elsewhere (see *www.wardriving.com*). To war drive, you need a vehicle, a computer or PDA, a wireless card, and some kind of an antenna that can be mounted on top of or positioned inside the car. If a WLAN has a range that extends beyond the building in which it is located, then an unauthorized user may be able to intrude into the network. The intruder can then obtain a free Internet connection and possibly can gain access to important data and other resources.

Eavesdropping refers to efforts by unauthorized users to access data traveling over wireless networks. Finally, in *radio-frequency (RF) jamming* a person or a device intentionally or unintentionally interferes with your wireless network transmissions.

The following solutions should be implemented to avoid these threats.

- Detect unauthorized access points with devices from among others, NetStumbler (*www.netstumbler.com*) or Kismet (*www.kismetwireless.net*).

- Block your SSIDs (the name of your wireless network), because they let war drivers know a wireless network is present.

- Encrypt wireless transmissions with Wi-Fi Protected Access (WPA). To gain access to WPA-encrypted information, users enter a virtually unbreakable password. (The earlier wireless encryption protocol—WEP—was notoriously easy to hack into.)

- Always know who is using your network and what they are doing with it. You must limit access to approved devices by programming their unique identity into your router. Monitoring software from AirMagnet (*www.airmagnet.com*), among others, further limits network access based on a user's physical location and IP address. In addition, it gives authorized users access only to the services you allow. This means, for example, that you can grant a visiting client access to the Internet but not to your corporate intranet.

- Implement a system that automatically shifts to different wireless channels when there is interference. As an alternative, design the network to automatically forward traffic to other access points when one point is jammed.

Before you go on . . .

1. Describe the four major threats to the security of wireless networks.
2. Describe the possible solutions to those threats.

What's in IT for me?

For the Accounting Major

Wireless applications help with inventory counting and auditing. They also assist in expediting the flow of information for cost control. Price management, inventory control, and other accounting-related activities can be improved by use of wireless technologies.

For the Finance Major

Wireless services can provide banks and other financial institutions with a competitive advantage. For example, wireless electronic payments, including micropayments, are more convenient (any place, any time) than traditonal means of payment, and they are also less expensive. Electronic bill payment from mobile devices is becoming more popular, increasing security and accuracy, expediting cycle time, and reducing processing costs.

For the Marketing Major

Imagine a whole new world of marketing, advertising, and selling, with the potential to increase sales dramatically. Such is the promise of mobile computing. Of special interest for marketing are location-based advertising as well as the new opportunities resulting from pervasive computing and RFIDs. Finally, wireless technology also provides new opportunities in sales force automation (SFA), enabling faster and better communications with both customers (CRM) and corporate services.

For the Production/Operations Management Major

Wireless technologies offer many opportunities to support mobile employees of all kinds. Wearable computers enable repair personnel working in the field and off-site employees to service customers faster, better, and at less cost. Wireless devices can also increase productivity within factories by enhancing communication and collaboration as well as managerial planning and control. In addition, mobile computing technologies can increase safety by providing quicker warning signs and instant messaging to isolated employees.

For the Human Resources Management Major

Mobile computing can improve HR training and extend it to any place at any time. Payroll notices can be delivered as SMSs. Self-service selection of benefits and updating of personal data can be extended to wireless devices, making these functions even more convenient for employees to handle on their own.

The MIS Function

MIS personnel provide the wireless infrastructure that enables all organizational employees to compute and communicate any time, anywhere. This convenience provides exciting, creative new applications for organizations to cut costs and improve the efficiency and effectiveness of operations (for example, to gain transparency in supply chains). Unfortunately, as we discussed earlier, wireless applications are inherently insecure. This lack of security is a serious problem that MIS personnel must deal with.

1. Discuss the various types of wireless devices and wireless transmission media.

A *pager* is a one-way, wireless messaging system that alerts the user and provides a message. *E-mail handhelds*, such as the BlackBerry, have a small display screen and a keypad for typing short messages. *Cellular telephones* use radio waves to provide two-way communication. *Personal digital assistants* (*PDAs*) are small, handheld computers capable of transmitting digital communications. *Smart phones* are digital appliances that combine the functionality of a PDA, a digital camera, and a digital cell phone.

Microwave transmission systems are widely used for high-volume, long-distance, point-to-point communication. Communication *satellites* are used in satellite transmission systems. The three types of satellite are geostationary-earth-orbit (GEO), medium earth orbit (MEO), and low earth orbit (LEO). *Radio* transmission uses radio-wave frequencies to send data directly between transmitters and receivers. *Infrared* light is red light not commonly visible to human eyes. The most common application of infrared light is in remote-control units for televisions and VCRs. Infrared transceivers are being used for short-distance connections between computers and peripheral equipment and LANs. Many portable PCs have infrared ports, which are handy when cable connections with a peripheral are not practical.

2. Describe Bluetooth, Wi-Fi, and WiMax.

Bluetooth is used to create small personal area networks. It can link up to eight devices within a 10-meter area using low-power, radio-based communication, and it can transmit up to 1 Mbps.

Summary

Wi-Fi has a range of about 300 feet and a data transfer rate up to 54 Mbps. The major benefits of Wi-Fi are its lower cost and its ability to provide simple Internet access. It is the greatest facilitator of the *wireless Internet*. Wi-Max has a wireless access range of up to 31 miles and a data transfer rate of up to 75 Mbps. It offers features such as voice and video.

3. Define mobile computing and mobile commerce.

Mobile computing is a computing model designed for people who travel frequently. *Mobile commerce* (*m-commerce*) is any e-commerce conducted in a wireless environment, especially via the Internet.

4. Discuss the major m-commerce applications.

Mobile financial applications include banking, wireless payments and micropayments, wireless wallets, and bill-payment services. Job dispatch is a major intrabusiness application. *Voice portals* and *mobile portals* provide access to information. Location-based applications include retail shopping, advertising, and customer service. Other major m-commerce applications include wireless *telemedicine* and *telemetry*.

5. Define pervasive computing and describe two technologies underlying pervasive computing.

Pervasive computing is invisible, everywhere computing that is embedded in the objects around us. Two technologies provide the infrastructure for pervasive computing: *radio-frequency identification* (*RFID*) and wireless sensor networks (*WSNs*).

RFID is the term for technologies that use radio waves to automatically identify the location of individual items equipped with tags that contain embedded microchips. WSNs are networks of interconnected, battery-powered, wireless devices placed in the physical environment to collect data from many points over an extended space.

6. Discuss the four major threats to wireless networks.

The four major threats to wireless networks are rogue access points, war driving, eavesdropping, and RF jamming. A rogue access point is an unauthorized access point to a wireless network. War driving is the act of locating WLANs while driving around a city or elsewhere. Eavesdropping refers to efforts by unauthorized users to access data traveling over wireless networks. Radio frequency (RF) jamming occurs when a person or a device intentionally or unintentionally interferes with wireless network transmissions.

Chapter Glossary

Bluetooth chip technology that enables short-range connection (data and voice) between wireless devices (220)

Cellular Telephones (also called cell phones); telephones that use radio waves to provide two-way communications (214)

Global Positioning System (GPS) a wireless system that uses satellites to enable users to determine their position anywhere on earth (217)

Hotspot a small geographical perimeter within which a wireless access point provides service to a number of users (222)

Infrared a type of wireless transmission that uses red light not commonly visible to human eyes (219)

Internet of Things a network that connects computers to objects (231)

Location-Based Commerce (l-commerce) mobile commerce transactions targeted to individuals in specific locations, at specific times (228)

Mesh Network a network composed of motes in the physical environment that "wake up" at intervals to transmit data to their nearest neighbor mote (232)

Microbrowser Internet browsers with a small file size that can work within the low-memory constraints of wireless devices and the low bandwidths of wireless networks (213)

Microwave Transmission a wireless system that uses microwaves for high-volume, long-distance, point-to-point communication (215)

Mobile Commerce (m-commerce) electronic commerce transactions that are conducted in a wireless environment, especially via the Internet (211)

Mobile Computing a real-time, wireless connection between a mobile device and other computing environments, such as the Internet or an intranet (211)

Mobile Portal a portal that aggregates and provides content and services for mobile users (228)

Mobile Wallet a technology that allows users to make purchases with a single click from their mobile devices (227)

Pager a one-way, wireless messaging system (214)

Personal Area Network a computer network used for communication among computer devices close to one person (220)

Personal Digital Assistant (PDA) a small, handheld computer that can transmit digital signals (215)

Pervasive Computing (also called ubiquitous computing) a computer environment where virtually every object has processing power with wireless or wired connections to a global network (211)

Propagation Delay the one-quarter second transmission delay in communication to and from geosynchronous satellites (216)

Radio Transmission uses radio-wave frequencies to send data directly between transmitters and receivers (219)

RFID (radio-frequency identification) technology a wireless technology that allows manufacturers to attach tags with antennas and computer chips on goods and then track their movement through radio signals (210)

Satellite Radio (also called digital radio) a wireless system that offers uninterrupted, near CD-quality music that is beamed to your radio from satellites (219)

Satellite Transmission a wireless transmission system that uses satellites for broadcast communications (216)

Short Message Service (SMS) a service provided by digital cell phones that can send and receive short text messages (up to 160 characters in length) (215)

Smart Phones a new class of digital communication appliances that combine the functionality of a personal digital assistant with that of a digital cell phone (215)

Telemetry the wireless transmission and receipt of data gathered from remote sensors (230)

Voice Portal a Web site with an audio interface (228)

Wireless telecommunications in which electromagnetic waves carry the signal between communicating devices. (211)

Wireless 911 911 emergency calls made with wireless devices (231)

Wireless Access Point an antenna connecting a mobile device to a wired local area network (222)

Wireless Application Protocol (WAP) the standard that enables wireless devices with tiny display screens, low-bandwidth connections, and minimal memory to access Web-based information and services (213)

Wireless Fidelity (Wi-Fi) a set of standards for wireless local area networks based on the IEEE 802.11 standard (222)

Wireless Local Area Network (WLAN) a computer network in a limited geographical area that uses wireless transmission for communication (222)

Wireless Network Interface Card a device that has a built-in radio and antenna and is essential to enable a computer to have wireless communication capabilities (222)

Wireless Sensor Network (WSN) networks of interconnected, battery-powered, wireless sensors placed in the physical environment (232)

Discussion Questions

1. Discuss how m-commerce can expand the reach of e-business.
2. Discuss how mobile computing can solve some of the problems of the digital divide.
3. List three to four major advantages of wireless commerce to consumers and explain what benefits they provide to consumers.
4. Discuss the ways in which Wi-Fi is being used to support mobile computing and m-commerce. Describe the ways in which Wi-Fi is affecting the use of cellular phones for m-commerce.
5. You can use location-based tools to help you find your car or the closest gas station. However, some people see location-based tools as an invasion of privacy. Discuss the pros and cons of location-based tools.
6. Discuss the benefits of telemetry in health care for the elderly.
7. Discuss how wireless devices can help people with disabilities.
8. Discuss the "battle" between Wi-Max and 3G cellular service.
9. Which of the applications of pervasive computing do you think are likely to gain the greatest market acceptance over the next few years? Why?

Problem-Solving Activities

1. Enter *www.kyocera-wireless.com* and view the demos. What is a smart phone? What are its capabilities? How does it differ from a regular cell phone?
2. Investigate commercial applications of voice portals. Visit several vendors (e.g., *www.tellme.com*, *www.bevocal.com*, etc.). What capabilities and applications are offered by the various vendors?
3. Using a search engine, try to determine whether there are any commercial Wi-Fi hotspots in your area. (*Hint:* Access *www.wifinder.com.*) Enter *www.wardriving.com*. Based on information provided at this site, what sorts of equipment and procedures could you use to locate hotspots in your area?
4. Explore wearable computers. Access *www.mobileinfo.com*, *www.xybernaut.com*, and *www.eg3.com*. Describe the products offered by these vendors. What are the capabilities of these products?

Internet Activities

1. Explore *www.nokia.com*. Prepare a summary of the types of mobile services and applications Nokia currently supports and plans to support in the future.
2. Enter *www.ibm.com*. Search for *wireless e-business*. Research the resulting stories to determine the types of wireless capabilities and applications IBM's software and hardware supports. Describe some of the ways these applications have helped specific businesses and industries.
3. Research the status of 3G and 4G cellular service by visiting *www.itu.int*, *http://4g.newstrove.com*, and *www.3gnewsroom.com*. Prepare a report on the status of 3G and 4G based on your findings.
4. Enter *www.mapinfo.com* and look for the location-based services demos. Try all the demos. Find all of the wireless services. Summarize your findings.
5. Enter *www.packetvideo.com* and *www.microsoft.com/mobile/pocketpc*. Examine their demos and products and list their capabilities.
6. Enter *www.onstar.com*. What types of *fleet* services does OnStar provide? Are these any different from the services OnStar provides to individual car owners? (Play the movie.)
7. Enter *http://gii.co.jp/english/cg11183_smart_appliances.html* and look for information about smart appliances. Also search *www.internethomealliance.com*.

Team Assignments

1. Each team should examine a major vendor of mobile devices (Nokia, Kyocera, Motorola, Palm, BlackBerry, etc.). Each team will research the capabilities and prices of the devices offered by each company and then make a class presentation, the objective of which is to convince the rest of the class why one should buy that company's products.
2. Each team should explore the commercial applications of m-commerce in one of the following areas: financial services, including banking, stocks, and insurance; marketing and advertising; manufacturing; travel and transportation; human resources management; public services; and health care. Each team will present a report to the class based on their findings. (Start at *www.mobiforum.org*.)
3. Each team should take one of the following areas—homes, cars, appliances, or other consumer goods like clothing—and investigate how embedded microprocessors are currently being used and will be used in the future to support consumer-centric services. Each team will present a report to the class based on their findings.

CASE # Philadelphia Adopts a Mesh Network

THE GOVERNMENT PROBLEM Cities as diverse as Philadelphia, Las Vegas, and Garland, Texas, are utilizing broadband wireless, or mesh, networks. These cities want to implement networks that offer more complete coverage, faster speeds, greater reliability, and easier deployment than conventional Wi-Fi or even WiMax networks. They also are hoping to reduce expenses.

The impetus for Philadelphia's mesh network was to meet the mayor's goal of overcoming the digital divide. This goal is crucial for a city such as Philadelphia, where

23 percent of its 1.5 million residents are below the poverty line, and 42 percent of city households still lack Internet access of any kind.

THE IT SOLUTION Philadelphia's solution is to implement a citywide mesh network. As we discussed, a mesh network differs from a conventional wireless network in that, if one mote stops working or is bogged down with too much traffic, the data are routed around it. Specifically, Philadelphia plans to blanket the city with 3,000 to 4,000 network motes, which will cover each of the city's 135 square miles with a Wi-Fi signal. These motes will transmit signals to Internet access points sprinkled throughout the city that either provide wireline access to the Internet or use WiMax to connect to the Internet. The motes will provide uniform coverage along all the streets, parks, and other open spaces of the city. The city is planning to contract with private organizations that would use the mesh network to extend inexpensive Internet access to homes and businesses.

It costs about $20 per household to install a mesh network in a neighborhood, compared to $700 to $1000 to bring in a wired broadband network such as DSL. Hopefully, these dramatic cost reductions will help the mayor to achieve his goal of overcoming the digital divide.

THE RESULTS The cost of building the city's portion of the wireless infrastructure will total only $10 million.

There are no large cell towers to construct. Instead, the network motes are small boxes that use very little electrical power and can be attached to city-owned light poles. The installation is a simple process. In addition, much of the infrastructure to which the Internet access points attach, such as fiber optic cable, is already installed.

One problem that is occurring, however, is "hopping." This term refers to the ability of every mote on the network to pass on signals. It turns out that each time the signal hops, some of the bandwidth is lost. An effective mesh network should have no more than three hops from a mote to an Internet access point. The city is still working to resolve this problem.

Sources: Compiled from E. Nee, "Municipalities Starting to Mesh," *CIO Insight*, March 22, 2005; C. Ellison, "Muni, Mesh Wireless Players Meet in Philadelphia," *eWeek*, April 29, 2005; and M. Douglas, "Some Cities Are in a Fine Mesh," *www.mrt.com*, March 1, 2004.

QUESTIONS

1. Discuss the implications of using technology to overcome the digital divide in Philadelphia. How successful do you think these efforts will be?
2. Even if cheap broadband access is made available to poverty-stricken neighborhoods, what types of devices will the people in these areas have to purchase to make use of the Internet? Will this be a problem? If so, how can this problem be addressed?

Interactive Learning

Business Unplugged: How to Build a Wi-Fi Network

Go to the Interactivities section on the *WileyPLUS* Web site and access Chapter 7: Wireless, Mobile Computing, and Mobile Commerce. There you will find an animated simulation of a Wi-Fi network, as well as some hands-on activities that visually explain business concepts in this chapter.

Pervasive Computing at Club IT

Go to the Club IT section of the *WileyPLUS* Web site to find assignments about using wireless technologies at Club IT.

wiley.com/college/rainer

Chapter 8

Chapter Preview

In this chapter we discuss the various systems that support organizations. We begin our discussion with transaction processing systems (TPSs), the most fundamental information systems within organizations. We continue our discussion by following a progression: information systems that support part of an organization (the functional area management information systems), information systems that support an entire organization (enterprise resource planning systems and customer relationship management systems), and finally information systems that span multiple organizations (supply chain management systems). We conclude with a look at the technologies that support interorganizational systems.

Organizational Information Systems

Introduction to Information Systems
R. Kelly Rainer, Jr., Efraim Turban, and Richard E. Potter. ISBN 978-0-471-7363-3
©2007 John Wiley & Sons, Inc.

Web Resources

wiley.com/college/rainer

Student Web Site
- Web Quizzes
- Links to relevant Web sites
- Lecture Slides in PowerPoint

WileyPlus
- Virtual Company assignments and Club IT Web site
- Interactive Learning Sessions
- Microsoft Excel and Access Exercises
- Software Skills Tutorials
- e-book

Learning Objectives

1. Describe transaction processing systems.

2. Describe management information systems and the support they provide for each functional area of the organization.

3. Describe enterprise resource planning systems.

4. Describe customer relationship management systems.

5. Describe supply chain management systems.

6. Discuss EDI and extranets.

What's in IT for me?

ACC FIN MKT POM HRM  MIS

241

VF Corporation Goes Global

The Business Problem

VF Corporation is the world's largest apparel maker, with annual sales of more than $6 billion. Many of the company's brand names are easily recognizable: Wrangler, Lee, Nautica, The North Face. Like many apparel companies, VF has globalized rapidly. Most of its materials and many of its finished products are now made outside the United States. In essence, VF has transformed itself from a manufacturing business to a sourcing business. A sourcing business is one that buys finished goods (in this case from over-

©AP/Wide World Photos

seas manufacturers) and sells them. Put simply, its strategy is to own brands, not machines.

VF has a growth strategy aimed at cost savings, customer service for big retail partners, and new products and acquisitions designed to reach more consumers and keep up with their changing tastes. In 2002, VF bought about $140 million worth of material from Asian producers. In 2005, it bought more than 10 times that amount. More than 50 percent of VF's products are now obtained from Mexico and Central America, with another 30 percent coming from Asia.

The migration of the U.S. textile and apparel industries to low-cost labor markets such as Mexico and China is a long-term process that has been encouraged by free-trade legislation such as NAFTA. This process has stretched VF's supply chain and redistributed its operations. Globalization also changed VF's distribution network. The company decided to reduce the number of distribution centers, currently 31 in the United States alone. They will move them from older locations near now-departed manufacturing plants to ports that can handle shipments from China and Latin America.

However, globalization presented VF with challenges as well as opportunities. Basically, the company lacked the IT systems to support this new kind of distributed, global corporation.

The IT Solution

VF was running a patchwork of legacy systems, which are older information systems, often developed in older computer languages such as COBOL. For this reason, it could not share data among the five groups of companies within VF, known as coalitions. The five coalitions are Jeanswear, Intimate Apparel, Outdoor, Sportsware, and Imageware. VF's overall plan was to create a core system, closely linked to VF's business processes, onto which new acquisitions could be added. VF chose an enterprise resource planning system from software vendor SAP and the supply chain management system from i2 (*www.i2.com*) for its first implementation: Jeanswear. This implementation went smoothly.

Unfortunately, the implementation for Intimate Apparel did not. There were problems with the way the software supported the products. SAP software at the time lacked the capacity to handle multiple garment sizes. After multiple delays, the implementation was shelved. Since that time, however, VF has smoothly integrated its Outdoor business and, the second time around, smoothly integrated Intimate Apparel as well.

VF is now implementing supply chain management software for all distribution centers, foreign and domestic, that are capable of handling products from any of the five coalitions. The company also is working closely with big retailers such as Wal-Mart, Target, and Sears to manage their inventories of VF products. This process is called *vendor-managed inventory*. VF also gathers data from these retailers to understand what customers around the world want to wear. Finally, VF helps these retailers with sales planning and product replenishment, down to the level of individual garment styles and colors in particular departments across the chains.

Using sales planning software from JDA Software Group supported by the enterprise resource planning system, VF is able to keep inventories lean but well matched to customer demand. The company can also analyze patterns at particular stores, factor in the demographics of an area, and plan accordingly at other stores that serve similar populations.

VF's technology strategy standardizes its supply chain and enterprise resource planning system, assimilates the acquisitions that have helped drive the company's expansion, and leverages sophisticated customer support to help drive further growth. VF has made the transition from a successful-but-stodgy manufacturer to a world-spanning enterprise. It has delivered strong growth and financial performance by sourcing and selling its products all over the world. Between 2002 and 2005, sales increased by 20 percent, and income from operations rose 30 percent. During that same period, VF stock doubled in price.

The opening case provides a timely illustration of many of the information systems discussed in this chapter. VF Corporation was forced by market and legislative pressures to globalize. As a result, the company had to develop information systems to support its operations and its global supply chain. VF implemented an enterprise resource planning system and a supply chain management system. Significantly, it was able to integrate the two systems, with outstanding corporate results. We discuss these systems (among others) in this chapter.

Sources: Compiled from: E. Cone, "Dressed for Success," *Baseline Magazine*, March 5, 2005; *www.vf.com*, accessed April 3, 2005; A. Zuckerman, "Integrating Security Compliance into Supply Chain Management Software," *World Trade Magazine*, April 1, 2005; E. Cone, "VF Corp—Inching Along," *Baseline Magazine*, October 2001; and *www.vf.com*, accessed April 22, 2005.

8.1 Transaction Processing Systems

Millions (sometimes billions) of business transactions occur in every organization every day. Examples of such transactions include a product produced, a service sold, a person hired, a payroll check produced, and so on. When you check out of Wal-Mart, every time one of your purchases is swiped over the bar code reader, that is one transaction.

Transaction processing systems (TPSs) monitor, collect, store, and process data generated from all business transactions. These data are inputs to the organization's database. In the modern business world this means they also are inputs to the functional information systems, decision support systems, customer relationship management, knowledge management, and e-commerce. TPSs have to efficiently handle high volume, avoid errors, handle large variations in volume (e.g., during peak times), avoid downtime, never lose results, and maintain privacy and security. Avoiding errors is particularly critical, because data from the TPSs are input into the organization's database and must be correct (remember: "garbage in, garbage out"). Figure 8.1 shows how TPSs manage data.

Regardless of the specific data processed by a TPS, a fairly standard process occurs, whether in a manufacturing firm, in a service firm, or in a government organization. First, data are collected by people or sensors and are entered into the computer via any input device. Generally speaking, organizations try to automate the TPS data entry as much as possible because of the large volume involved, a process called *source data automation*.

Next, the system processes data in one of two basic ways: *batch* or *online processing*. In **batch processing**, the firm collects data from transactions as they occur, placing them in groups or *batches*. The system then prepares and processes the batches periodically (say, every night).

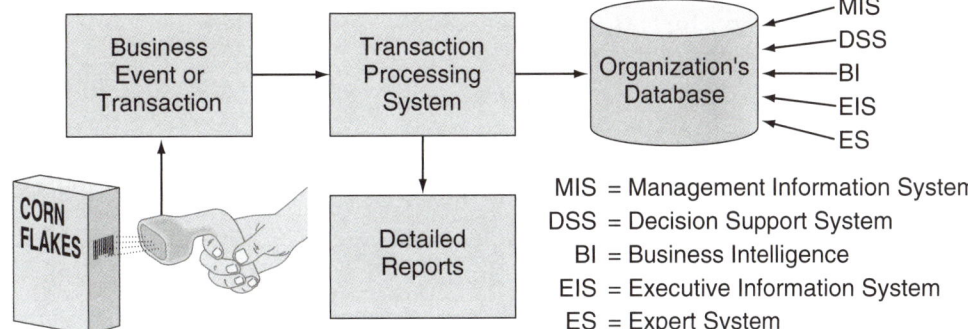

FIGURE 8.1
How transaction processing systems manage data.

MIS = Management Information System
DSS = Decision Support System
BI = Business Intelligence
EIS = Executive Information System
ES = Expert System

Traditional TPSs are centralized and run on a mainframe. However, innovations such as online transaction processing require a client/server architecture and may be Web-based. In **online transaction processing (OLTP)**, business transactions are processed online as soon as they occur. For example, when you pay for an item at a store, the system records the sale by reducing the inventory on hand by a unit, increasing the store's cash position by the amount you paid, and increasing sales figures for the item by one unit—by means of online technologies and all in real time.

IT's About Business 8.1 demonstrates how important TPSs are to an organization. It also illustrates how an error in a TPS can have far-reaching consequences.

IT's About Business

8.1 Software Error Costs Bank Millions

A foul-up at RBC Financial Group, Canada's largest bank (*www.rbc.com*), stifled payroll deposits and left as many as 10 million customers uncertain of their account balances. That error prompted an internal review of the bank's technology and processes. In addition, it will likely result in millions of dollars in damages. The problem, which took almost two weeks for RBC to correct, began when a single worker introduced a small number of faulty pieces of computer code into the bank's transaction processing system, which then began issuing error messages to users.

Bank accounts for millions of customers could not be properly updated, and payroll deposits could not be processed. The bank decided not to restart the software to complete the overnight updating process, to ensure that other banking systems would not be affected. That meant the bank essentially had two days' worth of transactions to process the next day. As transactions piled up with different dates, RBC's software had difficulty rectifying the multiple dates, forcing employees to process transactions manually.

RBC controls should have required that all new code be tested thoroughly. In addition, it should have restricted access to systems and required that work be done during off-peak periods. The problem serves as a warning to other banks that they must adopt processes to ensure that proper procedures for updating software are in place and are rigidly enforced. Banks should also expect to compensate customers when errors occur. For example, RBC is considering waiving service fees for the month. This move could result in about $123 million in lost revenues.

Adding insult to injury, RBC's woes also made the bank a target for hackers. Fraud operators took advantage of the computer glitch to launch a major phishing attack against the bank's customers over the Internet. In the "Dear Royal Bank Customer" e-mail, what looked like an official request asked for names, account numbers, and personal identifiers to verify customers' standing due to "increased fraudulent activity." Once customers opened the e-mail, went to a spoof Web site, and entered information, hackers could access their accounts.

Sources: Compiled from M. Duvall, "RBC's Account Imbalance," *Baseline Magazine*, July 1, 2004; "RBC Financial Group Automates Bank Statement Reconstruct Activities," *Information Builders Magazine*, Winter 2003; and *www.rbc.com*, accessed February 22, 2005.

QUESTIONS

1. What did RBC do incorrectly in the first place? That is, could RBC have foreseen the problem and put controls in place to prevent it? How?
2. Did RBC handle the problem properly? Why or why not?

Before you go on . . .

1. Define TPS.
2. List the key objectives of a TPS.

8.2 Functional Information Systems

Functional information systems, also called **management information systems (MISs)** and functional area information systems, provide information to managers (usually middle-level managers) in the functional areas. Managers use this information for support in planning, organizing, and controlling operations. The information is provided in routine reports such as daily sales, monthly expenditures, and weekly payrolls. (The term *MIS* is occasionally used as a blanket concept for all information systems combined—the same as IT by our definition. Historically, there were MIS departments in business organizations. Today, the broad concept is referred to as IS or IT, and MIS is reserved for the specific use described above.) As shown in Figure 8.1, the MISs access data from the corporate databases. However, to create management reports the MISs also use data from external databases.

MIS Reports

As we just discussed, each MIS generates reports in its functional area. The MIS also sends information to the corporate data warehouse and can be used for decision support. An MIS produces primarily three types of reports: routine, ad-hoc (on-demand), and exception. We examine each type below. In addition, IT's About Business 8.2 shows the importance of reports in regulatory compliance.

Routine reports are produced at scheduled intervals, ranging from hourly quality control reports to reports on monthly absenteeism rates. Although routine reports are extremely valuable to an organization, managers frequently need special information that is not included in these reports. Other times they need the information but at different times ("I need the report today, for the last three days, not for one week"). Such out-of-the routine reports are called **ad-hoc (on-demand) reports**. Ad-hoc reports also can include requests for the following types of information:

- **Drill-down reports**, which show a greater level of detail; for example, a manager might examine sales by region and decide to "drill down to more detail" to look at sales by store and then sales by salesperson.

- **Key-indicator reports**, which summarize the performance of critical activities; for example, a chief financial officer might want to watch cash flow and cash on hand.

- **comparative reports**, which compare, for example, performances of different business units or time periods.

Finally, some managers prefer **exception reports**. Exception reports include only information that falls outside certain threshold standards. To implement *management by exception,*

IT's About Business

8.2 Regulatory Compliance Places New Importance on Reports

Ingersoll-Rand (*www.irco.com*), an industrial equipment manufacturer, spent almost two years documenting each of the 100-plus internal controls and processes used to create the company's financial reports. Ingersoll-Rand had to have this documentation ready in January 2005 to meet the deadline for complying with the Sarbanes–Oxley Act.

Ingersoll-Rand started to work on compliance in March 2003. Alleged fraud committed by executives at Enron, Adelphia, and WorldCom prompted Securities and Exchange Commission (SEC) regulators to force about 300 companies with market capitalizations of more than $75 million to document the internal controls used to create financial reports.

The internal-control report assesses the control structure and procedures used at each step of the financial reporting process. The idea is that an independent auditor can now drill down from any piece of information in a financial report, such as sales, profits, and expenses, and track each individual component all the way back to the original transaction, payment, and employee who contributed to the final totals. In the end, the outside auditor will issue separate statements attesting to the company's general ledger and its control processes.

Failure to comply with this requirement will not result in any fines or criminal penalties. However, a qualified opinion, essentially a no-confidence vote from the auditor, could convince investors to sell their shares in the company. Further, Ingersoll-Rand's CEO could be fined $5 million personally and sentenced to as many as 20 years in prison if he signed off on a financial report that was accidentally or deliberately misleading or incorrect.

Analysts estimate that companies will spend roughly $1 million for every $1 billion in sales to make certain that they comply with the stipulations in Sarbanes–Oxley. For Ingersoll-Rand, this spending will total $10 million. Ingersoll-Rand states that it will spend most of the money on software for financial reporting and transaction processing.

Sources: Compiled from L. Barrett, "Ingersoll-Rand: Hidden Nuggets," *Baseline Magazine*, October 1, 2004; "Ingersoll-Rand Selects OpenPages SOX Express for Sarbanes–Oxley Compliance," *www.openpages.com*, November 22, 2004; *www.irco.com*, accessed April 2, 2005.

QUESTIONS

1. Do you think the Sarbanes–Oxley Act will help prevent further fraud? Support your answer.
2. Why did it take so long and cost so much for Ingersoll-Rand to become compliant with Sarbanes–Oxley? Do you think other companies will do the same, or is Ingersoll-Rand somehow distinct? Explain your answer.

"According to my Zip Code, I prefer non-spicy foods, enjoy tennis more than golf, subscribe to at least one news-oriented periodical, own between thirty and thirty-five ties, never buy lemon-scented products, and have a power tool in my basement, but none of that is true."

management first sets performance standards. Systems are then set up to monitor performance (via the incoming data about business transactions such as expenditures), compare actual performance to the standards, and identify predefined exceptions. Managers are alerted to the exceptions via exception reports.

We'll use sales as an example. First, management establishes sales quotas. The company then establishes an MIS that collects and analyzes all sales data. An exception report would identify only those cases where sales fell outside an established threshold (for example, more than 2 percent short of the quota). Expenditures that fell *within* the accepted range of standards would not be reported. By leaving out all "acceptable" performances, exception reports save managers time and help them concentrate on problem areas.

Information Systems for Specific Functional Areas

Traditionally, information systems were designed within each functional area, to support the area by increasing its internal effectiveness and efficiency. Typical function-specific systems are accounting, finance, marketing, operations (POM), and human resources management. Table 8.1 provides an overview of the activities that the functional information systems support. Also see Figure 8.2.

Historically, the functional area information systems were developed independently of one another, resulting in "information silos." These silos did not communicate with one another, and this lack of integration made organizations less efficient. This inefficiency was particularly evident in business processes that crossed the boundaries of functional areas. For example, developing new products involves all functional areas. Think of automobile manu-

Activities Supported by Functional Area Information Systems

Table 8.1

Accounting and Finance

Financial planning—availability and cost of money
Budgeting—allocates financial resources among participants and activities
Capital budgeting—financing of asset acquisitions
Managing financial transactions
  Handling multiple currencies
  Virtual close—ability to close books at any time on short notice
Investment management—managing organizational investments in stocks, bonds, real estate, and other investment vehicles
Budgetary control—monitoring expenditures and comparing against budget
Auditing—ensuring the accuracy and condition of financial health of organization
Payroll

Marketing and Sales

Customer relations—know who customers are and treat them like royalty
Customer profiles and preferences
Sales force automation—using software to automate the business tasks of sales, thereby improving the productivity of salespeople

Production/Operations and Logistics

Inventory management—how much inventory to order, how much inventory to keep, and when to order new inventory
Quality control—controlling for defects in incoming material and defects in goods produced
Materials requirements planning—planning process that integrates production, purchasing, and inventory management of interdependent items (MRP)
Manufacturing resource planning—planning process that integrates an enterprise's production, inventory management, purchasing, financing, and labor activities (MRP II)
Just-in-time systems—principle of production and inventory control in which materials and parts arrive precisely when and where needed for production (JIT)
Computer-integrated manufacturing—manufacturing approach that integrates several computerized systems, such as computer-assisted design (CAD), computer-assisted manufacturing (CAM), MRP, and JIT
Product life cycle management—business strategy that enables manufacturers to collaborate on product design and development efforts, using the Web

Human Resource Management

Recruitment—finding employees, testing them, and deciding which ones to hire
Performance evaluation—periodic evaluation by superiors
Training
Employee records
Benefits administration—medical, retirement, disability, unemployment, etc.

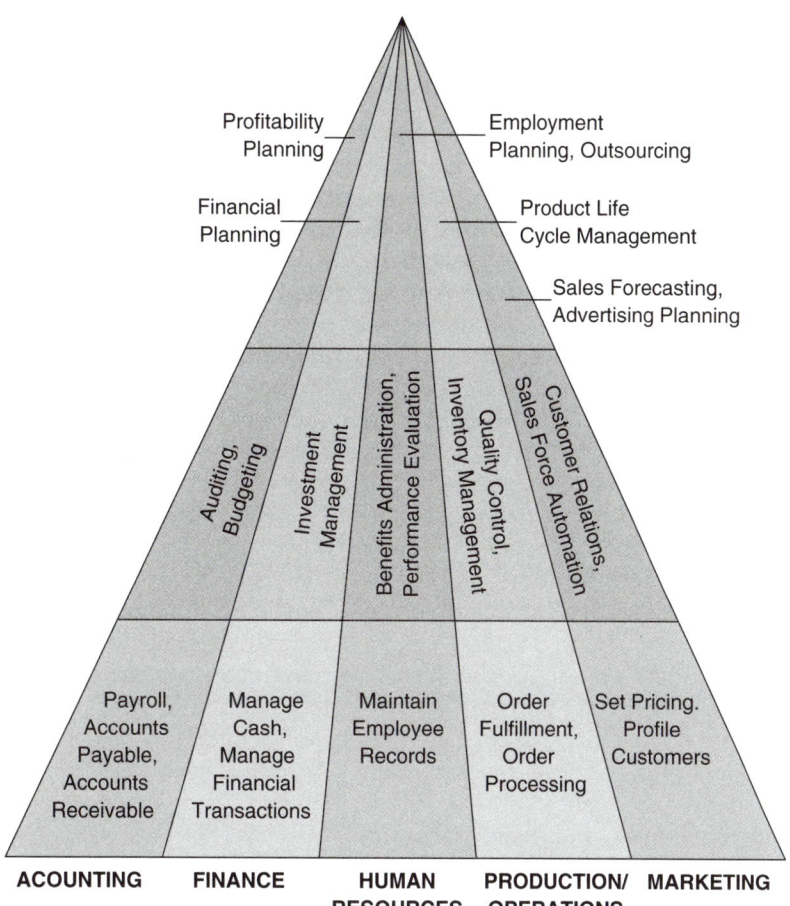

FIGURE 8.2
Examples of
information systems
supporting the
functional areas.

facturers. Developing a new automobile involves every functional area in the company, including design, engineering, production/operations, marketing, finance, accounting, and human resources. To solve their integration problems, companies developed enterprise resource planning systems. We discuss these systems in the next section.

Before you go on . . .

1. What is a functional area information system? List its major characteristics.
2. How does the MIS system support management by exception? How does it support on-demand reports?

8.3 Enterprise Resource Planning Systems

Enterprise resource planning (ERP) systems integrate the planning, management, and use of all resources of the organization. The major objective of ERP systems is to tightly integrate the functional areas of the organization, and to enable seamless information flows across the functional areas. Tight integration means that changes in one functional area are immediately reflected in all other pertinent functional areas. The advantages of an ERP system are demonstrated at Under Armour in IT's About Business 8.3.

IT's About Business

POM

8.3 Under Armour Puts an ERP System to Work

It is August 2001, at Under Armour (*www.underarmour.com*), a sports apparel company whose products are so cool that professional athletes wear them on TV without being paid to do so. Under Armour essentially created the market for "compression clothing," which makes athletes feel fresher by keeping light pressure on their muscles. Revenue has exploded, and the company is in desperate need of a system to manage orders, ship products, bill customers, and connect with suppliers. All the company's employees, including managers, spend time in the warehouse, packing boxes and shipping orders by hand. The back-order processing system is located in a big closet, with back orders clamped to clipboards, hundreds of them, hung on pegs.

To update this out-of-date system, Under Armour adopted an ERP system from Lilly Software Associates (*www.lillysoftware.com*). This system provides the basis for Under Armour's order-management and warehouse-management systems. It also offers inventory-planning capabilities, and it eliminates the manual work of printing orders, running them down to the warehouse, and handing them to the people who fill the boxes.

Under the ERP system, orders that come in via phone, fax, or e-mail are entered manually, and orders placed via electronic data interchange register automatically. (Electronic data interchange is the exchange of electronic documents from computer to computer without the use of paper. Therefore, no human intervention is necessary.) The orders are matched with a current inventory list. The system then produces orders that can be downloaded onto wireless handheld devices that warehouse workers use to pick up and scan the items on the order. The warehouse management segment of the application tracks a picker's location and turns on a light near the next item he is due to pick up. The pickers scan each item and then scan each box as it is filled. This way the system can register not only the orders but also when each order has been completed.

Large retailers make up 60 percent of Under Armour's business. The company deals with these customers with electronic document exchange. The remaining 40 percent of the company's business is with small retail stores. Under Armour handles these transactions via fax and telephone. This is not high-tech, but the small retailers appreciate Under Armour's efforts to take care of all its customers. Under Armour is now developing an extranet to handle their smaller customers more efficiently over the Internet.

Sources: Compiled from K. Fogarty, "Under Armour: No Sweat," *Baseline Magazine*, September 1, 2004; D. Navas, "Under Armour Gears Up for Triple Digit Growth," *Supply Chain Systems Magazine*, March 2003; and *www.underarmour.com* and *www.lillysoftware.com*, accessed April 2, 2005.

QUESTIONS

1. Why did Under Armour need an ERP system?
2. Why does Under Armour pay such close attention to its smaller customers?

ERP systems provide the information necessary to control the business processes of the organization. A **business process** is a set of related steps or procedures designed to produce a specific outcome. Business processes can be located entirely within one functional area, such as approving a credit card application or hiring a new employee. They can also span multiple functional areas, such as fulfilling a large order from a new customer.

ERP software includes a set of interdependent software modules, linked to a common database, that provide support for the internal business processes in the following functional areas: finance and accounting, manufacturing and production, sales and marketing, and human resources. The modules are built around predefined business processes and users access them through a single interface. Table 8.2 provides examples of the predefined business processes.

The business processes in ERP software are often predefined by the best practices that the ERP vendor has developed. **Best practices** are the most successful solutions or problem-solving methods for achieving a business objective.

Table 8.2

Business Processes Supported by ERP Modules

- *Financial and accounting processes:* general ledger, accounts payable, accounts receivable, fixed assets, cash management and forecasting, product-cost accounting, cost-center accounting, asset accounting, tax accounting, credit management, financial reporting
- *Sales and marketing processes:* order processing, quotations, contracts, product configuration, pricing, billing, credit checking, incentive and commission management, sales planning
- *Manufacturing and production processes:* procurement, inventory management, purchasing, shipping, production planning, production scheduling, material requirements planning, quality control, distribution, transportation, plant and equipment maintenance
- *Human Resources Processes:* personnel administration, time accounting, payroll, personnel planning and development, benefits accounting, applicant tracking, compensation, workforce planning, performance management

Although some companies have developed their own ERP systems, most organizations use commercially available ERP software. The leading ERP software vendor is SAP (*www.sap.com*), with its SAP R/3 package. Other major vendors include Oracle (*www.oracle. com*) and PeopleSoft (*www.peoplesoft.com*), now an Oracle company. (With more than 700 customers, PeopleSoft is the market leader in higher education.) For up-to-date information on ERP software, see *www.erpassist.com*.

Despite all of their benefits, ERP systems do have drawbacks. To begin with, they can be extremely complex, expensive, and time-consuming to implement. Also, companies may need to change existing business processes to fit the predefined business processes of the software. For companies with well-established procedures, this can be a huge problem. Finally, companies must purchase the entire software package even if they require only a few of the modules. For these reasons, ERP software is not attractive to everyone. IT's About Business 8.4 shows how Stanford University experienced these problems with its ERP implementation.

IT's About Business

8.4 ERP Problems at Stanford

Stanford University wanted to get rid of its 20-year-old mainframe software and advance to the latest financial and human-resources modules of ERP systems from Oracle and PeopleSoft. However, the process turned out to be extremely difficult.

Stanford spent more than seven years transferring its financial systems onto the Oracle financial modules. The project was supposed to be finished in 1999, but it experienced severe delays. These delays were caused in part by the huge amount of customization required by the software. In 2000, Stanford finally got part of the Oracle financial modules running. At that point the university set the remaining projects aside. It then started another project, installing PeopleSoft to manage student records and human resources systems. The PeopleSoft projects were delivered on time. However, faculty and students found the applications quite disruptive. For example, the modules interfered with Stanford's ability to issue correct paychecks and assign student housing. Finally, in 2002 the Faculty Senate called for independent oversight of Stanford's IT department.

One cause of these problems was that the Oracle and PeopleSoft applications were designed to be used by public companies, not decentralized educational institutions. For example, the ERP software had a single ship-to address in the purchasing module. This arrangement works well for a company like

IBM that is organized around a central receiving unit. However, it is not functional for a massive research university like Stanford where packages are delivered directly to numerous offices and labs.

Unfortunately, ERP vendors can be slow to recognize the pain their software can cause customers. For example, PeopleSoft was sued by the state of Ohio after a botched installation at Cleveland State University.

Stanford finally decided to change itself rather than change the software. So far, however, each project involving Oracle and PeopleSoft at Stanford has been different enough so that it is hard to establish best practices. The university must cope with "version upgrade gridlock." In other words, changing the version of the PeopleSoft package requires changing the version of the Oracle package, and vice versa. Stanford hopes that Oracle's purchase of PeopleSoft might help in this area by promoting compatible software.

Sources: Compiled from D. Gage, "Stanford University: Hard Lesson," *Baseline Magazine*; June 8, 2004; T. Wailgum, "Big Mess on Campus," *CIO Magazine*, May 1, 2005; and *www. stanford.edu*, *www.oracle.com*, and *www.peoplesoft.com*, accessed March 1, 2005.

QUESTIONS

1. Should Stanford simply have started fresh, rather than spending seven years trying to install Oracle financial modules?
2. Should Stanford have investigated other universities with ERP systems before beginning its implementation?
3. Should Stanford have had to pay for the difficulties in implementing the Oracle and PeopleSoft systems? Should Oracle and PeopleSoft have borne part of the costs?

During the late 1990s, companies began to extend ERP systems along the supply chain to suppliers and customers. These extended systems add functions to help companies manage customer interactions and relationships with suppliers and vendors. We discuss supply chain management systems in Section 8.5.

Before you go on . . .

1. Define ERP, and describe its functionalities.
2. List some drawbacks of ERP software.

8.4 Customer Relationship Management Systems

Customer relationship management (CRM) is an enterprisewide effort to acquire and retain customers. CRM recognizes that customers are the core of a business and that a company's success depends on effectively managing relationships with them. CRM focuses on building long-term and sustainable customer relationships that add value both for the customer and the company. (See *www.insightexec.com* and *www.crmassist.com*).

CRM includes a *one-to-one* relationship between a customer and a seller. To be a genuine one-to-one marketer, a company must be willing and able to change its behavior toward a specific customer, based on what it knows about that customer. So, CRM is basically a simple idea: *Treat different customers differently.* For example, "good" customers represent about 80 percent of a company's profits but only 20 percent of the company's customers.

It can cost many times more to acquire a new customer than to retain an existing customer. Therefore, CRM helps organizations keep profitable customers and maximize lifetime revenue from them.

Because a firm must be able to modify its products and services based on the needs of individual customers, CRM involves much more than just sales and marketing. Rather, smart companies encourage customers to participate in the development of products, services, and solutions. In order to build enduring one-to-one relationships in a CRM initiative, a company must continuously interact with customers *individually*. One reason so many firms are beginning to focus on CRM is that this kind of marketing can create high customer loyalty, which will increase the firm's profits. Significantly, for CRM to be effective, almost all other functional areas must become involved. IT's About Business 8.5 illustrates how Remington Arms used CRM to improve customer relations.

IT's About Business

8.5 Remington Takes Care of Its Customers

"Firearms are a lifestyle product," says the vice president of Remington Arms (*www.remington.com*). To nurture the relationship between Remington and its customers, the company must respond to endless queries about its products. The pool of information is deep and broad. Privately held Remington makes dozens of different models, and people expect the company to continue servicing guns that may last for generations. Remington does not sell firearms online. The company's products are highly regulated and expensive, and they are available in multiple configurations.

Approximately 27 million Americans are involved in hunting and shooting sports. During the late 1990s, however, Remington focused largely on huge national accounts like Wal-Mart. As a result, the company allowed its support for gun owners and small retailers to languish. The company decided to resolve its customer-relationship problems by creating a Web site that provided customers with detailed information and made it easier to buy and operate a Remington firearm. This Web site clearly involved knowledge management for complex products as well as customer relationship management. So, how does the Web site take care of Remington's customers?

Perhaps the most important strategy was to make the company's publications available online. Customer response was overwhelming. For example, the number of catalog downloads increased significantly, surpassing 3 million in 2004. At the same time, customer requests for paper catalogs declined from 23,000 in 2000 to 4,000 in 2004. During the same period the number of owner's manuals downloaded from the Web site increased from 62,000 to 802,000, while requests for printed manuals dropped from 14,000 to 4,800. The *Remington Quarterly*, a glossy magazine that used to cost about $100,000 per issue to produce, is now published online. Significantly, the number of readers has remained roughly the same.

Finally, customers downloaded almost 440,000 video clips, including safety and operating instructions and promotional footage, in 2004. As a result, Remington did not have to spend the $2.00 per tape to stock the videos.

Remington further helped its customers by compiling a database of about 11,000 of its dealers. The Web site has a locator program that sends customers to the nearest dealer. This application also has proved to be highly successful. In 2004 alone, 240,000 customers searched for the nearest dealer on the Web site, and 97 percent of them found a dealer located within 50 miles.

In fact, the Web site worked too well. Before Remington implemented the site, the company averaged about 50 e-mails per day. After it set up the site, e-mail traffic increased to more than 1,000 per day. As a result, the company's response time became much slower. E-mails that it used to respond to in a day or two now sat for a week or more. To speed up the response cycle, Remington put answers to frequently asked questions (FAQs) on its Web site. As with online publications, this approach proved highly successful. Since it took this step, the company has experienced a 30 percent reduction in phone calls and a 50 percent reduction in e-mail volume.

Sources: Compiled from E. Cone, "On Target," *Baseline Magazine*, March 1, 2004; M. Middlewood, "How Remington Self Serves Its Customers." *Mac News World*, June 22, 2004; L. Haber, "Putting a Lid on CRM Costs with Self-Service," *ZdNet UK*, July 16, 2002; and *www.remington.com*, accessed April 2, 2005.

QUESTIONS

1. Why does Remington need so much CRM on its Web site? *Hint:* Think of the particular characteristics of the company's products.
2. What benefits did Remington gain from its Web site?

Customer Relationship Management Applications

In the past, customer data were located in many isolated systems in various functional areas, such as finance, distribution, sales, service, and marketing. In addition, e-commerce generated huge amounts of customer data that were not integrated with the data in the functional area ISs.

CRM systems were designed to address these problems by providing information and tools to deliver a superior customer experience and to maximize the life time customer value for a firm. CRM systems integrate customer data from various organizational sources, analyze them, and then provide the results to both employees and customer touch points. A **customer touch point** is a method of interaction with a customer, such as telephone, e-mail, a customer service or help desk, conventional mail, a Web site, and a store.

Properly designed CRM systems provide a single, enterprisewide view of each customer. These systems also provide customers with a single point of contact within the enterprise as well as a unified view of the enterprise.

CRM systems provide applications in three major areas: sales, marketing, and customer service. Let's take a look at each one.

Sales   *Sales force automation (SFA)* functions in CRM systems make salespeople more productive by helping them focus on the most profitable customers. SFA functions provide such data as sales prospect and contact information, product information, product configurations, and sales quotes. SFA software can integrate all the information about a particular customer so that the salesperson can put together a personalized presentation for that customer.

Marketing.   CRM systems support marketing campaigns by providing prospect and customer data, product and service information, qualified sales leads, and tools for analyzing marketing and customer data. In addition, they enhance opportunities for cross-selling, up-selling, and bundling.

Cross-selling refers to the marketing of complementary products to customers. For example, a bank customer with a large balance in his or her checking account might be directed toward CDs or money-market funds. **Up-selling** is the marketing of higher-value products or services to new or existing customers. For example, if you are in the market for a television, a salesperson will show you a plasma-screen TV next to a conventional TV, in hopes that you will pay extra for a clearer picture. Finally, **bundling** is a type of cross-selling in which a combination of products is sold together at a lower price than the combined costs of the individual products. For example, your cable company might offer a package that includes basic cable TV, all the movie channels, and broadband Internet access, for a lower price than these services would cost individually. As another example, computer manufacturers or retailers often bundle a computer, monitor, and printer at a reduced cost.

Customer Service   Customer service functions in CRM systems provide information and tools to make call centers, help desks, and customer support staff more efficient. These functions often include Web-based self-service capabilities. Customer service can take many forms, as we see below.

- *Technical and other information and services.* CRM systems can personalize interactive experiences to induce a consumer to commit to a purchase or to remain a loyal customer. For example, General Electric's Web site (*www.ge.com*) provides detailed technical and maintenance information. In addition, it sells replacement parts for discontinued models. These types of parts and information are quite difficult to find offline. The ability to download manuals and solutions to common problems at any time is another innovation of Web-based customer service. Finally, customized information—such as product and warranty information—can be efficiently delivered when the customer logs on to the vendor's Web site. Not only can the customer pull (search and find) information as needed, but the vendor also can push (send) information to the customer.

- **Customized products and services.** Dell Computer revolutionized the purchasing of computers by letting customers configure their own systems. Many other online vendors now offer this type of mass customization. Consumers are shown prepackaged specials and are then given the option to custom-build products using product configurators.

- **Tracking account or order status.** Customers can view their account balances or check the shipping status of their orders at any time from their computers or cell phones. If you ordered books from Amazon, for example, you can find the anticipated arrival date. Many companies follow this model and provide similar services (see *www.fedex.com* and *www.ups.com*).

- **Personalized Web pages.** Many companies allow customers to create their own individual Web pages. These pages can be used to record purchases and preferences, as well as problems and requests.

- **FAQs.** FAQs are the simplest and least expensive tool for dealing with repetitive customer questions. Customers use this tool by themselves, which makes the delivery cost minimal. However, any nonstandard question requires an individual e-mail.

- **E-mail and automated response.** E-mail has become the most popular tool of customer service. Inexpensive and fast, e-mail is used mostly to answer inquiries from customers. However, firms also rely on e-mail to disseminate product and other information (e.g., confirmations) and to conduct correspondence regarding any topic.

- **Call centers.** One of the most important tools of customer service is the *call center*. Call centers are typically the "face" of the organization to its customers, as the following example demonstrates.

POM

Example

Efficiency at FedEx Call Centers Employees at FedEx call centers can handle a routine call in 20 seconds. They simply plug in a name, which leads to a Zip code, which in turn leads to a tracking number. With this system they can resolve a complicated complaint in less than 10 minutes.

Like many other companies, however, FedEx is trying to save money on customer service by making their customers use their Web site (*www.fedex.com*). For every caller that FedEx can divert to its Web site, the company saves as much as $1.87. The company's efforts to convince customers to use the Web site have experienced some success. The site handles an average of 60 million requests to track packages per month. These requests cost FedEx $21 million per year. In contrast, they would cost more than $1 billion if all those people called. At the same time, FedEx claims that its call centers handle 83,000 fewer calls per day than in 2000, a saving of $58 million per year.

Despite these changes, many customers still prefer to call and speak with a live person, especially if they think they have a problem. For this reason, FedEx spends $326 million per year on its call centers. FedEx call centers are designed around personal computers for each representative. Reps can pull up historical data on customers whenever they call. These data include customers' shipping histories, their preferences, and even images of their paper bills. As a result, FedEx reps can provide better, faster service to the company's customers. (*Sources:* Compiled from D. Gage, "FedEx: Personal Touch," *Baseline Magazine*, January 13, 2005; E. Rasmussen, "Executives' Guide to Call Center Excellence: Best Practices—FedEx: An Overnight Success Story," *www.destinationcrm.com*, February 2003; and *www.fedex.com*, accessed April 3, 2005.

8.5 Supply Chain Management Systems

A **supply chain** refers to the flow of materials, information, money, and services from raw material suppliers, through factories and warehouses, to the end customers. A supply chain also includes the *organizations* and *processes* that create and deliver products, information, and services to end customers.

The function of **supply chain management (SCM)** is to plan, organize, and optimize the supply chain's activities. Like other functional areas, SCM utilizes information systems. The goal of SCM systems is to reduce friction along the supply chain. Friction can involve increased time, costs, and inventories as well as decreased customer satisfaction. SCM systems, then, reduce uncertainty and risks by decreasing inventory levels and cycle time and improving business processes and customer service. All of these benefits contribute to increased profitability and competitiveness.

Significantly, SCM systems are a type of interorganizational information system. An **interorganizational information system (IOS)** involves information flows among two or more organizations. By connecting the information systems of business partners, IOSs enable the partners to perform a number of tasks:

- Reduce the costs of routine business transactions.
- Improve the quality of the information flow by reducing or eliminating errors.
- Compress the cycle time involved in fulfilling business transactions.
- Eliminate paper processing and its associated inefficiencies and costs.
- Make the transfer and processing of information easy for users.

Interorganizational systems that connect companies located in two or more countries are referred to as **global information systems**. Regardless of its structure, a company with global operations relies heavily on IT. The major benefits of global information systems for such organizations are effective communication at a reasonable cost and effective collaboration that overcomes differences in distance, time, language, and culture.

Issues in Global IOS Design

The task of designing any effective IOS is complicated. It is even more complex when the IOS is a global system, because of differences in cultures, economies, and politics among parties in different countries. Some countries are erecting artificial borders through local language preference, local regulation, and access limitations. Some issues to consider in designing global IOSs are cultural differences, localization, economic and political differences, and legal issues.

Cultural Differences *Culture* consists of the objects, values, and other characteristics of a particular society. It includes many different aspects ranging from tradition to legal and ethical issues to what information is considered offensive. When companies plan to do business in countries other than their own, they must consider the cultural environment.

Localization Many companies use different names, colors, sizes, and packaging for their overseas products and services. This practice is referred to as *localization*, which means that products and services are modified for each locality. In order to maximize the benefits of global information systems, the localization approach should also be used in the design and operation of such systems. For example, many Web sites offer different language and/or currency options, as well as special content.

Economic and Political Differences Countries also differ considerably in their economic and political environments. One result of such variations is that information technology infrastructures often differ from country to country. For example, many countries own the telephone services or control communications very tightly. France, for example, insisted for years that French should be the sole language on French Web sites. The country now permits Web sites to use other languages, but French still must appear in every site. China goes even further. The Chinese government controls the content of the Internet and blocks some Web sites from being viewed in the country.

Legal Issues   Legal systems differ considerably among countries. As a result, laws and rules concerning copyrights, patents, computer crimes, file sharing, privacy, and data transfer vary from country to country. All of these issues can affect what information is transmitted via global systems. For this reason, companies must consider them when they establish a global IS.

The impact of legal, economic, and political differences on the design and use of global information systems can be clearly seen in the issue of cross-border data transfer. The term **cross-border data transfer** refers to the flow of corporate data across nations' borders. Several countries, such as Canada and Brazil, impose strict laws to control this transfer. These countries usually justify their laws as protecting the privacy of their citizens, because corporate data frequently contain personal data. Other justifications are protecting intellectual property and keeping jobs within the country by requiring that data processing be done there.

The Structure and Components of Supply Chains

As we have shown, supply chains are IOSs that may be global. As a result, all considerations for IOSs and global IS apply to SCM systems. The term *supply chain* comes from a picture of how the partnering organizations are linked together. A typical supply chain, which links a company with its suppliers and its distributors and customers, is shown in Figure 8.3. Note that the supply chain involves three segments:

1. *Upstream*, where sourcing or procurement from external suppliers occurs
2. *Internal*, where packaging, assembly, or manufacturing takes place
3. *Downstream*, where distribution takes place, frequently by external distributors

The flow of information and goods can be bidirectional. For example, damaged or unwanted products can be returned, a process known as *reverse logistics*. Using the automobile industry as an example, reverse logistics would involve cars that are returned to dealers or recalled by the manufacturer because of defects.

Tiers of Suppliers   An examination of Figure 8.3 shows that there are several tiers of suppliers. As the diagram shows, a supplier may have one or more subsuppliers, and the subsupplier may have its own subsupplier(s), and so on. For example, with an automobile manufacturer, Tier 3 suppliers produce basic products such as glass, plastic, and rubber. Tier 2 suppliers use these inputs to make windshields, tires, and plastic moldings. Tier 1 suppliers produce integrated components such as dashboards and seat assemblies.

The Flows in the Supply Chain   There are typically three flows in the supply chain: materials, information, and financial. *Material flows* are the physical products, raw materials, supplies, and so forth that flow along the chain. Material flows also include *reverse* flows—returned products, recycled products, and disposal of materials or products. A supply chain thus involves a *product life cycle* approach, from "dirt to dust."

Information flows are all data related to demand, shipments, orders, returns, and schedules, as well as changes in any of these data. Finally, *financial flows* are all transfers of money, payments, credit card information and authorization, payment schedules, e-payments, and credit-related data.

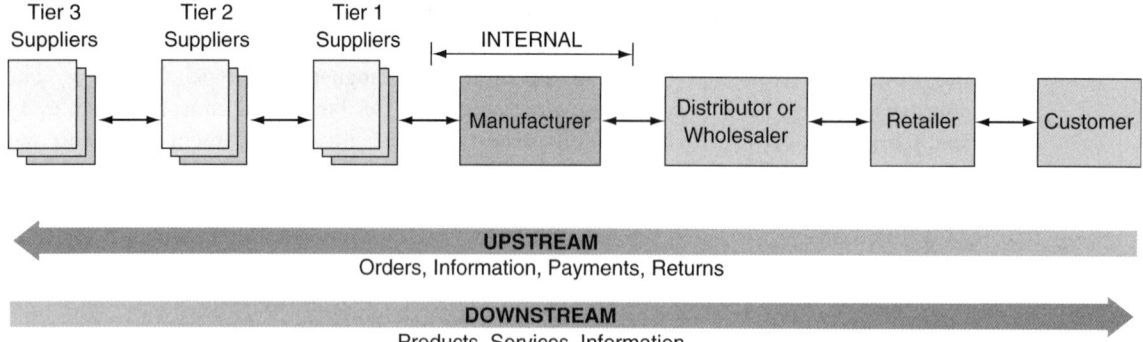

FIGURE 8.3   Generic supply chain.

All supply chains do not have the same number and types of flows. For example, in service industries there may be no physical flow of materials, but frequently there is a flow of information, often in the form of documents (physical or electronic copies). In fact, the digitization of software, music, and other content may result in a supply chain without any physical flow. Notice, however, that in such a case, there are two types of information flows: one that replaces materials flow (e.g., digitized software) and one that is the supporting information (orders, billing, etc). In managing the supply chain it is necessary to coordinate all the above flows among all the parties involved in the supply chain.

Problems along the Supply Chain

As we discussed earlier, problems, or friction, can develop within a supply chain. One major symptom of ineffective supply chains is poor customer service. In some cases, supply chains don't deliver products or services when and where customers—either individuals or businesses—need them. In other cases the supply chain provides poor-quality products. Other problems are high inventory costs and loss of revenues.

The problems along the supply chain stem mainly from two sources: (1) uncertainties, and (2) the need to coordinate several activities, internal units, and business partners. A major source of supply chain uncertainties is the *demand forecast*. Demand for a product can be influenced by numerous factors such as competition, prices, weather conditions, technological developments, and customers' general confidence. Another uncertainty is delivery times, which depend on factors ranging from production machine failures to road construction and traffic jams. In addition, quality problems in materials and parts can create production delays, which also lead to supply chain problems.

One of the major difficulties to properly setting inventory levels in various parts of the supply chain is known as the bullwhip effect. The **bullwhip effect** refers to erratic shifts in orders up and down the supply chain. Basically, customer demand variables can become magnified when viewed through the eyes of managers at each link in the supply chain. If each distinct entity makes ordering and inventory decisions with an eye to its own interest above those of the chain, then stockpiling can occur at as many as seven or eight locations along the supply chain. Research has shown that such hoarding has led in some cases to as many as 100 days of inventory that is waiting "just in case" (versus 10–20 days in the normal case).

In addition to all these factors, problems in supply chains can occur as a result of new technologies. The next example describes such a case.

Example

Supply Chain Failures Hamper Army in Iraq. Because of the failure of automated SCM systems in Iraq, U.S. Army combat units fighting there had to obtain key supplies such as lubricants and explosives by capturing them from enemy stockpiles. In addition, food supplies barely met demand, and stocks of ammunition and spare parts were nearly depleted during combat.

Military analysts found that the performance of supply chain operations "barely above subsistence levels" in large part because of problems with software based on RFID technology and network communications. The supply chain systems worked as expected until combat began in Iraq, after which the Army's network was quickly stretched too thin. The Army stress-tested its battlefield systems before the war. However, no testing could have fully prepared the Army to deal with fast-moving combat operations involving 150,000 troops and several million supply items. To resolve some of these problems, the Army is already working to replace its 13 core logistics systems with ERP software from SAP that is tailored specifically for defense operations. (*Sources:* Compiled from M. L. Songini, "Supply Chain System Failures Hampered Army Units in Iraq," *Computerworld*, July 26, 2004; "Supply Chains and the Army," *CNET News*, December 6, 2003; and *www.army.mil*, accessed April 2, 2005.)

Solutions to Supply Chain Problems

Supply chain problems can be very costly for companies, so organizations are motivated to find innovative solutions. During the oil crises of the 1970s, for example, Ryder Systems, a large trucking company, purchased a refinery to control the upstream part of the supply chain and ensure timely availability of gasoline for its trucks. Such a strategy is known as vertical integration. A general definition is that **vertical integration** occurs when a company buys its suppliers. (Ryder sold the refinery later, because (1) it could not manage a business it did not know and (2) oil became more plentiful.) In the remaining portion of this section we will look at some of the possible solutions to supply chain problems, many of which are supported by IT.

Using Inventories to Solve Supply Chain Problems Undoubtedly, the most common solution is *building inventories* as insurance against supply chain uncertainties. The main problem with this approach is that it is very difficult to correctly determine inventory levels for each product and part. If inventory levels are set too high, the costs of keeping the inventory will greatly increase. (Also, as we have seen, excessive inventories at multiple points in the supply chain can result in the bullwhip effect.) If the inventory is too low, there is no insurance against high demand or slow delivery times. In such cases, customers don't receive what they want, when they want or need it. The result is lost customers and revenues. In either event, the total cost—including the costs of maintaining inventories, the costs of lost sales opportunities, and the costs of developing a bad reputation—can be very high. Thus, companies make major attempts to optimize and control inventories.

Information Sharing Another common way to solve supply chain problems, and especially to improve demand forecasts, is *sharing information* along the supply chain. Such sharing can be facilitated by electronic data interchange and extranets.

One of the most notable examples of information sharing occurs between large manufacturers and retailers. For example, Wal-Mart provides Procter & Gamble with access to daily sales information from every store for every item P&G makes for Wal-Mart. This access enables P&G to manage the *inventory replenishment* for Wal-Mart's stores. By monitoring inventory levels, P&G knows when inventories fall below the threshold for each product at any Wal-Mart store. These data trigger an immediate shipment.

Such information sharing between Wal-Mart and P&G is done automatically. It is part of a vendor-managed inventory strategy. **Vendor-managed inventory (VMI)** occurs when a retailer does not manage the inventory for a particular product or group of products. Instead, the supplier manages the entire inventory process. P&G has similar agreements with other major retailers. The benefit for P&G is accurate and timely information on consumer demand for its products. Thus, P&G can plan production more accurately, minimizing the bullwhip effect.

Before you go on . . .

1. Define a supply chain and supply chain management (SCM).
2. List the major components of supply chains.
3. What is the bullwhip effect?
4. Describe solutions to supply chain problems.

8.6 Electronic Data Interchange and Extranets

Clearly, SCM systems are essential to the successful operation of many businesses. As we discussed, these systems—and IOSs in general—rely on various forms of IT to resolve problems. Three technologies in particular provide support for IOSs and SCM systems: electronic data interchange, extranets, and Web Services. We already discussed Web Services in Chapter 5. In this section we examine the other two technologies.

Electronic Data Interchange (EDI)

Electronic data interchange (EDI) is a communication standard that enables business partners to exchange routine documents, such as purchasing orders, electronically. EDI formats these documents according to agreed-upon standards (e.g., data formats). It then transmits messages using a converter, called a translator. The message travels over a value-added network (VAN) or the Internet. When the message is received, it is automatically translated into a business language.

The following are the major components of EDI:

- *EDI translators.* An EDI translator converts data into a standard format before it is transmitted.

- *Business transactions messages.* EDI primarily transfers messages about repetitive business transactions. These transactions include purchase orders, invoices, credit approvals, shipping notices, and confirmations.

- *Data formatting standards.* Because EDI messages are repetitive, it makes sense to use formatting (coding) standards.

EDI provides many benefits compared with a manual delivery system (see Figure 8.4). To begin with, it minimizes data entry errors, because each entry is checked by the computer. In addition, the length of the message can be shorter, and the messages are secured. EDI also reduces cycle time, increases productivity, enhances customer service, and minimizes paper usage and storage. In this way, EDI often serves as a catalyst and a stimulus to improve the standard of information that flows between and among organizations.

Despite all of the advantages of EDI, various factors prevented it from being more widely used. To begin with, implementing an EDI system involves a significant initial investment. In addition, the ongoing operating costs also are high, due to the use of expensive, private VANs. Another major issue for some companies is that the traditional EDI system is inflexible. For example, it is difficult to make quick changes, such as adding business partners. In

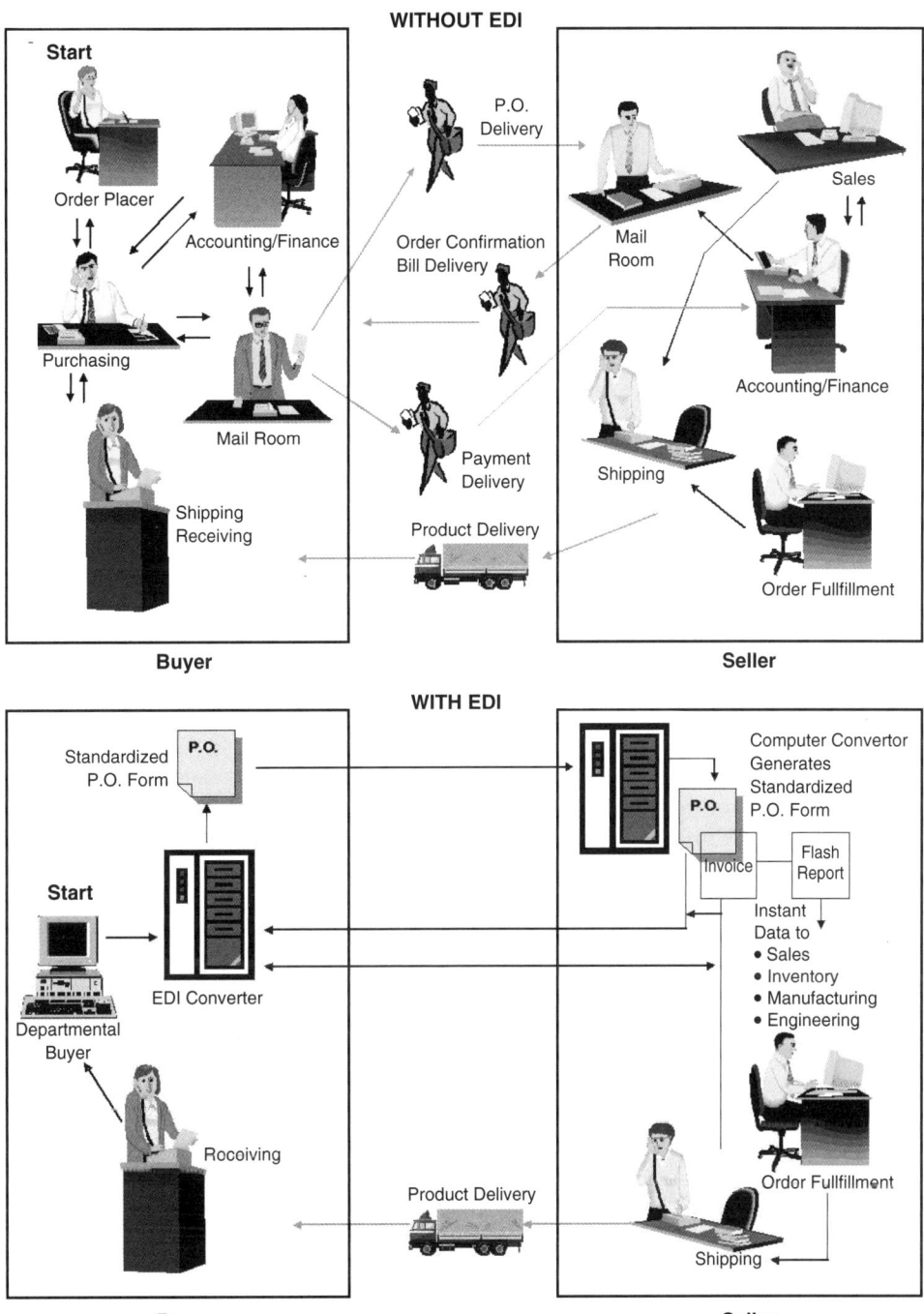

FIGURE 8.4
Comparing purchase order (PO) fulfillment with and without EDI. (*Source:* Drawn by E. Turban.)

addition, an EDI system requires a long startup period. Further, business processes must sometimes be restructured to fit EDI requirements. Finally, multiple EDI standards exist. As a result, one company may have to use several standards in order to communicate with different business partners.

Despite these limitations, EDI has changed the business landscape of many industries and large corporations. It is used extensively by large corporations, sometimes in a global network such as the one operated by General Electric Information System (which has more than 100,000 corporate users). Well-known retailers such as Home Depot, Toys R Us, and Wal-Mart would operate very differently without EDI, because it is an integral and essential element of their business strategies. IT's About Business 8.6 relates how one machinery manufacturer uses EDI in its operations.

Extranets

In building IOSs and SCM systems, it is necessary to connect the intranets of different business partners to build extranets. As we have discussed in previous chapters, extranets link business partners to one another over the Internet by providing access to certain areas of each other's corporate intranets (see Figure 8.5).

The main goal of extranets is to foster collaboration between business partners. An extranet is open to selected B2B suppliers, customers, and other business partners. These individuals access it through the Internet. Extranets enable people who are located outside a company to work together with the company's internally located employees. An extranet enables external business partners to enter the corporate intranet, via the Internet, to access data, place orders, check status, communicate, and collaborate. It also enables partners to perform self-service activities such as checking the status of orders or inventory levels.

IT's About Business

8.6 Murray Moves to Internet EDI

Murray, Inc. (now owned by Briggs and Stratton at *www.briggsandstratton.com*) is a manufacturer of snowblowers, lawn mowers, and recreational gear. To continue doing business with Wal-Mart, Murray needed to upgrade its IT infrastructure. Murray already used EDI to exchange business documents, such as purchase orders, invoices, and shipping notices, with Wal-Mart. However, Wal-Mart wanted to do EDI in a more modern way.

Over the past few years, Wal-Mart has used its clout to encourage its suppliers to shift to swapping EDI messages via the Internet rather than using VANs that incur per-message charges. Specifically, Wal-Mart now insists on using Internet EDI software that adheres to Applicability Statement 2 (AS2). AS2 describes how to create a connection and securely transport an EDI file over the Internet.

EDI will work only if both partners use the same data formats, a system known as data synchronization. Synchronizing data ensures that incompatible data will not be sent over EDI links between trading partners. In this way it will eliminate costly shipping discrepancies, and invoicing errors. The Uniform Code Council (UCC) has identified more than 150 attributes that can be used for item descriptions, such as color, size, item packaging type, and the number of items that form a case and a pallet. Wal-

Mart requires its suppliers to use UCCnet to synchronize item data.

Murray is a typical manufacturer, forced to find a technology balance that satisfies its retail customers who want to keep doing business the old way and those who want to adopt new processes. However, with EDI and data synchronization, Murray receives a number of benefits:

- Reduction in out-of-stock products
- Decrease in salesforce time spent communicating basic item information to retailers
- Reduction in time spent dealing with invoice disputes
- Reduction in inventory

Sources: Compiled from A. Bednarz, "The Art of Balancing E-Commerce Processes," *Network World*, February 7, 2005; A. Ackerman, "Ahead of the Game." *Consumer Goods Technology*, August 2003; and *www.briggsandstratton.com*, accessed April 2, 2005.

QUESTIONS

1. What is the relationship between Murray and Wal-Mart?

2. What is the relationship between EDI and data synchronization?

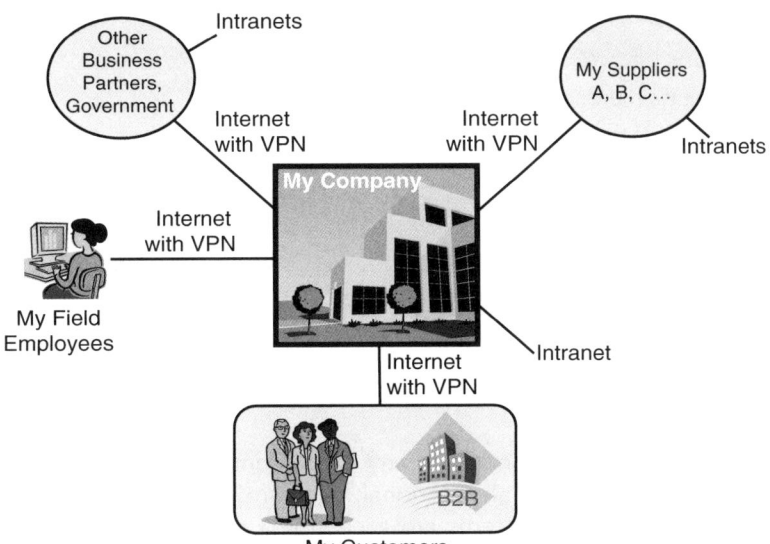

FIGURE 8.5
The structure of an
extranet.

Extranets use virtual private network (VPN) technology to make communication over the Internet more secure. The Internet-based extranet is far less costly than proprietary networks. It is a nonproprietary technical tool that can support the rapid evolution of electronic communication and commerce. The major benefits of extranets are faster processes and information flow, improved order entry and customer service, lower costs (e.g., for communications, travel, and administrative overhead), and overall improvement in business effectiveness.

Types of Extranets Depending on the business partners involved and the purpose, there are three major types of extranets. We discuss each one below, along with its major business applications.

A Company and Its Dealers, Customers, or Suppliers Such an extranet is centered around one company. An example would be the FedEx extranet that allows customers to track the status of a package. To do so, customers use the Internet to access a database on the FedEx intranet. By enabling a customer to check the location of a package, FedEx saves the cost of having a human operator perform that task over the phone.

An Industry's Extranet The major players in an industry may team up to create an extranet that will benefit all of them. For example, ANXeBusiness (*www.anx.com*) enables companies to collaborate effectively through a network that provides a secure global medium for business-to-business information exchange. The ANX Network is used for mission-critical business transactions by leading international organizations in aerospace, automotive, chemical, electronics, financial services, health care, logistics, manufacturing, transportaion and related industries. The ANX Network offers customers a reliable extranet and Virtual Private Network services.

Joint Ventures and Other Business Partnerships In this type of extranet, the partners in a joint venture use the extranet as a vehicle for communications and collaboration. An example is Bank of America's extranet for commercial loans. The partners involved in making such loans are a lender, loan broker, escrow company, title company, and others. The extranet connects lenders, loan applicants, and the loan organizer, Bank of America. A similar case is Lending Tree (*www.lendingtree.com*), a company that provides mortgage quotes for your home and also sells mortgages online. Lending Tree uses an extranet for its business partners (e.g., the lenders).

Before you go on . . .

1. Define EDI and list its major benefits and limitations.
2. Define an extranet and explain its infrastructure.
3. List and briefly define the major types of extranets.

What's in IT for me?

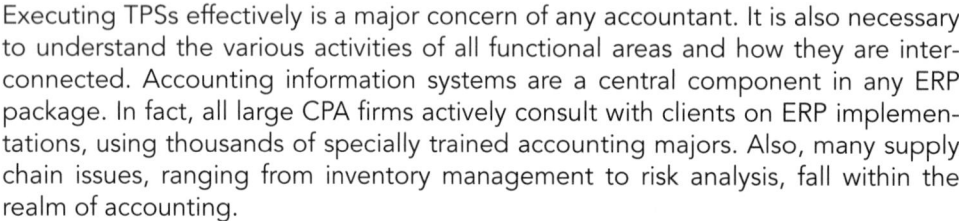

For the Accounting Major

Executing TPSs effectively is a major concern of any accountant. It is also necessary to understand the various activities of all functional areas and how they are interconnected. Accounting information systems are a central component in any ERP package. In fact, all large CPA firms actively consult with clients on ERP implementations, using thousands of specially trained accounting majors. Also, many supply chain issues, ranging from inventory management to risk analysis, fall within the realm of accounting.

Going further, accounting rules and regulations and cross-border transfer of data are critical for global trade. IOSs can facilitate such trade. Other issues that are important for accountants are taxation and government reports. In addition, creating information systems that rely on EDI requires the attention of accountants. Finally, fraud detection in global settings (e.g., transfers of funds) can be facilitated by appropriate controls and auditing.

For the Finance Major

IT helps financial analysts and managers perform their tasks better. Of particular importance is analyzing cash flows and securing the financing required for smooth operations. In addition, financial applications can support such activities as risk analysis, investment management, and global transactions involving different currencies and fiscal regulations.

Finance activities and modeling are key components of ERP systems. Flows of funds (payments), at the core of most supply chains, must be done efficiently and effectively. Financial arrangements are especially important along global supply chains, where currency conventions and financial regulations must be considered.

Many finance-related issues exist in implementing IOSs. For one thing, establishing EDI and extranet relationships involves structuring payment agreements. Global supply chains may involve complex financial arrangements, which may have legal implications.

For the Marketing Major

Marketing and sales expenses are usually targets in a cost-reduction program. Also, sales force automation not only improves salespeople's productivity (and thus reduces costs), but it also improves customer service.

The downstream segment of supply chains is where marketing, distribution channels, and customer service are conducted. An understanding of how downstream activities are related to the other segments is critical. Supply chain problems can reduce customer satisfaction and negate marketing efforts. It is essential, then, that marketing professionals understand the nature of such problems and their solutions. Also, learning about CRM, its options, and its implementation is important for designing effective customer services and advertising.

As competition intensifies globally, finding new global markets becomes critical. Use of IOSs provides an opportunity to improve marketing and sales. Understanding the capabilities of these technologies and their implementation issues will enable the marketing department to excel.

For the Production/Operations Management Major

Managing production tasks, materials handling, and inventories in short time intervals, at a low cost, and with high quality is critical for competitiveness. These activities can be achieved only if they are properly supported by IT. In addition, IT can greatly enhance interaction with other functional areas, especially sales. SCM is usually the responsibility of the POM department because it involves activities such as materials handling, inventory control, and logistics. Because they are in charge of procurement, production/operations managers must understand how their supporting information systems interface with those of their business partners. In addition, collaboration in design, manufacturing, and logistics requires knowledge of how modern information systems can be connected. Finally, supply chain collaboration frequently requires EDI agreements on data formats.

For the Human Resources Management Major

Human resources managers can increase their efficiency and effectiveness by using IT for some of their routine functions. Human resources personnel need to understand how information flows between the HR department and the other functional areas. Finally, the integration of functional areas via ERP systems has a major impact on skill requirements and scarcity of employees, which are related to the tasks performed by the HRM department.

Interactions among employees along the supply chain, especially between business partners from different countries, are important for supply chain effectiveness. It is necessary, therefore, for the HRM expert to understand the flows of information and the collaboration issues in SCM. In addition, the HRM manager is usually actively involved in setting up the CRM program, which may serve employees as well.

Preparing and training employees to work with business partners (frequently in foreign countries) requires knowledge about how IOSs operate. Sensitivity to cultural differences and extensive communication and collaboration can be facilitated with IT.

The MIS Function

The MIS function is responsible for the most fundamental information systems in organizations, the transaction processing systems. The TPSs provide the data for the databases. In turn, all other information systems use these data. MIS personnel develop applications that support all levels of the organization (from clerical to executive) and all functional areas. The applications also enable the firm to do business with its partners.

1. Describe transaction processing systems.

The backbone of most information systems applications is the transaction processing system. TPSs monitor, store, collect, and process data generated from all business transactions. These data provide the inputs into the organization's database.

2. Describe management information systems and the support they provide for each functional area of the organization.

The major business functional areas are production/operations management, marketing, accounting/finance, and human resources management. A management information system (MIS) is a system that is designed to support mid-level managers in functional areas. MISs generate reports (routine, ad-hoc, and exception) and provide information to managers regardless of their functional areas. Table 8.1 provides an overview of the many activities in each functional area supported by MISs.

3. Describe enterprise resource planning systems.

Enterprise resource planning (ERP) systems integrate the planning, management, and use of all of the organization's resources. The major objective of ERP systems is to tightly integrate the functional areas of the organization. This integration enables information to flow seamlessly across the various functional areas. ERP software includes a set of interdependent software modules, linked to a common database, that provide support for internal business processes.

4. Describe customer relationship management systems.

Customer relationship management (CRM) is an enterprisewide activity through which an organization takes care of its customers and their needs. It is based on the idea of one-to-one relationships with customers. CRM is conducted through many services, most of which are IT-supported, and many of which are delivered on the Web.

5. Describe supply chain management systems.

A supply chain refers to the flow of materials, information, money, and services from raw material suppliers, through factories and warehouses, to the end customers. A supply chain also includes the *organizations* and *processes* that create and deliver products, information, and services to end customers. The function of supply chain management (SCM) is to plan, organize, and optimize the supply chain's activities. A typical supply chain, which links a company with its suppliers and its distributors and customers, involves three segments: upstream, internal, and downstream.

6. Describe EDI and extranets.

EDI is a communication standard that enables the electronic transfer of routine documents, such as purchasing orders, between business partners. It formats these documents according to agreed-upon standards. It reduces costs, delays, and errors inherent in a manual document-delivery system.

Extranets are networks that link business partners to one another over the Internet by providing access to certain areas of one another's corporate intranets. The term *extranet* comes from "extended intranet." The main goal of extranets is to foster collaboration among business partners. The major benefits of extranets include faster processes and information flow, improved order entry and customer service, lower costs (e.g., for communications, travel, and administrative overhead), and overall improvement in business effectiveness.

Chapter Glossary

ad-hoc (on-demand) reports Nonroutine reports. (245)

batch processing TPS that processes data in batches at fixed periodic intervals. (243)

best practices The most successful solutions or problem-solving methods for achieving a business outcome. (249)

bullwhip effect Erratic shifts in orders up and down the supply chain. (257)

bundling A type of cross-selling in which a combination of products is sold together at a lower price than the combined costs of the individual products. (253)

business process A set of related steps or procedures designed to produce a specific outcome. (249)

comparative reports Reports that compare performances of different business units or time periods. (245)

cross-border data transfer The flow of corporate data across nations' borders. (256)

cross-selling The marketing of complementary products to customers. (253)

customer relationship management (CRM) An enterprisewide effort to acquire and retain customers, often supported by IT. (251)

customer touch point Any method of interaction with a customer. (253)

drill-down reports Reports that show a greater level of detail than is included in routine reports. (245)

electronic data interchange (EDI) A communication standard that enables the electronic transfer of routine documents between business partners. (259)

enterprise resource planning (ERP) Software that integrates the planning, management, and use of all resources in the entire enterprise. (248)

exception reports Reports that include only information that exceeds certain threshold standards. (245)

interorganizational information system (IOS) An information system that supports information flow among two or more organizations. (255)

global information systems Interorganizational systems that connect companies located in two or more countries. (255)

key-indicator reports Reports that summarize the performance of critical activities. (245)

management information system (MIS) A system that provides information to managers (usually mid-level) in the functional areas, in order to support managerial tasks of planning, organizing, and controlling operations. (245)

online transaction processing (OLTP) TPS that processes data after transactions occur, frequently in real time. (244)

routine reports Reports produced at scheduled intervals. (245)

supply chain The flow of materials, information, money, and services from raw material suppliers, through factories and warehouses, to the end customers; includes the organizations and processes involved. (255)

supply chain management (SCM) The planning, organizing, and optimization of one or more of the supply chain's activities. (255)

transaction processing system (TPS) Information system that supports routine, core business transactions. (243)

upselling The marketing of higher-value products and services to new or existing customers. (253)

vendor-managed inventory (VMI) Strategy in which the supplier monitors a vendor's inventory levels and replenishes products when needed. (259)

vertical integration Strategy of integrating the upstream part of the supply chain with the internal part, typically by purchasing upstream suppliers, in order to ensure timely availability of supplies. (258)

Discussion Questions

1. Why is it logical to organize IT applications by functional areas?
2. Describe the role of a TPS in a service organization.
3. Discuss the benefits of online self-service by employees and customers. How can these activities be facilitated by IT?

4. Distinguish between ERP and SCM software. In what ways do they complement each other? Relate them to system integration.
5. It is said that supply chains are essentially "a series of linked suppliers and customers; every customer is in turn a supplier to the next downstream organization,

until the ultimate end-user." Explain. Use of a diagram is recommended.
6. Explain the bullwhip effect. In which type of business is it most likely to occur? How can the effect be controlled?
7. Discuss why Web-based call centers are critical for a successful CRM.
8. Compare an EDI to an extranet and discuss the major differences.
9. Discuss the manner in which cross-border data transfer can be a limitation to a company that has manufacturing plants in other countries.

Problem-Solving Activities

1. Enter *www.resumix.yahoo.com*. Prepare a list of all the product's capabilities. As a job candidate, can you prepare your resume to be better processed by Resumix? How?
2. Identify the supply chain(s) and the flow of information described in the opening case. Draw it. Also, answer the following:
   a. Why was it necessary to use IT to support the change?
   b. Identify all the segments of the supply chain.
   c. Identify all supporting information systems in this case.
3. Go to a bank and find out the process and steps of obtaining a mortgage for a house. Draw the supply chain in this case. Explain how such a database can shorten the loan approval time. Compare your bank with *www.ditech.com* and *www.lendingtree.com*.
4. Enter *www.peoplesoft.com* and find material on CRM. Prepare a report.
5. General Electric Information Systems is the largest provider of EDI services. Investigate what services GEIS and other EDI vendors provide. If you were to evaluate their services for your company, how would you plan to approach the evaluation? Prepare a report.

Internet Activities

1. Examine the capabilities of the following (and similar) financial software packages: Financial Analyzer (from Oracle) and CFO Vision (from SAS Institute). Prepare a report comparing the capabilities of the software packages.
2. Surf the Internet and find information from three vendors on salesforce automation (try *www.sybase.com* and *www.salesforce.com*). Prepare a report on the state of the art.
3. Enter *www.microsoft.com/businessSolutions/Solomon/default.mspx*. View three of the demos in different functional areas of your choice. Prepare a report on the capabilities.
4. Enter *www.ups.com* and *www.fedex.com*. Examine some of the IT-supported customer services and tools provided by the company. Write a report on how UPS and FedEx contribute to supply chain improvements.
5. Enter *www.isourceonline.com* and *www.supplychaintoday.com*. Find information on the bullwhip effect and on the strategies and tools used to lessen the effect.
6. Enter *www.siebel.com*. View the demo on e-business. Identify all e-business–related initiatives. Why is the company considered as the leader of CRM software?
7. Enter *www.anntaylor.com* and identify the customer service activities offered there.
8. Enter *www.i2.com* and review the SCM products presented there. Examine the OCN Network and Rhythm. Write a report.
9. Enter *www.1edisource.com* and see the demo of WebSource. What are the benefits of this product?

Team Assignments

1. The class is divided into groups. Each group member represents a major functional area: accounting/finance, sales/marketing, production/operations management, and human resources. Find and describe several examples of processes that require the integration of functional information systems in a company of your choice. Each group will also show the interfaces to the other functional areas.

2. Each group is to investigate an HRM software vendor (Oracle, Peoplesoft, SAP, Lawson Software, and others). The group should prepare a list of all HRM functionalities supported by the software. Then each of the groups makes a presentation to convince the class that its vendor is the best.

3. Each group in the class will be assigned to a major ERP/SCM vendor such as SAP, PeopleSoft, or Oracle. Members of the groups will investigate topics such as: (a) Web connections, (b) use of business intelligence tools, (c) relationship to CRM and to EC, and (d) major capabilities by the specific vendor. Each group will prepare a presentation for the class, trying to convince the class why the group's software is best for a local company known to the students (e.g., a supermarket chain).

4. Create groups to investigate the major CRM software vendors, their products, and the capabilities of those products in the following categories. (Each group represents a topical area or several companies.)
   - Salesforce automation (Oracle, Onyx, Siebel, Saleslogix, Pivotal)
   - Call centers (LivePerson, NetEffect, Peoplesoft)
   - Marketing automation (Oracle, Pivotal, Nestor)
   - Customer service (Siebel, Broadvision, ATG)

   Start with *www.searchcrm.com* and *www.crmguru.com* (to ask questions about CRM solutions). Each group must present arguments to the class to convince class members to use the product(s) the group investigated.

5. Have each team locate several organizations that use IOSs, including one with a global reach. Students should contact the companies to find what IOS technology support they use (e.g., an EDI, extranet, etc.). Then find out what issues they faced in implementation. Prepare a report.

CASE The Museum of Modern Art Goes High-Tech

THE BUSINESS PROBLEM The Museum of Modern Art (MoMA) in Manhattan was having a problem with customer relations. In the past, when someone walked into MoMA and applied for membership, a volunteer would take the person's name, address, and payment information and type it into a dumb terminal (essentially just an electronic keyboard linked to a computer), line by line. If the volunteer typed in inaccurate information, the error would remain in the membership database. In addition, the old terminals lacked the ability to display graphics. Further, if someone wanted names and addresses of donors who gave to the annual fund in past years, a software developer had to spend as long as two days writing a program to get that information from the database.

The museum wanted to improve the collection and integration of information about visitors—from one-time museum goers, to longtime members or donors, to individuals who attend lectures, films, or classes, as well as MoMA store shoppers. MoMA attendance nosedived when the museum moved to Queens while the museum's home in Manhattan was being totally refurbished. Income from contributions, gifts, and grants dropped from $123 million to $65 million. Not surprisingly, then, MoMA wanted to win its customers back.

THE IT SOLUTION The museum developed a contact management application and a point-of-sale application. In the new system, MoMA membership volunteers use personal laptops with the familiar drop-down menus of the Windows operating system. Volunteers reduce transcription errors by clicking on options in those menus,

such as the menu to select a person's title. Also, an auto-fill feature generates the correct city and state once a Zip code is entered.

When someone becomes a member or a donor, MoMA collects basic information in a database. With this information, MoMA can get a better perspective on where members and donors live. If MoMA knows which neighborhoods contain a high proportion of members or donors, it can direct messages to those neighborhoods and expect better responses.

The museum has also placed nine 46-inch LCD (liquid crystal display) screens on the wall directly behind the ticket desk. The primary purpose of the screens is to display ticket prices and museum hours. They are also used to promote a popular event or a sale at a museum shop. Finally, the screens flash information about exhibitions, lectures, merchandise promotions, and restaurants.

THE RESULTS Having correct addresses before conducting a mailing saves MoMA a lot of money. The typical mailing—such as membership statements and invitations to special events—delivered to each of MoMA's 50,000 members costs about $37,500. On average, 15 percent of addresses in previous mailings were entered incorrectly. These errors cost MoMA more than $5,000 in wasted postage and materials.

In addition, individuals who enter the museum or one of its stores can now sign up for membership and get a permanent card immediately. Also, museum staff can instantly determine whether a shopper in a museum store qualifies for a discount.

The new applications provide MoMA with a single, holistic view of each member. As a result, the museum can cross-promote its merchandise, including books, posters, jewelry, and furniture. When someone makes a purchase, the salesperson scans his or her permanent card with a handheld wand. This enables the salesperson to address the member by name and know whether he or she is a longtime member, a donor, or a new member.

The results are encouraging. By 2004 the museum's revenue had increased to $115 million, which constituted a surplus.

Sources: Compiled from D. Dunn, "Renovated Art Museum Relies on IT," *Information Week*, March 18, 2005; E. Bennett, and A. M. Virzi, "Museum of Modern Art: Untitled Work." *Baseline Magazine*, December 1, 2004; and *www.moma.org*, accessed April 3, 2005.

QUESTIONS

1. Why did MoMA establish a contact management system?
2. What other IT could MoMA use to improve the customer experience?

Interactive Learning

Inventory Management: Taking a Look at the Supply Chain

Go to the Interactivities section on the *WileyPLUS* Web site for Chapter 8: Organizational Information Systems. There you will find an animated simulation of supply chain management, as well as some hands-on activities that visually explain the business concepts in this chapter.

Functional Systems at Club IT

Go to the Club IT section of the *WileyPLUS* Web site to find out how you can help the owners compile dollar and volume numbers more efficiently.

wiley.com/college/rainer

Chapter 10

Chapter Preview

Competitive organizations move as quickly as they can to acquire new information technologies (or modify existing ones) when they need to improve efficiencies and gain strategic advantage. Today, however, acquisition goes beyond building new systems in-house, and IT resources go beyond software and hardware. The old model in which firms built their own systems is being replaced with a broader perspective of IT resource acquisition that provides companies with a number of options. Companies now must decide which IT tasks will remain in-house, and even whether the entire IT resource should be provided and managed by other organizations. In this chapter we describe the process of IT resource acquisition from a managerial perspective. We pay special attention to the available options and how to evaluate them. We also take a close look at planning and justifying the need for information systems.

Acquiring IT Applications

Introduction to Information Systems
R. Kelly Rainer, Jr., Efraim Turban, and Richard E. Potter. ISBN 978-0-471-7363-3
©2007 John Wiley & Sons, Inc.

Chapter Outline

10.1 Planning for and Justifying IT Applications

10.2 Strategies for Acquiring IT Applications

10.3 The Traditional Systems Development Life Cycle

10.4 Alternative Methods and Tools for Systems Development

10.5 Outsourcing and Application Service Providers

10.6 Vendor and Software Selection

Learning Objectives

1. Describe the IT planning process.
2. Describe the IT justification process and methods.
3. Describe the SDLC and its advantages and limitations.
4. Describe the major alternative methods and tools for building information systems.
5. List the major IT acquisition options and the criteria for option selection.
6. Describe the role of ASPs.
7. Describe the process of vendor and software selection.

What's in **IT** for me?   ACC   FIN   MKT   POM   HRM   MIS

Systems Development in a Hurry

The Business Problem

AgriBeef (*www.agribeef.com*), a $500-million Idaho company with 1,100 employees, is in the business of beef ranching and distribution. The company did not want to continue using its old financial software because the software did not allow for automated recording of transactions among its 22 business units. Every time an order of meat was sold from one of its ranches to one of its distributing units, a clerk would have to type up a paper invoice and then cut a check to the other division. When an intercompany transaction occurred, that physical check was then

Source: Brand X Pictures/Media Bakery

deposited into the other company's account. At that point, all sales, cost of sales, inventory, and accounts payable and receivable transactions would be created. Finally, for consolidation purposes, those transactions would be manually entered and sent to the corporate controller for approval.

The company decided to implement a new financial information system and have it up and running by January 1. By going live at the beginning of a year (and also at the beginning of the company's fiscal year), AgriBeef would have to transfer only the balances in general ledger accounts. It would not have to convert the details of thousands of general ledger, accounts payable, and accounts receivable transactions that would otherwise accrue after January 1. In addition, the first quarter tends to be AgriBeef's busiest quarter. For this reason, if the company could not have the new system up and running on January 1, then it would have had to postpone the project until May or June. Unfortunately, even though they wanted to have a new system by January 1, AgriBeef executives did not decide on PeopleSoft until November, with only 42 days to go before January 1.

Lessons From
IT Failures

The IT Solution

For PeopleSoft, the January 1 deadline seemed unrealistic at best and potentially disastrous at worst. Implementing a new financial system often involves extensive configuration so that the system can report financial results in the manner to which a company has become accustomed. For PeopleSoft, knowing how complicated this can get, the definition of a "rapid" implementation was 12 weeks. Even this schedule was tight and involved a high degree of stress.

Nevertheless, PeopleSoft agreed to take on the project. It realized, however, that there might not be enough time to train AgriBeef's employees or to develop the 13 interfaces needed to draw information from existing AgriBeef systems and applications. In addition, it would have to limit the time devoted to testing and debugging the new system.

PeopleSoft immediately mobilized AgriBeef's four divisional controllers as "key users" of the effort. These people had been painfully slogging away for years with dozens of Excel spreadsheets generated from various financial systems every month and quarter to compile consolidated reports. Early in the process, the controllers agreed to a new numbering system for vendors and customers. That way, all of the accounts and billing statements would be uniform across the entire organization.

Originally, the plan called for six financial modules to be implemented by January 1. In fact, only the first four were implemented: general ledger, accounts payable, accounts receivable, and billing. Cash management and fixed asset management came later.

For the six-week implementation to be successful, AgriBeef had to make one crucial decision: to use PeopleSoft's software out of the box with no customization. This meant that AgriBeef had to make choices about how it would configure the PeopleSoft software from the existing options. In addition, AgriBeef employees had to be trained in half the time usually required. Normally, a customer would fly its key users into PeopleSoft university for four days of on-site training. For this project, PeopleSoft sent its consultants to Idaho for two days to lead a condensed boot camp at AgriBeef.

AgriBeef and PeopleSoft met the "drop dead" date. AgriBeef now recoups at least 200 staff-hours every month compiling the data for its financial reports. Transactions among business units are automated, and for the first time in the company's history every unit in the organization is using the same system.

The Results

The AgriBeef case demonstrates how a need for a new IT application arises: an organization is confronted with a serious business problem. The question then becomes which IT applications to implement and how to do it. The trend today is to use technology partners (PeopleSoft in this case) to buy or lease software from, to outsource the job to, or to work together with. In this case, PeopleSoft worked very closely with AgriBeef to develop the application that AgriBeef needed in a very short time frame.

What We Learned From This Case

This chapter focuses on the acquisition of IT systems. By "acquisition" we mean all of the approaches to obtaining systems: buying, leasing, and building. The acquisition issue is complex for several reasons. First, there is a large variety of IT applications, and they keep changing over time. Also, IT acquisition may involve several business partners. In addition, there is no single way to acquire IT applications. They can be developed in-house, obtained from a vendor, or developed through a combination of the two. Not surprisingly, then, organizations use different development methodologies and approaches to acquire their IT applications.

Sources: Compiled from L. Barrett, "AgriBeef: Cattle Drive," *Baseline Magazine*, November 1, 2004; "AgriBeef Company: Beefing Up Financial Systems Pays Off," *www.peopletalkonline.com*, July 2004; and *www.peoplesoft.com* and *www.agribeef.com*, last accessed March 11, 2005.

10.1 Planning for and Justifying IT Applications

Organizations must analyze the need for applications and then justify each application in terms of cost and benefits. The need for information systems is usually related to organizational planning and to the analysis of its performance vis-à-vis its competitors. The cost-benefit justification must look at the wisdom of investing in a specific IT application versus spending the funds on alternative projects.

When a company examines its needs and performance, it generates a prioritized list of both existing and potential IT applications, called the **application portfolio**. These are the applications that have to be added, or modified if they already exist. IT's About Business 10.1 describes the planning process.

IT's About Business

10.1 AFLAC Learns How to Plan Its IT Projects

In 2000, the American Family Life Assurance Co. (AFLAC) (*www.aflac.com*) had dozens of technology projects in everything from claims processing to financial analysis under development at once. AFLAC had decided to produce much of its software in-house but was not completing IT development projects on time. In 2001, the company instituted a planning process to identify dubious project ideas before they made it into the development queue.

The company created a planning cycle of six phases that it calls "gates." Gates 1 and 2 are where the greatest amount of thought and planning happen. About 75 percent of the ideas that emerge

(Continued)

from the business units get through Gate 1. In turn, 90 percent of the ideas that get through Gate 1 make it through Gate 2 and are then developed.

To get to Gate 1, a business manager comes to the IT project management office with an idea. They work together to: (1) develop the business case for the project; (2) determine what technology resources are needed, including any new software and the number of programmers; and (3) calculate the costs. If the initial study makes sense, the project reaches Gate 1, and the business manager presents the project to AFLAC's project steering committee. The Gate 1 meeting focuses on tangible goals, such as reducing the number of employees who deal with a single customer inquiry.

If the committee approves the project, it allocates about 25 percent of the estimated total project cost to develop the detailed business case and IT-impact statement required for Gate 2. The resulting analysis is summarized in a 10-page document of project goals, costs, and payback that is presented to the steering committee in the Gate 2 meeting. Getting

through Gate 2 is the most critical point in the life—or death—of a project.

Projects that survive Gate 2 go on to Gate 3 (design), Gate 4 (build and test), Gate 5 (installation), and Gate 6 (benefits assessment). In 2003, AFLAC completed just 9 projects. In contrast, in 2004, because projects were more carefully evaluated, the company completed all 40 of the projects that made it through Gate 2.

Sources: Compiled from K. Nash, "AFLAC: Duck Soup," *Baseline Magazine*, September 1, 2004; "AFLAC and Primavera: A Partnership for Success," *www.primavera.com*, accessed April 29, 2005; A. O'Donnell, "Worth the Effort: Tackling the New Project Management," *Insurance & Technology*, March 4, 2003; and *www.aflac.com*, accessed April 7, 2005.

QUESTIONS

1. Why are the gates so important to AFLAC?
2. What is the relationship between project management and systems development?

IT Planning

The planning process for new IT applications begins with analysis of the *organizational strategic plan*, as shown in Figure 10.1. The organization's strategic plan states the firm's overall mission, the goals that follow from that mission, and the broad steps necessary to reach these goals. The strategic planning process matches the organization's objectives and resources to meet its changing markets and opportunities.

The organizational strategic plan and the existing IT architecture provide the inputs in developing the IT strategic plan. As we discussed in Chapter 1, the *IT architecture* delineates the way an organization's information resources should be used to accomplish its mission. It encompasses both technical and managerial aspects of information resources. The technical aspects include hardware and operating systems, networking, data management systems, and applications software. The managerial aspects specify how managing the IT department will be accomplished, how functional area managers will be involved, and how IT decisions will be made.

The **IT strategic plan** is a set of long-range goals that describe the IT infrastructure and major IT initiatives needed to achieve the goals of the organization. The IT strategic plan must meet three objectives:

1. It must be aligned with the organization's strategic plan.
2. It must provide for an IT architecture that enables users, applications, and databases to be seamlessly networked and integrated.
3. It must efficiently allocate IS development resources among competing projects, so the projects can be completed on time and within budget and have the required functionality.

After a company has agreed on an IT strategic plan, it next develops the *IS operational plan*. This plan consists of a clear set of projects that the IS department and the functional

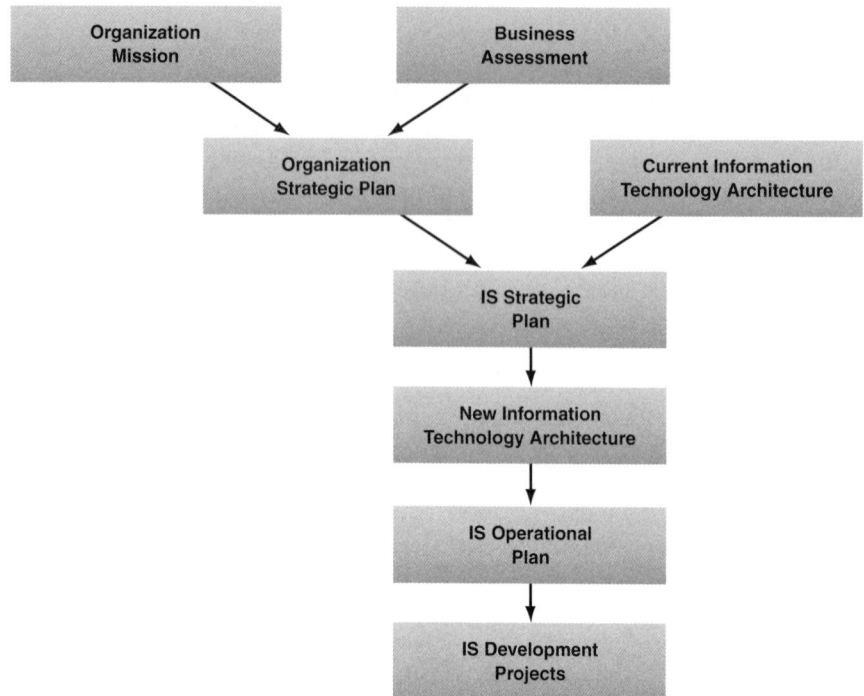

FIGURE 10.1
The information systems planning process.

area managers will execute in support of the IT strategic plan. A typical IS operational plan contains the following elements:

- *Mission*: The mission of the IS function (derived from the IT strategy).
- *IS environment*: A summary of the information needs of the functional areas and of the organization as a whole.
- *Objectives of the IS function*: The best current estimate of the goals of the IS function.
- *Constraints on the IS function*: Technological, financial, personnel, and other resource limitations on the IS function.
- *The application portfolio*: A prioritized inventory of present applications and a detailed plan of projects to be developed or continued during the current year.
- *Resource allocation and project management*: A listing of who is going to do what, how, and when.

Evaluating and Justifying IT Investment: Benefits, Costs, and Issues

As we already discussed, developing an IT plan is the first step in the acquisition process. All companies have a limited amount of resources available to them. For this reason they must justify investing resources in some areas, including IT, rather than in others. Essentially, justifying IT investment includes three functions: assessing the costs, assessing the benefits (values), and comparing the two. This comparison is frequently referred to as cost-benefit analysis. Cost-benefit analysis is not a simple task.

Assessing the Costs.   Placing a dollar value on the cost of IT investments may not be as simple as it sounds. One of the major challenges is to allocate fixed costs among different IT projects. *Fixed costs* are those costs that remain the same regardless of any change in the activity level. For IT, fixed costs include infrastructure cost, cost of IT services, and IT management cost. For example, the salary of the IT director is fixed, and adding one more application will not change it.

Another complication is that the cost of a system does not end when the system is installed. Costs for maintaining, debugging, and improving the system can accumulate over many years. In some cases they are not even anticipated when the company makes the investment. An example is the cost of the Y2K reprogramming projects that amounted to billions of dollars to organizations worldwide.

Assessing the Benefits.   Evaluating the benefits of IT projects is typically even more complex than calculating their costs. Benefits may be harder to quantify, especially because many of them are intangible (e.g., improved customer or partner relations or improved decision making). The fact that organizations use IT for several different purposes further complicates benefit analysis. In addition, to obtain a return from an IT investment, the technology must be implemented successfully. In reality, many systems are not implemented on time, within budget, or with all the features originally envisioned for them. Finally, the proposed system may be "cutting edge." In these cases there may be no previous evidence of what sort of financial payback the company can expect.

Conducting Cost-Benefit Analysis

After a company has assessed the costs and benefits of IT investments, it must compare the two. There is no uniform strategy to conduct this analysis. Rather, it can be performed in several ways. Here we discuss four common approaches: net present value, return on investment, breakdown analysis, and the business case approach.

Organizations often use *net present value (NPV)* calculations for cost-benefit analyses. Using the NPV method, analysts convert future values of benefits to their present-value equivalent by "discounting" them at the organization's cost of funds. They then can compare the present value of the future benefits to the cost required to achieve those benefits and determine whether the benefits exceed the costs. NPV analysis works well in situations where the costs and benefits are well defined or "tangible" enough to be converted into monetary values.

Another traditional tool for evaluating capital investment is *return on investment (ROI)*. ROI measures management's effectiveness in generating profits with its available assets. The ROI measure is a percentage, and the higher the percentage return, the better. ROI is calculated by dividing net income attributable to a project by the average assets invested in the project. In the case of IT, then, the company would divide the income generated by an IT investment to the costs of that investment. The greater the value of ROI, the more likely the company is to approve the investment.

Breakeven analysis determines the point at which the cumulative dollar value of the benefits from a project equals the investment made in the project.

One final method used to justify investments in projects is the *business case approach*. A business case is a written document that managers use to justify funding one or more specific applications or projects. In addition, a business case provides the bridge between the initial plan and its execution. Its purpose is not only to get approval and funding, but also to provide the foundation for tactical decision making and technology risk management. The business case approach is usually employed in existing organizations that want to embark on new IT projects. The business case helps to clarify how the organization can best use its resources to accomplish its IT strategy. It helps the organization to concentrate on justifying the investment. It also focuses on risk management and on how an IT project corresponds with the organization's mission.

Before you go on . . .

1. What are some problems associated with assessing the costs of IT?
2. What difficulties accompany the intangible benefits from IT?
3. Describe the NPV, ROI, and business case approaches.

10.2 Strategies for Acquiring IT Applications

If a company has successfully justified an IT investment, it must then decide how to pursue it. Companies have several options for acquiring IT applications. The major options are to buy the applications, to lease them, to develop them in-house, or to outsource them. In this section we discuss buying, leasing, and in-house development. We discuss one particular type of leasing (application service providers) and outsourcing in Section 10.5.

Buy the Applications (Off-the-Shelf Approach)

The standard features required by IT applications can be found in many commercial software packages. Buying an existing package can be a cost-effective and time-saving strategy compared with developing the application in-house. Nevertheless, the "buy" option should be carefully considered and planned to ensure that the selected package contains all of the features necessary to address the company's current and future needs. Otherwise such packages can quickly become obsolete.

In reality, a single software package can rarely satisfy all of an organization's needs. For this reason a company sometimes must purchase multiple packages to fulfill different needs. It then must integrate these packages with one another as well as with existing software.

IT's About Business 10.2 illustrates the benefits of purchasing existing software. Specifically, Vistakon—a division of Johnson & Johnson—used the buy option to streamline its order management process.

IT's About Business

10.2 Vistakon's New System in Europe

Vistakon (*www.jnjvision.com*) sells $1 billion of throw-away contact lenses every year. In Vistakon's business environment, speed is essential, and complexity rules. Vistakon has 25,000 stock-keeping units for its product. The company takes 15,000 orders per day around the world. As a result, Vistakon had to standardize the way it handled orders around the globe.

In August 2002, Vistakon operated 20 distribution centers and 20 customer service centers in Europe alone. It operated 60 computerized business sytems from 60 different suppliers. Managers of sales in the 20 countries in which Vistakon operated sent Excel spreadsheets at the end of each month to the company, where the results were manually imported into consolidated financial statements. Adding to this complexity, the differing legal and tax requirements of each country in which Vistakon operates had to be taken into account in every invoice and requisition.

Vistakon's primary goal was obtaining "absolute speed" in order management. To accomplish this mission, the company decided to standardize its operations based on a single software suite from SAP.

The estimated costs of acquiring and implementing the new system were substantial: $50 million. However, using a cost-benefit analysis, Vistakon calculated that if it were to reduce scattered operations and enforce a single system for processing orders, the benefits would be tangible. The company would save money in such diverse areas as inventory, streamlined planning, write-offs of obsolete products, and purchasing and technology costs. Thus, would receive payback on the IT investment in as little as two years. Having justified the investment, Vistakon purchased the software from SAP in 2003. Vistakon created project teams to handle technology and finance, including processes for converting orders into cash, issuing requisitions and making payments, getting products into stock, and converting data into a form the new systems could use. In the month preceding the instant when the new systems were turned on, members of these teams conducted training sessions on the new procedures. After the transition to the new system, the teams would coach employees.

Vistakon has not had to deal with any major system failures. The company now has just one distribution

---

center, one manufacturing facility, one "customer interaction center," and one order-taking system for all of Europe.

Sources: Compiled from T. Steinert-Threlkeld, "Vistakon: Far Sighted," *Baseline Magazine*, October 1, 2004; Anthony, S. "Mind over Merger." *Optimize*, February 2005; and *www.jnjvision.com* and *www.sap.com*, accessed April 9, 2005.

QUESTIONS

1. Why did Vistakon need a new ordering system? (*Hint:* Consider its product.)
2. Describe the implementation process for the new system.

The buy option is especially attractive if the software vendor allows the company to modify the technology to meet its needs. However, the option may not be attractive in cases where customization is the only method of providing the necessary flexibility to address the company's needs. It also is not the best strategy when the software is very expensive or is likely to become obsolete in a short time. The advantages and limitations of the buy option are summarized in Manager's Checklist 10.1. When the buy option is not appropriate, organizations consider leasing.

Lease the Applications

Compared with the buy option and the option to develop applications in-house, the "lease" option can save a company both time and money. Of course, leased packages (like purchased packages) may not always exactly fit the company's application requirements. However, vendor software generally includes the features that are most commonly needed by organizations in a given industry. It is common for interested companies to apply the 80/20 rule when evaluating vendor software. If the software meets 80 percent of the company's needs, then the company should seriously consider changing its business processes to resolve the remaining 20 percent. Many times this is a better long-term solution than modifying vendor software. Otherwise, the company will have to customize the software every time the vendor releases an updated version.

Manager's Checklist 10.1

Advantages and Limitations of the "Buy" Option

Advantages

- □ Many different types of off-the-shelf software are available.
- □ Software can be tried out.
- □ Much time can be saved by buying rather than building.
- □ The company can know what it is getting before it invests in the product.
- □ The company is not the first and only user.
- □ Purchased software may avoid the need to hire personnel specifically dedicated to a project.

Disadvantages

- □ Software may not exactly meet the company's needs.
- □ Software may be difficult or impossible to modify, or it may require huge business process changes to implement.
- □ The company will not have control over software improvements and new versions.
- □ Purchased software can be difficult to integrate with existing systems.
- □ Vendors may drop a product or go out of business.
- □ Software is controlled by another company with its own priorities and business considerations.
- □ Lack of intimate knowledge in the purchasing company about how the software works and why it works that way.

Leasing can be especially attractive to small-to-medium-size enterprises (SMEs) that cannot afford major investments in IT software. Large companies may also prefer to lease packages in order to test potential IT solutions before committing to heavy investments. Also, because there is a shortage of IT personnel with appropriate skills for developing custom IT applications, many companies choose to lease instead of developing software in-house. Even those companies that employ in-house experts may not be able to afford the long wait for strategic applications to be developed in-house. Therefore, they lease (or buy) applications from external resources to establish a quicker presence in the market.

Leasing can be done in one of two ways. The first way is to lease the application from a software developer and install it on the company's premises. The vendor can help with the installation and frequently will offer to contract for the support and maintenance of the system. Many conventional applications are leased this way. The second way, using an application service provider (ASP), is becoming more popular. We discuss ASPs in Section 10.5.

Develop the Applications In-House (Insourcing)

A third development strategy is to develop ("build") applications in-house. Although this approach is usually more time-consuming and may be more costly than buying or leasing, it often leads to a better fit with the specific organizational requirements. In-house development, however, is a challenging task, for several reasons. First, many applications are proprietary. Second, many people from outside the organization use these applications. Finally, these applications involve multiple organizations.

In-house development can make use of various methodologies. The basic, backbone methodology is the systems development life cycle (SDLC), which we discuss in the next section. In Section 10.4, we discuss the methodologies that complement the SDLC: prototyping, joint application development, rapid application development, and integrated computer-assisted systems development tools. We also discuss two other methodologies, end-user development and object-oriented development.

10.3 The Traditional Systems Development Life Cycle

The **systems development life cycle (SDLC)** is the traditional systems development method that organizations use for large-scale IT projects. The SDLC is a structured framework that consists of sequential processes by which information systems are developed. As shown in Figure 10.2, these processes are systems investigation, systems analysis, systems design, programming, testing, implementation, operation, and maintenance. Each process in turn consists of well-defined tasks. We consider all eight processes in this section.

Other models for the SDLC may contain more or fewer than the eight stages we present here. The flow of tasks, however, remains largely the same. In the past, developers used the **waterfall approach** to the SDLC. That is, tasks in one stage were completed before the work proceeded to the next stage. Today, however, design tools allow for greater flexibility than was true of the traditional approach.

Systems development projects produce desired results through team efforts. Development teams typically include users, systems analysts, programmers, and technical specialists. *Users* are employees from all functional areas and levels of the organization who interact with the system, either directly or indirectly. **Systems analysts** are information systems professionals who specialize in analyzing and designing information systems. Programmers are information systems professionals who modify existing computer programs or write new computer programs to satisfy user requirements. **Technical specialists** are experts on a certain type of technology, such as databases or telecommunications. All people who are affected by changes in information systems (users and managers, for example) are known as **systems stakeholders**. All stakeholders are typically involved in varying degrees and at various times in systems development.

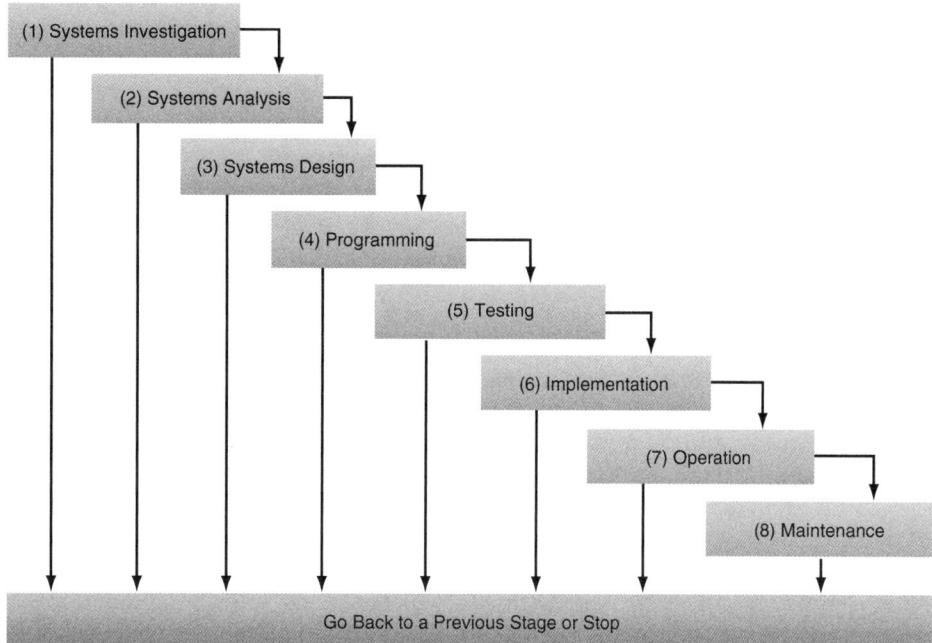

FIGURE 10.2

An eight-stage systems development life cycle (SDLC).

The SDLC has three major advantages: control, accountability, and error detection. An important issue in systems development is that the later in the development process that errors are detected, the more expensive they are to correct. The structured sequence of tasks and milestones in the SDLC thus makes error prevention and detection easier and saves money in the long run.

However, the SDLC does have disadvantages. Because of its structured nature, it is relatively inflexible. It is also time-consuming and expensive, and it discourages changes to user requirements once they have been established. Development managers who must develop large, enterprisewide applications must consider these disadvantages carefully. IT's About Business 10.3 illustrates how the FBI failed in developing a new information system.

Systems Investigation

The initial stage in a traditional SDLC is systems investigation. Systems development professionals agree that the more time they invest in understanding the business problem to be solved, the technical options for systems, and the problems that are likely to occur during development, the greater the chances of success. For these reasons, systems investigation begins with *the business problem* (or business opportunity), followed by the feasibility analysis.

Feasibility Study.   The main task in the systems investigation stage is the feasibility study. Organizations have three basic solutions to any business problem relating to an information system: (1) do nothing and continue to use the existing system unchanged, (2) modify or enhance the existing system, or (3) develop a new system. The **feasibility study** analyzes which of the three solutions best fits the particular business problem. This study determines the probability that the proposed systems development project will succeed. It also provides a rough assessment of the project's technical, economic, behavioral, and organizational feasibility, as we discuss below. The feasibility study is critically important to the systems development process because it can prevent organizations from making costly mistakes.

IT's About Business

Lessons From
IT Failures

10.3 New FBI System Fails

A top FBI official said that the bureau may have to scrap a computer program that so far has cost $170 million and was intended to be an important tool in fighting terrorism. Bureau officials expect to find that after four years in development, their much-touted Virtual Case File system does not work. They maintain, however, that a suitable replacement is commercially available.

Since the terrorist attacks of September 11, 2001, the FBI and contractor Science Applications International Corporation have been racing to complete the Virtual Case File system, which is intended to speed up the sharing of information. Counterterrorism information collected by agents through interviews and surveillance currently becomes available only after it is uploaded nightly into a system that is accessible to the nation's intelligence community. The current program requires FBI personnel to manually enter, print, sign, and scan their information into an "investigative data warehouse." Counterterrorism information collected by agents gets top priority and is entered into the system within 24 hours.

Information dealing with such matters as violent crime, organized crime, fraud, and other white-collar crime may take days to be shared throughout the law enforcement community. The Virtual Case File system was supposed to allow agents to pass along intelligence and criminal information in real time.

FBI officials said that they did not understand the rapidly changing state of technology. In fact, an entire system had to be developed to replace the antiquated FBI computer and record management systems. Officials also noted that the changed mission of the FBI after 9/11 (domestic counterterrorism now has the FBI's highest priority) added a burden to the system developers.

The FBI has been unsuccessful in developing its Virtual Case File system for several reasons: no coherent IT architecture for the Bureau, poor planning, scope creep, improper delegation of authority to outside contractors, and exclusion of users. The bottom line: four years of wasted effort and $170 million lost.

Sources: Compiled from T. Frieden, "FBI May Scrap $170 Million Project." *CNN.com*, January 15, 2005; "IT Infrastructure for 21st Century Crime," *www.fbi.gov*, April 2, 2004; J. Kumagai, "Mission Impossible?" *IEEE Spectrum Online*, *www.spectrum.ieee.org*, accessed May 22, 2005; and *www.saic.com*, accessed April 8, 2005.

QUESTIONS

1. Is four years too long to wait on a project? What guidelines would you propose so the FBI could have limited the expense and wasted time on this project?
2. What should the FBI do now? Buy the commercial package? Start a new in-house development project?

Technical feasibility determines if the hardware, software, and communications components can be developed and/or acquired to solve the business problem. Technical feasibility also determines if the organization's existing technology can be used to achieve the project's performance objectives.

Economic feasibility determines if the project is an acceptable financial risk and if the organization can afford the expense and time needed to complete the project. Economic feasibility addresses two primary questions: (1) Do the benefits outweigh the costs of the project? (2) Can the company afford the project? We have already discussed the commonly used methods to determine economic feasibility: net present value, return on investment, breakeven analysis, and the business case approach.

Behavioral feasibility addresses the human issues of the project. All systems development projects introduce change into the organization, and people generally fear change. Overt resistance from employees may take the form of sabotaging the new system (e.g., entering data incorrectly) or deriding the new system to anyone who will listen. Covert resistance typically occurs when employees simply do their jobs using their old methods.

Organizational feasibility refers to an organization's ability to accept the proposed project. Sometimes, for example, organizations cannot accept an affordable project due to legal or other constraints. In checking organizational feasibility, the firm should consider if the proposed project meets the criteria stated in the company's strategic plan.

Go/No-Go Decision. After the feasibility analysis is presented by the area manager for whom the system is to be developed and the IS project manager, a "Go/No-Go" decision is reached by the steering committee if there is one, or by top management in the absence of a committee. If the decision is "No-Go," the project either is put on the shelf until conditions are more favorable or it is discarded. If the decision is "Go," then the project proceeds, and the systems analysis phase begins.

Systems Analysis

Once a development project has the necessary approvals from all participants, the systems analysis stage begins. **Systems analysis** is the examination of the business problem that the organization plans to solve with an information system. This stage defines the business problem in more detail, identifies its causes, specifies the solution, and identifies the information requirements that the solution must satisfy. Understanding the business problem requires understanding the various processes involved. These processes are often complicated and interdependent.

The main purpose of the systems analysis stage is to gather information about the existing system in order to determine the requirements for an enhanced or new system. The end product of this stage, known as the "deliverable," is a set of *system requirements*.

Arguably the most difficult task in systems analysis is to identify the specific requirements that the system must satisfy. In this phase, the team must outline what information is needed, how much is needed, for whom, when, and in what format. Systems analysts use many different techniques to identify the information requirements for the new system. These techniques include interviews with users, direct observation, and document analysis ("follow the paper"). With direct observation, analysts observe users interacting with the existing system.

There are problems associated with eliciting information requirements, regardless of the method used. First, the business problem may be poorly defined. Second, the users may not know exactly what the problem is, what they want, or what they need. Third, users may disagree with one another about business procedures or even about the business problem. Finally, the problem may not be information related. Instead, it might require other solutions, such as a change in management or organizational structure. IT's About Business 10.4 illustrates the problems associated with gathering information requirements.

The systems analysis stage produces the following information: (1) strengths and weaknesses of the existing system, (2) functions that the new system must have to solve the business problem, and (3) user information requirements for the new system. Armed with this information, systems developers can proceed to the systems design stage.

Systems Design

Systems analysis describes what a system must do to solve the business problem. In contrast, **systems design** describes how the system will accomplish this task. The deliverable of the systems design phase is the *technical design* that specifies the following:

- System outputs, inputs, and user interfaces
- Hardware, software, databases, telecommunications, personnel, and procedures
- A blueprint of how these components are integrated

This output represents the set of *system specifications*.

IT's About Business

10.4 Information Requirements Cause Problems at the VA

The Veterans Administration (VA) Benefits Administration embarked on its new claims-processing, claims-tracking, and claims-payment system in 1986. Ten years later, the General Accounting Office (GAO) concluded that after "numerous false starts" and about $300 million, the VA had little to show for its efforts. Investigators cited a failure to identify the business requirements of the system.

Nevertheless, the VA tried again in 1996. The new initiative, called VetsNet, was expected to take two years and cost $8 million. Once again, the results were disappointing. By mid-2000, despite $100 million spent on VetsNet, the project was nowhere near completion.

In March 2002, a new project manager was brought in to fix the problem. His first move was to "freeze the requirements," telling all team members to take no additional suggestions on features or functions from the users. Previously, at the request of doctors and administrators, the project team had continued to change the number of fields to be displayed in menus on the VetsNet screens. Defining the project and holding firm is a key factor in the success of a project.

The freeze allowed the project team to assess how far away they were from final development of the system. The team then identified the "gaps," wrote whatever software was needed to finish the system, and tested the software to make sure all parts of the system worked.

The project moved back on track and was successfully delivered, albeit over time and over budget. By 2004, the number of claims waiting to be processed was cut almost in half from a peak of 420,603 in September 2001.

Sources: Compiled from J. McCormick, "Soldiering On," *Baseline Magazine*, April 4, 2004; P. Vasishtha, "Major Programs," *Government Computer News*, October 8, 2001; L. Margasak, "VA Upgrade Fails to Reduce Delays," The Associated Press, 2000; L. Gross, "VA Computer Upgrade Is a Bust," *Advance for Health Information Professionals*, May 1, 2000; and www.va.gov, accessed April 5, 2005.

QUESTIONS

1. What problems did VetsNet have? What were the causes of those problems?
2. How did the VA salvage the system?

Systems design encompasses two major aspects of the new system: logical and physical system design. **Logical system design** states *what* the system will do, using abstract specifications. **Physical system design** states *how* the system will perform its functions, with actual physical specifications. Logical design specifications include the design of outputs, inputs, processing, databases, telecommunications, controls, security, and IS jobs. Physical design specifications include the design of hardware, software, database, telecommunications, and procedures. For example, the logical telecommunications design may call for a wide area network that connects the company's plants. The physical telecommunications design will specify the types of communications hardware (computers and routers), software (the network operating system), media (fiber optics and satellite), and bandwidth (100 Mbps).

When both aspects of system specifications are approved by all participants, they are "frozen." That is, once the specifications are agreed upon, they should not be changed. Adding functions after the project has been initiated causes **scope creep**, which endangers the budget and schedule of a project. Scope creep occurs during development when users add to or change the information requirements of a system after those requirements have been "frozen." Scope creep occurs for two reasons. First, as users more clearly understand how the system will work and what their needs are, they request that additional functions be incorporated into the system. Second, after the design specifications are frozen, business conditions often change, leading users to request additional functions. Because scope creep is expensive, successful project managers place controls on changes requested by users. These controls help to prevent *runaway projects*—systems development projects that are so far over budget and past deadline that they must be abandoned, typically with large monetary loss.

Programming

Systems developers utilize the design specifications to acquire the software needed for the system to meet its functional objectives and solve the business problem. Although many organizations tend to purchase packaged software, many other firms continue to develop custom software in-house. For example, Wal-Mart and Eli Lilly design practically all of their software in-house.

If the organization decides to construct the software in-house, then programming begins. **Programming** involves translating the design specifications into computer code. This process can be lengthy and time-consuming, because writing computer code is as much an art as a science. Large systems development projects can require hundreds of thousands of lines of computer code and hundreds of computer programmers. These large-scale projects employ programming teams. These teams often include functional area users, who help the programmers focus on the business problem.

In an attempt to add rigor (and some uniformity) to the programming process, programmers use *structured programming* techniques. These techniques improve the logical flow of the program by decomposing the computer code into *modules*, which are sections of code (subsets of the entire program). This modular structure allows for more efficient and effective testing, because each module can be tested by itself. The structured programming techniques include the following restrictions:

- Each module has one, and only one, function.
- Each module has only one entrance and one exit. That is, the logic in the computer program enters a module in only one place and exits in only one place.
- Go To statements are not allowed.

Figure 10.3 diagrams a flowchart for a simple payroll application of structured programming. The figure shows the only three types of structures that are used in structured programming: sequence, decision, and loop. In the *sequence* structure, program statements are executed one after another until all the statements in the sequence have been executed. The *decision* structure allows the logic flow to branch, depending on certain conditions being met (decisions are represented by diamonds in the flowchart). The *loop* structure enables the software to execute the same program, or parts of a program, until certain conditions are met (e.g., until the end of the file is reached).

Testing

Thorough and continuous testing occurs throughout the programming stage. Testing is the process that checks to see if the computer code will produce the expected and desired results under certain conditions. Proper testing requires a large amount of time, effort, and expense. However, the costs of improper testing, which could possibly lead to a system that does not meet its objectives, are enormous.

Testing is designed to detect errors ("bugs") in the computer code. These errors are of two types: syntax and logic. *Syntax errors* (e.g., a misspelled word or a misplaced comma) are easier to find and will not permit the program to run. *Logic errors* permit the program to run but result in incorrect output. Logic errors are more difficult to detect, because the cause is not obvious. The programmer must follow the flow of logic in the program to determine the source of the error in the output.

As software increases in complexity, the number of errors increases, until it is almost impossible to find them all. This situation has led to the idea of *"good-enough" software*. This is

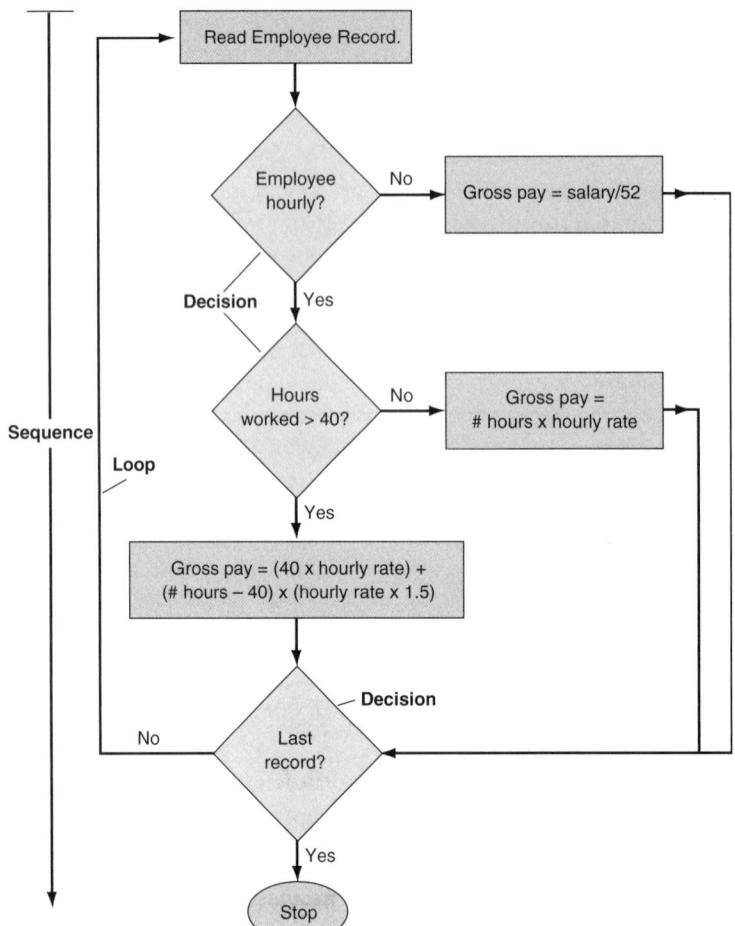

FIGURE 10.3
Flowchart diagram of
payroll application.

software that developers believe will meet its functional objectives although it contains errors in the code. That is, developers are convinced they have found all the "show-stopper" bugs. These are the serious errors that will cause the system to shut down or will cause catastrophic loss or corruption of data. The remaining errors should not affect the system's performance in any significant way.

Implementation

Implementation (or deployment) is the process of converting from the old system to the new system. Organizations use four major conversion strategies: parallel, direct, pilot, and phased.

In a **parallel conversion**, the old system and the new system operate simultaneously for a period of time. That is, both systems process the same data at the same time, and the outputs are compared. This type of conversion is the most expensive, and it has the least risk from a technology perspective, because both systems are operating. However, the possibility that employees will want to hold onto the old system and will covertly sabotage the new one is much greater than with the other methods. Parallel conversions are used with some very large systems.

In contrast, in a **direct conversion**, the old system is cut off and the new system is turned on at a certain point in time. This type of conversion is the least expensive. It is also the most risky if the new system doesn't work as planned. Because of these risks, few systems are implemented using direct conversion.

A **pilot conversion** introduces the new system in one part of the organization, such as in one plant or in one functional area. The new system runs for a period of time and is then assessed. If the assessment confirms that it is working properly, it is introduced in other parts of the organization.

Finally, a **phased conversion** introduces components of the new system, such as individual modules, in stages. Each module is assessed. If it works properly, then other modules are introduced until the entire new system is operational.

Operation and Maintenance

After the new system is implemented, it will operate for a period of time, until (like the old system it replaced) it no longer meets its objectives. Once the new system's operations are stabilized, *audits* are performed to assess the system's capabilities and to determine if it is being used correctly.

Systems need several types of maintenance. The first type is *debugging* the program, a process that continues throughout the life of the system. The second type is *updating* the system to accommodate changes in business conditions. An example is adjusting to new governmental regulations, such as changes in tax rates. These corrections and upgrades usually do not add any new functions. Instead, they simply help the system to continue meeting its objectives. In contrast, the third type of maintenance *adds new functions* to the existing system without disturbing its operation.

Before you go on . . .

1. Describe the feasibility study.
2. What is the difference between systems analysis and systems design?
3. Describe structured programming.
4. What are the four conversion methods?

10.4 Alternative Methods and Tools for Systems Development

There are a number of tools that are used in conjunction with the traditional systems development life cycle (SDLC). The first four tools that we discuss in this section are designed to supplement the SDLC and make various functions of the SDLC easier and faster to perform. These tools include prototyping, joint application development, integrated computer-assisted systems engineering, and rapid application development.

The alternative methods to developing systems are used instead of the SDLC. These methods include end-user development and object-oriented development.

Prototyping

The **prototyping** approach defines an initial list of user requirements, builds a prototype system, and then improves the system in several iterations based on users' feedback. Developers do not try to obtain a complete set of user specifications for the system at the outset, and they do not plan to develop the system all at once. Instead, they quickly develop a smaller version of the system known as a *prototype*. A prototype can take two forms. In some cases it contains only the components of the new system that are of most interest to the users. In other cases it is a small-scale working model of the entire system.

Users make suggestions for improving the prototype, based on their experiences with it. The developers then review the prototype with the users and use their suggestions to refine the prototype. This process continues through several iterations until either the users approve the system or it becomes apparent that the system cannot meet users' needs. If the system is viable, then the developers can use the prototype on which to build the full system. Developing screens that a user will see and interact with is a typical use of prototyping.

The main advantage of prototyping is that it speeds up the development process. In addition, prototyping gives users the opportunity to clarify their information requirements as they review iterations of the new system.

Prototyping also has disadvantages. Because it can largely replace the analysis and design stages of the SDLC in some projects, systems analysts may not produce adequate documentation for the programmers. This lack of documentation can lead to problems after the system becomes operational and needs maintenance. Prototyping can also generate an excess number of iterations. These iterations can actually consume the time that prototyping should be saving. In addition, there is a risk of getting into an endless loop of prototype revisions, as users may never be fully satisfied. Another drawback is the risk of *idiosyncratic design*. That is, the prototype may be revised based on the feedback of only a small group of users who are not necessarily representative of the entire user population.

Joint Application Design

Joint application design (JAD) is a group-based tool for collecting user requirements and creating system designs. JAD is most often used within the systems analysis and systems design stages of the SDLC. JAD involves a group meeting in which all users meet simultaneously with the analysts. It is basically a group decision-making process that can be done manually or on the computer. During this meeting, all users jointly define and agree on systems requirements. This process saves a tremendous amount of time.

The JAD approach to systems development has several advantages. First, the group process involves many users in the development process while still saving time. This involvement leads to greater support for the new system. In addition, it can improve the quality of the new system and make it easier to implement. In turn, this will reduce training costs.

The JAD approach also has disadvantages. First, it is very difficult to get all users to attend the JAD meeting. For example, in large organizations the users might literally be scattered all over the world. Second, the JAD approach has all the problems associated with any group process (e.g., one person can dominate the meeting, some participants may not contribute in a group setting, and so on). To alleviate these problems, JAD sessions usually have a facilitator who is skilled in systems analysis and design as well as in managing group meetings and processes. Also, the use of groupware (such as GDSS) can help facilitate the meeting.

Integrated Computer-Assisted Software Engineering Tools

Computer-aided software engineering (CASE) is a development approach that uses specialized tools to automate many of the tasks in the SDLC. The tools used to automate the early stages of the SDLC (systems investigation, analysis, and design) are called upper CASE tools. The tools used to automate later stages in the SDLC (programming, testing, operation, and maintenance) are called lower CASE tools. CASE tools that provide links between upper CASE and lower CASE tools are called **integrated CASE (ICASE) tools**.

CASE tools provide advantages for systems developers. These tools can produce systems with a longer effective operational life that more closely meet user requirements. They can also speed up the development process. Further, they help produce systems that are more flexible and adaptable to changing business conditions. Finally, systems produced using CASE tools typically have excellent documentation.

At the same time, however, initial systems produced by CASE tools are often more expensive to build and maintain. In addition, CASE tools require more extensive and accurate definition of user needs and requirements. Finally, CASE tools are difficult to customize. For this reason, they are sometimes difficult to use with existing systems.

Rapid Application Development

Rapid application development (RAD) is a systems development method that can combine JAD, prototyping, and integrated CASE tools to rapidly produce a high-quality system. In the first RAD stage, JAD sessions are used to collect system requirements, so that users are intensively involved early on. The development process in RAD is iterative, similar to prototyping. That is, requirements, designs, and the system itself are developed and then undergo a series, or sequence, of improvements. RAD uses ICASE tools to quickly structure requirements and develop prototypes. As the prototypes are developed and refined, users review them in additional JAD sessions. RAD produces functional components of a final system, rather than limited-scale versions. To understand how RAD functions and how it differs from SDLC, see Figure 10.4.

RAD methodologies and tools make it possible to develop systems faster, especially systems where the user interface is an important component. RAD can also improve the process of rewriting legacy applications.

End-User Development

Over the years, computers have become cheaper, smaller, and more widely dispersed throughout organizations. Today, almost everybody who works at a desk or in the field has a computer. One result of these developments is that many computer-related activities have shifted out into the work area. For example, end users now handle most of their own data entry. They create many of their own reports and print them locally, instead of waiting for them to arrive in the interoffice mail after a computer operator has run them at a remote data center. Users also provide unofficial training and support to other workers in their area. Finally, they design and develop an increasing number of their own applications, sometimes even relatively large and complex systems.

Beneficial as end-user development is to both workers and the organization as a whole, it has some limitations. End users may not be skilled enough in computers. This lack of skill can jeopardize quality and cost unless proper controls are installed. Also, many end users do not take enough time to document their work. In addition, they sometimes fail to take proper security measures. Finally, users often develop databases that cannot efficiently manage all of their production data.

Object-Oriented Development

Object-oriented development is based on a fundamentally different view of computer systems than the perception that characterizes traditional SDLC development approaches. Traditional approaches provide specific step-by-step instructions in the form of computer programs, in which programmers must specify every procedural detail. These programs usu-

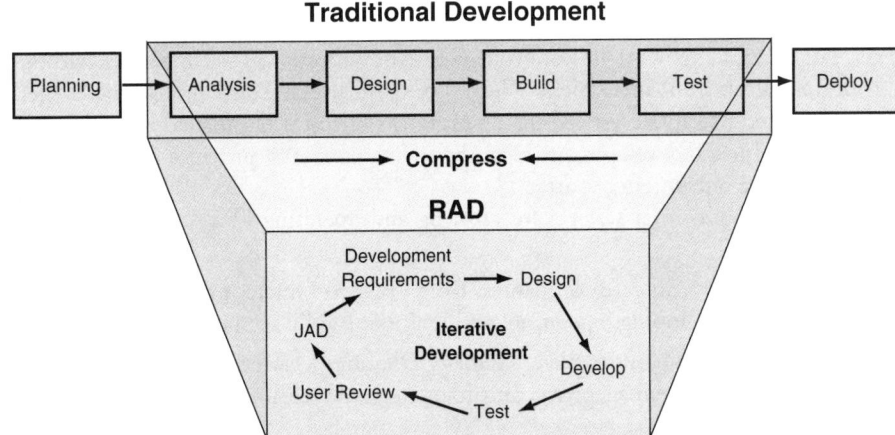

FIGURE 10.4
A rapid prototyping development process versus SDLC.
Source: datawarehouse-training.com/ Methodologies/ rapid-application-development.

ally produce a system that performs the original task but may not be suited for handling other tasks. This observation applies even when these other tasks involve the same real-world entities. For example, a billing system will handle billing but probably cannot be adapted to handle mailings for the marketing department or generate leads for the sales force. This is true even though the billing, marketing, and sales functions all use similar data, including customer names, addresses, and purchases. In contrast, an *object-oriented (OO) system* begins not with the task to be performed, but with the aspects of the real world that must be modeled to perform that task. Therefore, in the example above, if the firm has a good model of its customers and its interactions with them, this model can be used equally well for billings, mailings, and sales leads.

Object-Oriented Analysis and Design. The development process for an object-oriented system begins with a feasibility study and an analysis of the existing system. Systems developers identify the *objects* in the new system—the fundamental elements in OO analysis and design. Each object represents a tangible, real-world entity, such as a customer, bank account, student, or course. Objects have *properties*, or *data values*. For example, a customer has an identification number, name, address, account number(s), and so on. Objects also contain the *operations* that can be performed on their properties. For example, customer objects' operations may include obtain-account-balance, open-account, withdraw-funds, and so on. Operations are also referred to as *behaviors*.

In this way, object-oriented analysts define all the relevant objects needed for the new system, including their properties and operations. They then model how the objects interact to meet the objectives of the new system. In some cases, analysts can reuse existing objects from other applications (or from a library of objects) in the new system. This process saves the analysts the time they otherwise would spend coding these objects. In most cases, however, even with object reuse, some coding will be necessary to customize the objects and their interactions for the new system.

Before you go on . . .

1. Describe the tools that augment the traditional SDLC.
2. Describe the alternate methods that can be used for systems development, other than the SDLC.

10.5 Outsourcing and Application Service Providers

Small or medium-sized companies with few IT staff and limited budgets are best served by outside contractors. Acquiring IT applications from outside contractors or external organizations is called **outsourcing**. Large companies may also choose this strategy in certain circumstances. For example, they might want to experiment with new IT technologies without making a substantial up-front investment. They also might use outsourcing to protect their internal networks and to gain access to outside experts. Outsourcers can perform any or all of the tasks involved in IT development. IT's About Business 10.5 provides an example of how to manage a large outsourcing contract.

Several types of vendors offer services for creating and operating IT system including e-commerce applications:

- *Software houses*. Many software companies, from IBM to Oracle, offer a range of outsourcing services for developing, operating, and maintaining IT applications.

- *Outsourcers and others*. IT outsourcers, such as EDS, offer a variety of services. Also, the large CPA companies and management consultants (e.g., Accenture) offer some outsourcing services.

"Outsourcing? First door on your right."

© The New Yorker Collection 2005 Michael Shaw from cartoonbank.com. All Rights Reserved.

- **Offshoring.** As the trend to outsource is rising, so is the trend to do it offshore, particularly in India and China. Offshore outsourcing can save money, but it includes risks as well, such as sending sensitive corporate data overseas.

One of the most common types of IT outsourcing is the use of application service providers. An **application service provider (ASP)** is an agent or vendor who assembles the software needed by enterprises and packages the software with services such as development, operations, and maintenance. The essential difference between an ASP and an outsourcer is that an ASP manages application servers from a centrally controlled location rather than at a customer's site. The customer then accesses these applications via the Internet or VANs through a standard Web browser interface. Such an arrangement provides a full range of services for the company using the ASP. Applications can be sized to meet the needs of the customer, upgrades and maintenance can be centralized, physical security over the applications and servers can be guaranteed, and the necessary critical mass of human resources can be efficiently utilized.

The end-user businesses pay a monthly fee to the ASP for these services. In general, the fees include payment for the application software and hardware, as well as service and support. This support includes maintenance and upgrades. The fee can be fixed, or it can be based on utilization, such as the number of users or transactions.

IT's About Business

10.5 Procter & Gamble Outsources to Hewlett-Packard

Procter & Gamble's $3-billion technology services outsourcing pact with Hewlett-Packard meant that HP had to absorb P&G's data centers in Cincinnati, Singapore, and Brussels, along with P&G's network infrastructure and 2,000 P&G employees. With a 10,000-page contract and about 3,700 tasks to hand over, the companies adopted a "where is, as is" strategy in which HP initially just put P&G's technology operations and workers on its books. The key tasks of the outsourcing contract are revamping business processes and helping P&G effectively deploy wireless computing technology and radio frequency identification tagging. P&G evaluates HP's performance quarterly using criteria such as network uptime, data center availability, and response time on complaints, as well as qualitative measures on customer satisfaction.

P&G recognized that HP was a cultural match but was new to large outsourcing contracts. To assist HP, it implemented a "two-in-a-box" system. This setup paired an HP manager with a P&G counterpart to manage the transition on fronts such as human resources, technology infrastructure, and applications. HP's role was to figure out how to make the transition, with P&G assuming a support role. In areas where HP had little expertise, such as the contents of P&G's 5,000 global technology contracts with their various regulations and tax rules, P&G took the lead.

Sources: Compiled from L. Dignan, "P&G–HP Pact: Slow and Steady," *Baseline Magazine,* July 29, 2004; P. McDougall, "Procter & Gamble's Deal with HP Grows," *Outsourcing Pipeline,* August 16, 2004; K. Cushing, "Procter & Gamble's HP Deal Shows Mega IT Outsourcing Is Still Tempting Some," *Computer Weekly,* April 23, 2003; www.pg.com and www.hp.com, accessed April 6, 2005.

QUESTIONS

1. Compare the qualitative and quantitative sides of outsourcing contracts.
2. Discuss the "go slow" strategy that P&G and HP used in their outsourcing contract.

ASPs are especially active in enterprise computing and EC applications. These applications are frequently too complex for the customer to build and too cumbersome to maintain. Therefore, the major providers of ERP software, such as SAP and Oracle, now offer ASP options, as do IBM, Microsoft, and Computer Associates.

Leasing from an ASP is a particularly desirable option for SME businesses. Simply put, developing and operating IT applications in-house can be time-consuming and expensive for these entities. Leasing from ASPs offers such companies several advantages. First, it saves various expenses (such as labor costs) in the initial development stage. It also helps reduce both software maintenance and upgrading and user training costs over the long run. In addition, the company can select another software product from the ASP to meet its changing needs. This option saves the company the costs of upgrading the existing software. It also makes the company more competitive by reducing the time-to-market and enhancing the company's ability to adapt to changing market conditions.

Despite all these benefits, leasing from ASPs does have certain disadvantages. For example, many companies are concerned that ASPs don't offer adequate protection against hackers, theft of confidential information, and virus attacks. Also, leased software often does not provide the perfect fit for the desired application. Finally, the company must make certain that the speed of the Internet connection between the customer and the ASP is adequate to handle the requirements of the application, to avoid distortions in its performance.

We have discussed many methods that can be used to acquire new systems. Table 10.1 provides an overview of the advantages and disadvantages of these methods.

Advantages and Disadvantages of System Acquisition Methods

Table 10.1

Traditional Systems Development (SDLC)

Advantages
- Forces staff to systematically go through every step in a structured process.
- Enforces quality by maintaining standards.
- Has lower probability of missing important issues in collecting user requirements.

Disadvantages
- May produce excessive documentation.
- Users may be unwilling or unable to study the specifications they approve.
- Takes too long to go from the original ideas to a working system.
- Users have trouble describing requirements for a proposed system.

Prototyping

Advantages
- Helps clarify user requirements.
- Helps verify the feasibility of the design.
- Promotes genuine user participation.
- Promotes close working relationship between systems developers and users.
- Works well for ill-defined problems.
- May produce part of the final system.

Disadvantages
- May encourage inadequate problem analysis.
- Not practical with large number of users.
- User may not give up the prototype when the system is completed.
- May generate confusion about whether the system is complete and maintainable.
- System may be built quickly, which may result in lower quality.

(Continued)

Table 10.1

Advantages and Disadvantages of System Acquisition Methods (Continued)

Joint Application Design

Advantages
- Involves many users in the development process.
- Saves time.
- Greater user support for new system.
- Improved quality of the new system.
- New system easier to implement.
- New system has lower training costs.

Disadvantages
- Difficult to get all users to attend JAD meeting.
- JAD approach has all the problems associated with any group meeting.

Integrated Computer-Assisted Software Engineering

Advantages
- Can produce systems with a longer effective operational life.
- Can produce systems that closely meet user requirements.
- Can speed up the development process.
- Can produce systems that are more flexible and adaptable to changing business conditions.
- Can produce excellent documentation.

Disadvantages
- Systems often more expensive to build and maintain.
- Require more extensive and accurate definition of user requirements.
- Difficult to customize.

Rapid Application Development

Advantages
- Can speed up systems development.
- Users intensively involved from the start.
- Improves the process of rewriting legacy applications.

Disadvantages
- Produces functional components of final systems, but not final systems.

Object-Oriented Development

Advantages
- Objects model real-world entities.
- May be able to reuse some computer code.

Disadvantages
- Works best with systems of more limited scope; i.e., with systems that do not have huge numbers of objects.

End-User Development

Advantages
- Bypasses the IS department and avoids delays.
- User controls the application and can change it as needed.
- Directly meets user requirements.
- Increased user acceptance of new system.
- Frees up IT resources.
- May create lower-quality systems.

Disadvantages
- May eventually require maintenance from IS department.
- Documentation may be inadequate.
- Poor quality control.
- System may not have adequate interfaces to existing systems.

Outsourcing

Advantages
- Save costs.
- Rely on experts.
- Experiment with new information technologies.

Disadvantages
- Valuable corporate data in another company's control.
- During system development, programmers in another company could put malicious computer code (e.g., back doors) in applications.

Application Service Providers

Advantages
- Save costs.
- Reduces software maintenance and upgrades.
- Reduces user training.
- Makes the company more competitive by reducing time-to-market and enhances the company's ability to adapt to changing market conditions.

Disadvantages
- ASPs might not offer adequate security protection.
- Software might not be a perfect fit for the desired application.
- Company must make certain that the speed of the Internet connection between the customer and the ASP is adequate to handle the requirements of the application.

Table 10.1

Before you go on . . .

1. What types of companies provide outsourcing service?
2. Define ASPs, and discuss their advantages to companies using them.
3. List some disadvantages of ASPs.

10.6 Vendor and Software Selection

Few organizations, especially SMEs, have the time, financial resources, or technical expertise required to develop today's complex IT or e-business systems. As a result, business firms are increasingly relying on outside vendors to provide software, hardware, and technical expertise. As a result, selecting and managing these vendors and their software offerings has become a major aspect of developing an IT application. The following six steps in selecting a software vendor and an application package are useful.

Step 1: Identify Potential Vendors. Companies can identify potential software application vendors through various sources:

- Software catalogs
- Lists provided by hardware vendors

- Technical and trade journals
- Consultants experienced in the application area
- Peers in other companies
- Web searches

These sources often yield so many vendors and packages that the company must use some evaluation criteria to eliminate all but the most promising ones from further consideration. For example, it can eliminate vendors that are too small or have a questionable reputation. Also, it can eliminate packages that do not have the required features or are not compatible with the company's existing hardware and/or software.

Step 2: Determine the Evaluation Criteria.   The most difficult and crucial task in evaluating a vendor and a software package is to select a detailed set of evaluation criteria. Some areas in which a customer should develop detailed criteria are:

- Characteristics of the vendor
- Functional requirements of the system
- Technical requirements that the software must satisfy
- Amount and quality of documentation provided
- Vendor support of the package

These criteria should be set out in a **request for proposal (RFP)**. An RFP is a document that is sent to potential vendors inviting them to submit a proposal that describes their software package and explains how it would meet the company's needs. The RFP provides the vendors with information about the objectives and requirements of the system. Specifically, it describes the environment in which the system will be used, the general criteria that the company will use to evaluate the proposals, and the conditions for submitting proposals. The RFP may also request a list of current users of the package whom the company may contact. In some cases the RFP will describe in detail the form of response that the customer desires. Finally, it can require the vendor to demonstrate the package at the company's facilities using specified inputs and data files.

Step 3: Evaluate Vendors and Packages.   The responses to an RFP generate massive volumes of information that the company must evaluate. The goal of this evaluation is to determine the gaps between the company's needs (as specified by the requirements) and the capabilities of the vendors and their application packages. Often, the company gives the vendors and packages an overall score by (1) assigning an importance weight to each of the criteria, (2) ranking the vendors on each of the weighted criteria (say 1 to 10), and then (3) multiplying the ranks by the associated weights. The company can then shorten the list of potential suppliers to include only those vendors who achieved the highest overall scores.

Step 4: Choose the Vendor and Package.   Once the company has shortened the list of potential suppliers, it can begin negotiations with these vendors to determine how their packages might be modified to remove any discrepancies with the company's IT needs. Thus, one of the most important factors in the decision is the additional development effort that may be required to tailor the system to the company's needs or to integrate it into the company's computing environment. The company must also consider the opinions of both the users and the IT personnel who will have to support the system.

Several software selection methods exist. For a list of general criteria, see Manager's Checklist 10.2.

Criteria for Selecting a Software Application Package

Manager's Checklist 10.2

- ☐ Cost and financial terms
- ☐ Upgrade policy and cost
- ☐ Vendor's reputation and availability for help
- ☐ Vendor's success stories (visit their Web site, contact clients)
- ☐ System flexibility
- ☐ Ease of Internet interface
- ☐ Availability and quality of documentation
- ☐ Necessary hardware and networking resources
- ☐ Required training (check if provided by vendor)
- ☐ Security
- ☐ Learning (speed of) for developers and users
- ☐ Graphical presentation
- ☐ Data handling
- ☐ System-required hardware

Step 5: Negotiate a Contract.   The contract with the software vendor is very important. It specifies both the price of the software and the type and amount of support that the vendor agrees to provide. The contract will be the only recourse if either the system or the vendor does not perform as expected. It is essential, then, that the contract directly reference the request for proposal, because this is the vehicle that the vendor used to document the functionality supported in their system. Furthermore, if the vendor is modifying the software to tailor it to the company's needs, the contract must include detailed specifications (essentially the requirements) of the modifications. Finally, the contract should describe in detail the acceptance tests that the software package must pass.

Contracts are legal documents, and they can be quite tricky. For this reason, companies might need the services of experienced contract negotiators and lawyers. Many organizations employ software-purchasing specialists who assist in negotiations and write or approve the contract. These specialists should be involved in the selection process from the start.

Step 6: Establish a Service Level Agreement.   **Service level agreements (SLAs)** are formal agreements that specify how work is to be divided between the company and its vendors. These divisions are based on a set of agreed-upon milestones, quality checks, and what-if situations. They describe how quality checks will be made and what is to be done in case of disputes. SLAs accomplish these goals by (1) defining the responsibilities of both partners, (2) providing a framework for designing support services, and (3) allowing the company to retain as much control as possible over its own systems. SLAs include such issues as performance, availability, backup and recovery, upgrades, and hardware and software ownership. For example, the SLA might specify that the ASP have its system available to the customer 99.9 percent of the time.

Before you go on . . .

1. List the major steps of selection of a vendor and a software package.
2. Describe a request for proposal (RFP).
3. Describe SLAs.

What's in IT for me?

For the Accounting Major

Accounting personnel help perform the cost-benefit analyses on proposed projects. They may also monitor ongoing project costs to keep them within budget. Accounting personnel undoubtedly will find themselves involved with systems development at various points throughout their careers.

For the Finance Major

Finance personnel are frequently involved with the financial issues that accompany any large-scale systems development project (e.g., budgeting). They also are involved in cost-benefit and risk analyses. To perform these tasks they need to stay abreast of the emerging techniques used to determine project costs and ROI. Finally, because they must manage vast amounts of information, finance departments are also common recipients of new systems.

For the Marketing Major

In most organizations, marketing, like finance, involves massive amounts of data and information. Like finance, then, marketing is also a hotbed of systems development. Marketing personnel will increasingly find themselves participating on systems development teams. Such involvement increasingly means helping to develop systems, especially Web-based systems, that reach out directly from the organization to its customers.

For the Production/Operations Management Major

Participation on development teams is also a common role for production/operations people. Manufacturing is becoming increasingly computerized and integrated with other allied systems, from design to logistics to customer support. Production systems interface frequently with marketing, finance, and human resources. In addition, they may be part of a larger, enterprisewide system. Also, many end users in POM either develop their own systems or collaborate with IT personnel on specific applications.

For the Human Resources Management Major

The human resources department is closely involved with several aspects of the systems acquisitions process. Acquiring new systems may require hiring new employees, changing job descriptions, or terminating employees. Human resources performs all of these tasks. Further, if the organization hires consultants for the development project or outsources it, the human resources department may handle the contracts with these suppliers.

The MIS Function

Regardless of the approach that the organization uses for acquiring new systems, the MIS department spearheads it. If the organization chooses to buy the application, the MIS department leads in examining the offerings of the various vendors and in negotiating with the vendors. If the organization chooses to lease the application, the MIS department again examines vendor offerings and leads in negotiating with the vendors. If the organization chooses to develop the application in-house, the process falls to the MIS department. MIS analysts work closely with users to develop their information requirements, and then MIS programmers write the computer code, test it, and implement the new system.

Summary

1. Describe the IT planning process.

Information systems planning begins with reviewing the strategic plan of the organization. The organizational strategic plan and the existing IT architecture provide the inputs in developing the *IT strategic plan*, which describes the IT architecture and major IS initiatives needed to achieve the goals of the organization. The IT strategic plan may also require a new IT architecture, or the existing IT architecture may be sufficient. In either case, the IT strategic plan leads to the *IS operational plan*, which is a clear set of projects that will be executed by the IS/IT department and by functional area managers in support of the IT strategic plan.

2. Describe the IT justification process and methods.

The justification process is basically a comparison of the expected costs versus the benefits of each application. While measuring cost may not be complex, measuring benefits is, due to the many intangible benefits involved. Several methodologies exist for evaluating costs and benefits, including net present value, return on investment, breakeven analysis, and the business case approach.

3. Describe the SDLC and its advantages and limitations.

The systems development life cycle (SDLC) is the traditional method used by most organizations today. The SDLC is a structured framework that consists of distinct sequential processes: systems investigation, systems analysis, systems design, programming, testing, implementation, operation, and maintenance. These processes, in turn, consist of well-defined tasks. Some of these tasks are present in most projects, while others are present in only certain types of projects. That is, smaller development projects may require only a subset of tasks; large projects typically require all tasks. Using the SDLC guarantees quality and security, but it is slow and expensive.

4. Describe the major alternative methods and tools for building information systems.

A common alternative for the SDLC is quick prototyping, which helps to test systems. Useful prototyping tools for SDLC are JAD (for finding information needs) and RAD (which uses CASE tools). For smaller and rapidly needed applications, designers can use object-oriented development tools, which are popular in Web-based applications.

5. List the major IT acquisition options and the criteria for option selection.

The major options are buy, lease, and build (develop in-house). Other options are joint ventures and use of e-marketplaces or exchanges (private or public). Building in-house can be done by using the SDLC, by using prototyping or other methodologies, and it can be done by outsourcers, the IS department employees, or end users (individually or together).

6. Describe the role of ASPs.

ASPs lease software applications, usually via the Internet. Fees for the leased applications can be the same each month or can be based on actual usage (like electricity).

7. Describe the process of vendor and software selection.

The process of vendor and software selection is composed of six steps: identify potential vendors, determine evaluation criteria, evaluate vendors and packages, choose the vendor and package, negotiate a contract, and establish service level agreements.

Chapter Glossary

Application Portfolio The set of recommended applications resulting from the planning and justification process in application development. (305)

Application Service Provider (ASP) An agent or vendor who assembles the software needed by enterprises and packages them with outsourced development, operations, maintenance, and other services. (322)

Computer-Aided Software Engineering (CASE) Development approach that uses specialized tools to automate many of the tasks in the SDLC; upper CASE tools automate the early stages of the SDLC, and lower CASE tools automate the later stages. (319)

Direct Conversion Implementation process in which the old system is cut off and the new system is turned on at a certain point in time. (317)

Feasibility Study Investigation that gauges the probability of success of a proposed project and provides a rough assessment of the project's feasibility. (312)

Implementation (deployment) The process of converting from an old computer system to a new one. (317)

Integrated CASE (ICASE) Tools CASE tools that provide links between upper CASE and lower CASE tools. (319)

IT Strategic Plan A set of long-range goals that describe the IT infrastructure and major IT initiatives needed to achieve the goals of the organization. (306)

Joint Application Design (JAD) A group-based tool for collecting user requirements and creating system designs. (319)

Logical System Design Abstract specification of what a computer system will do. (315)

Object-Oriented Development Begins with aspects of the real world that must be modeled to perform a task. (320)

Outsourcing Use of outside contractors or external organizations to acquire IT services. (321)

Parallel Conversion Implementation process in which the old system and the new system operate simultaneously for a period of time. (317)

Phased Conversion Implementation process that introduces components of the new system in stages, until the entire new system is operational. (318)

Physical System Design Actual physical specifications that state how a computer system will perform its functions. (315)

Pilot Conversion Implementation process that introduces the new system in one part of the organization on a trial basis; when new system is working properly, it is introduced in other parts of the organization. (318)

Programming The translation of a system's design specifications into computer code. (316)

Prototyping Approach that defines an initial list of user requirements, builds a prototype system, and then improves the system in several iterations based on users' feedback. (318)

Rapid Application Development (RAD) A development method that uses special tools and an iterative approach to rapidly produce a high-quality system. (320)

Request for Proposal (RFP) Document that is sent to potential vendors inviting them to submit a proposal describing their software package and how it would meet the company's needs. (326)

Scope Creep Adding functions to an information system after the project has begun. (315)

Service Level Agreements (SLAs) Formal agreements regarding the division of work between a company and its vendors. (327)

Systems Analysis The examination of the business problem that the organization plans to solve with an information system. (314)

Systems Analysts IS professionals who specialize in analyzing and designing information systems. (311)

Systems Design Describes how the new system will provide a solution to the business problem. (314)

Systems Development Life Cycle (SDLC) Traditional structured framework, used for large IT projects, that consists of sequential processes by which information systems are developed. (311)

Systems Stakeholders All people who are affected by changes in information systems. (311)

Technical Specialists Experts on a certain type of technology, such as databases or telecommunications. (311)

Waterfall Approach SDLC approach in which tasks in one stage were completed before the work proceeded to the next stage. (311)

Discussion Questions

1. Discuss the advantages of a lease option over a buy option.
2. Why is it important for all business managers to understand the issues of IT resource acquisition?
3. Why is it important for everyone in business organizations to have a basic understanding of the systems development process?
4. Should prototyping be used on every systems development project? Why or why not?
5. Discuss the various types of feasibility studies. Why are they all needed?
6. What are the characteristics of structured programming? Why is structured programming so important?
7. Discuss the issue of assessing intangible benefits and the proposed solutions.
8. Why is the attractiveness of ASPs increasing?

Problem-Solving Activities

1. Enter *www.ibm.com* and find information about how IBM measures the ROI on WebSphere. Then examine ROI from CIOView Corporation (*www.CIOview.com*). Identify the variables included in the analysis (at both sites). Prepare a report about the fairness of such a tool.
2. Use an Internet search engine to obtain information on CASE and ICASE tools. Select several vendors and compare and contrast their offerings.
3. Use the Web to learn about analysis and design of intranets. What sort of sites have the most (and the most useful) information?

Internet Activities

1. Enter *www.ibm.com/software*. Find their WebSphere product. Read recent customers' success stories. What makes this software so popular?
2. Enter the Web sites of the GartnerGroup (*www.gartnergroup.com*), the Yankee Group (*www.yankeegroup.com*), and CIO (*www.cio.com*). Search for recent material about ASPs and outsourcing, and prepare a report on your findings.
3. Enter the Web site of IDC (*www.idc.com*) and find how the company evaluates ROI on intranets, supply chain, and other IT projects.
4. Visit the Web site of Resource Management Systems (*www.rms.net*) and take the IT investment Management Approach Assessment Self-Test (*www.rms.net/selftest.htm*) to compare your organization's IT decision-making process with those of best-practices organizations.
5. Enter *www.plumtree.com* and see how they conduct ROI on portals. List major elements of the analysis.

Team Assignments

1. Assessing the functionality of an application is a part of the planning process (Step 1). Select three to five Web sites catering to the same type of buyer (for instance, several Web sites that offer CDs or computer hardware), and divide the sites among the teams. Each team will assess the functionality of its assigned Web site by preparing an analysis of the different sorts of functions provided by the sites. In addition, the team should compare the strong and weak points of each site from the buyer's perspective.

2. Divide into groups, with each group visiting a local company (include your university). At each firm, study the systems acquisition process. Find out the methodology or methodologies used by each organization and the type of application each methodology applies. Prepare a report and present it to the class.

3. As a group, design an information system for a startup business of your choice. Describe your chosen IT resource acquisition strategy, and justify your choices of hardware, software, telecommunications support, and other aspects of a proposed system.

4. As a group, design an information system for a startup business of your choice. Describe your chosen systems development methodologies, and justify your choices of hardware, software, telecommunications support, and other aspects of the proposed system.

CASE Canada Has Trouble Developing a System

THE BUSINESS PROBLEM   Canada's new firearms act, passed in 1995, stiffened penalties for firearms offenses and called for the creation of a national computerized firearm registry. The law requires every gun owner to obtain a license and to undergo a background check. In addition, the owner must register every gun in his or her possession.

The country's gun lobby strongly opposed the registry, arguing that the monies required to develop and operate the system would be better spent fighting crime. The government responded that the costs would be offset by the licensing and registration fees. The projected net cost to taxpayers was to be very low.

Prior to 1995, Canada had a limited system of federal and provincial agencies in place to handle the licensing of new guns. Further, the government did not keep track of the estimated 7 million guns that already were in circulation. Initially, the federal government believed it could use the same agencies that issued firearm acquisition certificates to handle the registration. However, that plan did not work because several provinces, primarily those with strong hunting lobbies, refused to cooperate.

Faced with this opposition, the federal government was forced to assume total responsibility for the project. To do this it created a new agency to manage the program. This agency decided to include all violent incidents reported to police, whether they resulted in a criminal conviction or not, as grounds for further reviewing a license application. This process involved tapping into the computer records of every police agency in the country. In addition, it required placing information on any reported threats, domestic violence, or related incidents into a new database. This new database would provide inputs into the new firearm registry database, as would the Canadian Police database.

THE IT SOLUTION   The Canadian government awarded the contract to build the system to Electronic Data Systems from the United States and SHL Systemhouse from the United Kingdom. The heart of the system was a database to collect licensing and registration information, such as the make, model, caliber, and serial number of firearms. The companies also created an application to input information from mailed-in registration forms. This application would also connect this new database to the databases of law enforcement agencies across Canada.

Meanwhile, political arguing and pressure from the gun lobby and government officials prompted numerous changes to license and registry forms, rules, and processes. The development team eventually had to deal with more than 1,000 orders for changes to the system. Changes to the software required the developers to deal with 50 different department or agency computer systems, from the Royal Canadian Mounted Police to each provincial Ministry of Transportation for driver's license checks.

When the project was conceived, it was forecast that only 10 percent of applications would require follow-up by an employee. Instead, 90 percent of the applications required such follow-up. Some errors were deliberate: The gun lobby had encouraged people to fill out forms incorrectly.

THE RESULTS The firearm registry turned into a huge embarrassment. What was supposed to be a relatively modest IT project ballooned into a massive undertaking. As just one example, the government had claimed that it could recoup the vast majority of the development costs through registration fees. Instead, it decided to waive or eliminate most of the fees to encourage gun owners to comply.

At last count, the program had amassed more than $1 billion in costs. In fact, the system had become so cumbersome that an independent review board recommended that it be scrapped.

Sources: Compiled from M. Duvall, "Canada Firearms: Armed Robbery," *Baseline Magazine*, July 1, 2004; "Government of Canada Caps Costs of Registry and Improves Gun Crime Measures," *Public Safety and Emergency Preparedness Canada* (*www.psepc-sppcc.gc.ca*), May 20, 2004; and *www.eds.com* and *www.shl.com*, accessed March 15, 2005.

QUESTIONS

1. Discuss the problems of information requirements determination and scope creep in this case.
2. Should the government abandon the project?
3. Was it a good idea to build this system in the first place? Defend your answer by conducting a feasibility study of the case.

Interactive Learning

To Outsource or Not to Outsource?

Go to the Interactivities section on the *WileyPLUS* Web Site and access Chapter 10: Acquiring or Building IT Application and Infrastructure. There you will find some hands-on activities that help explore the implementation issues associated with outsourcing.

Acquiring Information Systems for Club IT

The assignments on the *WileyPLUS* Web site will ask you to make recommendations for overall improvements on how to upgrade the club's information management capabilities.

wiley.com/college/rainer

References

CHAPTER 1

Carr, D. "Cunard Line: Royal Treatment." *Baseline Magazine*, August 1, 2004.

Duvall, M. "Boston Red Sox: Backstop Your Business." *Baseline Magazine*, May 14, 2004.

Duvall, M. "Boston Red Sox: Backstop Your Business." *eWeek*, May 21, 2004.

Duvall, M., and K. Nash. "Albertson's: A Shot at the Crown." *Baseline Magazine*, February 5, 2004.

Esfahani, Elizabeth. "7-Eleven Gets Sophisticated." *Business 2.0*, January/February 2005.

Fitzgerald, M. "Branching Out." *CIO Insight*, January 5, 2005.

Rich, L. "Case Study: Pratt & Whitney." *CIO Insight*, June 1, 2004.

Rothfelder, J. "Better Safe Than Sorry: Blue Rhino Corp." *CIO Insight*, February 1, 2004.

Steinart-Threlkeld, T. "Trek Bicycle Corp: Tour de Force." *Baseline Magazine*, June 28, 2004.

www.albertsons.com, accessed January 19, 2005.

www.bluerhino.com, accessed March 4, 2005.

www.commerceonline.com, accessed March 3, 2005.

www.cunard.com, accessed March 1, 2005.

www.pratt-whitney.com, accessed February 27, 2005.

www.7-eleven.com, accessed March 10, 2005.

www.trekbikes.com, accessed March 3, 2005.

CHAPTER 2

Barrett, L., and D. F. Carr. "Eastman Kodak: Picture Imperfect." *Baseline Magazine*, September 1, 2004.

Briody, D. "Seize the Gate." *CIO Insight*, July 1, 2004.

Brooke, J. "Rural Cambodia, Though Far Off the Grid, Is Finding Its Way Online." *New York Times*, January 26, 2004.

Brown, S. F. "Send in the Robots." *Fortune*, January 24, 2005, pp. 140 [C]–140 [L].

Carey, J. "Big Brother's Passport to Pry." *BusinessWeek Online*, November 5, 2004.

Dignan, L. "Oh, Yeah, the Computers." *Baseline Magazine*, December 6, 2004.

Edwards, C. "Ready to Buy a Home Robot?" *BusinessWeek*, July 19, 2004; pp. 84–90.

"Finnish Army Drops Web Addicts." *BBC News*, August 5, 2004.

Freed, J. "The Customer Is Always Right? Not Anymore." *www.sfgate.com*, July 5, 2004.

Greenemeier, L. "Report Says IRS Software Program Is Not Doing the Job." *InformationWeek*, August 31, 2004.

Grossman, D. "Disappearing Hub: It's a Myth." *USA Today*, March 14, 2005.

Hancocks, P. "Scanner Creates Perfect-Fit Jeans." *CNN.com*, January 7, 2005.

"LAPD May Use Facial Recognition Software." *NewsMax Wires*, December 26, 2004.

"Kodak Posts Loss, Citing Costs of Shifts to Digital Photography." *New York Times*, April 23, 2005.

Lok, C. "Fighting Infections with Data." *MIT Technology Review*, October 2004, p. 24.

McKay, N. "Two-Faced and Tight-Fisted." *CIO Insight*, December 1, 2004.

Mullaney, T. J. "Real Estate's New Reality." *BusinessWeek*, May 10, 2004.

Nash, Kim. "Dollar General: 8 Days to Grow." *Baseline Magazine*, July 1, 2004.

Porter, M. E. *Competitive Advantage: Creating and Sustaining Superior Performance*, New York: Free Press, 1985.

Porter, M. E. "Strategy and the Internet." *Harvard Business Review*, March 2001.

Rothfeder, J. "Analysis: High Speed Compliance." *CIO Insight*, May 1, 2004.

381

"Sears Holding Corporation." *http://premium.hoovers.com*, March 14, 2005.

"Web Addiction Gets Conscripts Out of Army." *Reuters*, August 3, 2004.

http://company.monster.com/dgcorp/, accessed March 30, 2005.

www.bodymetrics.com, accessed March 21, 2005.

www.crownmedia.net, accessed March 22, 2005.

www.dollargeneral.com, accessed March 30, 2005.

www.gtaa.com, accessed February 22, 2005.

www.homegain.com, accessed March 3, 2005.

www.irs.gov, accessed March 31, 2005.

www.lendingtree.com, accessed March 3, 2005.

www.media.mit.edu, accessed March 12, 2005.

www.medmined.com, accessed March 17, 2005.

www.movaris.com, accessed March 22, 2005.

www.peoplesoft.com, accessed February 7, 2005.

www.pwc.com, accessed February 7, 2005.

www.sears.com, accessed March 21, 2005.

www.ziprealty.com, accessed March 3, 2005.

CHAPTER 3

"A Post-Privacy Future for Workers." *BW Online*, April 13, 2004.

Barrett, L., and S. Gallagher. "What Sin City Can Teach Tom Ridge." *Baseline Magazine*, April 4, 2004.

Biever, C. "Spam Being Rapidly Outpaced by Spim." *www.NewScientist.com*, March 26, 2004.

Cha, A. "Thieves Find Exactly What They're Looking For on eBay." *The Washington Post*, January 6, 2005.

Claburn, T. "Law Prompts Company to Disclose Data Breach." *InformationWeek*, February 21, 2005.

Cone, E., and S. Gallagher. "Cantor-Fitzgerald: Forty-Seven Hours." *Baseline Magazine*, October 29, 2001.

Dignan, L. "Hack to School." *Baseline Magazine*, September 1, 2004.

"Hacker Hits California-Berkeley Computer." *CNN.com*, October 10, 2004.

James, G. "Can't Hide Your Prying Eyes." *Computerworld*, March 1, 2004.

Jarvis, R. "Casinos Bet Big on RFID." *Business 2.0*, March 23, 2005.

Kerner, S. "Hilton's T-Mobile Hack a Password Wake-Up." *www.internetnews.com*, February 22, 2005.

Mark, R. "Teen's Extortion Plot Spims Out of Control." *Internetnews.com*, February 22, 2005.

McNichol, T. "Street Maps in Political Hues." *The New York Times*, May 20, 2004.

Morse, J. "Pair Admit Selling Stolen Goods on eBay." *The Enquirer*, June 24, 2004.

"Pop Culture." *Baseline Magazine*, September 8, 2004.

Roberts, P. "SCO Web Site Hack Mocks Company's Legal Claims." *Computerworld*, November 29, 2004.

Roberts, P. "MyDoom One Year Later: More Zombies, More Spam." *Computerworld*, January 27, 2005.

Schonfeld, E. "GPS-Tracked Car Insurance." *Business 2.0*, January/February, 2005, p. 49.

"Seller Charged over Stolen Goods on eBay." *ABC News Online*, February 2, 2005.

Sherriff, L. "Paris Hilton's Sidekick Hacked." *The Register*, February 21, 2005.

Sooman, D. "Fake FBI E-mail Carries Virus." *www.techspot.com*, February 24, 2005.

Sullivan, B. "Database Giant Gives Access to Fake Firms." *MSNBC News*, February 14, 2005.

"The ChoicePoint Incident." *Red Herring*, February 23, 2005.

"UK: Customised Car Insurance." *www.qualisteam.com/news/mar05/15-03-05-7.html*, March 10, 2005.

Weiss, T. "New Virus Being Distributed in Fake FBI E-mail." *Computerworld*, February 23, 2005.

http://lasvegas.about.com/cs/casinohotelsjobs/a/Security.htm, accessed March 3, 2005.

http://libraries.mit.edu/gis/teach/geocoding.html, accessed March 8, 2005.

www.fundrace.org, accessed March 8, 2005.

www.privacyrights.org/fs/fs7-work.htm, accessed March 7, 2005.

CHAPTER 4

Barrett, L. "Snyder's of Hanover: Twisted Logic." *Baseline Magazine*, January 16, 2004.

Booth, B. "Clean Data Is Good Business." *ComputerWeekly.com*, February 8, 2005.

Briody, D. "Toyota's Business Intelligence: Oh! What a Feeling." *CIO Insight*, October 1, 2004.

Briody, D. "Business Intelligence Beats Back Food Stamp Fraud." *CIO Insight*, December 1, 2004.

D'Agostino, D. "Expertise Management: Who Knows About This?" *CIO Insight*, July 1, 2004.

D'Agostino, D. "Data Management: Getting Clean." *CIO Insight*, August 1, 2004.

Dignan, L. "Diageo: Kindred Spirits." *Baseline Magazine*, December 1, 2004.

Hardy, Q. "Data of Reckoning." *Forbes*, May 10, 2004.

Kontzer, T. "Help Wanted: Expertise-Management Tools Locate Talent." *InformationWeek*, May 5, 2003.

Kwon, R. "Primer: The Virtual Database." *Baseline Magazine*, May 1, 2003.

Mearian, L. "MetLife Building Giant Customer Relational Database." *Computerworld*, January 1, 2002.

Nucleus Research. "ROI Case Study: Brio and Toyota Motor Sales." *Computerworld*, December, 2003.

"Procurement Perfected." *Infoconomy.com*, May 1, 2005.

Rothfeder, J. "Pay As You Go." *PC Magazine*, October 15, 2004.

"Satori Group Tears Open Snack Food Manufacturing Sector: Snyder's of Hanover, the #1 National Brand of Specialty Pretzels, Rolls with ProCube." *Business Wire*, January 16, 2003.

Soat, J. "Louisiana Fights Fraud with Mapping Software." *InformationWeek*, May 25, 2004.

Songini, M. "IBM Pushes Out Virtual Database Technology." *Computerworld*, February 6, 2003.

Virzl, A. M. "United Parcel Service: Sticky Fix." *Baseline Magazine*, February 5, 2004.

Wheatley, M. "Operation Clean Data." *CIO*, July 1, 2004.

www.dwl.com, accessed March 22, 2005.

www.metlife.com, accessed March 22, 2005.

www.ups.com, accessed March 25, 2005.

CHAPTER 5

"Advanced Auto Parts Opens." *Chesterton Tribune*, August 5, 2004.

Babcock, C. "Software's Next Step." *Wall Street Technology*, November 29, 2004.

"Big Challenges, Big Rewards." *www.cio.com*, March 9, 2005.

Carr, D. "The 100-Million-Mile Network." *Baseline Magazine*, February 6, 2004.

Dignan, L. "Diageo: Kindred Spirits." *Baseline Magazine*, December 1, 2004.

Duvall, M. "Screening Rooms." *Baseline Magazine*, March 1, 2004.

Fitzgerald, J. "Marketer's First Breakthrough: Itself." *Boston Herald*, January 24, 2005.

Fonda, D. "Downloading Hollywood." *Time*, February 14, 2005.

Kelleher, K. "66,207,896 Bottles of Beer on the Wall." *Business 2.0*, February 1, 2004.

Kelly, L. "Online Buying Means Business for Heinz." *Computing*, October 15, 2003.

Kirkpatrick, D., and Roth, D. "Why There's No Escaping the Blog." *Fortune*, January 10, 2005.

Lasswell, M. "Lost in Translation." *Business 2.0*, August 2004.

Metz, C. "The New Peer-to-Peer Players." *PC Magazine*, November 16, 2004.

"NewsEdge Desktop Applications Real-Time News Keeps British Aerospace Professionals on Top of Their World." *www.dialog.com/products/casestudies/british.shtml*, March 29, 2005.

Reynolds, P. "Packaging for Kids at Kellogg and Dannon." *www.packworld.com*, March 31, 2005.

Rojas, P. "Kryptonite Offers Free Upgrades for Easily Picked Bike Locks." *www.engadget.com*, September 19, 2004.

Serafin, T. "Hoping for a Bad Winter." *Forbes*, January 10, 2005.

Steinert-Threlkeld, T. "Say Hello to Your New Phone Company: You." *Baseline Magazine*, October 1, 2004.

"Torrentspy.com." *PC Magazine*, April 6, 2005.

Wells, M. "Have It Your Way." *Forbes*, February 14, 2005.

www.anheuser-busch.com, accessed March 3, 2005.

www.baeportal.datathree.com/, accessed April 3, 2005.

www.bhesc.org, accessed February 19, 2005.

www.infores.com/public/us/newsEvents/press, accessed March 3, 2005.

www.microsoft.com/resources/casestudies, accessed March 23, 2005.

www.workflowsystems.com, accessed February 17, 2005.

http://marsrovers.jpl.nasa.gov/home/, last accessed March 24, 2005.

http://babelfish.altavista.com, *www.google.com*, last accessed March 25, 2005.

CHAPTER 6

Baker, S. "The Online Ad Surge." *Business Week*, November 22, 2004; pp. 76–82.

Barrett, L., and T. Steinert-Threlkeld. "Procter & Gamble: Delivering Goods." *Baseline Magazine*, July 1, 2004.

Berner, R., and B. Grow. "Jewelry Heist." *Business Week*, May 10, 2004; pp. 82–83.

Buderi, R. "E-Commerce Gets Smarter." *MIT Technology Review*, April 2005; pp. 54–59.

"California Installs Wi-Fi Access at State Parks." *Reuters*, January 21, 2005.

Kellam, L. "P & G Rethinks Supply Chain." *Optimize Magazine*, October 2003.

McCarthy, K. "Microsoft Lawyers Threaten Mike Rowe." *The Register*, January 19, 2004.

"Microsoft Takes on Teen's Site MikeRoweSoft.com." *CNN.com*, January 19, 2004.

Mount, I. "Target's Not-So-Smart Cards." *Business 2.0*, September 2004.

Mullaney, T. "Checks Check Out." *Business Week*, May 10, 2004, pp. 83–84.

"No One Will Know You Are a Procrastinator." *PRNewswire*, December 16, 2004.

"Plastic Overtakes Checks." *http://moneycentral.msn.com*, December 6, 2004.

Schlough, B. "How IT Bolsters the Baseball Experience and Revenues." *CIO Insight*, October 1, 2004.

"Striking a Balance." *CIO Insight*, December 1, 2004.

"Target Taking Brains Out of Smart Cards." *Retail Merchandiser*, April, 2004.

www.bluenile.com, accessed March 11, 2005.

www.debeers.com, accessed March 11, 2005.

www.deluxe.com, accessed March 5, 2005.

www.diamondhelpers.com, accessed March 11, 2005.

www.ford.com, accessed February 21, 2005.

www.microsoft.com, accessed March 9, 2005.

www.mikerowesoft.com, accessed March 9, 2005.

www.pg.com, accessed March 12, 2005.

www.rei.com, accessed March 10, 2005.

www.returnexchange.com, accessed March 10, 2005.

www.sfgiants.com, accessed March 19, 2005.

www.staples.com, accessed March 10, 2005.

www.target.com, accessed March 17, 2005.

CHAPTER 7

Carr, D. F., and L. Barrett. "Philip Morris International: Smoke Screen." *Baseline Magazine*, February 1, 2005.

Cohen, P. "Panera Bread Goes Wi-Fi for Free." *MacWorld*, August 12, 2003.

Douglas, M. "Some Cities Are in a Fine Mesh." *www.mrt.com*, March 1, 2004.

Durman, P. "WiMax Technology Goes Live in Southwest England." *The Times Online*, February 6, 2005.

Ellison, C. "Muni, Mesh Wireless Players Meet in Philadelphia." *eWeek*, April 29, 2005.

Freedman, M. "Untapped Market." *Forbes*, January 10, 2005.

Greenemeier, L. "Jersey City Cops Add Video to Shoe Leather." *InternetWeek*, March 7, 2005.

Herskovitz, J. "Live, Digital Video Heading to U.S. Police Cars." *Reuters*, April 20, 2004.

Hoffman, T. "Smart Dust." *Computerworld*, March 23, 2003.

Judge, P. "Blending Wi-Fi and Bluetooth for a Tracking System." *Techworld*, July 2, 2004.

Mashberg, T. "Brown Goes Bluetooth." *MIT Technology Review*, June 2005.

Nee, E. "Municipalities Starting to Mesh." *CIO Insight*, March 22, 2005.

Nobel, C. "MCI Expands Wi-Fi Coverage." *eWeek*, March 22, 2005.

Ricadela, A. "Sensors Everywhere." *InformationWeek*, January 24, 2005.

Roberti, M. "Where RFID Is Happening." *RFID Journal*, January 26, 2004.

Schmidt, K. "Smart Dust Is Way Cool." *Science & Society*, February 16, 2004.

Schuman, E. "Circuit City's New Approach to Customer Service." *eWeek*, January 17, 2005.

Smith, B. "Police Drive into Next Gen." *Wireless Week*, August 1, 2003.

Smith, B. "Raising the RFID Profile." *Wireless Week*, December 15, 2003.

Ulanoff, L. "Bargain Hunting Online." *PC Magazine*, November 17, 2004.

www.boingo.com, accessed March 15, 2005.

www.btplc.com, accessed March 21, 2005.

www.circuitcity.com, accessed March 3, 2005.

www.dust-inc.com, last accessed March 11, 2005.

www.mci.com, accessed March 15, 2005.

www.saic.com, accessed March 11, 2005.

www.symbol.com, accessed April 4, 2005.

www.telabria.com, accessed March 21, 2005.

www.ups.com, accessed April 4, 2005.

www.xbow.com, accessed March 12, 2005.

CHAPTER 8

Ackerman, A. "Ahead of the Game." *Consumer Goods Technology*, August 2003.

Barrett, L. "Ingersoll-Rand: Hidden Nuggets." *Baseline Magazine*, October 1, 2004.

Bednarz, A. "The Art of Balancing E-Commerce Processes." *Network World*, February 7, 2005.

Bennett, E., and A. M. Virzi. "Museum of Modern Art: Untitled Work." *Baseline Magazine*, December 1, 2004.

Cone, E. "Dressed for Success." *Baseline Magazine*, March 5, 2005.

Cone, E. "On Target." *Baseline Magazine*, March 1, 2004.

Cone, E. "VF Corp—Inching Along." Baseline Magazine, October, 2001.

Dunn, D. "Renovated Art Museum Relies on IT." *Information Week*, March 18, 2005.

Duvall, M. "RBC's Account Imbalance." *Baseline Magazine*, July 1, 2004.

Fogarty, K. "Under Armour: No Sweat." *Baseline Magazine*, September 1, 2004.

Gage, D. "FedEx: Personal Touch." *Baseline Magazine*, January 13, 2005.

Gage, D. "Stanford University: Hard Lesson." Baseline Magazine; June 8, 2004.

Haber, L. "Putting a Lid on CRM Costs with Self-Service." *ZdNet UK*, July 16, 2002.

"Ingersoll-Rand Selects OpenPages SOX Express for Sarbanes-Oxley Compliance." *www.openpages.com*, November 22, 2004.

Middlewood, M. "How Remington Self Serves Its Customers." *Mac News World*, June 22, 2004.

Navas, D. "Under Armour Gears Up for Triple Digit Growth." *Supply Chain Systems Magazine*, March 2003.

Rasmussen, E. "Executives' Guide to Call Center Excellence: Best Practices—FedEx: An Overnight Success Story." *www.destinationcrm.com*, February 2003.

"RBC Financial Group Automates Bank Statement Reconstruct Activities." *Information Builders Magazine*, Winter 2003.

Songini, M. L. "Supply Chain System Failures Hampered Army Units in Iraq." *Computerworld*, July 26, 2004.

"Supply Chains and the Army." *CNET News*, December 6, 2003.

Wailgum, T. "Big Mess on Campus." *CIO Magazine*, May 1, 2005.

Zuckerman, A. "Integrating Security Compliance into Supply Chain Management Software." *World Trade Magazine*, April 1, 2005.

www.army.mil, accessed April 2, 2005.

www.briggsandstratton.com, accessed April 2, 2005.

www.fedex.com, accessed April 3, 2005.

www.irco.com, accessed April 2, 2005.

www.lillysoftware.com, accessed April 2, 2005.

www.moma.org, accessed April 3, 2005.

www.oracle.com, accessed March 1, 2005.

www.peoplesoft.com, accessed March 1, 2005.

www.rbc.com, accessed February 22, 2005.

www.remington.com, accessed April 2, 2005.

www.stanford.edu, accessed March 1, 2005.

www.underarmour.com, accessed April 2, 2005.

www.vf.com, accessed April 3, 2005.

CHAPTER 9

"Aetna Promotes Healthy Living While Controlling Costs with DB2 Data Warehouse." *http://www-306.ibm.com*, accessed April 6, 2005.

Balint, K. "Fair Isaac Corporation Products Protect Consumers, Companies." *San Diego Union Tribune*, May 19, 2005.

Barr, G. "Route Guide." *Houston Business Journal*, February 21, 2005.

Barrett, L. "San Jose Sharks: On Thick Ice." *Baseline Magazine*, May 14, 2004.

Baum, D. "Elie Tahari Ltd. Unveils New End-User Reporting Framework." *Information Builders Magazine*, Fall 2003.

Carr, D. "The Aetna Cure." *Baseline Magazine*, February 1, 2005.

Claburn, T. "Software Aggregates Medical Knowledge in Hopes of Averting Misdiagnoses." *InformationWeek*, December 22, 2004.

DeGroot, P. "WEBFOCUS Draws the Picture for Ford's Warranty Business." *Information Builders Magazine*, April 24, 2005.

Dignan, L. "Waste Management: Waste Not." *Baseline Magazine*, August 1, 2004.

Duvall, M. "Zarlink: Chipping Away." *Baseline Magazine*, August 1, 2004.

Enrado, P. "Buyer's Guide to DSS: Isabel Healthcare." *Healthcare IT News*, July, 2004.

Fainaru, S. "Programmed for Success." *Washington Post*, May 9, 2004.

"Fair Isaac Provides Both Credit Scores and Protection from Fraud." *NewsTarget.com*, May 19, 2005.

Gorry, G. A., and M. S. Scott-Morton. "A Framework for Management Information Systems." *Sloan Management Review*, v. 13, no. 1, Fall 1971.

Hackathorn, R. D., and P. G. W. Keen, "Organizational Strategies for Personal Computing in Decision Support Systems." *MIS Quarterly*, September 1981.

Leahy, T. "The Link to Better Business Performance Management." *Business Finance*, December 2004.

Leon, M. "Enterprise Business Intelligence Standardization Gains Steam." *Biz Intelligence Pipeline*, May 20, 2004.

McCormick, J. "Elie Tahari: Ready to Wear." *Baseline Magazine*, September 1, 2004.

Mintzberg, H. *The Nature of Managerial Work*. New York: Harper & Row, 1973.

Ohlson, K. "Elie Tahari Discovers Business Intelligence." *ADT Magazine*, April 27, 2005.

Ploskina, B. "The Gestalt of Data." *eWeek*, June 18, 2001.

Simon, H. *The New Science of Management Decisions*, rev. ed, Englewood Cliffs, NJ: Prentice-Hall, 1977.

www.aetna.com, accessed April 6, 2005.

www.autonomy.com, accessed April 5, 2005.

www.cognos.com, accessed April 4, 2005.

www.e-iit.com/news-detail2.asp, accessed April 5, 2005.

www.elietahari.com, accessed April 5, 2005.

www.fairisaac.com, accessed May 21, 2005.

www.ford.com, accessed April 6, 2005.

www.informationbuilders.com, accessed April 5, 2005.

www.internationalscouting.com, accessed April 2, 2005.

www.isabelhealthcare.com, accessed April 5, 2005.

www.sjsharks.com, accessed April 2, 2005.

www.wm.com, accessed April 5, 2005.

www.zarlink.com, accessed April 4, 2005.

CHAPTER 10

"AFLAC and Primavera: A Partnership for Success." *www.primavera.com*, accessed April 29, 2005.

"AgriBeef Company: Beefing Up Financial Systems Pays Off." *www.peopletalkonline.com*, July 2004.

Anthony, S. "Mind over Merger." *Optimize*, February 2005.

Barrett, L. "AgriBeef: Cattle Drive." *Baseline Magazine*, November 1, 2004.

Cushing, K. "Procter & Gamble's HP Deal Shows Mega IT Outsourcing Is Still Tempting Some." *Computer Weekly*, April 23, 2003.

Dignan, L. "P&G–HP Pact: Slow and Steady." *Baseline Magazine*, July 29, 2004.

Duvall, M. "Canada Firearms: Armed Robbery." *Baseline Magazine*, July 1, 2004.

Frieden, T. "FBI May Scrap $170 Million Project." *CNN.com*, January 15, 2005.

"Government of Canada Caps Costs of Registry and Improves Gun Crime Measures." *Public Safety and Emergency Preparedness Canada* (*www.psepc-sppcc.gc.ca*), May 20, 2004.

Gross, L. "VA Computer Upgrade Is a Bust." *Advance for Health Information Professionals*, May 1, 2000.

"IT Infrastructure for 21st Century Crime." *www.fbi.gov*, April 2, 2004.

Kumagai, J. "Mission Impossible?" *IEEE Spectrum Online*, *www.spectrum.ieee.org*, accessed May 22, 2005.

Margasak, L. "VA Upgrade Fails to Reduce Delays." *Associated Press*, 2000.

McCormick, J. "Soldiering On." *Baseline Magazine*, April 4, 2004.

McDougall, P. "Procter & Gamble's Deal with HP Grows." *Outsourcing Pipeline*, August 16, 2004.

Nash, K. "AFLAC: Duck Soup." *Baseline Magazine*, September 1, 2004.

O'Donnell, A. "Worth the Effort: Tackling the New Project Management." *Insurance & Technology*, March 4, 2003.

Steinert-Threlkeld, T. "Vistakon: Far Sighted." *Baseline Magazine*, October 1, 2004.

Vasishtha, P. "Major Programs." *Government Computer News*, October 8, 2001.

www.aflac.com, accessed April 7, 2005.

www.agribeef.com, accessed March 11, 2005.

www.eds.com, accessed March 15, 2005.

www.hp.com, accessed April 6, 2005.

www.jnjvision.com, accessed April 9, 2005.

www.peoplesoft.com, accessed March 11, 2005.

www.pg.com, accessed April 6, 2005.

www.saic.com, accessed April 8, 2005.

www.sap.com, accessed April 9, 2005.

www.shl.com, accessed March 15, 2005.

www.va.gov, accessed April 5, 2005.

Index

Preamble

- We all live in the midst of a complex interacting flux of changing events and ideas which unrolls through time. We call it 'everyday life', both personal and professional. Within that flux we frequently see situations which cause us to think: 'Something needs to be done about this, it needs to be improved.' Think of these as 'problematical situations', avoiding the word 'problem' since this implies 'solution', which eliminates the problem for ever. Real life is more complex than that!

- Soft Systems Methodology (SSM) is an organized way of tackling perceived problematical (social) situations. It is action-oriented. It organizes thinking about such situations so that action to bring about improvement can be taken.

- The complexity of problematical situations in real life stems from the fact that not only are they never static, they also contain multiple interacting perceptions of 'reality'. This comes about because different people have different taken-as-given (and often unexamined) assumptions about the world. This causes them to see it in a particular way. One person's 'terrorism' is another's 'freedom fighting'; one person sees a prison in terms of punishment, another sees it as seeking rehabilitation. These people have different *worldviews*. Tackling problematical situations has

---

Learning for Action: A Short Definitive Account of Soft Systems Methodology and its use for Practitioners, Teachers and Students, Peter Checkland and John Poulter. ISBN 978-0-470-02554-3 ©2006 John Wiley & Sons, Inc.

to accept this, and has to pitch analysis at a level that allows worldviews to be surfaced and examined. For many people worldviews are relatively fixed; but they can change over time. Sometimes a dramatic event can change them very quickly.

- All problematical situations, as well as containing different worldviews, have a second important characteristic. They always contain people who are trying to act *purposefully*, with intention, not simply acting by instinct or randomly thrashing about – though there is always plenty of that too in human affairs.

- The previous two points – the existence of conflicting worldviews and the ubiquity of would-be purposeful action – lead the way to tackling problematical situations. They underpin the SSM approach, a process of inquiry which, through social learning, works its way to taking 'action to improve'. Its shape is as follows:

    1. Find out about both the problematical situation and the characteristics of the intervention to improve it: the issues, the prevailing culture and the disposition of power within the overall situation (its politics). Ways of doing these things are provided.
    2. From the finding out, decide upon some relevant purposeful activities, relevant that is to exploring the situation deeply, and remembering that the ultimate aim is to define and take 'action to improve'. Express these relevant purposeful activities as activity *models*, each made to encapsulate a declared worldview, the model being a cluster of linked activities which together make up a purposeful whole. (For example, one model could express in terms of activities the notion 'prison' as if it were only 'a punishment system', another could express it as 'a rehabilitation system'.) Such models never describe the real world, simply because they are based on one pure worldview. They are devices, or tools, to explore it in an organized

way. Techniques for building and using such models have been developed.

3. Use the models as a source of questions to ask of the real-world situation. This provides a coherent structure to a discussion or debate about both the situation and how it might be changed, a discussion which will surface worldviews and generate ideas for change and improvement.

4. In the course of the discussion, continually bring together the results of the 'finding out' in (1) and the ideas for change in (3). The purpose now is to find changes which are both arguably *desirable* (given these models) but also culturally *feasible* for these people in this particular situation with its particular history, culture and politics. This is a process of seeking accommodations between different worldviews. That is to say, it is a process of finding versions of the to-be-changed situation which different people with conflicting worldviews could nevertheless *live with*. (Don't expect the worldviews to go away, nor wish that they would. Clashing worldviews, always present in human affairs, stimulate energy and ideas for change.)

- The elements (1) to (4) above constitute a *learning cycle*. They have necessarily been described linearly here but in use there is much iteration within the cycle as learning occurs. It is never followed in the flat-footed way in which it has been laid out here for explanatory purposes. Also it is apparent that it is essentially a group process leading to *group learning*. It is best carried out by people in the problematical situation itself, not left to an outside 'expert', though knowledgeable people can facilitate the process.

- Taking action to improve a problematical situation will of course itself change that situation, so that the learning cycle could in principle begin again. In any case the changing flux of everyday life will itself bring new events and new ideas, so that no human situation could ever be rendered static. In this sense SSM's learning cycle can be seen as never-ending. It ultimately offers a way of continuously managing any ongoing human situation. It does this by helping understanding of complex situations, encouraging multiple perspectives to be taken into account, and bringing rigour to processes of analysis, debate and taking 'action to improve'.

The seven points made above are presented pictorially in the following figure. (A diagram summarizing SSM's process of inquiry is also presented at the end of Chapter 6. That one refers to various tools and techniques described in Chapter 2.)

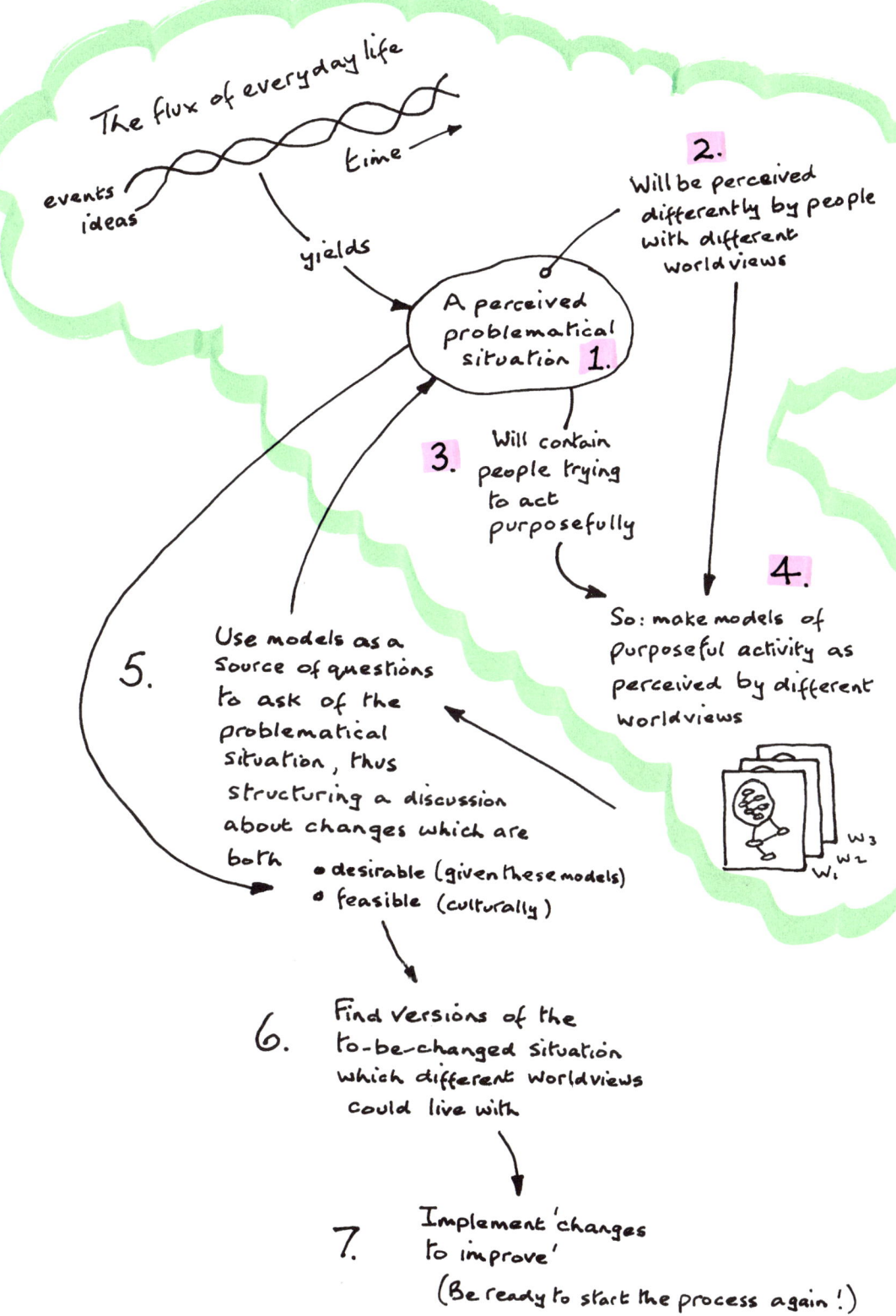

The flux of everyday life

events
ideas

time

yields

A perceived problematical situation **1.**

2. Will be perceived differently by people with different worldviews

3. Will contain people trying to act purposefully

4. So: make models of purposeful activity as perceived by different worldviews

W₃
W₂
W₁

5. Use models as a source of questions to ask of the problematical situation, thus structuring a discussion about changes which are both
• desirable (given these models)
• feasible (culturally)

6. Find versions of the to-be-changed situation which different worldviews could live with

7. Implement 'changes to improve'
(Be ready to start the process again!)

SSM's cycle of learning for action

1
A Skeleton Account of SSM

What is SSM?

The aim of the work which led to the development of Soft Systems Methodology (SSM) was to find a better way of dealing with a kind of situation we continually find ourselves facing in everyday life: a situation about which we have the feeling that 'something needs to be done about this'. We shall call such situations 'problematical', rather than describing them as 'problem situations', since they may not present a well-defined 'problem' to be 'solved' out of existence – everyday life is more complex than that! A company might feel that it needs to stimulate sales, perhaps by introducing a new product; or should they bid for the equity of a smaller rival? A university may feel that its student intake is too biased towards students from middle-class homes. What are the implications of changing that? A government may struggle to define legislation which would increase the feeling of security on the streets, given the threat of terrorism, without diminishing civil liberties. A local council may be receiving complaints that the delivery of its services is not sufficiently 'citizen-friendly'. What should it do? A head teacher may wonder how to decide whether to take on the responsibility for providing school meals (the school benefiting from any surplus generated) or to leave that function to the local education authority. An individual may develop a sense of unease about the future viability of the firm he or she works for, and wonder whether to look for a job elsewhere. All these are 'problematical situations'. They could be tackled in various ways: by appealing

Learning for Action: A Short Definitive Account of Soft Systems Methodology and its use for Practitioners, Teachers and Student, Peter Checkland and John Poulter. ISBN 978-0-470-02554-3
©2006 John Wiley & Sons, Inc.

to previous experience; intuitively; by randomly thrashing about (never a shortage of that in human situations); by responding emotionally; or they could be addressed by using SSM.

So what is it? It is an organized, flexible process for dealing with situations which someone sees as problematical, situations which call for action to be taken to improve them, to make them more acceptable, less full of tensions and unanswered questions. The 'process' referred to is an organized process of thinking your way to taking sensible 'action to improve' the situation; and, finally, it is a process based on a particular body of ideas, namely *systems* ideas.

That these ideas have proved themselves to be useful in dealing with the complexity of the social world is hardly surprising. Social situations are always complex due to multiple interactions between different elements in a problematical situation as a whole, and systems ideas are fundamentally concerned with the *interactions* between parts of a whole. So it is systems ideas which help to structure the thinking. (However, the way systems ideas are used within SSM is fundamentally different from the way they inform the various earlier systems approaches developed in the 1950s and 1960s, as we shall see below.)

In order to ensure that the previous two paragraphs are clear, we need to unpack them somewhat, and say a little more about the crucial elements within them, if this chapter is to fulfil its aim of presenting a broad-brush account of SSM as a whole. Four elements in the paragraphs above will be expanded: 'everyday life and problematical situations'; 'tackling such situations'; a 'flexible process', and 'the use of systems ideas'.

Everyday Life and Problematical Situations

As members of the human tribe we experience everyday life as being quite exceptionally complex. We feel ourselves to be carried along in an onrushing turbulent stream, a flux of happenings, ideas, emotions, actions, all mediated through the slippery agency of language, all continually changing. Our response to our immersion in this stream is not simply to experience it. Beyond that, we have an innate desire to try to see it, if we can, as *meaningful*. We *attribute* meaning to it – the ability to do this being one of the characteristics which marks us out as human. Part of this meaning attribution is to see chunks of the ongoing flux as 'situations'. Nothing is intrinsically 'a situation'; it is our perceptions which create them as such, and in doing that we know that they are not static; their boundaries and their content will change over time. Some of the situations we perceive, because they affect us in some way, cause us to feel a need to tackle them, to do something about them, to improve them.

Tackling Problematical Situations

As we tackle a situation we see as problematical, we are intervening in order to take action intended to bring about improvement. In order to do that sensibly we need to have a clear idea of what it is we are intervening in. This means having a clear view of the nature of the flux which constitutes everyday life. We have already described it as complex, changing, and having multiple strands: events, ideas, emotions, actions. To this we can add an answer to the question: What then happens when we intervene in a part of the flux seen as a problematical situation?

When we interact with real-world situations we *make judgements about them*: are they 'good' or 'bad', 'acceptable' or 'unacceptable', 'permanent' or 'transient'? Now, to make any judgement we have to appeal to some criteria or standards, these being the characteristics which define 'good' or 'bad' etc. for us. For example, an 'eco-warrior' would judge any economic activity 'good' only if it met the environmentalists' criteria for 'good', namely 'environmentally friendly' and 'sustainable'. A 'capitalist' would see an economic activity as 'good' if it were 'profitable'. And where do such criteria come from? They will be formed partially by our genetic inheritance from our parents – the kind of person we are innately – and, most significantly, from our previous experience of the world. Over time these criteria and the interpretations they lead to will tend to firm up into a relatively stable outlook *through which* we then perceive the world. We develop 'worldviews', built-in tendencies to see the world in a particular way. It is different worldviews which make one person 'liberal', another 'reactionary'. Worldviews cause one observer's 'terrorism' to be another's 'freedom fighting'. Such worldviews are relatively stable but can change over time. Thus a paranoid person whose worldview is 'this hostile world owes me a living' might become a more integrated member of society as a result of experiencing love and generosity.

This concept of worldview (the German *Weltanschauung* being the best technical word for it) is the most important concept in understanding the complexity of human situations, and indeed, the nature and form of SSM.

A Flexible Process

It is obvious from the argument so far that any approach able to deal with the changing complexity of real life will have to be flexible. It could never be reduced to a sequence of steps, which might be handed over to an intelligently programmed robot. It needs to be flexible enough to cope with the fact that every situation involving human beings is unique. The human world is one in which nothing ever happens twice, not in *exactly* the same way. This means that an approach to problematical human situations has to be a methodology rather than a method, or technique. A methodology, as the word indicates, is a logos of method; that is to say it is a set of ongoing principles which can be adapted for use in a way which suits the specific nature of each situation in which it is used. SSM provides a set of principles which can be both adopted and adapted for use in any real situation in which people are intent on taking action to improve it.

The Use of Systems Ideas

As stated above, systems ideas concern interaction between parts which make up a whole; also, the complexity of real situations is always to a large extent due to the many interactions between different elements in human situations. So it is not surprising that systems ideas have some relevance to dealing with real-world complexity (though they are only very rarely useful in *describing* that complexity).

The core systems idea or concept is that of an adaptive whole (a 'system') which can survive through time by adapting to changes in its environment. The concept is illustrated in Figure 1.1. A system S receives shocks from

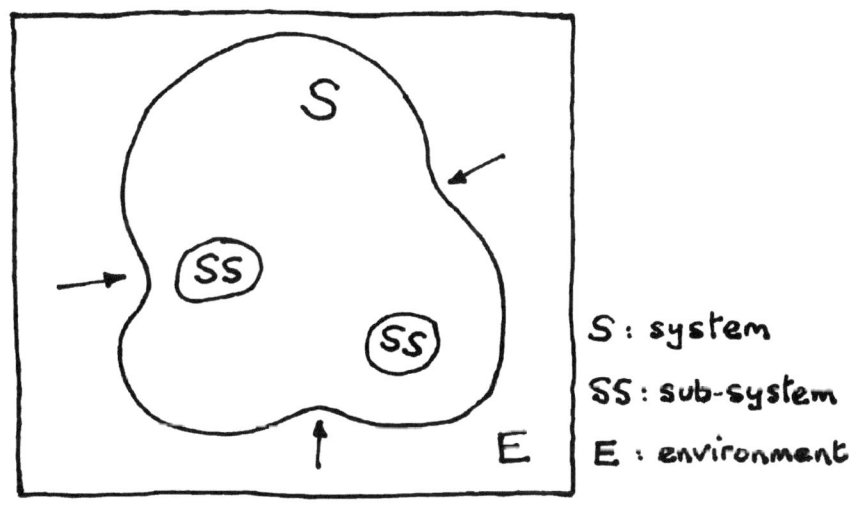

Survival of S through time requires:

o communication processes
o control processes
o structure in layers
o emergent properties of S as a whole

Figure 1.1 The core systems concept: an adaptive whole

its changing environment E. If it is to survive it requires *communication processes* (to know what is going on) and *control processes* (possible adaptive responses to the shocks). Also, the system may contain sub-systems SS, or may itself be seen by a different observer as only a sub-system of some wider system. The idea of a *layered structure* is thus fundamental in systems thinking. Finally, what is said to be a system must have some properties as a single whole, so-called *emergent properties*. (Thus the parts of a bicycle, when assembled correctly, and only then, produce a whole which has the emergent property of being a vehicle, the concept 'vehicle' being meaningful only in relation to the whole.) These four italicized phrases represent the core of systems thinking. So how can it be used here?

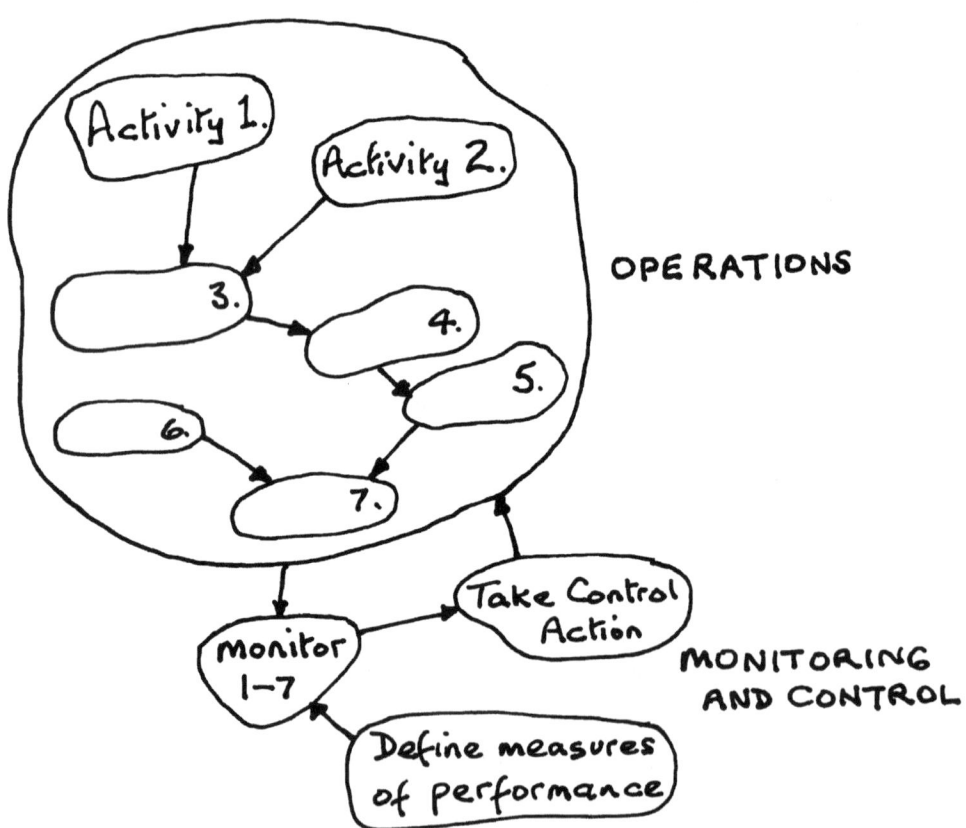

Figure 1.2 The general form of a purposeful activity model

The relevance of this kind of thinking to SSM emerged when it was realized that every single real-world problematical situation, whether in a small firm making wheelbarrows, a multi-national oil company, or in the National Health Service (which employs more than a million people) has one characteristic in common. All such situations contain people trying to act *purposefully*, not simply acting by instinct or splashing about at random. From this observation comes the key idea of *treating purposeful action as a system*. A way of representing purposeful action as a system, i.e. an adaptive whole (in line with Figure 1.1) was invented. Figure 1.2 shows its general form.

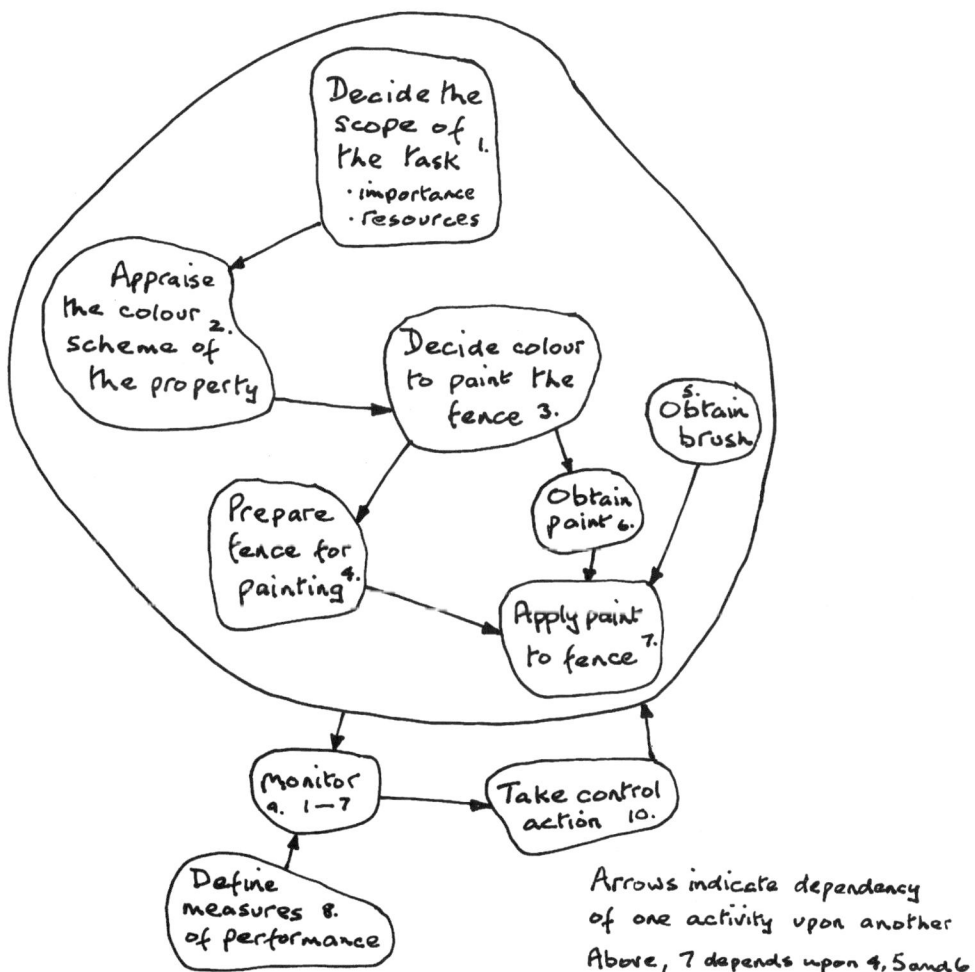

Figure 1.3 A simple example of an activity model: a system to paint the garden fence by hand painting

A logically linked set of activities constitute a whole – its emergent property being its purposefulness. The activities concerned with achieving the purpose (the operations) are monitored against defined measures of performance so that adaptive control action (to make changes) can be taken if necessary.

Figure 1.3 shows a trivial example to illustrate the concept. With regard to Figure 1.2, the 'measure of performance' might be the degree to which fence painting enhances the appearance of the property or, perhaps, 'good' or 'bad' might be defined according to whether or not the neighbours complain about it. This model, then, is a 'purposeful activity model'.

The model in Figure 1.3 is essentially within the worldview of whoever would do the fence painting. It is an instrumental model which spells out what is entailed in painting a garden fence. It could express the householder's worldview: 'I can do useful DIY jobs to improve my property.' However, if painting the fence were an issue in a real situation other worldviews would be relevant, even in an example as trivial as this – for example, in this case, those of the neighbours or the partner of the fence-painter. In general there will always be a number of worldviews which could be taken into account leading to a number of relevant models.

Suppose, for example, you were carrying out an SSM study of the future of the Olympic Games. For anything as complex as this global phenomenon it is obvious that it could be looked at from the perspective of worldviews attributed to the International Olympic Committee, the host country, the host city, the athletes, the athletes' coaches, the spectators, hot dog sellers, commercial sponsors, those responsible for security, television companies, a terrorist group seeking publicity for their cause, etc. This list could go on and on; there could never be a single model relevant to all these different interests.

An important consequence flows from this: these purposeful activity models *can never be descriptions* of (part of) the real world. Each of them expresses *one way of looking at and thinking about* the real situation, and there will be multiple possibilities. So how can such models be made useful? The answer is to see them as *devices* (intellectual devices) which are a source of *good questions to ask about the real situation*, enabling it to be explored richly. For example, we could focus on the differences between a model and the situation, and ask whether we would like activity in the situation to be more, or less, like that in the model. Such questioning organizes and structures a discussion/debate about the real-world situation, the purpose of that discussion being to surface different worldviews and to seek possible ways of changing the problematical situation for the better. This means finding an accommodation, that is to say a version of the situation which different people with different worldviews could nevertheless live with. Given the different worldviews which will always be present in any human situation, this means finding possible changes which meet two criteria simultaneously. They must be arguably *desirable*, given the outcomes of using the models to question the real situation, but must also be culturally *feasible* for these particular people in this particular situation with its unique history and the unique narrative which its participants will have constructed over time in order to make sense of their experience. Figure 1.4 illustrates this.

In summary, then, we have:

- a problematical real-world situation seen as calling for action to improve it;
- models of purposeful activity *relevant* to this situation (not describing it);
- a process of using the models as devices to explore the situation;
- a structured debate about desirable and feasible change.

This gives the bare bones of the process of SSM, whose shape can now be described.

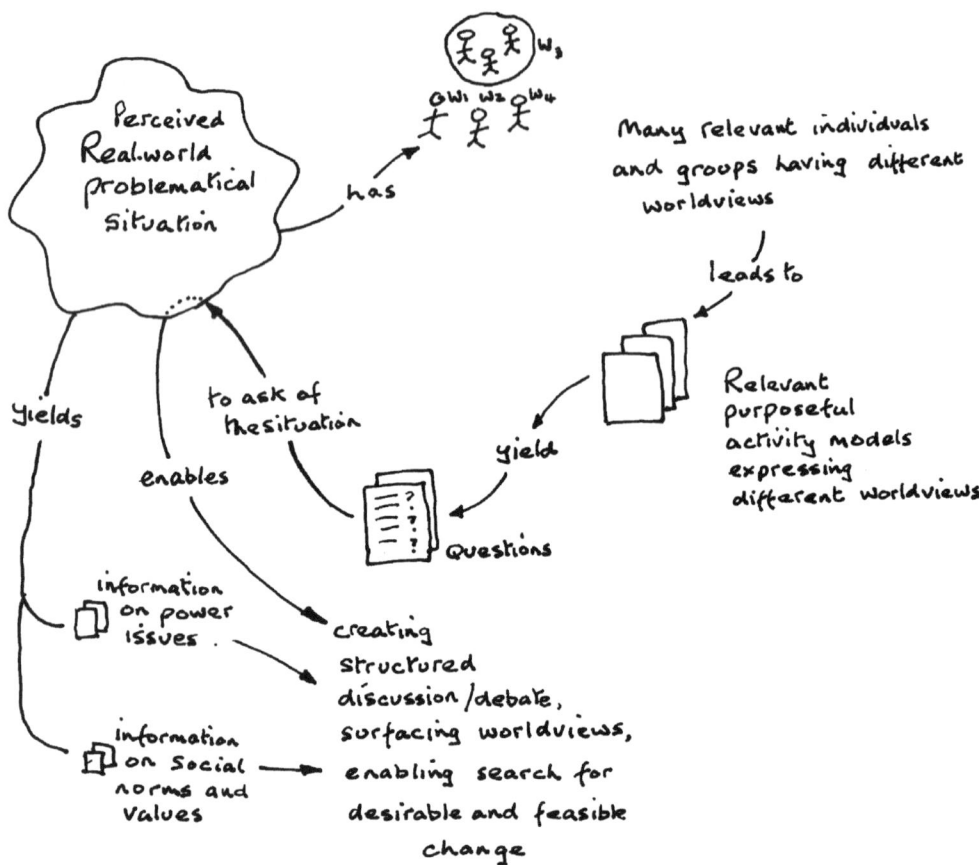

Figure 1.4 SSM's basic process

What is the SSM Process?

The SSM process takes the form of a cycle. It is, properly used, a cycle of learning which goes from finding out about a problematical situation to defining/taking action to improve it. The learning which takes place is social learning for the group undertaking the study, though each individual's learning will be, to a greater or lesser extent, personal to them, given their different experiences of the world, and hence the different worldviews which they will bring to the study. Taking action as a result of the study will of course change the starting situation into a new situation, so that in principle the cycle could begin again (a relevant system then being 'a system to make

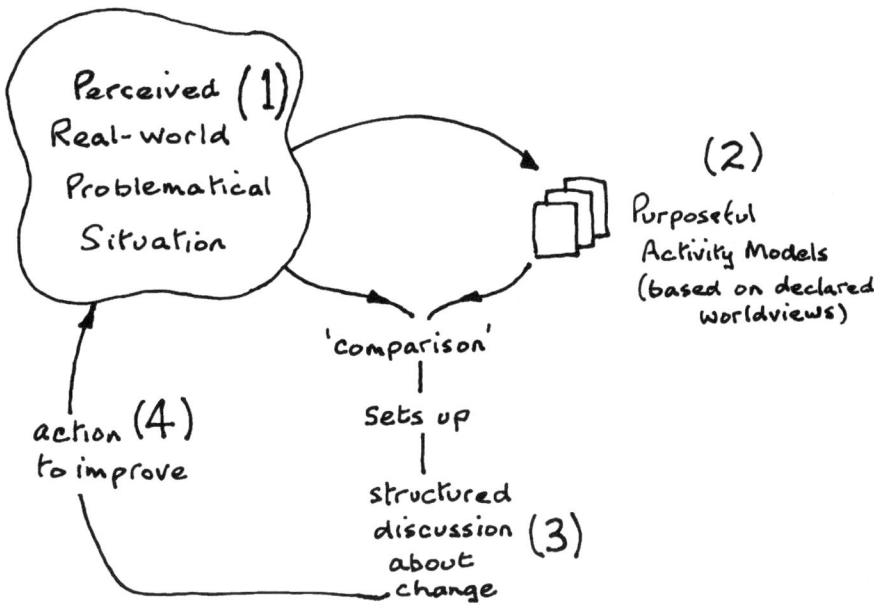

Figure 1.5 The iconic representation of SSM's learning cycle

these changes'). SSM is thus not only a methodology for a specially set-up study or project; it is, more generally, a way of managing any real-world purposeful activity in an ongoing sense.

The SSM cycle is shown in Figure 1.5, which eventually emerged as its classic representation. It contains four different kinds of activity:

1. Finding out about the initial situation which is seen as problematical.
2. Making some purposeful activity models judged to be relevant to the situation; each model, as an intellectual device, being built on the basis of a particular pure worldview.
3. Using the models to question the real situation. This brings structure to a discussion about the situation, the aim of the discussion being to find changes which are both arguably desirable and also culturally feasible in this particular situation.
4. Define/take the action to improve the situation. Since the learning cycle is in principle never-ending it is an arbitrary distinction as to whether the end of a study is taken to be defining the action or actually carrying

it out. Some studies will be ended after defining the action, some after implementing it.

This description of the cycle as activities (1) to (4) may give a false impression that we are describing a sequence of steps. Not so. Although virtually all investigations will be initiated by finding out about the problematical situation, once SSM is being used, activity will go on simultaneously in more than one of the 'steps'. For example, starting the organized discussion about the situation (3) will normally lead not only to further new finding out (1), perhaps focused on aspects previously ignored, but also to further new choices of 'relevant' systems to model. In real life, an investigation which sets out narrowly to improve, say, aspects of product distribution in a manufacturing company's distribution department, may well later sweep in issues concerning, perhaps, communications between production and marketing departments. Figure 1.6 illustrates a typical pattern of activity of the kind which emerges as an investigation digs deeper.

Figure 1.6 shows an on-going 'finding out' activity, three bursts of model building, discussion fed by both the models and the finding out, which itself leads to more finding out and more modelling. The final (fourth) burst of modelling shown here as an example follows from defining the 'action to improve' and would consist of purposeful activity models relevant to carrying out the action agreed.

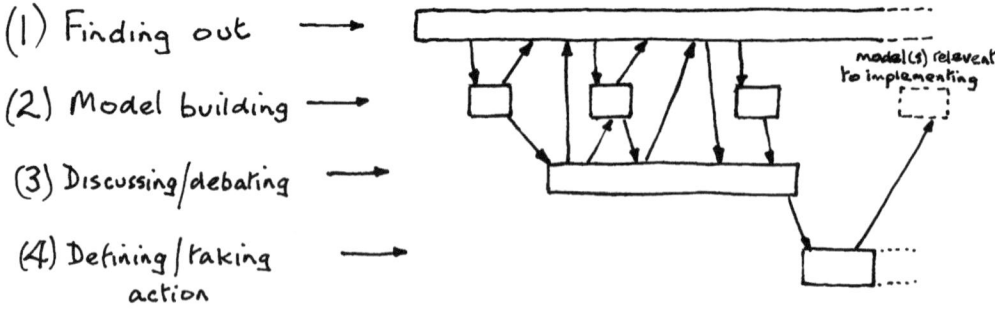

Figure 1.6 A typical pattern of activity during an SSM investigation

Finally, in describing the SSM cycle, we could add (though this is really a point from the end of this book) that as users of SSM become more sophisticated they treat Figure 1.5 not at all as a prescription to be followed, but as a model to make sense of their experience as they mentally negotiate their way through the problematical situation.

What Can SSM be Used for?

The application area for SSM is very broad. This is not due to megalo-mania on the authors' part. Rather it stems from the wide applicability of two key ideas behind SSM. One of these is to create a process of *learning your way* through problematical situations to 'action to improve' – a very general concept indeed. The other is the idea that you can make sure this learning is organized and structured by using, as a source of questions to ask in the real situation, models (systems models) of purposeful activity. This is because every real-world situation contains people trying to act pur-posefully, intentionally. It is the sheer generality of purposeful action – the core of being human – that makes the area in which SSM can be used so huge.

In Part Two, the stories of SSM use come from all sizes of company from small firms to large corporations, from organizations in both private and public sectors, including the National Health Service. Chapter 4 describes uses of SSM in the world of information systems and information tech-nology, where it is much used. This derives from the fact that for any purposeful activity model (Figure 1.3 being a noddy example) you can ask of each activity: What information would support doing this activity? And what information would be generated by doing it? Since information is what you get when you attribute meaning to data in a particular context, and meaning attribution depends upon worldview, SSM's strong emphasis on worldview explains its relevance to this field.

In summary, SSM can be used in any human situation which entails thinking about acting purposefully, and is especially useful in any situation in which it is helpful to lift the level of discussion from that of everyday opinions and dogma to that level at which you are asking: What taken-as-given worldview lies behind these assertions of opinion?

Is SSM Mature?

Obviously it is never possible to claim that the development of any approach to human inquiry is 'finished', though some features of any such process may become so taken-as-given as to appear permanent. For example, in the inquiry process of natural science, if you are testing a new drug you give some patients the drug while others receive a placebo. The difference between the group ingesting the drug and the so-called 'control' group taking the placebo tells you what effects the drug produces (given a statistically significant sample size). This pattern would seem to be a permanent feature of scientific experiment. In applied social science, where SSM sits, the situation is less definite. Nevertheless, after hundreds of studies the core processes of SSM do now appear to be well-established, though the application area continues to expand. In the early days each significant study was likely to cause some rethinking of the process itself; but such changes became increasingly rare over the 30-year development period. We now regard it as a mature process.

The most recent addition to the literature about its development describes the use of SSM both in relation to the perceived *content* of the situation in question – SSM (c) – and in relation to the *process* of carrying out the inquiry itself – SSM (p) – (described in Chapter 2). This is in a paper published in 2006. But this is a case of the literature lagging behind practice, as these twin uses of SSM have been recognized and exploited by those developing the approach since the early 1980s.

So SSM is now considered mature enough to justify writing this book.

How was SSM Created?

The classic way of doing research comes from natural science: set up a hypothesis and then test it experimentally. It is not easy to transfer this model of research to the gloriously rich social and human arena, though strenuous efforts to do that have been made over many years. SSM was developed using an alternative model of research, one more suitable for social research at the level of a situation, group or organization, namely 'action research'. In this kind of research you accept the great difficulty of 'scientific' experimental work in human situations, since each human situation is not only unique, but changes through time and exhibits multiple conflicting worldviews. Hence the pattern for the action researcher is to enter a human situation, *take part* in its activity, and use that experience as the research object. In order to do that, to do more than simply return from the research with a one-off story to tell, it is necessary to declare in advance the intellectual framework you, the researcher, will use to try to make sense of the experience gained. Given such an explicit framework, you can then describe the research experience in the well-defined language of the framework. This makes it possible for anyone outside the work to 'recover' it, to see exactly what was done and how the conclusions were reached. This 'recoverability' requirement is obviously not as strong as the 'repeatability' criterion for scientific findings within natural science. But then, human situations are very much more complex than the phenomena studied in physics and chemistry labs! It is the declared framework and the recoverability criterion which clearly separate accounts of well-organized action research from novel writing – which, alas, too much published social research resembles.

In the action research which produced SSM the initial declared framework was the Systems Engineering approach developed by the Bell Telephone Company from their own case histories. Systems Engineering (SE) is a process of naming a 'system' (assumed to be some complex object which exists or could exist in the real world), defining its objectives, and then using an array of techniques developed in the 1950s and 1960s to 'engineer' the system to meet its objectives. This framework was rapidly found to be poverty-stricken when faced with the complexity of human situations. It was too thin, not rich enough to deal with fizzing social complexity.

The SE framework was modified (and enriched) in the light of and in direct response to real-life experiences. Eventually, we had in our hands an adequately rich framework, but it was far removed from the starting point in SE. It became known as Soft Systems Methodology. It then took some time for even its pioneers to realize just how radical the shift had been from SE to SSM. Having introduced the notion of 'worldview' – essential in dealing with human social complexity – we were thereafter thinking of systems models not as descriptions of something in the real world but simply as devices (based on worldview) to organize a debate about 'change to bring about improvement'. That was the key step in finding our way to SSM. This important shift in thinking is not abstruse, but it turns out to be very difficult for many people to grasp, simply because everyone is so used to the casual everyday-language use of the word 'system'. In ordinary talk we constantly refer to complex chunks of the everyday world as systems, even though they do not come close to meeting the requirements of that concept. We speak of 'the education system', 'health-care systems', 'the prison system', etc. using the word 'system' simply to indicate a chunk of reality which seems to be very complex but is, in some vague sense, a whole, something which might be better 'engineered'. Figure 1.7 gives a visual indication of the shift in thinking as SE was transformed into SSM.

At the starting point (SE) in Figure 1.7 (which ignores worldviews), 'systems' are names for things in the world which, given precise objectives, can be engineered to achieve them. At the end point (which accepts different world-

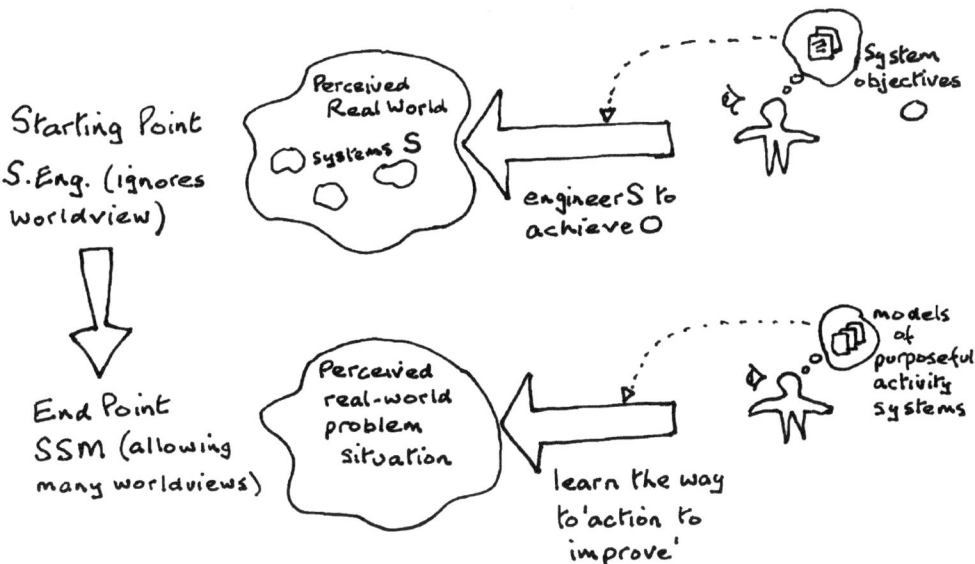

Figure 1.7 The shift in thinking entailed in developing SSM

views), 'systems' are devices used in a learning process to define desirable and feasible 'action to improve'.

Once the end point in Figure 1.7 was reached, and the SSM framework had been established, it was further developed, modified and honed in a few hundred new experiences. Out of this came a model which captures all of these developmental experiences. The model, known as the LUMAS model, is shown in Figure 1.8. (It is in fact a generic model for making sense of any real-world application of any *methodology*, remembering that that word covers a set of principles which need to be embodied in an application tailored to meet the unique features of a particular situation.)

LUMAS stands for Learning for a User by a Methodology-informed Approach to a Situation. In order to 'read' this model, start from the user (U) in the centre. He or she, perceiving a problem situation (S) and appreciating the methodology (M), tailors the latter to the former to produce the specific approach (A) to be used in this situation (S). This not only produces an improved situation but also yields learning (L). This will change the user,

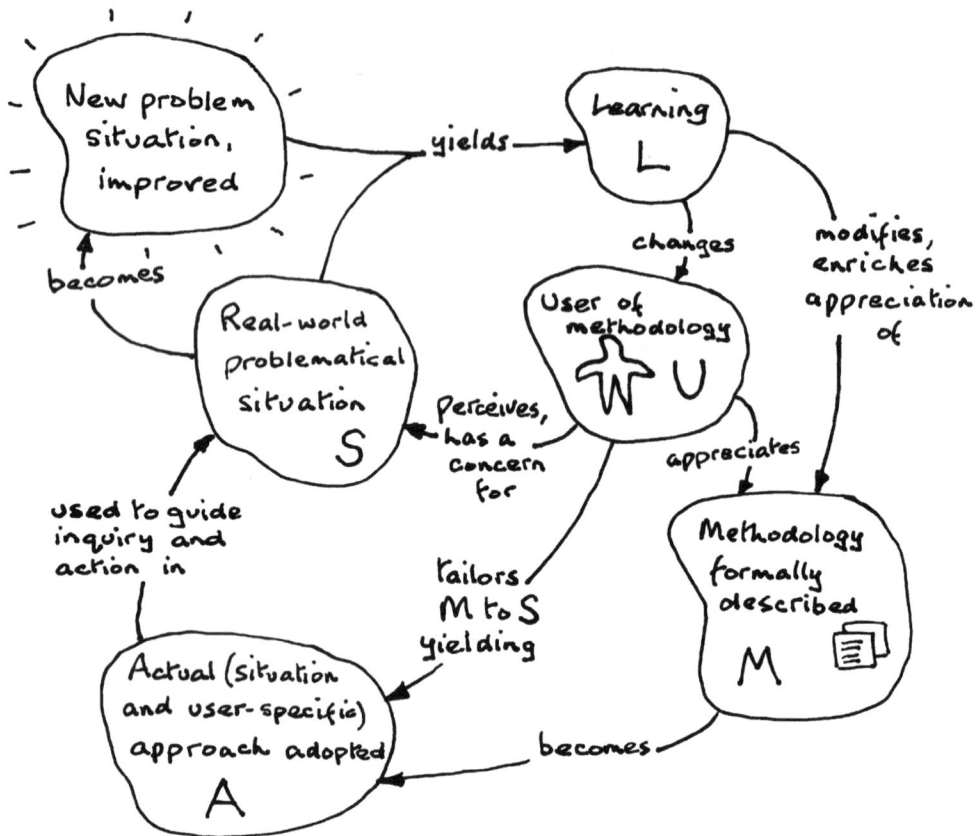

Figure 1.8 The LUMAS model – Learning for a User by a Methodologically-informed Approach to a Situation

who has gained this experience, and may also modify or enrich appreciation of the methodology. Every use of SSM can in principle be described in the language of this model. It is the gradually diminishing activity, over the years, of development occurring along the arrow which links L and M that makes it legitimate to describe SSM as mature.

How Does SSM Differ from Other Systems Approaches?

As described above, changes had to be made to Systems Engineering when it proved too blunt an instrument to deal with the complexity of human situations. Those changes explain SSM's difference from the other systems approaches developed in the 1950s and 1960s. SE is an archetypal example of what is now known as 'hard' systems thinking. Its belief is: the world contains interacting systems. They can be 'engineered' to achieve their objectives. This is the stance not only of SE; this thinking also underpins classic Operational Research, RAND Corporation 'systems analysis', the Viable System Model, early applications of System Dynamics and the original forms of computer systems analysis. None of these approaches pays attention to the existence of conflicting worldviews, something which characterizes all social interactions. In order to incorporate the concept of worldview into the approach being developed, it was necessary to abandon the idea that the world is a set of systems. In SSM the (social) world is taken to be very

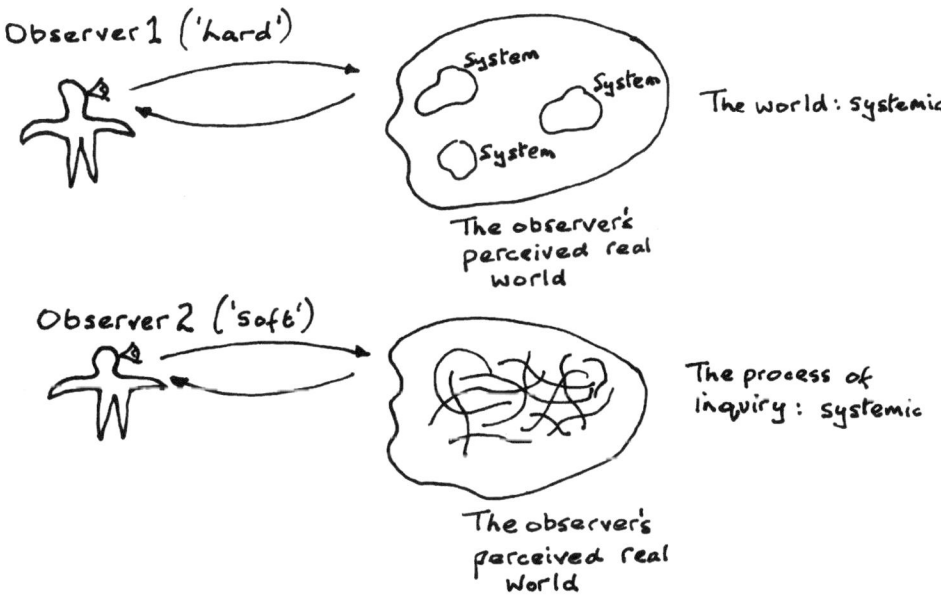

Observer 1 'I spy systems which I can engineer.'

Observer 2 'I spy complexity and confusion; but I can organize exploration of it as a learning system.'

Figure 1.9 The 'hard' and 'soft' systems stances

complex, problematical, mysterious, characterized by clashes of worldview. It is continually being created and recreated by people thinking, talking and taking action. However, our coping with it, our process of inquiry into it, can itself be organized as a learning *system*. So the notion of systemicity ('systemness') appears in the process of inquiry into the world, rather than in the world itself. This shift created 'soft' as opposed to 'hard' systems thinking, the different stances adopted by the two being shown in Figure 1.9, itself another version of Figure 1.7.

This brings us to the end of a skeletal account of SSM as a whole. The next chapter expands on this, describing the techniques used in the cyclic process in detail. Meanwhile it seems worthwhile to try to summarize the broad account of SSM in a couple of sentences.

> SSM is an action-oriented process of inquiry into problematical situations in the everyday world; users learn their way from finding out about the situation to defining/taking action to improve it. The learning emerges via an organized process in which the real situation is explored, using as intellectual devices – which serve to provide structure to discussion – models of purposeful activity built to encapsulate pure, stated worldviews.

2
A Fleshed-out Account of SSM

Introduction

The previous chapter has answered the basic question about SSM, namely: What is it? And it has provided some context concerning its development, its application area and its crucial difference from the earlier systems approaches from the 1950s and 1960s. In this chapter the focus is on 'how' rather than 'what': How exactly does the user move through the learning cycle of SSM, shown in Figure 1.5, in order to define useful change? Which techniques for finding out, modelling and using models to question the real situation have shown themselves robust enough to survive in many different circumstances, so that they have become part of the classic approach?

The account here will follow the four basic activities of the broad-brush account (finding out, modelling, using the models to structure debate, and defining/taking action), with the usual reminder that activity in any project using SSM will reflect the kind of pattern shown in Figure 1.6 rather than a stately linear progress.

The SSM Learning Cycle: Finding Out

Four ways of finding out about a problematical situation have survived many tests and become a normal part of using SSM. In the language of SSM they

Learning for Action: A Short Definitive Account of Soft Systems Methodology and its use for Practitioners, Teachers and Student, Peter Checkland and John Poulter. ISBN 978-0-470-02554-3
©2006 John Wiley & Sons, Inc.

are known as 'making Rich Pictures' and carrying out three kinds of inquiry, known as 'Analyses One, Two and Three'. These focus, respectively, on the intervention itself, a social analysis (What kind of 'culture' is this?) and a political analysis (What is the disposition of power here?). They will be described in turn.

(Readers anxious to reach the stories of SSM use might turn to the first few case histories described in Part Two, but all the accounts there use the terms and language carefully defined here, so a little patience might well be worthwhile!)

Making Rich Pictures

Entering a real situation in order first to understand it and then to begin to change it in the direction of 'improvement' calls for a particular frame of mind in the user of SSM. On the one hand the enquirer needs to be sponge-like, soaking up as much as possible of what the situation presents to someone who may be initially an outsider. On the other hand, although holding back from imposing a favoured pattern on the first impressions, the enquirer needs to have in mind a range of 'prompts' which will ensure that a wide range of aspects are looked at. Initially two dense and cogent questions were used as a prompt:

- What resources are deployed in what operational processes under what planning procedures within what structures, in what environments and wider systems, by whom?
- How is resource deployment monitored and controlled?

Certainly, if you can answer these questions you know quite a lot about the situation addressed. But these questions did not survive as a formal part of SSM. (The problem with them is that when they were formulated, in the early days of SSM development, the thinking of the pioneers had not sufficiently divorced itself from thinking of the world as a set of systems.

The questions imply intervention in some real-world system – hence the references to 'wider systems' and to monitoring and control – rather than the intervention being addressed to *a situation*.) The questions would no doubt have been changed eventually as the true nature of SSM was realized. However, what happened instead was that the questions were dropped because the phrase 'rich picture' quickly moved from being a metaphor to being a literal description of an account of the situation *as a picture*.

The rationale behind this was as follows. The complexity of human situations is always one of multiple interacting relationships. A picture is a good way to show relationships; in fact it is a much better medium for that purpose than linear prose. Hence as knowledge of a situation was assembled – by talking to people, by conducting more formal interviews, by attending meetings, by reading documents, etc. – it became normal to begin to draw simple pictures of the situation. These became richer as inquiry proceeded, and so such pictures are never finished in any ultimate sense. But they were found invaluable for expressing crucial relationships in the situation and, most importantly, for providing something which could be tabled as a basis for discussion. Users would say: 'This is how we are seeing your situation. Could we talk you through it so that you can comment on it and draw attention to anything you see as errors or omissions?'

In making a Rich Picture the aim is to capture, informally, the main entities, structures and viewpoints in the situation, the processes going on, the current recognized issues and any potential ones.

Here is a real-world problematical situation described in a paragraph of prose:

> The newly appointed headteacher of an 11s-to-18s school, which
> has overspent its budget in the last year or two, finds herself, in
> her first term, facing an issue concerning the provision of school
> meals. Currently these are provided by the county education authority

through their catering services company, the contract being renewed annually. A member of that company who is leaving to set up her own catering company urges the headteacher to make a contract with her instead of the county, suggesting the school could save money on this. Some staff members agree with this, others want to stick with the status quo. Some parents, alerted by a national debate about school meals, want more nutritious meals as long as they don't cost more. Pupils say: 'We like burgers and chips.' The school governors are discussing this issue; the Chairman, himself MD of a catering company, is urging the headteacher to be entrepreneurial and to take on responsibility for the provision of school meals, believing this could be profitable for the school.

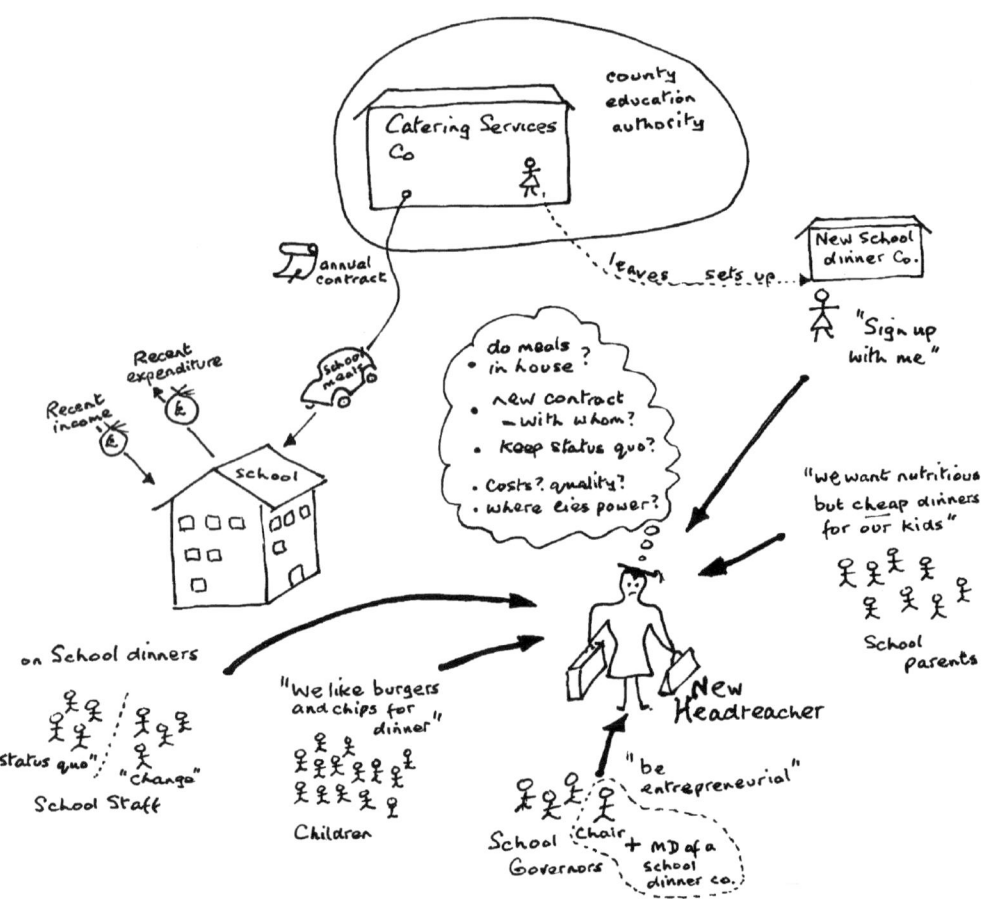

Figure 2.1 A Rich Picture of the situation described in the text

Figure 2.1 represents this situation in a Rich Picture. Our point is that this picture is a more useful piece of paper than the prose account. It could lead to a better-than-usual level of discussion because not only can it be taken in as a whole, but also it displays the multiple *relationships* which the headteacher has to manage, not just immediately, but through time. That is the power of such pictures, though we have to remember that however rich they are they could be richer, and that such pictures record a snapshot of a situation which will itself not remain static for very long. Wise practitioners continually produce such pictures as an aid to thinking. They become a normal way of capturing impressions and insights.

Carrying Out Analysis One (the Intervention Itself)

Whenever SSM is used to try and improve a problematical situation three elements – the methodology, the use of the methodology by a practitioner and the situation – are brought together in a particular relationship, namely that shown in Figure 2.2. The practitioner will adapt the principles and

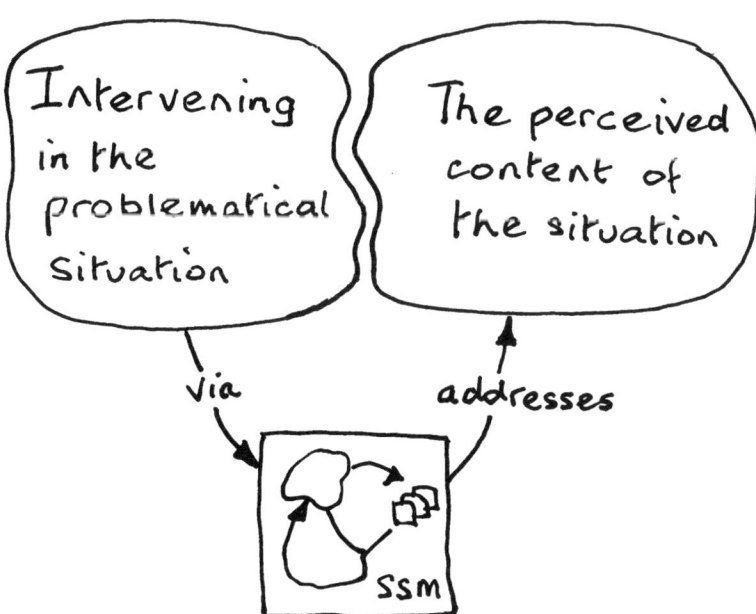

Figure 2.2   The three elements in any SSM investigation

techniques of the methodology to organize the task of addressing and inter-vening in the situation, aiming at taking action to improve it. In developing SSM, this process was organized in a sequence of real situations, and it was quickly found useful to think about Figure 2.2 in a particular way. Three key roles were always present:

1. There was some person (or group of persons) who had *caused the inter-vention to happen*, someone without whom there would not be an inves-tigation at all – this was the role 'client'.
2. There was some person (or group of persons) who were *conducting the investigation* – this was the role 'practitioner'.
3. Most importantly, whoever was in the practitioner role could choose, and list, a number of people who could be regarded as being *concerned about or affected by the situation and the outcome* of the effort to improve it – this was the role 'owner of the issue(s) addressed'.

It is important to see why these are named as 'roles' rather than particular people. It is because one person (or group) might be in more than one role. For example, if the headteacher in the Rich Picture (Figure 2.1) were to herself carry out an SSM-based study of her complex situation, she would not only be both 'client' and 'practitioner', she would also be one of the people in the list of 'issue owners' who care about the outcome. Some-times a manager who causes an intervention to take place delegates detailed involvement in it to others, and so is only in the role 'client'. In this case the person(s) in the 'practitioner' role needs to take steps to ensure that the 'client' is kept informed about the course of the intervention so that the outcome when it emerges does not come as a big surprise. In every case the 'practitioner' needs to make sure that the resources available to carry out the investigation are in line with its ambition. Don't undertake a study of 'the future of the A-level examination in British education' if you have only got one man and a boy to work on it between now and next Thursday.

SSM's 'Analysis One', then, consists of thinking about the situation displayed in Figure 2.2 in the way shown in Figure 2.3, asking: Who are in the roles 'client' and 'practitioner'? and Who could usefully be included in the list of 'issue owner'?

Much learning came out of the simple thinking which led to this 'Analysis One'. For example, it was always useful to think about the client's aspirations for the intervention. They should always be taken seriously but should not be the sole focus of the work done. Thus, the person(s) in the 'client' role should be in the list of possible 'issue owners' but should very definitely not be the only one in the list. In this connection it was interesting to hear a

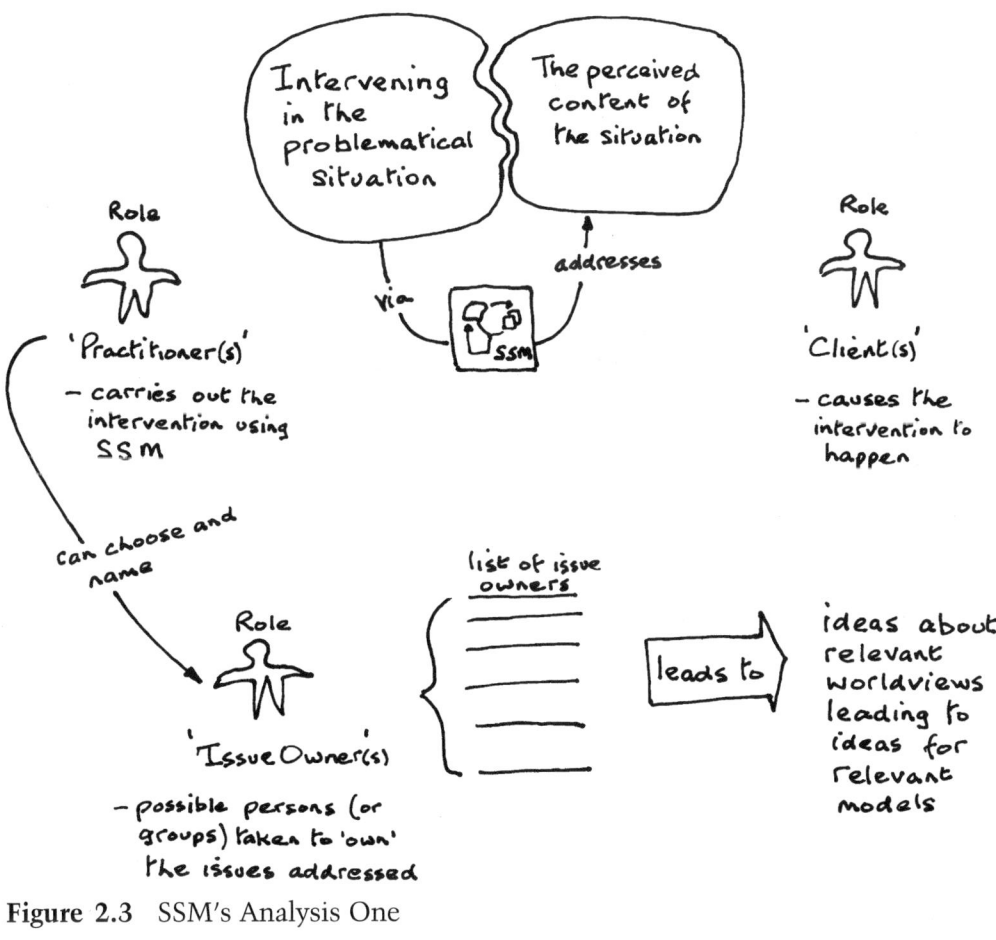

Figure 2.3   SSM's Analysis One

senior manager from the RAND Corporation declare, some years ago, 'The RAND analyst places his or her expertise at the disposal of a real-world decision-taker who has to be a legitimate holder of power.' In the language of Figure 2.3 this was to declare that for RAND the client *is* the issue owner, full stop. This cuts off all the richness which comes from the practitioner compiling a list of persons or groups who *could be taken to be* issue owners; for it is that list which introduces multiple worldviews. They in turn open up the chance of a richness of learning at a deep level for all involved in the intervention, leading, perhaps, to major change. The RAND manager's statement would define the practitioner as only a servant to the legitimately powerful. In the situation shown in Figure 2.1, for example, 'issue owners' might include: the headteacher; the school governors, staff and pupils; parents; the county education authority and their catering services company; other catering companies, etc. The many worldviews from such a list give a chance that the richness of the inquiry can cope with the complexity of the real situation. They suggest ideas for 'relevant' activity models, ones likely to be insightful.

Some final learning, which is important in understanding SSM as a whole, comes from the fact that the person(s) in the 'practitioner' role can include *themselves* in the list of possible 'issue owners'. Normally SSM is thought of as a means of addressing the problematical content of the situation, which will include would-be purposeful action by people in the situation. It *is* that, of course. However, the practitioner(s) is about to carry out another purposeful activity, that of *doing the study*, which is a task always associated with the practitioner role. Carrying out the investigation can be thought about, and planned, using models relevant to doing this. Thus SSM can be applied both to grappling with the content of the situation and to deciding how to carry it out. These two kinds of use of the methodology are known as 'SSM (c)' and 'SSM (p)' – c for content, p for process. Use of SSM (p) often leads to the first models made in the course of an intervention being models related to doing the study. This will be illustrated in Part Two

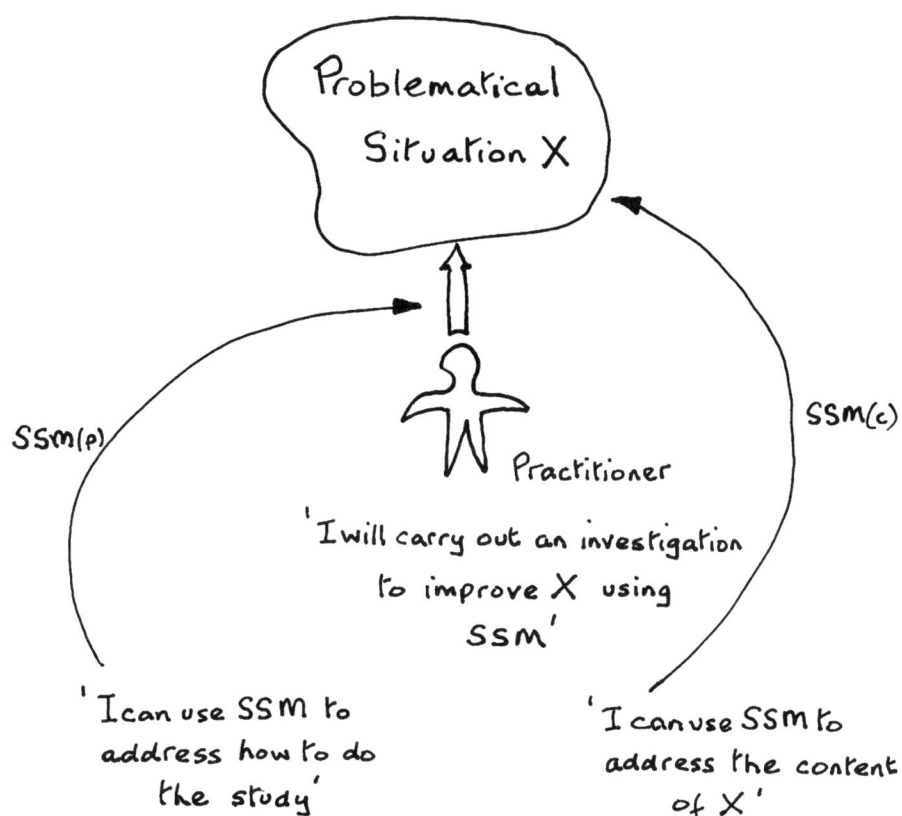

Figure 2.4 SSM(p) concerned with the process of using SSM to do the study and SSM(c) concerned with the problematical content

(Chapter 3, Case 1, Figure 3.1). Meanwhile Figure 2.4 illustrates these two ways of using SSM.

Carrying Out Analysis Two (Social)

It might seem obvious that if you are going to intervene in, and change, a human situation, you ought to have a clear idea about what it is you are intervening in. You should have some sense of what you take 'social reality' to be. However, this is not too obvious! The Management Science field, for example, tries to get by through concentrating almost entirely on the *logic* of situations, even though the motivators of much human action lie outside logic, in cultural norms or emotions. So, if we are to be effective in social situations, we have to take 'culture' seriously and decide what we mean by it. This is especially important for SSM as an action-oriented approach. If we are to learn our way to practical action which will improve a situation under investigation, then the changes involved in 'improvement' have to be not only arguably desirable but also *culturally feasible*. They need to be possible for these particular people, with their particular history and their particular ways of looking at the world. We have to understand the local 'culture', at a level beyond that of individual worldviews.

This might be straightforward if there were an agreed definition of exactly what we mean by 'culture'. However, there is no agreed definition, though the concept is much discussed by anthropologists, sociologists and people writing in the management literature. By the 1950s, a survey (by Kluckhohn and Kroeber) found 300 different definitions, and no agreement has been reached since then! In spite of that, everyone has a general, diffuse sense of what the word means. If you say 'This is a "can-do" culture', or 'This is a buttoned-up culture', or assert that 'The Civil Service is a punishment-avoiding, rather than a reward-seeking culture' then it will be accepted that you have said something meaningful. To anyone familiar with the society in question, those statements will have conveyed some sense of the 'feel', or 'flavour', of the situation: its social texture. In order to pin down such feelings more firmly, in a way which makes practical sense, SSM makes use of a particular model. This is a model which does not claim the status of rounded theory, but it has proved itself useful in situations from small firms dominated by individuals to large corporations which develop and (partially) impose their own norms.

The model is at the same time simple (you can keep it in your head) but also subtle. It consists of only three elements – roles, norms, values – but the subtlety comes from the fact that none of these elements is static. Each, over time, continually helps to create and modify the other two elements, as shown in Figure 2.5.

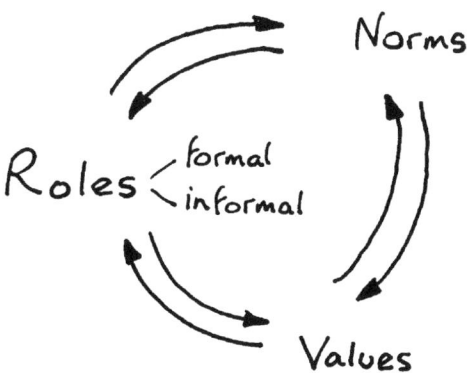

each arrow means:

'creates and recreates'

Figure 2.5 SSM's model for getting a sense of the social texture of a human situation

Together the three elements help to create the social texture of a human situation, something which will both endure *and* change over time. Consider the three elements in turn.

Roles are social positions which mark differences between members of a group or organization. They may be formally recognized, as when a large organization has, say, a chief executive, directors, department heads, section heads and members of sections. But in any local culture informal roles also develop. Individuals may develop a reputation as 'a boat-rocker', or 'a licensed jester' – someone who can get away with saying things others would suppress. The informal roles which are recognized in a given culture tell you a lot about it.

Norms are the expected behaviours associated with, and helping to define, a role. Suppose you told a friend you were going to meet 'the vice-chancellor of a UK university' next day. If you returned from the meeting and said that the VC sat picking her teeth, with her feet on the table, and was very foul-mouthed, your friend would be flabbergasted. Such behaviour is way outside the expected behaviour of someone in the role of VC in British society.

Values are the standards – the criteria – by which behaviour-in-role gets judged. In all human groups there is always plenty of gossip related to this. People love to discuss behaviour in role and reach judgements which praise or disparage: 'He's a very efficient town clerk who services committees well'; 'She's an ineffective vice-chancellor who won't take decisions.'

It is obvious from these definitions that the three elements – roles, norms, values – are closely related to each other, dynamically, and that they change over time as the world moves on. Anyone who has ever been promoted within an organization will know that occupying the new role changes them, as they adopt a new perspective appropriate to the role. Equally, how they enact the new role will have its effect, in future, on the local norm – the behaviour which people expect from whoever fills that role. The elements also change over time at a macro level. For example, when the authors were growing up in British society the worst role for a young woman to find herself in was to be an unmarried mother. At that time, society judged harshly the behaviour which led to this. Not any more; the social stigma attached to the role has disappeared in the UK over the last 50 years.

So how exactly is the model of linked roles, norms and values in Figure 2.5 used in SSM? At the start of an intervention open a file marked 'Analysis Two'. Then, every time you interact with the situation – talking to people informally, reading a document, sitting in a meeting, conducting an inter- view, having a drink in the pub after work – ask yourself afterwards whether that taught you anything about the roles, norms and values which are taken seriously here and characterize this particular group. Record the finding in the 'Analysis Two' file. Carry on doing this throughout the engagement, and

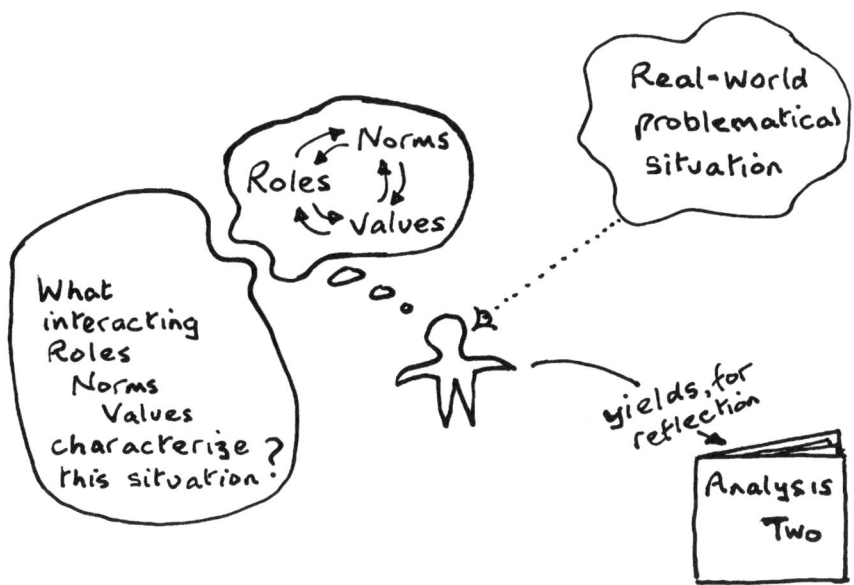

Figure 2.6 SSM's Analysis Two

put a date on every entry so that later on you can recover the progress of your learning, and reflect upon it. Figure 2.6 summarizes Analysis Two.

Carrying Out Analysis Three (Political)

The experienced reader will have noticed that so far in this discussion of 'Finding Out' about a problematical situation we have made no mention of the *politics* of a situation, which arc always powerful in deciding what does or does not get done. That is the focus of Analysis Three: to find out the disposition of power in a situation and the processes for containing it. That is always a powerful element in determining what is 'culturally feasible', politics being a part of culture not addressed directly in the examination of roles, norms and values of Analysis Two.

The 'political science' literature contains many models – usually fairly complex ones – which set out to express the nature of politics. The model used in SSM, in Analysis Three, does not come from that literature but from some basic ideas found in the work of the founding father of the field: Aristotle.

Aristotle argues that in any society (for him, the Greek city-state) in which human beings constantly interact, different interests will be being pursued. If the society as a whole is to remain coherent over time, not breaking up into destructive factions, then those differing interests will have to be accommodated; they will never go away. Accommodating different interests is the concern of politics; this entails creating a power-based structure within which potentially destructive power-play in pursuit of interests can nevertheless be contained. This is a general requirement in all human groups which endure, not only in societies as a whole. There will be an unavoidable political dimension in companies, in international sport, in health-care provision, in the local tennis club – in fact in any human affairs which involve deliberate action by people who can hold different worldviews and hence pursue different interests.

Analysis Three in SSM asks: How is power expressed in this situation? This is tackled through the metaphor of a 'commodity' which embodies power. What are the 'commodities' which signal that power is possessed in this situation? Then: What are the processes, by which these commodities are obtained, used, protected, defended, passed on, relinquished, etc? Figure 2.7 summarizes Analysis Three. The commodities which indicate power in human groups are, of course, many and various. There is a link here to Analysis Two, since occupying a particular role embodies power: the chief constable has more power than a detective sergeant, by virtue of his role. Other common commodities of power include, for example: personal charisma; membership of various committees in organizations; having regular access to powerful role-holders; in knowledge-based settings, having intellectual authority and reputation; having authority to prepare the minutes of meetings – a chore, perhaps, but it gives you some power! Many commodities of power derive from information. Having access to important information, or being able to prevent others from having access to certain information, is a much-used commodity of power in most organizations.

A dramatic example of an unusual commodity of power in a specific SSM project was revealed when two managers in a consultancy company were being interviewed as a pair. They began to disagree with each other and, in a deliberate bit of power-play, one of them suddenly said: 'You say that, but you're NKT; I'm KT.' This local private language within this company referred to those partners who 'knew Tom' and those, more recent joiners, who 'never knew Tom', Tom being the charismatic founder of the company, now deceased. This taught those facilitating this use of SSM that there was an unstated but very real hierarchy here. The KTs, Tom's original disciples, were much more influential than the come-lately NKTs. This indicated that the only changes likely to be culturally feasible in this situation would be those supported by the KTs, whose power stemmed from their association with the charismatic Tom. This is an interesting example of a commodity of power which would gradually fade over time. And this itself reminds us that, as with Analysis Two, Analysis Three deals with elements which are continually being redefined as life moves on.

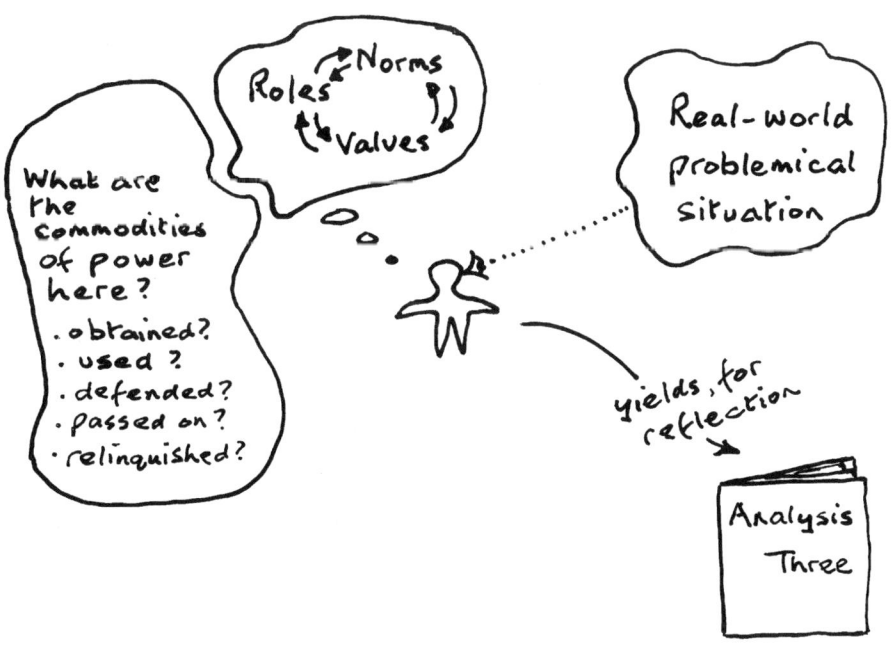

Figure 2.7 SSM's Analysis Three

The way of doing this analysis echoes that of Analysis Two: open a file and record in it – with a date – any learning gained about power and the processes through which it is exercised. Do this, and reflect upon it, over the whole course of an investigation.

The SSM Learning Cycle: Making Purposeful Activity Models

As explained in Chapter 1, in order to ensure that learning can be captured, SSM users create an *organized* process of enquiry and learning. They do this by making models of purposeful activity and using them as a basis for asking questions of the real-world situation. This kind of model is used because every human situation reveals people trying to act purposefully. Since each model is built according to a declared single worldview (e.g. 'the Olympic Games from the perspective of the host city') such models could never be descriptions of the real world. They model *one way* of looking at complex reality. They exist only as devices whose job is to make sure the learning process is not random, but organized, one which can be recovered and reflected on. This section describes how to make these devices.

The task is to construct a model of a purposeful 'activity system' viewed through the perspective of a pure, declared worldview, one which has been fingered as relevant to this investigation. In order to do that we need a statement describing the activity system to be modelled. Such descriptions are known in SSM as Root Definitions (RDs), the metaphor 'root' conveying that this is only one, core way of describing the system. A too-simple example would be: 'A system to paint the garden fence'. Here the worldview is unclear, and it is obvious that a richer description would lead to a richer outcome when the model is used as a source of questions to ask of the real situation. A number of ways of enriching an RD have shown themselves to be useful. For example, we could more richly express the RD above as:

'A householder-owned and staffed system to paint the garden fence, by hand-painting, in keeping with the overall decoration scheme of the property in order to enhance the appearance of the property'. This makes clear that the model takes a householder's worldview as given, and that that particular householder believes in DIY activity to improve it. In addition it not only describes *what* the system does (paint the fence); it also says *how* (by hand-painting) and *why* (to enhance the appearance of the property). (Also the worldview assumes a link between painting and improving appearance.) Clearly this would lead to a richer questioning of the real situation to which this purposeful activity was thought to be relevant as a device to structure the questioning.

The whole set of guidelines of this kind – there to help the modelling process – will now be described. They are set out in Figure 2.8; the five numbered elements in the figure will be described in turn.

1. The formula followed in enriching the fence-painting RD above is always helpful, and can apply to every RD ever written. It is known in SSM as 'the PQR formula': do P, by Q, in order to help achieve R, where PQR answer the questions: What? How? and Why? PQR provides a useful shape for any and every RD. Remember, though, in using PQR, that if the formula is complete, with all three elements defined, then the transforming process is captured in Q, the declared 'how'. In the simple example above the Q is 'hand-painting' (not simply 'painting'). Also, though it is not an issue in this example, the model builder has to be able to defend Q as a plausible 'how' for the 'what' defined by P. If you were to write 'define health-care needs' as P and then define Q *only* as 'by asking patients for their views' this would not be easily defensible.

2. The PQR formula allows you to write out the RD as a statement. This always describes the purposeful activity being modelled as a transformation process, one in which some entity (in the example an 'unpainted fence') is transformed into a different state (here, a 'painted fence'). Any purposeful

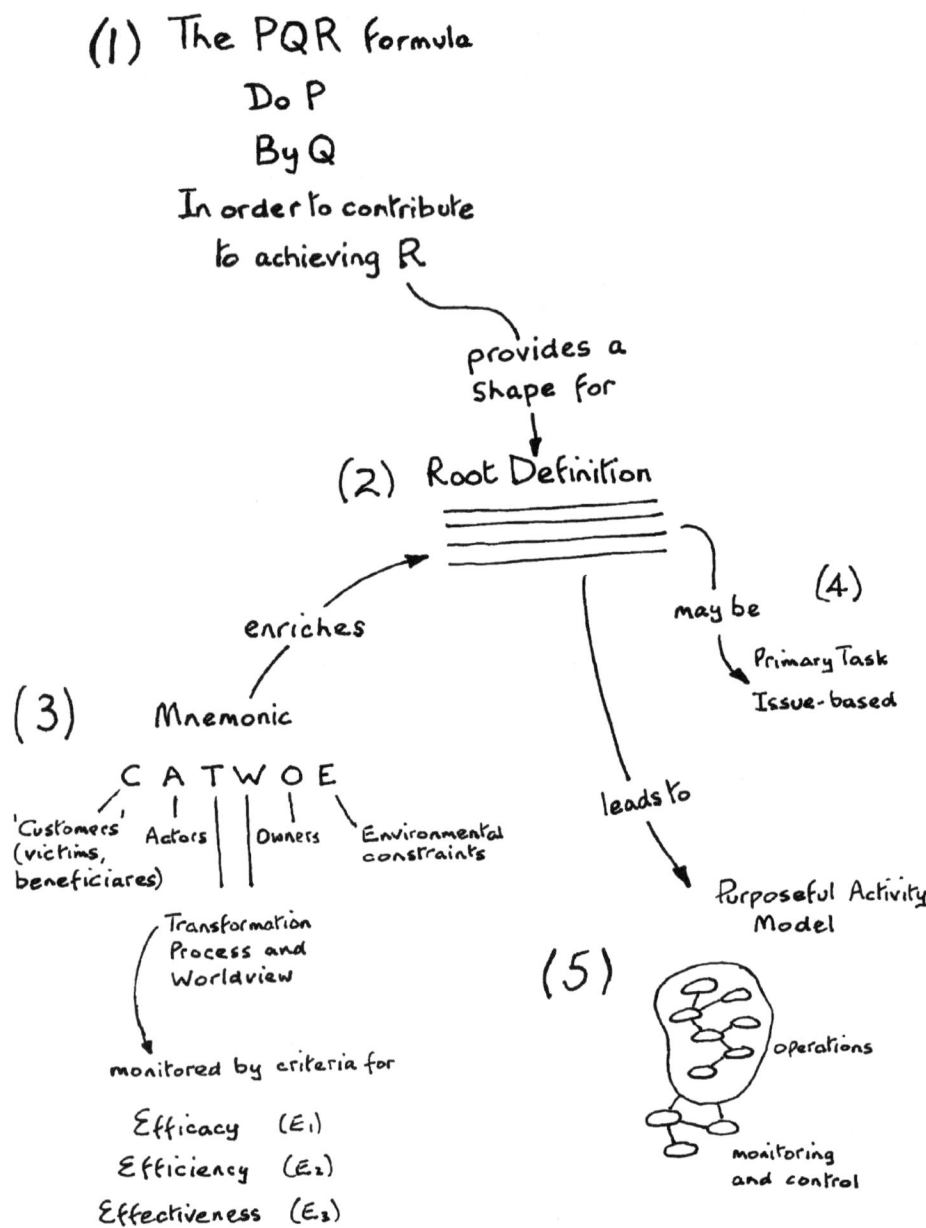

Figure 2.8 Guidelines which help with building models of purposeful activity

activity you can think of can be expressed in this way, which is useful because it makes model building a straightforward process. For complex activities the entity being transformed will probably be best expressed in an abstract way, for example: 'the health-care needs of Coketown citizens' transformed into 'the health-care needs of Coketown citizens met'. But the idea of purposeful activity as a transformation always holds, whether the transformation is concrete or abstract. Putting together the activities needed to describe the transforming process (i.e. 'building the model') can begin when an RD is complete, but before moving on to this, elements 3 and 4 in Figure 2.8 should be considered. They further enrich the modelling and improve it as a source of questions to ask in the real situation.

3. When the idea of working with RDs as a source of models was being developed, a further enrichment of the thinking came from having, as a reference, a completely general model of any purposeful activity. (This was a way of declaring exactly what we meant by 'purposeful activity'.) The general model is shown in Figure 2.9. It contains elements which can usefully be thought about for any purposeful (transforming) activity.

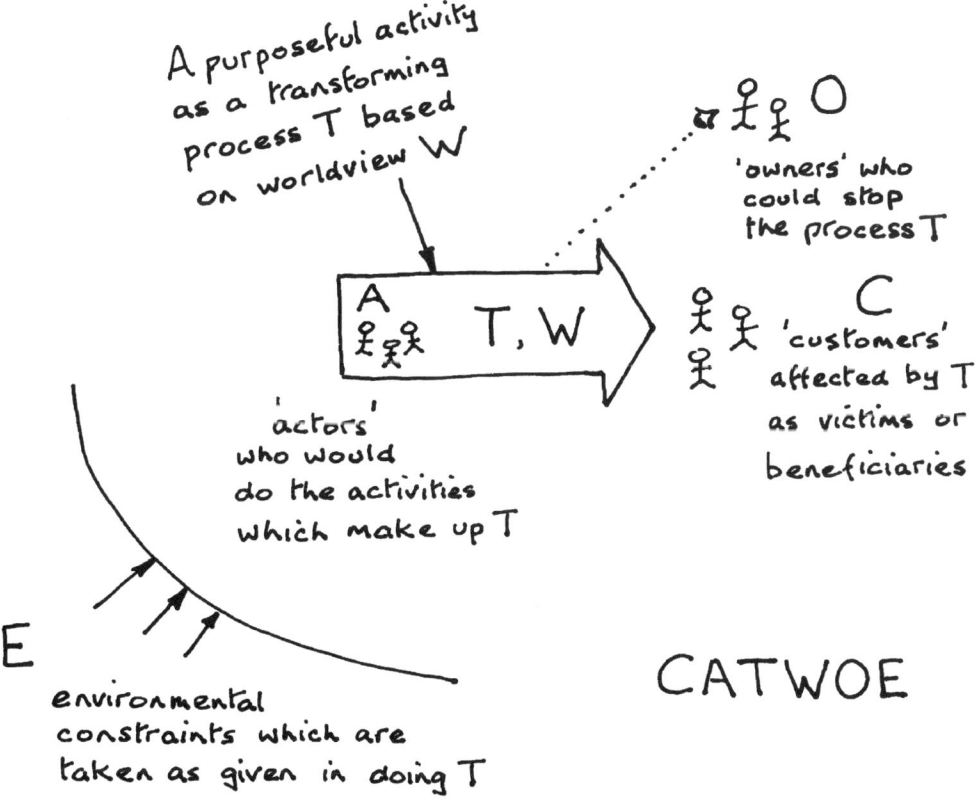

Figure 2.9 A generic model of any purposeful activity, which yields the mnemonic CATWOE

The model provides the mnemonic CATWOE, defined as in Figure 2.9. The concept here is that purposeful activity, defined by a transformation process and a worldview (a T and a W):

- will require people (A) to do the activities which make up T;
- will affect people (C) outside itself who are its beneficiaries or victims (C for 'Customers');
- will take as given various constraints from the environment outside itself (E) (such as a body of law, or a finite budget);
- could be stopped or changed by some person or persons (O) who can be regarded as 'owning' it.

Many people find it useful, when model building, to start the process by defining first T and W, then the other CATWOE elements. Experience suggests, though, that it is still useful to write out the RD as a statement which gives a holistic account of the concept being modelled.

Finally, within the guideline which CATWOE provides, it is useful to think ahead to the model and ask yourself: What would be the measures of performance by which the operation of the notional system would be judged? Thinking out what those criteria would be really sharpens up the thinking about the purposeful activity being modelled. Three criteria are relevant in every case, and should always be named. We need:

- criteria to tell whether the transformation T is working, in the sense of producing its intended outcome, i.e. criteria for *efficacy*;
- criteria to tell whether the transformation is being achieved with a minimum use of resources, i.e. criteria for *efficiency*; and
- criteria to tell whether this transformation is helping achieve some higher-level or longer-term aim, i.e. criteria for *effectiveness*.

In the case of the simple fence-painting system the criteria address, respectively, the questions: Does this count as 'a painted fence' (human judgement would decide)? Is the painting being done with minimum use of the resources of materials and time (these might be expressed as costs)? and Does the painted fence enhance the appearance of the property (again human judgement would decide)? These three criteria are always independent of each other. Thus, for example, the purposeful act of taking a drug to relieve your headache might be efficacious if the headache goes. But it could be inefficient if the drug cost too much or was very slow-acting. And it could also be ineffective, medically, if treating the symptom of the headache was unwise because the headache actually signalled a more serious complaint.

These 'three Es' will always be relevant in building any model, but in particular circumstances other criteria might also apply, such as *elegance* (Is this a beautiful transformation?) or *ethicality* (Is this a morally correct transformation?). The judgement is yours as to what criteria are needed.

4. The final consideration in Figure 2.8 when formulating RDs prior to model building concerns RDs as a whole. Are they 'Primary Task' or 'Issue-based' definitions? This useful distinction (though it does not affect model building technique) arose through experience, like most developments in SSM. In the early days, when the legacy of Systems Engineering hung heavy over the new approach, the models built were always of purposeful activity of a kind that was present in the real world in the form of departments, divisions, sections, etc.; that is to say it was institutionalized. Thus, if working in a company with functional sections – production, marketing, research and development, etc. – we would in the early days of developing SSM make models only of a production system, a marketing system, an R&D system, etc. In these cases the boundary of the models we built would coincide with internal organizational boundaries. This is not 'wrong', but it puts limitations on the thinking of the team carrying out the investigation, which may go unnoticed. Every organization has to carry out many, many purposeful activities as it goes about its business. Only a few of these can be

captured in the organization structure as departments, etc. These organizational boundaries are, in the last analysis, arbitrary, and could be changed.

Experience quickly showed that to stimulate the thinking of everyone involved in the investigation it was useful to make models of purposeful activity whose boundaries *cut across organizational boundaries*. These are 'Issue-based' models from 'Issue-based' RDs, models whose boundaries do not coincide with organizational boundaries. When such models are used to ask questions in the situation, interest and attention are always increased. This brings in broader considerations than is the case with a model which accepts organizational boundaries as a given. This is because the questions about what departments, sections, etc. should exist, and what their boundaries should be are always bound up in the power-play going on in organizations. That catches everyone's attention!

As a generalization we can suggest one choice of Issue-based RD which is always worth considering. In virtually all organized human groups there will always be contentious issues concerned with allocating resources. This is something which affects all members, leads to wide discussion, and is not usually assigned as an activity to a particular sub-group. An issue-based model based on transforming unallocated into allocated resources will be worth considering as a stimulant in most investigations. The general rule is: never work exclusively with either Primary Task (PT) or Issue-based (IB) RDs. Most investigations will best feature a mixture of both types.

5. Earlier in this chapter, in section 2 above, model building was described as 'putting together the activities needed to describe the transforming process', in other words defining and linking the activities needed to achieve the transforming process. Given the guidelines provided by PQR, an RD, CATWOE, the 3Es and PT/IB, this task should not be a difficult

one. The only skill called for is logical thinking. The most common error – even among logical thinkers – is to take your eye off the root definition and start modelling some real-world version of the purposeful activity being modelled. In work in a medium-sized manufacturing company, concerned with various issues regarding product distribution, it was easier for the SSM practitioners to build relevant models than it was for the distribution manager. He kept slipping into modelling the current ways of working in his department rather than the concepts in RDs. If you do this, of course, you find yourself not questioning current practice but comparing X with X – not very profitable!

People find their own way of making the selected relevant models, but a logical sequence to follow, or to refer to if in difficulty, is as follows:

(1) Assemble the guidelines: PQR, CATWOE, the RD, etc.

(2) Write down three groups of activities – those which concern the thing which gets transformed (the 'unpainted fence', or the 'health needs of the citizens of Coketown', in the examples above); those activities which *do* the transforming; and any activities concerned with dealing with the transformed entity (e.g. judging if it improves the appearance of the property, in the fence-painting example); this will give you a cluster of activities.

(3) Connect the activities by arrows which indicate the dependency of one activity upon another; for example, you can't *use* a raw material to make something before you've *obtained* it, so an arrow goes from an 'obtain' activity to the 'use' activity. In Figure 1.3 activity 7 (paint the fence) depends upon both activities 4, 5 and 6, since you can't paint the fence until you've obtained both brush and paint and prepared the fence.

(4) Add the three monitoring and control activities, which always have the structure shown in Figures 1.2 and 1.3.

(5) Check the model against the guidelines. Ask yourself: Does every phrase in the RD lead to something in the model? And: Can every activity in

the model be linked back to something in the RD or CATWOE, etc.? If the answer to both questions is 'Yes', then you have a defensible model. Note that the word used here is 'defensible' rather than 'correct'. This is because everyday words have different connotations for different people. Competent SSM practitioners working from the same RD might well produce somewhat different models; this is because they are interpreting the words in the RD, etc. somewhat differently. The important thing is that you can defend your model as representing what is in your RD, PQR, CATWOE, etc.

Figure 2.10 summarizes the model building process.

Finally, on model building, there is one more guideline worth taking seriously. *Aim* to capture the activity in the operational part of the model in 'the magical number 7 ± 2' activities (but do break the 'rule' if necessary). This famous phrase comes from a celebrated paper in cognitive psychology. George Miller, based on laboratory work, suggests that the human brain may have the capacity to cope with around seven concepts simultaneously. Whether or not this is true it is certainly the case that a set of 7 ± 2 activities can be thought about holistically. If the number seems low, this is not a problem. Any activity in a model can itself, at a more detailed level, become the source of an RD and a model. Thus, in Figure 1.3, activity 6 (obtain paint) could itself be expanded into a model which set out the connected, more-detailed activities which together combine to constitute 'obtain paint' – activities concerned with checking out suppliers, their prices, selecting one, etc. If this model were built, its activities would be numbered 6.1, 6.2, 6.3, etc. since they all derive from activity 6 in the parent model. In this way coherence is maintained no matter how many levels it may be necessary to go to in a particular investigation. In the authors' experience of more than a hundred studies it has never been necessary to expand beyond two levels below that of the parent model, and even then expanding only a few activities at the lower levels.

1. Assemble guidelines :   TandW
   PQR ; PT/$_{1B}$
   CATWOE , $E_1 E_2 E_3$

2. Starting from T and W name the purposeful action as a transformation:

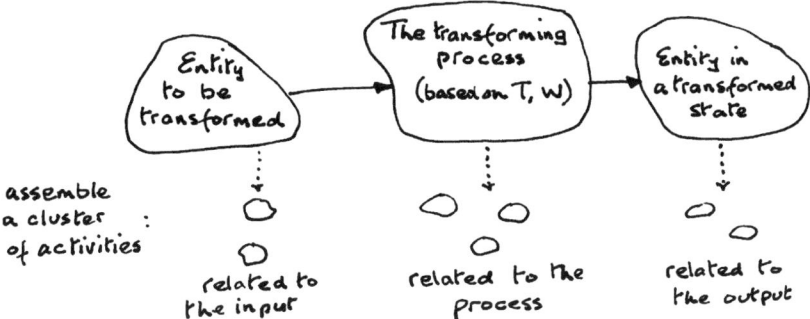

assemble
a cluster   :
of activities

3. Structure the activities according to dependency of one
   on another

aim for 7±2

4. Add the monitoring and control activities

5. Check the mutual dependency of guidelines and model

Figure 2.10 A logical process for building SSM's activity models

The first model presented here, to illustrate the idea of purposeful activity models, was that in Figure 1.3. This was presented without a Root Definition, but now that this has been defined (above) we can present part of the model in a more developed form. This is done in Figure 2.11 which makes one particular change. It would have been possible to include in the 'operations' part of the model an activity such as 'ascertain the judgement about the enhanced appearance of the property'. Another way of bringing in the R of PQR (the higher-level, or longer-term aim of the transforming process,

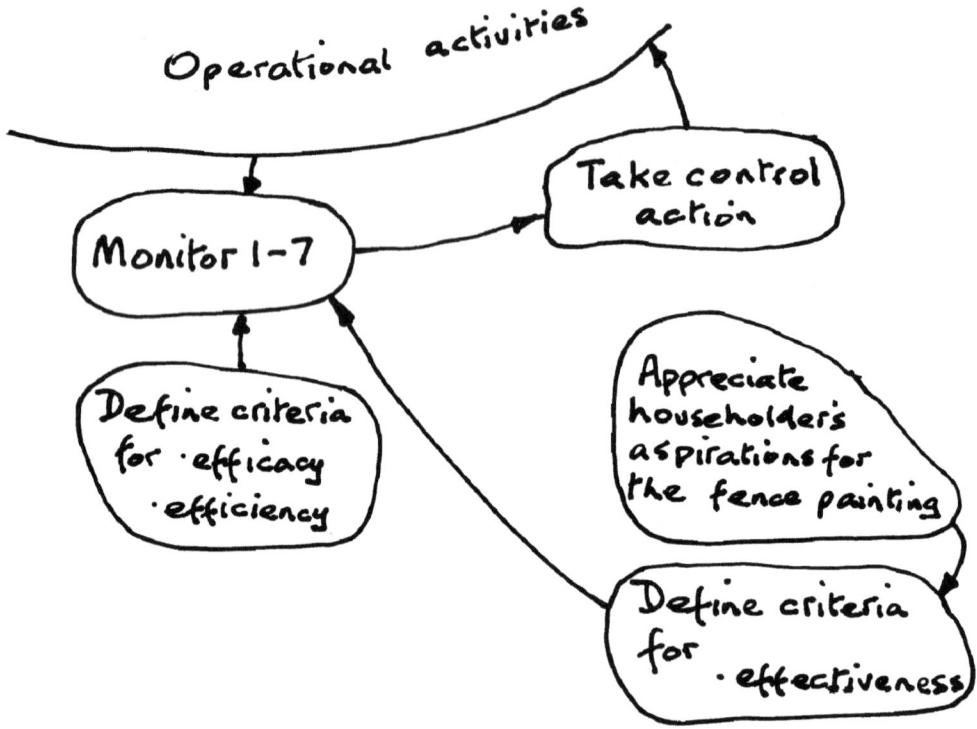

Figure 2.11 A variant of part of the model in Figure 1.3

judged by the criteria for effectiveness) is shown in Figure 2.11. The monitoring and control activity has been split into two, with the monitoring for effectiveness having the added activity: 'Appreciate householder's aspirations for the fence painting.' This leaves open who would make the judgement about the hoped-for enhancement of the appearance of the property – the householder? his or her partner? the neighbours? a prospective purchaser? This is probably, in this instance, the most elegant way of bringing all the elements in the guidelines into the model.

Appendix C carries an example of model building which starts from a Root Definition and 'talks through' the whole process for that definition. In general, the best way to learn about activity modelling is to have a look at examples and then have a go. And do remember that even rough-and-ready models can be helpful in real situations.

The SSM Learning Cycle: Using Models to Structure Discussion about the Situation and its Improvement

When we enter a problematical situation and start drawing rich pictures and carrying out preliminary versions of Analyses One, Two and Three, we begin to build up what can become a rich appreciation of the situation. This appreciation – helped especially by the list of possible 'issue owners' from Analysis One – enables us to begin to name some models which might be helpful in deepening our understanding of the situation and beginning to learn our way to taking 'action to improve'. Having built a hopefully relevant model or two, we are then ready to begin the structured discussion about the situation, and how it could be changed, which will eventually lead to action being taken. The models are the devices which enable that discussion to be a structured rather than a random one.

In everyday situations, typical discussions among professionals are characterized by a remarkable lack of clarity. In a typical 'management' discussion in an organization, unless there is a chairperson of near-genius, different voices will be addressing different issues; different levels, from the short-term tactical to the long-term strategic, will be being addressed; different speakers will assume different timescales. The resulting confusion will then provide splendid cover for personal and private agendas to be advanced. Use of the models to help structure discussion enables us to do rather better than this.

Structure to the discussion is provided by using the models as a source of questions to ask about the situation. This phase of SSM has usually been referred to as a 'comparison' between situation and models, but this wording is truly dangerous if it is taken to imply that the discussion focuses on deficiencies in the situation when set against the 'perfect' models. *The models do not purport to be accounts of what we would wish the real world to be like.* They could not, since they are artificial devices based on a pure worldview, whereas human groups are always characterized by multiple conflicting worldviews (even within one individual!) which themselves change over time – sometimes slowly, sometimes remarkably quickly. (It is those conflicting worldviews which are the fundamental cause of the confusion in most 'management' discussion.)

No, the purposeful activity models simply enable our organized discussion to take place. From the model we can define a set of questions to ask. For example: 'Here is an activity in this model; does it exist in the real situation? Who does it? How? When? Who else could do it? How else could it be done?' . . . etc. Or: 'This activity in the model is dependent upon these other two activities; is it like this in the real situation?' There is no shortage of possible questions, and practitioners quickly develop the knack of passing in a light-footed way over many possibilities and resting on those questions which are likely to generate attention, excitement or emotion. The questions can be about activities or the dependence of one activity upon another or upon the measures of performance by which purposeful activity is judged.

A general finding is that groups find it very difficult to answer questions derived from the measures of performance in a model. 'What criteria would indicate the degree to which this activity (either individual, or the set of operational activities as a whole) is efficacious, efficient and effective?' This is usually a difficult question to answer in most real-world situations, due to their complexity, but it usefully draws attention to the need for organized processes of monitoring, something which is often given scant attention in organizations of all kinds. At a broader level, the fact that a given model is based upon a declared (pure) worldview will draw attention to other, usually implicit, worldviews which may underlie what is actually going on in the situation. This may serve to define other relevant models worth building and also helps to raise the level of discussion to that at which previously taken-as-given assumptions are now questioned. This will usually wake up anyone who is sleep-walking through the discussion, not least because differences of worldview always provoke *feelings*, not simply mental activity. (Also, incidentally, experience in developing SSM suggests that the stimulation of emotion is probably, for most people, a powerful trigger for significant learning to occur.)

In practice, several ways of conducting the questioning of the situation have emerged. An informal approach is to have a discussion about improving the situation in the presence of the models. If some relevant models are on flip charts on the wall, they can be referred to and brought into the discussion at appropriate moments. This has been found useful in situations in which detailed discussion of the SSM approach is inappropriate or is not feasible for cultural reasons. It was effective in a situation in a giant publishing/printing company which was characterized by an operation – publishing, printing and selling consumer magazines – which combined two very separate cultures who found it difficult to appreciate each other's worlds. The editor/publisher culture contained people very different from those in the printing culture, though they worked in the same company. Models which related to the whole operation of commissioning material, editing and assembling magazine issues, printing them and marketing them, proved useful here as a background, rather than as a source of specific detailed questioning. They were on flip charts on the wall, and could be referred to during discussion.

A more formal approach, probably the most commonly used, is to create a chart matrix as in Figure 2.12. The model provides the left-hand column, consisting of activities and connections from the model, while the other axis contains questions to ask about those elements (which may vary depending on the investigation underway). The task is then to fill in the matrix by answering the questions. Case 1 in Chapter 4 illustrates a question-matrix from an SSM investigation.

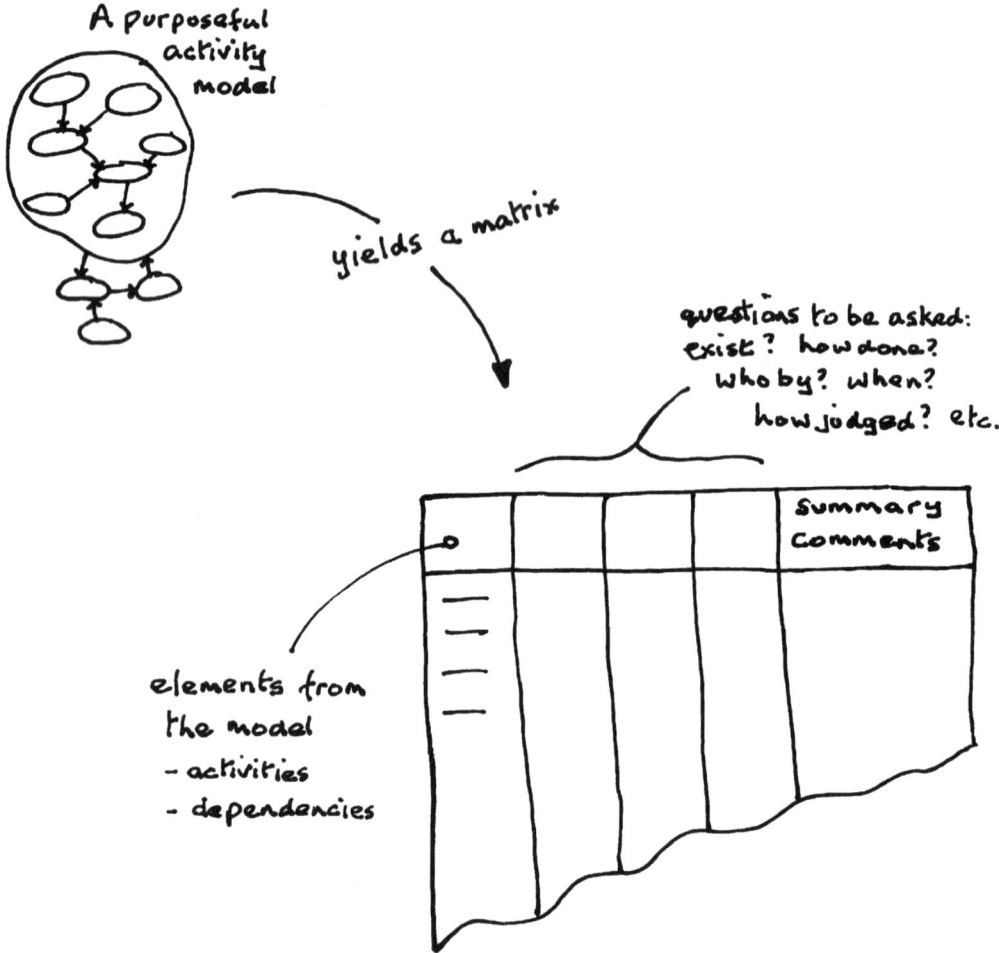

Figure 2.12 A formal process for using models to question the real-world situation

An important warning here is that this process should not be allowed to become mechanical drudgery. This is where a light-footed approach is needed, glancing quickly at many activities and questions, making judgements, and avoiding getting bogged down. Experience quickly develops this craft skill. In fact, experience suggests that this business of seeking to avoid plodding through every cell in the matrix itself helps develop insights into 'the real issues in this situation' – though such judgements have to be tested.

A third way of using models to question reality is to use a model as a basis for writing an account of how some purposeful action would be done

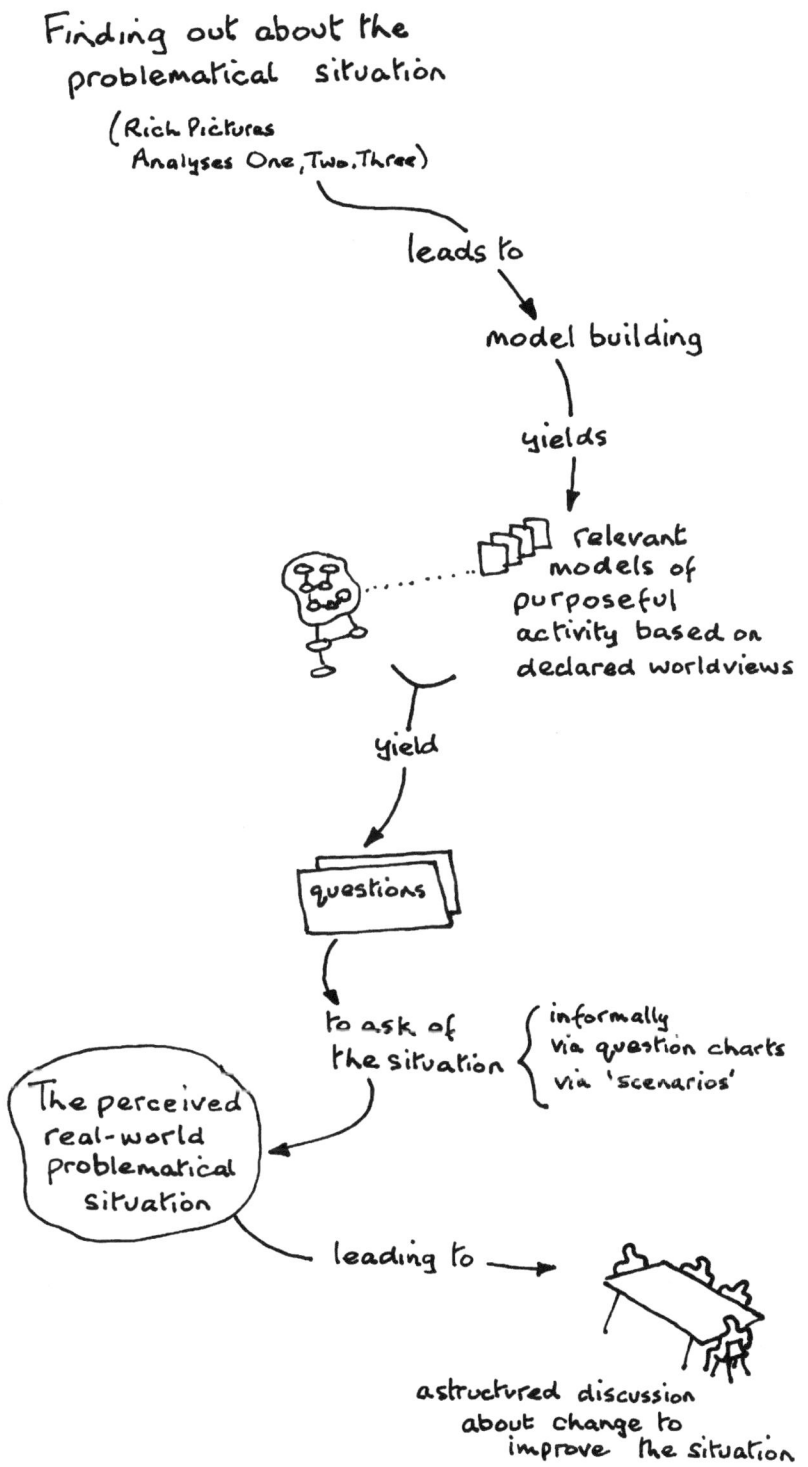

Finding out about the
problematical situation

(Rich Pictures
Analyses One, Two, Three)

leads to

model building

yields

relevant
models of
purposeful
activity based on
declared worldviews

yield

questions

to ask of
the situation

informally
via question charts
via 'scenarios'

The perceived
real-world
problematical
situation

leading to →

a structured discussion
about change to
improve the situation

Figure 2.13 The role of models in SSM summarized

according to the model, and comparing this story, or scenario, with a real-world account of something similar happening in the real world. For example, work with SSM was carried out in a chemical company which treated every plant start-up as if it were the first they had ever carried out. It was very useful in that situation to make a basic generic model of 'a system to start up a new chemical plant' and then write a story from this pure (instrumental) model which could be compared with the real-world stories of previous plant start-ups, usually stories of delays and cock-ups. The company was right in saying that every plant start-up revealed unique features. But this work also showed that it was useful to have a generic model to hand when planning for a new start-up. This model could then be enriched by new experiences, so that the chance of future surprises in plant start-up could be diminished.

Figure 2.13 summarizes different ways of using models in the context of SSM as a whole.

Whichever way the models are used to structure discussion, the aim is the same: to find a version of the real situation and ways to improve it which different people with different worldviews can nevertheless *live with*. Outside of the arbitrary exercise of power, this is the necessary condition which must be met in any human group if agreed 'action to improve' is to be defined.

The SSM Learning Cycle: Defining 'Action to Improve'

When describing the discussion/debate in SSM, much – perhaps most – of the secondary literature about the approach makes a remarkable and fundamental error. It assumes that the purpose of the discussion/debate is to find *consensus*. It is a 'remarkable' mistake in that anyone who had read the primary literature with care would not make it, and it is 'fundamental' because, in order to cope with the complexity of human affairs, SSM uses a much more subtle idea than 'consensus'. It works with the idea of finding an *accommodation* among a group of people with a common concern. This does not abandon the possibility of consensus; rather it subsumes it in the more general idea of accommodation. A true consensus is the rare, special case among groups of people, and usually occurs only with respect to issues which are trivial or not contentious; issues which people do not feel particularly strongly about. In the general case, however, because individuals enter the world with different genetic dispositions and then have different experiences in the world, there will always be differences of opinion resulting from different worldviews. So, if a group of people are to achieve agreed corporate action in response to a problematical situation, they will have to find an accommodation. That is to say they will have to find a version of the situation which they can all live with. These accommodations will of course involve either compromise or some yielding of position. A compromise may give no member of the group all they personally would look for in action to improve the situation. But finding an accommodation is usually a necessary condition for moving to deciding 'what we will now do' in the situation.

The idea of finding accommodations is probably most familiar to us in our personal lives. Any family, as long as it is not of the classic Victorian kind, run by a (male) tyrant who decides everything, will have to continually find versions of the family situation which the different members can accept and live with. This is a necessary characteristic if families are to stick together over a long period. But the idea is also relevant to our professional lives, and to public life. A dramatic illustration of the latter is provided by some British political history. In the UK in the 1970s there were a number of major strikes in the coal industry, the disputes usually involving pay. One of those strikes lasted for a year. Now, the interesting thing about these disputes was that they were conducted within an accommodation between the two sides, the Coal Board and the National Union of Miners (NUM). Although the miners were on strike, members of the NUM nevertheless went down every mine in the country, every day, in order to keep the pumps running, since if you don't continuously pump water out of a coal mine you lose the mine. Although both sides regretted, but were prepared to have the dispute, there was an accommodation between them at a higher level: neither was prepared to live with the idea of the conflict destroying the whole industry. (It took political action to do that some years later!)

This view taken within SSM – that consensus is rare in human affairs, due to clashing worldviews – is not to be regretted. Clashing worldviews, always present, are a source of strong feelings, energy, motivation and creativity. If you find that the models you've built are not leading to *energetic* discussion, abandon them and formulate some more radical Root Definitions.

As discussion based on using models to question the problematical situation proceeds, worldviews will be surfaced, entrenched positions may shift, and possible accommodations may emerge. Any such accommodation will entail making changes to the situation, if it is to become less problematical, and discussion can begin to focus on finding some changes which are both arguably desirable and culturally feasible. In practical terms it is a good idea not to try and discuss the abstract idea 'accommodation' directly. It is best approached obliquely through considering what changes might be made in the situation and what consequences would follow. The relations between accommodations, consensus and changes is summarized in Figure 2.14, and the practical way forward in seeking accommodation is by exploring possible changes and noting reactions to them.

In doing this it is best to think richly about change in human situations, separating the concept into three parts for analytical purposes, even though any significant change in real situations will usually entail all three elements. These are: making changes to *structures*; changing *processes* or procedures; and changing *attitudes*.

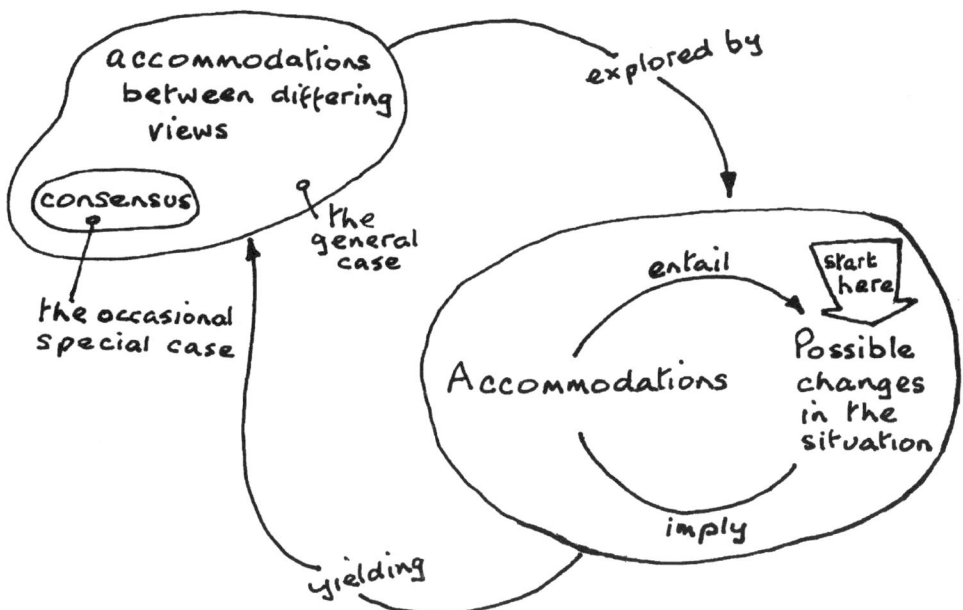

Figure 2.14 Seeking accommodations or (rarely) consensus by exploring implications of possible changes

Obviously the easiest element to change is structure, which can often be done by decree through the exercise of legitimate power. Researchers have noted, for example, that large organizations tend to reorganize themselves structurally about every 18 months to two years. In the UK, governments have imposed structural change upon the National Health Service more than 20 times since it was established in 1948. That is the easy part, for governments. But of course new structures usually require both new processes and new attitudes on the part of those carrying out the processes or being affected by them. Organizations (and governments) find it much harder to think out the necessary new processes; and no one can be sure, in a unique social situation, about what to do to change attitudes in a particular direction. (In our current culture, obsessed with economics, the usual mechanism for trying to change attitudes is to provide material incentives, but this reflects acceptance of a bleak model of human beings as creatures responding only to sticks and carrots. Human beings are more complex than that.)

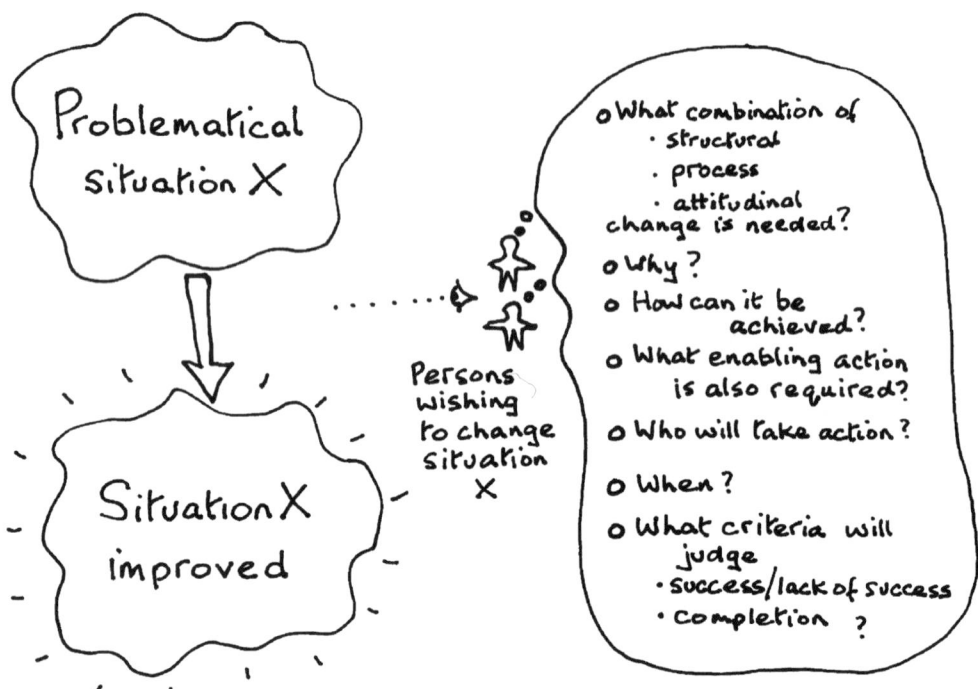

Figure 2.15 SSM's stance on introducing change in human situations

Figure 2.15 illustrates the stance on 'change' taken within SSM. It represents a reminder of things to think about when considering changes which are both desirable and feasible. It is self-explanatory, but two points are worth making. There is a question concerning the 'enabling action' which may be necessary if a potential change is to be accepted. This recognizes the social *context* in which any change will sit. Because of this context, introducing the change may require other action, enabling action, which is not directly part of the change itself. For example, when working within the UK National Health Service for the first time, in the early 1970s, the authors quickly found that in an acute hospital no proposed change would get accepted unless it had the support of senior hospital consultants. Shifts in the disposition of power have now modified that, but at that time in the history of the NHS, enabling action to secure the support of senior doctors was essential if any change of any kind was to occur in a hospital! The second point concerns trying to define the criteria by which a change can be judged as 'completed' and 'successful/unsuccessful'. This point has already been made above in connection with asking about 'monitor-and-control' activities in a real situation: well worth doing, but don't expect people in the situation to have any ready answers.

As we come to the end of this chapter's exposition of a 'fleshed-out' account of SSM, the discussion has become less detailed, in the sense that there are more detailed guidelines for finding out about a real-world situation, and building models used to question it, than there are for taking action to improve the situation. This is inevitable, and is due simply to the fact that no human situation is ever exactly the same as any other. Once we start exploring the real complexity of a human situation, not simply its logic, then formulae, algorithms and ready-made solutions are not available. Even guidelines become fewer. That being so, it seems helpful to give here, ahead of Part Two of this book, a real example of these ideas about change in action.

In the work mentioned above in the publishing–printing industry, the company carried out both of these major activities in selling a large range of consumer magazines. Publishing and printing were organizationally separate, and were in the hands of two very different cultures: on the one hand 'media-folk', on the other 'technologists'. There were many issues in the company concerning investment, pricing, and the placing and scheduling of work. For example, the printers thought of themselves as 'jobbing printers', making no distinction between printing one of the company's titles or that of a competitor. Publishers had ill-defined freedom to print within the company or externally. There were many rows about 'where to print', for example. This was an occasion in which the least-formal way of using models to question the situation was used: discussion in the presence of the models, which were on flip charts on the walls. In the discussion stimulated by the models the end point finally reached, subsequently approved by the board, was that there should be structural change. A new unit within the company was set up. This unit was centrally placed, and was staffed (part-time – it was not permanently in session) by people from both publishing and printing. This structural change was just about culturally feasible (where a fully integrated magazine-producing operation was out of the question) and the processes within the new unit were defined. As far as changes of attitude were concerned, the chief executive, who understood the difficulties of forcing change of that kind, wrote in the in-house company 'newspaper': 'Primarily the new unit is concerned with trying to develop a more effective relationship between our publishers and printers.' He was hoping that each of the two cultures would, through working together on some issues, begin to see the world through the eyes of the other.

The Whole SSM Learning Cycle Revisited: Seven Principles, Five Actions

Before moving on to accounts of SSM in action, in Part Two, we can now summarize the whole learning cycle of the SSM approach. In a concise account of SSM, which is as spare as we can make it, seven principles lead to five actions. These are based only on findings which, through many experiences over a long period, always turned out to be helpful. They are the end product of the several hundred cycles through the LUMAS model in Chapter 1 (Figure 1.8).

The seven principles which underlie SSM are set out first.

1. The idea 'real-world problem' is subsumed in the broader concept of 'real-world *problematical situation*'; that is to say, a real situation which someone thinks needs attention and action.

2. All thinking and talking about problematical situations will be conditioned by the *worldviews (Weltanschauungen)* of the people doing the thinking and talking. These worldviews are the internalized taken-as-given assumptions which cause us to see and interpret the world in a particular way (one observer's 'terrorism' being another's 'freedom fighting').

3. Every real-world problematical situation will contain people trying to act *purposefully*, with intent. This means that *models of purposeful activity*, in the form of systems models built to express a particular worldview, can be used as *devices* to explore the qualities and characteristics of any problematical human situation.

4. *Discussion and debate* about such a situation can be *structured* by using the models in (3) as a source of questions to ask about the situation.

5. Acting to improve a real-world situation entails finding, in the course of the discussion/debate in (4), *accommodations* among different world-views. An accommodation entails finding a version of the situation addressed which different people, with different worldviews, can nevertheless live with.

6. The *inquiry* created by principles (1) to (5) is in principle a *never-ending process of learning*. It is never-ending since taking action to improve the situation will change its characteristics. It becomes a new (less problematical) situation, and the process in (3), (4) and (5) could begin again. Learning is never finished!

7. Explicit organization of the process which embodies principles (1) to (6) enables and embodies *conscious critical reflection* about both the situation itself and also about the thinking about it. This reflection, which leads to learning, can (and should) take place prior to, during and after intervening in the situation in order to improve it. The process thus itself virtually ensures *reflective practice* by those who make use of it. Once the practitioner has internalized the SSM process, so that he or she no longer has to stop and ask questions about it ('Remind me again, what did PQR stand for?') then reflective practice becomes built-in too. The SSM user becomes a reflective practitioner.

These seven principles clearly underlie the four actions which define the classic shape of SSM in Figure 1.5: finding out about a problematical situation;

making models relevant to exploring it, based on different worldviews; questioning the situation using the models, in order to find desirable and feasible change; and defining/taking action to change the situation for the better. The seventh principle itself defines a fifth action which ensures cycling round the primary four, namely critical reflection on the whole process. This fifth action is at a different level from the other four. It is *about* the other four, i.e. at a meta-level. It is the activity which ensures that the lessons learned are captured, in the way that the LUMAS model of Figure 1.8 indicates. Figure 2.16 expresses these five activities at their two levels.

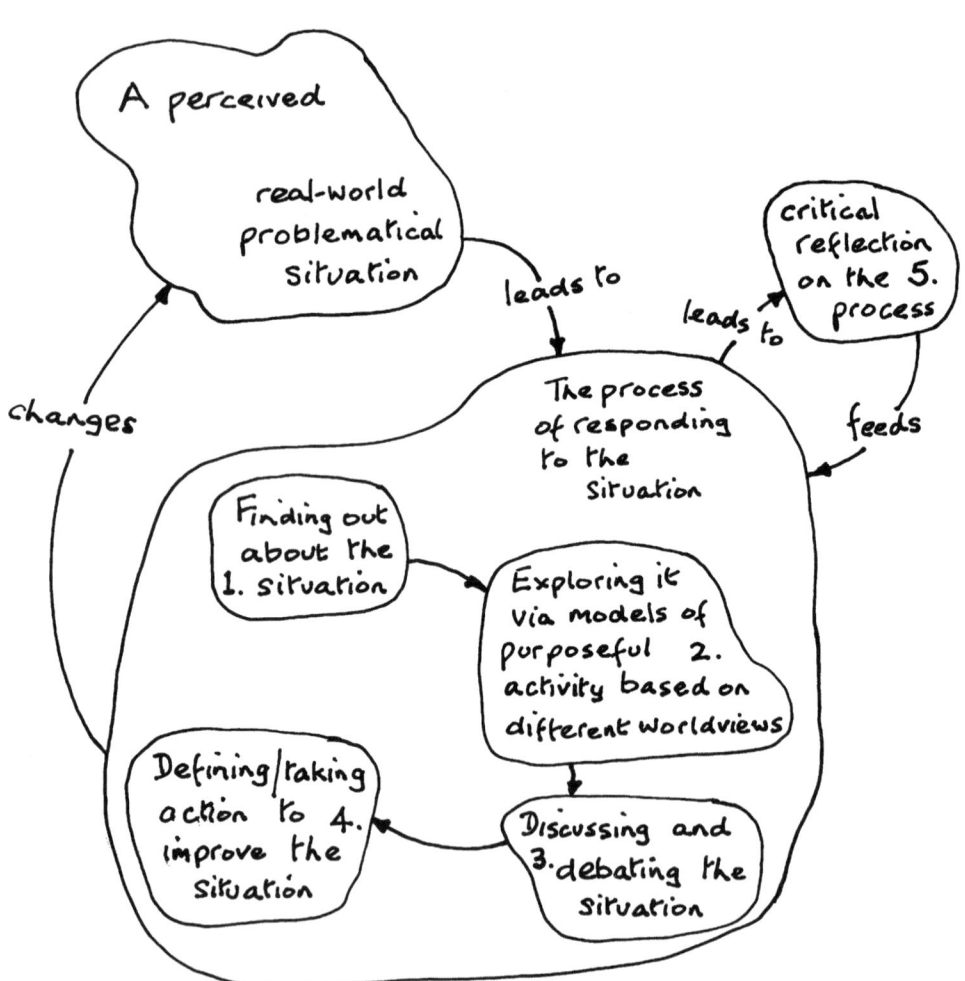

Figure 2.16 The five activities which flow from SSM's seven principles

Finally, in completing this more detailed account of SSM, it is worth re-emphasizing some of its core ideas. It does not seek 'solutions' which 'solve' real-world problems. Those ideas are a mirage when faced with real-life complexity, with its multiple perceptions and agendas. Instead SSM focuses on the process of engaging with that complexity. It offers an organized process of thinking which enables a group of people to learn their way to taking 'action to improve'; and it does that by means of a well-defined, explicit process which makes it possible to recover the course of the thinking which leads to action. This makes sure that every use of the approach produces learning which will accumulate over time, leaving the user better equipped to cope with future complexities.

Part Two now provides examples of these ideas in action in situations of many different kinds.

Part IV | Organizational Applications

▶ 7. Transaction Processing, Functional Applications, and Integration
8. Enterprise Systems
9. Interorganizational and Global Information Systems

Chapter

7

Transaction Processing, Functional Applications, and Integration

Learning Objectives

After studying this chapter, you will be able to:

❶ Relate functional areas and business processes to the value chain model.

❷ Identify functional management information systems.

❸ Describe the transaction processing system and demonstrate how it is supported by IT.

❹ Describe the support provided by IT and the Web to production/operations management, including logistics.

❺ Describe the support provided by IT and the Web to marketing and sales.

❻ Describe the support provided by IT and the Web to accounting and finance.

❼ Describe the support provided by IT and the Web to human resources management.

❽ Describe the benefits and issues of integrating functional information systems.

❾ Describe how IT supports compliance, especially that of SOX.

Integrating *IT*

 **ACC**
 FIN
 MKT
 POM
 HRM
 IS
 SVC

257

Information Technology for Management: Transforming Organizations in the Digital Economy, 6th Edition
Efraim Turban, Dorothy Leidner, Ephraim McLean, and James Wetherbe. ISBN 978-0-471-78712-9
©2008 John Wiley & Sons, Inc.

WIRELESS INVENTORY MANAGEMENT SYSTEM AT DARTMOUTH-HITCHCOCK MEDICAL CENTER

The Problem

Dartmouth-Hitchcock Medical Center (DHMC) is a large medical complex in New Hampshire with hospitals, a medical school, and over 600 practicing physicians in its many clinics. DHMC was growing rapidly and was encountering a major problem in the distribution of medical supplies. These supplies used to be ordered by nurses. But nurses are usually in short supply, so having nurses spending valuable time ordering supplies left them less time for their core competency—nursing. Furthermore, having nurses handling supply orders led to inventory management problems: Busy nurses tended to overorder in an effort to spend less time in managing inventory. On the other hand, they frequently waited until the last minute to order supplies, which led to costly rush orders.

SVC

POM

One solution would have been to transfer the task of inventory ordering and management to other staff, but doing so would have required hiring additional personnel and the DHMC was short on budget. Also, the coordination with the nurses to find what was needed and when, as well as maintaining the stock, would have been cumbersome.

What the medical center needed was a solution that would reduce the burden on the nurses, but also reduce the inventory levels and the last-minute, expensive ordering. Given the size of the medical center, and the fact that there are over 27,000 different inventory items, this was not a simple task.

The Solution

DHMC realized that their problem was related to the supply chain, and so it looked to IT for solutions. The idea the DHMC chose was to connect wireless handheld devices with a purchasing and inventory management information system. Here is how the new system works (as of the summer of 2002): The medical center has a wireless LAN (Wi-Fi) into which handhelds are connected. Information about supplies then can be uploaded and downloaded from the devices to the network from anywhere within the range of the Wi-Fi. In remote clinics without Wi-Fi, the handhelds are docked into wireline network PCs.

For each item in stock a "par level" (the level at which supplies must be reordered) was established, based on actual usage reports and in collaboration between the nurses and the materials management staff. Now nurses simply scan an item when it is consumed, and the software automatically adjusts the recorded inventory level. When a par level is reached for any inventory item, an order to the supplier is generated automatically. Similarly, when the inventory level at each nursing station dips below the station's par level, a shipment is arranged from the central supply room to that nursing station. The system also allows for nurses to make restocking requests, which can be triggered by scanning an item. The system works for the supplies of all non-nursing departments as well (e.g., human resources or accounting). Overall, the Wi-Fi system includes over 27,000 line items.

The system is integrated with other applications from the same vendor (PeopleSoft Inc., now an Oracle company). One such application is Express PO, which enables purchasing managers to review standing purchase orders, e-procurement, and contract management.

The Results

Inventory levels were reduced by 50 percent, paying for the system in just a few months. Materials purchasing and management now are consistent across the enterprise, the last-minute, sometimes expensive ordering, has been eliminated, the time spent by nurses on ordering and tracking materials has been drastically reduced, and access to current information has been improved. All of this contributed to reduced costs and improved patient care.

Sources: Compiled from Grimes (2003), and *peoplesoft.com* (now at *Oracle.com*; material no longer available online).

258

Lessons Learned from This Case

The DHMC case provides some interesting observations about implementing IT: First, IT can support the routine processes of inventory management, enabling greater efficiency, more focus on core competencies, and greater satisfaction for employees and management. The new system also helped to modernize and redesign some of the center's business processes (e.g., distribution, procurement), and was able to support several business processes (e.g., operations, finance, and accounting), not just one. Although the system's major application is in inventory management, the same software vendor provided ready-made modules, which were *integrated* with the inventory module and with each other (for example, with purchasing and contract management). The integration also included connection to suppliers, using the Internet. This IT solution has proven useful for an organization whose business processes cross the traditional functional departmental lines. (In this case nursing is considered operations/production, and so is inventory control; purchasing and contract management are in the finance/accounting area.)

Functional information systems get much of their data from the systems that process routine transactions (*transaction processing systems, TPSs*). Also, many applications in business intelligence, e-commerce, CRM, and other areas use data and information from two or more functional information systems. Therefore, there is a need to integrate the functional systems applications among themselves, with the TPS, and with other applications. These relationships are shown in Figure 7.1, which provides a pictorial view of the topics discussed in this chapter. (Not shown in the figure are related applications discussed in other chapters, such as e-commerce and knowledge management.)

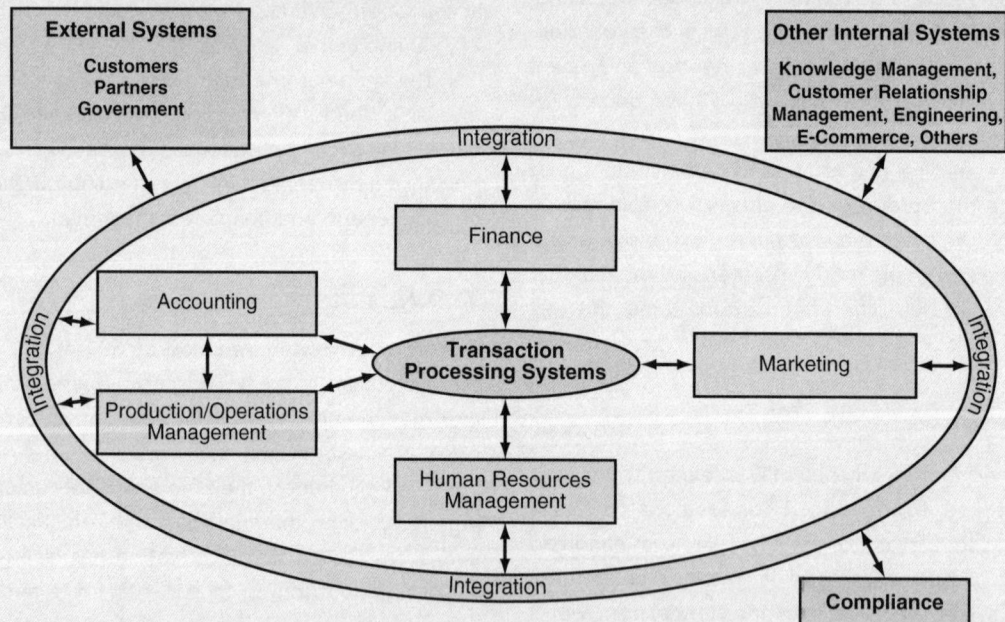

Figure 7.1 The functional areas, TPS, and integration connection. Note the flow of information from the TPS to the functional systems. Flow of information between and among functional systems is done via the integration component.

259

7.1 Functional Information Systems

The major functional areas in many companies are the production/operations, marketing, human resources, accounting, and finance departments. (See the value chain model in Chapter 13 for their role.) Traditionally, information systems were designed within each functional area, to support the area by increasing its internal effectiveness and efficiency. However, as we will discuss in Chapters 8 and 9, the traditional functional hierarchical structure may not be the best structure for some organizations, because certain business processes involve activities that are performed in several functional areas. Suppose a customer wants to buy a particular product. When the customer's order arrives at the marketing department, the customer's credit needs to be approved by Finance. Someone (usually in the production/operations area) checks to find if the product is in the warehouse. If it is there, then someone needs to pack the product and forward it to Shipping, which arranges for delivery. Accounting prepares a bill for the customer, and Finance may arrange for shipping insurance. The flow of work and information between the different departments may not work well, creating delays or poor customer service.

One possible solution is to restructure the organization. For example, the company can create cross-functional teams, each responsible for performing a complete business process. Then, it is necessary to create appropriate information systems applications for the restructured processes. In other cases, the company can use IT to create minor changes in the business processes and organizational structure, but this solution may not solve problems such as lack of coordination or an ineffective supply chain. One other remedy may be an *integrated approach* that keeps the functional departments as they are, but creates an integrated supportive information system to facilitate communication, coordination, and control. The integrated approach is discussed in Section 7.7.

Before we demonstrate how IT facilitates the work of the functional areas, and makes possible their integration, we need to look at the characteristics of the functional areas.

**MAJOR
CHARACTERISTICS
OF FUNCTIONAL
INFORMATION
SYSTEMS**

Functional information systems share the following characteristics:

- **Composed of smaller systems.** A functional information system consists of several smaller information systems that support specific activities performed in the functional area (e.g., recruiting and promotions in HRM).
- **Integrated or independent.** The specific IS applications in any functional area can be integrated to form a coherent departmental functional system, or they can be completely independent. Alternatively, some of the applications within each area can be integrated across departmental lines to match a business process.
- **Interfacing.** Functional information systems may interface with each other to form the organization-wide information system such as ERP (Chapter 8). Some functional information systems interface with the environment outside the organization. For example, a human resources information system can collect data about the labor market.
- **Supportive of different levels.** Information systems applications support the three levels of an organization's activities: *operational, managerial,* and *strategic* (see Chapter 2).

An illustration of the IS applications in the production/operations area is provided in Online File W7.1. Other functional information systems have a similar basic structure.

In this chapter we describe some representative functional IT applications. However, since information systems applications receive much of the data that they process from the corporate *transaction processing system* or are integrated with it, we deal with this system first.

7.2 Transaction Processing Information Systems

The core operations of organizations are enabled by transaction processing systems.

COMPUTERIZATION OF ROUTINE TRANSACTION PROCESSES

In every organization there are business transactions that provide its mission-critical activities. Such transactions occur when a company produces a product or provides a service. For example, to produce toys, a manufacturer needs to order materials and parts, pay for labor and electricity, create a shipment order, and bill customers. A bank that maintains the toy company's checking account must keep the account balance up-to-date, disperse funds to back up the checks written, accept deposits, and mail a monthly statement.

Every transaction may generate additional transactions. For example, purchasing materials will change the inventory level, and paying an employee reduces the corporate cash on hand. Because the computations involved in most transactions are simple and the transaction volume is large and repetitive, such transactions are fairly easy to computerize.

The *transaction processing system* (TPS) monitors, collects, stores, processes, and disseminates information for all routine core business transactions. These data are input to functional information systems applications, as well as to data warehouse, customer relationship management (CRM), and other systems. The TPS also provides critical data to e-commerce, especially data on customers and their purchasing history.

Transaction processing occurs in all functional areas. Some TPSs occur within one area, others cross several areas (such as payroll). Online File W7.2 provides a list of TPS activities by the major functional areas. The information systems that automate transaction processing can be part of the departmental systems, and/or part of the enterprisewide information systems. For a comprehensive coverage of TPSs, see Wikipedia (2006) and Subrahmanyam (2002).

OBJECTIVES AND EXAMPLES OF TPS

The primary goal of a TPS is to provide all the information needed by law and/or by organizational policies to keep the business running properly and efficiently. Specifically, a TPS has to efficiently handle high volume, avoid errors, be able to handle large variations in volume (e.g., during peak times), avoid downtime, never lose results, and maintain privacy and security. To meet these goals, a TPS is usually automated and is constructed with the major characteristics listed in Table 7.1.

Examples of Computerized TPSs. Here are some examples of TPSs:

- American Airlines (AA) and American Express partnered to offer passengers the convenience of in-flight card payments. A pilot program in 2005 led to AA customers' use of their credit and charge cards to purchase sandwiches, drinks, or headsets. Wireless, handheld devices process the transactions. The new system, which accepts most major credit and debit cards, became available across the entire fleet in June 2006 (*Cheapflights.com,* 2006). Other airlines use a similar device. These systems are so successful that cash is not accepted any more.

- To process companies' tax returns faster and with fewer errors, the U.S. government (and other governments) mandate electronic filing. Furthermore, a preliminary analysis by smart programs identifies potential cheaters.

TABLE 7.1	The Major Characteristics of a TPS

- Typically, *large amounts of data* are processed.
- The *sources of data are mostly internal,* and the output is intended mainly for an *internal audience.* This characteristic is changing somewhat, since trading partners may contribute data and may be permitted to use TPS output directly.
- The TPS processes information on a *regular basis:* daily, weekly, biweekly, and so on.
- *High processing speed* is needed due to the high volume.
- The TPS basically *monitors and collects current or past data.*
- Input and output *data are structured.* Since the processed data are fairly stable, they are formatted in a standard fashion.
- A *high level of detail* (raw data, not summarized) is usually observable, especially in input data but often in output as well.
- *Low computation complexity* (simple mathematical and statistical operations) is usually evident in a TPS.
- A high level of *accuracy, data integrity, and security* is needed. Sensitive issues such as privacy of personal data are strongly related to TPSs.
- *High reliability* is required. The TPS can be viewed as the lifeblood of the organization. Interruptions in the flow of TPS data can be fatal to the organization.
- *Inquiry processing* capacity is a must. The TPS enables users to query files and databases (sometimes in real time).

- Many organizations allow their employees to electronically enter changes in their personnel files (e.g., change of address, having a new baby). Furthermore, many companies allow employees to electronically select fringe benefits packages.

Specific objectives of a TPS may include one or more of the following: to allow for efficient and effective operation of the organization, to provide timely documents and reports, to increase the competitive advantage of the corporation, to provide the necessary data for tactical and strategic systems, to ensure accuracy and integrity of data and information, and to safeguard assets and security of information. It is also important to remember that TPSs must closely interface with many IT initiatives, especially with e-payment, e-procurement, and e-marketing.

ACTIVITIES AND METHODS OF TPS

Regardless of the specific data processed by a TPS, a fairly standard process occurs, whether in a manufacturer, in a service firm, or in a government organization. First, raw data are collected by people or sensors (or data are already in files), and then the data are entered into the computer via any input device. Generally speaking, organizations try to automate the TPS data entry as much as possible because of the large volume involved.

Next, the system processes data in one of two basic ways: *batch* or *online processing.* In **batch processing,** the firm collects data from transactions as they occur, and stores them. The system then prepares and processes the collected data periodically (say, once every night). Batch processing is particularly useful for operations that require processing for an extended period of time. Once a batch job begins, it continues until it is completed. In **online processing,** data are processed as soon as a transaction occurs, possibly even in *real time* (instantly).

To implement online transaction processing, *master transaction files* containing key information about important business entities are placed on hard drives, as an operational database (see Figure 7.2) where they are directly accessible.

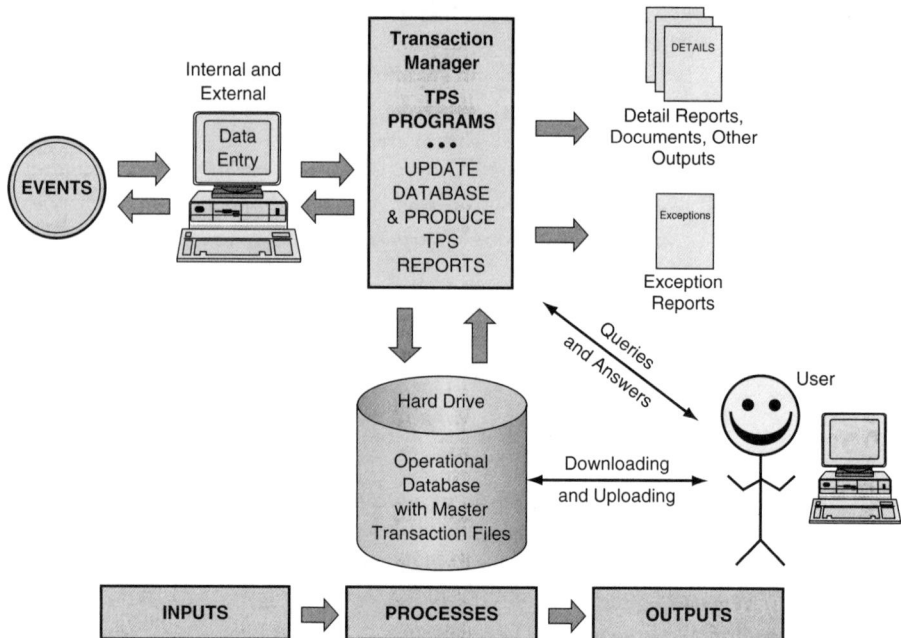

Figure 7.2 The flow of information in transaction processing.

The *transaction files* containing information about business activities, such as orders placed by customers, are also held in online files until they are no longer needed for everyday transaction processing activity. This ensures that the transaction data are available to all applications, and that all data are kept up-to-the-minute. These data can also be processed and stored in a data warehouse. The entire process is managed by a *transaction manager* (see Subrahmanyam, 2002, for details).

The flow of information in a typical TPS is shown in Figure 7.2. An event, such as a customer purchase, is recorded by the TPS program (e.g., by a barcode reader). The processed information (output) can be either a report or an activity in the database. In addition to a scheduled report, users can query the TPS for nonscheduled information (such as, "What was the impact of our price cut on sales during the first five days, by day?"). The system will provide the appropriate answer by accessing a database containing transaction data (see bidirectional arrows in Figure 7.2).

WEB-BASED AND ONLINE TRANSACTION PROCESSING SYSTEMS

Transaction processing systems may be fairly complex, involving customers, vendors, telecommunications, and different types of hardware and software. Traditional TPSs are centralized and run on a mainframe. In **online transaction processing (OLTP),** transactions are processed as soon as they occur. For example, when you pay for an item at a POS at a store, the system records the effects of the sale by instantly reducing the inventory on hand by a unit, increasing the store's cash position by the amount you paid, and increasing sales figures for the item by one unit. For more on OLTP see Chapter 11.

With OLTP and Web technologies such as a portal and an extranet, suppliers can look at the firm's inventory level or production schedule in *real time*. The suppliers themselves, in partnership with their customers, can then assume responsibility for inventory management and ordering in what is known as vendor-managed inventory (VMI); see Chapter 9. Customers too can enter data into the TPS to track orders and even query it directly, as described in *IT at Work 7.1.*

IT at Work 7.1

Modernizing the TPS Cuts Delivery Time and Saves Money

MKT   POM   ACC

Here are some examples of how modernizing transaction processing systems has saved time and/or money:

Kinko's (a FedEx company). Each time you make a copy at Kinko's, a copying transaction and a payment transaction occur. In the past you received a device (a card, the size of a credit card) and inserted it into a control device attached to the copy machine, and it recorded the number of copies that you made. Then you stood in line to pay: The cashier placed the device in a reader to see how many copies were made. Your bill was computed, with tax added. Kinko's cost was high in this system, and some customers were unhappy about standing in line to pay for only a few copies. Today, using Kinko's new system, you insert your credit card (or a stored-value card purchased from a machine) into a control device, make the copies, print a receipt, and go home. You no longer need to see a Kinko's employee to complete your purchase.

Carnival Line. Carnival Line, the operator of cruise ships, needs to rapidly process sometimes over 2,500 people leaving the ship at the ports of call, and later returning to the ship. The company used to use printed name lists with room for checkmarks. Today, passengers place a smart card into a reader. This way the company knows who left the ship and when, and who returns. Each smart-card reader can process over 1,000 people in 30 minutes. In the past it was necessary to use 10–15 employees to process the people leaving and returning to the ship, and it took almost an hour. Today, one person supervises two card readers for less than 30 minutes.

California Department of Motor Vehicles. The California DMV processes 15 million vehicle registration fees each year. To smooth the process, the DMV is using a rule-based expert system that calculates the fees (see *blazesoft.com* for details).

UPS Store. Seconds after you enter an address and a Zip code into a terminal at UPS delivery outlets at a UPS Store, a shipping label and a receipt are generated. Your shipping record stays in the database, so if you send another package to the same person, you do not need to repeat the address again.

Sprint Inc. Using an object-oriented approach, Sprint Inc. has improved its order processing for new telephones. In the past it took a few days for a customer to get a new telephone line; with its new system, Sprint can process an order in only a few hours. The order application itself takes less than 10 minutes, experiences fewer errors, and can be executed on electronic forms on a salesperson's desktop or laptop computer.

For Further Exploration: Could Kinko's operate completely without employees at their outlets? What effect does Carnival's smart-card reader have on security? Whose time is being saved at UPS and Sprint?

TYPICAL TASKS IN TRANSACTION PROCESSING

Transaction processing exists in all functional areas. Here we describe in some detail one application that crosses several functional areas—order processing.

Order Processing. Orders for goods and/or services may flow from customers to a company by phone, on paper, or electronically. Fast and effective order processing is recognized as a key to customer satisfaction. Orders can also be internal—from one department to another. Once orders arrive, an order processing system needs to receive, document, route, summarize, and store the orders. A computerized system can also track sales by product, by zone, by customer, or by salesperson, providing sales or marketing information that may be useful to the organization. As described in Chapter 6, more and more companies are providing systems for their salespeople that enable them to enter orders from a business customer's site using wireless notebook computers, PDAs, or Internet-enabled smart phones (see Minicase 2). Some companies spend millions of dollars reengineering their order processing as part of their transformation to e-business. IBM, for example, restructured its procurement system so its own purchasing orders are generated quickly and inexpensively in its e-procurement system.

Orders can be for services as well as for products. Otis Elevator Company, for example, tracks orders for elevator repair. The processing of repair orders is done

IT at Work 7.2

Automatic Vehicle Location and Dispatch System in Singapore

SVC   POM   GLOBAL

Taxis in Singapore are tracked by a *global positioning system* (GPS), which is based on the 24 satellites originally set up by the U.S. government. The system allows its users to get an instant fix on the geographical position of each taxi equipped with GPS (see the figure).

Here's how the system works: Customer orders are usually received via cell phone, regular telephone, fax, or e-mail. Customers can also dispatch taxis from special kiosks (called CabLink) located in shopping centers and hotels. Other booking options include portable taxi-order terminals placed in exhibition halls. Frequent users enter orders from their offices or homes by keying in a PIN number over the telephone. That number identifies the user automatically, together with his or her pickup point. Infrequent customers use an operator-assisted system.

Once an order has been received, the system finds a vacant cab nearest the caller, and a display panel in the taxi alerts the driver to the pickup address. The driver has 10 seconds to push a button to accept the order. If he does not, the system automatically searches out the next-nearest taxi for the job.

The system completely reengineered taxi order processing. First, the transaction time for processing an order for a fre-

quent user is much shorter, even during peak demand, since they are immediately identified. Second, taxi drivers are not able to pick and choose which trips they want to take, since the system will not provide the commuter's destination. This reduces the customer's average waiting time significantly, while minimizing the travel distance of empty taxis. The system increases the capacity for taking incoming calls by 1,000 percent, providing a competitive edge to those cab companies that use the system. It also reduces misunderstanding between drivers and dispatchers, and driver productivity increased since they utilize their time more efficiently. Finally, customers who use terminals do not have to wait a long time just to get a telephone operator (a situation that exists during rush hours, rain, or any other time of high demand for taxis). Three major taxi companies with about 50,000 taxis are connected to the system.

Sources: Compiled from Liao (2003) and *entersingapore.com* (2006).

For Further Exploration: What TPS tasks do computers execute in this order processing system? What kinds of priorities can be offered to frequent taxi customers?

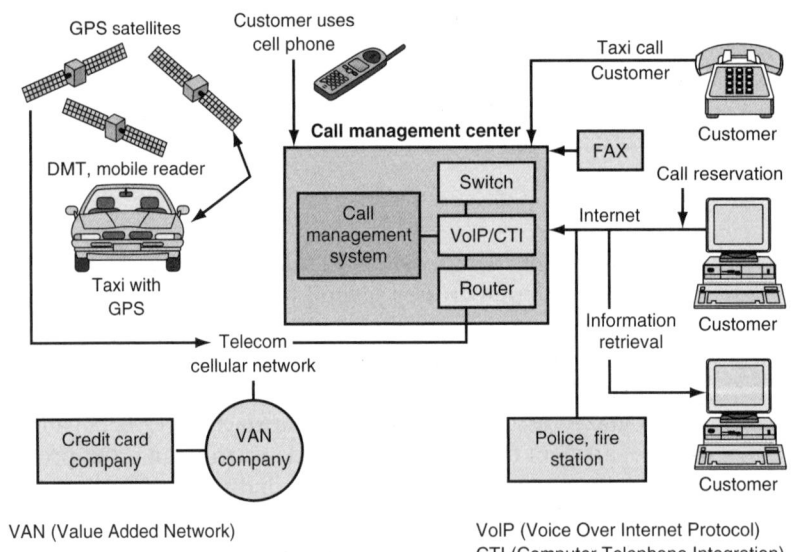

Location tracking of taxicabs in Singapore.

via wireless devices that allow effective communication between repair crews and Otis physical facilities. Orders also can be processed by using innovative IT technologies such as global positioning systems; see *IT at Work 7.2.*

Other TPS Activities. Other typical TPS activities are summarized in Table 7.2 (page 266). Most of these routine tasks are computerized.

TABLE 7.2	Typical TPS Activities
Activities	**Description**
The ledger	The entire group of an organization's financial accounts. Contains all of the assets, liabilities, and owner's (stockholders') equity accounts.
Accounts payable and receivable	Records of all accounts to be paid and those owed by customers. Automated system can send reminder notes about overdue accounts.
Receiving and shipping records	Transaction records of all items sent or received, including returns.
Inventory-on-hand records	Records of inventory levels as required for inventory control and taxation. Use of barcodes improves ability to count inventory periodically.
Fixed-assets management	Records of the value of an organization's fixed assets (e.g., buildings, cars, machines), including depreciation rate and major improvements made in assets, for taxation purposes.
Payroll	All raw and summary payroll records.
Personnel files and skills inventory	Files of employees' history, evaluations, and record of training and performance.
Reports to government	Reports on compliance with government regulations, taxes, etc.
Other periodic reports and statements	Financial, tax, production, sales, and other routine reports.

WHAT IF TPS FAILS?

TPSs deal with the core activities of the organization. Their failure can cause a disaster. Several years ago, the U.S. Social Security Administration had some major TPS failures, as did insurance companies, hospitals, and banks. One might think that a large financial institution should be immune from IT failure, but this was not the case with TIAA/CREF, as illustrated in *IT at Work 7.3*.

IT at Work 7.3

The TIAA-CREF Computerized Reporting Failed

TIAA-CREF is a huge company serving the retirement, insurance, investment, and other needs of teachers and professors. It is one of the largest financial institutions of its kind.

In September 2005, thousands of TIAA-CREF members were unable to access funds from their own accounts. Clients were unable to withdraw funds or receive under- or overpayments in their pensions. The company assured clients that this was just a small delay due to the IT platform upgrade. However, according to Boucher-Fergusen (2006a), the problems lingered for months and expanded to inflow of money as well. The problem resulted from an attempt to introduce a powerful new platform, called Open Plan Solutions, whose objectives were to bring together fixed annuities, variable annuities, mutual funds, and homegrown platforms onto a single, connected platform with:

- **Flexible,** state-of-the-art record keeping
- **Streamlined** enrollment process
- **Comprehensive** remittance services

- **Improved** Web-based institutional reporting on accumulations, transactions, and salary reduction agreements
- **New** and improved participant quarterly statements

The problems included synchronization issues between the company's Web access software and the record-keeping system during the batch transaction processing. In other words, the new system was not in sync with the old one. By April 2006, the problem became a disaster (Boucher-Ferguson, 2006b) because of the inability to solve all the integration problems fast enough. At that time, the company set up a new cross-functional team to catch issues before they escalated. By the time this book was written (July 2006), major progress had been made, but some problems still persist.

Sources: Compiled from Boucher-Ferguson (2006a, 2006b) and from *tiaa-cref.org* (2006).

For Further Exploration: If such a giant finance company had such problems, what about small companies? Could proper IT planning (Chapter 13) have prevented the problem? What are the damages to TIAA/CREF?

**TRANSACTION
PROCESSING
SOFTWARE**

There are dozens of commercial TPS software products on the market. Many are designed to support Internet transactions. (See a sampler of TPS software products and vendors in Online File W7.3.)

The problem, then, is how to evaluate so many software packages. In Chapter 15, there is a discussion on software selection that applies to TPS as well. But the selection of a TPS software product has some unique features. Therefore, one organization, the Transaction Processing Performance Council (*tpc.org*), has been trying to assist in this task. This organization is conducting *benchmarking* for TPS. It checks hardware vendors, database vendors, middleware vendors, and so forth. Recently it started to evaluate e-commerce transactions (*tpc.org/tpcw;* there, see "transactional Web e-commerce benchmark"). Also, the organization has several decision support benchmarks (e.g., TPC-App, TPC-H, and TPC-R).

7.3 Managing Production/Operations and Logistics

POM

The *production and operations management* (POM) function in an organization is responsible for the processes that transform inputs into useful outputs (see Figure 7.3). In comparison to the other functional areas, the POM area is very diversified and so are its supporting information systems. It also differs considerably among organizations. For example, manufacturing companies use completely different processes than do service organizations, and a hospital operates much differently from a university. (Look again at Online File W7.1 for an example of the complexity of the POM field. Note that the internal interfaces are on the left and the external ones on the right.)

Because of the breadth and variety of POM functions, here we present three IT-supported POM topics: in-house logistics and materials management, planning production/operations, and computer-integrated manufacturing (CIM).

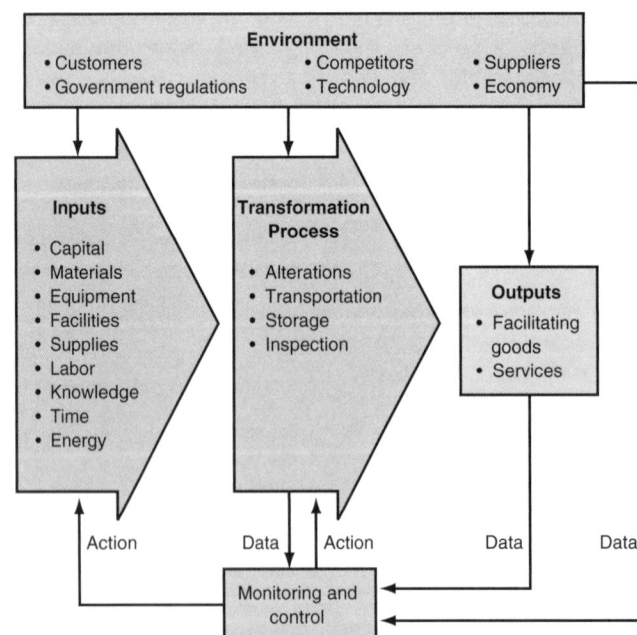

Figure 7.3 The production/operations management functions transform inputs into useful outputs. (*Source:* J. R. Meredith and S. M. Shafer, *Operations Management.* New York: Wiley, 2002. Reprinted by permission of John Wiley & Sons, Inc.)

**IN-HOUSE
LOGISTICS AND
MATERIALS
MANAGEMENT**

Logistics management deals with ordering, purchasing, inbound logistics (receiving), and outbound logistics (shipping) activities. In-house logistics activities are a good example of processes that cross several functional departments. Both conventional purchasing and e-procurement result in incoming materials and parts. The materials received are inspected for quality and then stored. While the materials are in storage, they need to be maintained until distributed to those who need them. Some materials are disposed of when they become obsolete or their quality becomes unacceptable.

All of these activities can be supported by information systems (Robb, 2003 and Ho, 2004). For example, many companies today are moving to some type of e-procurement (Chapter 5). Scanners, RFID, and voice technologies, including wireless ones, can support inspection, and robots can perform distribution and materials handling. Large warehouses use robots to bring materials and parts from storage, whenever needed. The parts are stored in bins, and the bins are stacked one above the other (similar to the way safe deposit boxes are organized in banks). Whenever a part is needed, the storekeeper keys in the part number. The mobile robot travels to the part's "address," takes the bin out of its location (e.g., using magnetic force), and brings the bin to the storekeeper. Once a part is taken out of the bin, the robot is instructed to return the bin to its permanent location. In intelligent buildings in Japan, robots bring files to employees and return them for storage. In some hospitals, robots even dispense medicines. An example of a parts-tracking system is provided by Carr (2005).

Inventory Management. *Inventory management* determines how much inventory to keep. Overstocking can be expensive; so is keeping insufficient inventory. Three types of costs play important roles in inventory decisions: the cost of maintaining inventories, the cost of ordering (a fixed cost per order), and the cost of not having inventory when needed (the shortage or opportunity cost). The objective is to minimize the total of these costs.

Two basic decisions are made by operations: when to order, and how much to order. Inventory models, such as the economic order quantity (EOQ) model, support these decisions. Dozens of models exist, because inventory scenarios can be diverse and complex. A large number of commercial inventory software packages to automate the application of these models are available at low cost. More and more companies are improving their inventory management and replenishment, better meeting customers' demand (Amato-McCoy, 2002c).

Many large companies (such as Wal-Mart) allow their suppliers to monitor the inventory level and ship when needed, eliminating the need for sending purchasing orders. Such a strategy, in which the supplier monitors inventory levels and replenishes when needed, is called **vendor-managed inventory (VMI)** (Chapter 8). The monitoring can be done by using mobile agents over the Internet. It also can be done by using Web Services, as Dell Computer is doing. An emerging solution is the use of RFIDs (Chapter 9).

Reducing inventories and managing them properly is a major objective of supply chain management (Chapter 8).

Quality Control. Manufacturing quality-control systems can be standalone systems or can be part of an enterprisewide total quality management (TQM) effort. They provide information about the quality of incoming materials and parts, as well as the quality of in-process semifinished and finished products. Such systems record the results of all inspections. They also compare actual results to metrics. One such matrix is the Six Sigma (Chapter 8).

Quality-control data may be collected by Web-based sensors and interpreted in real time, or they can be stored in a database for future analysis. Also, RFIDs can be used to collect data. Periodic reports are generated (such as percentage of defects, percentage of rework needed), and management can compare performance among departments on a regular basis or as needed.

Web-based quality control information systems are available from several vendors (e.g., HP and IBM) for executing standard computations such as preparing quality control charts. First, manufacturing data are collected for quality-control purposes by sensors and other instruments. After the data have been recorded, it is possible to use Web-based expert systems to make interpretations and recommend actions (e.g., to replace equipment).

PLANNING PRODUCTION/ OPERATIONS

The POM planning in many firms is supported by IT. Some major areas of planning and their computerized support are described here. An automatic defect-reporting system is described by Duvall (2005).

Just-in-Time Systems. In mass customization and build-to-order production, the just-in-time concept is frequently used. **Just-in-time (JIT)** is an approach that attempts to minimize waste of all kinds (of space, labor, materials, energy, and so on) and to continuously improve processes and systems. For example, if materials and parts arrive at a workstation *exactly when needed,* there is no need for inventory, there are no delays in production, and there are no idle production facilities or underutilized workers. Many JIT systems are supported by software from vendors such as HP, IBM, CA, and Cincom Systems. For how IT works with JIT, see Gillium et al. (2005).

As of 2001, car manufacturers were rapidly adopting a make-to-order process. To deliver customized cars quickly and with cost efficiency, manufacturers need a JIT system. Oracle, PeopleSoft, and other vendors offer a demand-driven *lean manufacturing,* which is a derivative of JIT (see Gillium et al., 2005).

Project Management. A *project* is usually a one-time effort composed of many interrelated activities, costing a substantial amount of money, and lasting for weeks or years. The management of a project is complicated by the following characteristics.

- Most projects are unique undertakings, and participants have little prior experience in the area.
- Uncertainty exists due to the generally long completion times.
- There can be significant participation of outsiders, which is difficult to control.
- Extensive interaction may occur among participants.
- The many interrelated activities make changes in planning and scheduling difficult.
- Projects often carry high risk but also high profit potential.

The management of projects is enhanced by computerized project management tools such as the *program evaluation and review technique* (PERT) and the *critical path method* (CPM). For example, developing Web applications is a major project, and several IT tools are available to support and help manage these activities (see Project Net from *citadon.com*). Merrill-Lynch uses such computerized tools to plan and manage its main projects, significantly improving resource allocation and decision making. For project cost estimation using special software, see Vijayakumar (2002). Project management can be streamlined through online solutions, as demonstrated by Perkins-Munn and Chen (2004). Microsoft offers several project management tools (e.g., Project and Enterprise Project Management).

Other areas. Many other areas of planning production and operations are improved by IT. For example, Lee and Chen (2002) developed a Web-based production planning optimization tool. Factory layout planning and design also have been greatly improved due to IT tools (Benjaafar et al., 2002).

Korolishin (2003) describes a Web-based system at Office Depot that matches employee scheduling with store traffic patterns to increase customer satisfaction and reduce costs. Parks (2004b) describes how Schurman Fine Papers (a retailer and manufacturer of greeting cards and specialty products) uses special *warehouse management software* to improve forecasting and inventory processes. Its two warehouses distribute products to over 30,000 retail stores.

COMPUTER-INTEGRATED MANUFACTURING

Computer-integrated manufacturing (CIM) is a concept or philosophy that promotes the integration of various computerized factory systems. CIM has three basic goals: (1) the *simplification* of all manufacturing technologies and techniques, (2) *automation* of as many of the manufacturing processes as possible, and (3) *integration and coordination* of all aspects of design, manufacturing, and related functions via computer hardware and software. Typical technologies to be integrated are flexible-manufacturing systems (FMSs), JIT, MRP, CAD, CAE, and group technology (GT). For details see Online File W7.4.

The major advantages of CIM are its comprehensiveness and flexibility. These are especially important in business processes that are being completely restructured or eliminated. Without CIM, it may be necessary to invest large amounts of money to change existing information systems to fit the new processes. For an example of how a furniture company uses CIM, see *kimball.com* (click on Kimball Electronics). For more on a unified framework for integrated manufacturing see Zaremba and Morel (2003).

7.4 Managing Marketing and Sales Systems

MKT

In Chapters 1 through 6 we emphasized the increasing importance of a customer-focused approach and the trend toward customization. How can IT help? First we need to understand how products reach customers, which takes place through a series of marketing entities known as *channels*.

Channel systems (in marketing) are all the systems involved in the process of getting a product or service to customers and dealing with all customers' needs. The complexity of channel systems can be observed in Figure 7.4 (page 272), where six major marketing systems are interrelated.

Channel systems can link and transform marketing, sales, procurement, logistics and delivery, and other activities. Added market power comes from the integration of channel systems with the corporate functional areas. The problem is that a change in any of the channels may affect the other channels. Therefore, the supporting information systems must be coordinated or even integrated.

Channel-driven advantages are (1) transaction speed (real-time response) because of the interactive nature of the process, (2) global reach, (3) reduced costs, (4) multimedia content, and (5) reliability.

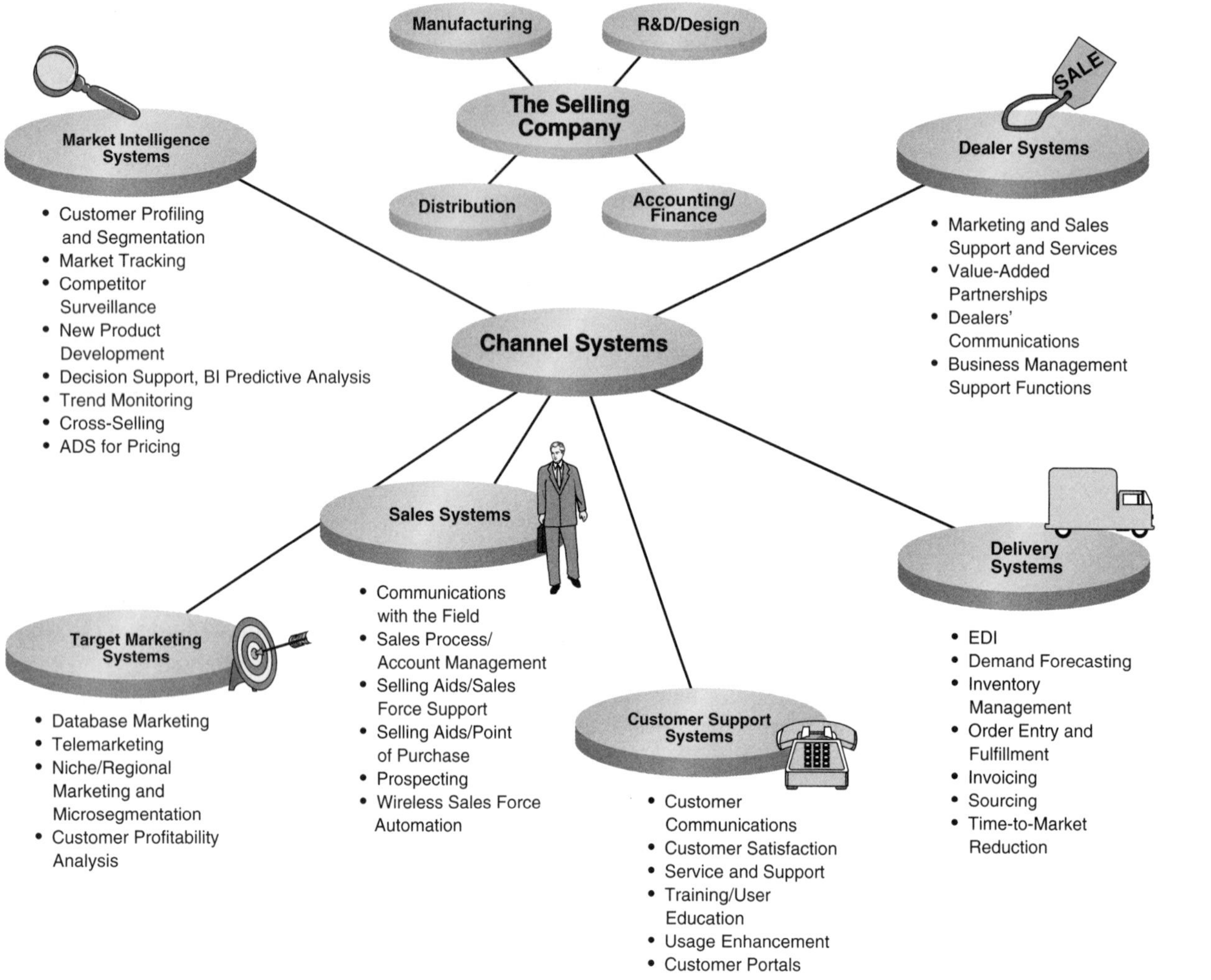

Figure 7.4 Marketing channel systems.

We describe only a few of the many channel-system activities here, organizing them into three groups: customer relations, distribution channels and in-store innovations, and marketing management. A fourth topic, telemarketing and online shopping, is presented in Online File W7.5.

"THE CUSTOMER IS KING/QUEEN"

It is essential for companies today to know who their customers are and to treat them like royalty. New and innovative products and services, successful promotions, customization, and world-class customer service are becoming a necessity for many organizations. In this section we will briefly describe a few activities related to *customer-centric* organizations. More are described in Chapter 8, where customer relationship management (CRM) is presented.

Customer Profiles and Preference Analysis. Information about existing and potential customers is critical for success. Sophisticated information systems have been developed to collect data on customers, their demographics (age, gender, income level), and preferences. For example, shoppers' in-store activities can be monitored and then analyzed to better arrange the layouts and employees' scheduling. Analysis of shopping habits can help in organizing layouts of stores and carts (see Nishi, 2005).

Prospective Customer Lists and Marketing Databases. All firms need to know who their customers are, and IT can help create customer databases of both existing and potential customers. It is possible today to purchase computerized lists from several sources and then merge them electronically. These prospective-customer lists then can be analyzed and sorted by any desired classification for direct mailing, e-mailing, or telemarketing. Customer data can be stored in a corporate database or in special marketing databases (Chapter 3) for future analysis and use. For how Sears uses a marketing database, see Amato-McCoy (2002b). For example, Staples, Inc. uses software to identify its profitable customers as well as those who try to get refunds for shoplifted items or other kinds of refund fraud.

Mass Customization. Increasingly, today's customers want customized products. Some manufacturers offer different product configurations, and in some products dozens of options are available. The result is *mass customization,* as practiced successfully by Dell Computer and many other companies (see Appendix 2A). Customization is possible both in manufactured goods and in services.

Wind (2001) analyzed the impact of customization on marketing and the resultant changes (see Online File W 7.6). As shown throughout this book, these changes are being supported by IT. For example, the Web can be used to expedite the ordering and fulfillment of customized products, as demonstrated in *IT at Work 7.4,* about building a Jaguar.

IT at Work 7.4

Build Your Jaguar Online

MKT GLOBAL

Prospective Jaguar car buyers can build, see, and price the car of their dreams online. As of October 2000, you can configure the car at *jaguar.com* in real time. Cars have been configured online since 1997, but Jaguar was the industry's first to offer comprehensive services, delivered in many languages.

Using a virtual car, users can view more than 1,250 possible exterior combinations, rotating the car through 360 degrees, by moving directional arrows. As you select the model, color, trim, wheels, and accessories, both image and price information automatically update. The design choices are limited to current models. Up to 10 personalized car selections per customer can be stored in a "virtual garage." Customers can "test" virtual cars and conduct comparisons of different models. Once the buyer makes a decision, the order is forwarded to a dealer of his or her choice.

Like most other car manufacturers, Jaguar will not let you consummate the purchase online. To negotiate price, customers can go to a Jaguar dealer or use Auto By Tel (*autobytel.com*), which connects nearby dealers to the customer. However, Jaguar's system helps get customers to the point of purchase. It helps them *research* the purchase and

explore, price, and visualize options. Customers thus familiarize themselves with the Jaguar before even visiting a showroom. The ability to see a 3-D photo of the car is an extremely important customer service. Finally, the order for the customer-configured car can be transmitted electronically to the production floor, reducing the time-to-delivery cycle.

The IT support for this innovation includes a powerful configuration database integrated with Jaguar's production system (developed by Ford Motor Company and Trilogy Corp.) and the "virtual car" (developed by Global Beach Corp.).

As of mid-2000, most car manufacturers had introduced Web-based make-to-order systems. In order to avoid channel conflicts, these systems typically involve the dealers in the actual purchase. All major car manufacturers are attempting to move some part of car ordering to the Web.

Sources: Compiled from *jaguar.com* press releases (October–November 2000); *ford.com* (2006) (go to Services); and *autobytel.com* (2006).

For Further Exploration: Why would manufacturers be interested in the Web if the actual purchase is done at the dealers' site?

Mass customization is not for everyone, and it does have several limitations (Butcher, 2006). The major limitations are that it requires a highly flexible production technology, an elaborate system for eliciting customers' wants and needs, and strong direct-to-customer logistics system. Another limitation is cost: Some people are unable or unwilling to pay even the slightly higher prices that customization often entails. Butcher (2006) provides some guidelines for how to overcome these limitations.

Personalization. Using cameras, retailers can find what people are doing while they visit physical stores. Similarly, tracking software can find what people are doing in a virtual store. This technology provides information for real-time marketing and is also used in m-commerce (see Chapter 6). Personalized product offers then are made, based on where the customer spent the most time and on what he or she purchased. A similar approach is used in Web-based *cross-selling* (or *up-selling*) efforts, in which advertising of related products is provided. For example, if you are buying a car, car insurance is automatically offered (see Johnson, 2006).

Advertising and Promotions. The Internet opens the door to a new advertising medium. As was shown in Chapter 5, online advertising, mainly via e-mail and targeted banners, is growing rapidly. Innovative methods such as viral marketing (Reda, 2002) are possible only on the Internet. Wireless and pervasive computing applications also are changing the face of advertising (Chapter 6). For example, in order to measure attention to advertising, a mobile-computing device from Arbitron (see Portable People Meter at *arbitron.com*) is carried by customers. Whoever is wearing the device automatically logs advertising seen or heard any time, anywhere in their daily movements.

DISTRIBUTION CHANNELS AND IN-STORE INNOVATIONS

Organizations can distribute their products and services through several delivery channels. For instance, a company may use its own outlets or distributors. Digitizable products can be distributed online, or can be delivered on CD-ROMs. Other products can be delivered by trucks or trains, with the movement of goods monitored by IT applications. The Web is revolutionizing distribution channels. Here we look at some representative topics relating to distribution channels.

Improving Shopping and Checkout at Retail Stores. The modern shopper is often pressed for time, and most are unhappy about waiting in long lines. Using information technology, it is possible to reengineer the shopping and the checkout process, as illustrated in Chapter 6. Additional examples are:

- An information kiosk enables customers to view catalogs in stores, conduct product searches, and even compare prices with those of competitors. Kiosks at some stores (e.g., 7-Eleven stores in some countries) can be used to place orders on the Internet. (For details about use of in-store kiosks, see Online File W7.7.) In Macy's you can check the current price on computerized screens with barcode readers.
- Some stores that have many customers who pay by check (e.g., large grocery stores, Costco, Wal-Mart stores) have installed check-writers. All you have to do is submit the blank check to the cashier, who runs it through a machine attached to the cash register. The machine prints the name of the store as the payee and the amount, you sign the check, and in seconds the check is validated, your bank account is debited, and you are out of the store with your merchandise.

U-Scan kiosk.

- The Exxon Mobil Speedpass allows customers to fill their tanks by waving a token, embedded with an RFID device, at a gas-pump sensor. Then the RFID starts an authorization process, and the purchase is charged to your credit card. Customers no longer need to carry their Mobil credit cards (See *mobil.com/speedpass.*)
- An increasing number of retailers are installing self-checkout machines. For example, Home Depot in 2003 added self-checkouts in their stores. Not only does the retailer save the cost of employees' salaries, but customers are happier for saving time. (And some enjoy "playing cashier" briefly.) A major vendor is U-Scan, which is used in many supermarkets (see photo). Soon, RFIDs will improve the process even further.

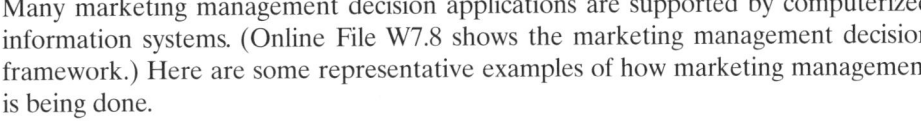

MARKETING MANAGEMENT

Many marketing management decision applications are supported by computerized information systems. (Online File W7.8 shows the marketing management decision framework.) Here are some representative examples of how marketing management is being done.

Pricing of Products or Services. Sales volumes are largely determined by the prices of products or services. Price is also a major determinant of profit. Pricing is a difficult decision, and prices may need to be changed frequently. For example, in response to price changes made by competitors, a company may need to adjust its prices or take other actions. Checking competitors' prices is commonly done by retailers. But instead of carrying paper and pen, one can use wireless price checkers (e.g., PriceMaster Plus, from SoftwarePlus). These devices make data collection easy.

Pricing decisions are supported by a number of computerized systems. Many companies are using business analytical processing to support pricing and other marketing decisions (see Chapters 11 and 12). In Chapter 2 we discussed the optimization models used to support prices at Longs Drug Stores and others (see Online File W2.1). Web-based comparison engines enable customers to select a vendor at the price they want, and they also enable vendors to see how their prices compare with others. For an example of price optimization, see Rapt (2006) and Chapter 12. For more on price optimization, see Parks (2004a).

Salesperson Productivity. Salespeople differ from each other; some excel in selling certain products, while others excel in selling to a certain type of customer or in a certain geographical zone. This information, which is usually collected in the sales and marketing TPS, can be analyzed, using a comparative performance system in which sales data by salesperson, product, region, and even the time of day are evaluated. Actual current sales can be compared to historical data and to standards. Multidimensional spreadsheet software facilitates this type of analysis. Assignment of salespeople to regions and/or products and the calculation of bonuses can also be supported by this system.

In addition, sales productivity can be boosted by Web-based systems. For example, in a Web-based call center, when a customer calls a sales rep, the rep can look at the customer's history of purchases, demographics, services available where the customer lives, and more. This information enables reps to work faster, while providing better customer service (see Minicase 2).

Productivity Software. **Sales automation software** is especially helpful to small businesses, enabling them to rapidly increase sales and growth. Such Web-based software (e.g., from *salesforce.com*) can manage the flow of messages and assist in writing contracts, scheduling, and making appointments. Of course it also provides word processing and e-mail, and it helps with mailings and follow-up letters. Electronic stamps (e.g., *stamps.com*) can assist with mass mailings.

Profitability Analysis. In deciding on advertising and other marketing efforts, managers often need to know the profit contribution of certain products and services. Profitability information for products and services can be derived from the cost-accounting system. For example, profit performance analysis software available from IBM, Oracle, SAS, and Microstrategy, Inc. is designed to help managers assess and improve the profit performance of their line of business, products, distribution channels, sales regions, and other dimensions critical to managing the enterprise. Northwest Airlines, for example, uses expert systems to set prices based on profitability. They also use a similar system to audit tickets and for calculating commissions to travel agents.

New Products, Services, and Market Planning. The introduction of new or improved products and services can be expensive and risky. An important question to ask about a new product or service is, "Will it sell?" An appropriate answer calls for careful analysis, planning, and forecasting. These can best be executed with the aid of IT because of the large number of determining factors and the uncertainties that may be involved (e.g., using predictive analysis, Chapter 11). Market research also can be conducted on the Internet. A related issue is the speed with which products are brought to market. An example of how Procter & Gamble expedites the time-to-market by using the Internet is provided in *IT at Work 7.5*.

IT at Work 7.5

Internet Market Research Expedites Time-to-Market at Procter & Gamble   MKT

For decades, Procter & Gamble (P&G) and Colgate-Palmolive have been competitors in the market for personal care products. Developing a major new product, from concept to market launch, used to take over 5 years. First, a concept test was done; the companies sent product photos and descriptions to potential customers, asking whether they might buy it. If the feedback was negative, they tried to improve the product concept and then repeated the concept testing. Once positive response was achieved, sample products were mailed out, and customers were asked to fill out detailed questionnaires. When customers' responses met the companies' internal hurdles, the company would start with mass advertising on television and in magazines.

However, thanks to the Internet, it took P&G only three-and-a-half years to get Whitestrips, the teeth-brightening product, onto the market and to a sales level of $200 million a year—considerably quicker than other oral care products. In September 2000, P&G threw out the old marketing test model and instead introduced Whitestrips on the Internet, offering the product for sale on P&G's Web site. The company spent several months studying who was coming to the site and buying the product; it collected responses to online questionnaires, which was much faster than the old mail-outs.

The online research, which was facilitated by data mining conducted on P&G's huge historical data (stored in a data warehouse) and the new Internet data, revealed the most enthusiastic groups. These included teenage girls, brides-to-be, and young Hispanic Americans. Immediately, the company started to target these segments with appropriate advertising. The Internet created a product awareness of 35 percent, even before any shipments were made to stores. This "buzz" created a huge demand for the product by the time it hit the shelves.

From this experience, P&G learned important lessons about flexible and creative ways to approach product innovation and marketing. The whole process of studying the product concept, segmenting the market, and expediting product development has been revolutionized.

Sources: Compiled from Buckley (2002), and from *pg.com* (accessed July 2006).

For Further Exploration: How did the Internet decrease time-to-market in this situation? What is the role of data mining? Why is so much testing needed?

Web-Based Systems in Marketing. The use of Web-based systems in support of marketing and sales has grown rapidly, as demonstrated by the P&G case. A summary of some Web-based impacts is provided in Online File W7.8.

Other Applications. Many other applications exist. For example, Howarth (2004) describes the use of IT to reduce theft in stores.

Marketing activities conclude the *primary* activities of the value chain. Next we look at the functional systems that are *secondary* (support) activities in the value chain: accounting/finance and human resources management.

7.5 Managing the Accounting and Finance Systems

ACC

FIN

A primary mission of the accounting/finance functional area is to manage money flows into, within, and out of organizations. This is a very broad mission since money is involved in all functions of an organization. Some repetitive accounting/financing activities such as payroll, billing, and cash management were computerized as early as the 1950s. Today, accounting/finance information systems are very diverse and comprehensive. Note that while in universities accounting and finance are separate departments, in the real world they are frequently united in one department.

The general structure of an accounting/finance system is presented in Online File W7.9. It is divided into three levels: strategic, tactical, and operational. Information technology can support almost all the activities listed, as well as the communication and collaboration of accounting/finance with internal and external environments. We describe selected activities in the rest of this section.

FINANCIAL PLANNING AND BUDGETING

Appropriate management of financial assets is a major task in financial planning and budgeting. Managers must plan for both the acquisition of financial resources and their use. Financial planning, like any other functional planning, is tied to the overall organizational planning and to other functional areas. It is divided into short-, medium-, and long-term horizons, much like activities planning. Financial analysts use Web resources and computerized analytics (Chapters 11 and 12) to accomplish the organization's financial planning and budgeting activities.

Financial and Economic Forecasting and Budgeting. Knowledge about the availability and cost of money is a key ingredient for successful financial planning. Especially important is the projection of cash flow, which tells organizations what funds they need and when, and how they will acquire them. This function is important for all firms, but is especially so for small companies, which tend to have little financial cushion. Inaccurate cash flow projection is the number-one reason why many small businesses go bankrupt. Availability and cost of money depend on corporate financial health and the willingness of lenders and investors to infuse money into the company.

Financial and economic analysis can be facilitated by intelligent systems such as neural computing (Chapter 12). Many software packages are available for conducting economic and financial forecasting, which are frequently available for a fee, over the Internet.

Budgeting. The best-known part of financial planning is the annual budget, which allocates the financial resources of an organization among participants and activities. The budget is the financial expression of the organization's plans. It allows management to allocate resources in the way that best supports the organization's mission and goals. IT enables the introduction of financial logic and efficiency into the budgeting process.

Software Support. Several software packages, many of which are Web-based, are available to support budget preparation and control (e.g., Budget 2000 from PROPHIX Software, and budgeting modules from Oracle and Capterra.com) and to facilitate communication among all participants in the budget preparation.

Example: Software support for budgeting is available from PROPHIX. The key benefits of the package are: a familiar Windows Explorer interface, customizable flexibility that supports a variety of budgeting templates, a controlled database that secures data and allows for multiple user accessibility, and various data manipulation tools for complicated budgeting.

PROPHIX's New Model Wizard creates a new budgeting model in seconds. Using the Account Manager, the Dimension Manager, and the Import Data modules, individual companies' distinctive account and organization structures are populated with data at the beginning of the budgeting process. PROPHIX has multicurrency budgeting capabilities ensuring precision to budgets by adjusting exchange rates based on business exposure and risk. More accurate reporting is achieved through the conversion and consolidation of multiple currencies into the company's home currency (*Prophix.com,* 2006).

Since budget preparation may involve both top-down and bottom-up processes, modeling capabilities in some packages allow the budget coordinator to take the top-down numbers, compare them with the bottom-up data from the users, and reconcile the two.

The major benefits of using budgeting software are that it can: reduce the time and effort involved in the budget process, explore and analyze the implications of organizational and environmental changes, facilitate the integration of the corporate strategic objectives with operational plans, make planning an ongoing, continuous process, and automatically monitor exceptions for patterns and trends.

Capital Budgeting. *Capital budgeting* is the financing of asset acquisitions, including the disposal of major organizational assets. It usually includes a comparison of options, such as keep the asset, replace it with an identical new asset, replace it with a different one, or discard it. The capital budgeting process also evaluates buy-versus-lease options.

Capital budgeting analysis uses standard financial models, such as net present value (NPV), internal rate of return (IRR), and payback period (all presented in Chapter 14), to evaluate alternative investment decisions. Most spreadsheet packages include built-in functions of these models.

MANAGING FINANCIAL TRANSACTIONS

An accounting/finance information system is also responsible for gathering the raw data necessary for the accounting/finance TPS, transforming the data into information, and making the information available to users, whether aggregate information about payroll, the organization's internal reports, or external reports to stockholders or government agencies.

Many packages exist to execute routine accounting transaction processing activities. Several are available free on the Internet (try *tucows.com*). Many software packages are integrated. In these integrated systems, the accounting/finance activities are combined with other TPSs such as those of marketing and production and operations management. The data collected and managed for the accounting/finance transaction processing system are also inputs for the various functional information systems.

One such integrated system is MAS 90 ERP, MAS 200 ERP, and Sage MAS 500 ERP (from *bestsoftware.com*). It is a collection of standard accounting modules, as

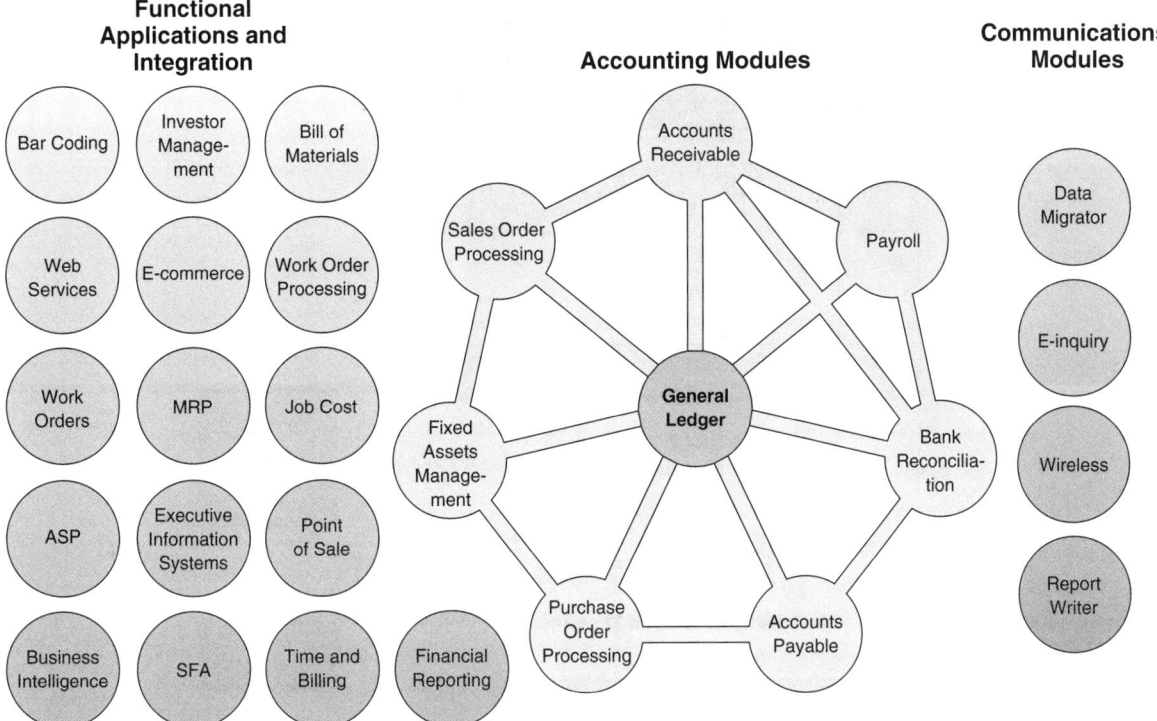

Figure 7.5 Integrated accounting/business software.

shown in Figure 7.5 (the "wheel" in the diagram). Communication and inquiry modules (right side) support the accounting modules. The user can integrate as many of the modules as needed for the business. On the left side is a list of other business processes and functional applications that can interface with accounting applications. Note that the software includes an e-commerce module, which provides dynamic Web access to MAS 90. This module includes account and order inquiry capabilities as well as a shopping cart for order entry. The 2006 version of MAS 90 includes modules for business intelligence, e-commerce, CRM, sales force automation (SFA), and financial reporting.

Another integrated accounting software package is *peachtree.com*, which offers a sales ledger, purchase ledger, cash book, sales order processing, invoicing, stock control, job casting, fixed-assets register, and more. Other accounting packages can be found at *2020software.com* and *findaccountingsoftware.com*.

The accounting/finance TPS also provides a complete, reliable audit trail of all transactions transmitted through the network. This feature is vital to accountants and auditors. (For more, see the "Control and Auditing" section below.)

XBRL: Extensible Business Reporting Language. **XBRL** is a programming language and an international standard for electronic transmission of business and financial information. As of September 2005, it can be used to file financial reports electronically with the SEC and FDIC. With XBRL all the company's financial data are collected, consolidated, published, and consumed without the need to use Excel spreadsheets. Figure 7.6 illustrates how XBRL works. Such submission allows government analysts to validate information submitted in hours instead of two to three weeks.

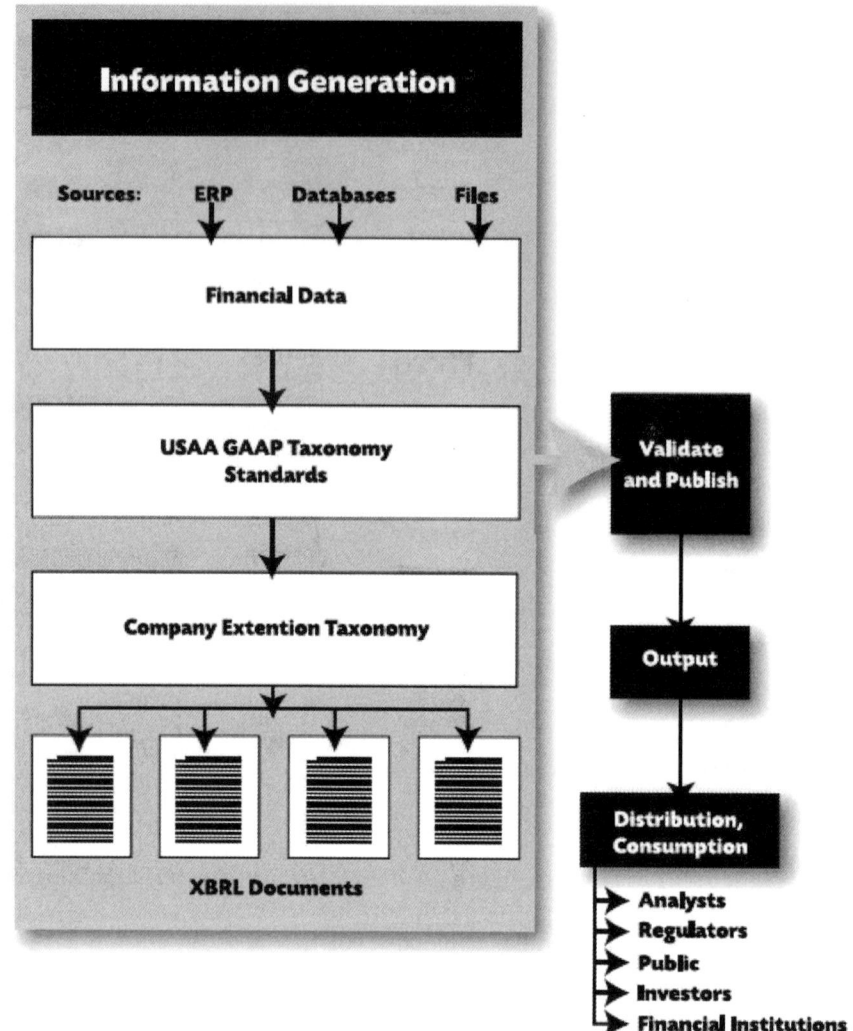

Figure 7.6 How XBRL works.

The U.S. government agencies plan to mandate the use of XBRL. According to Malykhina (2006), the Federal Financial Institutions Examination Council found that XBRL helps banks:

- Generate cleaner data, including written explanations and supporting notes.
- Produce more accurate data with fewer errors that require follow-up by regulators.
- Transmit data faster to regulators and meet deadlines.
- Increase the number of cases and amount of information that staffers can handle.
- Make information available faster to regulators and the public.
- Address issues and concerns in their filings rather than after the fact.

For additional applications in financial transactions, see Online File W7.10.

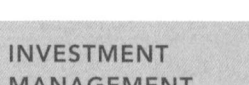

INVESTMENT MANAGEMENT

Effective investment management is a difficult task, both for individuals and for corporations. For one thing, there are thousands of investment alternatives. On the New York Stock Exchange alone, there are more than 2,000 stocks, and millions of possible combinations for creating portfolios. Investment decisions are based on economic and financial forecasts and on various multiple and conflicting objectives (such as high yield, safety, and liquidity). The investment environment also includes opportunities in other countries. Another factor that contributes to the complexity of investment management is that investments made by many organizations are subject to complex regulations and tax laws. Finally, investment decisions need to be made quickly and frequently. Decision makers can be in different locations, and they need to cooperate and collaborate. Therefore, computerization is especially popular in financial institutions that are involved in investments. Many other banks and financial institutions have similar systems, especially for portfolio management. An example is Opti-Money, which is successfully used in Israel (see Avriel et al., 2004). Companies today conduct shareholders' votes online and send reports to shareholders. Brokers attempt to replace all paper reports with electronic ones.

In addition, data-mining tools and neural networks (Chapter 12) are used by many institutional investment managers to analyze historical databases, so they can make better predictions. For a data-mining tool, see *wizsoft.com*. Some typical financial applications of neural computing are provided in Online File W7.11.

The following are the major areas of support that IT can provide to investment management.

Access to Financial and Economic Reports. Investment decisions require managers to evaluate financial and economic reports and news provided by federal and state agencies, universities, research institutions, financial services, and corporations. There are hundreds of Web sources, many of which are free; a sampling is listed in Online File W7.12. Most of these services are useful both for professional investment managers and for individual investors.

Financial Analysis. Financial analysis can be executed with a spreadsheet program, or with commercially available ready-made decision support software (e.g., see *tradeportal.com/matrixsuite.asp*). Or it can be more sophisticated, involving intelligent systems. Other information technologies can be used as well. For example, Morgan Stanley and Company uses virtual reality on its intranet to display the results of risk analysis in three dimensions. Seeing data in 3-D makes it easier to make comparisons and intuitive connections than would seeing a two-dimensional chart or spreadsheet data.

One area of analysis that is becoming popular is referred to as **financial value chain management (FVCM).** According to this approach, financial analysis is combined with operations analysis. All financial functions are analyzed (including international trades). Combining financial and operations analysis provides better financial control. For example, if the organization runs its operations at a lower-than-planned level, it is likely to need less money; if it exceeds the operational plan, it may well be all right to exceed the budgeted amounts for that plan. For details see *Aberdeen.com* (2002).

CONTROL AND AUDITING

A major reason organizations go out of business is their inability to forecast and/or secure sufficient *cash flow*. Underestimated expenses, overspending, financial mismanagement, and fraud can lead to disaster. Good planning is necessary, but not sufficient, and must be supplemented by skillful control. Control activities in organizations take many forms, including control and auditing of the information systems themselves (see Chapter 16). Information systems play an extremely important role in supporting organizational control, as we show throughout the text. Specific forms of financial control are presented next.

Risk Analysis. Companies need to analyze the risk of doing business with partners or in other countries. Giving credit to customers can be risky, so one can use products such as FICO (from *fairisaac.com*) for calculating risk. Also see @RISK for Excel from *palisade.com*.

Budgetary Control. Once the annual budget has been decided upon, it is divided into monthly allocations. Managers at various levels then monitor departmental expenditures and compare them against the budget and operational progress of the corporate plans. Simple reporting systems summarize the expenditures and provide *exception reports* by flagging any expenditure that exceeds the budget by a certain percent or that falls significantly below the budget. More sophisticated software attempts to tie expenditures to program accomplishment. Numerous software programs can be used to support budgetary control; most of them are combined with budget preparation packages from vendors such as *outlooksoft.com, clarifysystems. com,* and *capterra.com*.

Auditing. The major purpose of auditing is to ensure the accuracy and condition of the financial health of an organization. Internal auditing is done by the organization's accounting/finance personnel, who also prepare for external auditing by CPA companies.

IT can facilitate auditing. For example, intelligent systems can uncover fraud by finding financial transactions that significantly deviate from previous payment profiles. Also, IT provides real-time data whenever needed (see *oracle.com*).

Financial Ratio Analysis. A major task of the accounting/finance department is to watch the financial health of the company by monitoring and assessing a set of financial ratios. These ratios are mostly the same as those used by external parties when they are deciding whether to invest in an organization, loan money to it, or buy it. But internal parties have access to much more detailed data for use in calculating financial ratios.

The collection of data for ratio analysis is done by the transaction processing system, and computation of the ratios is done by financial analysis models. The *interpretation* of the ratios, and especially the prediction of their future behavior, requires expertise and is sometimes supported by expert systems.

Profitability Analysis and Cost Control. Many companies are concerned with the profitability of individual products or services as well as with the financial health of the entire organization. Profitability analysis DSS software (see Chapter 12) allows accurate computation of profitability. It also allows allocation of overheads. One way to control cost is by properly estimating it. This is done by special software; see Vijayakumar (2002).

Profitability Management from Hyperion provides potent multidimensional and predictive analysis, and proven query, reporting, and dashboard functionality with ease-of-use and deployment. See Chapter 11, Figure 11.2 for illustrations of Hyperion's dashboards. The solution delivers powerful, insightful activity-based cost analysis and what-if modeling capabilities to help create and test new business strategies. Sophisticated business rules are stored in one place, enabling

A Closer Look 7.1

Expense and Spend Management Automation

ACC   FIN

Companies are interested in controlling all types of expenses, not just for travel. For these purposes there are several specialized IT programs. Most notable are those from Ariba.com. Ariba Spend Management software provides tools to analyze spending, buy products and services from suppliers via the Web, host online auctions (to reduce purchasing prices), and manage the bid process for prospective suppliers. Ariba even provides software tools to save money on SOX compliance as well as allocating resources for online sourcing.

Another company that provides tools for **spend management** and analysis is Ketera Technologies (*ketera.com*). They also provide procurement and sourcing services (e.g., automating interactions with suppliers). Finally, they provide a repository for contracts and manage approval workflow.

Frictionless Commerce (*frictionless.com*) provides software to analyze spending transactions to see whether purchases are being made with suppliers that have negotiated contracts (SRM Explorer). Online auctions and RFP are managed by Enterprise Sourcing.

About a dozen other companies provide tools for expense and spend management. Some relate it to compliance software.

---

analyses and strategies to be shared easily across an entire enterprise (*Hyperion. com*, 2006).

Expense Management Automation. Expense management automation (EMA) refers to systems that automate data entry and processing of travel and entertainment expenses. These expenses can account for 20 percent of the operating expenses of large corporations (Degnan, 2003). EMA systems (by companies such as Captura, Concur, Extensity, and Necho) are Web-based applications that replace the paper forms and rudimentary spreadsheet. These systems let companies quickly and consistently collect expense information, enforce company policies and contracts, and reduce unplanned purchases of airline and hotel services. The software forces travelers to be organized before a trip starts. In addition to benefits to the companies, employees also benefit from quick reimbursement (since expense approvals are not held up by sloppy or incomplete documentation). (For details, see "What EMA systems now offer. . . ," 2002.)

For more on expense and spend management automation, see *A Closer Look 7.1*.

Several more applications in the financial/accounting area are described in Online File W7.13. Many more can be found at Reed et al. (2001).

7.6 Managing Human Resources Systems

HRM

Developments in Web-based systems increased the popularity of human resources information systems (HRISs) as of the late 1990s. Initial HRIS applications were mainly related to transaction processing systems. (For examples, see Thomas and Ray, 2000; and Bussler and Davis, 2001–2002.) In recent years, as systems generally have been moved to intranets and the Web, so have HRIS applications, many of which can be delivered via an HR portal. Many organizations use their Web portals to advertise job openings and conduct online hiring and training. Gomez-Mejia et al. (2007) describe the impact of the Internet on acquiring, rewarding, developing, protecting, and retaining human resources. Their findings are summarized in Online File W7.14. Perhaps the biggest benefit to companies of human relations IT services is the release of HR staff from intermediary roles (e.g., by self-services, such as self-entry of an address change), so they can focus on strategic planning and human resources organization and development. In the following sections we describe in more detail how IT facilitates the management of human resources (HRM).

RECRUITMENT	*Recruitment* is finding employees, testing them, and deciding which ones to hire. Some companies are flooded with viable applicants, while others have difficulty finding the right people. Information systems can be helpful in both cases. Here we present some examples.

Using the Web for Recruitment. With millions of resumes available online, it is not surprising that companies are trying to find appropriate candidates on the Web, usually with the help of specialized search engines. Also, hundreds of thousands of jobs are advertised on the Web (see Field, 2006). Many matching services exist (see Internet Exercise 3). Online recruiting is able to "cast a wide net" to reach more candidates faster (Field, 2006), which may bring in better applicants. In addition, the costs of online recruitment are lower. Other benefits of online recruitment for employers, plus some disadvantages, are shown in Online File W7.15.

Recruitment online is beneficial for candidates as well. They are exposed to a larger number of job offerings, can get details of the positions quickly, and can begin to evaluate the prospective employer. To check the competitiveness of salary offerings, or to see how much one can make elsewhere in several countries, job candidates can go to *monster.com*.

As more companies expand operations overseas, global recruiting is becoming a vexing problem. Companies simply have problems finding qualified people, especially engineers and salespeople. Using the Internet to recruit from other countries is becoming popular, yet it requires expertise (see Shah, 2006).

Example: Field (2006) provides an example of recruiting by Finish Line Corp. In a 12-month period, more than 330,000 candidates applied for employment with the company; more than 75 percent of them applied online. Using screening software (by Unicru), 112,154 candidates were eliminated immediately. More than 60,000 hours of store managers' time were saved because of the reduction in the number of interviews conducted.

For a complete analysis of and guidelines for e-recruitment, see Field (2006).

HRM Portals and Salary Surveys. One advantage of the Web is the large amount of information related to job matching. There are also many private and public HR-related portals. The portal is a search engine, an index of jobs, posted on corporate-member sites. For example, several large companies (e.g., IBM, Xerox, GE) created jointly with 120 companies a career portal called DirectEmployer.com. Commercial, public online recruiters, such as Monster.com, help corporate recruiters find candidates for difficult-to-fill positions. For details see *JobCentral.com.*

Another area for HR portals is salary surveys. Salary surveys help companies determine how much to pay their employees. Companies used to pay consultants up to $10,000 for a one-time survey (Bussler and Davis, 2001–2002). Now they can conduct such surveys themselves by utilizing free data from vendors such as Salary.com (check "What you are worth"). Salary Wizard Pro covers pay scales in small businesses.

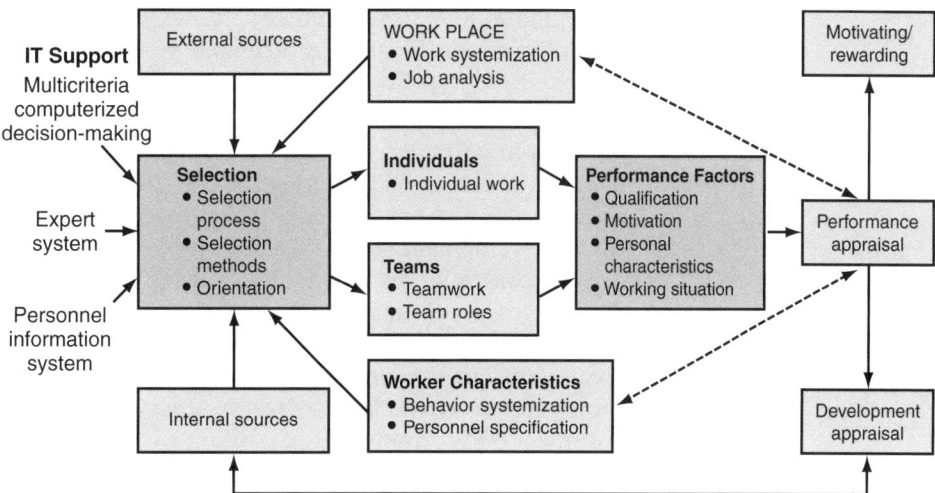

Figure 7.7 Intelligent personnel selection model. (*Source:* Jareb and Rajkoric, 2001.)

Employee Selection. The human resources department is responsible for screening job applicants, evaluating, testing, and selecting them in compliance with state and federal regulations. The process of employee selection can be very complex since it may involve many external and internal candidates and multiple criteria. To expedite the testing and evaluation process and ensure consistency in selection, companies use information technologies such as Web-based expert systems. Figure 7.7 shows the multiple criteria involved in employee selection and illustrates the role of an expert system in this process and in related tasks such as performance appraisal.

HUMAN RESOURCES MAINTENANCE AND DEVELOPMENT

Once recruited, employees become part of the corporate human resources pool, which needs to be maintained and developed. Some activities supported by IT are the following.

Performance Evaluation. Most employees are periodically evaluated by their immediate supervisors. Peers or subordinates may also evaluate others. Evaluations are usually recorded on paper or electronic forms. Using such information manually is a tedious and error-prone job. Once digitized, evaluations can be used to support many decisions, ranging from rewards to transfers to layoffs. For example, Cisco Systems is known for developing an IT-based human capital strategy (Chatman et al., 2005). Many universities evaluate professors online. The evaluation form appears on the screen, and the students fill it in. Results can be tabulated in minutes. Corporate managers can analyze employees' performances with the help of expert systems, which provide systematic interpretation of performance over time.

Wage review is related to performance evaluation. For example, Hewlett-Packard's Atlanta-based U.S. Field Services Operations (USFO) Group has developed a paperless wage review (PWR) system. The Web-based system uses intelligent agents to deal with quarterly reviews of HP's 15,000 employees. (A similar system is used by most other groups, covering a total of 150,000 employees.) The agent software lets USFO managers and personnel access employee data from both the personnel and functional databases. The PWR system tracks employee review dates and automatically initiates the wage review process. It sends wage review forms to first-level managers by e-mail every quarter.

Training and Human Resources Development. Employee training and retraining is an important activity of the human resources department. Major issues are planning of classes and tailoring specific training programs to meet the needs of the organization and employees. Sophisticated human resources departments build a career development plan for each employee. IT can support the planning, monitoring, and control of these activities by using workflow applications.

IT also plays an important role in training (see discussion on e-learning in Chapter 17, and Harris, 2005). Some of the most innovative developments are in the areas of *intelligent computer-aided instruction* (ICAI) and application of multimedia support for instructional activities. Instruction is provided online at 38 percent of all Fortune 1,000 corporations, according to OmniTech Consulting ("Web Breathes Life," 1988). Training salespeople is an expensive and lengthy proposition. To save money on training costs, companies are providing sales-skills training over the Internet or intranet. Online File W7.16 provides examples of the variety of employee training available on the Internet and intranets. Interesting implementations of computer-based training at Shoney's are reported by McKinley (2003) and at Sheetz convenience stores by Korolishin (2004b).

Training can be improved using Web-based video clips. For example, using a digital video-editing system, Dairy Queen's in-house video production department produced a higher-quality training video at 50 percent lower cost than by outsourcing it. The affordability of the videos encourages more Dairy Queen franchisees to participate in the training program. This improves customer service as well as employee skill. For tools for online training, see *Softsim.com* and Camtasia from *Techsmith.com*.

Mobile devices are increasingly being used for training as well as for performance improvement (Gayeski, 2004). Finally, training can be enhanced by virtual reality. Intel, Motorola, Samsung Electronic, and IBM are using virtual reality (Chapter 11) to simulate different scenarios and configurations. The training is especially effective in complex environments where mistakes can be very costly (see Boisvert, 2000).

HUMAN RESOURCES PLANNING AND MANAGEMENT	Managing human resources in large organizations requires extensive planning and detailed strategy (Gomez-Mejia, 2007). In some industries, labor negotiation is a particularly important aspect of human resources planning and it may be facilitated by IT. For most companies, administering employee benefits is also a significant part of the human resources function. Here are some examples of how IT can help.

Personnel Planning and HR strategies. The human resources department forecasts requirements for people and skills. In some geographical areas and for overseas assignments it may be difficult to find particular types of employees. In such cases the HR department plans how to find (or develop from within) sufficient human resources. Also, compliance with regulations regarding safety and privacy is facilitated by IT (Section 7.8).

Large companies develop qualitative and quantitative workforce planning models. Such models can be enhanced if IT is used to collect, update, and process the information. Radio Shack uses special software to develop HR strategies (see Reda, 2004, for details).

Benefits Administration. Employees' contributions to their organizations are rewarded by salary/wage, bonuses, and other benefits. Benefits include those for health and dental care as well as contributions for pensions. Managing the benefits system can be a complex task, due to its many components and the tendency of organizations to allow employees to choose and trade off benefits ("cafeteria style"). In large companies, using computers for self-benefits selection can save a tremendous amount of labor and time for HR staff (see *iemployee.com*).

Providing flexibility in selecting benefits is viewed as a competitive advantage in large organizations. It can be successfully implemented when supported by computers. Some companies have automated benefits enrollments. Employees can self-register for specific benefits using the corporate portal or voice technology. Employees self-select desired benefits from a menu. Payroll pay cards are now in use in numerous companies, such as Payless Shoes, which has 30,000 employees in 5,000 stores (see Korolishin, 2004a). The system specifies the value of each benefit and the available benefits balance of each employee. Some companies use intelligent agents to assist the employees and monitor their actions. Expert systems can answer employees' questions and offer advice online. Simpler systems allow for self-updating of personal information such as changes in address, family status, and so on. Self-entry saves money for the company and is usually more accurate.

For a comprehensive resource of HRM on the Web, see *shrm.org/hrlinks*.

Employee Relationship Management. In their effort to better manage employees, companies are developing *human capital management* (HCM), facilitated by the Web, to streamline the HR process. These Web applications are more commonly referred to as **employee relationship management (ERM).** For example, self-services such as tracking personal information and online training are very popular in ERM. Improved relationships with employees results in better retention and higher productivity. ERM technologies and applications are very similar to those of customer relationship management (CRM), which we discuss in Chapter 8. For an example in the U.S. Navy, see Online File W7.17.

7.7 Integrating Functional Information Systems

Functional information systems can be built in-house, they can be purchased from large vendors (such as Computer Associates, Best Software Inc., Microsoft, Oracle, or IBM), or they can be leased from application service providers (ASPs). In any of these cases, there is a need for their integration with other information systems, including databases.

REASONS FOR INTEGRATION

For many years most IT applications were developed in the functional areas, independent of each other. Many companies developed their own customized systems that dealt with standard procedures to execute transaction processing/operational activities. These procedures are fairly similar, regardless of what company is performing them. Therefore, the trend today is to buy commercial, off-the-shelf functional applications or to lease them from ASPs. The smaller the organization, the more attractive such options are. Indeed, several hundred commercial products are available to support each of the major functional areas.

Development tools are also available to build custom-made applications in a specific functional area. For example, there are software packages for building financial applications, a hospital pharmacy management system, and a university student registration system. Some software vendors specialize in one or a few areas. For example, Lawson Software concentrates on retailing (see Minicase 1), and Oracle's strength is in HRM.

However, to build information systems along business processes (which cross functional lines) requires a different approach. Matching business processes with a combination of several functional off-the-shelf packages may be a solution in some areas. For example, it may be possible to integrate manufacturing, sales, and accounting software if they all come from the same software vendor (as shown in the opening case). However, combining existing packages from several vendors may not be practical or effective. To build applications that will easily cross functional lines and reach separate databases often requires new approaches such as Web Services and integrated suites, such as Oracle 9i (McCullough, 2002).

Information systems integration tears down barriers between and among departments and corporate headquarters and reduces duplication of effort. For example, Palaniswamy and Frank (2000) studied five ERP systems and found in all cases that better cross-functional integration was a critical success factor.

One of the key factors for integration, especially with business partners, is agreement on appropriate standards (see *openapplications.org*). Integration can be done by middleware (Technology Guide 2) and by Web Services (Technology Guide 6).

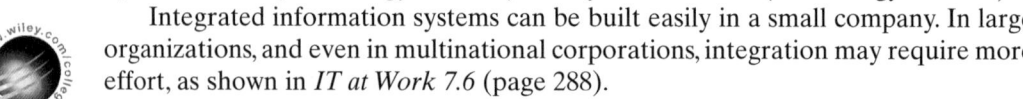

Integrated information systems can be built easily in a small company. In large organizations, and even in multinational corporations, integration may require more effort, as shown in *IT at Work 7.6* (page 288).

Another approach to integration of information systems is to use ERP software (Chapter 8). However, ERP requires a company to fit its business processes to the software. As an alternative to ERP, companies can choose the *best-of-breed systems* on the market, or use some of their own home-grown systems and integrate them. The latter approach may not be simple, but it may be more effective.

By whatever method it is accomplished, integrating information systems helps to reduce cost, increase employees' productivity, and facilitate information sharing and collaboration, which are necessary for improving customer service.

INTEGRATION OF FRONT-OFFICE WITH BACK-OFFICE OPERATIONS

In Chapters 2 and 5 we discussed the need to integrate front-office with back-office operations. This is a difficult task. It is easier to integrate the front-office operations among themselves and the back-office operations among themselves (which is basically what systems such as MAS 90 are doing).

Software from various vendors offers some front-office and back-office integration solutions. Oracle Corp., for example, is continuously expanding its front-office software, which offers a capability of connecting back-office operations with it. To do so, the software uses new integration approaches, such as process-centric integration. **Process-centric integration** refers to integration solutions designed, developed, and managed from a business-process perspective, instead of from a technical or middleware perspective. The Oracle 9i product, for example, offers not only internal integration of the back office and front office, but also integration with business partners (see McCullough, 2002). Among its capabilities are:

• **Online field sales:** a Web-based customer management application.

IT at Work 7.6

Software Helps Cirque du Soleil

MKT POM

Cirque du Soleil is a Canada-based traveling circus. Using IT, the circus is able to entertain more people each year than the Red Sox and Yankees combined (over seven million in 2005, in four continents). How do they do it? First, this is no ordinary circus. It features astonishing acrobatics and Broadway-caliber music and dance in 11 different shows (in addition to traditional circus and opera). All this is done by 20,000 performers and 3,500 management employees who are constantly on the move using 250 tractor-trailers. Twenty thousand performers are scheduled and transported with all the stage equipment and costumes that are constantly changing. The company grew very rapidly between 2000 and 2005, and several problems were created as a result of the rapid growth.

The logistics of people, transportation, accommodations, food, supplies, and so on, in hundreds of different cities each year, for several traveling groups is fairly difficult. And there are 200 different applications in all functional areas, from finance to POM, accounting, marketing, and human resources management. These applications were unable to share data, threatening the productivity of people and causing delays, problems, and unnecessary expenses. For example, if an employee gets sick, how quickly can a replacement be found? What is done if equipment is lost, or a tractor-trailer is delayed?

The problem was compounded by the rapid growth of the business and the frequent changes in programs and plans.

Because of the unique nature of the business, most of the applications were done in-house. For example, special software was needed to make or buy costumes and to assign artists to the "make" job. In addition, the company installed ERP, for human resources management, production scheduling, logistics, and finance. Even the medical records of the performers were tracked. To enable the various applications communicating with each other, the company implemented IBM WebSphere Business Integration software to connect all of its disparate systems and applications. The integrated system replaced the manual work of the production managers, who do an inventory whenever a group arrives at a destination. If something was missing, several people were engaged in finding a replacement. Now due to data sharing, there are very few cases of missing items. Furthermore, IBM WebSphere helped cut the development time for new applications, as well as the modification time of existing applications, by about 25 percent. Also, time to connect new business software to the intranet has been reduced by 20 percent. All this helped increase productivity. In 2001, there were 65 tickets sold per employee, but by 2005 the total was about 200.

Sources: Compiled from Barrett (2005b) and from IBM (2005).

For Further Exploration: Why was it necessary to integrate the functional applications? Could the company grow so rapidly otherwise?

- **Service contracts:** contract management and service options.
- **Mobile sales and marketing:** wireless groupware for connecting different management groups.
- **Call center and telephony suite:** a Web-based call center.
- **Internet commerce:** an order-taking and payment unit interconnected with ERP back-office applications. It is also tightly connected to the call center for order taking.
- **Business intelligence:** identification of most-valuable customers, analysis of why customers leave, and evaluation of sales forecast accuracy.

Another integration software product is IBM's WebSphere architecture, which includes front office (WebSphere Portal), back office, and supportive infrastructure. Special software for integrating front- and back-office applications is provided by Best Software.

Many other vendors offer complete enterprise packages. For example, SAP-AG, in its ERP R/3 product, offers more than 70 integrated modules, as will be shown in Chapter 8.

7.8 How IT Supports Compliance

Regulatory compliance refers to an organization's activities conducted to meet federal, state, and other regulatory requirements, and relevant laws. As of 2002, the issue of compliance occupies the mind of management and is listed as one of the top five topics of concern both for CEOs and CIOs.

According to D'Agostino (2005), U.S. companies are spending an average of $4 million per company each year on their SOX compliance alone (see Chapter 1). Gartner Inc. estimated that in 2006 about 80 percent of all large and medium U.S. corporations employed a *chief compliance officer.*

THE MAJOR TOPIC: SOX

The SOX Act of 2002, Title III, Section 302, states:

> (4) The signing officers (A) are responsible for establishing and maintaining internal (financial) controls, (B) have designed such internal controls to ensure that material information relating to the issuer. . . is made known, (C) have evaluated the effectiveness of the internal controls . . . , and (D) have presented their conclusions about the effectiveness of the internal controls. (*Openpages.com,* 2006)

To many, this statement is confusing, intimidating, and overwhelming. Several vendors and management consultants developed software and guidelines for how to comply with SOX. For more on SOX, see Marchetti (2005). For an example of implementation, see Online File W7.18.

THE COMPLIANCE PROCESS

Several vendors and consultants recommended appropriate compliance processes. For example, Symantec Corp., in special advertising sections in *eWeek,* and *Baseline* (several times during 2005 and 2006), recommends the following eight steps (*Baseline,* December 15, 2005):

1. Establish compliance leadership and hire a compliance officer.
2. Know the compliance mandates, including international regulations.
3. Document and measure policy compliance, using such tools as Symantec Enterprise Security Manager.
4. Master information retention and retrieval. Leverage tools such as VERITAS Enterprise Vault to ensure data are properly archived and can be easily discovered.
5. Develop and review your business continuity plan.
6. Identify all critical applications, and don't overlook mobile CRM applications—which are prone to system theft and data loss.
7. Test the contingency plan at least quarterly.
8. Partner wisely with IT vendors that provide access to senior compliance experts.

For details see *information-integrity.com. CIO Advisor Searchcio.com* (Executive Guide section) offers several guides on how to handle compliance (e.g., budgeting for compliance). D'Agostino (2005) cited a Gartner Inc. recommendation that cost-effective compliance requires:

- **Organizational support.** Compliance officers, compliance committees, and internal auditor functions will be essential to doing business. Without the assignment of responsibility, there can be no real compliance.
- **Process control methodology.** Using open, accessible, and peer-reviewed frameworks for risk management and different kinds of control—whether inside or outside the IT organization—will make compliance regimes more transparent to outsiders.

- **Content control.** The only indisputable trail of evidence—of right practice or wrongdoing—comes through the electronic and paper records that companies keep and 99.9 percent of companies need to work on this area of compliance management.

The following seven steps are suggested by Gartner Inc.:

1. **Establish** the scope of the compliance effort. (*Pitfall: Not adequately delineating lines of responsibility.*)
2. **Assign** employees to specific compliance-related tasks. (*Pitfall: "But I already have a day job!"*)
3. **Screen** personnel to ensure job functions don't overlap. (*Pitfall: Personnel screening not connected to program goals.*)
4. **Communicate and train** employees on good compliance practices. (*Pitfall: Lack of an auditable training record.*)
5. **Monitor** ongoing compliance efforts and consider improvements. (*Pitfall: Risk assessment disconnected from business goals.*)
6. **Enforce** corporate policies and rules around compliance. (*Pitfall: Belief that reporting and oversight is enough.*)
7. **Prevent** policy breaches through monitoring and enforcement. (*Pitfall: Lack of attention to prevention and anticipation.*)

In its performance management suite, Geac Computer Corp. (a Golden Gate Capital company) offers a detailed technology checklist for effective performance management and regulatory compliance.

To execute these and similar steps in the compliance process, supportive software is needed.

SOFTWARE FOR COMPLIANCE

The following three types of technologies are suggested by D'Agostino (2005):

1. Management tools such as automated control testing and workflow.
2. Identity and authentication tools for change management and segregation of duties.
3. Content management software for records and e-mail archiving.

These are usually supported by software and computerized process.

Almost all major software vendors (e.g. IBM, HP, SAP Ag, Microsoft, AXentis, Symantec) offer compliance solutions, especially for SOX (see Armour, 2005). The basic purpose of the software is to automate compliance activities.

Example: According to Spangler (2006), compliance tracking was one of the top-10 IT projects in 2006. For example, in order to comply with SOX, BMO Financial Group (a Canadian financial services company whose subsidiaries include Chicago-based banking firm Harris) must confirm that users have appropriate access privileges to minimize "segregation of duties" conflicts that create opportunities for fraud (e.g., if an employee somehow had the ability to cut himself a check without authorization). Fraud is discussed in greater detail in Chapter 16.

In fall 2005, Harris installed software from Logical Apps to automate checks for such conflicts, based on rules about which job functions are allowed to have certain change privileges. The software also records changes to the accounts-payable system, such as if the amount of an invoice were altered, and lets support staffers configure the system, but prevents unauthorized changes. The software cut the time to monitor conflicts and system security from two months to about a week.

To cope with changing regulations or internal policies, Ilog.com also offers rule-based compliance software in its business solutions. Cybersource.com offers software called Export Compliance that automatically checks all the details involved when a request for export is made to ensure compliance with U.S. government regulations (e.g., restrictions). Finally, according to Popkin (2002), *business process modeling* (Chapter 8) can be used to improve regulatory compliance.

Also see Group Assignment #4 at the end of this chapter.

7.9 Managerial Issues

1. Integration of functional information systems. Integration of existing stand-alone functional information systems is a major problem for many organizations. Although client/server architecture is more amenable to integration than legacy systems, there are still problems of integrating different types of data and procedures used by functional areas. Also, there is an issue of willingness to share information, which may challenge existing practices and cultures.

2. Priority of transaction processing. Transaction processing may not be an exotic application, but it deals with the core processes of organizations. It must receive top priority in resource allocation, balanced against innovative applications needed to sustain competitive advantage and profitability, because the TPS collects the information needed for most other applications.

3. Finding innovative applications. Tools such as Lotus Notes, corporate portals, and Web-based business intelligence enable the construction of many applications that can increase productivity and quality. Finding opportunities for such applications can be best accomplished cooperatively by end users and the IS department.

4. Using the Web. Web-based systems should be considered in all functional areas. They are effective, cost relatively little, and are user friendly. In addition to new applications, companies should consider conversion of existing applications to Web-based ones.

5. Systems integration. Although functional systems are necessary, they may not be sufficient if they work independently. It is difficult to integrate functional information systems, but there are several approaches to doing so. In the future, Web Services could solve many integration problems, including connecting to a legacy system.

ETHICS

6. Ethical issues. Many ethical issues are associated with the various topics of this chapter. Professional organizations, relating to the functional areas (e.g., marketing associations), have their own codes of ethics. These codes should be taken into account in developing functional systems. Likewise, organizations must consider privacy policies. Several organizations provide comparisons of privacy policies and other ethics-related topics. For an example, see *socap.org*.

HRM applications are especially prone to ethical and legal considerations. For example, training activities that are part of HRM may involve ethical issues in recruiting and selecting employees and in evaluating performance. Likewise, TPS data processing and storage deal with private information about people, their performance, etc. Care should be taken to protect this information and the privacy of employees and customers.

For more on business ethics as it applies to topics in this chapter, see *ethics. ubc.ca/resources/business*.

Integrating *IT*

For the Accounting Major

Executing TPSs effectively is a major concern of any accountant. It is also necessary to understand the various activities of all functional areas and how they are interconnected and supported by IT. Also, many supply chain management issues, ranging from inventory management to risk analysis, fall within the realm of accounting.

Other accounting tasks are taxation, auditing, and government reports. They all can be improved with appropriate accounting software. Appropriate controls and auditing can eliminate fraud and are executed with software.

For the Finance Major

IT helps financial analysts and managers perform their tasks better. Of particular importance is analyzing cash flows and securing the financing required for smooth operations. In addition, financial applications can support such activities as risk analysis, investment management, and global transactions involving different currencies and fiscal regulations.

A major area of concern for the finance department is compliance with SOX. Many innovative software packages can help here. Also, financial performance, budgeting and its analysis, and many more finance activities can be facilitated with IT.

For the Human Resources Management Major

Human resources managers can increase their efficiency and effectiveness by using IT for some of their routine functions. Using the Web for recruiting, for example, has revolutionized the HRM area. Human resources personnel need to understand how information flows between the HR department and the other functional areas.

Preparing and training employees to work with business partners (frequently in foreign countries) requires knowledge about how IT collaboration software operates. Finally, compliance with government safety regulations and other human resources–related requirements can be facilitated by IT software.

For the IS Major

The IS function is responsible for the shared enterprise information systems infrastructure, and the transaction processing systems. TPSs provide the data for the databases. In turn, all other information systems use these data. IS personnel develop applications that support all levels of the organization (from clerical to executive) and in all functional areas (or they work with vendors that develop them). The applications also enable the firm to work better with its partners.

For the Marketing Major

Due to increased competition, marketing decisions about advertising, promotions, and pricing become critical, and in many cases require software support. E-CRM is frequently a critical success factor. In addition, marketing and sales expenses are usually targets in a cost-reduction program. Also, sales force automation not only improves salespeople's productivity (and thus reduces costs), but also improves customer service.

As competition intensifies globally, finding new global markets and global partners becomes critical. Use of electronic directories, for example, provides an opportunity to improve marketing and sales. Understanding the capabilities of marketing and sales support technologies and their implementation issues will enable the marketing department to excel.

For the Production/Operations Management Major

Managing production tasks, materials handling, and inventories in short time intervals, at a low cost, and with high quality is critical for competitiveness. These activities can be achieved only if they are properly supported by IT. Because they are in charge of procurement, production/operations managers must understand how their supporting information systems interface with those of their business partners. In addition, collaboration in design, manufacturing, and logistics requires knowledge of how modern information systems can be connected. Finally, on-demand manufacturing must be done at a competitive cost. Optimization with appropriate computerized analysis is very helpful.

Key Terms

Batch processing *262*
Channel systems *270*
Computer-integrated manufacturing (CIM) *270*

Employee relationship management (ERM) *286*
Expense management automation (EMA) *282*

Financial value chain management (FVCM) *280*
Just-in-time (JIT) *269*
Online processing *262*

Chapter Highlights

(Numbers Refer to Learning Objectives)

❶ Information systems applications can support many functional activities. Considerable software is readily available on the market for much of this support (for lease or to buy).

❷ The major business functional areas are production/operations management, marketing, accounting/finance, and human resources management.

❸ The backbone of most information systems applications is the transaction processing system (TPS), which keeps track of the routine, mission-central operations of the organization.

❹ The major area of IT support to production/operations management is in logistics and inventory management: JIT, mass customization, and CIM.

❺ Marketing and sales information systems deal with all activities related to customer orders, sales, advertising and promotion, market research, customer service, and product and service pricing. Using IT can increase sales, customers' satisfaction, and profitability.

❻ Financial information systems deal with topics such as investment management, financing operations, raising capital, risk analysis, and credit approval.

❻ Accounting information systems also cover many non-TPS applications in areas such as cost control, taxation, and auditing.

❼ Most tasks related to human resources development can be supported by human resources information systems. These tasks include employee recruitment and selection, hiring, performance evaluation, salary and benefits administration, training and development, labor negotiations, and work planning.

❼ Web-based HR systems are extremely useful for recruiting and training.

❽ Integrated functional information systems are necessary to ensure effective and efficient execution of activities that cross functional lines or that require functional cooperation.

❽ Integrating applications is difficult; it can be done in different ways, such as buying off-the-shelf applications from one vendor or using special connecting software known as middleware. A promising new approach is that of Web Services.

❾ Compliance can be very time consuming and expensive, especially SOX. Using software makes it possible to expedite the process and eliminate errors.

Virtual Company Assignment

Transaction Processing at The Wireless Café

Go to The Wireless Café's link on the Student Web Site. There you will be asked to think about the business activities and transactions, other than cooking, that the restaurant engages in. You will be asked to consider types of transaction processing applications that could be implemented at The Wireless Café.

Instructions for accessing The Wireless Café on the Student Web Site:

1. Go to *wiley.com/college/turban.*
2. Select Turban/Leidner/McLean/Wetherbe's *Information Technology for Management, Sixth Edition.*
3. Click on Student Resources site, in the toolbar on the left.
4. Click on the link for Virtual Company Web site.
5. Click on Wireless Café.

Online Resources

More resources and study tools are located on the Student Web Site and on WileyPLUS. You'll find additional chapter materials and useful Web links. In addition, self-quizzes that provide individualized feedback are available for each chapter.

Questions For Review

1. What is a functional information system?
2. List the major characteristics of a functional information system.
3. What are the objectives of a TPS?
4. List the major characteristics of a TPS.
5. Distinguish between batch and online TPS.
6. Explain how the Web enables mass customization.
7. Describe spend management.
8. Define XBRL.
9. Describe VMI.
10. Define CIM, and list its major benefits.
11. Define channel systems.
12. Define JIT, and list some of its benefits.
13. What is product/customer profitability?
14. Describe some tactical and strategic accounting/finance applications.
15. List some budgeting-related activities.
16. List some EC activities in finance.
17. List IT-supported recruitment activities.
18. How can training go online?
19. Explain human resources information systems.
20. Describe the need for application integration.
21. Describe regulatory compliance.

Questions for Discussion

1. Why is it logical to organize IT applications by functional areas?
2. Describe the role of a TPS in a service organization.
3. Why are transaction processing systems a major target for restructuring?
4. Which functional areas are related to payroll, and how does the relevant information flow?
5. Discuss the benefits of Web-based TPS.
6. It is said that in order to be used successfully, MRP must be computerized. Why?
7. The Japanese implemented JIT for many years without computers. Discuss some elements of JIT, and comment on the potential benefits of computerization.
8. Describe the role of computers in CIM.
9. Explain how Web applications can make the customer king/queen.
10. Why are information systems critical to sales-order processing?
11. Describe how IT can enhance mass customization.
12. Describe how XBRL can help banks.
13. Describe cost-effective compliance.
14. Discuss how IT facilitates the budgeting process.
15. Why is risk management important, and how can it be enhanced by IT?
16. Compare bill presentment to check re-presentment. How are they facilitated by IT?
17. How can the Internet support investment decisions?
18. Describe the benefits of an accounting integrated software such as MAS 90; compare it to MAS 200.
19. Discuss the role IT plays in support of auditing.
20. Investigate the role of the Web in human resources management.
21. Geographical information systems are playing an important role in supporting marketing and sales. Provide some examples not discussed in the text. (See Chapter 11.)
22. Discuss the need for application integration and the difficulty of doing it.
23. Discuss the approaches and reasons for integrating front-office with back-office operations.
24. Discuss why some of the services provided by *iEmployee.com* are considered support to on-demand workforce management solutions.

Exercises and Projects

1. Review the Dartmouth-Hitchcock Medical center case. Assume that RFID tags cost 5 cents each. How might use of RFID tags change the supply chain management? Would the new system at the medical center still be needed? Write a report on your conclusions.
2. The chart shown in Figure 7.3 portrays the flow of routine activities in a typical manufacturing organization. Explain in what areas IT can be most valuable.
3. Argot International (a fictitious name) is a medium-sized company in Peoria, Illinois, with about 2,000 employees.

The company manufactures special machines for farms and food-processing plants, buying materials and components from about 150 vendors in six different countries. It also buys special machines and tools from Japan. Products are sold either to wholesalers (about 70) or directly to clients (from a mailing list of about 2,000). The business is very competitive.

The company has the following information systems in place: financial/accounting, marketing (primarily information about sales), engineering, research and development, and inventory management. These systems are independent of each other although they are all connected to the corporate intranet.

Argot is having profitability problems. Cash is in high demand and short supply, due to strong business competition from Germany and Japan. The company wants to investigate the possibility of using information technology to improve the situation. However, the vice president of finance objects to the idea, claiming that most of the tangible benefits of information technology are already being realized.

You are hired as a consultant to the president. Respond to the following:

a. Prepare a list of 10 potential applications of information technologies that you think could help the company.

b. From the description of the case, would you recommend any portals? Be very specific. Remember, the company is in financial trouble.

c. How can Web Services help Argot?

4. Enter *extensity.com*. Take the demo. Prepare a list of all the product's capabilities.

Group Assignments and Projects

1. Each group should visit (or investigate) a large company in a different industry and identify its channel systems. Prepare a diagram that shows the components shown in Online File W7.8. Then find how IT supports each of those components. Finally, suggest improvements in the existing channel system that can be supported by IT technologies and that are not in use by the company today. Each group presents its findings.

2. The class is divided into groups of four. Each group member represents a major functional area: production/operations management, sales/marketing, accounting/finance, and human resources. Find and describe several examples of processes that require the integration of functional information systems in a company of your choice. Each group will also show the interfaces to the other functional areas.

3. Each group investigates an HRM software vendor (Oracle, SAP, Lawson Software). The group prepares a list of all HRM functionalities supported by the software. Then the groups make a presentation to convince the class that its vendor is the best.

4. Each group is assigned to a compliance vendor(s). Document the regulation they are dealing with and the capabilities of the software offered.

Internet Exercises

1. Surf the Net and find free accounting software (try *shareware.com, rkom.com, tucows.com, passtheshareware.com,* and *freeware-guide.com*). Download the software and try it. Write a report on your findings.

2. Enter the site of Federal Express (*fedex.com*) and learn how to ship a package, track the status of a package, and calculate its cost. Comment on your experience.

3. Finding a job on the Internet is challenging; there are almost too many places to look. Visit the following sites: *careerbuilder.com, careermag.com, hotjobs.yahoo.com, jobcenter.com,* and *monster.com*. What do these sites provide you as a job seeker?

4. Enter the Web site *tps.com* and some of those listed in Online File W7.3, and find information about software products available from those sites. Identify the software that allows Internet transaction processing. Prepare a report about the benefits of the products identified.

5. Enter *sas.com* and access revenue optimization there. Explain how the software helps in optimizing prices.

6. Enter *hyperion.com/downloads/profitability_management.pdf,* and download the brochure on profitability management. Prepare a summary.

7. Enter *iemployee.com* and find the support they provide to human resources management activities by IT. View the demos and read the white paper by Shah (2006). Prepare a report.

8. Enter *softsim.com* and view the demo of the product. Do you think it is a valuable tool?

9. Enter *authorial.com* and *successfactors.com*. Examine their software products and make a comparison.

10. Examine the capabilities of the following financial software packages: TekPortal (from *teknowledge.com*), Financial Analyzer (from Oracle), and CFO Vision (from SAS Institute). Prepare a report comparing the capabilities of the software packages.

11. Surf the Internet and find information from three vendors on sales force automation (try *sybase.com* first). Prepare a report on the state of the art.

12. Enter *teknowledge.com* and review the products that help with online training (training systems). What are the most attractive features of these products?

13. Enter *microsoft.com/dynamics/sl/default.mspx*. View three of the demos in different functional areas of your choice. Prepare a report on the capabilities.

14. Enter *sagesoftware.com*. Identify functional software, CRM software, and e-business software products. Are these standalone or integrated? Explain.

Minicase 1

Dollar General Uses Integrated Software

ACC   HRM

Dollar General (*dollargeneral.com*) operates more than 6,000 general stores in the United States, fiercely competing with Wal-Mart, Target, and thousands of other stores in the sale of food, apparel, home-cleaning products, health and beauty aids, and more. The chain doubled in size between 1996 and 2002 and has had some problems in addition to the stiff competition, due to its rapid expansion. For example, moving into new states means different sales taxes, and these need to be closely monitored for changes. Personnel management also became more difficult with the organization's growth. An increased number of purchasing orders exacerbated problems in the accounts payable department, which was using manual matching of purchasing orders, invoices, and what was actually received in the "receiving" department before bills were paid.

The IT department was flooded with requests to generate long reports on topics ranging from asset management to general ledgers. It became clear that a better information system was needed. Dollar General started by evaluating information requirements that would be able to solve the above and other problems that cut into the company's profit.

A major factor In deciding which software to buy was the integration requirement among the existing information systems of the various functional areas, especially the financial applications. This led to the selection of the Financials suite (from Lawson Software). The company started to implement applications one at a time. Before 1998, the company installed the suite's asset management, payroll, and some HR applications which allow the tens of thousands of employees to monitor and self-update their benefits, 401k contributions, and personal data (resulting in big savings to the HR department). After 1998, the accounts payable and general ledger modules of Lawson Software were activated. The accounting modules allow employees to route, extract, and analyze data in the accounting/finance area with little reliance on IT personnel. During 2001–2003, Dollar General moved into the sales and procurement areas, thus adding the marketing and operation activities to the integrated system.

Here are a few examples of how various parts of the new system work: All sales data from the point-of-sale scanners of some 6,000 stores are pulled each night, together with financial data, discounts, etc., into the business intelligence application for financial and marketing analysis. Employee payroll data, from each store, are pulled once a week. This provides synergy with the sales audit system (from STS Software). All sales data are processed nightly by the STS System, broken into hourly journal entries, processed and summarized, and then entered into the Lawson's general ledger module.

The original infrastructure was mainframe based (IBM AS 400). By 2002, the 800 largest suppliers of Dollar General were submitting their bills on the EDI. This allowed instantaneous processing in the accounts payable module. By 2003, service providers, such as utilities, were added to the system. To do all this the system was migrated in 2001 from the old legacy system to the Unix operating system, and then to a Web-based infrastructure, mainly in order to add Web-based functionalities and tools.

A development tool embedded in Lawson's Financials allowed users to customize applications without touching the computer programming code. This included applications that are not contained in the Lawson system. For example, an employee-bonus application was not available at Lawson, but was added to Financial's payroll module to accommodate Dollar General's bonus system. A customized application that allowed additions and changes in dozens of geographical areas also solved the organization's state sales-tax collection and reporting problem.

The system is very scalable, so there is no problem in adding stores, vendors, applications, or functionalities. In 2003, the system was completely converted to Web-based, enabling authorized vendors, for example, to log on the Internet and view the status of their invoices by themselves. Also, the Internet/EDI enables small vendors to use the system. (An EDI is too expensive for small vendors, but the EDI/Internet is affordable.) Also, the employees can update personal data from any Web-enabled desktop in the store or at home. Future plans call for adding an e-purchasing (procurement) module using a desktop purchasing model (see Chapter 5).

Sources: Compiled from Amato-McCoy (2002a) and *lawson.com* (accessed May 2004).

Questions for Minicase 1

1. Explain why the old, nonintegrated functional system created problems for the company. Be specific.

2. The new system cost several million dollars. Why, in your opinion, was it necessary to install it?

3. Lawson Software Smart Notification Software (*lawson. com*) is being considered by Dollar General. Find information about the software and write an opinion for adoption or rejection.

4. Another new product of Lawson is Services Automation. Would you recommend it to Dollar General? Why or why not?

Minicase 2

Musco Food Uses IT to Improve Sales and Operations

MKT   POM

Musco Food Corp. (*muscofood.com*) is a distributor of food products (meats, cheese, olive oil, and other deli-need products) in Queens, New York. It has only an eight-man sales force who visit customers and, until recently, showed them a paper catalog and took orders orally ("Just give us the same as last time," or "I need fourteen cases of Italian cheese"). The salesman then went to his car and called a customer service employee, who then typed the information into the company's computerized order processing system that generated the order to the warehouse for preparation and delivery, and an invoice for the customer.

The system was in place for about 10 years; however, mistakes occurred about five times a week. The quantity ordered differed from that delivered. Either the customer service employee made a mistake or the salesman forgot the exact number while walking to his car. In either case, customers were unhappy, inventories were incorrect, and expensive rush orders (order corrections) had to be made.

Salesman productivity was low and other expenses were too high. In addition, price changes and promotions that might be of interest to specific customers were not communicated in time. Finally, inventory availability was not known in real time.

Using Treo smart phones (from *Palm.com*) that display product images and order entry e-forms, the salesmen struggled at the beginning to pull up the products and enter orders. However, after a few weeks, the salesmen became experts in locating a product out of more than 1,000 in the e-catalog. Now, an order is punched in the minute it is expressed by the customer. An electronic invoice is generated in seconds and shown to the deli owner for verification on the spot. Also, the customer service representatives who used to enter the orders in the computers are not needed. Instead, they have been retrained to help locate new customers. The wireless Treo enters the order information directly to the corporate computer system. In addition, the Treo provides instant access to pricing changes and promotions. The salesmen can check, in real time, any customer accounts receivable balance. Finally, real-time inventory availability can be checked at the customer's site.

Each salesman now visits six instead of five customers on an average day. Orders get instant attention from the warehouse employees. Most important, errors, correcting trips, and expenses have been reduced by over 50 percent for an annual savings of $25,000. Finally, the process fulfillment time takes one to two instead of three days. The system paid for itself in just a few months.

Sources: Compiled from Barrett (2005a) and from *Palm.com* (2006).

Questions for Minicase 2

1. Identify the real-time activities.
2. How is customer service improved?
3. Which functional information systems need to be integrated to support the new system?
4. Which types of errors were eliminated?
5. Enter *sco.com/products/meinc* and identify the software on the back end (order fulfillment).

References

Aberdeen.com, "Best Practices in Streamlining the Financial Value Chain: Top Seven FVCM Implementations," Aberdeen Group, 2002, *aberdeen.com/summary/report/other/FVCMBestPracticesReport10. asp* (accessed July 2006).

Amato-McCoy, D. M., "Dollar General Rings Up Back-Office Efficiencies with Financial Suite," *Stores,* October 2002a.

Amato-McCoy, D. M., "Sears Combines Retail Reporting and Customer Databases on a Single Platform," *Stores,* November 2002b.

Amato-McCoy, D. M., "Linens 'n Things Protects Inventory Investment with Supply Planning Suite," *Stores,* November 2002c.

autobytel.com (accessed July 2006).

Avriel, M., et al., "Opti-Money at Bank Hapoalim," *Interfaces,* January–February 2004.

Barrett, L., "Dial-a-Deli," *Baseline,* November 2005a.

Barrett, L., "Juggling Act," *Baseline*, June 2005b.

Benjaafar, S. et al., "Next Generation Factory Layouts," *Interfaces,* November–December 2002.

Buckley, N., "E-Route to Whiter Smile," *Financial Times,* August 26, 2002.

Bussler, L., and E. Davis, "Information Systems: The Quiet Revolution in Human Resource Management," *Journal of Computer Information Systems,* Winter 2001–2002.

Butcher, D. R., "Mass Customization: A Leading Paradigm in Future Manufacturing," February 14, 2006.

Carr, D. F., "Leaner Machine," *Baseline*, June 2005.

Chatman, J., C. O'Rielly, and V. Chang, "Cisco Systems: Developing a Human Cupid Strategy," *California Management Review,* Winter 2005.

Cheapflights.com, "Plastic Purchases Onboard American Airlines," May 4, 2006, *news.cheapflights.com/airlines/2006/05/plastic_purchas.html#more* (accessed July 2006).

D'Agostino, D., "A Rock and a Hard Place," *Baseline,* August 2005.

Degnan, C., "Best Practices in Expense Management Automation," Special Report. Boston: Aberdeen Group, January 2003, *ofm.wa.gov/ roadmap/modeling/expense/Aberdeen_BestPractices_Spend_ Management.pdf* (accessed July 2006).

Duvall, M., "Lemon Aid," *Baseline*, June 2005.

Entersingapore.com, "Public Transport," *entersingapore.info/sginfo/ public-transport.php* (accessed July 2006).

Field, K., "High Speed Hiring," *Chain Store Age,* June 2006.

ford.com (accessed July 2006).

Fujitsu Corp. (sponsor), "Smart Stores," advertising supplement, *Stores,* January 2004.

Gayeski, D., "Going Mobile," *TD,* November 2004.

Gibson, S., "Tech Behind the Trophy," *e-Week*, November 29, 2004.

Gillium, D., et al., *The Quantum Leap: Next Generation—The Manufacturing Strategy for Business*. Fort Lauderdale, FL: J. Ross Publishers, 2005.

Gomez-Mejia, L., et al., *Managing Human Resources,* 5th ed. Upper Saddle River: NJ, Prentice Hall, 2007.

Grimes, S., "Declaration Support: The B.P.M. Drumbeat," *Intelligent Enterprise*, April 23, 2003.

Harris, P., "Training's New Wave," *TD*, August 2005.

Ho, G. T. S., et al., "An Intelligent Information Infrastructure to Support the Streamlining of Integrated Logistics Workflow," *Expert Systems*, July 2004.

Howarth, B., "To Catch a Thief," *BRW*, January 15–21, 2004.

Hyperion.com, "Profitability Management from Hyperion," *hyperion. com/solutions/project/profitability_management/index.cfm* (accessed July 2006).

IBM, "Increasing Cirque du Soleil's Agility," *IBM.com,* July 1, 2005, *www-1.ibm.com/businesscenter/smb/us/en/contenttemplate/gcl_xmlid/ 33893/nav_id/resources* (accessed July 2006).

jaguar.com (accessed July 2006).

Jareb, E., and V. Rajkovic, "Use of an Expert System in Personnel Selection," *Information Management,* July–December 2001.

Johnson, S., "Five Components of Personalization," *iMediaConnection,* April 6, 2006, *imediaconnection.com/content/8952.asp* (accessed July 2006).

Korolishin, J., "Meeting the Employee Scheduling Challenge," *Stores,* September 2003.

Korolishin, J., "Payroll Pay Cards Pay Off at Payless," *Stores*, February 2004a.

Korolishin, J., "Sheetz Keeps Tab on Training Compliance via Web Portal," *Stores,* February 2004b.

Kroll, K. M., "Video-Based Systems Seek Cleaner Focus on Store Traffic," *Stores,* April 2002.

Lawson.com (accessed July 2006).

Lee, Y. M., and E. J. Chen, "BASF Uses a Framework for Developing Web-Based Production-Planning Optimization Tools," *Interfaces,* November–December 2002.

Liao, Z., "Real Time Tax: Dispatching Using GPS," *Communications of the ACM*, May 2003.

Malykhina, E., "XBRL: More Than a Must-Do," *Information Week*, May 29, 2006.

Marchetti, A. M., *Beyond Sarbanes-Oxley Compliance*. Hoboken NJ: Wiley, 2005.

Maxemchuk, N. F., and D. H. Shur, "An Internet Multicast System for the Stock Market," *ACM Transactions on Computer Systems,* August 2001.

McCullough, D. C., *Oracle 9i*. New York: Hungry Minds, 2002.

McKinley, E., "Multicasting Solution Ushers in New Era of Computer-Based Training," *Stores,* April 2003.

Meredith, J. R., and S. M. Shafer, *Operations Management*. New York: Wiley, 2002.

Nishi, D., "Market-Basket Mystery," *Retail Technology Quarterly*, May 2005.

Openpages.com, "Sarbanes-Oxley Act of 2002: Title III, Section 302— Corporate Responsibility for Financial Reports," *openpages.com/ solutions/sarbanes-oxley/sarbanes-oxley-sec302.asp* (accessed July 2006).

Palm.com, "Musco Food Corp. Expand Customer Base with Treo Smartphones," *solutions.palm.com/regac/success_stories* (accessed July 2006).

Palaniswamy, R., and T. Frank, "Enhancing Manufacturing Performance with ERP Systems," *Information Management Journal,* Summer 2000.

Parks, L., "Making Sure the Price Is Right" (price optimization), *Stores,* August 2004a.

Parks, L., "Schurman Fine Papers Racks Up Labor Savings," *Stores,* February 2004b.

Perkins-Munn, T. S., and Y. T. Chen, "Streamlining Project Management Through Online Solutions," *Journal of Business Strategy*, January 2004.

pg.com (accessed July 2006).

Popin, J., "Improving Regulatory Compliance with Business Process Modeling," *Business Integration Journal*, June 2005.

Prophix.com, "Features: Budgeting," *prophix.com/solutions/prophix_ features.php#Budgeting* (accessed July 2006).

Rapt.com, "Case Study: Delivering Profit-Optimal Prices for Configured Products," 2006, *rapt.com/cases/high_tech-hp.htm* (accessed July 2006).

Reda, S., "Digital Signage Helps Tesco Inform, Entertain and Boost Sales," *Stores*, March 2005.

Reda, S., "Evelyn Follit Fuses Technology, Business, and HR Strategies," *Stores,* March 2004.

Reda, S., "Word-of Mouth Marketing Enjoys New Life as Potent Online Advertising Strategy," *Stores,* October 2002.

Reed, C. et al., *eCFO: Sustaining Value in New Corporations*. Chichester, U.K.: Wiley, 2001.

Shah, S., *The Five Foundations of Next Generation HRO Technology*, a white paper from *iemployee.com* (downloaded July 2006).

Spangler, T., "The Top Ten Projects in 2006," *Innovations*, Issue 2, 2006 (supplement to *Baseline* and *eWeek*).

Subrahmanyam, A., "Nuts and Bolts of Transaction Processing: A Comprehensive Tutorial," *subrahmanyam.com...articles/transactions/NutsAndBoltsOfTP.html* (no longer available online).

TIAA CREF, *Annual Report 2005.* tiaa-cref.org, July 2006. Available for download at *tiaacref.org/about/governance/corporate/topics/annual_reports.html* (accessed October 2006).

Thomas, S. L., and K. Ray, "Recruiting and the Web: High-Tech Hiring," *Business Horizons*, May–June 2000.

Turban, E. et al., *Electronic Commerce 2008.* Upper Saddle River, NJ: Prentice Hall, 2008.

Vijayakumar, S., "Improving Software Cost Estimation," *Project Management Today,* May 2002.

Virzi, A. M., "Cleaning Up" *Baseline*, September 2005.

"Web Breathes Life into Medical Firm's Training Program," *Internet Week,* July 27, 1988, *internetwk.com/search/results.jhtml?query Text_Omnitech&site_id_3* (no longer available online).

"What EMA Systems Now Offer Accounting Departments" *Accounting Department Management & Administration Report,* February 2002.

Wikipedia.org, "Transaction Processing Systems," *en.wikipedia.org/wiki/Transaction_Processing_System* (accessed July 2006).

Zaremba, M. B., and G. Morel, "Integration and Control of Intelligence in Distributed Manufacturing," *Journal of Intelligent Manufacturing,* February 2003.

Web Page Design

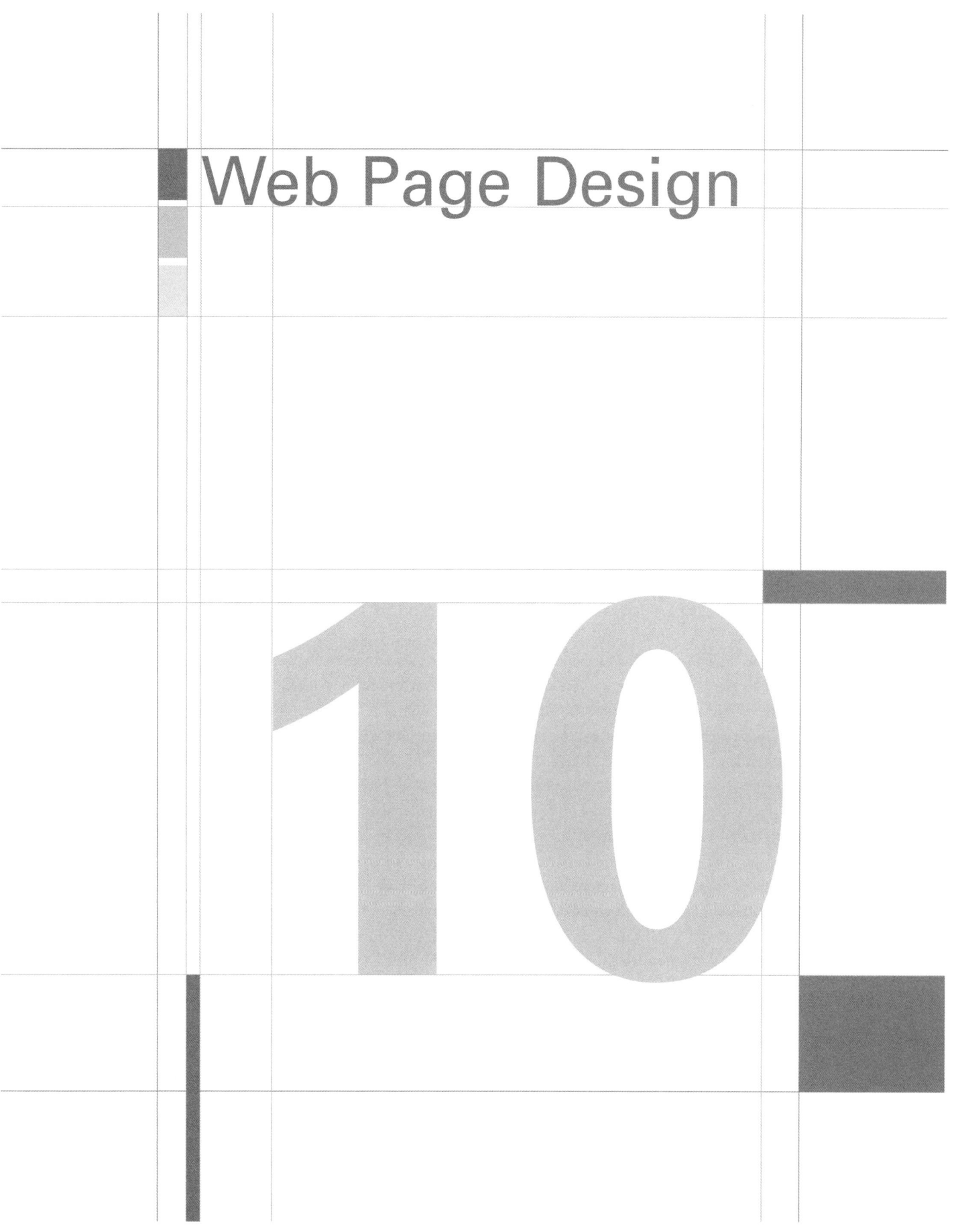

Web Design: A Complete Introduction
Nigel Chapman and Jenny Chapman. ISBN 978-0-470-06089-6
©2006 Nigel Chapman and Jenny Chapman

Clear layout, good use of contrast, sensitive use of colour, a well-informed but practical approach to typography, and an appropriate choice and presentation of images and time-based media should all work together to convey a Web site's content positively and effectively to as broad a range of users as possible, and in a way that makes the least demands on the visitor. With the exception of people who cannot see at all, all users will benefit from good visual design.

No Web designer can afford to ignore the basic principles of visual design and visual communication, because every Web page implements them – some very badly, with the result that the site fails to convey its content or is hard to use – and some very well, with the result that the site is easy to use and understand, popular with users, and likely to attract repeat visits. Above all, visual design should work to make Web sites more usable, more accessible and more successful. Very often, the principles which lead to the achievement of these goals also result in more attractive sites.

It is not the purpose of this book to teach graphic design, partly because space does not allow us to cover this specialist subject anything like adequately here (that would require a whole book in itself), and partly because many Web designers will have little to do with graphic design in practice. We therefore limit our coverage to those general principles of usability, visual communication and visual design which are fundamental to the practice of good Web design as a whole, and which are implemented in markup and stylesheets. Even if you never do any visual design work yourself, but work as part of a team with specialist graphic designers, it is important to be able to understand what their requirements are and why. In turn, you also need to be able to communicate to the graphic designers how and why their visual ideas may or may not be appropriate for implementation on a Web page.

Remember that, on the Web, structure and content should be separated from presentation. Whereas graphic designers working in print media are accustomed to developing a structure visually, on the Web structure is already explicitly present in markup, and so – in addition to ensuring usability and the effective communication of content – it is also the job of visual design to express that inherent structure clearly, through CSS rules that control the layout and appearance of the elements of the page. The hierarchy which is already defined by the page's markup should be expressed through the appearance and position of elements on the page, by the use of such attributes as size, colour and spacing. Ideally, this visual presentation and the explicit structure will work hand-in-hand. This ideal situation falls down in the face of the limited repertoire of elements provided by XHTML, which are not always adequate to express the appropriate structure of a page. The use of `class` and `id` attributes to provide hooks for styling is a way of getting round this shortcoming and, at the same time, creating ad hoc markup to express the true structure, so in a sense, the visual design does contribute to the development of the structure.

Visual Communication

The basic principles of visual design have been developed through hundreds of years' accumulated experience in print media. But, as we have repeatedly stressed, the Web is a new medium, with profound differences from printed media. This unfortunately renders many of the practices of print-based visual design inappropriate or impractical, above all because the size and shape of a Web page, and the appearance of many elements in it, may be determined by the browser and the user in ways which the designer cannot foresee. Nevertheless, some of the fundamental principles of visual design apply in all contexts where content is being conveyed visually, and the use of stylesheets allows the designer at least to indicate, if not to determine absolutely, the way that they wish the page to appear.

Visual Design for Usability

The notion, prevalent in some circles, that visual design is just concerned with trivial ornamentation which is not really necessary – 'eye candy' as it is disparagingly referred to – is wholly mistaken. Neglect of visual design is one of the main factors that lead to Web sites being hard to use.

An enormous amount has been written about *usability* in the context of Web design, and a great deal of advice has been put forward by self-proclaimed experts on the subject. Some of this advice is valuable, some is trite; some of it is based on ideas that are almost certainly wrong, or on inadequate models and invalid statistical analyses, whereas some is based on common sense and ideas that most people would agree are right. So how do you sort out the useful guidelines from the rest?

Usability is a vague term which relates to something that cannot be quantified. Furthermore, owing to substantial variation among users in the global community, a site that is usable for some may be quite unusable by others, so it makes no sense to talk about the usability of a Web page or site as though it were an absolute fixed measure. Nor does it help to think of an average user. As we asked back in Chapter 1, what gender is the average user? We can go much further and ask, what educational level have they achieved? What physical difficulties or limitations do they experience? How familiar are they with the conventions of the World Wide Web? What language do they speak? The list of potential questions is long, but the answer is clear: there is no average user, and there is no such thing as a Web page or site which is usable in the abstract. The most beautifully designed and functional site might be completely unusable by someone in Africa for the simple reason that it is written entirely in Japanese. And yet in Japan that same site might be considered particularly easy to use. Even if we eliminate language entirely and rely solely on images, there will be some people who cannot see those images, and some who do not understand them.

All usability experts advocate user testing, but they generally draw their test group from their own nation, and often from a very much smaller community of people – perhaps only a handful. While the results of a small test may provide broad qualitative results that may be adequate for certain types of commercial or corporate enterprise with a restricted target audience, there are many other types of site for which they will be a very poor guide. (Published claims that tests on no more than twenty participants are sufficient to produce quantitatively meaningful results are based on hopelessly naive statistical analyses, and should not be taken seriously.)

Usability is concerned with several aspects of Web design, notably function, structure, accessibility, and visual presentation. Once again we must stress that – so far as it is possible to ensure – a Web site must work properly and without errors on all browsers, it must be navigable and coherent, and it must be made accessible to all potential users. Clearly, if a site fails in any of these respects then it is not fully usable, but we deal with these aspects of Web design in other chapters of this book. In this chapter, therefore, we will only look at the way usability may be controlled by visual design.

Experience in the field of interface design in general has shown that both familiarity and memory play an important role in usability, and visual design plays an important role in ensuring that page elements are familiar or memorable. Although some usability guidelines suggest that the purpose of functional features should be intuitively obvious, that is clearly an inappropriate objective. For example, without previous experience or instruction we cannot intuit that an underlined piece of text is a link to another document; there is no inherent reason why it should be, and no precedent. On the contrary, in printed and hand-written media, underlining has traditionally been used for emphasis – even to the extent that it is conventionally used by students to draw attention to important passages in books they are studying – so a Web novice would probably make a completely wrong assumption about underlined text on a Web page. But the widespread establishment of this type of textual formatting as a convention for links ensures that it quickly becomes familiar in the context of the Web once the user has learned the convention. And this convention is visual – we see the underlining, and instantly recognize its meaning. It is a wholly visual sign. We can understand this better when we realize that assistive technologies do not tell their users that a piece of text is underlined; instead, they simply say what it is, for example 'link'. In an XHTML document, the fact of something's being a link is determined by mark-up, but it is conveyed to the user by visual or spoken convention. We will return to the role of signs shortly, in the section on *Gestalt Principles and Semiotics*.

Many different visual factors work together to make a site usable. One look at a Web page should be sufficient to convey to a sighted user where the navbar is and where the links will lead; where the search box is and how to use it; who owns the site; what type of content is being presented; and – if the site has a specific function such as e-commerce – how to operate all aspects of that function (for example, how to order goods and services, how to check what has been ordered, and how to pay). It is not sufficient that all of these elements are present somewhere on the page; it is necessary that they are presented in a way that makes each one easy to find, identify or use.

Figure 10.1 shows a simple, usable Web page, which draws both on current conventions and fundamental visual design principles to present all its elements in a clear and obvious way. The company logo appears at the top of the page, because the top of the page will always be seen. The logo identifies the owner of the site and should tell the user something about what kind of site it is (for example, it might be the logo and name of a university). Whether it is positioned on the right or left should be determined by the reading conventions of the language in which the site's content is written. The search box also appears at the top of the page, with the box in which search terms should be entered distinguished from the search button by use of contrast and colour. It has become conventional to place the search box at the top because it provides a function which is so frequently used. A white background was chosen for this top area, to keep it simple, legible and apart from the rest of the page whose function is different. It also works to create a visual balance and link with the large

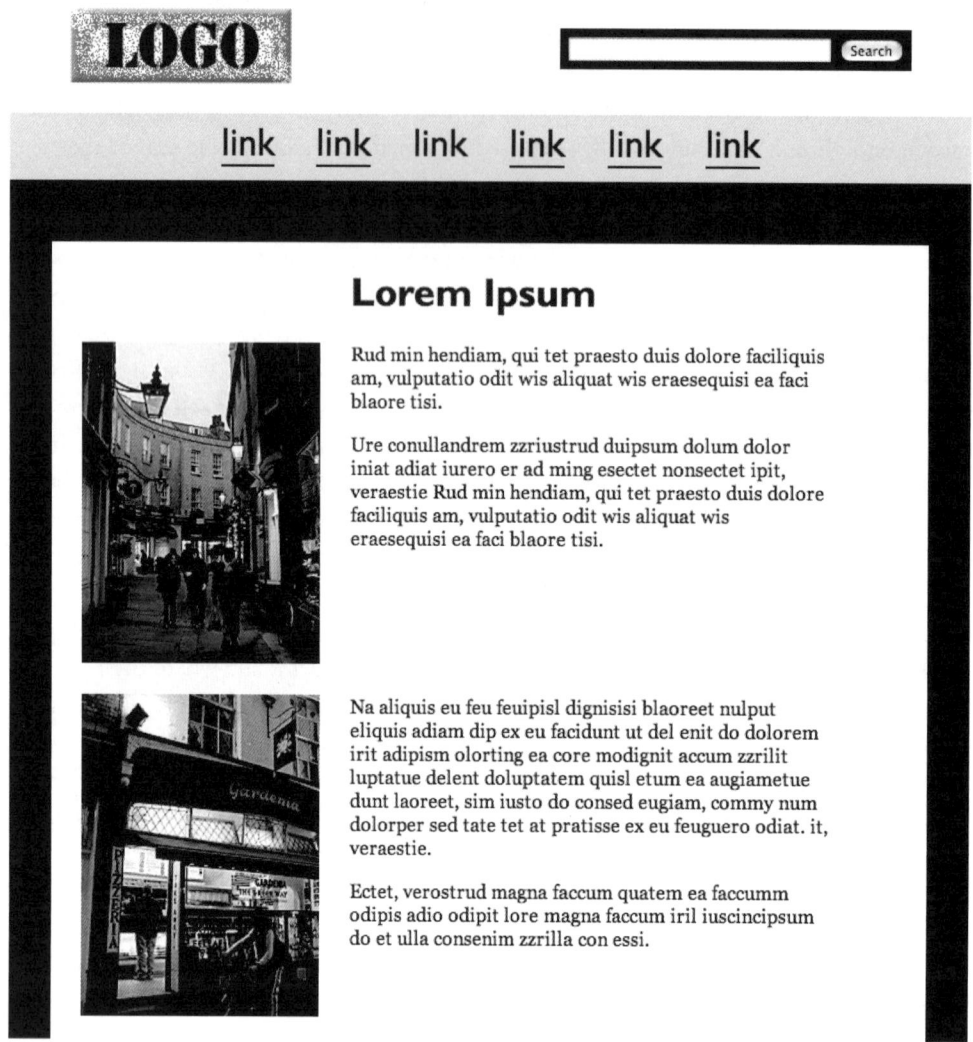

Figure 10.1 A usable Web page

white area lower down, so that the parts of the page do not become too detached from one another.

Immediately below the logo and search box we find the navbar. This is set apart from the rest of the page by being placed on an area of contrasting colour and tone, to ensure that users with all levels of vision can easily identify it. (It also scales up cleanly to a very large size, without wrapping, when magnified – unlike the logo, which is a GIF image.) We will

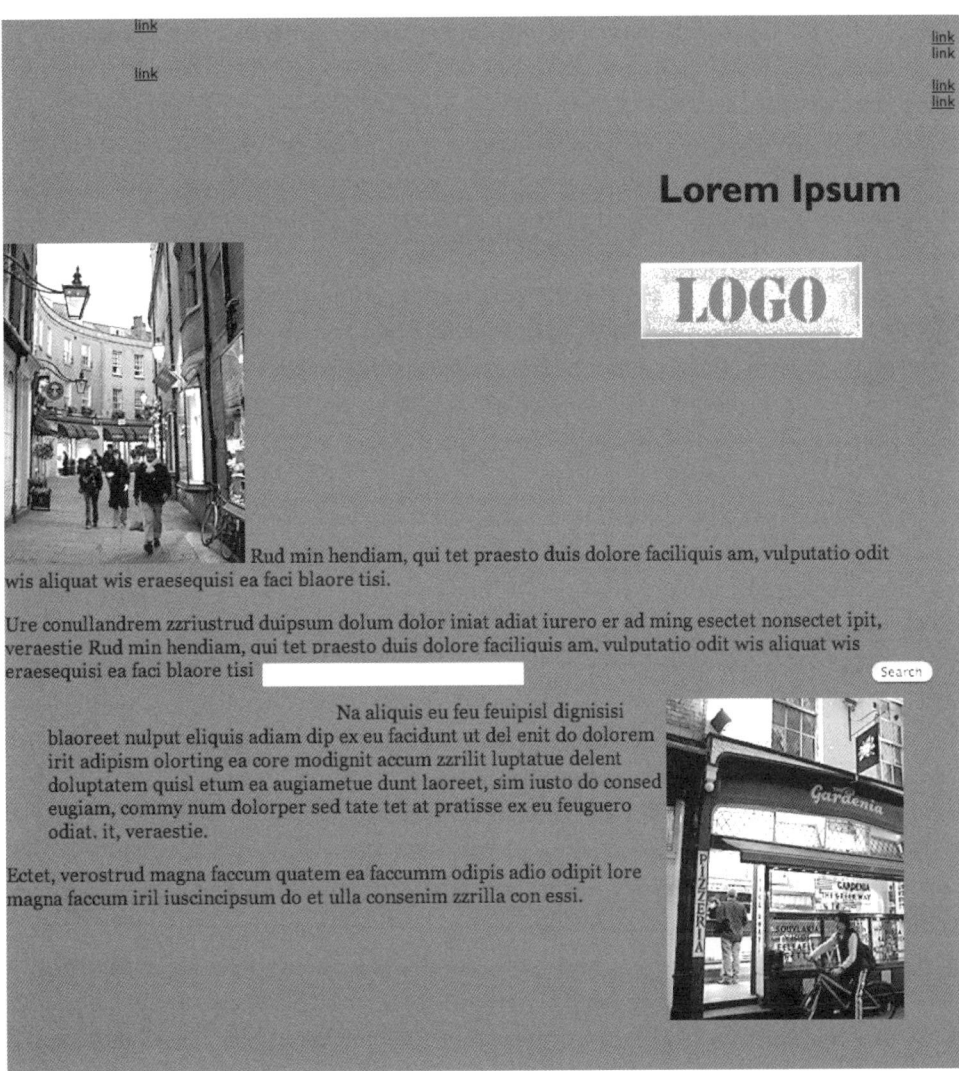

Figure 10.2 A less usable Web page

discuss the composition and presentation of the navbar itself further in the next section, but its position as a bar across the page near the top has become a matter of convention. It is usual now either to position the navbar in the way shown in Figure 10.1, or down one or other side of the page.

For this example we have chosen a centred design for the main content of the page. There is no strong inherent virtue in this choice, but it is a popular means of presentation at the time of writing, and has the benefit of looking the same whether users are accustomed to organizing their screens from right to left or from left to right. It also means that the content is displayed in the centre of the window, no matter how wide or narrow that window may be. (It would not be such a good choice, however, where the amount of content to be presented required a multi-column layout.) The box which contains the content has a white background as this provides the highest contrast with the black text (and thus maximum legibility) and makes the photographic images stand out well without any risk of colour clash. As we will see later on, however, it is not necessary to use quite such a stark contrast as this in order to achieve good legibility. Within the white box, the content has been laid out on a simple grid, aligning the photographs and the blocks of text in a way that makes it easy to see which elements go together. The heading has been set apart at the top of the page, in a larger size, to make it clear that it is the heading for the content below.

Finally, the main background to the page has been set to a fairly dark tone which harmonizes pleasantly with the other colours, and which acts to make the white content box stand out and 'advance' visually towards the user. The choice of the same colour that is used for the search box and navbar text works to make the whole page more visually coherent and to indicate to the user that all the elements are part of a single whole, and allows the background to remain unremarkable, as it should do. The choice of a radically different background colour – bright pink or sky blue, for example – would have acted to break up the parts of the page and suggest that there might be something special about the background (some particular reason for choosing bright pink), which sends a misleading message to the user.

To illustrate what might happen if all the visual design principles that governed the design of the page in Figure 10.1 were ignored, we created a second, unusable page, shown in Figure 10.2. Functionally the two pages are identical. They both have the same links, a search box and a company logo, and they both present exactly the same information. But one is clear and simple to use (if not very exciting) and the other is not. The markup for the two pages is essentially the same. The only difference between them is their visual design, which is controlled by different stylesheets.

The way in which elements are visually organized and grouped on the page, familiarity with visual conventions and signs, the use of visual hierarchies to make it clear which elements are the most important on a page, the use of alignment, the avoidance of confusing visual complexity, the choice of suitable colours with adequate tonal contrast where appropriate, and the choice of suitable fonts (so far as that can be controlled), all play a role in making our simple Web page usable and visually coherent. We discuss each of these design issues in turn in the rest of this chapter.

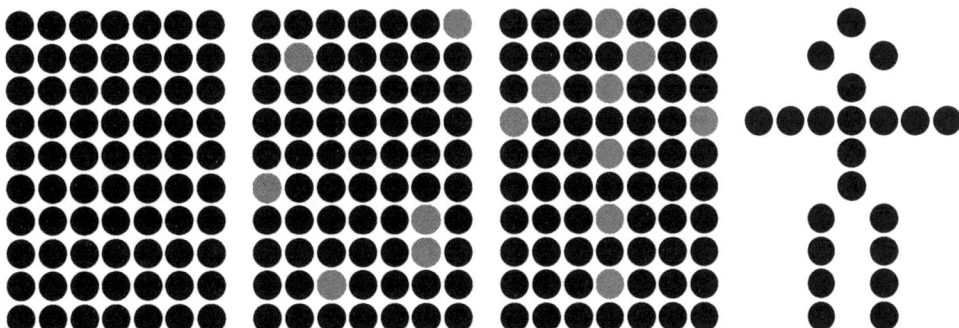

Figure 10.3 Gestalt principles of visual perception

Gestalt Principles and Semiotics

Gestalt

Gestalt principles of visual design are derived from the theories of gestalt psychology, which were applied to the study of visual perception in the 1930s and 1940s in order to investigate how the human brain tends to organize the visual information that reaches the eyes. Although we are able to identify the parts of a visual image separately – for example, we can see that each of the four images in Figure 10.3 is actually composed from individual dots – we nevertheless tend to organize visual information into patterns and structures, rather than concentrating on each piece of discrete information – each object – in the visual field. Looking again at Figure 10.3 the image on the far right immediately stands out, because the we see that the arrangement of dots forms a crude drawing of a human figure, a symbol which is likely to be recognizable by almost all people and cultures. This universal recognition of the human figure is so strong that it is almost impossible to see this image simply as a collection of dots.

In the image on the far left of Figure 10.3, however, we can discern no symbolic pattern. Here we simply see a field of dots, but we percieve that they are aligned into a perfectly regular grid. If we stare at this image for a while we may perhaps see the regular lattice pattern formed by the negative white space between the dots, rather than that formed by the dots themselves.

The perception of patterns and structures is determined by various factors, but particularly by the grouping of objects in a visual field. Our recognition of grouping is in turn determined by the proximity of elements, by similarity between elements, by symmetry, by the distinction between figure and ground, and by closure – that is, by the brain's ability to infer a complete visual pattern or image from incomplete information. These gestalt principles of visual perception are often summed up by the adage that the whole is greater than and different from the sum of the parts.

In the field of black dots on the left of Figure 10.3, we perceive grouping as a result of the similarity between the elements (the dots are identical), proximity (the dots are close to one another, and the whole group is set apart from its surroundings by some white space), and a distinction between figure (black dots) and ground (white background) – although with some effort we can make the white lattice pattern (the ground) seem dominant. We can organize this particular image no further, but this sort of non-symbolic ordering is not without value in itself. Figure 10.4 shows how these Gestalt principles work in a tiled background for a Web page, composed from the repetition of a logo. When the logo is repeated many times we perceive it simply as a pattern. Like the field of black dots, the background is composed of a collection of identical objects laid out in close proximity in a structured grid. We therefore perceive the result not as a collection of parts but as a whole pattern.

In the second and third images in Figure 10.3 (counting from the left), some of the dots have been coloured red. Looking at these two fields of dots we immediately attempt to organize the red ones into some kind of visual structure or pattern. In the second image, however, there is no pattern to be found – there is neither any meaningful symbol nor any discernible abstract pattern to be seen in this particular arrangement. The human brain works in such a way that this can make this image the most frustrating of the four; we try in vain to find a visual structure, and may expend unwarranted time and effort on this attempt.

The third image is more satisfying, however. With a little effort we can see a symbol in this image, composed from the arrangement of the red dots. This demonstrates one of the most interesting principles of gestalt theory: closure. Almost half of the dots in the arrow shape are in fact black and not red – nearly half of the visual information that says 'arrow' to us is in fact missing. And yet we can see the arrow without much difficulty, and do not try to arrange the red dots into another visual pattern. The brain completes the pattern implied by the dots that are coloured red in such a way that we can almost see a complete red arrow if we stare at this image.

The gestalt visual principles illustrated in Figure 10.3 are of considerable importance to the Web desginer. First, we need to realize that the user's brain is going to be looking for patterns. This means that a user will find a Web page easy to use if its elements are arranged in accordance with gestalt principles, and difficult and frustrating to use if no visual structure or order can be perceived. Some social networking sites presently allow the creation of personal

Figure 10.4 The whole is different from and greater than the sum of its parts

pages by their users, without imposing any design guidelines. Without sufficient attention to design principles, some of these pages can be very difficult to use, like the example shown in Figure 10.5. (This particular page extends downwards below the part illustrated for some considerable distance.) While it is up to the individual to determine how they wish to represent themselves on a personal Web page (after all, chaos might be a deliberate choice), this sort of design can make pages unusable (and in this type of case, probably inaccessible too). The fault does not lie in the separate elements that comprise the page, but in the way that they are arranged (or not) into a whole. In this particular case the design fails not only with respect to gestalt principles, but also on grounds of legibility as a result of poor colour and contrast, and over-complexity. In this case the whole is greater than the sum of the parts only in achieving a sense of chaos and confusion which the parts themselves lacked. The result acts in a way that actually detracts from any merits which the individual parts might have had.

Even the component parts of a Web page may themselves be constructed according to gestalt principles. We have seen how this might work in a background (in Figure 10.4) but it is often most obvious in the navbar. The convention has become so well established that users are unlikely to stop to think about this, which is as it should be. However, as we saw in Figure 10.2, there is no structural reason why a navbar should appear as a coherent whole. The types of menu and navbar that we are used to seeing and constructing owe their concept to gestalt principles of visual design. In a contemporary navbar, links are usually all presented in the same font, in the same size and colour, in close proximity to one another, and organized into an ordered structure. In the case of complex multi-level navbars, additional use of the principles is usually made in order to make it clear which upper-level element relates to which lower-level ones. The use of a coloured tab metaphor, adapted from office filing

Figure 10.5 Design chaos

Technical Detail

Navbars, Gestalt and Markup

The navbar is an excellent example of gestalt principles in operation which also illustrates the relationship between document structure and visual structure.

The very earliest Web sites had no navbars; HTML had (and XHTML 1.0 has) no element type suitable for grouping together a set of links. But designers seeking to make the links that define the top-level structure of a site conspicuous and easy to find soon came up with the idea of grouping them together in a distinctive style and a consistent position. This is a pure application of the gestalt principles of visual design.

This purely visual grouping led to the emergence of the navbar as a concept. This led Web designers to start using ad hoc markup to delimit navbars: first, a table, then a `div` element, finally a consensus has emerged that navbars should be marked up as unordered lists. They aren't, though. It is only with the inclusion of the `nl` (navigation list) element in the XHTML 2 proposal that markup has been provided to specify navbars as structural elements. The relationship between document structure and visual structure is not just one way.

conventions, has become very popular for this purpose. We recognize the pattern easily, and understand that each tab is a separate link to a collection of pages (or even other links) which belong together in some way. Although the navbar is made up of many separate parts, we recognize it as a whole; we visualize a navbar as a single object because of the way that the parts are presented visually.

In the same way, the designer should ensure that any visual components of a Web page that are linked conceptually will also seem linked visually, as this makes the page much easier to comprehend. If a weather forecasting site offers a set of predictions for temperature, precipitation, wind speed, etc., then these should be presented and organized on the page in a way that is visually coherent. This may be so intuitively obvious that few people will stop to think about it, but imagine how confusing it would be if the symbol for 'heavy rain' was a different size, a different colour, or even of a different design each time it appeared. To simplify matters further, suppose the forecast was provided in text only, set out in a table with a row for each of the next seven days (which we assume will be very wet), but that the font

Monday	**Heavy Rain**
Tuesday	Heavy Rain
Wednesday	HEAVY RAIN
Thursday	**Heavy Rain**
Friday	**Heavy Rain**
Saturday	*Heavy Rain*
Sunday	*Heavy Rain*

Figure 10.6 Confusing absence of similarity

for 'heavy rain' was different almost every time it appeared, as in Figure 10.6. Users would assume that there was some reason for the difference – that one day's heavy rain was going to be somehow different from the next, and that the two occurrences of the same font signified some similarity. But if every occurence of heavy rain was in the same font, size and colour, users simply recognize the pattern.

Semiotics

Because the human brain so readily organizes visual information into patterns, it is important to understand when these patterns may have meaning, and to avoid the accidental creation of visual patterns or signs that could have some unintended meaning. For example, it would be inappropriate to arrange a set of images on a page in a single column which crossed a single row in the centre, unless you intended to make use of the sign of the cross for some specific reason. Gestalt theory tells us that users will see the cross sign because of the grouping of the images; **semiotics** (or semiology, as it is known in Europe) tells us that those who recognize it will interpret that sign in a particular way and infer some meaning from it.

Semiotics was originally concerned with the way in which natural language is built up out of meaningless phonemes into whole words that have meaning. For example, the word 'elephant' is understood by all who know English and are familiar with the relevant creature to refer to the animal 'elephant'. When they hear or read the word, they think of an elephant. In the terminology of semiotics we say that the word is the **signifier**; the elephant itself is what is **signified**. The relationship between the signifier and the signified is arbitrary, and we only understand it through knowledge of the specific system within which it operates – in this case, the English language. (The word for 'elephant' in languages other than English is of course quite different, and yet the same animal is signified.)

This approach to the understanding of how meaning is created was extended to cover visual language and the way that we understand images and graphic signs. The analysis of images is of considerable importance in graphic design, but it is not directly relevant to the work of most Web designers, although it is useful to have some familiarity with this when designing sites whose content includes images. (Those who are interested in this field of study will find suggestions for further reading on the book's supporting Web site.) But the meaning of signs and symbols does concern Web designers. One of the simplest examples is the use of underlining to indicate hypertext links. As we observed earlier in this chapter, the association between the underline and the function of linking to another document (or another part of the page, perhaps) is entirely arbitrary, and has been established by convention. In semiotic terms the underline is the signifier, and the act of jumping to somewhere if we click on that underlined term is what is signified. In this case the situation is slightly complicated by the text that is involved; the text that is underlined should tell us something about what we are likely to find if we click, so the text acts in conjunction with the underlining symbol. The problem with underlining links, however, was that it used an existing signifier – the underline – for a new purpose. Underlining in hand-written and printed media had long been used to signify emphasis, and in the early years of the Web some designers continued to use it for this purpose, carrying on a long-established convention. But it soon became clear that using the same signifier to signify two completely separate things just could not work. Users were quite naturally confused. So usability experts started to prescribe that underlining must *only* be used for links to avoid confusion, and this has now become standard practice.

Not all of the uses of signs in Web design have become so well defined, however. Consider the simple arrow – the basic sign that we recognized in the third image in Figure 10.3. Arrows of various designs (though not usually made up of dots) are quite often used on Web pages, most frequently in the vestigial form of arrowheads. It is not enough that the user recognizes the sign; if a page is to be usable it has to be absolutely clear what that sign means. It is confusing to the user if the same signifier – an arrowhead – relates to several different signifieds, that is, if it has several different meanings. However, this is quite often seen in practice. For example, the use of arrowheads pointing to the right and left at the bottom of a page probably mean 'go to next page' and 'go to previous page' in a sequence of pages, and clicking on the arrow will perform that function. Arrowheads used to separate breadcrumbs indicate the page's place in the site's hierarchical structure; in this case clicking on an arrow will achieve nothing at all as it serves only as a sign, not as a link. Arrowheads used in the context of a time-based media player are conventionally connected with player controls, but the symbols for these differ. It is not always obvious what clicking on each sign using an arrowhead in this context will achieve, but it is very unlikely to link to another document. In a quite different context, arrowheads are frequently used for pop-down menus, in which case

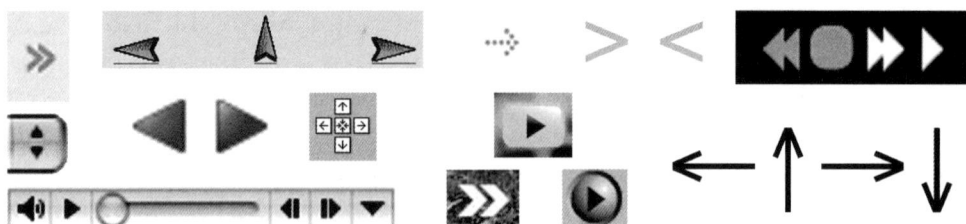

Figure 10.7 Arrows, signifying

the user is expected to click on the arrowhead beside a menu item to reveal the sub-menu. And, at the time of writing, at least one major European e-commerce site is using arrowheads in menus simply to point to each of the menu items. Figure 10.7 illustrates some of the many forms this sign can take on the Web.

In each of the cases above the designer of the page (or the media player) is relying upon a combination of convention, context and user experience to convey the meaning of the sign accurately to the user. But all three of these factors require that the user has some pre-existing knowledge to draw on, which might not always be the case. It is important to remember that the connection between visual symbols and what they signify is arbitrary (just like the connection between the word 'elephant' and the animal). We cannot expect a user to intuit or guess what a sign will mean, except on the basis of experience. An arrow may mean many things; at any time it could come to be associated with a new meaning. For this reason usability experts are now trying to insist upon standard symbols for particular purposes, but this seems both overly prescriptive and slightly desperate. It would also require that every user is able to distinguish clearly between a range of different arrows, for example, and that all designers world-wide adhere to this 'code', which in practice is unlikely to happen.

The use of symbols in Web design is therefore both contentious and subject to change. If we look back over the past few years we can see that a number of symbols once commonly used have already been largely (though not completely) abandoned. It used to be common to see a simple graphic of an envelope used on a navbar as a link for 'contact us', and a crude graphic of a house for 'home'. Simplified drawings of shopping carts or baskets are still very widely used on e-commerce sites to signify 'view my shopping basket', and variations on this theme can be found, from almost indecipherable graphic of a large, bright pink bag to an elegantly simplified line drawing of a wire basket of the kind commonly used in supermarkets. When a designer uses one of these signs they are relying upon the user's recognizing what it is and what it means. But once again it is vital to remember that the connection between the sign and what is signified is arbitrary. After all, in almost every case the basket or cart is illustrated empty, when in fact it is a link to view the contents. The sign is therefore positively misleading if interpreted literally.

Current thinking about good design practice tends to the view that designers should avoid the use of symbols of the sort we have been discussing above. Although the reasons for avoiding signs which may be potentially confusing are clear, there are two good reasons for retaining at least some of them in Web design. The Web is a global community of people who speak many different languages, and who will therefore have difficulty understanding links that are only in text form. The use of a symbol such as a shopping cart, if sufficiently widely established as a convention, transcends language barriers (it is, for example, the only understandable link on the Japanese version of a well-known online bookstore's site, if you cannot read Japanese or the very few labels in English). And there are some cases where it is virtually impossible to think of an adequate alternative for a sign or symbol. The underlining of hypertext links is one; certainly it would be possible to think of an alternative, such as putting a circle around each link, but that is simply to change to the use of a different sign. The use of arrowheads for pop-down menus is another. It is difficult to see how to indicate that a menu can be popped down without the use of some symbol, and again the symbol serves to transcend barriers of language.

So although signs should always be used cautiously and with due thought, it is not necessarily the case that they should simply be avoided.

Layout

Even if you just place images and blocks of text randomly on a page, people looking at it will see them as being visually related to each other, simply because they are all presented within the space of their browser window. As we have seen, some relationships work to convey an impression of order, but others convey a disorganized or chaotic effect which interferes with usability. Some elements need to be visually grouped together, while others require to be clearly separated. It is therefore important to pay attention to every Web page's layout – how the elements are placed on the page, which can be controlled, as we described in Chapter 4, by CSS positioning properties.

Layout Grids

Graphic designers frequently use a *layout grid* to help organize the elements of a page in a way which is visually structured and coherent, and this device is also of value in Web design, even though Web pages have no fixed dimensions. A layout grid is a geometrical division of the page that can be used to control the placement of text blocks and images. Figure 10.8

Figure 10.8 Layout grids

shows some examples. Simple grids, such as the two on the left, divide the page into areas, such as text blocks and margins. More complex grids, such as the one on the right, define a framework, into which different-sized blocks can be placed. But a grid does more than define alignments. As the example on the left of Figure 10.8 shows, elements can be aligned but still look untidy and not clearly grouped. For example, we cannot tell by a quick glance whether the text between the images belongs with the image above or below it – to discover this we either need to read the text or check the top or bottom image. The way in which the images appear on the right-hand side but the text is aligned to the left interferes further with our ability to recognize grouping. The eye also has to move repeatedly backwards and forwards across the page from image to text. Contrast this with the example on the right of Figure 10.9. Even though the images are not all of the same width, the strict left-alignment of the images and text blocks in two columns is sufficient to make the page look ordered, while the top-alignment of each block of text with the relevant image, combined with their proximity, makes it possible for us to recognize without difficulty how the blocks of text and images are grouped – that is, to see at a glance which bit of text belongs with which image. As in earlier examples, the two pages in fact present the same information and have the same function; the only difference lies in their appearance, which makes one more usable (and more pleasing to look at) than the other. (You will note that the more usable page is also a lot shorter; a good layout grid often helps make the most efficient use of space.)

Although alignment is of great importance in creating visual coherence, the grid's additional function of defining regions is what makes it such a powerful tool for visual organization. As long as the same grid is used throughout a Web site's design, different combinations of images and text blocks can be used on different pages, while preserving a feeling of uniformity throughout. Users will recognize the same overall pattern and groupings, even though the

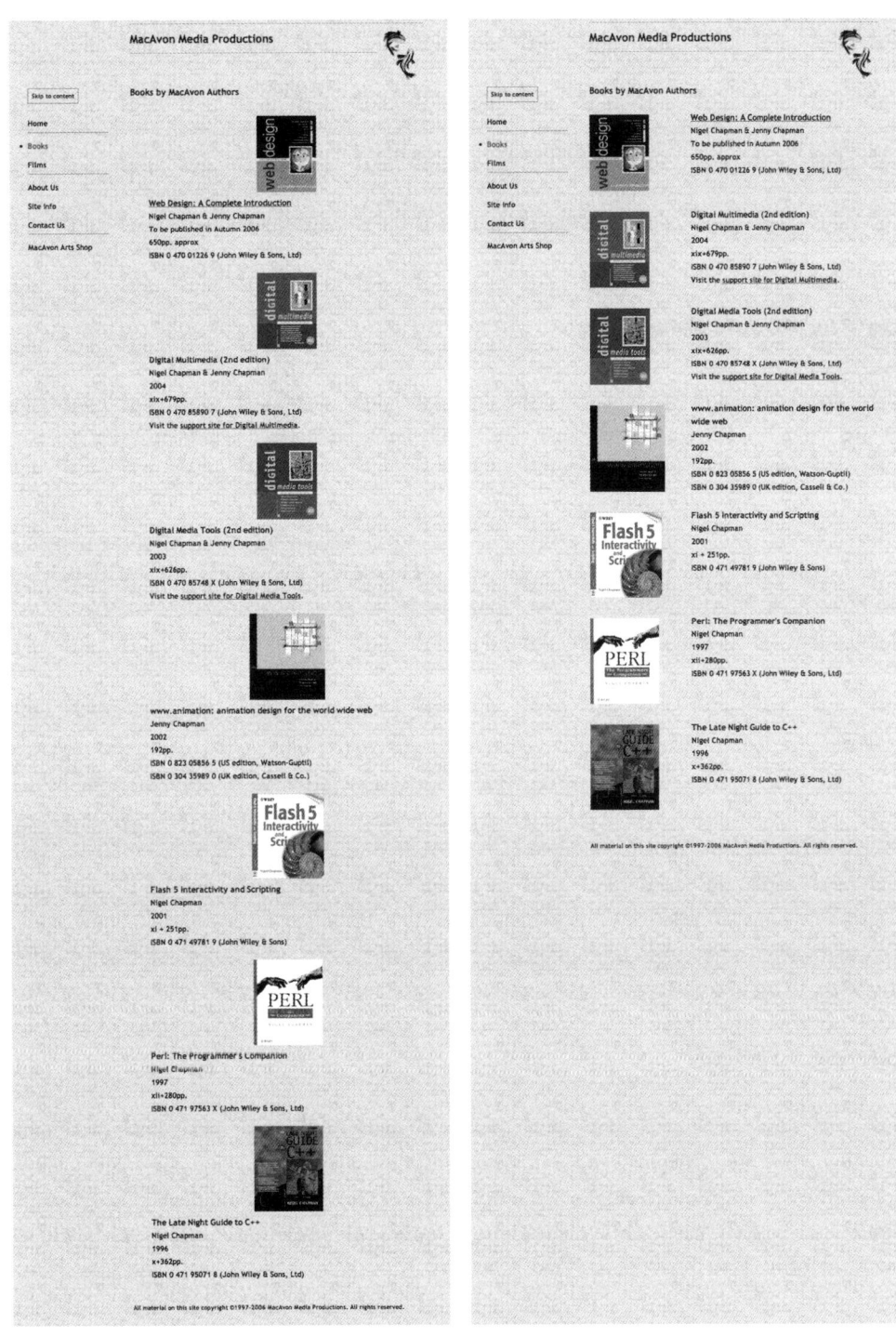

Figure 10.9 Alignment and a grid

Units	Changing font size	Changing window size
px, pt, pc, mm, cm, in	No effect	No effect
em, ex	Lengths change proportionally	No effect
%	No effect, unless the parent element's length is specified in em or ex	Lengths change proportionally, unless the parent element's length is specified absolutely or in em or ex

Table 10.1 Units in flexible layouts

elements change, and this helps give the site a particular identity. It also makes it easier to use, as we remember where particular types of elements were placed on previous pages and look for them in the same place again.

Although the grid is a powerful design element, the grid itself normally remains invisible – we see only the resulting visual structure that it imposes on layout, and not the supporting structure itself. The grid is exceptional, therefore, in that it is an abstraction – unlike visual design elements such as typography or colour.

Grids are often based on ratios, such as $\sqrt{2}$ or the Golden Ratio, to create elements with pleasing proportions. Many books have been written on the subject of creating layout grids to create harmonious pages. However, there is a serious problem in applying established guidelines for layout grids to the design of Web pages: we never know how tall or wide a page will be, because users have screens of different sizes and they can resize their browser windows. Nor do we necessarily know how big any element on a page will be, because sizes might be defined in relative units, which depend on the font size or window dimensions. Trying to create a fixed grid layout based on the geometry of a page is not going to work for the Web. (This hasn't stopped designers trying, and creating pages that force some users to scroll horizontally, others to see vast areas of blank space, and others to see a mess of overlapping text and images.)

However, all is not lost. Grids aren't an end in themselves, they are just a means of creating alignment and grouping, and enforcing uniformity. If you abandon rigid geometrical constraints, it is possible to employ a modified type of grid that accommodates the dynamic dimensions of Web pages, while maintaining a framework for vertical and horizontal alignments. This leads to flexible – or 'fluid' – layouts.

Flexible Layouts

A flexible layout abandons the idea of the elements on a page having fixed width and height in favour of allowing them to change their dimensions to accommodate changes in the size of the browser window and font. The way in which elements behave when either of these changes occurs depends on the units that have been used to specify their size. Table 10.1 summarizes the behaviour of lengths specified using the various units available in CSS.

The case of percentage units perhaps requires a little explanation. When a width or height is specified as a percentage, it is interpreted as a percentage of the corresponding dimension of the containing box. If the containing box is the entire window, the element will shrink and expand proportionally when the window is resized, but it will be unaffected by changes in font size. If, however, the containing box is itself defined in absolute terms, so that it doesn't change size, the enclosed box which is defined as a percentage will not change either. Similarly, if the containing box is defined using em or ex units, so that it changes size when the font size changes, the enclosed box will do so too, maintaining its proportion. A box which is not at the top level, and whose dimensions are specified using percent, might change size when the window is resized only if it is enclosed in another box defined using percentage units.

To make matters more complicated, many Web pages contain a mixture of textual elements and images, with perhaps some embedded time-based media objects. It is normally a bad idea to use anything other than absolute units to define the width and height of images, because if the size changes – when the window is resized or the font size altered – the image will be resampled to scale it to the new size. Web browsers make an appalling job of resampling. Even if a new generation of browsers were to employ better resampling algorithms, they would still have to work with the image at screen resolution, whereas most images are originally prepared at higher resolution, and only downsampled to screen resolution when they are exported for the Web. If you care at all about image quality, you will want to ensure that the size of all bitmapped images is fixed in absolute units to the size at which the images were originally saved. Embedded animations and video often cannot be resized at all, because the plug-ins used to play them are not capable of resizing. As a result of these considerations, many pages consist of a mixture of liquid elements, whose size can change, and fixed elements, whose size cannot change.

Lorem ipsum dolor sit amet, consectetur adipisicing elit, sed do eiusmod tempor incididunt ut labore et dolore magna aliqua. Ut enim ad minim veniam, quis nostrud exercitation ullamco laboris nisi ut aliquip ex ea commodo consequat. Lorem ipsum dolor sit amet, consectetur adipisicing elit, sed do eiusmod tempor incididunt ut labore et dolore magna aliqua. Ut enim ad minim veniam, quis nostrud exercitation ullamco laboris nisi ut aliquip ex ea commodo consequat.

Lorem ipsum dolor sit amet, consectetur adipisicing elit, sed do eiusmod tempor incididunt ut labore et dolore magna aliqua. Ut enim ad minim veniam, quis nostrud exercitation ullamco laboris nisi ut aliquip ex ea commodo consequat. Lorem ipsum dolor sit amet, consectetur adipisicing elit, sed do eiusmod tempor incididunt ut labore et dolore magna aliqua. Ut enim ad minim veniam, quis nostrud exercitation ullamco laboris nisi ut aliquip ex ea commodo consequat.

Figure 10.10 The default display of a single column layout

Single-Column Layouts

There is much to be said on grounds of simplicity for adopting a layout consisting of a single column. Understanding how single-column layouts behave also provides an insight into more complex layouts.

You will get a single-column page if you do nothing about layout in your stylesheet. It will look terrible, like Figure 10.10. (The coloured background shows the extent of the page in a browser window 800 pixels wide.)

There are many things wrong with the way browsers display XHTML documents by default in the absence of stylesheets, but in the context of layout, there are two in particular that make the result unacceptable. The lines are too long and they go too close to the edge of the window. Both are easily rectified.

People find it hard to read text that is laid out in very long lines. There is a great deal of experimental and anecdotal evidence to suggest that, for continuous text, lines must be short enough to be read without excessive eye movements so that after reading each line it is easy to find the beginning of the next. While there is some doubt about the effect on reading speed of long lines presented on screen – some research suggests that it is actually increased – there is no doubt that most people feel more comfortable with shorter lines. In accordance with our guideline of making it nice, therefore, we advocate avoiding long lines of text.

There is no agreement on a precise definition of what constitutes an excessively long line. The size at which a line becomes too long to be read comfortably can depend on the font family, type size, leading and margins, as well as on the user. Style guides advocate various measures: one traditional formula is 'an alphabet and a half', that is, 39 characters, but 72 characters is also often quoted. Some recommendations express the length as 10 to 12 words, which (in English) equates to around 50 or so characters. A broad consensus is that any

Lorem ipsum dolor sit amet, consectetur adipisicing elit, sed do eiusmod tempor incididunt ut labore et dolore magna aliqua. Ut enim ad minim veniam, quis nostrud exercitation ullamco laboris nisi ut aliquip ex ea commodo consequat. Lorem ipsum dolor sit amet, consectetur adipisicing elit, sed do eiusmod tempor incididunt ut labore et dolore magna aliqua. Ut enim ad minim veniam, quis nostrud exercitation ullamco laboris nisi ut aliquip ex ea commodo consequat.

Lorem ipsum dolor sit amet, consectetur adipisicing elit, sed do eiusmod tempor incididunt ut labore et dolore magna aliqua. Ut enim ad minim veniam, quis nostrud exercitation ullamco laboris nisi ut aliquip ex ea commodo consequat. Lorem ipsum dolor sit amet, consectetur adipisicing elit, sed do eiusmod tempor incididunt ut labore et dolore magna aliqua. Ut enim ad minim veniam, quis nostrud exercitation ullamco laboris nisi ut aliquip ex ea commodo consequat.

Figure 10.11 Restricting the column's width

value between 40 and 60 characters is likely to work, depending on the associated factors we just mentioned. The lower end of this range will usually look more elegant than the higher, which will, of course, be more efficient at fitting text into a given amount of vertical space.

In 16pt Verdana, a fairly generous font for a Web page, a line containing 55 characters is about 450 pixels wide. Most laptop screens and desktop monitors are at least 1024 pixels wide, and it is unlikely that many users will use browser windows that narrow by choice, so for most people, the default layout of a page will be too wide – usually much too wide. We must therefore constrain the width using a stylesheet.

In CSS there is no unit that allows you to express a length in characters, but em is fairly closely related in most fonts. 1em is usually between 1.5 and 2 characters. Therefore, a line length of 30 em should give you the required 40 to 60 characters in any conventional font. Figure 10.11 shows the effect of the following CSS rule on the width of our text:

```
body { width: 30em; }
```

This sets the width in terms of the size of the default font. Any elements, such as headings, set at a larger size will have fewer characters per line.

Setting the *measure* (as the text width is technically called) in em units means that it will scale with the font size. In other words, blocks of text will get wider on the screen if the font size is increased, and narrower if it is decreased. If a large font is used, or the user has opened a narrow window, text may grow to occupy an unreasonable proportion of the window. It may even exceed the width of the window, requiring horizontal scrolling to read.

One way of preventing this is to set a maximum width, expressed as a percentage. If the maximum is set in a rule for the body element, it will be computed as a percentage of the window. Hence, a better rule would be:

```
body {
    width: 30em;
    max-width: 85%;
}
```

The measure is constrained to a reasonable number of characters, but if it begins to fill the window, text will reflow in shorter lines so that horizontal scrolling is avoided. (The value of 85% is essentially arbitrary; any value below 100% will avoid the scrollbars.)

A different approach to setting the measure is to concentrate on the proportion between the text and the window, instead of the number of characters in each line. From this point of view, it makes sense to define the body measure as a percentage. The text will then occupy a constant proportion of the window's width. If the font size is increased, the text will reflow, but the boundary of the box containing it won't jump around. If the measure is a large proportion of the window, there is a risk that lines will get too long to be comfortably readable, as happens if no width is specified. To prevent this, a maximum width can be specified, this time in em units. For instance,

```
body {
    width: 50%;
    max-width: 40em;
}
```

On the face of it, very narrow windows will cause a layout of this sort to break, especially if a large font size is used. In practice, browsers prevent their users making windows so narrow that no text will fit in them.

The third way of specifying the measure is in absolute units, such as px.[†] The line length never accommodates itself to any changes in font size or window width. In the case of a single column layout, this may be acceptable behaviour, provided the width is chosen so that it will accommodate reasonable font sizes and windows, but it is an increasingly risky strategy, as more devices with small screens, such as PDAs, are being used to access the Web.

[†] Technically, px is a relative unit in CSS, but on any particular monitor it behaves as an absolute unit as long as the resolution is not changed.

Lorem ipsum dolor sit amet, consectetur adipisicing elit, sed do eiusmod tempor incididunt ut labore et dolore magna aliqua. Ut enim ad minim veniam, quis nostrud exercitation ullamco laboris nisi ut aliquip ex ea commodo consequat. Lorem ipsum dolor sit amet, consectetur adipisicing elit, sed do eiusmod tempor incididunt ut labore et dolore magna aliqua. Ut enim ad minim veniam, quis nostrud exercitation ullamco laboris nisi ut aliquip ex ea commodo consequat.

Lorem ipsum dolor sit amet, consectetur adipisicing elit, sed do eiusmod tempor incididunt ut labore et dolore magna aliqua. Ut enim ad minim veniam, quis nostrud exercitation ullamco laboris nisi ut aliquip ex ea commodo consequat. Lorem ipsum dolor sit amet, consectetur adipisicing elit, sed do eiusmod tempor incididunt ut labore et dolore magna aliqua. Ut enim ad minim veniam, quis nostrud exercitation ullamco laboris nisi ut aliquip ex ea commodo consequat.

Figure 10.12 Centring the column with auto margins

At present, though, fixed absolute widths seem to be the most commonly encountered, probably because Web authoring software usually generates them by default.

Any of these methods will set the text width to a more readable size than the default, but they all leave the text jammed against the left edge of the window.

To fix this, we can add either padding or margins to the body element. It doesn't really matter which we use at this stage, although using the margin properties avoids some potential problems with early versions of Internet Explorer. One option is to set the left and right margins to auto. This divides any horizontal window space shich is not occupied by text equally, so that the text block is automatically centred in the window, no matter how wide the window is. (At the time of writing this type of layout is quite commonly seen on the Web.) For instance, the following CSS rule leads to the display illustrated in Figure 10.12:

```
body {
    width: 50%;
    max-width: 40em;
    margin: 0 auto;
}
```

A popular variation on this approach, much favoured by bloggers, uses slightly more elaborate markup, and takes advantage of the fact that margins are transparent, to centre the page's content on a contrasting background. An extra, semantically unnecessary, div element is placed around the content, so the outline of the document looks like this:

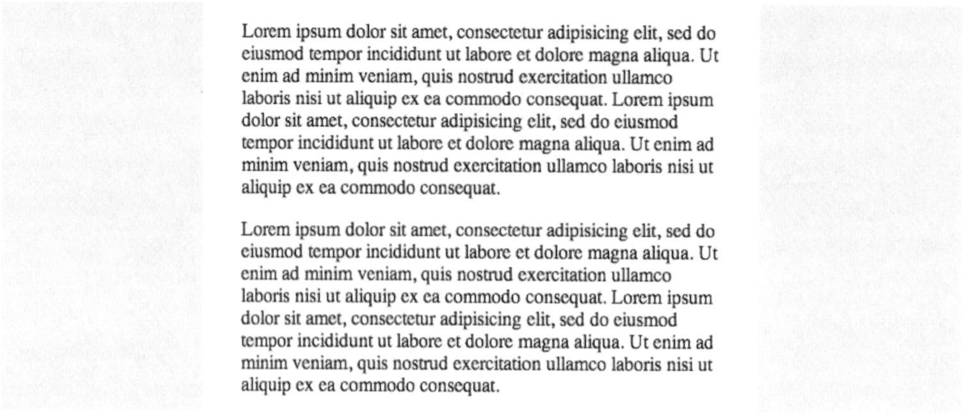

Lorem ipsum dolor sit amet, consectetur adipisicing elit, sed do eiusmod tempor incididunt ut labore et dolore magna aliqua. Ut enim ad minim veniam, quis nostrud exercitation ullamco laboris nisi ut aliquip ex ea commodo consequat. Lorem ipsum dolor sit amet, consectetur adipisicing elit, sed do eiusmod tempor incididunt ut labore et dolore magna aliqua. Ut enim ad minim veniam, quis nostrud exercitation ullamco laboris nisi ut aliquip ex ea commodo consequat.

Lorem ipsum dolor sit amet, consectetur adipisicing elit, sed do eiusmod tempor incididunt ut labore et dolore magna aliqua. Ut enim ad minim veniam, quis nostrud exercitation ullamco laboris nisi ut aliquip ex ea commodo consequat. Lorem ipsum dolor sit amet, consectetur adipisicing elit, sed do eiusmod tempor incididunt ut labore et dolore magna aliqua. Ut enim ad minim veniam, quis nostrud exercitation ullamco laboris nisi ut aliquip ex ea commodo consequat.

Figure 10.13 Centring the column as a div

```
<body>
   <div id="content">
   page content
   </div>
</body>
```

The automatic margins are then applied to the div, which is thus centred in the window. A little padding is also added, to prevent the text jamming against the edge of the div's box, which will now be visible. Contrasting background colours are applied to the div and body, and the body's margin is set to zero, producing the result shown in Figure 10.13:

```
#content {
   background-color: #FCE5D2;
   width: 50%;
   max-width: 40em;
   padding: 1em 2em;
   margin: 0 auto;
}

body {
   margin: 0;
   background-color: #B6D6ED;
}
```

You could use a background image for a more elaborate effect, and a non-zero body margin if you didn't want the content to butt up against the top of the window.

However, there is no particularly good reason to centre the content area of a page; you may prefer to use asymmetrical margins. (Our thesaurus lists the following synonyms for asymmetrical: lopsided, unsymmetrical, uneven, unbalanced, crooked, awry, askew, skew, misaligned; disproportionate, unequal, irregular; informal, cockeyed, wonky. This suggests that asymmetry may be perceived in a somewhat negative manner, but in visual design this is not necessarily the case.) Generally, pages which read from the left will seem more readable and more pleasing if the right margin is wider than the left, whereas pages which read from the right should have a wider left margin.

The margins' width may be specified in any of the units available in CSS, depending on how you want them to behave when the window is resized or the font size is varied. There is a case for not using em units for margins: if the margin gets wider when the font size is increased, even less text will fit within the window. Using percentage margins maintains their proportions; using absolute sizes maintains a fixed distance around the text. Either may be desirable depending on the rest of the page design.

Although we have illustrated the possibilities for margins with the content width set as a percentage, the same techniques are applicable to widths defined as ems or using absolute units.

Two- and Three-Column Layouts

Single-column layouts are simple to design and implement and can be elegant, but they do not make efficient use of the available space, and they impose a monolithic structure on the page which is not always appropriate. Adding extra columns helps to overcome these limitations.

Before considering how to place columns side by side, we need to look at how they might be used. In books, magazines and especially newspapers, columns are often used to allow type to be set on narrow measures within a wide page. The text flows from one column to the next, so each column is read from top to bottom in turn, as indicated in Figure 10.14. This is rarely an effective use of columns on a Web page. Although the wide windows typical of browsers appear to lend themselves to this arrangement, there is no way of knowing how deep a window will be, so there is no way for the user to know where the bottom of a column will be found. The darker background area in Figure 10.14 shows a probable extent of a window on a conventionally shaped monitor. Here, having the text laid out in imitation of a multi-column magazine spread requires the user to scroll to the bottom of each column

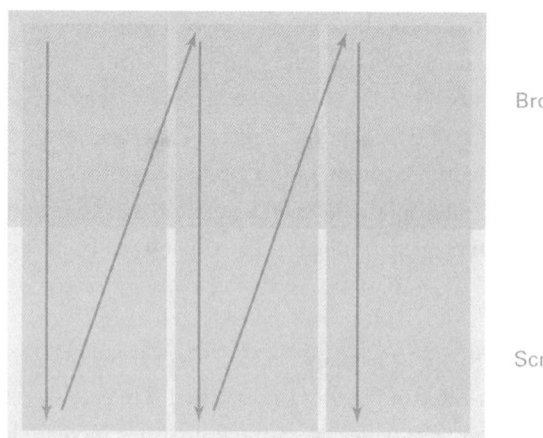

Browser window

Scrolled area

Figure 10.14 Linked text columns

and then back up to the top of the next. This frequently happens when several columns are used to hold linked text like this.

Columns in Web pages are therefore better used in a different way, generally with a main column carrying the body text or main content, and others holding material that is relevant to, but separate from, it. This material might consist of a separate story, illustrative images, hypertext links to related material, called-out quotes from the main text, digressive material (like traditional sidebars), advertisements or navigation aids. The columns should break up the horizontal space in a proportion which is pleasing, appropriate to their content, and which assists in making the page more usable by separating elements in a visually clear way. In most cases the main column will be significantly wider than subsidiary columns, both to indicate by its scale that it contains the main content, and to convey an appropriate visual balance to the page. However, this is not to say that a narrow column necessarily contains material of lesser importance. A vertically oriented navbar is hardly unimportant, but it fits conveniently into a narrow width, and a narrow navbar, with compact buttons or text, conforms to user expectations and is likely to be more usable. Users without sight impairment will often quickly recognize a feature such as a navbar by its typical layout; diverging from the norm may be interesting in some contexts, but it will compromise usability.

In practice, the proportion of the page which each column occupies can only be judged by eye once typical content has been added, but arithmetic can provide some starting points. Figure 10.15 shows some typical ways of dividing up a page horizontally. The first two examples use columns of equal width, a design which is only really suitable for cases where the

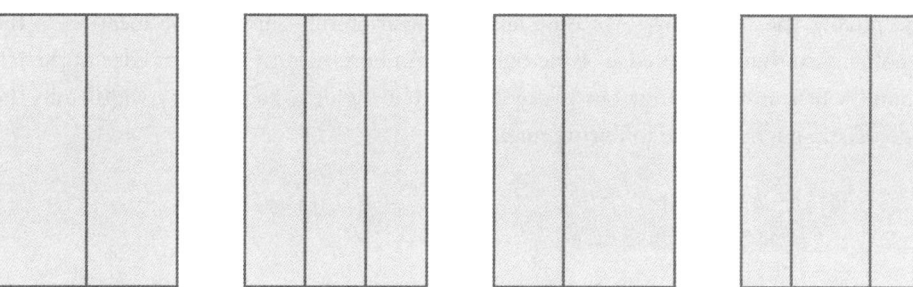

Figure 10.15 Column ratios

content of each column has equal importance, because identity in size conveys a sense of identity of importance to the user. The two asymmetrical cases are based on division by the Golden Ratio (approximately 1.618), which has long been held to produce a visually pleasing proportion. (It is also mathematically pleasing, since, in the two-column case, the ratio of the width of the larger column to the whole page is the same as the ratio of the widths of the smaller and larger columns.)

We'll begin by considering two-column layouts that use a separate `div` element for each column. That is, the document has the following structure:

```
<body>
   <div id="left">
   contents of left column
   </div>
   <div id="right">
   contents of right column
   </div>
</body>
```

With each column isolated in its own `div`, it is easy to set their widths and apply distinctive backgrounds to each, if that is desired. An explicit separator between the columns can be provided by setting a border on the right edge of the left column (or the left edge of the right), and CSS rules using contextual selectors can be used to style the contents of the two columns separately. All we need to do is place the two columns side by side, instead of one after the other, as they would be displayed by default.

There are two ways of achieving the desired placement.

Conceptually, the simpler way is to use absolute positioning – just set the location of the two columns so that the left edge of the right column butts against the right edge of the left column. A first attempt to lay out two columns that divide a page of any width into the Golden Ratio might use the following rules:

```
#left,#right {
    position: absolute;
    top: 0;
    margin:0;
    padding:0 2%;
}
#left {
    width: 34%;
    left: 0;
}
#right {
    width: 58%;
    left: 38%;
}
```

Both the elements are absolutely positioned. We have added a little padding to separate their contents, and rounded up the percentage values for the Golden Ratio to whole numbers, since most browsers fail to deal correctly with percentages that are not integers. The total width of the wider right column should thus be 62% of the page, leaving 38% for the left column, so the left property of the right column is set to that value. Subtracting the padding, the content widths of the two columns are 58% and 34%, since each has left and right padding of 2%, making 4% in all. (Recall from Chapter 4 that both content width and padding expressed using percentage units are calculated as a percentage of the enclosing box.)

The widths of the two columns can be expressed in any CSS units, depending on how you want them to behave when the font or window size is changed. There is nothing to stop you mixing units – a fixed width column for images and a zoomable text column in ems, for instance – but the left property of the right hand column has to be computable from the dimensions of the left column. This means, for instance, that you can't apply a fixed 12px of padding to a left column whose content width is 25%. There is no way in CSS2 to set the left property to 25%+24px. (In CSS3 there will be.)

For cases where you want to combine a fixed-width column with one that flexes when the window is resized, you can use the value auto for the width of the latter. For example, the following rules will give you a left column that is always 250px wide, with 10px of padding on each side, and a right column whose width adjusts itself to fill the rest of the window, no matter how big or small the window is:

```
#left,#right {
    position: absolute;
    top: 0;
    padding: 0 10px;
    margin:0;
}
#left {
    width: 250px;
    left: 0;
}
#right {
    width: auto;
    left: 270px;
}
```

These techniques using absolute positioning can be extended in a trivial way to layouts with three or more columns. Notice that because the elements are being absolutely positioned, it doesn't matter what order they appear in the source document. It will always be possible to place the most important content first, so that skip links will not be necessary for screen reader users.

The alternative way of creating a two-column layout is to float one column to the left or right, leaving the other in the normal flow. As we explained in Chapter 4, the margin on the element that is not floated should be set to a wide enough value to accommodate the floating element. For instance, the last example could be implemented using the following rules:

```
#left,#right {
    padding: 0 10px;
    margin:0;
}
#left {
    width: 250px;
    float:left;
}
#right {
    width: auto;
```

```
        margin-left: 270px;
    }
```

The code is slightly simpler than the previous version, and floats work more reliably in more browsers than absolute positioning does. It would, of course, be possible to float the right column to the right, instead of floating the left column to the left.

It is important to remember that the floated material must come before the material it floats by. This may sometimes force you to put less important elements, such as navbars, before the main content, leading to a requirement for skip links. If you need to place material, such as a page footer, below both columns, it will be necessary to set its `clear` property.

As with the absolute positioning techniques, any units can be used, and units can be mixed, providing it is possible to obtain a value for the left margin from the dimensions of the left column.

Note that a column is a visual component of the laid-out page. Each column may or may not correspond to an element of the source document. Hitherto, we have used a `div` to group together some elements to form a separate column; it is also possible for several floated elements to be aligned so that they appear to be placed in a column. Since, by default, the top of a floated box is aligned with the first line of text that follows it, using floats provides a way of adding horizontal alignment to the vertical alignment of columns. Consider, for instance, a document with the following outline:

```
<body>

<p>
<img class="left" src="url1" alt="first image"/>
    Text of first paragraph
</p>
<p>
<img class="left" src="url2" alt="second image"/>
    Text of second paragraph
</p>
<p>
    Text of third paragraph
</p>
<p>
<img class="left" src="url3" alt="third image"/>
    Text of fourth paragraph
```

Floats, Margins and Internet Explorer

There is a strange and nasty bug in versions of Internet Explorer for Windows, at least up to IE6. If a block element (for example, a `div` or `p`) is floated and has a non-zero (positive or negative) margin, the width of the margin on the side that the element is floated to is doubled. (That is, if the element is floated left, its left margin is doubled.) Although this won't affect the floated layouts described in the text (`img` is an inline element) it would have a disastrous effect on any similar layouts using floated `div` elements, for example, as pull-quotes.

The workround is as strange as the bug. Set the `display` property of the floated element to `inline`. When the element is floated, it is converted to a block irrespective of the value of this property, so correct browsers are not affected. In IE, though, the margin is no longer doubled.

```
</p>
<p>
    Text of fifth paragraph
</p>
```

We can easily define a CSS rule that floats all the images to the left. Provided all the images are the same size, we can also set their width explicitly, and add a negative left margin, so that they are all moved leftwards from the place they would normally occupy. That would be the left edge of the content region of the box for the body element. If we add a margin to the body sufficient to accommodate our floated images, all the images will move out into this margin to form a column. Figure 10.16 shows how the elements of the page would be placed by the following CSS rules:

```
.left {
   padding: 0;
   width: 250px;
   float:left;
   margin: 0 0 10px -270px;
}
body {
   margin: 0 0 0 270px;
}
```

Figure 10.16 Floating several elements into a left column

Extending the float techniques to three columns is not straightforward, except for the simplest cases. For instance, three fixed-width columns, defined in absolute units, can be created by applying wide margins to both sides of the page, floating one column to the left and one to the right, leaving the third one alone to occupy the middle. Considerable ingenuity has been expended in devising ways of using floats for three-column layouts that allow you to use a mixture of units for the columns' dimensions. We will not describe the solutions that have been put forward, since they are elaborate and do not seem to offer any improvement over the use of absolute positioning, unless, perhaps, you need to support some older browsers.

Arbitrary Grid Layouts

Grids with more than three columns are best treated as a framework which can be used to align elements on the page, horizontally as well as vertically. Broadly speaking, there are two ways of using a grid for layout of this sort, which we will call dense and sparse. These possibilities are illustrated in Figure 10.17.

In a dense layout, most of the grid cells are filled with text or images (or embedded time-based media objects). The widths of these elements are chosen so that they occupy one or more grid cells, with standard margins around them. The result is similar to some newspaper layouts. Using a dense layout will tend to create a cluttered effect, but it does allow you to pack a lot of information into a small space. Sometimes, clutter might be appropriate or necessary, for instance in a classified ad site or a gallery of thumbnail images.

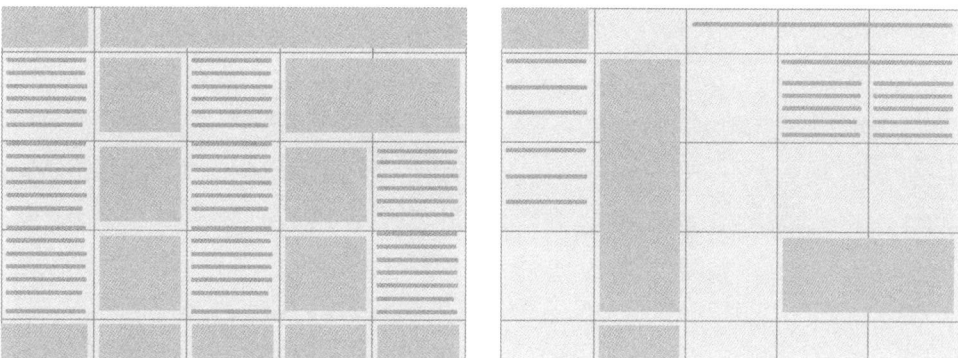

Figure 10.17 Dense and sparse grid layouts

A sparse layout leaves many of the cells empty, creating negative spaces around the elements in the filled cells. By placing those elements on the grid, though, related elements can be connected visually by their alignment and proximity. For example, in the sparse layout in Figure 10.17, the tall narrow image (indicated by an orange rectangle) naturally leads downwards to the small image at the bottom below it.

If you don't care about what happens when users resize their browser window or increase the font size, grid layouts can be implemented very easily using absolute positioning, some simple arithmetic and a bit of trial and error. Web authoring programs, such as Dreamweaver, allow you to lay out blocks on a grid just by dragging out rectangles on the screen. They then generate stylesheet rules that set the position and size of div elements that correspond to each box you have drawn in px units.

This approach to layout is paper-based thinking, and cannot be recommended, except for pages consisting of nothing but images, which, as we explained before, should never be resized. Once textual elements are incorporated, as they almost always are, you should start thinking about flexible layouts, otherwise a user with poor eyesight will find that when they increase the font size, text overflows its box, and users who prefer narrow windows will be forced to scroll horizontally.

There is no totally satisfactory solution to creating flexible complex grid layouts. One way to approach the problem is by breaking it into two: a layout for narrow windows and small screens, and a layout that accommodates font size changes. A stylesheet switcher can be used to select one or the other, as described in Chapter 7. Multiple columns are never going to fit

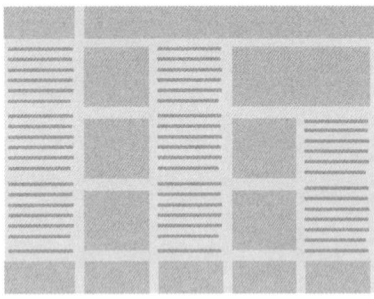 

Figure 10.18 A zooming layout

in a narrow window, so one style should remap the grid to a single-column layout. This leaves the style for wide screens with the problem of accommodating font size changes only.

If all the widths and heights of the elements on the grid and their horizontal and vertical coordinates are specified in em units, you will end up with a zooming layout. That is, when the font size is increased, all dimensions are increased and objects are moved, so that the entire page is bigger in both directions but maintains the same proportions. (See Figure 10.18.) Images must be placed inside some other element, usually a `div`, so that the space around them can be zoomed while the image itself remains the same size. It is advisable to allow some space around each image at its default size (that is, using your default font settings) in case somebody makes the font smaller and causes the layout to shrink.

If your page was wide to begin with, letting it expand in both directions may lead to users' needing to scroll horizontally, which is unpopular. Vertical scrolling, on the other hand, is something that most people accept as necessary, so it may be preferable to design your layout so that it only ever expands vertically, while remaining the same width.

This is done by using absolute widths for all the elements and their horizontal coordinates (i.e. their `left` or `right` property), reserving relative units for the heights and vertical coordinates (`top` property). When the font size is increased, text boxes will get higher to accommodate the extra lines that will result when the larger text reflows. (See Figure 10.19. Both pages are exactly the same width.)

Emerging Technology

CSS3 Template-Based Layouts

There are very good reasons for not using `table` elements to lay out Web pages, but it cannot be denied that tables provide a good approximation to grids – they consist of rows and columns, after all – which absolutely positioned elements don't really. The CSS3 *Advanced Layout Module* Working Draft proposes a new positioning scheme for CSS that provides a simple mapping of a grid layout to rows and columns, without requiring the abuse of markup that table-based layouts lead to.

In brief, the `display` property can be set to a template that defines a collection of grid cells, named by letters. The `position` property for elements of the document can then be set to one of these letters, with the effect of positioning the element inside the corresponding cell of the grid. The following simple example shows how this will work:

```
body { display: "aaa"
               "bcd"; }
#navbar { position: a; }
#left { position: b; }
#main { position: c; }
#right { position: d; }
```

The page is divided into a 3×2 grid. The three cells of the top row are merged into a single region, because all three cells have the same letter. The element with `id` equal to `navbar` is then placed in that row, with the three cells of the lower row being filled with three other elements.

It is possible to specify the size of some or all of the cells in any CSS units. If no sizes are given, the cells are all set to the same size.

The proposed display model will simplify the construction of grid-based layouts considerably if and when it is correctly implemented in browsers, but, given the record of browsers' implementing CSS2, that may be some way off.

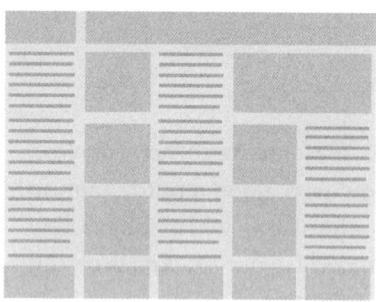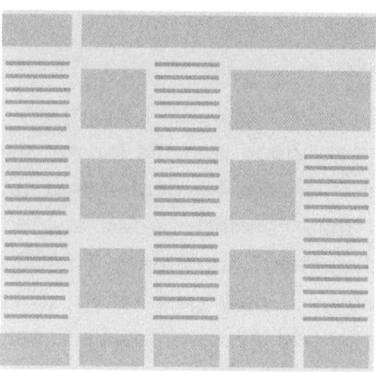

Figure 10.19 A stretching layout

Whether you choose to have a zooming layout or one that stretches vertically only, you will need to work out the dimensions and heights of all your elements in order to use absolute positioning. This can only be done by measurement: you must lay out the boxes and fill them with the actual text of the page, using the font at the size specified in your stylesheet. This can conveniently be done in a Web authoring program, or mocked up in a graphics program. You will have to convert the measurements, which will be in absolute units, to em units, using the font size.

Why can't you just set the boxes' widths to a pre-determined value, and set the `height` property to `auto`, so that the boxes will be as tall as they need to be? If you do so, and therefore don't know the actual height of any particular box, you cannot know where to position any boxes that lie below it. Allowing what you believe to be plenty of space is a risky business – few things look worse on a Web page than text crashing into material that is supposed to be below it.

To use automatic box heights, you need a layout based on floated elements instead of absolute positioning. The float algorithm means that, if several elements are floated to the left, they will line up next to each other. Any following element that has its `clear` property set to `left` will be positioned below all the floated elements. Hence, a row of a grid can be made by floating all the cells in it to the left, and then the next row can be started with an element that clears its left edge. For sparse layouts, extra margins can be applied where necessary to create gaps in the rows. Each row will be as high as the tallest cell it contains. There is no need to know how tall each row is, but the elements must appear in the same order in the XHTML source as they are to appear on the grid (reading left to right, top to bottom).

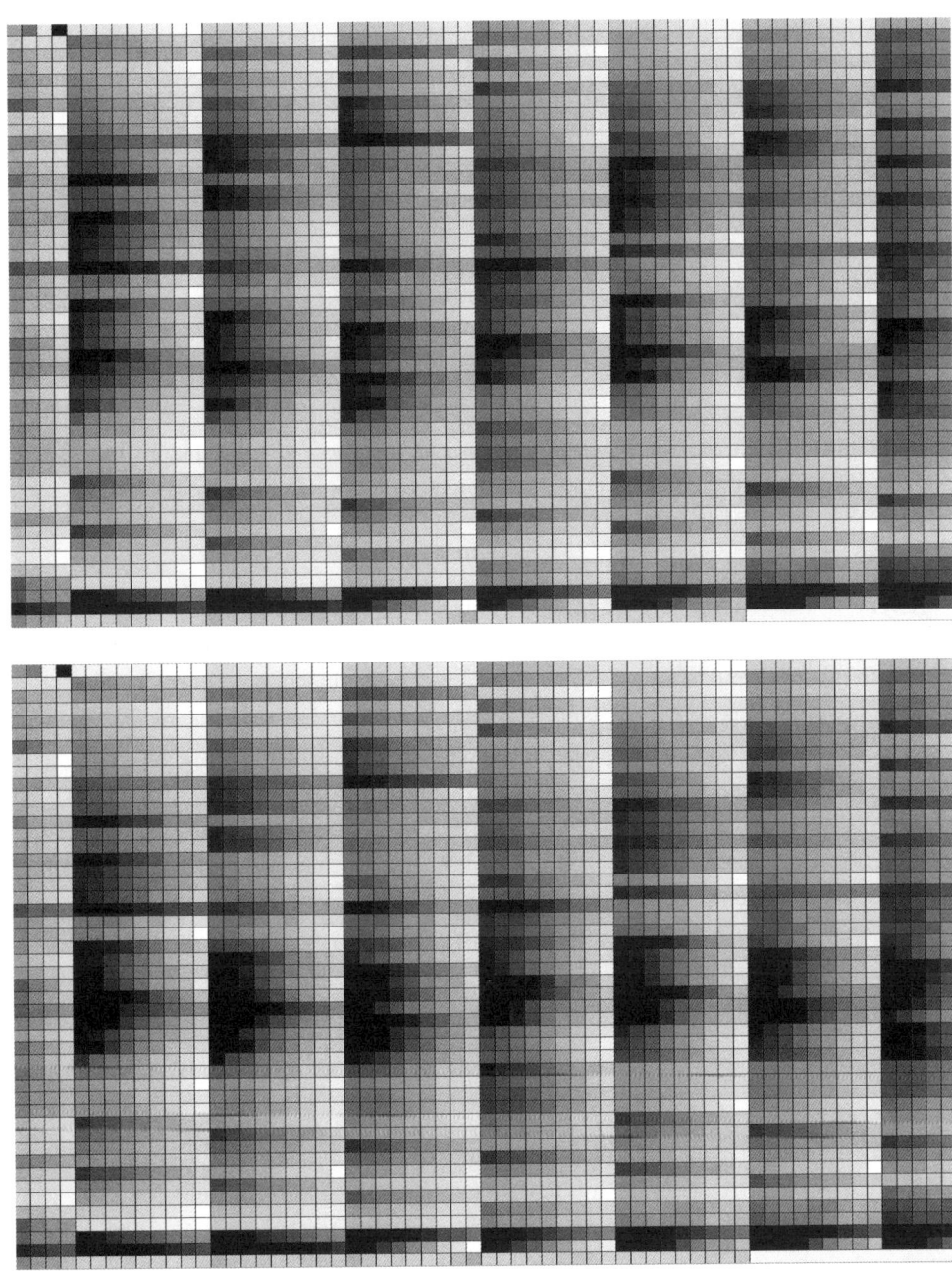

Figure 10.20 Colours and tones

This method lends itself well to columns whose widths are defined as percentages of the window, where that is possible. If any other units are used, then it is essential that the width of the body is also specified, otherwise there is a possibility that the rows will wrap within the window, if it is not wide enough to accommodate them. This will completely ruin the layout.

Colour and Tone

We have discussed many aspects of colour for Web design in Chapters 5 and 9, so we will not repeat here what has already been said. However, when thinking about the visual design of Web pages, colour obviously plays an important role which has to be considered by the designer. Every element on a Web page, including the text, will be assigned some colour, even if it is only black or white; there can be no such thing as a visual element which is colourless. (There will always be some other coloured element underneath transparent areas.)

Colour in Web Page Design

As we saw in Chapter 5, computer displays use an RGB colour space which includes millions of different colours. However, in reality it is improbable that anyone can perceive the subtle distinctions between all these possible colours. Even in the much more limited table of just a few thousand colours shown in Figure 10.20 it is difficult to distinguish many of the colour samples from one another, although in fact no two are identical. When we consider that it is also impossible to know how any colour we might specify in a stylesheet will be seen on a user's computer (different screens and personal settings result not just in slight variations but in completely different colours being seen), we realize that it is not worthwhile being too particular about chosing one subtle shade of a colour in preference to another. This can be very frustrating to graphic designers who are used to having much tighter control over colour in print media, but on the Web this problem is unavoidable and there is no way round it, nor will there ever be for as long as people view Web pages from different machines and have control over display settings.

In practice this means that although we need to think carefully about colour, we should do so in fairly broad terms, and not worry about minor distinctions between hues or tones. Even then, however, it can be very difficult to choose colours. Figure 10.21 shows the same Web page with a range of different coloured backgrounds (please check the example pages on the supporting Web site to see the actual colours). On a Web page like the simple one illustrated here, which has only two small graphics and fairly sparse text, there is a great deal of screen space available between the elements conveying the content. This means that when we fill

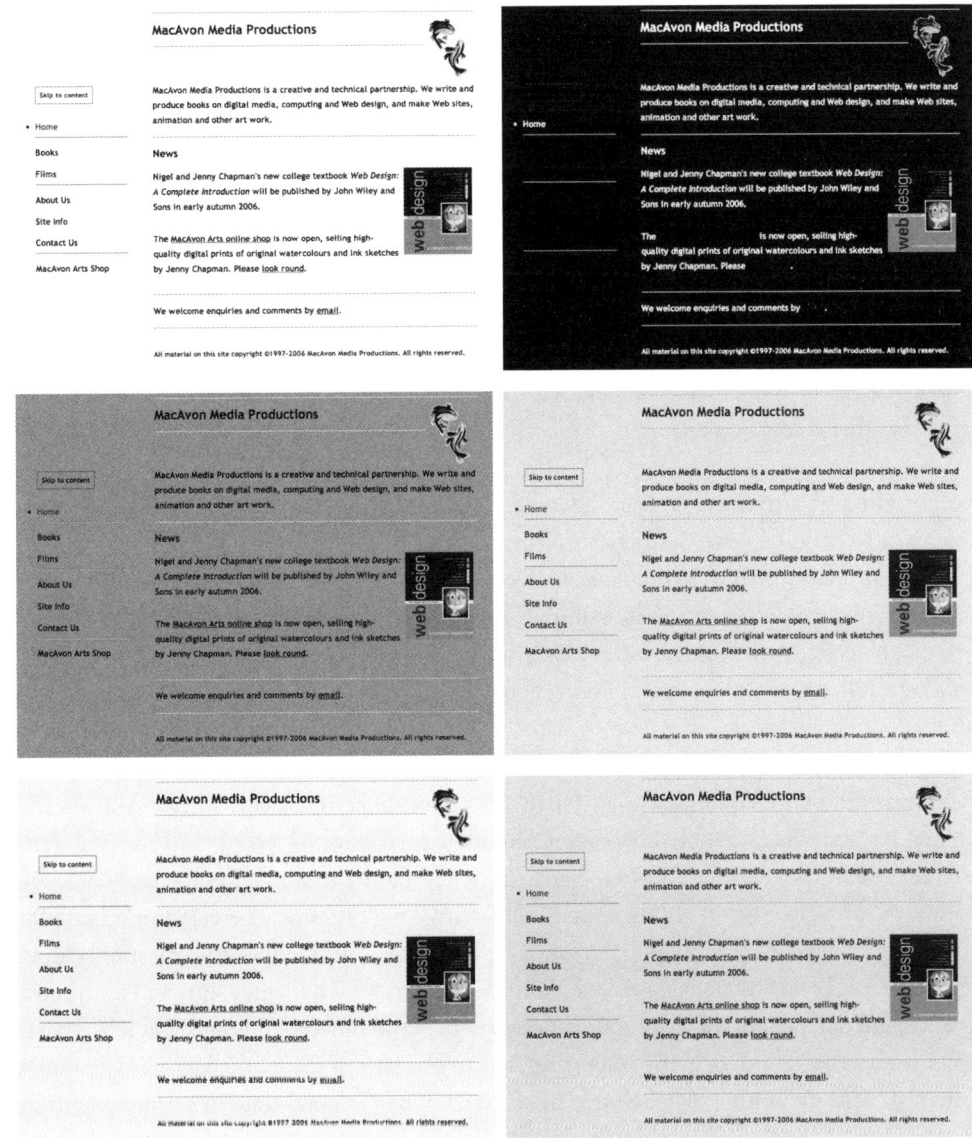

Figure 10.21 The effect of different background colours

that space with colour, that colour is the dominant visual element in our browser window – it occupies by far the largest proportion of the page's available space – and it will therefore have a significant impact on any viewer who does not suffer problems with vision.

With the exception of the change of text colour for greater legibility in the example at top right of Figure 10.21 there is no difference between the six pages other than the background colour. Why does a change of colour seem to give the page a different character? If we viewed them all in greyscale there would be little discernible difference in character, despite the variations in tone, except for the page (top right) with the very dark background. (Grey is generally perceived as 'neutral' which is why it is used by designers who wish to avoid imparting any particular character – other than neutrality – to their sites.) Colours other than greys, however, generally evoke some kind of emotive response. Various theories about this have been put forward, but we will not discuss them here because many are contentious, and most are culturally insensitive. (For example, when it is suggested that black is a funereal colour it exhibits ignorance of the fact that in many cultures black does not play this role, whereas other colours do).

So it is impossible to discuss colour differences like those illustrated in Figure 10.21 without reference to personal taste, aesthetics, cultural differences and fashion, and these are imprecise factors upon which to base colour decisions. However, they are also powerful influences upon personal responses to visual material, and cannot simply be ignored. The one thing you can be certain of is that, given a wide enough sample of people around the world, there will be a full range of different opinions about which colour works best, or which colours and colour combinations they like or hate, and this will tend to vary between cultures as well as between individuals. Despite what anyone might claim to the contrary, there is no right answer when it comes to colour (apart from issues affecting accessibility). And yet the colours chosen affect not only how easy it is to use a page, but how people will respond to it, because responses to colour are often emotive – and for a site that requires to get its message across, or to be effective in selling something, emotive responses may be very important. On top of personal taste, fashion and convention play a role. (Why do we roll out a red carpet for VIPs to walk on and not a green one? Why do bankers wear dark grey suits and not yellow ones?) And once again, there are wide differences between different cultures. On a Web site, what seems a garish riot of many colours to users in one part of the world may seem a normal colour scheme in another; what seems the epitome of muted good taste in certain countries may seem excessively dull and boring elsewhere.

As there is so much variation both culturally and personally in response to colours it is impossible to arrive at any general guidelines for the choice of colours in Web design, and any that are proposed must be liable to change as fashions and conventions change. It is therefore prudent to be wary of people or services which claim to tell you right answers about colour choices. For example, there are a number of 'colour schemers' available online or even to purchase. You may find some helpful, but the colour schemes they provide are of very variable quality, give no consideration to cultural or emotive feelings about colour, and usually ignore the necessity for the use of good tonal contrast in Web design. (And because the RGB colour space is not perceptually uniform, it is not possible just to lighten or darken a colour without altering the perceived hue, so to be useful a scheme must actually specify the colours in the precise tones you require.)

There is one aspect of human response to colour that we can consider more precisely, however. As human brains and eyes work in roughly the same way the world over, we can investigate how colour combinations are perceived (in people with standard colour vision) – how the presence of one colour affects perception of another, and so on. Painters in the late 19th century experimented with placing dots of colours side by side to create optical mixing – that is, new colours mixed in the brain rather than on the canvas. In the same way that if you actually mix blue and yellow paint together you will get green, if you put sufficient small dabs of pure blue and pure yellow paint on a canvas in very close proximity you will see not blue and yellow but green.

You are probably also familiar with the concept of the afterimage: if you stare at an area of pure colour for a while and then look away you will 'see' an area of the same shape but in the *complementary* colour. For example, if you stare hard at a yellow patch you will see a violet one, or if you stare at a something light blue you will see an orange afterimage, and so on. If you place small grey squares on strong plain-coloured backgrounds (of equal brightness to the grey) and look at them for a while each grey square will seem to take on a tinge of the colour which is complementary to the background, although of course they do not change in fact.

In other words, the brain plays some funny tricks on us. For example, the yellow and red squares in Figure 10.22 are all of exactly the same size, but they don't look it. (The black and white frames are of identical sizes too.) We say that a colour seems to advance or recede, according to whether it looks nearer and larger, or further away and smaller. (Unfortunately,

Figure 10.22 The effect of colour combinations on perception of size

however, while most people experience this phenomenon to some extent, there does not seem to be universal agreement on which colours advance and which recede in particular circumstances, so once again be wary of anyone offering prescriptive rules about this.)

Figure 10.23 illustrates the way in which the same colour is perceived differently when combined with a range of other colours. The colour of the red frame shape is identical in all three cases, and yet it not only seems to have a different hue when superimposed upon different coloured backgrounds, it also seems to be brighter or duller and more lifeless, according to the colour upon which it is superimposed. You may also find that the size of the red shape seems to vary too.

When using colour in Web design, therefore, there are many factors to consider, and no easy answers. The only aspect of colour which we can be reasonably confident of exploiting to good effect for all users is tonal value.

Contrast and Tonal Values

We have already discussed the implications of colour choices for accessibility in Chapter 9, and advised that to make pages more accessible for people with any kind of vision problems – and more usable for all – good tonal contrast should be used. But what is good tonal contrast? Two colours are said to have high contrast if there is a great difference between their brightness; the greatest contrast, therefore, is between black and white. They will have low contrast if their brightness is very similar, regardless of their hue. It is conventional to refer to colours with the highest levels of brightness as 'light', and colours with the lowest levels as 'dark'. (In RGB representation the darkest tones in each colour component have the lowest numerical values, and the lightest have the highest values.) While it is certainly not always necessary to use maximum contrast on a Web page, it is advisable to use high

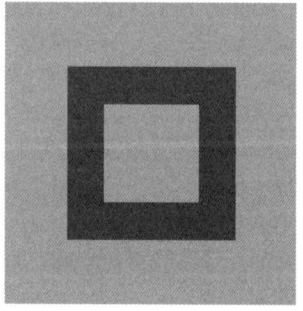

Figure 10.23 The effect of colour combinations on perception of colour

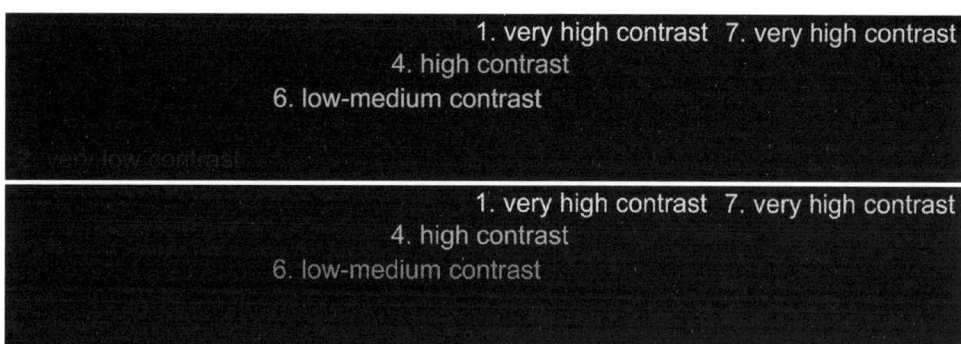

Figure 10.24 Tonal contrast

contrast between text and background, and at least medium contrast between any other elements which need to be readily distinguished from one another.

However, it isn't always easy to judge the tonal values of colours, and some people naturally find this much more difficult than others. In the lower part of Figure 10.19 we showed an approximation of the tonal values of the several thousand colours above, by converting the colour chart to greyscale. You will notice that most colours convert to a grey which is neither very light nor very dark. Just as we cannot perceive the subtle nuances of hue that distinguish one colour in the upper chart from another, we cannot always see differences in tonal value either, and can even completely misjudge the relative brightness of colours.

Figure 10.24 shows seven colours presented as text, first on a light apricot background and then on a dark blue background. As we have observed, the same colour may look different when presented in conjunction with certain other colours, so to make it clear which colours are in fact the same in the two cases, each one has been assigned a number from 1 to 7. (Colours with the same number are identical.) Each fully-coloured version in this example (the first and third bands in the figure) has then been reproduced in greyscale to show the tonal values more clearly (in the second and fourth bands respectively). Many people will find some of the results surprising. For example, people with good colour vision may feel that the red text (5) and the bright blue text (6) stand out quite well against the dark blue background, while in fact the tonal contrast is not good. The red colour (5), in particular, offers almost no contrast with the dark blue. And on the light apricot-coloured background the bright blue text (6) seems really quite striking, but the contrast is only moderate. In this case the red (5) offers significantly better contrast than the bright blue, even though both hues are very clearly differentiated from the apricot background. On this light background the orange (4) seems to stand out quite well against the pale apricot colour, but in fact the contrast is barely adequate for good legibility. For text on this background a darker tone of the same colour would have been a much better choice, but if the two colours were each being used as background for two different areas on a page, such as the main body text and the navbar, the contrast would be acceptable. The level of contrast required will therefore vary with the purpose of the element to be coloured.

In all cases, however, it is prudent to test the tonal contrast of any colour scheme by convert-ing either your display or your colour space (in Photoshop or a similar program) to greyscale. If, having done this, you can easily read or distinguish the different elements on your Web page, then your tonal contrast is adequate for good usability and accessibility.

Typography

Many of the subtle points that distinguish fine typography in print are largely irrelevant to Web designers, because they depend on being able to use specific fonts. Unless and until the downloading feature of CSS Web fonts is widely implemented, it will not be possible to assert that any particular font will be used when a page is displayed. It will depend on whether the user has got that font installed on their system. (Even if font downloading is a possibility, it will also depend on whether the user has overridden your stylesheets with their own.) There is thus little point in carefully adjusting inter-word spacing and tracking by hand, even though CSS provides means of doing so. What works for one font probably won't work for a different one, so for some visitors to your site, such adjustments may do more harm than good.

There are, however, some typographical adjustments that should be considered. They pro-vide ways to express the structure of a page visually, by the use of contrasting typographical properties. Font size and weight have a natural ordering, from smallest to largest and from lightest to heaviest, respectively, which provides one possible way of arranging type hierar-chically. This hierarchical arrangement will reflect the structure of the page as expressed in its XHTML markup.

Typography for Reading

It would be quite possible to set an entire page in a single font family, style, weight and size and – provided you paid attention to line length and leading – the result would be perfectly readable. However, text can convey its message more clearly with the aid of typography. For the most part, this means using typographical contrasts to mark out different elements that serve particular functions. In particular, emphasis can be denoted typographically. We can also use the same style for different pieces of text which serve the same purpose on a page, in accordance with gestalt principles of similarity.

Before considering variations in type properties, we must look at the question of which font settings to use for the bulk of the text on a page – the standard values from which any changes will differ. A simple choice is the user's defaults. This choice would mean that you do not specify any font family, size, weight or style, except for elements, such as headings, that you want to distinguish typographically. The reasoning behind this would be that, although you don't know what the page will look like in any particular user's browser, you can be sure that it will respect any choices they have made about fonts.

There are two flaws in this reasoning. First, many users do not know how to change their default fonts, or can't be bothered to do so. The defaults do not represent a choice that these users have made, but one made for them by a browser designer. (And for the majority of users, this is Microsoft, not a company known for its aesthetic sense.) Second, as a designer, you ought to know more about fonts and typography than ordinary Web users do. Even if a user has made a deliberate choice of font, it may not have been a good choice. Even if it was a good choice in general, it may not suit a particular page.

We therefore recommend that a `font-family` declaration should be used to set a default font for use in all elements. As we described in Chapter 4, the value of the `font-family` property is a list of fonts. It should begin with the font that you think should ideally be used for the page. This may be followed by a more widely available approximation, then one of the fonts listed in Chapter 4 that are almost universally available, and finally a generic font family. For instance,

```
font-family: "Lucida Grande",Univers,Verdana,sans-serif;
```

The question of whether to specify a font size is a more difficult one to answer. Although it is probably true (there is no real way of knowing for sure) that the majority of users leave the browser default settings alone, and have not made a deliberate choice of font size,

Lorem ipsum dolor sit amet, consectetur adipisicing elit, sed do eiusmod tempor incididunt ut labore et dolore magna aliqua. Ut enim ad minim veniam, quis nostrud exercitation ullamco laboris nisi ut aliquip ex ea commodo consequat. Duis aute irure dolor in reprehenderit in voluptate velit esse cillum dolore eu fugiat nulla pariatur. Excepteur sint occaecat cupidatat non proident, sunt in culpa qui officia deserunt mollit anim id est laborum.
Lorem ipsum dolor sit amet, consectetur adipisicing elit, sed do eiusmod tempor incididunt ut labore et dolore magna aliqua. Ut enim ad minim veniam, quis nostrud exercitation ullamco laboris nisi ut aliquip ex ea commodo consequat.

Lorem ipsum dolor sit amet, consectetur adipisicing elit, sed do eiusmod tempor incididunt ut labore et dolore magna aliqua. Ut enim ad minim veniam, quis nostrud exercitation ullamco laboris nisi ut aliquip ex ea commodo consequat.

Duis aute irure dolor in reprehenderit in voluptate velit esse cillum dolore eu fugiat nulla pariatur. Excepteur sint occaecat cupidatat non proident, sunt in culpa qui officia deserunt mollit anim id est laborum.

Lorem ipsum dolor sit amet, consectetur adipisicing elit, sed do eiusmod tempor incididunt ut labore et dolore magna aliqua. Ut enim ad minim veniam, quis nostrud exercitation ullamco laboris nisi ut aliquip ex ea commodo consequat.

Lorem ipsum dolor sit amet, consectetur adipisicing elit, sed do eiusmod tempor incididunt ut labore et dolore magna aliqua. Ut enim ad minim veniam, quis nostrud exercitation ullamco laboris nisi ut aliquip ex ea commodo consequat.

Duis aute irure dolor in reprehenderit in voluptate velit esse cillum dolore eu fugiat nulla pariatur. Excepteur sint occaecat cupidatat non proident, sunt in culpa qui officia deserunt mollit anim id est laborum.

Lorem ipsum dolor sit amet, consectetur adipisicing elit, sed do eiusmod tempor incididunt ut labore et dolore magna aliqua. Ut enim ad minim veniam, quis nostrud exercitation ullamco laboris nisi ut aliquip ex ea commodo consequat.

Figure 10.25 The effect of varying the vertical space between paragraphs

there will be some people who have changed the default to suit their eyesight and display resolution. Should you then take the view that you, as a designer, know better, as we recommend that you do in the case of font families? No definitive rule is possible, but generally the answer is 'probably', provided that your choice is informed by considerations of users' likely needs, and not just by the superficial appearance of the page. In particular, don't use tiny text. (On a Web page, unlike a book, 10pt is tiny. 14pt or 16pt will display without seeming particularly huge at most common resolutions. Even 21pt only looks fashionably chunky.) You must remember that many people do not have perfect vision, and others may be using very small screens, so users may need to increase or decrease the font size in their browsers. You therefore need to devise your layout accordingly, as we discussed earlier.

You can set default font characteristics for all elements using a CSS rule with * as the selector. The font family, size and other settings will be used for all elements, unless a specific rule overrides them.

The reason for overriding the default font characteristics is to provide contrast that distinguishes different types of element. We have several typographical attributes at our disposal for emphasizing (and de-emphasizing) text: spacing, position, font family, style, size and weight. All of these, as we showed in Chapter 4, can be controlled by CSS.

To begin with, consider the use of vertical spacing. Figure 10.25 shows the same three paragraphs, set with different amounts of vertical space between them. (This is done in the

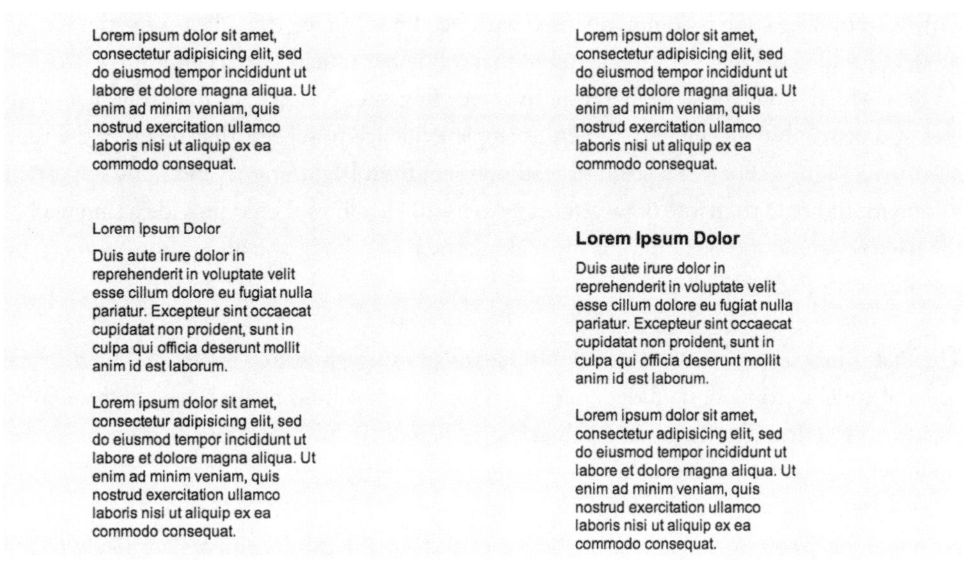

Lorem ipsum dolor sit amet, consectetur adipisicing elit, sed do eiusmod tempor incididunt ut labore et dolore magna aliqua. Ut enim ad minim veniam, quis nostrud exercitation ullamco laboris nisi ut aliquip ex ea commodo consequat.

Lorem Ipsum Dolor

Duis aute irure dolor in reprehenderit in voluptate velit esse cillum dolore eu fugiat nulla pariatur. Excepteur sint occaecat cupidatat non proident, sunt in culpa qui officia deserunt mollit anim id est laborum.

Lorem ipsum dolor sit amet, consectetur adipisicing elit, sed do eiusmod tempor incididunt ut labore et dolore magna aliqua. Ut enim ad minim veniam, quis nostrud exercitation ullamco laboris nisi ut aliquip ex ea commodo consequat.

Lorem ipsum dolor sit amet, consectetur adipisicing elit, sed do eiusmod tempor incididunt ut labore et dolore magna aliqua. Ut enim ad minim veniam, quis nostrud exercitation ullamco laboris nisi ut aliquip ex ea commodo consequat.

Lorem Ipsum Dolor

Duis aute irure dolor in reprehenderit in voluptate velit esse cillum dolore eu fugiat nulla pariatur. Excepteur sint occaecat cupidatat non proident, sunt in culpa qui officia deserunt mollit anim id est laborum.

Lorem ipsum dolor sit amet, consectetur adipisicing elit, sed do eiusmod tempor incididunt ut labore et dolore magna aliqua. Ut enim ad minim veniam, quis nostrud exercitation ullamco laboris nisi ut aliquip ex ea commodo consequat.

Figure 10.26 Spacing and styling of headings

stylesheet by using different values for the `margin-bottom` property, with `margin-top` set to zero.) The example on the left shows the effect of setting the space to zero. In the absence of any gap between them, it is hard to perceive the paragraphs as separate elements. In the middle, we show the effect of a space equal to the line height (1.2em in this case). That is, we have left a single blank line between paragraphs. The elements are clearly separated visually, but remain sufficiently close together to be perceived as a connected series. In contrast, when the space between paragraphs is increased to the equivalent of four lines, as it is on the right, the visual connection between the paragraphs is diminished, and the individuality of each one is emphasized. For text intended to be read continuously, this is undesirable, but where each paragraph may stand alone, using exaggerated spacing like this can be a simple and effective way of isolating each one and deliberately preventing their being perceived as a connected sequence.

It follows that two elements can be visually combined by making the space above the first greater than that below it, as shown on the left of Figure 10.26. The single line `Lorem Ipsum Dolor` is clearly attached to the following paragraphs and separated from the first. The relevant CSS rules used here are:

```
p { margin: 0 0 1.2em 0; }
h1 { margin: 3em 0 0.6em 0; }
```

This pattern of spacing is commonly used with headings (hence the selector for the second rule). A heading belongs with the material that follows it; it marks the beginning of a logical division which should be separated from the preceding one. The spacing does that, but headings also demand some emphasis. There is ample evidence to suggest that much of the time most users skim Web pages instead of reading them from beginning to end. Any important information should therefore draw attention to itself. Headings should provide a summary of the page's content and organization. By making them stand out, you allow users to grasp the essence of the page at a glance.

The first things that probably come to mind for emphasizing headings are increasing the type size and weight. You will doubtless have seen big bold headings many times, both on Web pages and in print. The example on the right of Figure 10.26 shows the effect of increasing the heading's size by a factor of 1.2, and using a bold font.

Although only certain sorts of scientific paper and some legal documents are likely to use the full range of six levels of heading provided by XHTML, many pages will need two or possibly three levels. For two levels of heading, it is appropriate to use two sizes, reflecting their relative importance. For a third level, it may be better to use some other typographical effect, as we will describe later.

Making them big and bold is not the only way to make headings stand out, however. If the body text is set left-aligned with a significant margin, using a negative text indent on headings will make them stand out from the body, drawing attention to themselves. If the body text is justified, headings can be centred or right-aligned. These three possibilities are illustrated in Figure 10.27. There is a risk in either centring or right-aligning, that if the heading is roughly the same width as the following paragraph, its alignment will not be visually distinctive. In accordance with gestalt principles of grouping, instead of being clearly demarked, the heading may look as if you had meant to line it up with the following paragraph and had failed. This is particularly likely to happen if the body text is set with a ragged right margin, or if the first line of the paragraph following the heading is indented, so you should combine centred and right-aligned headings with justified text without indented first lines. Centred headings tend to look old-fashioned, although they remain popular in North America. (The technique sometimes used in print of altering the tracking to make the heading fit exactly over the paragraph cannot be applied on Web pages, because it will fall apart if a different font is substituted in the browser.)

This is by no means the end of what can be achieved with spacing. Where a wide left margin is being used, headings can be pulled out into it to line up with the following paragraph,

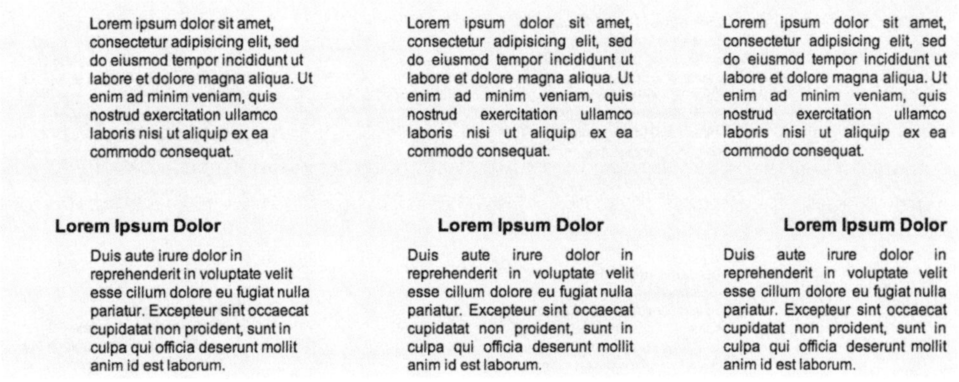

Lorem ipsum dolor sit amet, consectetur adipisicing elit, sed do eiusmod tempor incididunt ut labore et dolore magna aliqua. Ut enim ad minim veniam, quis nostrud exercitation ullamco laboris nisi ut aliquip ex ea commodo consequat.

Lorem ipsum dolor sit amet, consectetur adipisicing elit, sed do eiusmod tempor incididunt ut labore et dolore magna aliqua. Ut enim ad minim veniam, quis nostrud exercitation ullamco laboris nisi ut aliquip ex ea commodo consequat.

Lorem ipsum dolor sit amet, consectetur adipisicing elit, sed do eiusmod tempor incididunt ut labore et dolore magna aliqua. Ut enim ad minim veniam, quis nostrud exercitation ullamco laboris nisi ut aliquip ex ea commodo consequat.

Lorem Ipsum Dolor

Duis aute irure dolor in reprehenderit in voluptate velit esse cillum dolore eu fugiat nulla pariatur. Excepteur sint occaecat cupidatat non proident, sunt in culpa qui officia deserunt mollit anim id est laborum.

Lorem Ipsum Dolor

Duis aute irure dolor in reprehenderit in voluptate velit esse cillum dolore eu fugiat nulla pariatur. Excepteur sint occaecat cupidatat non proident, sunt in culpa qui officia deserunt mollit anim id est laborum.

Lorem Ipsum Dolor

Duis aute irure dolor in reprehenderit in voluptate velit esse cillum dolore eu fugiat nulla pariatur. Excepteur sint occaecat cupidatat non proident, sunt in culpa qui officia deserunt mollit anim id est laborum.

Figure 10.27 Exdented, centred and right-aligned headings

just as images can. The following rule is one way of achieving this effect. (As we showed in Chapter 4, similar effects can be achieved by floating the heading.)

```
h1 {
    font-weight: bold;
    font-size: 220%;
    line-height: 115%;
    margin: 3em 0 -2.2em -6.5em;
    width: 6em;
    color: white;
}
```

Note that it is necessary to set the width of the heading, as well as its margins, to ensure that it wraps within the margin area.

Use of negative bottom margins but a smaller exdent allows a heading to overlap the following paragraph. This may sound undesirable, but with a suitable choice of colour and type size, it can provide a visually striking style of heading, which is nonetheless readable and effective at drawing readers' attention to itself.

Colour should, as we explained in Chapter 9, never be used as a signifier on its own, but it can effectively be used in conjunction with other properties to distinguish headings. Tonal contrast will help to make the heading stand out. In Figure 10.28, which also illustrates the two preceding examples, the neutral background allows both the body text in black and the heading in white to be read easily, and the contrast immediately distinguishes the heading.

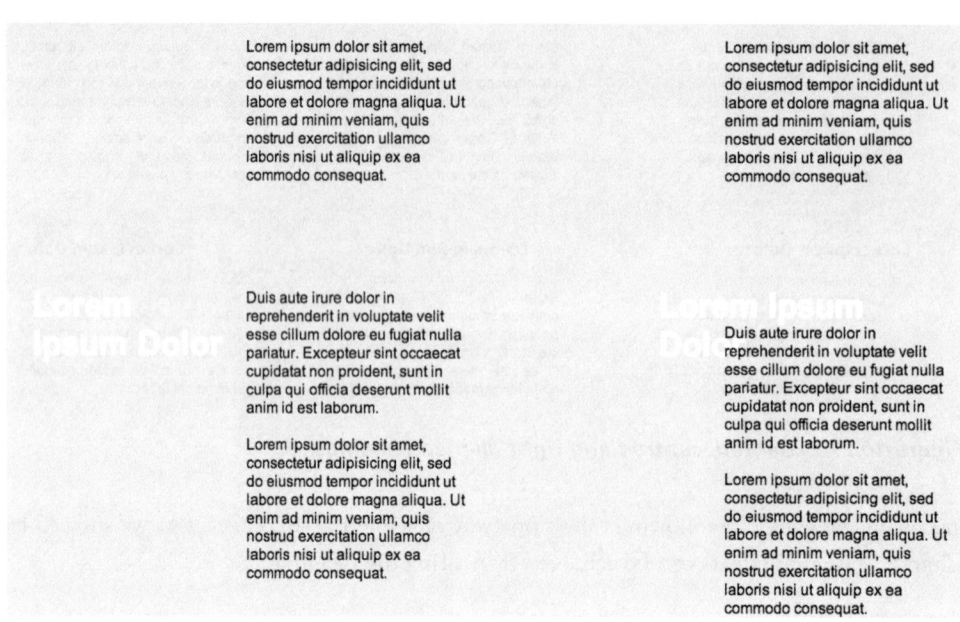

Figure 10.28 Pulled and overlapped headings

Font style also provides a means of denoting headings: they can be italicized. However, on its own, italicization provides only a minor contrast, so it does not often work for important distinctions. But it may be appropriate for lower level headings (h3 and perhaps h2 elements).

Italics are more often used when inline text must be emphasized. In XHTML, the em and strong elements provide the markup for two intensities of inline emphasis. The conventional rendering of these elements uses an italic version of the body font for emphasis and a bold weight for strong emphasis. For sites with a serious character and for purely informative prose these conventions are appropriate and safe, although if you find that italic text does not work well on screen, bold can be used for both, since the distinction between emphasis and strong emphasis is rarely meaningful. (It is unknown in print typesetting.)

Colour can be used for textual emphasis, but only with care. In the first place, the same considerations apply here as to the use of colour in headings. You should choose colours that provide good tonal contrast, and possibly augment the colour with some other distinction, such as bold or italic. Additionally, you should be aware that many users are likely to assume that coloured text denotes a link, and will therefore try to click on it. Most Web designers reserve coloured text for this purpose and so avoid using it for emphasis. For the same reason, underlining and background highlighting are best avoided for this purpose.

be achieved hierarchy
may changing size and
visual through weight

be achieved
hierarchy may
changing **size** and
visual through
weight

Figure 10.29 Expressing hierarchical emphasis through type size

In less conventionally typeset pages, font size can be used as an indicator of emphasis. This approach might lend itself to the two levels, em and strong, being manifested as two sizes, but more levels can be used to good effect. Figure 10.29 shows how changing the size of words within a word cloud places them into a visual ranking, which is absent when the words are all the same size. You will probably find it necessary to increase the leading to allow for larger words, and you will also find that the mixture of type sizes interferes with justification, so this approach is best used with ragged margins or, as we have done here, centred text.

The way in which we perceive the relative importance of elements on a page – that is, the visual hierarchy – does not depend on size and weight alone in an obvious way. The examples in Figure 10.30 show that the interaction between size, colour and space is sometimes complex. In the version at the top left, the big bold text is clearly the most important, but simply by adding a colour, as in the version at the top right, the smaller word, in its vast blank space, acquires more importance and draws the eye towards it (but only providing you have good colour vision). The two lower examples show that by partitioning the space or altering the contrast between the text and backgrounds, subtle shifts in emphasis can be achieved.

We have implicitly assumed so far that each page is typeset using a single font family. This is a safe and reliable but dull approach to typographic design. All the members of a font family are designed to work well together visually, so there is no risk of creating undesirable visual conflicts, as there can be when fonts from different families are combined. However, by restricting yourself to a single font family you are denying yourself a dimension of contrast and interest, which, when used appropriately, can provide a valuable design element. In particular, it is common practice in print design, to use a display font (see Chapter 4) for headings. In books, headings are often set in a sans serif font, with a serifed font being used

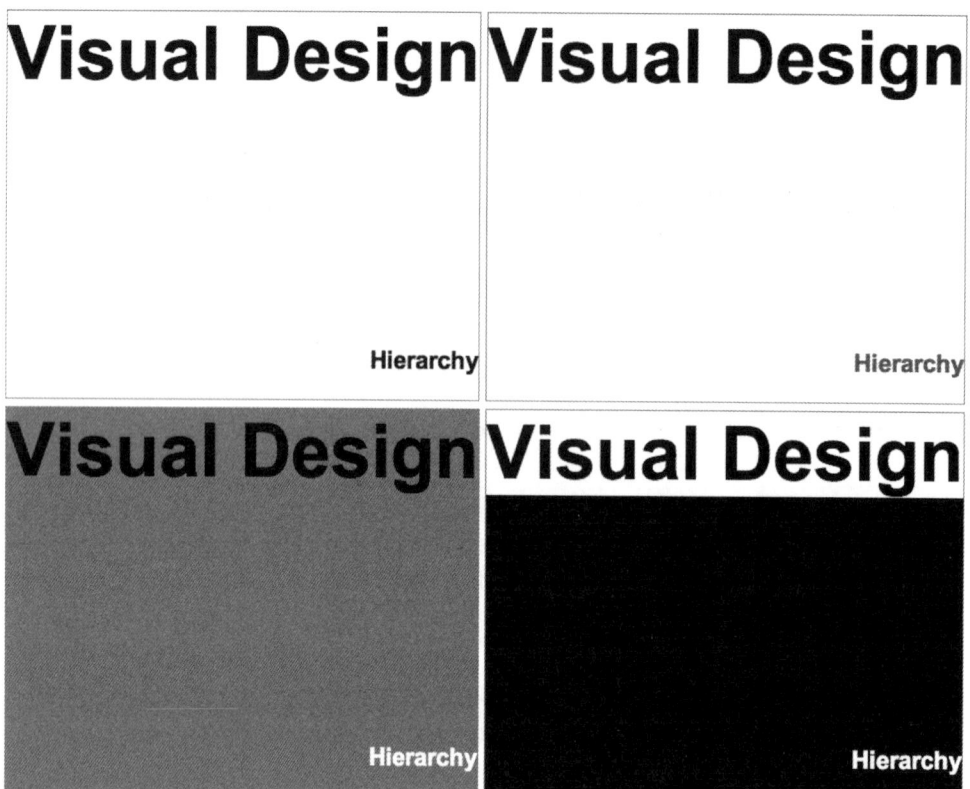

Figure 10.30 Visual hierarchy

for the body text. In addition to the basic contrast of glyph shapes created by using different fonts, differences in x-height and other font metrics can cause elements set in different faces to appear to have different size and weight, even though they don't.

We have repeated *ad nauseum* that on the Web you cannot be sure which fonts a user will see. It isn't even the case that the generic families `serif` and `sans-serif` will necessarily produce serifed and sans serif fonts on the user's screen – most browsers allow their users to choose any font to be used for each generic family. The majority of users probably don't know how to do so, however, so although it is the case that if you specify that headings should be set in Officina Sans with body text in Bembo, there is not much chance that they will be, if you add `sans-serif` and `serif` to the font list for those elements, you can reasonably expect that some of the distinction between the font families will be retained. For the benefit of those users who do set both the `serif` and `sans-serif` generic families to a font like Verdana, say, you should also use colour, size or weight to ensure that headings can still be distinguished.

Alternatively, you can employ the more drastic expedient described in the next section.

GIF Text

In graphic design, type is considered to be a visual element, albeit one of a special kind because it can convey meaning through its linguistic content. The same text set in different fonts may be more or less readable or attractive and may alter the balance and appearance of a complete page for better or worse. For these reasons, the careful choice of fonts has been a major part of the job of the graphic designer and book designer. But as we have repeatedly explained, on the Web you cannot dictate the precise fonts that will be used.

There is a way round this problem, but it is not one that should be used casually. Type may be prepared in a graphics application and saved as a GIF image, which can be embedded in a Web page. In Chapter 9 we pointed out that GIF text should only be used where really necessary, because the use of images for text can present accessibility problems.

In Chapter 9 we showed a naive way of using GIF text as a heading:

```
<h1><img src="heading.gif" alt="Medieval Web Design"></h1>
```

This produces the desired result, but the alt-text is not treated in the same way that the text content of an h1 element normally is: screen readers may read it in a special way, and search engine robots may not index it properly.

There is a more elaborate way of using GIF text that – while not 100% satisfactory – does avoid these problems. The basic idea is to use the GIF as a background image for the element it replaces. For this example, the heading would use conventional markup, with no img element, but it would be given an id attribute to hang some special styling on:

```
<h1 id="head">Medieval Web Design</h1>
```

In the associated stylesheet, the image originally used in the content of the heading is applied as a background. The size of the heading is explicitly set to match that of the image. Here, the use of absolute units is essential.

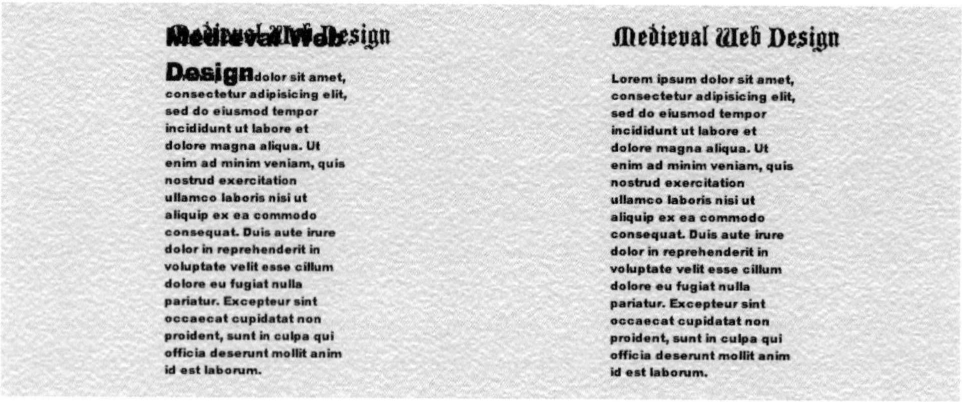

Figure 10.31 Using GIF type as a background

```
#head {
    background-image: url(heading.gif);
    width: 191px;
    height: 26px;
}
```

The result of applying this rule is the horrible mess shown on the left of Figure 10.31. To achieve the desired result, it is necessary to hide the text of the heading, leaving only the background image.

Several different ways of doing this have been devised. The most obvious is to set the `display` property to `none`. This has the effect of generating nothing for the content of the `h1` element. Unfortunately, most popular screen readers therefore do not speak the content, so this approach is actually worse from an accessibility point of view than using an `img` element inside the `h1`. A better approach is to add the following declaration to the rule for `#head`:

```
text-indent: -50em;
```

The effect is to move the text `Medieval Web Design` so far to the left that it moves off the page, leaving the element's background behind, as it were, giving the result shown on the right of Figure 10.31. By using em units here, we guarantee that the displacement will always be big enough, no matter how much the font size is increased or decreased.

This is an improvement over the other approaches. Despite the physical displacement, screen readers and robots will treat the heading in the normal way on the basis of the markup, but sighted readers will see the text displayed in the special medieval font. There is, unfortunately, one fairly unlikely combination of circumstances under which the heading is not displayed in any form. We leave it to you to determine what this is as an exercise.

GIF text is often used for buttons and the elements of navbars. The usual approach is to place an `img` element inside an `a` element, as we originally did for headings. JavaScript is frequently used to create a rollover effect by replacing the image with a different one – perhaps with some effect, such as a drop shadow, applied to it. However, the CSS technique just described can also be used for links and buttons. Applying a large negative `text-indent` does not change the area of the element that receives `click` and other events; this is still the visible area occupied by the element, so the GIF text will respond to mouse events as required. You can only apply a `text-indent` to a block element, but buttons and links in navbars usually are blocks, or else are floated, in which case their `display` property can safely be set to block. (The element will be treated as if it was anyway.)

A background GIF will never scale, so readers with poor vision will not be able to blow up GIF text. You should therefore never use a GIF for small type. The technique is not really suitable for extended pieces of text. Here, the content is paramount, and the ability to scale text and to allow it to reflow within a liquid layout is valuable, so it makes sense to use ordinary CSS styling – if you wish to insist that all text be typeset exactly as the designer envisaged, the Web is not the medium for you.

GIF text is therefore best reserved for headings, navbar links, logos and those Web pages where the type is being used less as a medium for language than as a graphic, visual object in its own right. In such cases, vector graphics programs such as Illustrator can be used not only to set type in whatever esoteric font you choose, but also to apply kerning and tracking with precision and to set the type on a path or inside a shape. Type can also be combined with other graphic objects, before being rasterized and exported as a GIF image. (Possibly, in the future, SVG will be used to create such effects, while still making the text accessible.)

Key Points

Visual Design

Neglect of visual design is one of the main factors that lead to Web sites being hard to use.

Usability is concerned with function, structure, accessibility, and visual presentation.

Familiarity and memory play an important role in usability; visual design can ensure that page elements are familiar or memorable.

Elements must be presented in a way that makes each one easy to find, identify or use.

Gestalt principles of visual design are derived from theories about how the human brain organizes visual information.

The perception of patterns and structures is determined by by the grouping of objects in a visual field.

Proximity, similarity, symmetry, the distinction between figure and ground, and closure all contribute to our perception of grouping.

Closure is the brain's ability to infer a complete visual pattern or image from incomplete information.

The whole is greater than and different from the sum of the parts.

Semiotics is the study of systems of signs.

The relationship between the signifier and the signified is arbitrary, and can only be understood through knowledge of the system within which the sign operates.

Web pages incorporate signs, such as underlining for links, whose meaning depends on convention.

Web designers rely on a combination of convention, context and user experience to convey the meaning of signs accurately to the user.

Layout

A layout grid is a geometrical division of the page, used to control the placement of text blocks and images.

Grids create alignment and define regions, which can be used for similar purposes on all pages to help create an impression of uniformity.

Web pages must use flexible layouts, since the height and width of the page and regions within it are not fixed.

The way in which elements behave when the window is resized or the font size is changed depends on the units that have been used to specify their dimensions.

The length of lines of text should be restricted to roughly 30em using a stylesheet.

> A max-width expressed in % will restrict the width to avoid the need for scrollbars if very large fonts are used.

Setting the measure in % units maintains the proportion between text and the window.

Setting left and right margins to `auto` centres a single column in the browser window, however wide it is.

> Centring a `div` within the `body` can produce contrasting margins.

Multi-column layouts on the Web usually have a main column holding the primary content, with separate columns used to hold separate related material or images.

> Layouts with multiple linked columns of text are awkward to read on Web pages.

Two-column layouts can be created either using absolute positioning or by floating one of the columns beside the other.

There is no totally satisfactory solution to creating flexible complex grid layouts.

Specifying the dimensions and coordinates of the elements on a grid in em units results in a zooming layout.

Specifying the width and x-coordinates in absolute units results in a stretching layout.

Colour and Tone

Because of the characteristics of computers and Web pages, precise control over colours is not possible.

Colour may influence users responses to Web pages; an individual's reponse to particular colours may be emotive and/or determined by cultural conventions, personal taste and fashion.

There is therefore wide personal and cultural diversity among the responses to any particular colour or combination of colours.

Combinations of colour affect the way the size of coloured objects and colour itself is perceived. The same colour will not look the same in every context.

Good tonal contrast makes pages more accessible and usable, but tonal values are not always easy to see.

Tonal contrast should be checked by converting to greyscale.

Typography

Web designers can never rely on particular fonts being available to all users, so many fine points of typography are irrelevant to Web design.

A `font-family` declaration should be used to set a default font for use in all elements, since users' defaults may not be appropriate.

If a font size is specified for the body text, it should not be very small.

The vertical space between paragraphs determines whether they are seen as individual elements or as a sequence.

Placing a heading close to the following paragraph makes it clear that the heading belongs with what follows it.

Increased font weight and size can be used to emphasize headings.

In order to set them apart from body text, headings may be exdented, centred, right-aligned, pulled out into the margin or overlapped with the following text.

Contrasting colour can also be used to draw attention to headings.

Italic and boldface are conventional indicators of emphasis.

Type size can impose a hierarchy on textual elements.

Visual hierarchy can be expressed in more subtle and creative ways.

GIF type allows the designer full control over fonts and typography, but must be used judiciously to avoid accessibility problems.

CSS rules can be used to allow GIF type to co-exist with ordinary markup for better accessibility.

Exercises

Test Questions

1. Why is visual design so important a factor in determining the usability of a Web page?

2. What is the probability that a randomly chosen group of twenty people will include somebody with defective red-green colour vision? (State any assumptions you make about what constitutes a random selection.) What can you deduce about the reliability of usability studies based on groups of that size?

3. List all the visual design faults evident in the Web page illustrated in Figure 10.2.

4. In what ways are gestalt theories of visual perception relevant to the design of Web pages? List at least two common elements in Web design that depend on these principles and explain how they utilize them.

5. Explain what is meant by the signifier and the signified in semiotic terminology. Under what circumstances do Web designers need to take the meaning of signs into account?

6. On page 566, we remarked, 'This hasn't stopped designers trying [to create fixed grid layouts], and creating pages that force some users to scroll horizontally, others to see vast areas of blank space, and others to see a mess of overlapping text and images.' Explain how each of these problems might come about.

7. Suppose you have a div inside a div inside a div at the top level. For all combination of em, % and mm widths, what will happen to the inmost div when (a) a user increases the font size, (b) a user stretches the browser window? Note any adverse effects that may occur.

8. Explain how you would centre a navbar that was twice as wide as the text measure across a centred one-column layout.

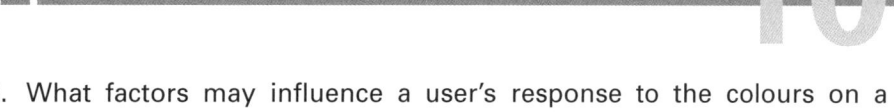

9. What factors may influence a user's response to the colours on a Web page?

10. If you specify colours for page elements in a stylesheet, what will determine whether a user will see the same colours that you see when you preview the result on your screen?

11. Why is good tonal contrast important in the visual design of Web pages? Which elements on a Web page should contrast most strongly with each other, and why?

12. What can you do to make one piece of text stand out from the rest of a page?

13. What will happen to a heading with GIF type as its background and a negative text indent if a user with a browser that supports CSS turns images off? Is this likely to happen?

Discussion Topics

1. If search engines returned a thumbnail-sized screenshot of each Web page when you conducted a search, how would that affect your approach to the visual design of Web pages?

2. When should iconic symbols, such as arrows, icons for home page and email, and so on, be used on Web pages? Give reasons for your answer.

3. Can you think of use for a layout with three columns not all of the same width, where the widest was not in the middle?

4. Should a Web designer be concerned with colour?

5. It is said that Web users frequently skim the text of pages, instead of reading them carefully from beginning to end. How would you ensure that when they do so, they see the essential textual content on the page?

Practical Tasks

1. Find a Web page or site that you believe makes good use of the principles of visual design we have discussed in this chapter. Analyze how each aspect of the design works, and explain why. If there is some room for improvement, make suggestions for ways to improve the design further.

2. Find a Web page or site that you think is very poorly designed, and identify all the ways in which the design could be improved. If the page is not too complex, create a simple working version of your improved design with mocked-up content.

3. This exercise should be done by a group. Each person should look at the six screenshots in Figure 10.20, and, without consulting the others, rate them in order of prefered colour. Then, all members of the group should compare their preferences and explain what they like and dislike about each background colour. Is there a consensus, either about which colours are preferable, or about why?

4. Find a page on the World Wide Web with lots of different colours on it. Write down a list of the colours according to their tonal value, in order from lightest to darkest. Put your screen into greyscale and see if your assessment was correct.

5. Design a two-level navbar, with at least seven items on the upper level, which exhibits good visual coherence and usability.

6. Design a Web page for displaying advertisements for job vacancies. Each job should be described in a few short sentences. For example, 'Contract Web designer required for three month project in insurance sector. PHP experience vital. CSS preferred. Payment negotiable.' Your page should display several such announcements in such a way that each is clearly delimited and readable. Devise some way of classifying the types of job, and use suitable visual devices to make the classification clear to somebody reading the page.

CHAPTER

2

Setting Up Your Web Site

You start a project in Dreamweaver by setting up a local site on your computer and then creating the first Web page of the site. This chapter shows you how to set up your Web site.

Teach Yourself VISUALLY™ Macromedia® Dreamweaver® 8
Janine Warner. ISBN 978-0-7645-9998-9
©2006 Wiley Publishing Inc.

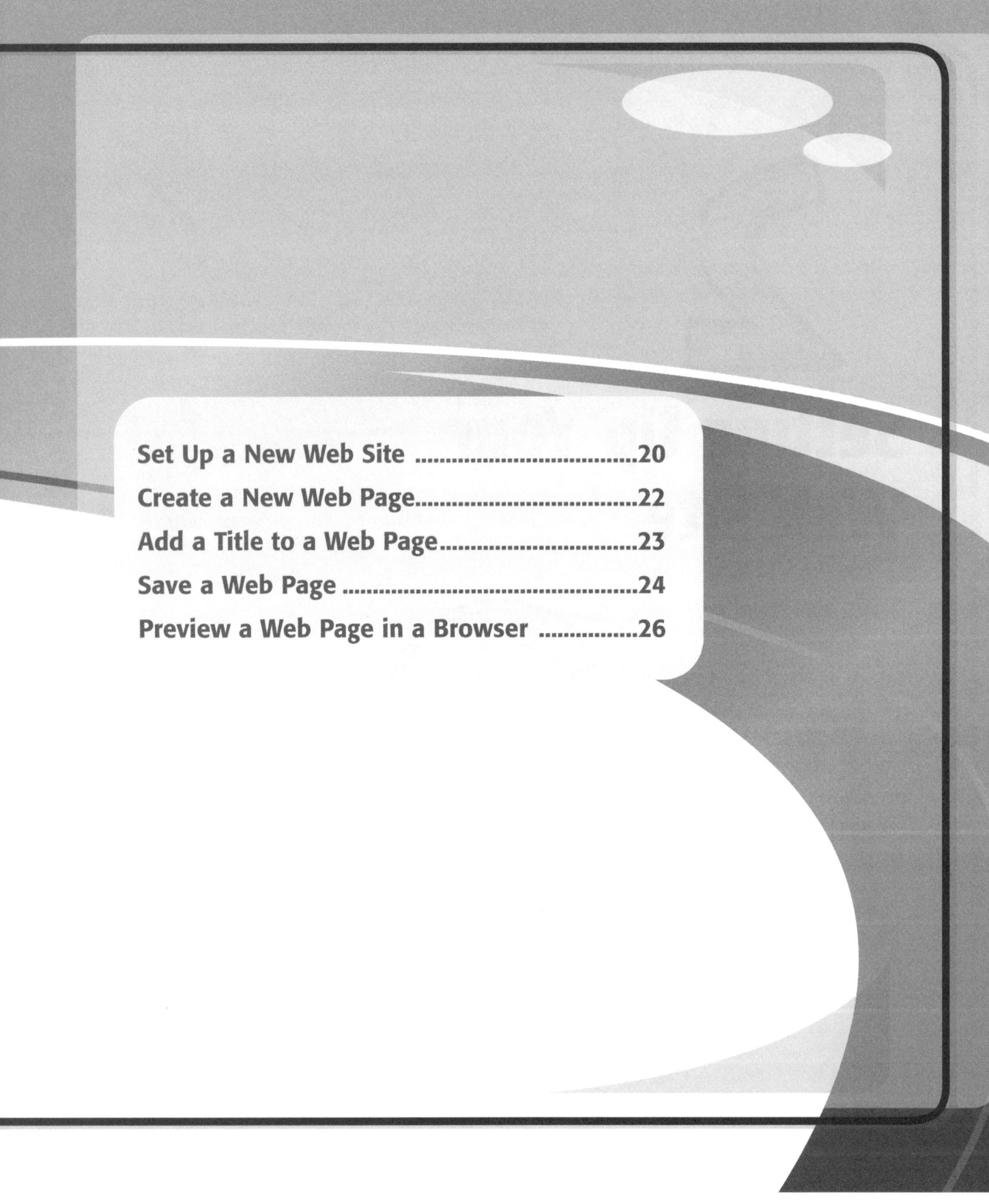

Set Up a New Web Site

Before you create your Web pages, you need to define your site in Dreamweaver. You must create a folder on your local hard drive where you can store your HTML, images, and other files. Defining a local site enables you to manage your Web page files in the Site window. For more information on the Site window, see Chapter 14.

① Click the **Manage Sites** link in the Files panel.

The Manage Sites dialog box appears.

② Click **New**.

③ Click **Site**.

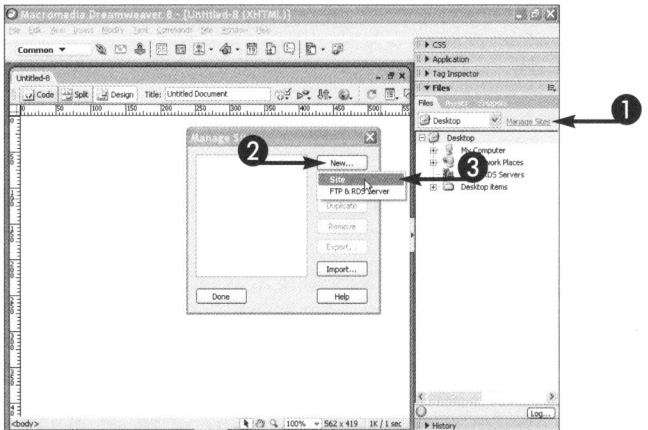

The Site Definition dialog box appears.

④ Click the **Advanced** tab.

⑤ Type a name for your site.

⑥ Click the Folder icon (🗀) to search for your Web site folder.

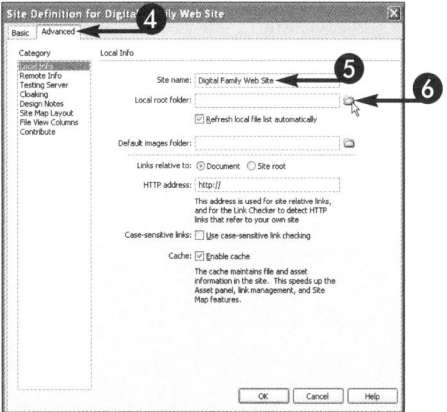

20

The Choose local root folder dialog box appears.

7 Click here and select the folder that stores your Web pages.

● You can create a new folder by clicking 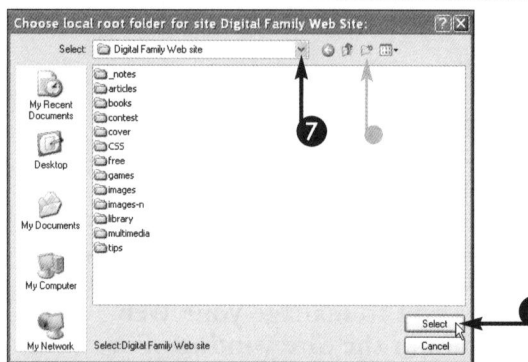 and then selecting that folder.

8 Click **Select**.

9 Click 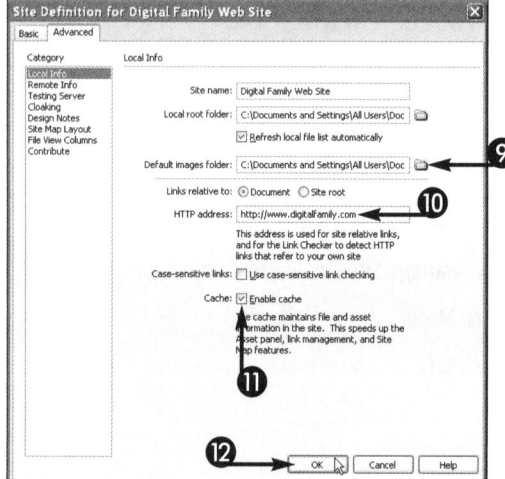 and select the folder where you want to store the images for your Web site.

10 Type the URL (Web address or domain name) of your Web site.

11 Click this option to enable the cache, which makes it faster to create links (☐ changes to ✓).

12 Click **OK**.

13 In the Manage Sites Window, click **Done**.

TIP

Why is it important to keep all of my Web site files in a main folder on my computer?

Keeping everything in the same folder enables you to easily transfer your Web site files to a Web server without changing the organization of the files. If you do not organize your Web site files on the Web server in the same way they are organized on your local computer, then hyperlinks may not work, and images may not display properly. For more information about working with Web site files, see Chapter 14.

21

Create a
New Web Page

A new feature in Dreamweaver 8 is the initial Start Page. There are many useful shortcuts on this page, including some for creating a new Web page.

① Click **File**.

② Click **New.**

The New Document dialog box appears.

③ Click **Basic page**.

④ Click **HTML**.

⑤ Click **Create**.

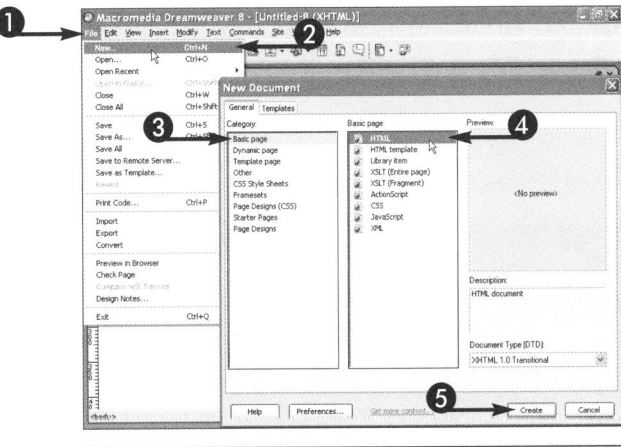

● An Untitled Document window appears.

Note: The page name and filename are untitled until you save them.

You can also create preformatted pages by choosing the Page Designs category in the New Document dialog box.

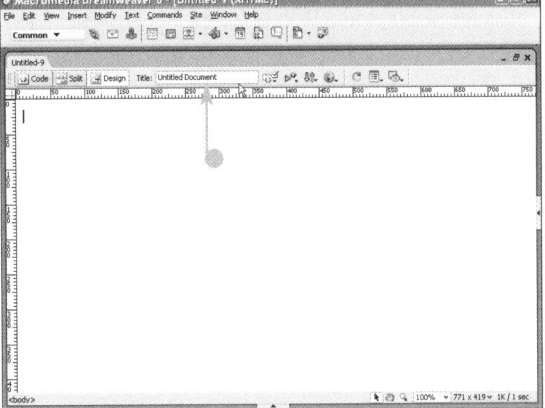

22

Add a Title to a Web Page

A Web page title appears in the title bar when the page opens in a Web browser. The title helps search engines to index pages with more accuracy, and is saved in a user's Bookmark list if they bookmark your Web page.

Add a Title to a Web Page

① Type a name for your Web page in the Title text box.

② Press **Enter** (**Return**).

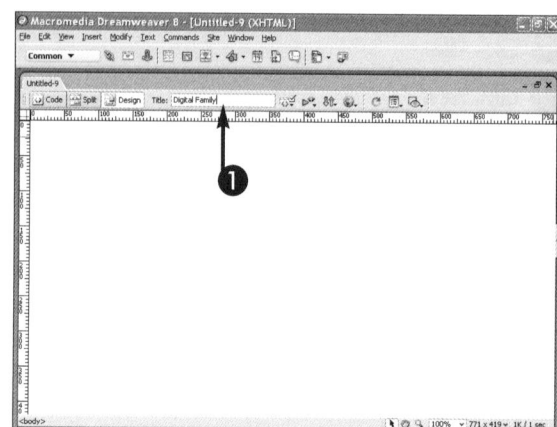

● The Web page title appears in the title bar when the page displays in a Web browser.

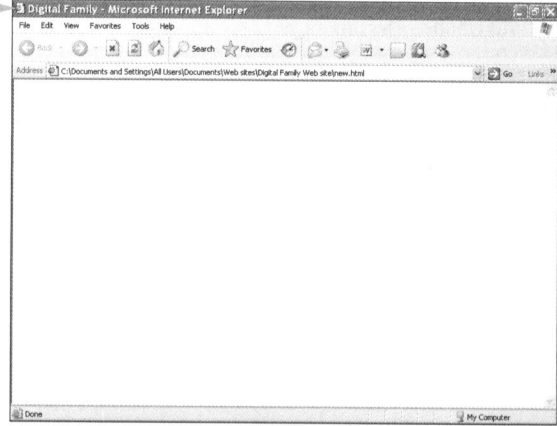

23

Save a
Web Page

You should save your Web page before closing the program or transferring the page to a remote site. It is also a good idea to save all of your files frequently to prevent work from being lost due to power outages or system failures. For more information about connecting to remote sites, see Chapter 14.

Save a Web Page

SAVE YOUR DOCUMENT

1 Click **File**.

2 Click **Save**.

● You can click **Save As** to save an existing file with a new filename.

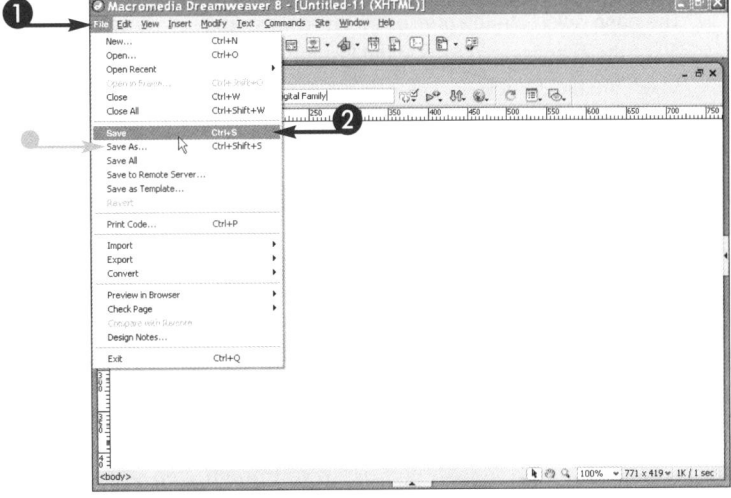

If you are saving a new file for the first time, then the Save As dialog box appears.

3 Click here and select your local site folder.

4 Type a name for your Web page.

Your local site folder is where you want to save the pages and other files for your Web site.

5 Click **Save**.

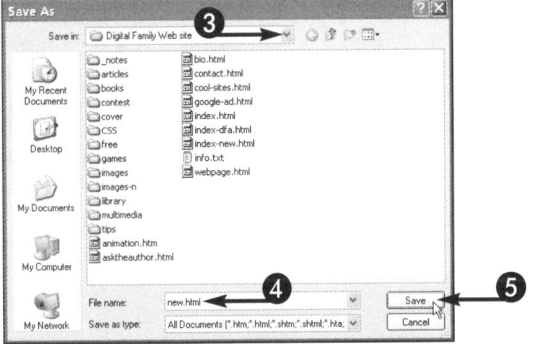

24

● Dreamweaver saves the Web page, and the filename and path appear in the title bar.

● You can click **X** to close the page.

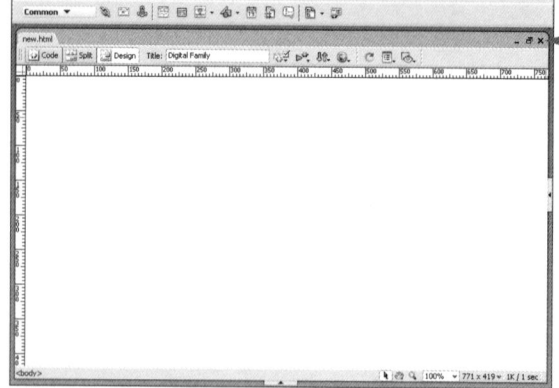

REVERT A PAGE

① Click **File**.

② Click **Revert**.

The page reverts to the previously saved version. All of the changes made since the last time you saved the file are lost.

Note: If you exit Dreamweaver after you save a document, Dreamweaver cannot revert to the previous version.

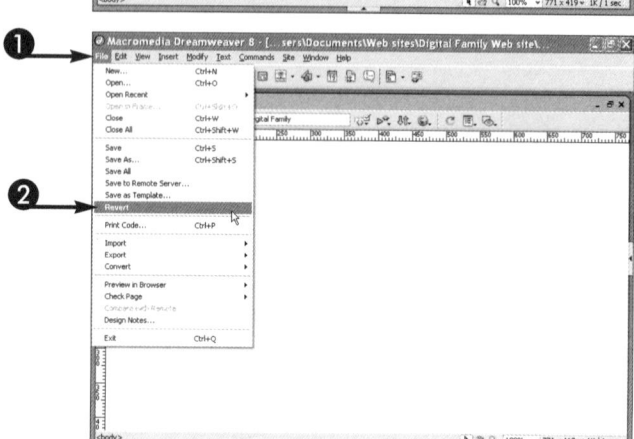

Why should I name the main page of my site index.html?

You should name your main Web site or home page index.html because that is the filename that most Web servers open first when a user types a domain name into a Web browser. If you name your main page index.html and it does not open as your first page when your site is on the server, then check with your system administrator or hosting service.

25

Preview a Web Page in a Browser

You can see how your Web page will appear online by previewing it in a Web browser. The Preview in Browser command works with any Web browser that is installed on your computer. Although Dreamweaver does not ship with Web browser software, Internet Explorer is preinstalled on most computers.

Preview a Web Page in a Browser

① Click **Preview in Browser** (🌐).

② Click a Web browser from the drop-down menu that appears.

You can also preview the page in your primary Web browser by pressing F12.

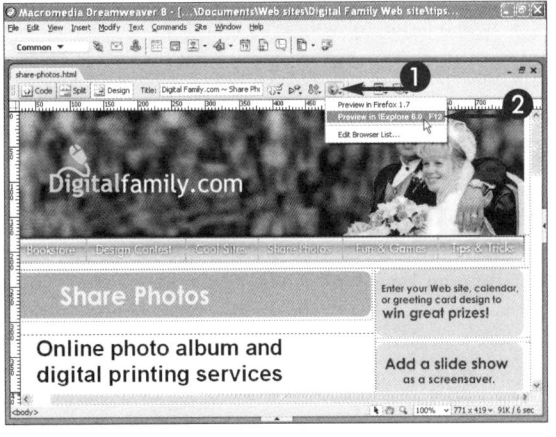

Your Web browser launches and opens the current page.

The file has a temporary filename for viewing in the Web browser.

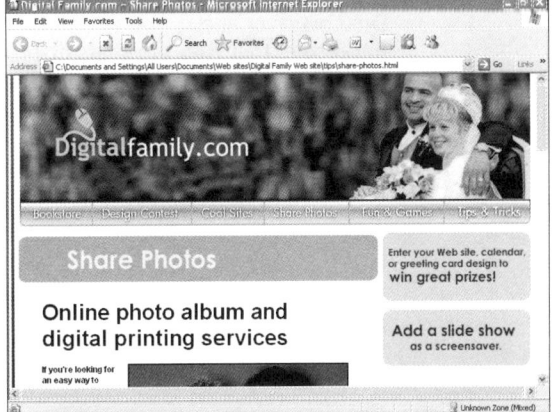

26

ADD/REMOVE BROWSER

① Click **File**.

② Click **Preview In Browser**.

③ Click **Edit Browser List**.

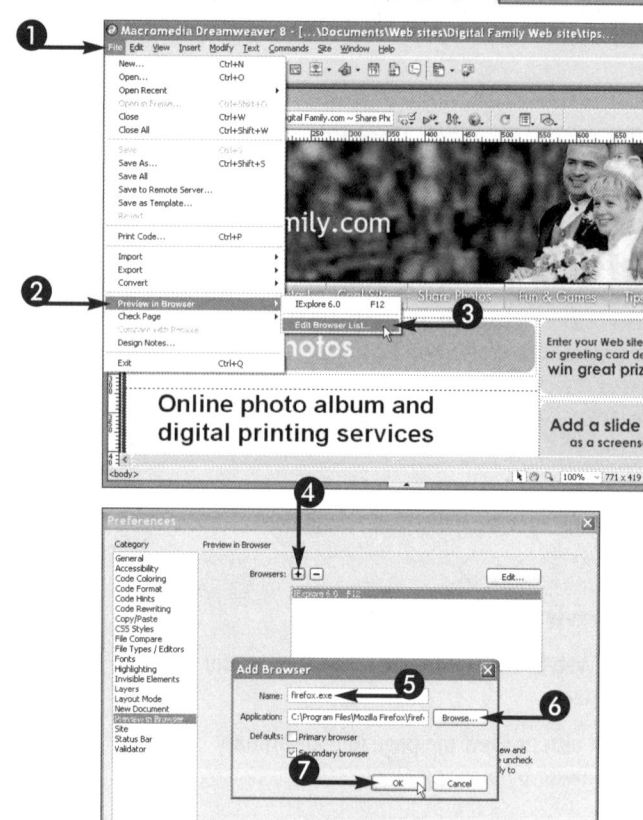

The Preferences dialog box appears.

④ Click ⊞ to open the Add Browser dialog box.

⑤ Type a name for your Web browser.

⑥ Click **Browse** and select a Web browser for your computer.

⑦ Click **OK** to close the Add Browser dialog box.

⑧ Click **OK** to close the Preferences dialog box.

The newly added Web browser appears in the browser list.

Why can I use more than one Web browser for previews?

Dreamweaver allows you to add more than one Web browser because not all Web browsers display Web pages the same way; for example, Lynx is a text-based Web browser. By using the browser list, you can easily test your Web page in a different Web browser with just a few mouse-clicks.

CHAPTER 7

Creating Hyperlinks

Links, also called hyperlinks, are used to connect related information. Using Dreamweaver, you can create links from one page to another in your Web site, or to other Web sites on the Internet, and you can also create e-mail links and image maps. This chapter shows you how to use both text and images as hyperlinks.

Teach Yourself VISUALLY™ Macromedia® Dreamweaver® 8
Janine Warner. ISBN 978-0-7645-9998-9
©2006 Wiley Publishing Inc.

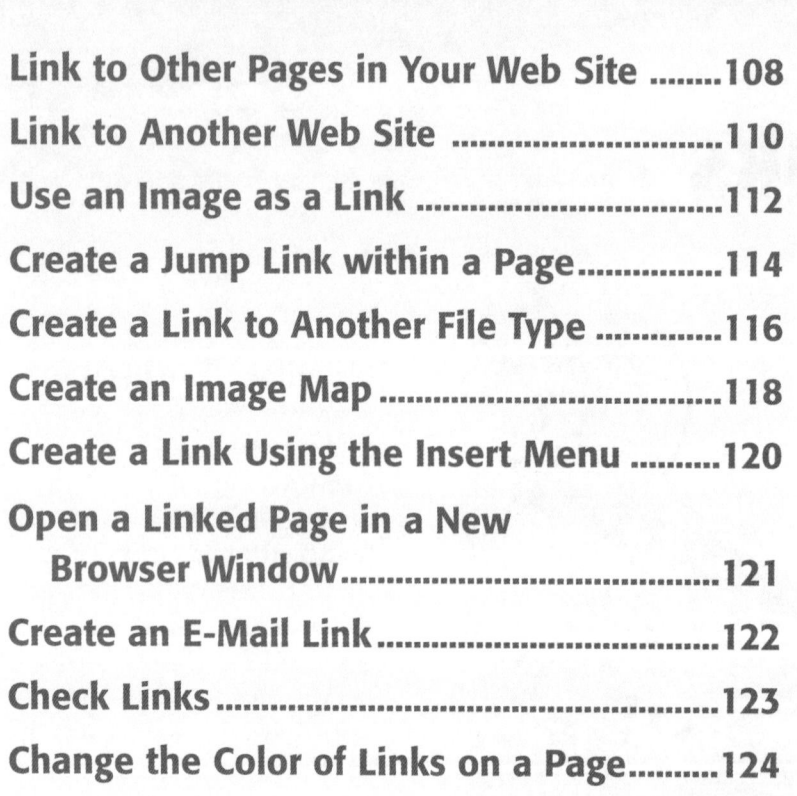

Link to Other Pages in Your Web Site

Dreamweaver allows you to create a link from one page in your Web site to another page, thus making it easy for visitors to navigate your Web site.

Link to Pages in Your Web Site

① Click and drag to select the text that you want to turn into a link.

Note: To link an image, see Chapter 6.

② Click the **Link** 📁 in the Properties inspector.

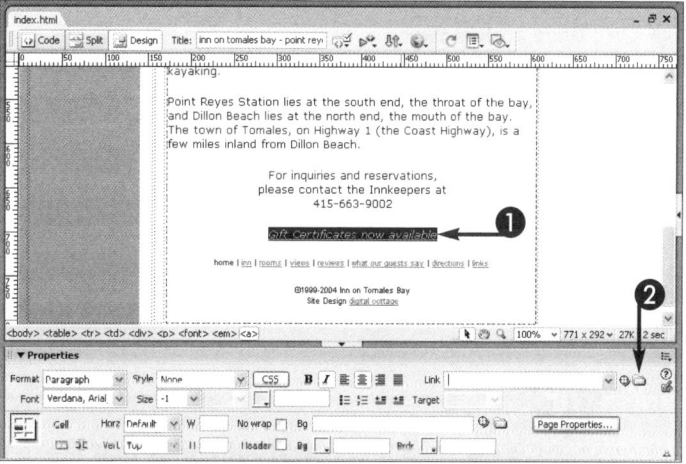

The Select File dialog box appears.

③ Click here and select the folder that contains the destination page.

④ Click the HTML file to which you want to link.

⑤ Click **OK**.

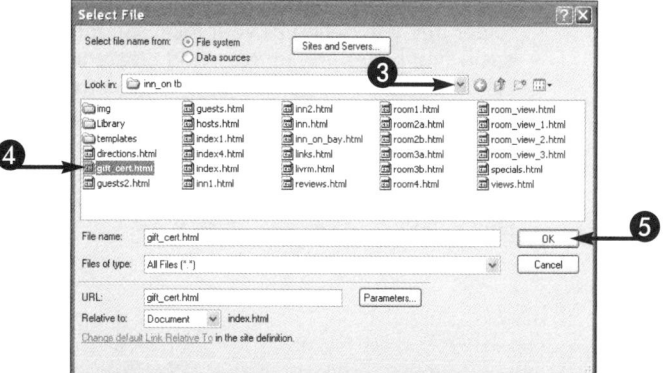

● The new link appears in color and underlined.

Note: Links are not clickable in the Document window.

● You can click test the link by previewing the file in a Web browser, such as Firefox or Internet Explorer.

Note: For more on viewing a page in a Web browser, see Chapter 2.

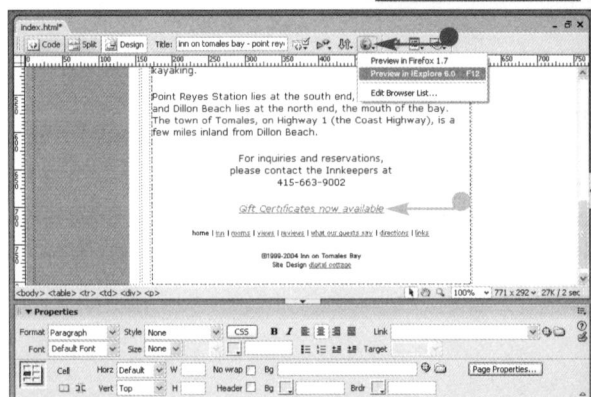

OPEN AND EDIT A LINKED PAGE

① Click anywhere on the text of the link whose destination you want to open.

② Click **Modify**.

③ Click **Open Linked Page**.

The link destination opens in a Document window allowing you to edit that document.

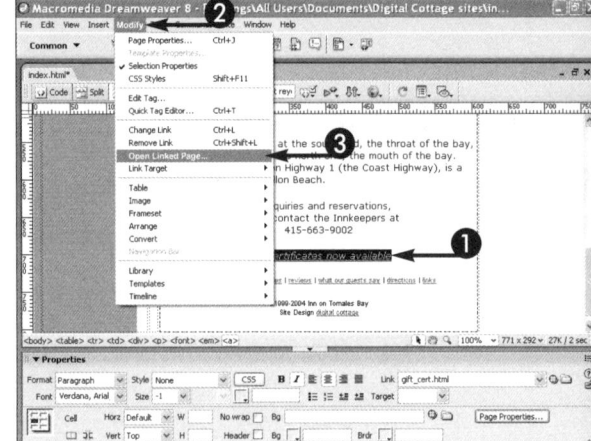

 TIP

How should I organize the files that make up my Web site?

You should keep the files that make up your Web site in one main folder that you define as your local site folder. This allows you to easily find pages and images, and create links between your pages. It also ensures that all of the links work correctly when you transfer the files to a live Web server. If you have many pages under one section, you can create subfolders to further divide the file structure of your site. You may also want to create a separate file for images. For more on setting up your Web site, see Chapter 2. For more on transferring files to a Web server, see Chapter 14.

109

Link to Another Web Site

You can link from your Web site to any other Web site on the Internet, giving your visitors access to additional information and providing valuable references to related information.

Link to Another Web Site

1 Click and drag to select the text that you want to turn into a link.

2 Type the Web address of the destination page, including the **http://**, in the Link field in the Properties inspector.

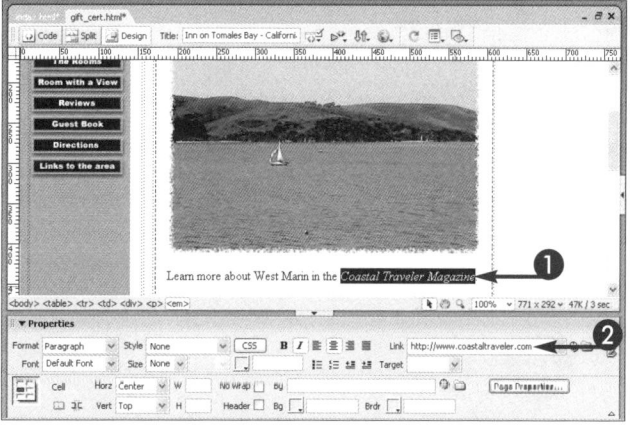

● The new link appears in a color and underlined.

Note: Links are not clickable in the Document window.

● You can test the link by previewing the file in a Web browser.

Note: To preview a Web page in a Web browser, see Chapter 2.

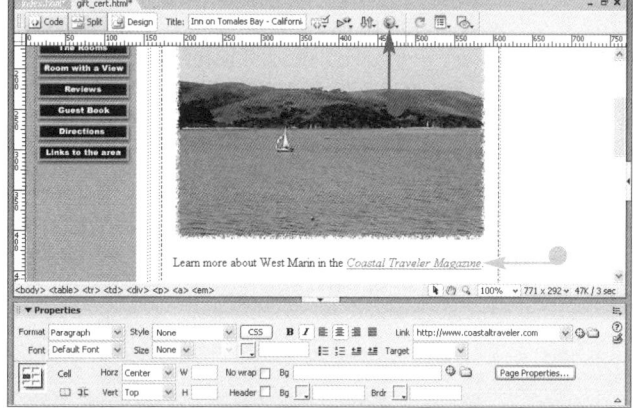

110

When you test the link in a Web browser while you are connected to the Internet, it should open the linked site, even if the link page is still on your hard drive.

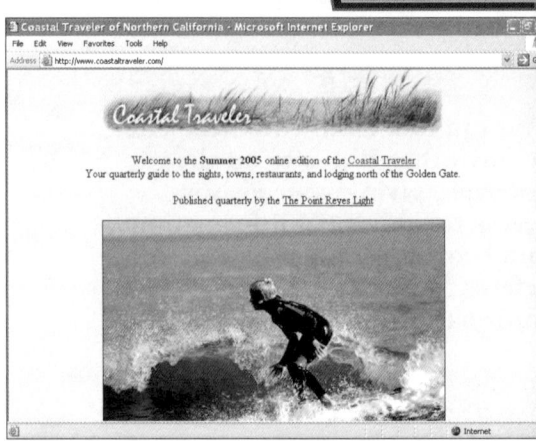

REMOVE A LINK

① Select the text of the link that you want to remove.

② Click **Modify**.

③ Click **Remove Link**.

Dreamweaver removes the link, and the text no longer appears in a color and underlined.

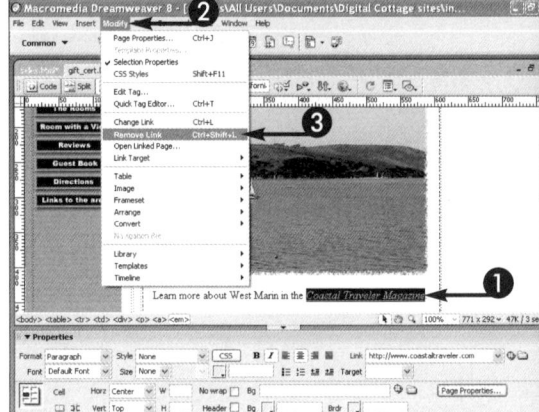

TIP

How do I ensure that my links to other Web sites always work?

You do not have control over the Web pages on other Web sites to which you have linked. If you have linked to a Web page whose file is later renamed or taken offline, your viewers receive an error message when they click the link on your Web site. Maintain your Web site by periodically checking your links. You can also use software or Web site tune-up services, such as www.netmechanic.com to perform this check for you. Although neither single method can bring back a Web page that no longer exists, both methods combined can tell you which links you need to remove or update.

111

You can use an image to create a
link to another page or Web site
in much the same way that you
create a link with text. Using
images as links is a very common
way to build a Web site's main
navigation system, for example
using a row of images that link
to all of the main pages of the
Web site.

Use an Image as a Link

CREATE AN IMAGE LINK

1️⃣ Click the image that you want to turn into a link.

2️⃣ Click the **Link** 🖻 in the Properties inspector.

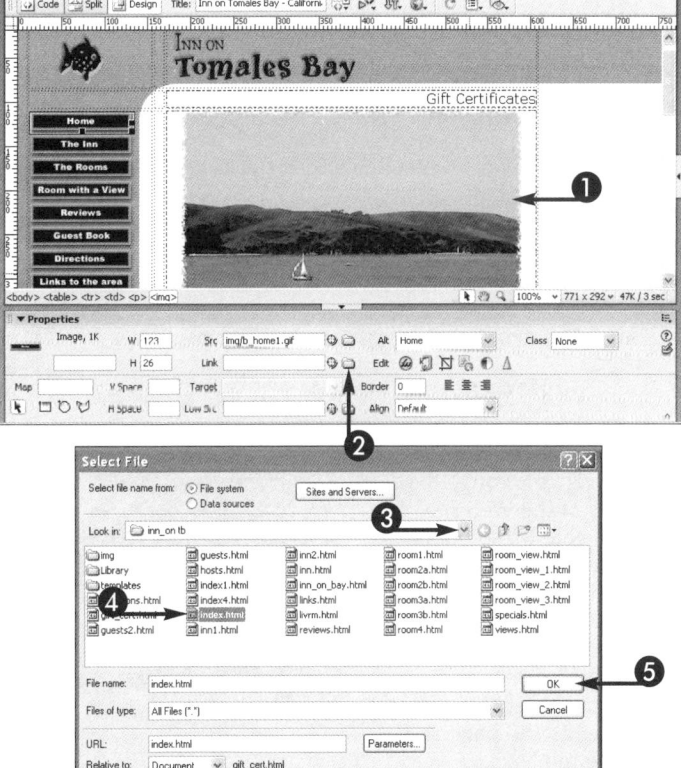

The Select File dialog box appears.

3️⃣ Click here and select the folder that contains the destination page.

4️⃣ Click the HTML file to which you want to link.

5️⃣ Click **OK**.

Your image becomes a link.

● Dreamweaver automatically inserts the filename and path to the linked page.

● You can test the link by previewing your page in a Web browser.

Note: To preview a page in a Web browser, see Chapter 2.

REMOVE A LINK FROM AN IMAGE

❶ Click a linked image.

❷ Click **Modify**.

❸ Click **Remove Link**.

Dreamweaver removes the link.

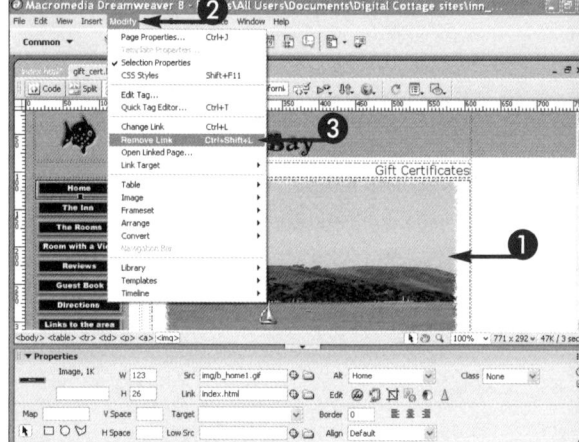

How do I create a navigation bar for my Web page?

Many Web sites include sets of images that act as link buttons on the top, side, or bottom of each page. These button images allow viewers to navigate through the pages of the Web site. You can create these button images by using an image-editing program such as Adobe Photoshop or Macromedia Fireworks, and then use Dreamweaver to insert them into the page and create the links.

How will visitors to my Web site know to click an image?

When a visitor rolls a cursor over an image that serves as a link, their cursor turns into a hand. You can make it clearer which images are linked by putting links in context with other content, and by grouping links to let visitors know that images are clickable.

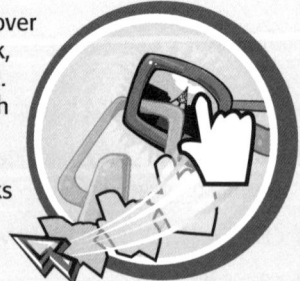

113

Create a Jump Link within a Page

You can create a link to other content on the same page. Same-page links, often called *jump links* or *anchor links*, are commonly used on long pages when you want to provide an easy way to navigate to relevant information lower on the page.

You create a jump link by first placing a named anchor where you want the link to go to and then linking from the text or image to the named anchor point.

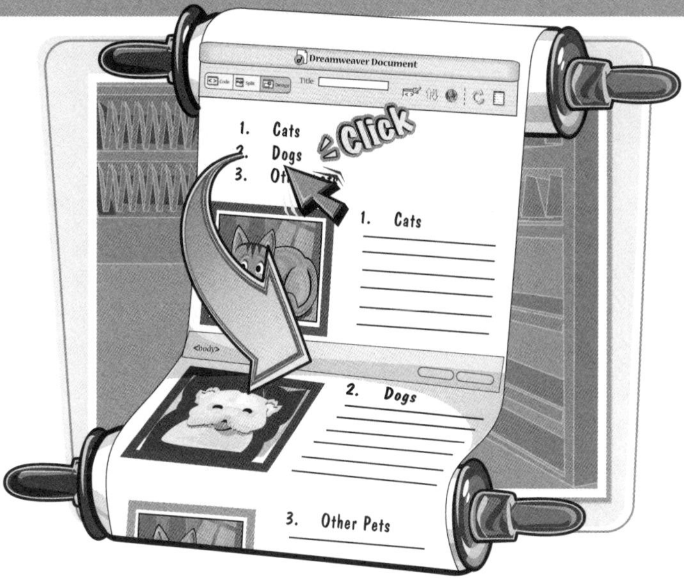

Create a Jump Link within a Page

1. Position the mouse where you want to insert the named anchor.
2. Click **Insert**.
3. Click **Named Anchor**.

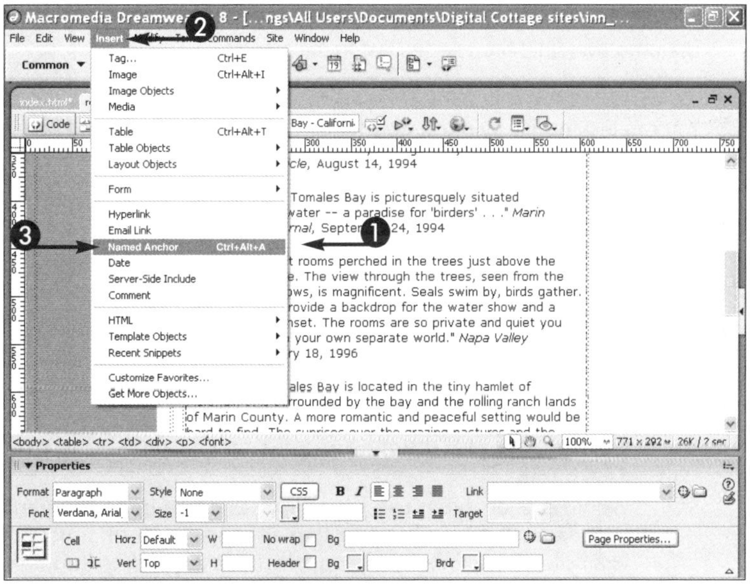

The Named Anchor dialog box appears.

4. Type a name for the anchor.
5. Click **OK**.

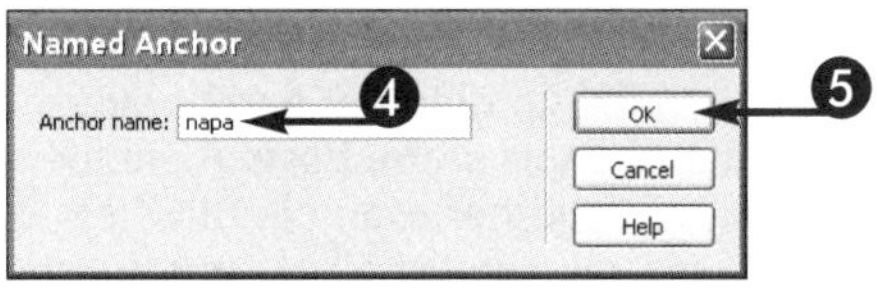

● An anchor appears in the Document window.

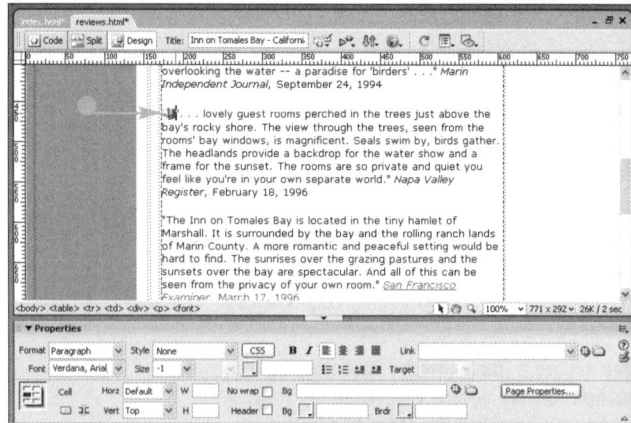

6 Click and drag to select the text that you want to link to the anchor.

7 In the Link field in the Properties inspector, type a pound sign (**#**), followed by the name of the anchor.

Dreamweaver links the selected text to the named anchor.

● You can test the link by previewing the file in a Web browser.

Note: *To preview a Web page in a Web browser, see Chapter 2.*

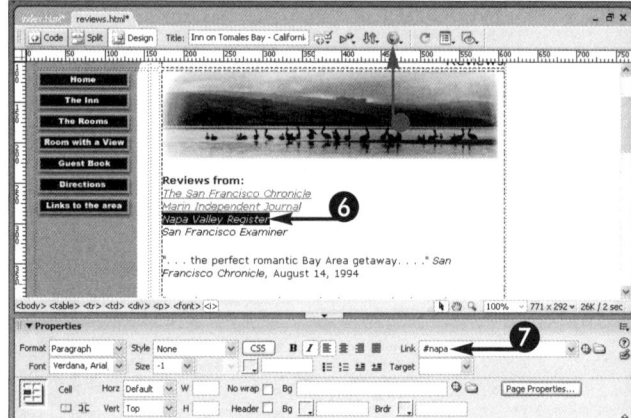

 Why would you create a jump link to something on the same page?
Web designers often use jump links, or same-page hyperlinks, to make it easier to find text that appears lower on a page. For example, these links are frequently used as Back to Top links that bring you to the beginning of a page when you click a link lower on the page. If you have a Web page that is a glossary, same-page links allow you to link to different parts of the glossary from a link menu at the top of the page. A Frequently Asked Questions (FAQ) page is another example of when to use same-page links, because you can list all of your questions at the top of the page to make it easier to find the answers.

115

Create a Link to Another File Type

Links do not have to lead just to other Web pages. You can also link to other file types, such as image files, word processing documents, PDF files, and multimedia files. Many of these files require their own players, but as long as your visitor has the required program, the file opens automatically when the user clicks the link.

Create a Link to Another File Type

① Click and drag to select the text that you want to turn into a link.

② Click the **Link** ▭ in the Properties inspector.

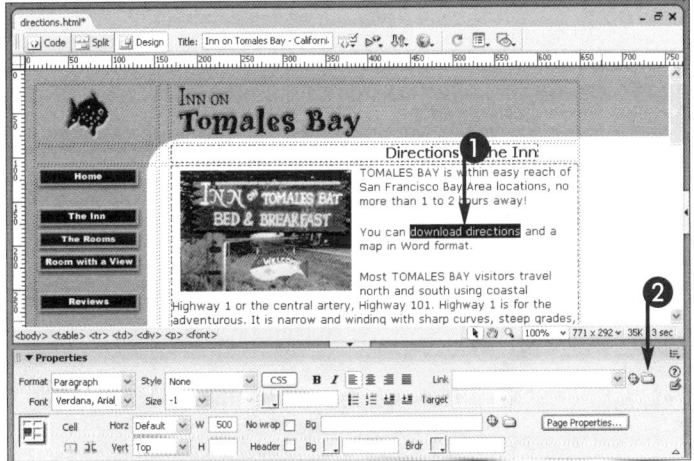

The Select File dialog box appears.

③ Click here and select the folder that contains the destination file.

④ Click the file to which you want to link.

⑤ Click **OK**.

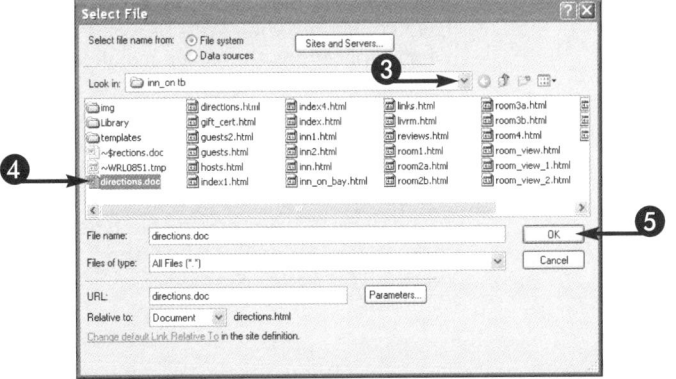

● The new link appears in a color and underlined.

Note: Links are not clickable in the Document window.

● You can test the link by previewing the file in a Web browser.

Note: To preview a page in a Web browser, see Chapter 2.

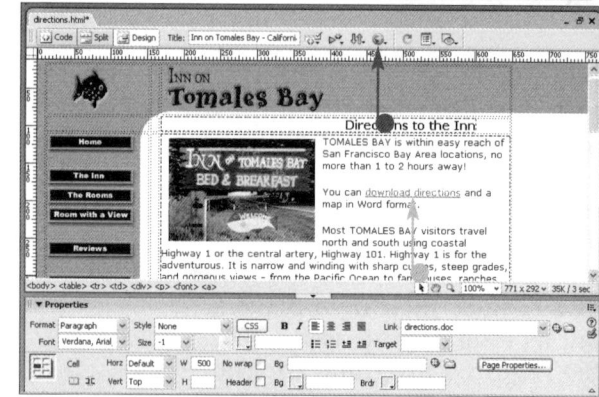

When you click the link in a Web browser, the linked file opens.

In this example, a Word document opens in Microsoft Word.

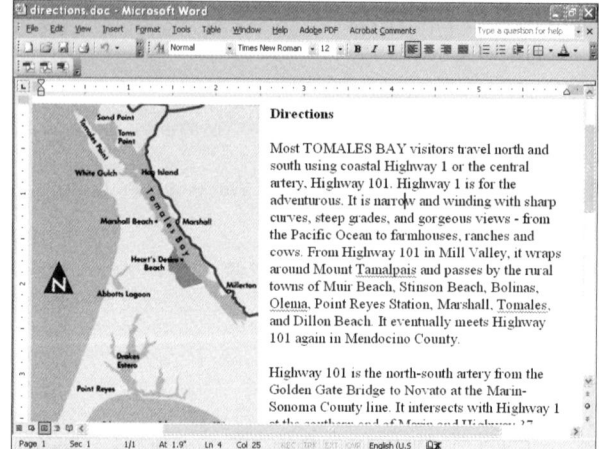

 TIP

How do users see files that are not HTML documents?

What users see when they click links to other types of files depends on how they have configured their Web browser and what applications they have installed on their computer. For example, if you link to a QuickTime movie (which has a .mov file extension), your visitors need to have a player that can display QuickTime movies. It is always good practice to include a link to the player for any special file type, to make it easy for users to find and download it if they choose.

117

Create an Image Map

You can link different areas of an image to different pages with an image map. First, you define areas of the image, called hotspots, using Dreamweaver's image-mapping tools, and then you turn them into links.

Create an Image Map

1 Click an image.

2 Type a name for the image map.

Note: You cannot use spaces or special characters in an image map name.

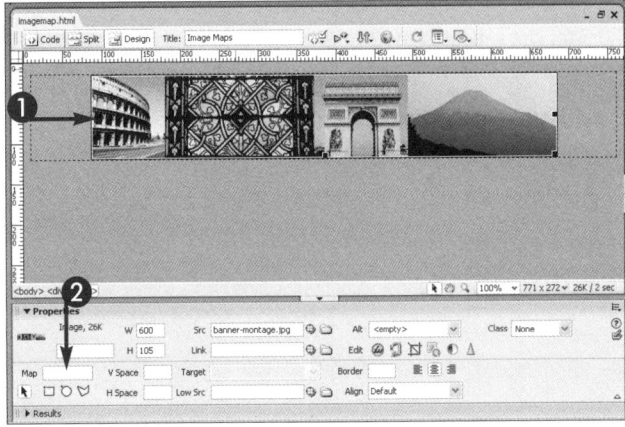

The name appears in the map field.

3 Click a drawing tool.

You can create rectangular shapes with the ▢ tool, oval shapes with the ◯ tool, and irregular shapes with the ◌ tool.

4 Draw an area on the image using the tool that you selected.

You can repeat Steps **3** to **8** to create as many hotspots as you want.

To delete a hotspot, select it, and then press Delete.

5 Click the **Map** ▢.

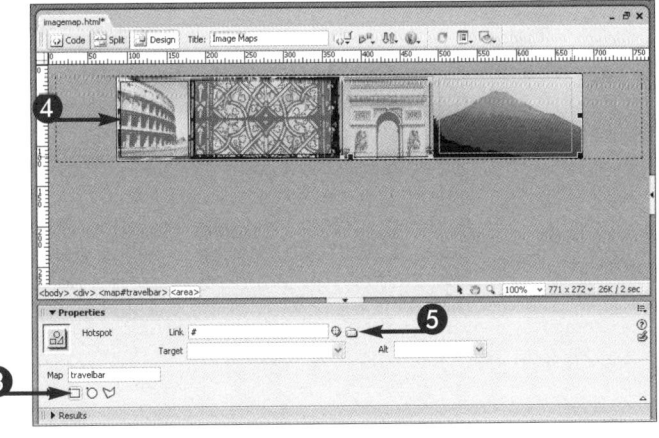

118

The Select File dialog box appears.

⑥ Click here and select the folder that contains the destination file.

⑦ Click the file to which you want to link.

⑧ Click **OK**.

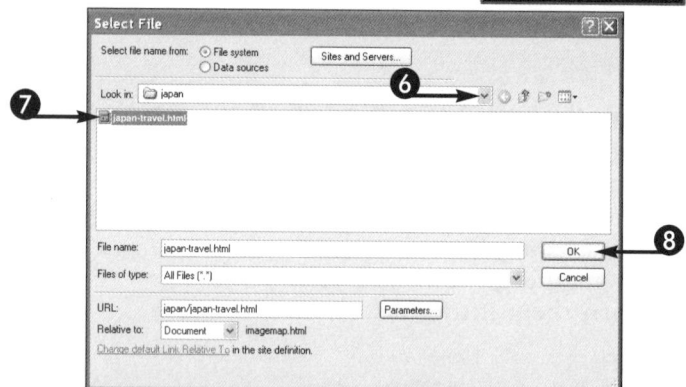

● The area defined by the selected shape links to the selected file. In this example, the image of the mountain links to a page about Japanese travel.

You can repeat Steps **3** to **8** to add other linked areas to your image.

The image-map shapes do not appear when you open the page in a Web browser.

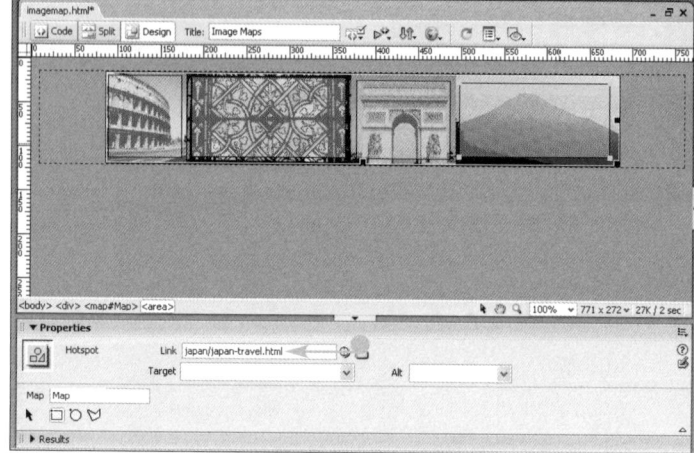

 TIP

Can image maps be used for geographical maps that link to multiple locations?

An interactive geographical map, such as a map of Latin America, is a common place to see hotspots in action. You can create one by adding a graphic image of a map to your Web page and then defining a hotspot over each location to which you want to link. Use the Polygon tool (⬠) to draw around boundaries that do not follow a square shape. Finally, assign a different link to each hotspot.

Create a Link Using the Insert Menu

Dreamweaver provides multiple options for creating links. For example, you can create links quickly and easily using either the Properties inspector or the Insert menu.

Your Web pages only display in the Files panel if you have set up your site in Dreamweaver, an important first step that is covered in Chapter 2.

Create a Link Using the Insert Menu

Note: Arrange your workspace so that both the Document window and Files panel are visible for this task.

1 Click and drag to select the text that you want to turn into a link.

2 Click **Insert**.

3 Click **Make Link**.

The Select File dialog box appears.

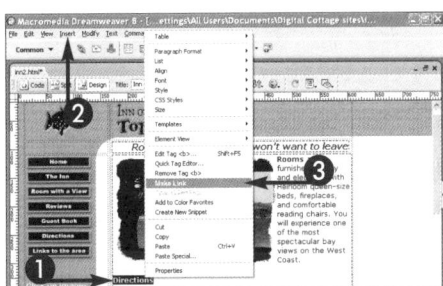

4 Click here and select the folder that contains the page to which you want to link.

5 Click the file name.

6 Click **OK**.

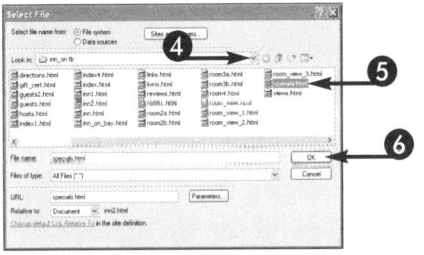

● The new link appears in color and underlined.

● The destination file displays in the Link field in the Properties inspector.

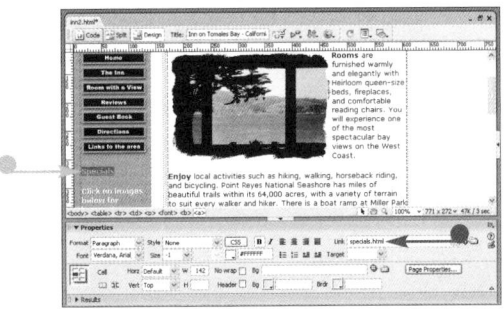

120

Open a Linked Page in a New Browser Window

You can create a link that when clicked, opens a new browser window to display the destination page.

Opening a new browser window allows a user to keep the previous Web page open.

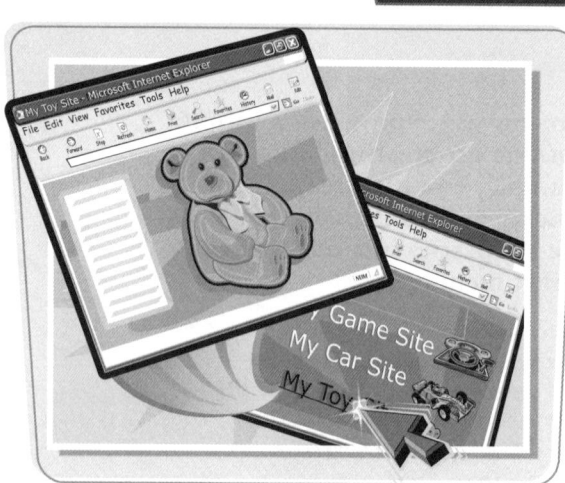

Open a Linked Page in a New Browser Window

1 Click and drag to select the link that you want to open in a new browser window.

2 Click the **Target** ⊡.

3 Click **_blank**.

4 Click ⊙ to preview the page in a Web browser.

Note: To preview a page in a Web browser, see Chapter 2.

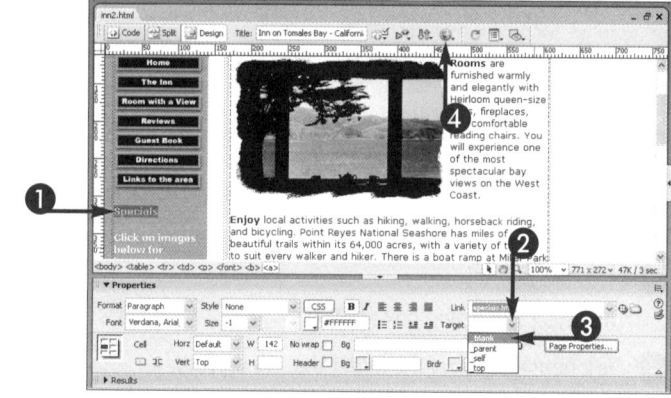

5 Click the link.

The link destination appears in a new browser window.

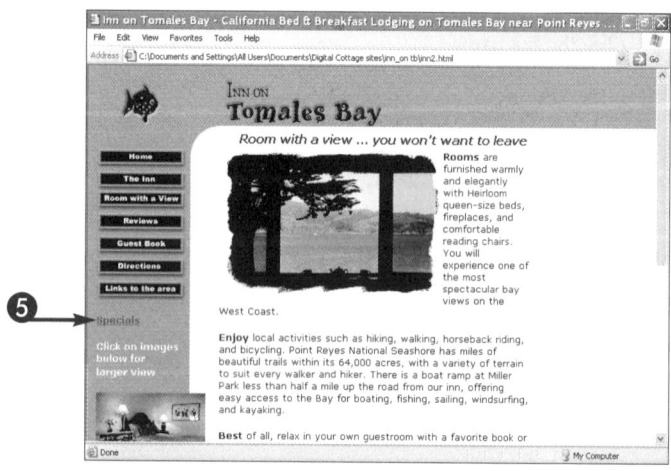

You can create an e-mail link in your Web page. When a user clicks the link, it launches an e-mail program on the user's computer, creates a message, and inserts the e-mail address into the Address field.

Create an E-Mail Link

1 Click to select the text or image that you want to turn into an e-mail link.

2 Click **Insert**.

3 Click **Email Link**.

The Email Link dialog box appears, with the selected text in the Text field.

4 Type the e-mail address to which you want to link.

5 Click **OK**.

Dreamweaver creates your e-mail link.

To test the link, you can preview the page in a Web browser.

122

Check Links

You can automatically verify the links on a Web page. Using Dreamweaver's link-testing features, you can also receive a report that lists any links that are broken.

There are many ways in which links can become broken. Dreamweaver makes it easy to find and fix them.

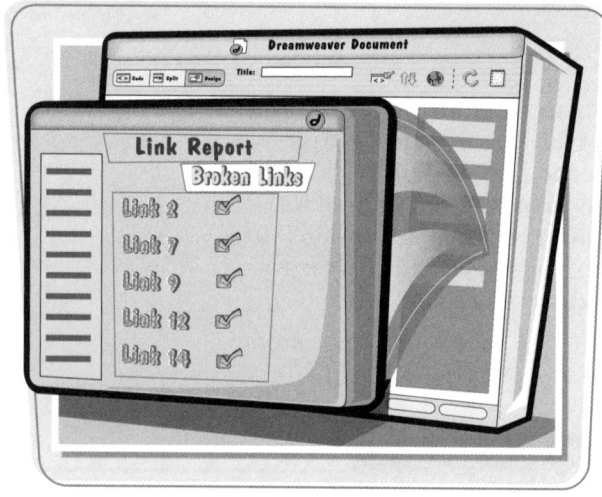

Check Links

① Click **File**.

② Click **Check Page**.

③ Click **Check Links**.

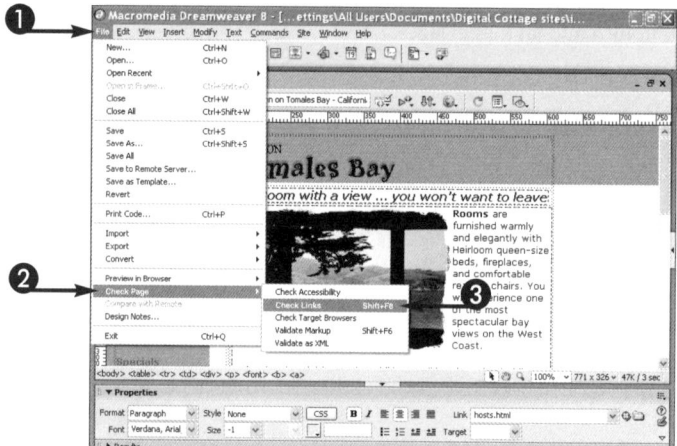

● Dreamweaver checks the local links and lists any broken links that it finds in the Results panel.

Note: Dreamweaver cannot verify links to Web pages on external sites.

● You can edit a broken destination or image file by selecting it, and then using the Browse 📁 to locate the correct file.

You can also double-click the page to open it.

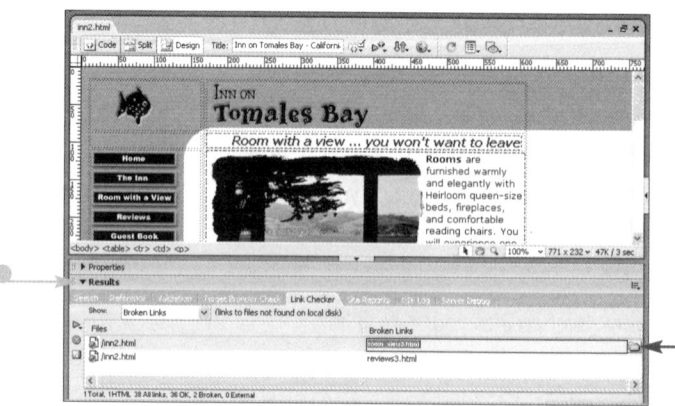

123

Change the Color of Links on a Page

You can change the color of the links on your Web page to make them match the visual style of the other text and images on your page.

Change the Color of Links on a Page

① Click **Modify**.

② Click **Page Properties**.

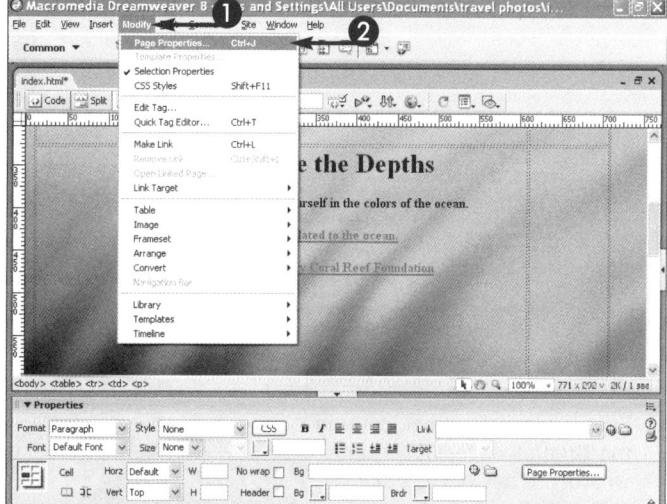

The Page Properties dialog box appears.

③ Click **Links**.

④ Click the **Link color** 🔲 (⇗ changes to ✐).

⑤ Click a color from the menu using the ✐ tool.

● You can click the **System Color Picker** (🔲) to select a custom color, or to specify no color.

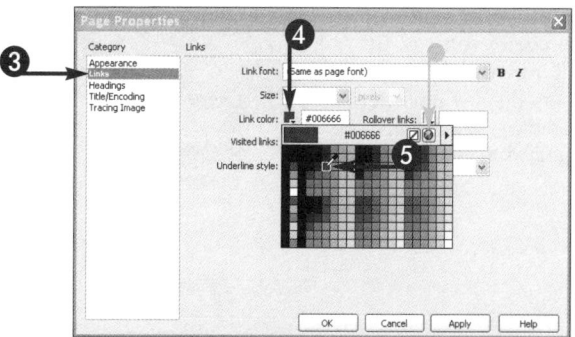

124

The color menu closes.

6 Click 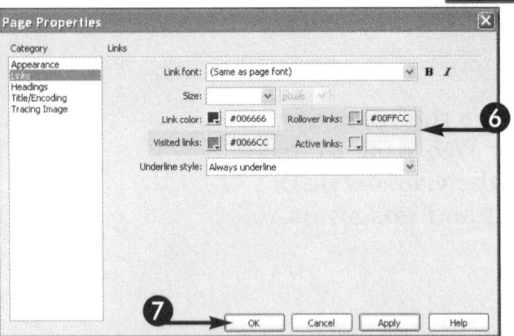 and select the colors for Visited links, Rollover links, and Active links.

This example defines the links with a hex number, but you can specify common colors on your Web page with their names. For example, you can specify the colors red or blue, instead of choosing the colors from the color menu.

Note: To change the color of links, see Chapter 5.

7 Click **OK**.

When you preview the page in a Web browser, the links display in the specified color.

Note: To preview a page in a Web browser, see Chapter 2.

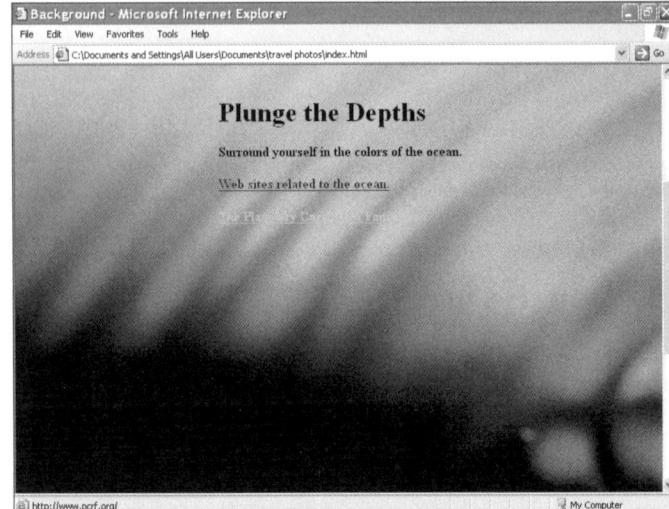

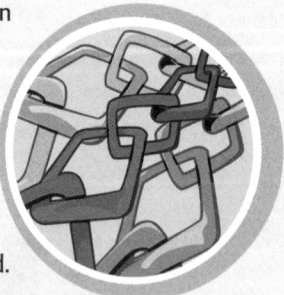

What color will my links be if I do not choose colors for them?

Blue is the default link color in the Dreamweaver Document window. What viewers see when the page opens in a Web browser depends on their browser settings. By default, most Web browsers display unvisited links as blue, visited links as purple, and active links as red.

How can I override the link colors that I set?

Sometimes you may need to change the color of a linked word to something other than the set link color of a page — if it is set against a different background color or you want it to stand out better, for example. Select the text and use the Font  in the Properties inspector to select a color. Once changed, the text always appears in that color, even after it is visited.

125

CHAPTER

8

Using Tables to Design a Web Page

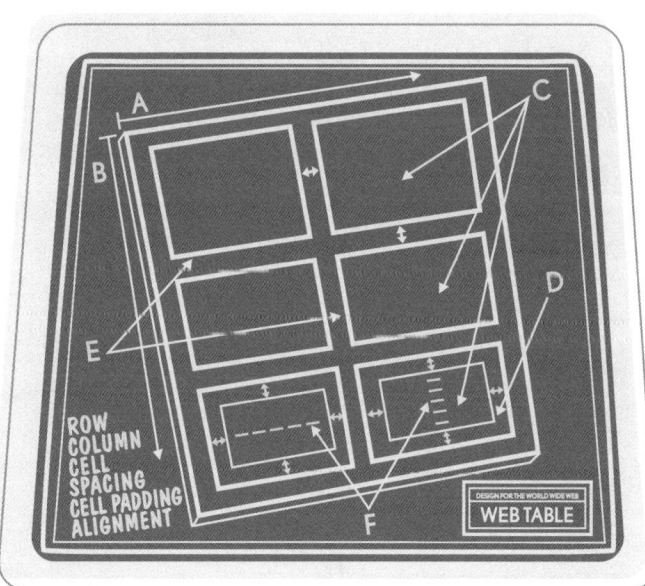

Tables enable you to arrange text, images, and other elements on your Web pages, and to create complex designs, even within the constraints of HTML. This chapter shows you how to create and format tables.

Teach Yourself VISUALLY™ Macromedia® Dreamweaver® 8
Janine Warner. ISBN 978-0-7645-9998-9
©2006 Wiley Publishing Inc.

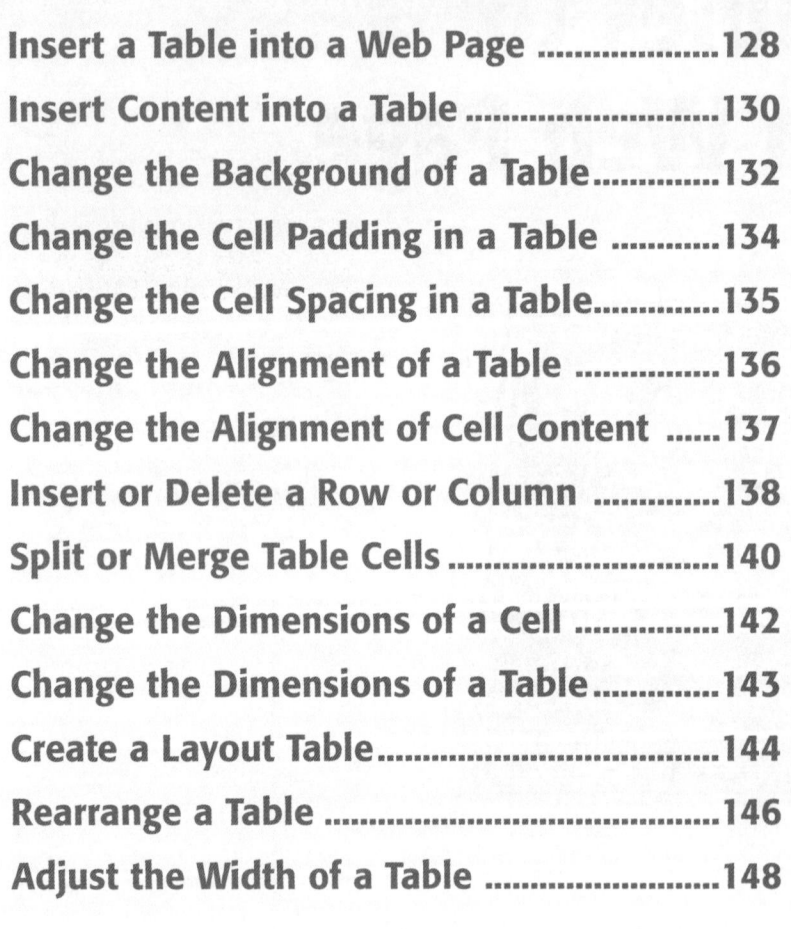

Insert a Table into a Web Page

You can use tables to organize and design pages that contain financial data, text, images, and multimedia. Dreamweaver's layout features allow you to create simple tables for tabular data or complex tables to create sophisticated layouts and designs.

Insert a Table into a Web Page

① Position the mouse ⌕ where you want to insert a table.

By default, the cursor snaps to the left margin. However, you can insert tables between existing elements on a page, and you can control table alignment.

② Click **Insert**.

③ Click **Table**.

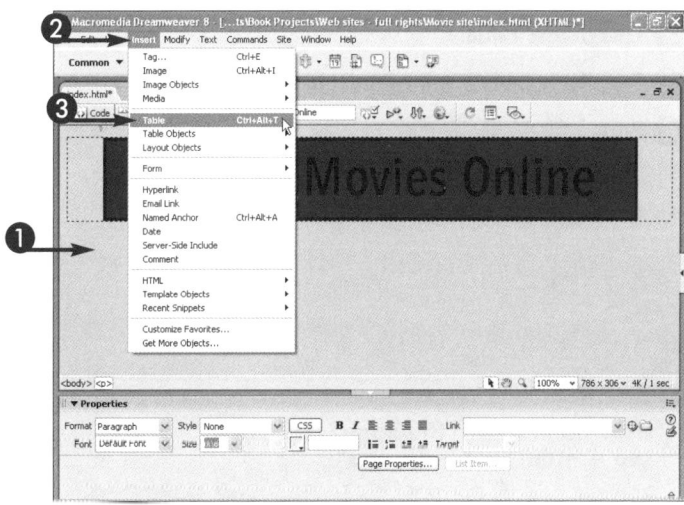

The Table dialog box appears.

④ Type the number of rows and columns that you want in your table.

⑤ Type the width of your table.

You can set the width in pixels, or as a percentage of the page, by clicking ⊡ and selecting your choice of measurements.

⑥ Type a border thickness in pixels.

⑦ Click **OK**.

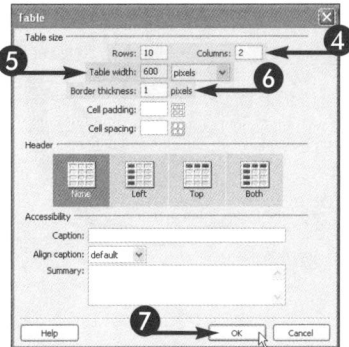

128

● An empty table appears, aligned to the left by default.

● You can click here and select a different alignment.

TURN OFF TABLE BORDERS

1 Click ▾.

2 Click **Select Table**.

3 Type the number **0** in the Border field.

4 Press `Enter` (`Return`).

When you view the page in a Web browser, the dashed table border disappears.

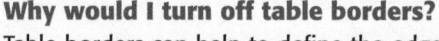

TIPS

How do I change the appearance of the content inside my table?

You can specify the size, style, and color of text inside a table in the same way that you format text on a Web page. Likewise, you can control the appearance of an image inside a table in the same way that you can control it outside a table. For more on formatting text, see Chapter 5, and for more on images, see Chapter 7.

Why would I turn off table borders?

Table borders can help to define the edges of a table and organize columnar data, such as a financial report. However, if you want to use a table to arrange photos and text within the design of your page, then you can have a cleaner layout if you set the border to zero so that it becomes invisible. Because most users do not want a border, Dreamweaver's default setting is zero. You can set it to one pixel for a slim border, or try five or ten if you want a thick border.

129

Insert Content into a Table

You can fill the cells of your table with the same content that you would insert on a Web page. This content can include text, images, multimedia files, form elements, and other tables.

Insert Content into a Table

INSERT TEXT

1 Click to place your mouse ⬚ inside a table cell.

2 Type text into the cell.

Note: To format your text, see Chapter 5.

INSERT AN IMAGE

1 Click inside a table cell.

2 Click **Image** (▣).

The Select Image Source dialog box appears.

3 Click here and select the folder that contains your image.

4 Click an image file.

5 Click **OK**.

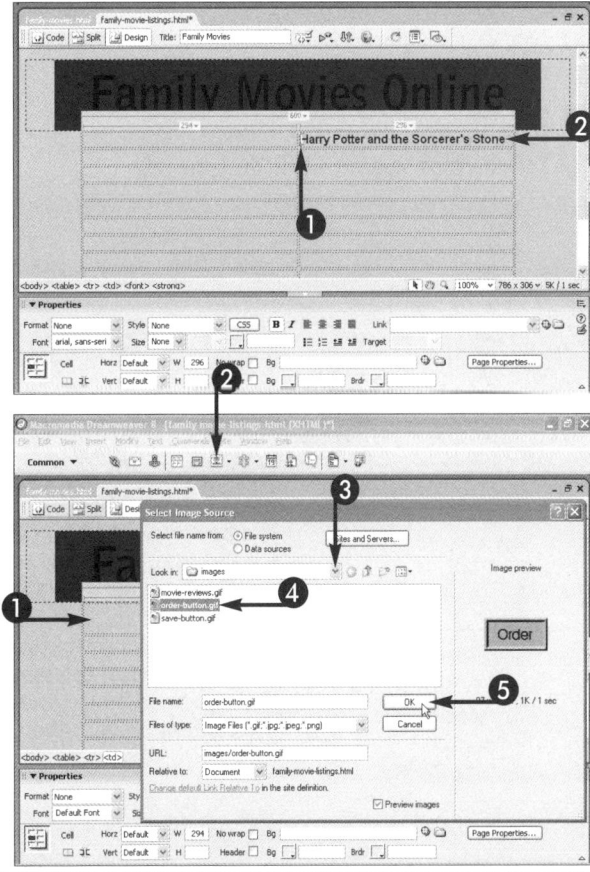

130

● The image appears in the table cell.

● If the image is larger than the cell, the cell expands to accommodate the image.

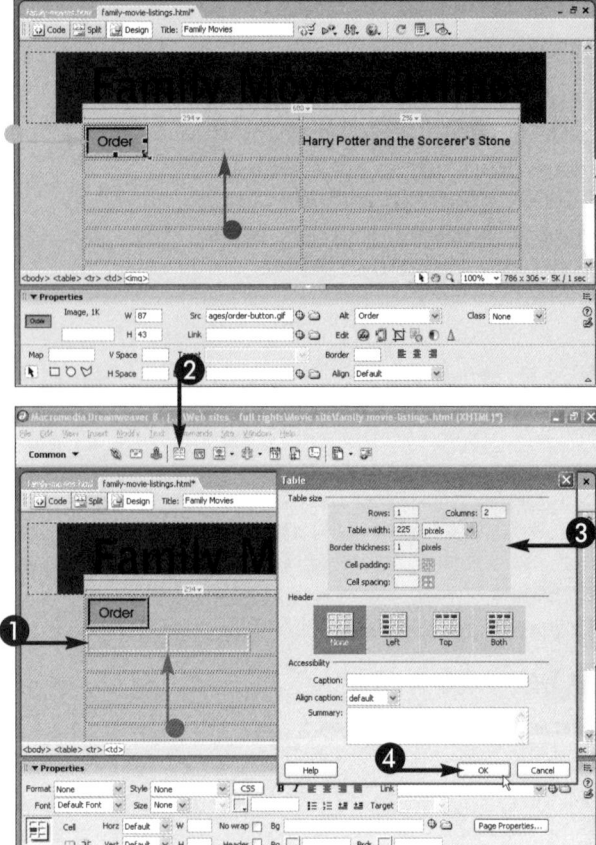

INSERT A TABLE WITHIN A TABLE

1 Click inside a table cell.

2 Click **Table** (▦).

The Table dialog box appears.

3 Type values in the fields to define the characteristics of the table.

4 Click **OK**.

● The new table appears within the table cell.

TIP

How can I add captions to images on my Web page?

The best way to add a caption to the top, bottom, or side of an image is by creating a two-celled table. Place the image in one cell and the caption in the other. You can then adjust the size and alignment of the table to position the captioned image within the rest of the content on your Web page.

131

Change the Background of a Table

You can change the background of a table, or only change the background of a cell, a row, or a column. This is a great way to add a design element or to call attention to a section of a table. Just like the background of a Web page, you can change the background color of a table, or fill the background of a table with an image. For more on Web page backgrounds, see Chapter 7.

Change the Background of a Table

① Click to select a table or individual cell, or click and drag to select a row or column of cells.

② Click the **Background** 🔲 to open the color menu (⌖ changes to 🖉).

③ Click a color.

● You can click the **System Color Picker** (🔘) to select a custom color.

● You can delete the contents of the color field to specify no color.

● The color fills the background of the selected cells.

● You can also type a color name or a color code into the Color field.

Note: To change the font color of a Web page, see Chapter 5.

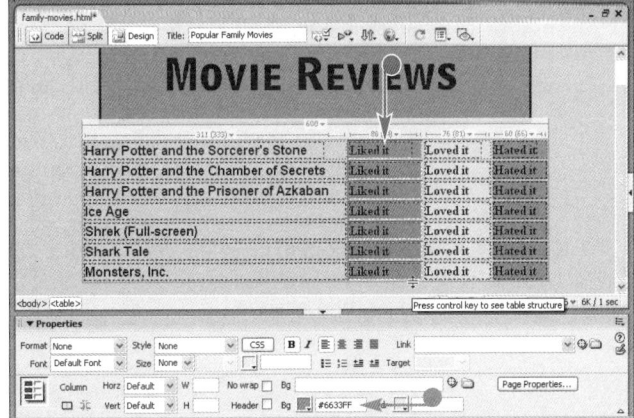

132

ADD A BACKGROUND IMAGE TO A TABLE

1️⃣ Click a corner to select a table or cell, or click and drag to select multiple cells.

2️⃣ Click the **Background Image** 🖼 in the Properties inspector.

The Select Image Source dialog box appears.

3️⃣ Click here and select the folder that contains your image.

4️⃣ Click an image file.

5️⃣ Click **OK**.

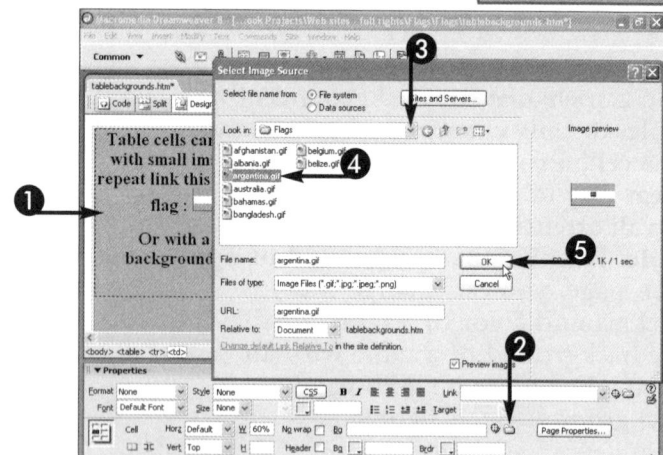

● The table or cell background fills with the image.

If the cell space is greater than the image size, then the image tiles fill the available area.

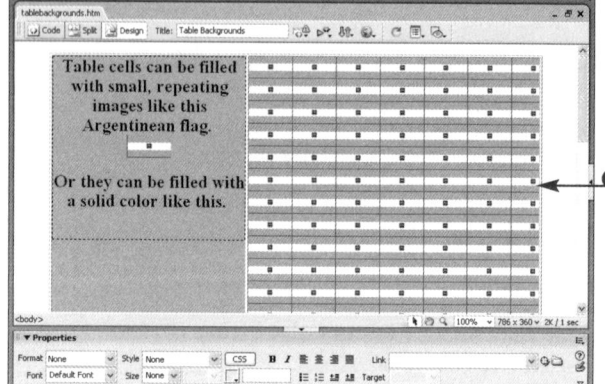

 TIP

How can I change the background of a table cell?

Click inside a cell and then specify the background color using the Background Color 🎨, or insert a background image by clicking 🖼 and selecting an image from the Image Source dialog box. You can give each cell a different background or use one color to create an appearance of a solid area. You can also fill a cell with one large image in the background. You can then add text and other elements over the background.

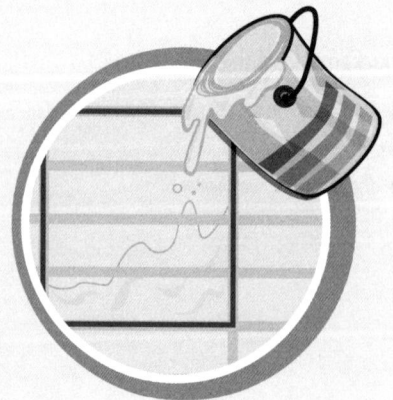

Change the Cell Padding in a Table

You can change the cell padding to add space between a table's content and its borders.

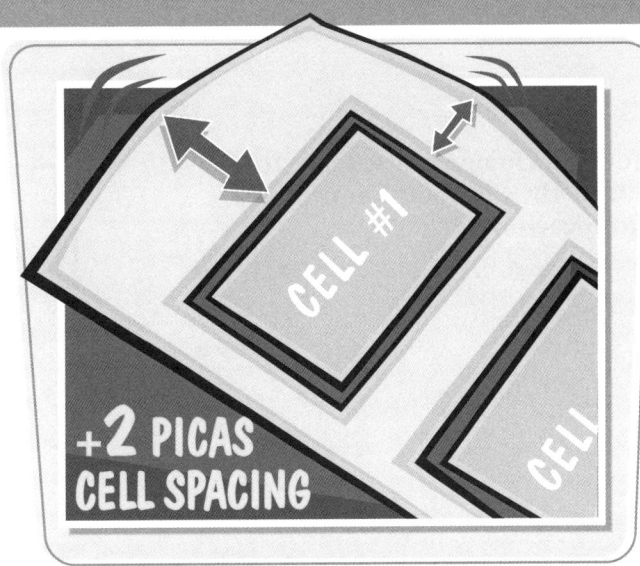

Change the Cell Padding in a Table

1 Click the top left corner of the table to select it.

2 In the CellPad field in the Properties inspector, type the amount of padding in pixels.

3 Press Enter (Return).

● The space changes between the table content and the table borders.

Note: *Adjusting the cell padding affects all of the cells in a table. You cannot adjust the padding of individual cells by using the CellPad field.*

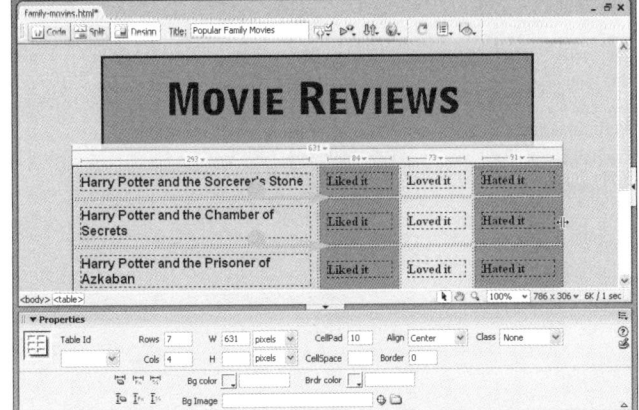

You can change cell spacing to adjust the distance that cells are from each other.

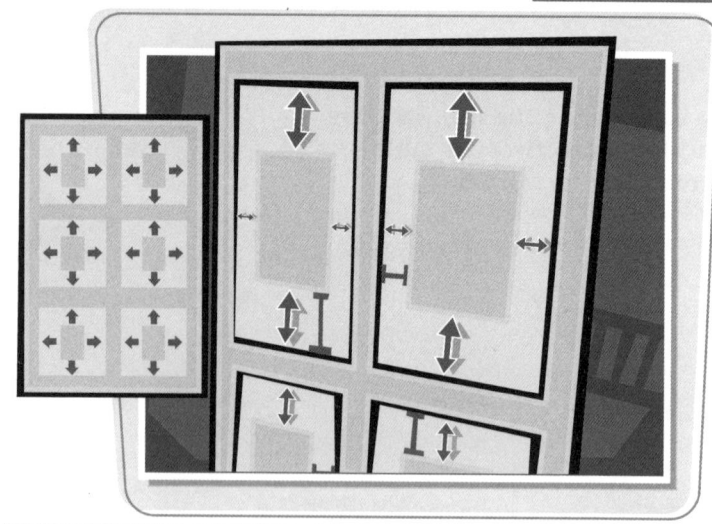

Change the Cell Spacing in a Table

① Click the top left corner of the table to select it.

② In the Cell Space field, type the amount of spacing in pixels.

● The cell spacing changes.

● You can change the width of the table or a column by clicking and dragging the cell borders.

Note: Adjusting the cell spacing affects all of the cell borders in the table. You cannot adjust the spacing of individual cell borders by using the CellSpace field.

135

Change the Alignment of a Table

You can change the alignment of a table and wrap text and other content around it, much like you would do with images and other elements.

Change the Alignment of a Table

① Click the top left corner of the table to select it.

② Click the Align ⬇.

③ Click an alignment option.

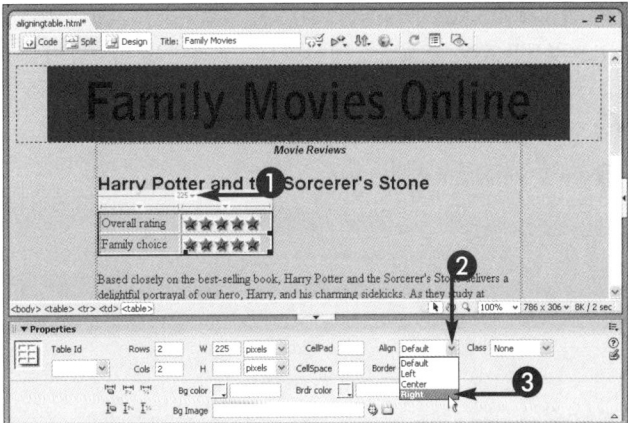

● The table aligns in the page.

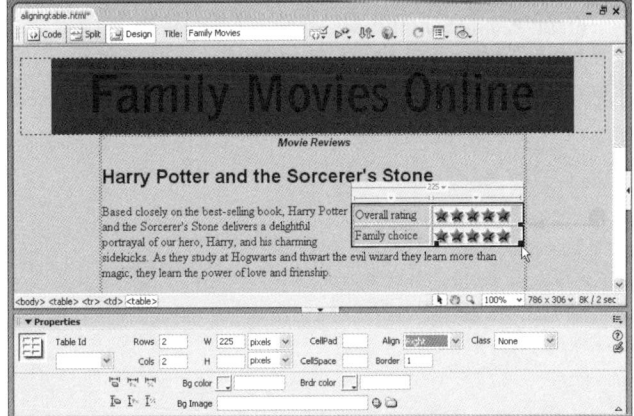

You can align the content in your table cells horizontally and vertically to center elements or move them to the top or bottom of a cell.

Change the Alignment of Cell Content

1 Click and drag to select the entire column.

You can press **Shift** + click, or click and drag, to select multiple cells.

2 Click the Horizontal ⊡.

3 Click a horizontal alignment.

● The content aligns.

In this example, horizontal alignment was set to center for four cells simultaneously.

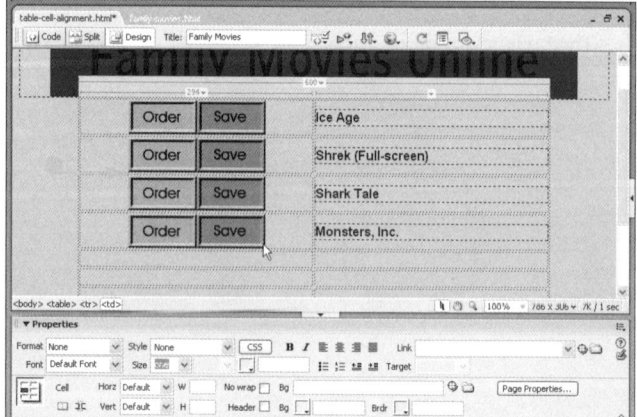

Insert or Delete a Row or Column

You can insert cells into your table to add content or create space between elements. You can also delete rows or columns to remove them when they are not needed.

Insert a Row or Column

❶ Click the top left corner of the table to select it.

❷ Type the number of rows and columns that you want in the Properties inspector.

❸ Press **Enter** (**Return**).

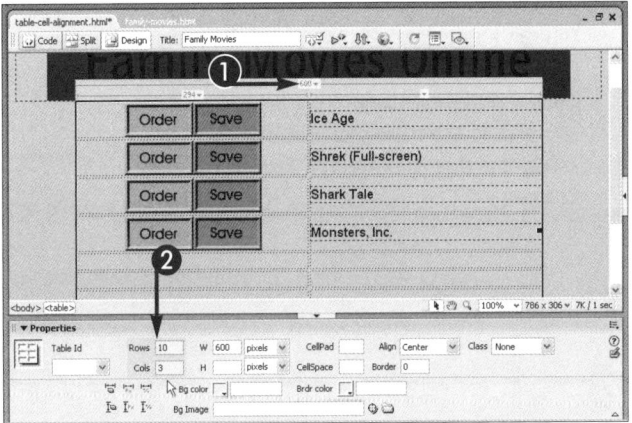

● Empty rows or columns appear in the table.

To add a row or column in the middle of a table, right-click inside an existing cell, click **Table**, and then click **Insert Row or Column** from the menu that appears. You can also click **Modify**, then click **Table**, and then click **Insert Row or Column**.

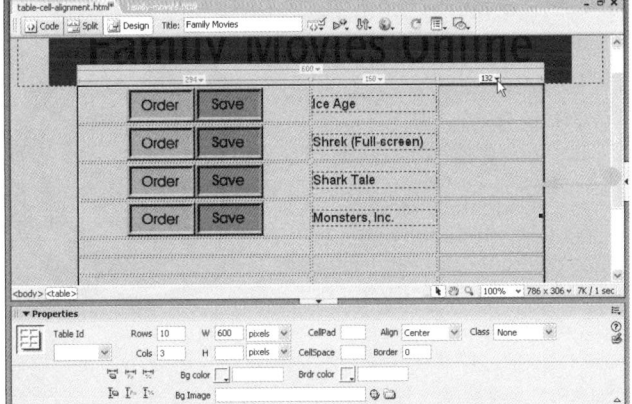

138

Delete a Row or Column

❶ Press `Shift` + click, or click and drag, to select the cells that you want to delete.

❷ Press `Delete`.

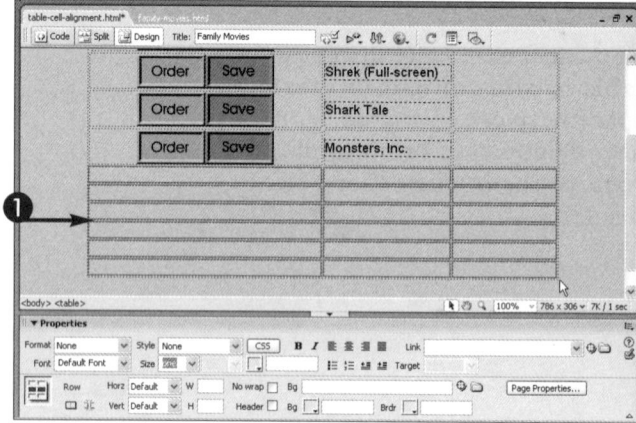

● The selected table cells disappear.

Note: The content of a cell is deleted when you delete a cell.

You can also delete cells by right-clicking inside the cells, then clicking **Table**, and then clicking **Delete Row** or **Delete Column** from the menu that appears. You can also click **Modify**, then click **Table**, and then click **Delete Row** or **Delete Column**.

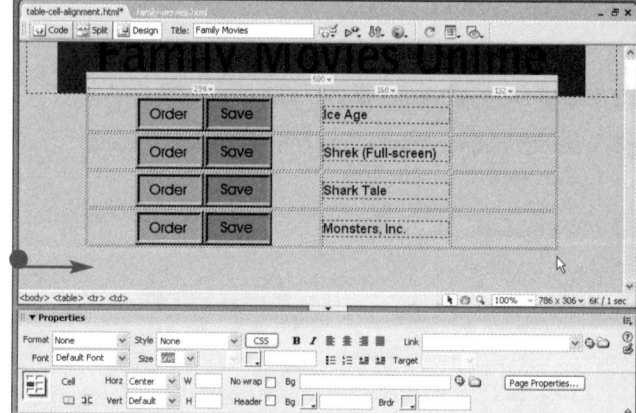

What happens to the content of a deleted cell?

Dreamweaver does not warn you if the cells that you are deleting in a table contain content. This is because Dreamweaver assumes that you also want to delete the cell content. If you accidentally remove content when deleting rows or columns, you can click **Edit** and then click **Undo** to undo your last action.

How do I move content around a table?

You can move the contents of a table cell by clicking to select any image, text, or element in the cell and then dragging it out of the table or into another cell. You can also use copy and paste to move content from one cell to another, or to another part of a page.

139

Split or Merge Table Cells

You can create more elaborate page designs by splitting or merging cells in a table to create larger cells adjacent to smaller ones. You can then insert text, images and other content into the cells.

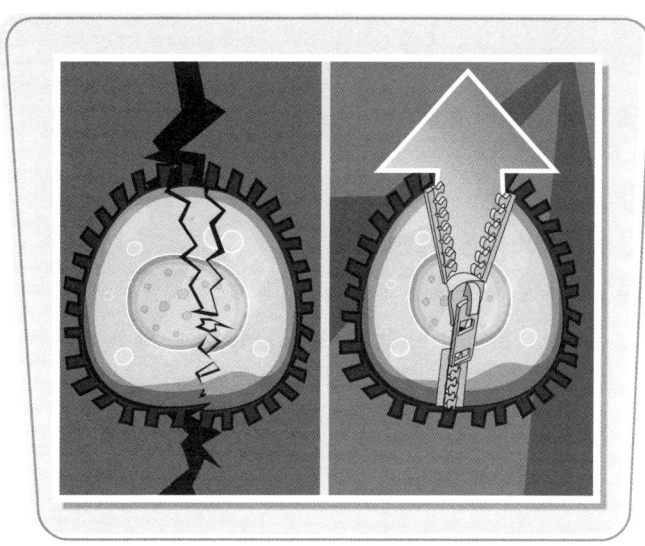

Split a Table Cell

① Click to place your cursor in the cell that you want to split.

② Click **Modify**.

③ Click **Table**.

④ Click **Split Cell**.

● You can also split a cell by clicking **Split Cell** (⬚) in the Properties inspector.

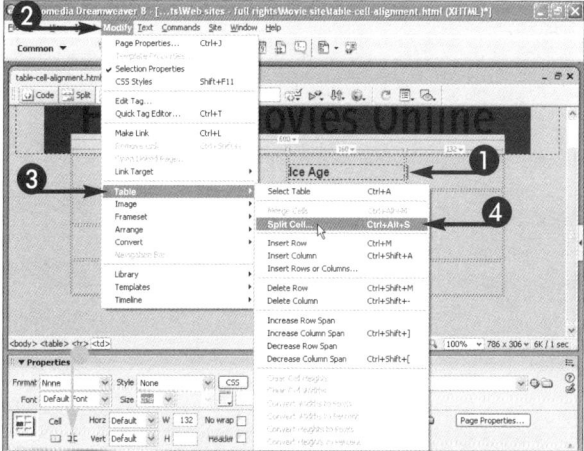

The Split Cell dialog box appears.

⑤ Click **Rows** or **Columns** to split the cell (○ changes to ◉).

⑥ Type the number of rows or columns.

⑦ Click **OK**.

● The table cell splits.

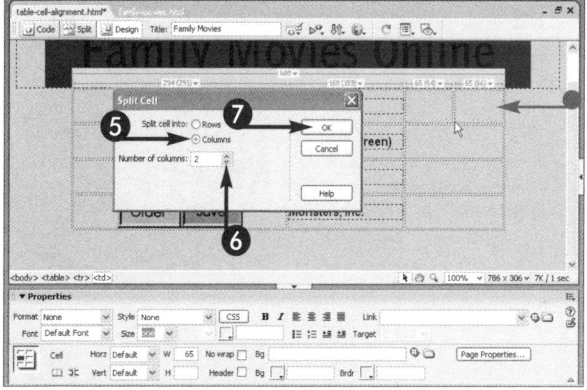

140

Merge Table Cells

① Click and drag to select the cells that you want to merge.

② Click **Modify**.

③ Click **Table**.

④ Click **Merge Cells**.

● You can also merge cells by clicking **Merge Cells** (▢) in the Properties inspector.

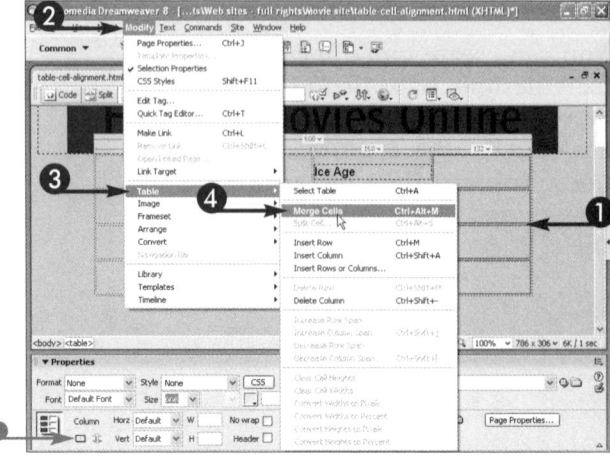

● The table cells merge.

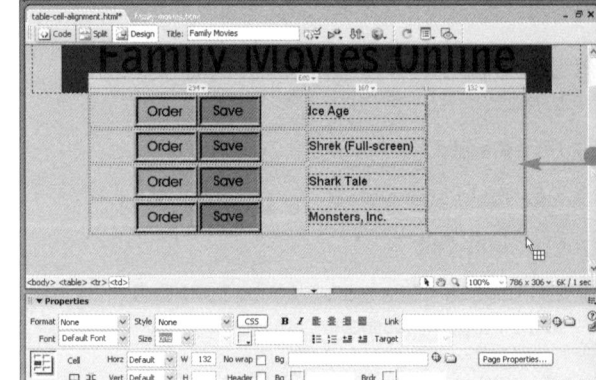

TIPS

Can I merge any combination of table cells?

No. The cells must have a rectangular arrangement. For example, you can merge all of the cells in a two-row-by-two-column table. However, you cannot select three cells that form an *L* shape and merge them into one cell.

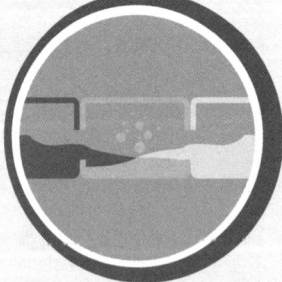

Can I add as many cells as I want?

Yes, just make sure that your final table design displays well on a computer monitor. For example, although it is common to design Web pages that are long and require visitors to scroll down, it can be confusing to create overly wide pages that require scrolling right or left.

141

Change the Dimensions of a Cell

You can change the dimensions of individual table cells to better accommodate their content. As you enlarge and reduce cells, you can create more complex tables for more precise design control.

① Click to select the edge of a cell and drag to adjust the size.

● You can also enter a size in the Properties inspector.

You can also specify a percentage of the table size instead of specifying pixels. For example, you can type **25** percent in the width or height box.

② Press `Enter` (`Return`).

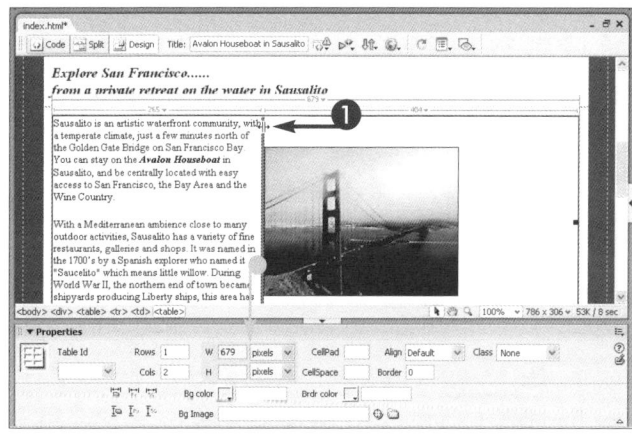

● The cell and its contents readjust to its new dimensions.

Note: *Cell dimensions may be constrained by content. For example, Dreamweaver cannot shrink a cell smaller than the size of the content that it contains.*

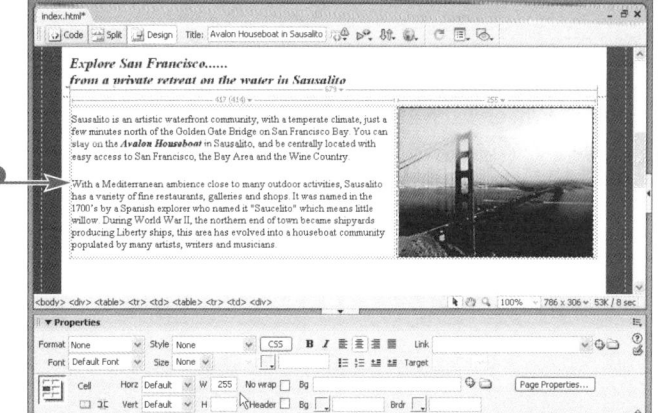

142

You can change the dimensions of your entire table. This is a good technique for ensuring that your content fits well within your Web page.

Change the Dimensions of a Table

① Click the top left corner of the table to select it.

② Type a width and height.

③ Click here and select the width setting in pixels, or a percentage of the screen.

④ Press **Enter** (**Return**).

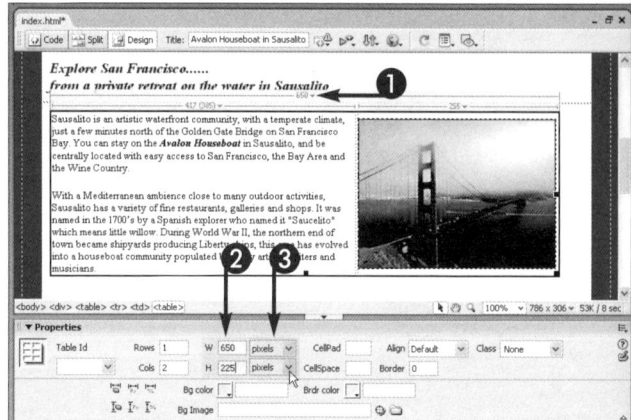

● The table readjusts to its new dimensions.

Note: *Table dimensions may be constrained by content. For example, Dreamweaver cannot shrink a table smaller than the size of the content that it contains.*

If a height or width is not specified, the table automatically adjusts to fit the space that is available on the user's screen.

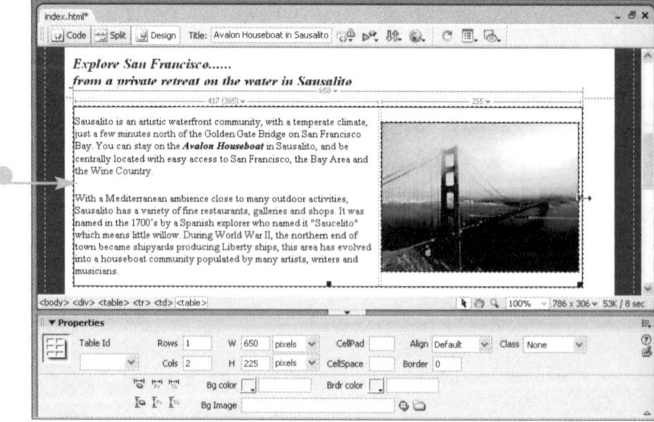

143

Create a
Layout Table

You can create tables to better control the design of a Web page. Dreamweaver makes this easier with its table layout features, which allow you to click and drag to draw tables and cells anywhere on a page.

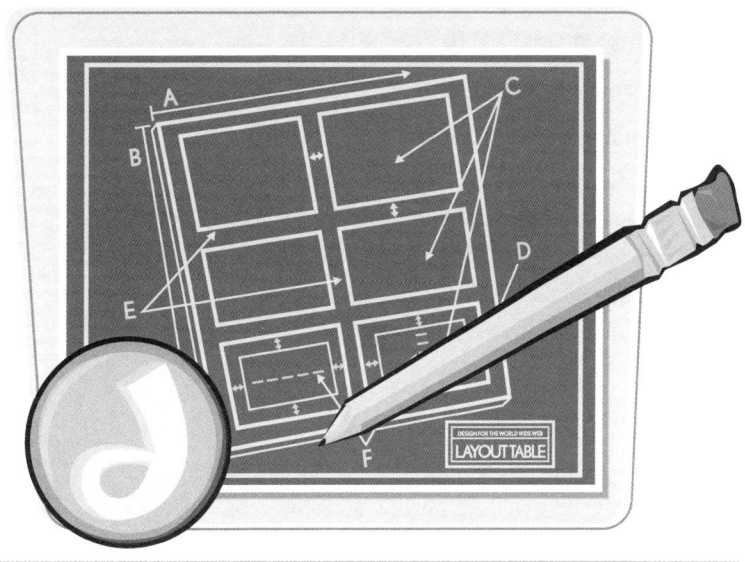

Create a Layout Table

① Click here and select **Layout** from the Insert bar.

The Layout options appear in the Insert bar.

② Click **Layout**.

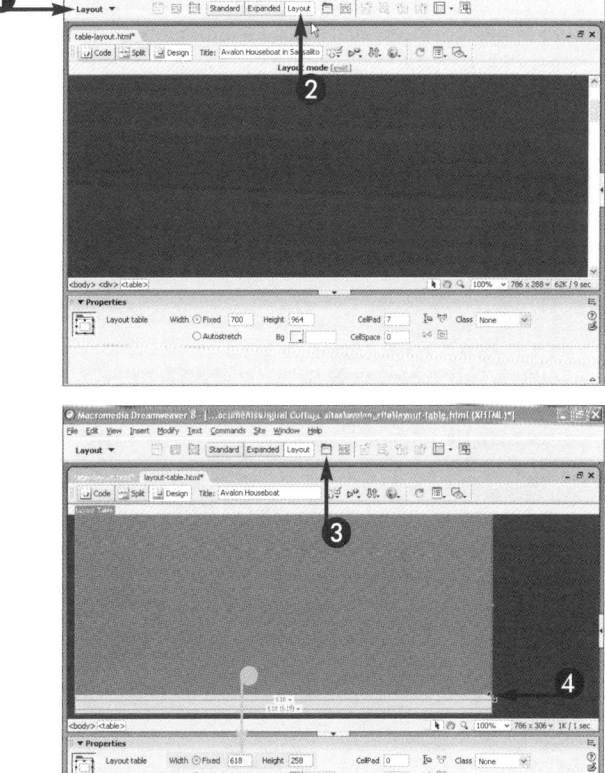

③ Click **Layout Table** (□) (↙ changes to ↖).

④ Click and drag the mouse ↖ to create a table.

The outline of a table appears.

● You can specify the exact size of the table in the Properties inspector.

144

5 Click **Layout Cell** (▣) (⌖ changes to ⌖).

6 Click and drag inside the table to create a Layout Cell.

The attributes of the cell appear in the Properties inspector.

● You can adjust the size and position of a cell by clicking and dragging its edge or by clicking the center of the border where the dots appear.

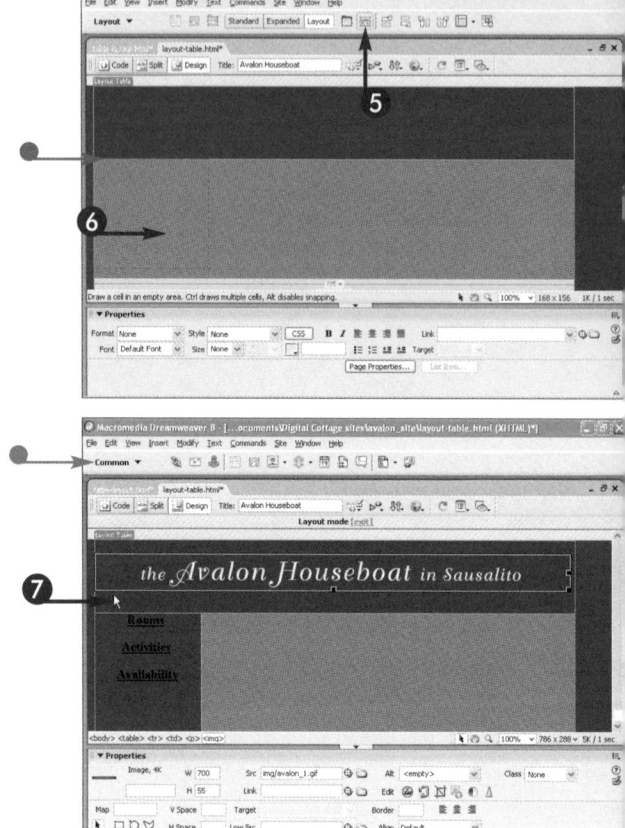

7 Click to position your mouse ⌖ in the cell, and add content as you would anywhere else on the page.

Note: To insert content, see the section "Insert Content into a Table" in this chapter.

● You can click the **Common** option in the Insert bar to access the Insert Image (▣) and other buttons.

Although you can insert content in Layout view in the same way as you do in Standard view, it is easier to tab around a table in Standard view.

What can I do to draw my layout table cells more precisely?

It is easy, you just click and drag to create tables and cells in Layout view anywhere on the page. In Standard Layout view, you have to merge and split cells to try to position a cell, which makes it much harder to be precise. Click **Layout** on the Insert Layout bar to use Layout view.

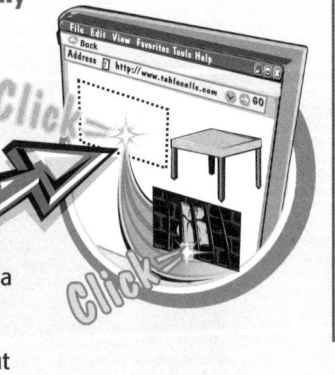

Can I create a cell anywhere I want?

In Layout view, you can draw table cells anywhere inside a table. Simply click and drag to create a cell. Dreamweaver fills in any necessary cells as it creates a complex table in the background, with spacers to control the exact positioning of elements in your page design.

145

Rearrange a Table

In Layout or Standard view, you can easily change the size of the cells in a table. You can also click and drag to move content from one cell in a table to another cell or table.

Rearrange a Table

MOVE THE CONTENTS OF A CELL OR TABLE

1️⃣ Click to select an element, such as an image.

2️⃣ Click and drag the content to the desired location.

Note: *Do not click and drag a handle, or you risk resizing the element or the table cell.*

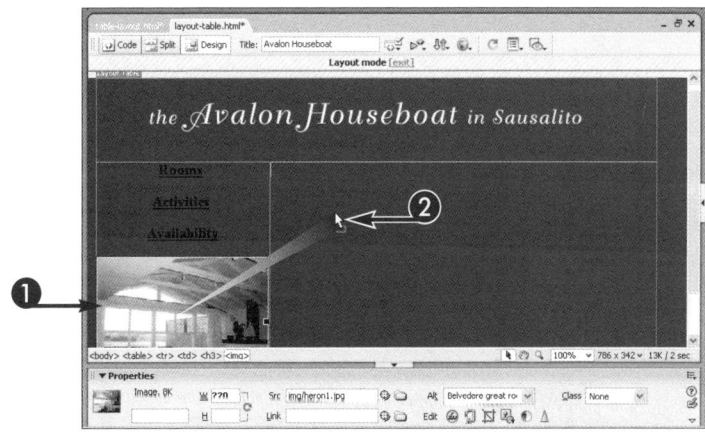

● The content appears in the new location.

Undefined cells in the table adjust their sizes to make room for the content of the cell.

146

CHANGE THE SIZE OF A TABLE OR A CELL

1. Click the edge of the table or an individual cell (⇖ changes to ⟷).
2. Click and drag a side or corner handle to the desired size.

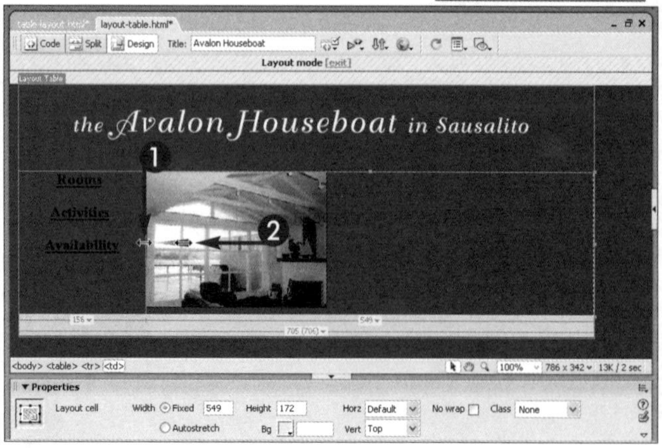

- The table or cell resizes.

***Note:** You cannot overlap cells in a table.*

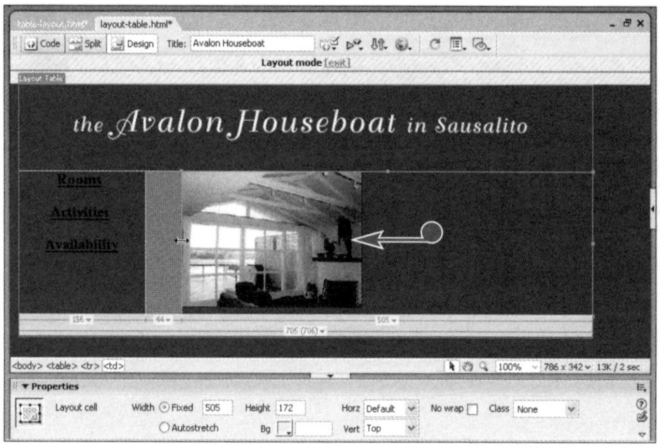

TIPS

How do I delete a cell in Layout view?

Click the edge of the cell to select it and then press Delete. Dreamweaver replaces the space with gray, non-editable cells that it uses as space holders to maintain the placement of other cells.

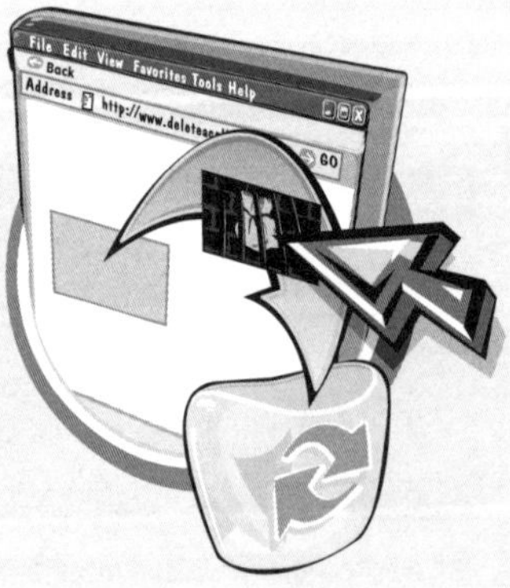

How do I delete a table in Layout view?

Click ▾ and click **Select Table** to select an entire table, and then press Delete. If you decide that you want to change the design, then you may find that it is easier to delete a table and start over than to make adjustments to an existing one.

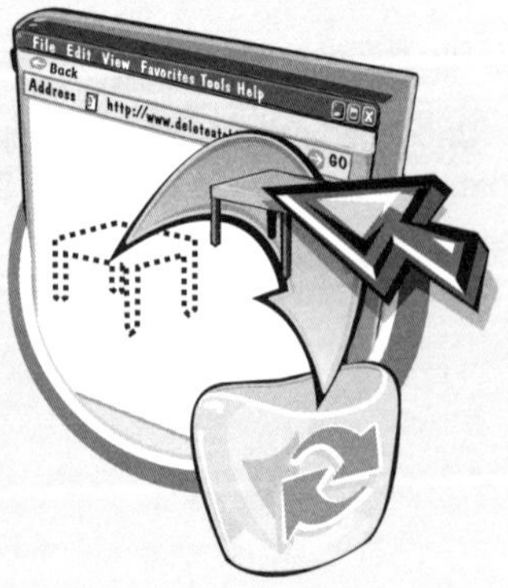

Adjust the Width of a Table

You can specify the size of a table using percentage instead of pixels. As a result, the table automatically adjusts to fit a user's browser window size.

When you define a table size as a percentage, it adjusts to fill that percentage of a user's browser window.

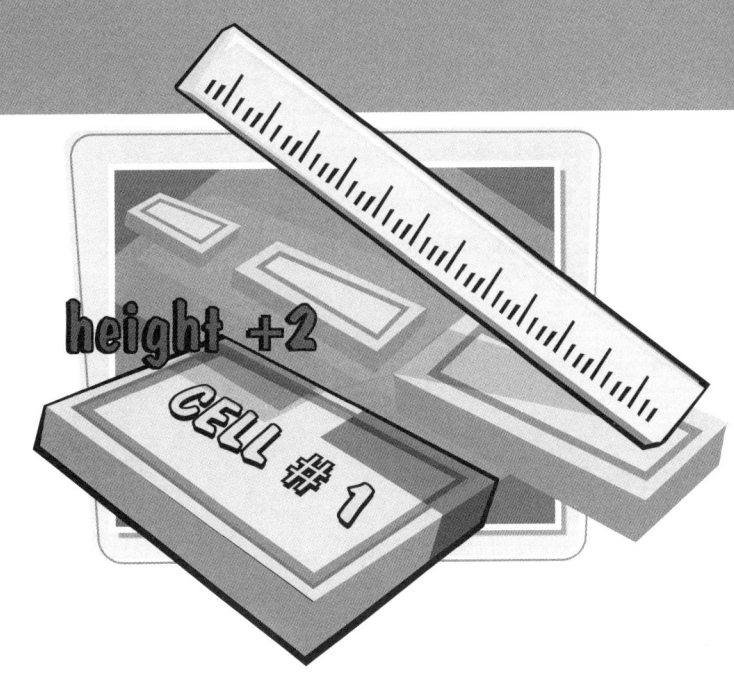

Adjust the Width of a Table

CREATE A FIXED-WIDTH COLUMN

① Click **Layout** in the Layout bar to change to Layout view.

② Click at the top or bottom of a column.

③ Click **Add Spacer Image** from the menu that appears.

If your site lacks a spacer image file that it can reference, a dialog box appears asking whether you want to create one. Click **OK**.

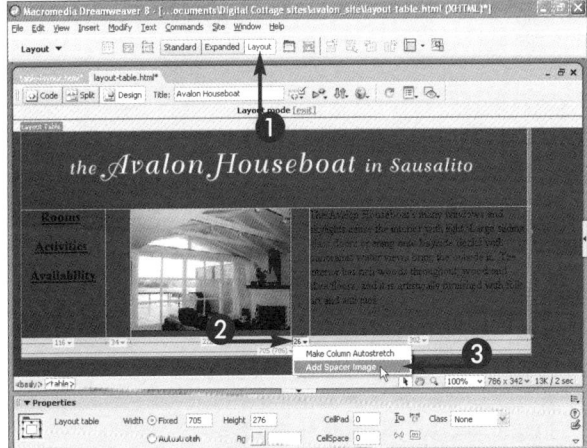

● A spacer image is inserted into the cell to maintain a fixed width.

Spacer images are transparent so that they do not appear in the display.

● A bar appears at the bottom of the cell containing the spacer image, indicating the size of the image.

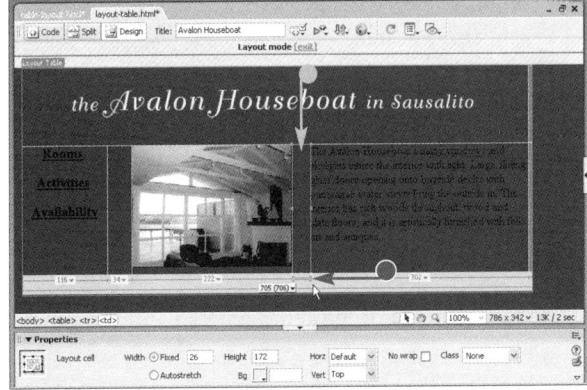

148

CREATE AN AUTOSTRETCH COLUMN

1 Click at the top or bottom of a column.

2 Click **Make Column Autostretch** from the menu that appears.

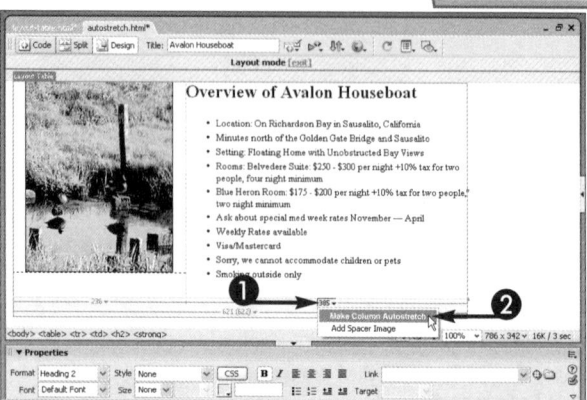

● Dreamweaver sets the column size to automatically adjust to fill up any available space on the screen.

● To see the autostretch effects in your browser window, resize the window.

Note: To preview a page in a Web browser, see Chapter 2.

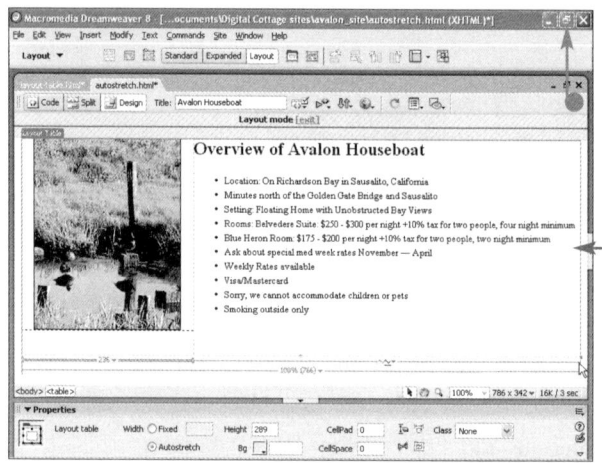

What is a spacer image?

A *spacer image* is a transparent GIF image file that is used as a filler to invisibly control spacing on a Web page. Essentially, you insert a spacer image into a table cell and then use the height and width attributes to control the size. The invisible image ensures that blank spaces on your page remain consistent. This is important because browsers sometimes display elements closer together if there is no text or image to prevent tightening up the design.

How do you make a spacer image?

Although Dreamweaver automatically creates spacer images, you can create your own in an image-editing program, such as Adobe Photoshop. Create a new image and set the background color to transparent. Save it as a GIF file in your Web site 🗔. An ideal size for a spacer image is 10 x 10 pixels; however, it can be any size. You can resize it in Dreamweaver to fit the space that you want to fill.

149